THE CHRONICLER'S GENEALOGIES

Society of Biblical Literature

Academia Biblica

Steven L. McKenzie,
Hebrew Bible/Old Testament Editor

Number 28

THE CHRONICLER'S GENEALOGIES
Towards an Understanding of
1 Chronicles 1–9

THE CHRONICLER'S GENEALOGIES
Towards an Understanding of
1 Chronicles 1–9

James T. Sparks

Society of Biblical Literature
Atlanta

THE CHRONICLER'S GENEALOGIES
Towards an Understanding of
1 Chronicles 1–9

Copyright © 2008 by the Society of Biblical Literature

All rights reserved. No part of this work may be reproduced or transmitted in any form or by any means, electronic or mechanical, including photocopying and recording, or by means of any information storage or retrieval system, except as may be expressly permitted by the 1976 Copyright Act or in writing from the publisher. Requests for permission should be addressed in writing to the Rights and Permissions Office, Society of Biblical Literature, 825 Houston Mill Road, Atlanta, GA 30329, USA.

The Greek and Hebrew text in this work were produced using the fonts supplied in BibleWorks 7. BWHEBB, BWHEBL, BWTRANSH [Hebrew]; BWGRKL, BWGRKN, and BWGRLI [Greek] Postcript® Type 1 and TrueType fonts Copyright © 1994–2006 BibleWorks, LLC. All rights reserved. These Biblical Greek and Hebrew fonts are used with permission and are from BibleWorks, software for Biblical exegesis and research.

Library of Congress Cataloging-in-Publication Data

Sparks, James T., 1955–
   The chronicler's genealogies : towards an understanding of 1 Chronicles, 1–9 / James T. Sparks.
      p. cm. — (Academia biblica ; no. 28)
   Includes bibliographical references and index.
   ISBN 978-1-58983-365-4 (paper binding : alk. paper)
   1. Bible. O.T., Chronicles, 1st, 1–9—Commentaries 2. Genealogy in the Bible. I. Title.
   BS1345.53.S68 2008b
   222'.6306—dc22
                              2008022527

Printed in the United States of America on acid-free, recycled paper conforming to ANSI/NISO Z39.48-1992 (R1997) and ISO 9706:1994 standards for paper permanence.

DEDICATION

This book is dedicated to the two most important people in my life:

My wonderful wife Stephanie, and my son James.

TABLE OF CONTENTS

TABLE OF FIGURES xiii
LIST OF ABBREVIATIONS xv
ACKNOWLEDGEMENTS xvii

CHAPTER 1
INTRODUCTION 1
The Trouble with Genealogies 1
    Approaches to the Genealogies 5
    Wilson's Study of Tribal Genealogies 9
    Genealogical Terms and Terminology 14
Determining the Purpose of the Chronicler's Genealogies 21
The Structure of the Genealogical Section 23
    Balance 24
    Inversion 24
    Intensification 25
Chiasm as an Aid to Understanding 25
The Chiastic Structure of 1 Chronicles 1–9 29
    Balance 29
    Inversion 30
    Intensification 31
The Central Theme of 1 Chronicles 1–9 31
Procedure 33

CHAPTER 2
F: 1 CHRONICLES 6:48–49: THE CULTIC PERSONNEL IN THEIR DUTIES 35
Introduction 35
The Limits of the Section 35
The Contrasting Functions of Levites and Sons of Aaron 40
The Centrality of Cultic Functions 42
Atonement: The Purpose of the Cult 45
The Place of Moses 51
Presentation of Moses and David 56
The Future of Moses and David 61
Conclusion 61

CHAPTER 3
F1: 1 CHRONICLES 6:35–38 [6:50–53]: THE CULTIC LEADERS 63
The Place of the Passage in the Genealogies 63
The List of the Sons of Aaron 64
Interpretations of the List of the Sons of Aaron 66

    A High Priest List 66
    The Legitimization of Zadok 67
Conclusion 83

Chapter 4
E: 1 Chronicles 6:1–47: The Descendants of Levi 85
Introduction 85
Structure 85
The Order of Listing 88
    Clarifying Notes for Figure 4.9 88
    Observations on the Data 89
Form of the Lists 94
    Samuel as Levite 97
The Relationship between the Lists of Levites and Singers 99
    The Gershomite Lists 99
    The Kohathite Lists 102
    Amminadab: The Son of Kohath? 105
1 Chronicles 5:27–41 [6:1–15]: A High Priest List? 107
    The Structure of the List of the Sons of Aaron 115
The Purpose of the Lists of the Sons of Levi 118
Conclusion 122

Chapter 5
E1: 1 Chronicles 6:54–81: The Descendants of Levi in Their Land . 125
Introduction 125
The Relation of 1 Chronicles 39–66 [6:54–81] to Joshua 21 129
    1 Chronicles 6 is Shorter Than the List in Joshua 21 132
    1 Chronicles 6 is More Disordered and "Natural" than Joshua 21 135
    MT 1 Chronicles 6 Is Closer to the LXX Joshua 21 than to
        MT Joshua 21 140
    Textual Evidence for the Priority of Joshua 21 150
The Function of the List in 1 Chronicles 6 153
Conclusion 162

Chapter 6
D: 1 Chronicles 4:24–5:26: Tribes of Israel in Victory
    and Defeat 163
The Structure of the Lists 164
Sources 169
The Battle Accounts 174
"To This Day" and the Chronicler's Plan 178
Conclusion 184

Chapter 7
D1: 1 Chronicles 7:1–40: Tribes of Israel in Defeat and Restoration 185
Introduction 185
Structure and Content of 1 Chronicles 7 185
The Armies of Yahweh 189
The People of Yahweh in Their Generations and in Their Land 194
    Naphtali 195
    Manasseh 195
    Ephraim 197
    The Land 200
Retribution upon the Wicked and the Provision of a Godly Warrior 201
    The Deaths of Ezer and Elead 201
    The Genealogy of Joshua 203
Restoration and Rebuilding 205
Concluding Observations 207
    Excursus 1: The Place of Dan 209

Chapter 8
C: 1 Chronicles 2:3–4:23: Judah: the Tribe of King David 215
Introduction 215
Content of the Judahite Genealogy 217
    Familial Terminology in the Judahite Genealogy 218
    Leaders of Judahite Communities 220
    Domestic Terminology in the Judahite Genealogy 222
    Retribution in the Judahite Genealogy 223
    Foreign Elements in the Judahite Genealogy 224
Understanding the Structure of the Judahite Genealogy 227
    Random Textual Growth 228
    A Chiastic Structure 229
The Judahite Genealogy as Presenting Alternative Paths 236
The Focus on Jerahmeel 244
Judah: First among His Brothers 247
Concluding Observations 249

Chapter 9
C1: 1 Chronicles 8:1–40: Benjamin: the Tribe of King Saul 251
Introduction 251
Content of the Benjaminite Genealogy 252
    Familial Terminology 253
    Leaders 253

    Domestic Terminology 253
    Retribution 254
    Foreign Elements 255
    Observations on the Content of the Benjaminite Genealogy 256
The Structure of the Benjaminite Genealogy 257
    The Significance of the Benjaminite Structure 258
Concluding Observations on Benjamin 261
    Excursus 2: The Conflicting Genealogies of the Sons of Benjamin 262

CHAPTER 10
B AND B1: 1 CHRONICLES 2:1–2; 9:1A: "ALL ISRAEL" 269
Introduction 269
The Text of 1 Chronicles 9:1a 270
The Book of the Kings of Israel and Judah 273
All Israel 278
The Order of the Sons of Israel 285
Conclusion 287

CHAPTER 11
THE CHRONICLER'S USE OF HIS SOURCES 291
Introduction 291
The Chronicler as Copier of His Source Material 296
The Chronicler as Editor of His Source Material 301
The Chronicler as Summariser of His Source Material 302
The Chronicler as Interpreter of His Source Material 305
The Chronicler: Changing the Emphasis of His Source Material 308
Conclusions and Implications 313
Types of Differences between 1 Chronicles 1 and Genesis 314

CHAPTER 12
A: 1 CHRONICLES 1:1–54: THE WORLD BEFORE ISRAEL 319
Introduction 319
What 1 Chronicles 1 Is Not 320
    First Chronicles 1 as Commentary 321
    First Chronicles 1 as Presenting "Divine Election" 321
    First Chronicles 1 as Encouragement to the Postexilic Community 322
What 1 Chronicles 1 Is 324
The Barrenness of 1 Chronicles 1 326
Concluding Observations 331

CHAPTER 13
A1: 1 CHRONICLES 9:1B–34: ISRAEL RE-ESTABLISHED 333
Introduction 333
Determining the Chronicler's Source 333
The Relationship between 1 Chronicles 9 and Nehemiah 11 337
    The Similarities between the Texts 338
    The Differences between the Texts 340
    Concluding Observations on the Similarities and Differences 348
The Common Form of the Texts 349
The Purpose of 1 Chronicles 9 350
Settlers or Resettlers? 353
Concluding Observations 357

CHAPTER 14
CONCLUSION 359
Introduction 359
The Chiastic Structure of 1 Chronicles 1–9 359
    Balance 359
    Inversion 360
    Intensification 360
    Observation 362
Implications for Future Research 362
    The Priority of the Cult 363
    Community Support for the Cult 364
    The Davidic Kings 365
    The Place of the Persian Kings in the Chronicler's Yehud 366
    All Israel 367
Final Comments 367

BIBLIOGRAPHY 369
INDEX OF AUTHORS 383

TABLE OF FIGURES

Figure 1.1: Genealogical Depth and Breadth 18
Figure 1.2: The Chiastic Structure of 1 Chronicles 1–9 29
Figure 3.1: Ezekiel and the Zadokites 69
Figure 3.2: Priestly Families in 1 Chronicles 9 // Nehemiah 11 74
Figure 3.3: Priestly Genealogies in Chronicles; Ezra; Nehemiah 77
Figure 3.4: The Family of Eli 81
Figure 4.1: Parallel Texts of the Sons of Levi 87
Figure 4.2: The Order of Listing in Nehemiah 92
Figure 4.3: The Family of Samuel 96
Figure 4.4: The Gershomite lists 100
Figure 4.5: The Kohathite Lists 104
Figure 4.6: Persons Given the Title "High/Chief Priest" 109
Figure 4.7: The Sons of Aaron 110
Figure 4.8: מָעַל/מַעַל in Chronicles 119
Figure 4.9: The Order of Listing in the Postexilic Community 123
Figure 5.1: The Order of Joshua 21 // 1 Chronicles 6 Compared 135
Figure 5.2: The Four Scenarios of Textual Relationship of
            Joshua 21 // 1 Chronicles 6 143
Figure 5.3: LXX Joshua 21 = MT 1 Chronicles 6 Against MT Joshua 21 .. 144
Figure 5.4: MT Joshua 21 = MT 1 Chronicles 6 Against LXX Joshua 21 .. 145
Figure 5.5: Joshua 21 MT = Joshua 21 LXX Against 1 Chronicles 6 MT .. 146
Figure 5.6: Different Town Names in the Levitical Town Lists 149
Figure 5.7: Towns Named in the Different Levitical Towns Lists 158
Figure 6.1: Order of Presentation in the Simeonite and Transjordan Lists . 165
Figure 6.2: The Cities of the Tribe of Simeon 168
Figure 6.3: The Transjordanian Tribal Allotments 169
Figure 6.4: The Source of 1 Chronicles 5:3 170
Figure 6.5: The Clans of Simeon 171
Figure 7.1: The Chiastic Structure of 1 Chronicles 7 186
Figure E1.1: The Offspring of Dan and Naphtali 211
Figure 7.2: Building Texts 213
Figure 8.1: Familial Terms in the Genealogies of the Sons of Israel 219
Figure 8.2: אָב as Town Leader in the Genealogies 221
Figure 8.3: The Chronicler's Sources for the Judahite Genealogy 233
Figure 8.4: Williamson's Structure of the Judahite Genealogy 234
Figure 8.5: The Structure of the Jabez Narrative 241

Figure 8.6: The Alternate Paths of the Judahite Genealogy 244
Figure 9.1: The Structure of the Benjaminite Genealogy 258
Figure E2.1: Variations in Names in the Benjamin Traditions 264
Figure E2.2: Genesis 46:21 (MT) 265
Figure E2.3: Genesis 46:21 (LXX) 266
Figure E2.4: Numbers 26:38–41 266
Figure E2.5: 1 Chronicles 7:6–11 267
Figure E2.6: 1 Chronicles 8:1–7 268
Figure 10.1: Book of the Kings 274
Figure 10.2: "All Israel"—Identical to the Chronicler's Source 279
Figure 10.3: "All Israel"—the Chronicler's Unique and Added Material ... 280
Figure 10.4: "All Israel"—Modified from the Chronicler's Source 282
Figure 10.5: "All Israel"—Removed by the Chronicler 282
Figure 10.6: Which Kingdom is "All Israel" 284
Figure 10.7: The Recorded Order of the Sons of Israel 289
Figure 11.1: McIver's Group Organisation 292
Figure 11.2: Parallel Passages in 1 Chronicles 1 and Genesis 297
Figure 11.3: Sequences of Exactly the Same Sixteen or More Words 298
Figure 11.4: Sequences of Exactly the Same Sixteen or More Words
              with Allowances for Plené Spelling and Misreading Letters .. 298
Figure 11.5: Sequences of Exactly the Same Sixteen or More Words
              with Allowances for Minor Variations 299
Figure 11.6: The Chronicler Following Genesis Rather than J/P 301
Figure 11.7: Plené Spelling 314
Figure 11.8: Misread Letters 315
Figure 11.9: Conjunction ו 315
Figure 11.10: Transposed Letters 316
Figure 11.11: Alternate Word Endings 316
Figure 11.12: Preposition 316
Figure 11.13: Direct Object Marker 316
Figure 11.14: "These"/ אֵלֶּה 316
Figure 11.15: Additional Words 317
Figure 11.16: Alternate Words 317
Figure 12.1: Oeming's Narrowing Focus on the Temple 332
Figure 13.1: 1 Chronicles 9 // Nehemiah 11 335
Figure 13.2: Similar Names in the Lists 339
Figure 13.3: Group Totals 342

LIST OF ABBREVIATIONS

AB	Anchor Bible
AJBI	*Annual of the Japanese Biblical Institute*
AmAnthr	*American Anthropologist*
ATJ	*Ashland Theological Journal*
BA	*Biblical Archeologist*
BEATAJ	Beiträge zur Erforschung des Alten Testaments und des antiken Judentums
Bib	*Biblica*
BN	*Biblische Notizen*
BWA(N)T	Beiträge zur Wissenschaft vom Alten (und Neuen) Testament
CBQ	*Catholic Biblical Quarterly*
CC	Continental Commentary
ConBOT	Coniectanea biblica: Old Testament Series
DCH	*Dictionary of Classical Hebrew*
FAT	Forschungen zum Alten Testament
FOTL	Forms of Old Testament Literature
HAT	Handbuch zum Alten Testament
HTR	*Harvard Theological Review*
IBC	Interpretation: A Bible Commentary for Teaching and Preaching
ICC	International Critical Commentary
IDBSup	*The Interpreter's Dictionary of the Bible: Supplementary Volume*
JAOS	*Journal of the American Oriental Society*
JBL	*Journal of Biblical Literature*
JQR	*Jewish Quarterly Review*
JSOT	*Journal for the Study of the Old Testament*
JSOTSup	Journal for the Study of the Old Testament: Supplement Series
JSPSup	Journal for the Study of the Pseudepigrapha: Supplement Series
JTS	*Journal of Theological Studies*
K&D	Keil & Delitzsch
LS	*Louvain Studies*
NAC	The New American Commentary

NCB	New Century Bible
NICOT	New International Commentary on the Old Testament
NIDOTTE	*New International Dictionary of Old Testament Theology and Exegesis*
OTL	Old Testament Library
SBLDS	Society of Biblical Literature Dissertation Series
SBLSymS	Society of Biblical Literature Symposium Series
SJOT	*Scandinavian Journal of the Old Testament*
SSN	Studia semitica neerlandica
TDOT	*Theological Dictionary of the Old Testament*
TOTC	Tyndale Old Testament Commentary
TynBul	*Tyndale Bulletin*
VT	*Vetus Testamentum*
VTSup	Supplements to Vetus Testamentum
WBC	Word Biblical Commentary
WTJ	*Westminster Theological Journal*
ZAW	*Zeitschrift für die alttestamentliche Wissenschaft*

ACKNOWLEDGEMENTS

Any work of this length, which has occupied a person's life for the period in which it has been worked upon, owes its completion to the efforts and encouragement of many people.

As the bibliography attests, I owe much to those individuals who have grappled with the meaning and understanding of the Hebrew Bible in general, and the work of the Chronicler in particular. Although I have only personally met a handful of these individuals, their works have informed, stimulated, and challenged my thinking. I have not always agreed with their conclusions, but I have always appreciated their scholarship, and their commitment to understanding and explaining the Biblical text.

To my PhD supervisor, Dr. Jim Trotter, I owe an unpayable debt of thanks for his encouragement, patience, understanding, and guidance through the ups and the many downs of the past years. Without his ongoing support, this work would not have been accomplished.

To Sabine Wiertz, my German teacher at Central TAFE in Perth, who patiently tried to teach me the German language so that I might understand the works of Oeming, Rudolph, Rothstein and Hänel, Kartveit, and others, I say "danke für alle deine Hilfe." She, of course, is not to be blamed for any mistranslations or misunderstandings of the German text encountered.

I am grateful to my good friend Philip Friend who proofread the entire text. He also is not to be blamed if I ignored or overlooked his advice.

My friend of many years, Stan Sheldon, bought me a new computer so that I might be able to produce this work. I am grateful for his kindness.

A special word of thanks is due to Leigh Andersen of the *Society of Biblical Literature*, who patiently guided the editing process of this work. Without her careful observation and attention to detail, this book could not have been completed.

To Len and Maxine Kenny, who supported me financially and with ongoing prayer and encouragement throughout my undergraduate and post-graduate studies, I say "thank you." Most of all, I am grateful to them for allowing me to marry their only daughter.

Finally, to my wonderful wife Stephanie, who has done so much, and put up with so much, to help me achieve this goal, I can only say, "I love you immensely for all that you have done, and for all that you are."

CHAPTER 1
INTRODUCTION

THE TROUBLE WITH GENEALOGIES

Any reader confronting the books of 1 and 2 Chronicles has two major issues with which to contend. First, much of Chronicles already appears in the canonical works of Samuel and Kings, thus giving the reader a sense of *déjà vu*. Since the reader may already be familiar with an account that is in many respects similar to the text of Chronicles, he/she will be tempted to read Chronicles as a supplement to that with which they are already familiar. This results in the varying accounts being "harmonised" into one, unified text,[1] often with the reader making the text of Chronicles subordinate to the texts of Samuel/Kings. The unfortunate consequence is that the reader fails to appreciate the Chronicler's own message.[2]

---

[1] On the tendency throughout history to supplement the other canonical texts on the basis of Chronicles, or to harmonise the divergent viewpoints, see Matt Patrick Graham, *The Utilization of 1 and 2 Chronicles in the Reconstruction of Israelite History in the Nineteenth Century* (SBLDS 116; Atlanta: Scholars Press, 1990), 1–8. This viewpoint is reflected in the LXX name for Chronicles, παραλειπομενων, or, "the things omitted." For a discussion of the various titles given to the work in antiquity, see Gary N. Knoppers and Paul B. Harvey, "Omitted and Remaining Matters: On the Names Given to the Book of Chronicles in Antiquity," *JBL* 121 (2002): 227–243.

[2] I use the term "Chronicler" in this work to refer only to the author of the books of Chronicles. Although scholars in the first two thirds of the twentieth century generally held to the literary unity of Chronicles/Ezra/Nehemiah, this view was challenged in the latter part of that century. Noth was so certain of the unity of the works he stated, "the work of the Chronicler has come down to us as a literary unity . . . in contrast with our analysis of the Deuteronomic History, there is no need to start with a demonstration of the work's literary unity." This view has been seriously challenged, and many have come to recognise Chronicles and Ezra/Nehemiah as separate works: Sara Japhet, "The Supposed Common Authorship of Chronicles and Ezra-Nehemiah Investigated Anew," *VT* 18 (1968): 330–371; Sara Japhet, "The Relationship between Chronicles and Ezra-Nehemiah," in *Congress Volume: Leuven 1989* (ed. J. A. Emerton; Leiden: Brill, 1991); Mark A. Throntveit, "Linguistic Analysis and the Question of Authorship in Chronicles, Ezra and Nehemiah," *VT* 32 (1982): 201–216; H. G. M. Williamson, *Israel in the Books of Chronicles* (Cambridge: Cambridge University Press, 1977). It may be fair to say that the traditional view is no longer the majority view, although there are a number of writers who still hold to the unity of Chronicles/Ezra/Nehemiah. For a defence of the traditional view see Peter R. Ackroyd, "Chronicles-Ezra-Nehemiah: The Concept of Unity," in *The Chronicler in His Age* (*Journal for the Study of the Old Testament Supplement 101*; Sheffield: Sheffield Academic Press, 1991); Joseph Blenkinsopp, *Ezra-Nehemiah* (OTL;

The second major problem, which is in fact the first to be confronted by readers, is the first nine chapters of 1 Chronicles. These nine chapters are primarily genealogies, and to most readers consist of one long, daunting list of names.³ Some of these names are familiar to readers of the Hebrew Bible, while others are new and obscure. Whether familiar or not, these long lists of names can present an insurmountable barrier to those attempting to read Chronicles, resulting in the individual either "giving up," or instead simply skipping over the first nine chapters in order to reach the narrative beginning in 1 Chr 10.

To many readers, these lists of names seem unnecessary and irrelevant. There is no apparent meaning or purpose behind them or their presence within the text. There is no apparent teaching or doctrine to encourage or challenge the reader who approaches the text from a position of faith. Within faith communities, rarely are the genealogies the subject of sermons,⁴ and more rarely are they the subject of devotional study and reflection,⁵ and are totally absent from the lectionary.

This problem with the genealogies is recognised by commentators as well. Williamson says, "few biblical passages are more daunting to the modern reader than the opening chapters of 1 Chronicles."⁶ McKenzie recognises that such long genealogies are foreign to many modern Westerners when he says, "Understandably, modern readers find ancient genealogies – especially one of this length and detail – difficult to appreciate and often skip over them."⁷ Pratt has also commented, "the first chapters of Chronicles challenge the endurance of

---

Philadelphia: Westminster/John Knox Press, 1988), 47–54; John W. Wright, "The Legacy of David in Chronicles: The Narrative Function of 1 Chronicles 23–27," *JBL* 110 (1991): 229–242, esp. 241 note 31.

³ This was made clear to me by a friend who, after her first attempt to read Chronicles, told me, "It is so boring. It is just names."

⁴ The only sermon the author has ever heard which used the genealogies as the basic text, is one he himself preached.

⁵ One notable exception is Bruce H. Wilkinson, *The Prayer of Jabez* (Sisters: Multnomah, 2000), which focuses primarily upon 1 Chr 4:9–10. As will be discussed at a later point, Wilkinson's interpretation of the text is founded upon a misunderstanding of the Hebrew. See especially the studies of Larry Pechawer, *The Lost Prayer of Jabez* (Joplin: Mireh, 2001); R. Christopher Heard, *Echoes of Genesis in 1 Chronicles 4:9–10: An Intertextual and Contextual Reading of Jabez's Prayer* (2002) [cited August 21, 2006]); available from www.purl.org/jhs. See also the utilisation of Jabez in a liturgical setting in, Elaine Heath, "Jabez: A Man Named Pain: An Integrative Hermeneutical Exercise," *ATJ* 33 (2001): 7–16.

⁶ H. G. M. Williamson, *1 and 2 Chronicles* (NCB; Grand Rapids: Eerdmans, 1982), 38.

⁷ Steven L. McKenzie, *1–2 Chronicles* (AOTC; Nashville: Abingdon Press, 2004), 59.

most modern readers. At first glance, we are tempted to pass over these ancient lists and genealogies as irrelevant."[8]

Although those approaching the text from within the Christian tradition may find some comfort in Tuell's words, "it may help a Christian reader, tempted to despair at this welter of ancient ancestors and family gossip, to recall that the New Testament begins in much the same way (Matt 1:1–17)"![9]

It is probable that many readers would agree with Knoppers when he says:

> If one were to take a poll in a contemporary context, requesting respondents to name their favourite subjects, it would be unlikely that listening to rehearsals of long genealogies would be listed as their most preferred leisure activity. Indeed, people in the modern world may find the intense fascination of ancients with the past puzzling. Why would individuals in ancient Mediterranean societies display such an avid interest in the lineages and stories of their predecessors in bygone eras?[10]

One of the issues which comes to the fore through the statements of each of these authors is the differences in thought between "ancient" and "modern" readers. Modern people view the world and their place within it differently to those who lived within the ancient world, and, often, the modern method of viewing the world is assumed to be superior.[11] However, both modern and ancient cultures possess a world-view which gives individuals within that society an understanding of who they are, as well as how and where they fit within their own societies and cultures. The struggle that many modern people have in respect to 1 Chr 1–9 arises not because the ancients were strange, or because the customs, viewpoints, and means of expression of the ancients bring "difficulties," "despair," and "puzzlement." These are in fact the result of the struggle that modern readers have in placing themselves into the world-view and cultural understanding of the ancients and being able to view the world through the eyes of the ancients. To appreciate and value 1 Chr 1–9, the Chronicler's genealogies, the modern reader must develop the ability to view the genealogies as an ancient reader or hearer would, and to appreciate the genealogies on their own terms,

---

[8] Richard L. Pratt, *1 and 2 Chronicles* (Fearn, Ross-shire: Christian Focus Publications, 1998), 62.

[9] Steven S. Tuell, *First and Second Chronicles* (IBC; Louisville: John Knox Press, 2001), 17.

[10] Gary N. Knoppers, *1 Chronicles 1–9* (AB 12; New York: Doubleday, 2004), 245.

[11] Kraft complains about "western culture's tendency to *interpret history evolutionarily*, with western culture at the top and all other cultures judged to be inferior because (we think) they represent stages of culture that we have outgrown," Charles H. Kraft, *Christianity in Culture: A Study in Dynamic Biblical Theologizing in Cross-Cultural Perspective* (Maryknoll: Orbis Books, 1979), 228 (italics his).

rather than imposing modern viewpoints and understandings of what genealogies are, or are not.

This dichotomy is not, however, one that exists simply between ancient and modern. It can also be seen to exist between those who classify themselves as Western, and those who do not. Kraft relates the following story:

> A conversation between a Gentile and a Jewish student of Old Testament studies at Brandeis University illustrates the same point. The Gentile asked the Jewish student what his favourite passage of Scripture was. His immediate response was, 'The first eight chapters of First Chronicles'. These are Hebrew genealogies. From my (Gentile) point of view I have often wondered why God allowed so much space in his Word to be 'wasted' on such trivia. But to a Hebrew (and to many other kinship-oriented societies around the world) genealogical lists of this nature demonstrate in the clearest way the specificity of God's love and concern that lies at the heart of the Gospel.[12]

This story illustrates the fact that "culture," even within the world of the twenty-first century, is not monolithic. There is no "one way" of viewing the world, and there is no one way of interpreting texts. Each culture interprets texts within the framework of its own values and worldview. The culture to which an individual belongs is the prism through which that individual values, orders, and interprets the world in which they find themselves. Kraft further recounts his experiences when, as a Christian missionary teacher in Africa, he sought to teach what he viewed as the "epitome of God's revelation to humanity" and discovered to his surprise that the people "with whom I worked actually saw many aspects of God's message more clearly in the Old Testament than in the book of Romans."[13]

Herein lies the major problem that modern Western readers have experienced in approaching and in appreciating the genealogies in the Bible in general, and the extended genealogical section contained in 1 Chr 1–9 in particular. It becomes far too easy to approach such texts from the perspective of twenty-first century Westerners, and to view the genealogies from that perspective.[14] As such, they do

---

[12] Kraft, *Christianity*, 229.

[13] Kraft, *Christianity*, 228.

[14] This could, of course, be extended to include white, western, middle class males. Each of these characteristics has shaped a view of the world, and therefore shaped the interpretation of the text. Within this it is interesting to note that of all the commentaries on Chronicles to which I had access, only one, by Sara Japhet, was written by a woman. It would be beneficial to explore the differences that arise in the interpretation of Chronicles in general, and the genealogies in particular, on the basis of gender, religious affiliation, country of origin, and indeed, the century in which one wrote. A new work which arrived too late to bring into full consideration in respect to the issue of the genealogies, is the

often appear dry, convoluted, repetitive, confusing, and at times contradictory. However, it should not be concluded that simply because modern Westerners view them as such, that that is what the genealogies are. Instead, we must seek to comprehend the genealogies in the terms in which the author presented and intended them to be read.

APPROACHES TO THE GENEALOGIES

The above approach lies behind the negative assessment of the genealogies of 1 Chr 1–9 in Wellhausen's analysis.[15] Wellhausen approached the genealogies from the perspective of a nineteenth century historian, looking for items of historical value within them. When the Chronicler's genealogies could not attain the criteria for historical validity set by Wellhausen, he dismissed them as being from "later times," and therefore of no value.[16] In respect to the Chronicler's genealogies as a whole, he stated:

> It is certain that quite as many [of the genealogies] have been simply invented; and the combination of the elements . . . dates, as both form and matter show, from the very latest period. One might as well try to hear the grass growing as attempt to derive from such a source as this a historical knowledge of the conditions of ancient Israel.[17]

What Wellhausen failed to do is to ask himself whether or not he was asking the right questions of the text. Wellhausen was asking questions properly shaped by nineteenth century Western culture. As such, Wellhausen's questions would have been appropriate in the evaluation of a nineteenth century Western text. The difficulty is, the Chronicler's work is not a nineteenth century Western text. By failing to recognise that his cultural viewpoint was at odds with the cultural viewpoint of the text he was seeking to evaluate, Wellhausen failed to ask the right questions and, consequently, Wellhausen was unable to come to or discover satisfying answers.[18]

---

contribution on Chronicles by Nupanga Weanzana, in the one volume work: Tokunboh Adeyemo, ed., *Africa Bible Commentary* (Nairobi: WordAlive Publishers, 2006). This work by seventy African scholars seeks to interpret and explain the text of the Bible from within an African context.

[15] Julius Wellhausen, *Prolegomena to the History of Israel* (Atlanta: Scholars Press, 1994), 211–222.

[16] Wellhausen, *Prolegomena*, 211.

[17] Wellhausen, *Prolegomena*, 215.

[18] "The danger is always to let the text serve the reader's own needs or ideologies, so that the reader entrenches his or her own position (unconsciously, of course) by not recognizing his or her own subjectivity during the reading process," Gerrie F. Snyman, "A

Wellhausen, however, is not alone in these negative appraisals of the Chronicler's genealogies. Adam Welch rejected the possibility that these genealogies were an original part of the Chronicler's work for they "have no unity among themselves and are not integrally related to the rest of the book,"[19] and again, "they are a collection of loose material . . . [which] when they are removed, the unity of design in the Chronicler's work becomes apparent."[20]

For Welch, not only were the genealogies later additions to the text and included for some unknown reason, but they also masked the true purpose of the Chronicler's work, a purpose which can only be identified when these later genealogical additions have been removed. Once the genealogical material was removed Welch identified an *historical* text which, "dealt with the period of the kingdom in Judah from the time of its foundation by David to that of its collapse under Zedekiah."[21]

Other writers have followed Welch in rejecting the originality of the genealogies within the Chronicler's work, suggesting, as did Welch, that they are later additions to the text, incorporated at some stage within the longer textual history of Chronicles.[22] Freedman, Cross, and Newsome all suggest that the original work of the Chronicler was produced during the early postexilic era as part of the program of support for Zerubbabel in his work of building the second temple, as well as support for Zerubbabel as a descendant of David to the leadership of the community.[23] They have suggested that the Chronicler was

---

Possible World of Text Production for the Genealogy in 1 Chronicles 2.3–4.23," in *The Chronicler as Theologian: Essays in Honor of Ralph W. Klein* (ed. M. Patrick Graham, et al. *Journal for the Study of the Old Testament Supplement 371*; London: T&T Clark International, 2003), 34.

[19] Adam C. Welch, *Post-Exilic Judaism: The Baird Lecture for 1934* (Edinburgh: William Blackwood & Sons, 1935), 185. He repeats the same opinion in Adam C. Welch, *The Work of the Chronicler: Its Purpose and Its Date: The Schweich Lectures 1938* (London: Oxford University Press, 1939), 1.

[20] Welch, *Post-Exilic Judaism*, 186.

[21] Welch, *Work*, 1. Although it would be fair to conclude that Welch would term the text of Chronicles as an "historical" work, this should not be taken to suggest that he would conclude that it was thereby "historically accurate." He viewed Chronicles as a tendentious text, written and revised to present a particular view and understanding of present society as illustrated through incidents, some contrived by the Chronicler himself, in the past.

[22] David N. Freedman, "The Chronicler's Purpose," *CBQ* 23 (1961): 436–442; Frank Moore Cross, "A Reconstruction of the Judean Restoration," *JBL* 94 (1975): 4–18; James D. Newsome, "Toward a New Understanding of the Chronicler and His Purposes," *JBL* 94 (1975): 201–217.

[23] Freedman, "Purpose," 441; Cross, "Reconstruction," 14; Newsome, "New Understanding," 216.

influenced in his views by the prophets Haggai and Zechariah who called Zerubbabel Yahweh's "signet ring" (Hag 2:23; cf. Jer 22:24), or the "branch" (Zech 6:9–14; cf. Jer 23:5–6).[24] To this "original" work of the Chronicler were added the memoirs of Ezra/Nehemiah and, in the final stage of textual growth, the genealogical section.[25]

There are three primary reasons why Freedman, Cross, and Newsome reject the Chronicler's genealogies as being original to the text. First, they have an *a priori* commitment to a theory of textual development that demands that anything contrary to their interpretation of the text must be a later textual addition. Second, and most significantly for our purposes here, they failed to appreciate the purpose and function of genealogies in the ancient world in general. Third, they express an unwillingness to examine the Chronicler's genealogies in their own right as a unified text. These second and third issues will be investigated in detail in this work.

Even among scholars from previous generations who did accept some of the genealogies as being original to the text, there was a general tendency to suggest that a core of genealogical material present to the Chronicler's work had been supplemented to such an extent by later revisers, that the end result bore no resemblance to what the Chronicler had penned.

---

[24] Freedman, "Purpose," 441; Newsome, "New Understanding," 216.

[25] There is no exact agreement as to the process by which the Chronicler's work was expanded. Freedman does not define the full extent of the original work, but does indicate that Ezra/Nehemiah were added a later time, and that at "about the same time" that Ezra/Nehemiah were added, 1 Chr 1–9 were also included, "Purpose," 441. Cross states that the text developed in three stages: Chr_1, consisting of 1 Chr 10 – 2 Chr 34, plus the *Vorlage* of 1 Esdras 1:1–5:65 (=2 Chr 34:1–Ezra 3:13). To this was added the *Vorlage* of 1 Esdras, which resulted in Chr_2. The final stage, Chr_3, came with the addition of the Nehemiah memoir and 1 Chr 1–9, "Reconstruction," 11–14. These conclusions are not far from the suggestion of Welch, to whom neither Freedman, Cross, or Newsome refer. Welch also argues that Chronicles developed in three stages. The first is the work of the "author," who wrote immediately after the return, and was supportive of the temple cult, particularly of the ark of the covenant, and the Davidic monarchy. Second is the work of the "annotator" who "belonged to the generation which followed the Return from Exile," and who had never experienced "exile," *Work*, 155, and the fuller discussion in pages 149–160. The "annotator" or "reviser" did not fully agree with everything written by the "author," but subjected the work "to a careful and thorough revision" (page 150), particularly in the actions of the reforming kings (page 151), and in the significance of the ark (page 153). The "annotator" was influenced by, and followed the teachings of the "law which the Lord delivered unto Moses" (page 154), and his additions and corrections are consistent with what the law of Moses taught, whereas the "author" deferred to the presence, practice, and commands of the great Kings. The final stage in the production of Chronicles was the inclusion of the genealogies.

Characteristic of these proposals is that of Noth, who stated about 1 Chr 1–9, "in the form in which it has come down to us the condition of this section is one of unusually great disorder and confusion, but for this . . . Chr. cannot be held responsible. Here again it is innumerable genealogies and lists which have been subsequently added in to Chr.'s work."[26]

For Noth, the Chronicler primarily utilised existing canonical sources. This suggests that Noth viewed the Chronicler as an historian in the modern sense as one who compiled his work on the basis of factual, authoritative texts. As such, any content which was not based upon such texts, could not be the work of a historian, and consequently must be a later addition. According to Noth, the Chronicler's main sources were Genesis, from which the Chronicler gleaned his lists in 1 Chr 1, and Num 26 which provided the lists of the sons and grandsons of Israel.[27] The only section of the genealogies which Noth ascribes to the Chronicler is 1 Chr 2:9–15 because the Chronicler "manifests a particular interest in the figure of David,"[28] and a list of high priests and their duties.[29] For Noth, the Chronicler's original format, based upon Num 26, had been obscured by later redactors so that only a portion of what the Chronicler included regarding the tribes remained, while the Chronicler's original list had been displaced.[30]

Similar to Noth is the view of Rudolph, who is equally dismissive of much of the material in the current text of 1 Chr 1–9.[31] Although Rudolph's proposed "original" material is slightly different to that of Noth,[32] he follows the same basic suggestion that, "the Chronicler has taken the statements in the genealogical part predominately from the Pentateuch,"[33] although he does allow that some material may come from non-canonical sources.[34] In this way, Rudolph, like

---

[26] Martin Noth, *The Chronicler's History* (JSOTSup 50; trans. H. G. M. Williamson; Sheffield: Sheffield Academic Press, 1987), 36, and his fuller discussion in pages 36–42. Noth accepts only 1 Chr 1; 2:1–5, 9–15; 4:24; 5:3; 6:1–4 [16–19], 34–38 [49–53]; 7:1, 12–13, 20; 8:1 as being the Chronicler's work.

[27] Noth, *Chronicler's History*, 36–38. He further states that "the Pentateuch was practically the only source at Chr.'s disposal," (page 52).

[28] Noth, *Chronicler's History*, 38–39.

[29] Noth, *Chronicler's History*, 42.

[30] Noth, *Chronicler's History*, 37–38. For a critique of Noth's use of Num 26, see Magnar Kartveit, *Motive und Schichten der Landtheologie in I Chronik 1–9* (ConBOT 28; Stockholm: Almqvist & Wiksell International, 1989), 23–30.

[31] Wilhelm Rudolph, *Chronikbücher* (HAT 21; Tübingen: Paul Siebeck, 1955), 1–2.

[32] Rudolph allows 1 Chr 1:1–4a, 24–27, 28–31, 34b, 35–42; 2:1–9, 10–17, 25–33, 42–50aα; 4:24–27; 5:1–3; 6:1–9 [16–24], 4–15 [29–30]; 7:1–2a, 3, 12a, 12b, 13, 14–19, 20; 9:1a, as being original.

[33] "Die Angaben im genealogischen Teil der Chr sind überwiegend aus dem Pentateuch geschöpft," Rudolph, *Chronikbücher*, x.

[34] Rudolph, *Chronikbücher*, xii.

Noth, essentially indicated that the Chronicler only had written sources available, and that most of these were to be found within those writings which were to become the Hebrew Bible. Consequently, anything that was not to be found within these sources was considered to be a later addition to the text.

Although it is impossible to address every aspect of Noth and Rudolph's positions, it is clear that neither of these men approached the genealogies of 1 Chr 1–9 on the basis of the function and purpose of genealogies in the ancient Near East. It is instead clear that both allowed criteria from their own time period to dominate their understandings of the text. In this respect both Noth and Rudolph follow the path of Wellhausen, Welch, Freedman, Cross, and Newsome as individuals who allow criteria from other times and cultures to become the dominant matrix through which the text of 1 Chr 1–9 is viewed and interpreted.

WILSON'S STUDY OF TRIBAL GENEALOGIES

A significant change in how the Biblical genealogies are to be understood arose with the work of Wilson.[35] Although other writers had begun to view the Biblical genealogies on their own terms,[36] or on the basis of comparison with other ancient Near Eastern literature,[37] Wilson brought the insights of anthropological and sociological studies into how genealogies actually work within modern tribal societies to bear on the question of the function, meaning and purpose of Biblical and other ancient Near Eastern genealogies.

---

[35] Robert R. Wilson, *Genealogy and History in the Biblical World* (New Haven: Yale University, 1977); Robert R. Wilson, "The Old Testament Genealogies in Recent Research," *JBL* 94 (1975): 169–189; Robert R. Wilson, "Between 'Azel' and 'Azel': Interpreting the Biblical Genealogies," *BA* 42 (1979): 11–22.

[36] Marshall D. Johnson, *The Purpose of the Biblical Genealogies with Special Reference to the Setting of the Genealogies of Jesus* (Eugene: Wipf and Stock, 2002).

[37] J. R. Bartlett, "The Edomite King-List of Genesis XXXVI. 31–39 and 1 Chron I. 43–50," *JTS* 16 (1965): 301–314; Abraham Malamat, "King Lists of the Old Babylonian Period and Biblical Genealogies," *JAOS* 88 (1968): 163–173; Thomas C. Hartman, "Some Thoughts on the Sumerian King List and Genesis 5 and 11B," *JBL* 91 (1972): 25–32; Abraham Malamat, "Tribal Societies: Biblical Genealogies and African Lineage Systems," *AES* 14 (1973): 126–136; Karin R. Andriolo, "A Structural Analysis of Genealogy and Worldview in the Old Testament," *AmAnthr* 75 (1973): 1657–1669; Jack M. Sasson, "A Genealogical 'Convention' in Biblical Chronography?," *ZAW* 90 (1978): 171–185; Piotr Michalowski, "History as Charter: Some Observations on the Sumerian King List," in *Studies in Literature From the Ancient Near East by Members of the American Oriental Society Dedicated to Samuel Noah Kramer* (ed. Jack M. Sasson; New Haven: American Oriental Society, 1984).

Working from the starting point that, "fruitful hypotheses are most likely to be drawn from sources that are geographically as close to Israel as possible,"[38] Wilson concentrated his comparative study upon the genealogies within tribal African and Arabic societies, rather than upon "Chinese, Polynesian, European, or American societies," because being closer geographically to the land of ancient Israel, they would be more likely to reflect aspects of the customs and practices of ancient Israel than would other, more geographically distant tribal societies.

Significantly for our purposes, Wilson concluded that:

> the data we have collected so far casts considerable doubt on the proposition that oral genealogies function primarily as *historical* records. Nowhere in our study of genealogical function did we see genealogies created or preserved only for *historiographic* purposes. Rather, we saw that oral genealogies usually have some sociological function in the life of the society that uses them.[39]

The importance of this conclusion for understanding the Biblical genealogies cannot be overestimated. Wellhausen had dismissed the genealogies because, in his view, they were not "historical."[40] Wilson's observations, however, indicate that tribal genealogies are not created for the purpose of "history" or "historiography." Genealogies are instead created for domestic,[41] politico-jural,[42] or religious reasons,[43] although there is often not a clear distinction between these areas, with one area often overlapping with another.[44]

Genealogies operating within the domestic sphere are created to govern and express social relationships and "sanction the social order of the tribe."[45] They help in resolving domestic disputes,[46] as well as helping to "regulate an individual's daily behaviour" and "other areas of his domestic life."[47]

Within the politico-jural sphere, genealogies express not the social, but the political relationships and power structures within a society.

---

[38] Wilson, *Genealogy*, 17.
[39] Wilson, *Genealogy*, 54. Italics mine. Note, however, Wilson's caveat, "there may be major differences in the formal and functional characteristics of oral and written" genealogies (page 55).
[40] Wellhausen, *Prolegomena*, 215.
[41] Wilson, *Genealogy*, 38–40.
[42] Wilson, *Genealogy*, 40–44.
[43] Wilson, *Genealogy*, 44–45.
[44] Wilson, *Genealogy*, 37–38.
[45] Wilson, *Genealogy*, 38.
[46] Wilson, *Genealogy*, 38.
[47] Wilson, *Genealogy*, 39.

When genealogies are used in some way as charters of a society's organization of people and territory, the genealogies function politically, and because the stability of the political structure is assured by the existence of legal authority and of law enforcement mechanisms, the genealogies that validate the political order have jural dimensions as well.[48]

Genealogies operating in the religious sphere may be used within an ancestor cult as a means of gaining or retaining the assistance of the ancestors with the problems facing the lineage in the present.[49] Genealogies used in the religious sphere may also indicate the legitimate successor to an office. This could be that of a cultic official, or even of a divinely appointed king who must justify, through his genealogy, his right to rule.[50]

What Wilson's study made evident, is that nowhere are genealogies created simply to give a history. This is not to suggest that genealogies are entirely artificial with no relation to some historical reality. What this does mean is that genealogies were not created primarily for the purpose of declaring historical reality.

Nor should it be thought that genealogies, because they were not created to present history, are for that reason non-historical. Genealogies may, "in fact contain a great deal of accurate information."[51] Even tendentiously created genealogies must contain a kernel of historically accurate information, otherwise the society in which they were created would have rejected their claims to be accurate reflections of the domestic, political or religious structures, and they would have ceased to be used or retained.[52] Wilson notes that although "genealogies are not created or preserved for strictly historiographic purposes,"[53] they are:

> nevertheless considered to be accurate statements of past domestic, political, and religious relationships. A society may knowingly manipulate a genealogy, and rival groups within the society may advance conflicting tendentious genealogies, but once the society agrees that a particular version of the genealogy is correct, that version is cited as historical evidence to support contemporary social

---

[48] Wilson, *Genealogy*, 40.
[49] Wilson, *Genealogy*, 44; cf. Nupanga Weanzana, "1 and 2 Chronicles," in *Africa Bible Commentary* (ed. Tokunboh Adeyemo; Nairobi: WordAlive Publishers, 2006), 480.
[50] Wilson, *Genealogy*, 45.
[51] Wilson, *Genealogy*, 55.
[52] Wilson, *Genealogy*, 55.
[53] Wilson, *Genealogy*, 54.

configurations. Only the fact that genealogies are considered to be accurate historical records permits them to be used as charters.[54]

Genealogies then can be considered to be a different type of history to that expected within Western society. They are not the history of the modern, Western historian with his/her quest for objective facts. They are instead the subjective reflections of the changing social, political and religious relationships exhibited within a society. Yet, even when they do not provide accurate historical information about the past they recount, they do provide information about the context in which they were created.

Wilson's study then does not give support to the viewpoints of those who approach, and reject, the genealogies from a purely modern historical position.

Wilson's study may appear, however, to lend some support to the view of Noth and Rudolph that there had been an original "core" text which was subsequently expanded upon by later editors. Wilson has observed that, at times, "entire lineages may be grafted into a foreign lineage structure."[55] It may therefore be argued that the textual growth postulated by Noth and Rudolph is reflective of later groups seeking to establish their *bona fides* as true members of the society by attaching their lineages to portions of the Chronicler's original genealogical text.

Although this is a possibility, there are several points which speak against it. First, it must be recognised that Wilson's study indicates that when one lineage seeks to attach itself genealogically to another, it is always a lineage which is *external* to the second lineage, that is, not a part of the second lineage, which seeks to join itself to that second lineage. In the context of 1 Chr 1–9, this would mean that it would be a lineage *external* to Judah which would seek to attach itself to Judah. Likewise, it would be non-Simeonites who would seek to allign themselves to Simeon, etc.

Although it is possible that later groups placed their lineage founders into a genealogical relationship with Israel, the essential question to be asked within a post-Chronistic context is "Why would they?" What circumstances within the late Persian, and more probably the early Hellenistic period if additions to the text after the Chronicler are envisioned, would prompt outsiders to seek to be affiliated with the community in Yehud by associating themselves genealogically with "Israel" or with one of the twelve tribes?

One option would be the desire for religious affiliation within the temple community. Ezra 4:1–2 (cf. 2 Kgs 17:24–33), suggests the possibility that some of the people of Samaria viewed themselves as the religious descendants of the

---

[54] Wilson, *Genealogy*, 54–55.
[55] Wilson, *Genealogy*, 32. See also the discussion on "foreign elements" within the Judahite genealogy in chapter 8.

northern tribes through their worship of Yahweh. This being the case, these individuals could have sought to justify their inclusion within the temple community through attaching themselves to one of the ancient tribes who formerly occupied that land. Although possible, Ezra 4:2 makes it clear that the author of Ezra, and if this account has an historical base the Samarians themselves, viewed the Samarians as foreigners who were brought into the land, not natives who could claim a genealogical right to inclusion within the temple community.

Another option is the desire for political affiliation. However, if the purpose of these additions were to facilitate political links, then it would be more reasonable to propose that genealogical links to the secular tribes of Judah and Benjamin would be sought, instead of the more distant, and currently non-existent, former enemies. Attaching oneself to one of these non-existent tribes would not present itself as a viable option if one was seeking to be included in Yehud, with its dominant associations with Judah, Benjamin and Levi.

The second observation that speaks against the theory of textual growth, is that some of the material which has been proposed as additions to the text are not genealogies as such, but are military muster lists of the various tribes.[56] These lists were created and operative within the military sphere, and represent not clan or lineage founders, but military heroes and leaders. As such, they do not present domestic or even political relationships (although military exploits are related to political power), and are therefore inadequate in establishing a genealogical link between a later group and one of the tribes of Israel.

Third, few of the genealogies which are presented within 1 Chr 1–9 extend into the period of the Chronicler's lifetime. Of those genealogies that are in the present text, one terminates at the exile (Jehozadak, 1 Chr 5:41 [6:15]), two may extend into the exilic period, although no time indicators are given (Sheshan: 1 Chr 2:34–41; Ner: 1 Chr 8:33–39), while only one genealogy clearly extends into the postexilic era (Solomon, 1 Chr 3:10–24). Although Wilson's study has shown that when one lineage attaches itself to another, it is important to place "the founder of the grafted lineage in the proper position on the host lineage's genealogy,"[57] it is also important to show how the people in the present are linked to that grafted lineage founder. It is therefore insufficient to proclaim that "person X" is related to "person Y." It must also be explained how "person Z" is related to "person X" in order to establish "person Z's" right to be associated with the community.

---

[56] This includes 1 Chr 5; 7:1–5, 6–10, 30–40. "The weight of evidence thus inclines us to consider the genealogies of Issachar, Benjamin, Asher and the Transjordanian tribes as being at least in part based on actual lists of military leaders and war heroes," Johnson, *Purpose*, 65. These portions will be discussed at the appropriate places in chapters 6 and 7.

[57] Wilson, *Genealogy*, 32.

Fourth, Wilson has indicated that when one lineage does seek to graft itself onto another lineage, the grafted lineage is "never completely assimilated" into the lineage it seeks to join, and "this fact is usually expressed in the genealogy in some way."[58] This is not the case in the genealogies of 1 Chr 1–9. Taken as a unit, each of the genealogies present within 1 Chr 1–9 is well situated in its respective location in the text. None appears out of place, and there is nothing in the text of 1 Chr 1–9 to indicate that some lineages have been grafted in and are therefore not fully assimilated. Although it has been suggested that some of the lineages in the Judahite genealogy (1 Chr 2:3–4:23), are non-Judahite in origin,[59] it must also be recognised that this judgment is based not on the content of the genealogies themselves, but upon the historical narratives contained in either the Pentateuch or the Deuteronomistic History. The genealogies themselves give no indication that these lineages are not fully assimilated into the various tribes to which they are attached.

Consequently, although on first impressions Wilson's study may appear to support the textual growth hypothesis of Noth and Rudolph, a closer examination indicates that the theory that the text of 1 Chr 1–9 originally consisted of a small core which was supplemented by subsequent editors, is contrary to genealogical practice, as delineated by Wilson.

GENEALOGICAL TERMS AND TERMINOLOGY

Before continuing, it would be helpful to define the terms and terminology which are used in the discussion of genealogies. Since his work has become the standard in the discussion of the Biblical genealogies, the definitions here will be based upon those given by Wilson. They will be accompanied, where possible, with illustrations drawn from 1 Chr 1–9.

Genealogy

Wilson defines a genealogy as, "a written or oral expression of the descent of a person or persons from an ancestor or ancestors."[60]

This indicates that a genealogy may have either one person (1 Chr 7:25–27), or many persons (1 Chr 2:1–2), as its goal. Likewise, a genealogy can have either one parent or both parents (1 Chr 2:18–20), as its starting point.

The relationship that exists between two persons can be expressed either *internally* (X the son of Y the son of Z), or *externally* (the sons of X: Y and Z).[61]

---

[58] Wilson, *Genealogy*, 32. Although he refers specifically to an individual rather than a group, the principle probably still applies.

[59] See the fuller discussion on the Judahite genealogy, chapter 8.

[60] Wilson, *Genealogy*, 9.

[61] Wilson, *Genealogy*, 10.

An example of *external* expression is found in 1 Chr 8:30, "the sons of Asher: Imnah, Ishvah, Ishvi, and Beriah." In this example, the relationship that exists between the persons named is given externally to the list of names itself. An example of an *internal* expression is 1 Chr 6:35–38 [6:50–53]:

> These were the descendants of Aaron: Eleazar his son, Phinehas his son, Abishua his son, Bukki his son, Uzzi his son, Zerahiah his son, Meraioth his son, Amariah his son, Ahitub his son, Zadok his son and Ahimaaz his son.

Although this list is introduced by an external expression "these are the descendants of Aaron," each name in the list is internally connected to the name that proceeds it by means of a kinship term.

It is also to be observed that while a genealogy must consist of at least two generations, it may also be quite long. Although indicating that normally a genealogy does not exceed ten to fourteen generations, Wilson indicates that in some tribes who maintain specialised genealogies, such as king lists, genealogies have exceeded thirty generations.[62] The genealogy from Solomon to the sons of Elioenai (1 Chr 3:10–24), consists of twenty-six generations,[63] as also does the genealogy from Levi to Jehozadak (1 Chr 5:27–41 [6:1–15]). The Assyrian King List and the genealogy of the Hammurapi dynasty are even longer.[64] Wilson points out, however, that the most common maximal length of an oral genealogy is ten to fourteen generations.[65]

One important observation made by Wilson is that, "because a genealogy is an expression of a person's descent, it must express or imply a kinship relationship between the persons named in it."[66]

And again, "without this expression of the kinship relationship, the names simply constitute a list and are not a genealogy."[67]

If a genealogy does not link the names in some way by the use of kinship terms (father, mother, son, daughter, brother, sister), then it is not a genealogy, but only a list of names. Examples of this are found in 1 Chr 1:1–4, 24–27 where

---

[62] Wilson, *Genealogy*, 26.

[63] The LXX allows for the possibility of four additional generations, taking the total to 30, Knoppers, *1 Chronicles 1–9*, 334.

[64] Malamat, "King Lists," 172.

[65] Wilson, *Genealogy*, 21. In this respect it must be noted that the Assyrian King List, the genealogy of the Hammurapi dynasty, and the king list of 1 Chr 3, are all written genealogies. The act of writing gives greater opportunity to create longer genealogies, for issues of memory that relate to oral genealogies do not apply.

[66] Wilson, *Genealogy*, 9.

[67] Wilson, *Genealogy*, 10.

a series of names are given, but no kinship relationships are presented. Consequently, these verses are only a list, and not a genealogy.[68]

Segmented Genealogy

Genealogies appear in two basic forms. The first of these is the *segmented* genealogy. "When a genealogy expresses more than one line of descent from a given ancestor, then it will exhibit segmentation or branching. We will refer to this type of genealogy as a *segmented genealogy*, and each of its component lines or branches will be called a segment."[69]

Segmented genealogies relate different persons or groups to one another by reference to a common ancestor. First Chronicles 2–8 represents one, large, segmented genealogy with the common ancestor "Israel." It begins with the primary ancestor, Israel, and his twelve sons (1 Chr 2:1–2), and in the following chapters gives various details for most of these twelve sons. Each individual tribe is presented as just one segment of the larger, segmented, genealogy of Israel. Further, the Judahite genealogy (1 Chr 2:3–4:23), is itself a segmented genealogy of the primary ancestor,[70] Judah, as represented through his three sons, Shelah, Perez, and Zerah (1 Chr 2:3–4).

A shorter example is found in 1 Chr 1:8–13, the descendants of Ham. Ham, the primary ancestor, is listed in 1 Chr 1:8 with his four sons, Cush, Mizraim, Put and Canaan. In the following verses, the descendants of three of these sons, Cush (1 Chr 1:9–10), Mizraim (1 Chr 1:11–12), and Canaan (1 Chr 1:13–16), are detailed. These three sons provide different segments listing the descendants of the primary ancestor, Ham. It is also to be recognised, that the Hamite genealogy is itself a segment within the larger genealogy of the descendants of Noah (1 Chr 1:4), and his sons Japhet (1 Chr 1:5–7), Ham, and Shem (1 Chr 1:17–23).

Linear Genealogy

The second form in which a genealogy may be written is a *linear* genealogy. "If the genealogy expresses only one line of descent from a given ancestor, then it will exhibit no segmentation, and we will refer to it as a *linear genealogy*."[71]

A linear genealogy relates only one person to an ancestor, but not to any of his/her other relations. A linear genealogy may, at times, present only one person

---

[68] It will be suggested in Chapters 11 and 12, where these texts are discussed, that the Chronicler probably assumed his reader's familiarity with these genealogies, and therefore assumed that his reader's would supply the kinship terms. However, these two texts, as they stand in the Chronicler's work, are lists, and not genealogies.

[69] Wilson, *Genealogy*, 9. Italics his.

[70] Contra the assertion of Snyman, "Possible World," 46, who says that "the genealogy of 1 Chron. 2.3–4.23 is mainly linear."

[71] Wilson, *Genealogy*, 9. Italics his.

per generation (1 Chr 2:36–41), or at other times more than one person per generation, as in the genealogy of Ner which includes the four sons of Saul (1 Chr 8:33), but will only trace the descendants of one of those persons, while ignoring the descendants of the remaining ones. Thus, in the genealogy of Ner, although four of Saul's sons are mentioned, only the descendants of Jonathan are traced (1 Chr 8:34). Further, although Micah has four sons, only the descendants of Jehoaddah are traced (1 Chr 8:35–36). Siblings, both brother and sister, may be named on the same level in a linear genealogy, but what sets a linear genealogy apart from a segmented genealogy, is that a linear genealogy only traces the descendants of one segment, while a segmented genealogy will trace the descendants of two or more segments.

Linear genealogies may also be presented in two forms. They may be *descending*, tracing descent from parent to child, or they may be *ascending*, tracing the ancestry from child to parent. Although descending genealogies are the most common, ascending genealogies do regularly occur (1 Chr 9:4, 11).

It is also possible for the same genealogical relationships to be expressed by both an ascending and descending genealogy. First Chronicles 6:7–13 [6:22–28] presents a descending genealogy from Kohath to Abijah[72] while 1 Chr 6:18–23 [6:33–38] presents an ascending genealogy from Heman, through Joel, to Israel through Kohath. While the exact purpose of these two genealogies will be discussed later,[73] they both present slight variations on the theme of the legitimate holder of an office. Descending genealogies indicate that the last persons named are the rightful heirs and successors of the first person named, while the ascending genealogy seeks to legitimate the first person named within his position because he can make a direct genealogical connection between himself and the last person named.

Depth and Breadth

Genealogies can be defined in terms of depth and breadth. Genealogical *depth* refers to the number of generations in the past who are included within the genealogy,[74] while genealogical *breadth* refers to the number of segments which relate themselves to the primary ancestor. These terms can be illustrated as follows in Figure 1.1:

---

[72] Although the NIV of 1 Chr 6:28 includes "Joel" this is not found in the MT. Joel is included on the basis of 1 Chr 6:18 [6:33].

[73] See Chapter 4.

[74] Wilson, *Genealogy*, 21.

Figure 1.1: Genealogical Depth and Breadth

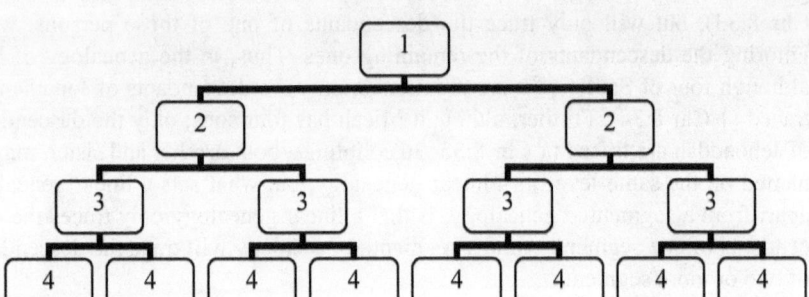

In Figure 1.1, levels one through four represent genealogical *depth*. Each person in level four can trace their ancestry back three generations to the lineage founder. Individually, levels two, three, and four, represent genealogical *breadth* as the genealogy of the primary ancestor expands through the passage of time. A linear genealogy will contain only genealogical depth, while a segmented genealogy contains both depth and breadth, as it relates differing genealogical segments to a common ancestor.

Fluidity

One of the greatest challenges that genealogies present is their ability to change their details in differing and changing circumstances. Wilson terms this change *fluidity*.[75]

One of the causes of fluidity may be the different context in which different genealogies are operating. As mentioned above, Wilson has identified that genealogies operate within the domestic, politico-jural, and religious spheres. The genealogical relationships expressed in these varying spheres relate to different functions in society, and they therefore may be expressed in different terms. In the broader genealogy of Ram, David is simply one of the many sons of Jesse (1 Chr 2:10–17), indistinguishable from any of his brothers. In the king list, all of the kings of Judah and their exilic and postexilic descendants looked to David as their primary ancestor (1 Chr 3:1–23). In the king list, David is without father, brothers, sisters or nephews, while in the genealogy of Ram, David has all of these. In the genealogy of Ram, David is the youngest and has no children, while in the king list David is the lineage founder and has many children. These two different lists, however, operate in different spheres. The genealogy of Ram operates as one segment of the larger domestic Judahite segmented genealogy, which is itself part of the still larger Israelite segmented genealogy, while the

---

[75] Wilson, *Genealogy*, 27–36.

politico king list is an amalgam of lists of David's sons, heading up a list of Davidic kings. It is the differing purposes for which the lists are used which determines the different forms and details.

Wilson notes:

> a lineage functioning in the domestic sphere may have a different structure from the same lineage functioning in the political or religious spheres. As a result, the lineage genealogy must also alter its form in order to continue to reflect the lineage structure in various contexts. This fact may cause several conflicting genealogies to exist at the same time, but each one can be considered accurate in its own context.[76]

Apart from operating within different contexts, Wilson notes three primary reasons why changes in genealogies may occur over time. First, the expressed relationship between persons may change.[77] This is evidenced in 1 Chr 8:33, where Ner is said to be the father of Kish, the father of Saul. However, in 1 Sam 14:50–51 Ner is expressly said to be Saul's uncle, while the father of Kish and Ner is Abiel. The precise reason why these genealogies are different is uncertain, but it cannot be assumed that if one is "historical" then the other must be "unhistorical." It is better to conclude that both are "historical" within the contexts in which they were created. That these genealogies are contradictory (for Ner cannot be both the father and brother of Kish), is not important for they were not created for modern historical purposes. Wilson indicates that this type of change sometimes occurs through changes in power and status within a lineage,[78] and it is therefore possible that these different genealogies reflect this type of change.[79]

The second reason the accepted genealogy is changed is when further persons or families are added to the society.[80] This may be reflected through the addition of a single name, such as is found in the LXX of Gen 10:22, 24; 11:12–13 with the addition of Καιναν, a tradition also followed in Luke 3:36. The reasons behind this change are uncertain, but it is an example of fluidity. At other times, an entire lineage may be grafted onto a genealogy. On the basis of other data,

---

[76] Wilson, *Genealogy*, 46–47.
[77] Wilson, *Genealogy*, 30.
[78] Wilson, *Genealogy*, 31.
[79] Snyman indicates "in apartheid South Africa genealogies were important in order to prove one's purity of race. In the post-apartheid period, it has become quite customary to prove the opposite, in order to indicate some kind of link to Africa so as to claim African citizenship," "Possible World," 36–37. In other words, the change in power structures brought about the necessity to change genealogies to properly reflect, and conform to, the new power structures.
[80] Wilson, *Genealogy*, 31.

rather than the genealogies of 1 Chr 1–9 themselves, it is reasonable to conclude that Jerahmeel (1 Chr 2:25–33; cf. 1 Sam 27:10; 30:29), was a non-Judahite tribe which attached itself to Judah at some point in time.[81] This being the case, the descendants of Jerahmeel were grafted into Judah, which necessitated a revision of the Judahite genealogies. This revision is an example of fluidity and is reflected in 1 Chr 1–9. If a genealogy of Judah prior to the grafting in of Jerahmeel were available for comparison, a different genealogical structure would be evident. However, once Jerahmeel was incorporated into Judah, the old genealogy no longer reflected the current domestic relationships, and so lapsed into non-use and disappeared.[82]

The final means by which genealogies express fluidity is through *telescoping*, or the loss of names from a genealogy over time.[83] Wilson indicates that when names are lost from a lineage:

> seldom are names lost from the lower levels of the genealogy, for these contain the names of living people. Similarly, the levels at the top of the genealogy contain the names of the lineage founder and his children. These names are usually firmly fixed in the mythology dealing with the origin of the lineage and thus serve as points of lineage unity.[84]

As a consequence, "names are most likely to be omitted in the middle levels of the genealogy."[85] Wilson gives seven reasons why names may be omitted:[86]
1. the lineage segment has been destroyed through war, famine, etc.
2. the lineage produced no children, and thus was not remembered.

---

[81] See the discussion in chapter 8.

[82] As noted above (note 58), and stated by Wilson, in such a case the genealogy gives some indication that the grafted lineage had not been fully assimilated into the tribe lineage group, Wilson, *Genealogy*, 32. That this does not occur in the text of 1 Chr 1–9 as we have it may reflect further changes, and thus greater assimilation of Jerahmeel, over a longer period of time, or it may reflect the actions of the Chronicler or some intermediate scribe.

[83] Wilson, *Genealogy*, 32–36. Cf. the genealogy of Adaiah in 1 Chr 9:12; Neh 11:12. The genealogy in Chronicles is shorter through the omission of three middle generations. More recent generations (those within the living memory of the current generation), and the clan's founder (Pashhur son of Malkijah) are identical. Middle generations are omitted, they are not altered, resulting in generations being "lost."

[84] Wilson, *Genealogy*, 33.

[85] Wilson, *Genealogy*, 33. This observation makes it clear that one cannot use the genealogies as a means of determining chronological time periods. As some, perhaps many, generations may have been omitted, genealogies of themselves provide no safe criteria for determining time.

[86] Wilson, *Genealogy*, 33–36.

3. the lineage split off and attached itself to a different lineage, and therefore its original lineage had no reason to retain it within their own.
4. the names were simply forgotten, perhaps because the person was unimportant.
5. the name was deliberately suppressed, perhaps because that person had brought shame to the lineage, or because the living sought to elevate their own status through connecting themselves to a greater person in the past.
6. the name no longer had a function in the lineage.
7. more than one person shared the name or title, and thus the two merged into one.

As can be observed, there are many reasons why a genealogy may change over time. What is important to recognise is that each succeeding genealogy is an accurate reflection of the domestic, political or religious relationships operative at the time the genealogy was created. As such, genealogies taken from different time periods, or from different spheres of operation within the same time period, may appear to contradict one another. This should not be taken to mean that they are in conflict, for the society that created them would not see them in conflict when utilised in their proper context.[87]

This is an important observation to keep in mind when analysing the Chronicler's genealogies in 1 Chr 1–9 or other genealogies which have their origins in the ancient Near East.

DETERMINING THE PURPOSE OF THE CHRONICLER'S GENEALOGIES

It is clear from the foregoing discussion that genealogies were not created for purely historical purposes, but were created to reflect the domestic, political and religious relationships which existed within a society. This, however, presents another question: what relationships are the Chronicler's genealogies presenting?

In some respects the Chronicler's genealogies present the overall domestic relations of Israel. First Chronicles 2–8 gives an extended segmented genealogy of Israel and his sons and therefore express the domestic relationships which existed in the history of Israel.

This observation, however, is neither complete, nor fully satisfactory. Although 1 Chr 2–8 is a large segmented genealogy, the majority of the

---

[87] "Although it is true that different groups may produce tendentious genealogies at the same time in order to establish their own pre-eminence, once the society determines the 'accurate' genealogy, it becomes the accepted reflection of society, and the others are forgotten," Wilson, *Genealogy*, 29–30.

individual lineages do not give the appearance of genealogies created within the domestic sphere. Some are political (1 Chr 3), others are religious (1 Chr 6), while still others are military lists (1 Chr 5; 7:1–5, 6–10, 30–40).

Neither do these genealogies appear to express relationships at any one time period, but contain data from a number of periods. There are references to the periods of Hezekiah (1 Chr 4:41), Saul (1 Chr 5:10), Jotham and Jeroboam (1 Chr 5:17). They refer to the exile of the Transjordanian tribes (1 Chr 5:26), as well as the exile of Judah a century and a half later (1 Chr 5:41 [6:15]). There are also references to exilic and postexilic people (1 Chr 3:17–24) and society (1 Chr 9).

This diversity makes it apparent that the Chronicler's genealogies would never have operated as a united genealogy within the societies of Israel, Judah, or Yehud, for they do not express the relationships within the society at any one point. If, however, the Chronicler's genealogies are not the reflection of a society's relationships at a particular point in time, and are not the result of haphazard growth as suggested by Noth, this only leaves the conclusion that the Chronicler's genealogies are a literary construction of the Chronicler himself.[88] If this conclusion is accepted, then this indicates that the current content, arrangement, and structure are the result of the deliberate plan and purpose of the Chronicler, as he shaped the overall work.

Furthermore, if the genealogies are a literary construct, then their meaning and purpose are not to be found in the individual genealogies but in the overall literary structure of the genealogical section. The individual genealogies then become building blocks, by which the overall structure and meaning are created by the Chronicler, but the meaning is not to be found in the individual blocks read and analysed in isolation from one another, but in the total structure created by the combination of all the genealogies.

It is not necessary for our purposes here to speculate about the sources of the Chronicler's material. It is clear that he gleaned some material from works which were later incorporated into the Hebrew Bible. He may have found some of his material in official archives or from traditional accounts maintained by families or groups. Indeed, he could have created some of the genealogies without consulting a reliable source. What is important for understanding the Chronicler's purposes is not the origins of his genealogical material, but what he does with it. The overall structure rather than the origins of the individual components is the vital factor.

---

[88] Unless, that is, one wants to assume that the Chronicler found the genealogies as they are here recorded in an otherwise unknown source and incorporated them into his work. The end result is, however, the same. The genealogies are a literary construct, created for a particular purpose by an author.

Therefore, because the Chronicler's genealogies should be viewed as a literary construct they must also be investigated in literary terms and searched for literary clues as to their structure and their meaning.

THE STRUCTURE OF THE GENEALOGICAL SECTION

It has long been recognised that *Chiasmus* (named from the Greek letter X because of the typical crossover pattern that it exhibits) was a common phenomena not only in the literature of the Hebrew Bible, but also in literature throughout the ancient Near East.[89]

John Welch describes chiasmus as, "a two-part structure or system in which the second half is a mirror image of the first, i.e. where the first term recurs last, and the last first."[90]

A chiasm can be as simple as one sentence, or can exist in a larger, more complex literary structure covering many chapters within the Hebrew Bible.[91] One short example is Gen 1:27:

    A   so God created humanity
      B   in his own image
      B^1 in the image of God
    A^1 he created them

---

[89] See the various essays in: John W. Welch, ed., *Chiasmus in Antiquity* (Heldesheim: Gerstenberg Verlag, 1981).

[90] John W. Welch, "Introduction" in *Chiasmus in Antiquity* (ed. John W. Welch; Hildesheim: Gerstenberg Verlag, 1981), 10. Boda has recently presented a strong word of caution about the need for strict criteria in determining the presence of a chiasm. He identifies four areas where errors in identification are prone to happen: (1) errors in symmetry (2) errors in subjectivity (3) errors in probability (4) errors in purpose. M. J. Boda, "Chiasmus in Ubiquity: Symmetrical Mirages in Nehemiah 9," *JSOT* 71 (1996): 55–70.

[91] See, for example, the discussion of the flood narrative in Gen 6–9 in Gordon J. Wenham, *Genesis 1–15* (WBC 1; Dallas: Word, 1987), 155–158, 167–169. Williamson, however, in a personal letter, indicates that "by definition, a chiasm can only have four elements . . . however this misuse [of the term] has become widespread in biblical studies." It is also when discussing larger chiastic structures that issues of terminology come to the fore. Graham makes a distinction between a "chiasm" and a "concentric structure." He suggests that "in chiasmus there is an equal pairing of elements" (ABCCBA), while in a "concentric structure there is a central element that separates the paired elements" (ABCBA). M. Patrick Graham, "Aspects of the Structure and Rhetoric of 2 Chronicles 25," in *History and Interpretation: Essays in Honour of John H. Hayes* (ed. M. Patrick Graham, et al.*Journal for the Study of the Old Testament Supplement 173*; Sheffield: Sheffield Academic Press, 1993), 81, Note 9.

In light of Welch's definition there are two important things to note. First, there is a "two-part structure": the first half reading, "so God created humanity in his own image," and the second, "in the image of God he created them." Second, the second half of the structure repeats the essential idea of the first half in reverse order.[92] Welch indicates that this repetition can be "complementary as well as antithetical," that is, it can either repeat the corresponding idea, using either the same or similar words, or it can repeat by means of contrasting words.[93]

Welch further states that chiasmus depends upon three items being present: "balance, inversion, and intensification."[94]

BALANCE

This refers to two separate, yet related, items. First, a chiastic structure is in balance when the two halves contain the same, or nearly the same, number of elements. Thus a structure is not in balance when the first half contains six elements or levels and the second half only three. Second, a chiastic structure is in balance when the two halves, and perhaps even the various elements within those halves, are generally similar in the quantity of their content. In the example from Gen 1:27 it can be seen that both halves contain the same number of elements and that the overall size of each half is about the same.

INVERSION

Inversion refers to the appearance of the same or related terms in the two halves, however in reverse order. This is more clearly observed in the Hebrew text of Gen 1:27:

A וַיִּבְרָא אֱלֹהִים אֶת־הָאָדָם
B בְּצַלְמוֹ
B¹ בְּצֶלֶם אֱלֹהִים
A¹ בָּרָא אֹתוֹ

Elements A // A¹ both contain the verb ברא (created) while the noun הָאָדָם (humanity) is represented by the pronoun אתו. Both elements B and B¹ contain the noun צֶלֶם (image) and the possessive ו in בְּצַלְמוֹ in element "B" is represented by

---

[92] Watson, however, points out that there is not always a strict reversal or complete repetition of content. See his full discussion and explanation in Wilfred G. E. Watson, "Chiastic Patterns in Biblical Hebrew Poetry," in *Chiasmus in Antiquity* (ed. John W. Welch; Hildesheim: Gerstenberg Verlag, 1981), especially 123–136.

[93] Welch, "Introduction," 9.

[94] Welch, "Introduction," 10.

the noun אֱלֹהִים (God) in element B¹. It can be observed as well, in keeping with the previous point, that the structure remains "balanced" in that no element is grossly disproportional in size to its corresponding element.

INTENSIFICATION

The inverted structure, and the verbal and thought repetition that it presents, constitutes what Welch called "intensification." This occurs through "building to a climax at the center, as well as by strengthening each element individually upon its chiastic repetition."[95] This indicates that words and ideas are not stated once but are repeated in such a way that the fundamental ideas that the author seeks to relate are reemphasised for the sake of his readers/hearers. In elements A // A¹ these ideas are "God, created, humanity/them," while in elements B // B¹ the emphasis falls on "his image // image of God." Further, through the process of inversion, the pivot point, which is the central point at which the repetition begins (in the example of Gen 1:27 this is element B // B¹) the reader/hearer is able to discern that central idea which the author seeks to relate. In our example, this is "his image // the image of God."

CHIASM AS AN AID TO UNDERSTANDING

The presence of a chiastic structure is not to be considered as simply a literary device. It is also to be recognised as a memory aid in relation to what has been said, as well as enabling individuals to recognise what is most significant in an account, without being directly told, "this is important." This is true not only in literate societies, but especially in preliterate or semiliterate societies where the ability to read and write is possessed by only a select few, and these normally in the service of the politically or religiously powerful.

As the majority of persons in ancient societies would be hearers of texts, rather than readers of texts, aids to memory, such as intensification, as well as aids to recognition of what is significant, such as inversion, would be powerful tools in the hands of writers and storytellers in their attempts to relate and emphasise information to and for their hearers.[96]

---

[95] Welch, "Introduction," 10.

[96] Some important examples of texts being read to groups of hearers are: Exod 24; Josh 8:34–35; 2 Kgs 22:10; Neh 8; Jer 36. Even though modern readers possess a written text, the Hebrew Bible itself acknowledges the reality that the majority of the people in ancient Israelite society, possibly including the kings themselves, would not be capable of reading these texts, but would require others to read the texts to them.

As Welch states:

> An emphatic focus on the center can be employed by a skillful composer to elevate the importance of a central concept . . . Meanwhile, the remainder of the system can be used with equal effectiveness as a framework through which the author may compare, contrast, juxtapose, complement, or complete each of the flanking elements in the chiastic system.[97]

As such, not only is the centre vital for emphasizing what is central to the author's purposes, but each supporting flanking element helps to support that essential thesis, while at the same time further explaining, clarifying and strengthening the ideas presented by the chiastic element which appears on the same level. Each step enables not only readers, but especially hearers, to better understand the central and supporting arguments of the author. As Chapell says, "listeners do not have the opportunity to back up and reread what you just said."[98] Chiastic structuring, however, enables hearers to rehear a main point, for it is repeated by the speaker. Chapell goes on to say:

> The repetition of key terms in a consistent order is an audio cue that another major idea is being presented. Hundreds of sentences and sentence fragments whistle past listeners' ears during a sermon, so, when congregants hear something that orients their thought to earlier expressions, they have the landmarks they need to keep navigating the message.[99]

In his study of *Chiasmus in Hebrew Biblical Narrative*, Yehuda T. Radday makes three suggestions regarding the presence of chiasm in the Hebrew Bible:

> Many narrative sections of Scripture are chiastically built . . . Biblical authors and/or editors placed the main idea, the thesis, or the turning point of each literary unit, at its centre . . . The beauty and completeness of the chiastic construction bears a direct correlation to age: the older [the biblical narrative is] the more chiastic.[100]

In relation to the second point, Radday states:

---

[97] Welch, "Introduction," 10.

[98] Bryan Chapell, *Christ-Centered Preaching: Redeeming the Expository Sermon* (Grand Rapids: Baker Books, 1994), 133.

[99] Chapell, *Christ-Centered Preaching*, 134.

[100] Yehuda T. Radday, "Chiasmus in Hebrew Biblical Narrative," in *Chiasmus in Antiquity* (ed. John W. Welch; Hildesheim: Gerstenberg Verlag, 1981), 51. See, however, Boda's fourth concern, "errors in purpose," where he questions the presupposition that the centre of a chiasm is its most important point, without however, expanding upon this concern, "Chiasmus," 58, 67.

the books of the Bible are silent as to the express purposes for which they were written. . . If the importance of the central passage is properly recognised, however, all we have to do in order to find the answer to this question is open the book to its middle and read.[101]

As a result of his studies Radday concludes that 1 and 2 Chronicles, "are not chiastic and thus it appears that when they were written, chiasm was no longer *en vogue*."[102]

Two things may be said in response to this conclusion. First, after the publication of Radday's essay, several works were published which showed the presence of chiasmus within the narrative of Chronicles, the possession of which may have forced Radday to reassess his conclusions.[103] Further examples have more recently been observed. This indicates that Radday's initial conclusion regarding the absence of chiasm in Chronicles is incorrect.

Second, Radday exhibits a clear bias against the literary nature of genealogies in general when he states, "very few will dispute that the Hebrew Bible, *except for several undistinguished* parts *such as genealogies*, is literature of the highest rank."[104]

It is therefore probable that Radday's otherwise valuable search for chiastic phenomena in the Hebrew Bible did not adequately take into account the genealogical section of 1 Chr 1–9. It is also probable that this bias against the literary nature of genealogies caused him to overlook the earlier observations of Curtis.[105]

---

[101] Radday, "Chiasmus," 51.

[102] Radday, "Chiasmus," 52. This conclusion does, however, appear to be contradicted by his observation that while Chronicles (which he proposes was written around 400 B.C.E.) contains no chiasm, Daniel (which he dates to around 160 B.C.E.) does contain elements of chiasm. Radday, "Chiasmus," 53. Watson rejects the possibility that the presence or absence of chiasmus can be used to date a work because "many 'late' books preserve archaic material or deliberately use archaism. Also, much of the OT has undergone at least one editorial re-working," "Chiastic Patterns," 118.

[103] H. G. M. Williamson, "Sources and Redaction in the Chronicler's Genealogy of Judah," in *Studies in Persian Period History and Historiography* FAT 38; Tübingen: Mohr Siebeck, 2004); Raymond B. Dillard, "The Chronicler's Solomon," *WTJ* 43 (1981): 289–300; Andrew E. Hill, "Patchwork Poetry or Reasoned Verse? Connective Structure in 1 Chronicles XVI," *VT* 33 (1983): 97–100; Mark A. Throntveit, *When Kings Speak: Royal Speech and Royal Prayer in Chronicles* (SBLDS 93; Atlanta: Scholars Press, 1987), 118; Isaac Kalimi, *The Reshaping of Ancient Israelite History in Chronicles* (Winona Lake: Eisenbrauns, 2005), 215–231.

[104] Italics mine. Radday, "Chiasmus," 50.

[105] Edward L. Curtis and Albert A. Madsen, *A Critical and Exegetical Commentary on the Books of Chronicles* (ICC; Edinburgh: T&T Clark, 1910), 82. In his observations of the genealogies of Judah, Curtis states that the Chronicler: "first he gives his primary

Welch indicates that, "the task of understanding the meaning of a writing is never complete until its formular aspects as well as its thought contents have been grasped."[106]

It is the author's proposal here that 1 Chr 1–9 is a deliberately constructed chiasm which through the placing of "the main idea, the thesis, or the turning point . . . at its center," reveals the "key to meaning" of both the chiastically structured genealogical section as well as to the Chronicler's work as a whole.[107] It is only through the recognition of the chiastic structure and the deliberate interpretation of the genealogical section as a chiastic structure, that the purpose and function of the genealogical section can be appreciated within the context of the Chronicler's entire work.

While some scholars have rejected the notion of a chiastic structure in the genealogies, suggesting instead that they show a "progressive development" from the beginning until the end,[108] others have been open to the presence of a chiasmus either in the entire genealogical structure[109] or in individual components of the genealogies.[110] However, as far as I have been able to ascertain, no author has yet understood the interpretive implications of this recognition of the structuring of the genealogical section as a chiasm.[111] It is this task which is here attempted.

---

genealogical material . . . then appends supplementary matter . . . concerning each in reverse order."

[106] Welch, "Introduction," 11–12.

[107] Radday, "Chiasmus," 51.

[108] Simon J. De Vries, *1 and 2 Chronicles* (FOTL 11; Grand Rapids: Eerdmans, 1989), 22. Manfred Oeming, *Das wahre Israel: die "genealogische Vorhalle" 1 Chronik 1–9* (BWA(N)T 128; Stuttgart: Kohlhammer, 1990), 210, suggests that this progression is "World, Israel, Jerusalem, Temple."

[109] Williamson, *Chronicles*, 38. Williamson, however, speaks broadly of only three sections: the people of the world to the time of Israel; the descendants of Israel; and the Judeans of the present day (so also Pratt, *Chronicles*, 63). Knoppers' work on the genealogies was published after the present author had observed the chiastic structure of 1 Chr 1–9. Knoppers' structure is slightly different, and he fails to account for the sons of Israel (1 Chr 2:1–2) or for the captivity of Judah (1 Chr 9:1), *1 Chronicles 1–9*, 261.

[110] Williamson, "Sources," 113–114.

[111] Johnstone, to whom I am indebted for drawing my attention to the centrality of the Levites and the significance of the priestly function as indicated in the genealogies, does not acknowledge the presence of a chiasm. In Johnstone's scheme, Judah (with Simeon attached!) and Benjamin form the outer layers of Israel, not because their inclusion complements and expands upon one another, but only because they survived until the fall of the southern kingdom and make up the majority of the postexilic community. These two major tribes enclose "the more vulnerable elements" to secure their continued existence, in theory if not in practice, within Israel. He does highlight, however, "the centrality of Levi.

THE CHIASTIC STRUCTURE OF 1 CHRONICLES 1–9

The chiastic structure of 1 Chr 1–9 is shown in Figure 1.2.

Figure 1.2: The Chiastic Structure of 1 Chronicles 1–9

A   1 Chr 1:1–53: The world before Israel
  B   1 Chr 2:1–2: The sons of Israel
    C   1 Chr 2:3 – 4:23: Judah – the tribe of King David
      D   1 Chr 4:24 – 5:26: Tribes of Israel in victory and defeat
        E   1 Chr 6:1–47: The descendants of Levi
          F   1 Chr 6:48–49: The cultic personnel in their duties
          F^1 1 Chr 6:50–53: The cultic leaders
        E^1 1 Chr 6:54–81: The descendants of Levi in their land
      D^1 1 Chr 7:1–40: Tribes of Israel in defeat and restoration
    C^1 1 Chr 8:1–40: Benjamin – the tribe of King Saul
  B^1 1 Chr 9:1a: "All Israel" counted
A^1 1 Chr 9:1b–34: Israel re-established[112]

Even within the individual levels of this structure, evidence of chiastic structuring can be observed. Although not naming it as such, Curtis noted the chiastic structuring of 1 Chr 2:3–4:23.[113] The same will be observed in the discussion of 1 Chr 7:1–40. Chiasm is also to be observed in 1 Chr 5:1–3a.[114]

The first question to be addressed is whether this structure meets the criteria set by Welch, that a chiasm must exhibit balance, inversion, and intensification.

BALANCE

The proposed structure of 1 Chr 1–9 is made up of two halves of six levels each, with the sixth level (level F // F^1) operating as the pivot point for the entire structure. Each level in the first half has its corresponding level in the second

---

The role of the Levites is, in the Chronicler's view, quite literally, central to Israel's life." William Johnstone, *Chronicles and Exodus: An Analogy and Its Application* (JSOTSup 275; Sheffield: Sheffield Academic Press, 1998), 108.

[112] It will be noticed that 1 Chr 9:35–44 is not included within the chiastic structure of the genealogical section. This section, which is a near repetition of 1 Chr 8:29–38, properly introduces the death of Saul contained in 1 Chr 10.

[113] Curtis and Madsen, *Chronicles*, 82; see also Williamson, "Sources," 113–114.

[114] Kalimi, *Reshaping*, 228. It is to be noted that, although the Chronicler shaped the overall genealogica structure chiastically, and it is suggested that he shaped some of the individual levels chiastically, he did not shape all of the levels thus. Why this is so is uncertain. It is possible that his available source material or theme at a particular point did not lend itself to such shaping.

half. Furthermore, each of the levels, with one exception, is of approximately the same length as its corresponding level.[115]

The exception is levels C // C^1, which relate the tribal details of Judah and Benjamin from whom the royal lines of David and Saul arose. These are clearly not balanced, since the Hebrew text of 1 Chr 2:3 – 4:23 contains approximately 1013 words while 1 Chr 8:1–40 have about 306 words.

It is tempting to speculate that the list of Judah's descendants had been corrupted through a series of textual additions. It is to be noted that the text of 1 Chr 2:3–17, which recounts the immediate descendants of Judah down to David and his family (134 words), and the list contained in 1 Chr 3, which relates David's descendants (199 words), combine for a total of 333 words, about the length of the Benjaminite genealogy in 1 Chr 8 (306 words).

The Judahite lists will be investigated in greater detail later, and therefore final judgement on this issue will be reserved until that time. At this point it may be safest to recognise that the Judahite genealogies themselves contain several chiastic structures which would preclude relegating much of the material to the status of "additions and textual corruptions." Williamson has observed a chiastic structure within the Judahite genealogies as a whole as well as within lists in 1 Chr 2–4.[116] It is also to be noted that the list of the sons of David in 1 Chr 3:1–8 has been deliberately amended from the corresponding lists in 2 Sam 3:2–5 and 5:13–16, in order to place Solomon as the central figure.

Therefore, while recognizing that the corresponding levels of the Judahite and Benjaminite genealogies are not exactly balanced, the overall structure of 1 Chr 1–9 meets Welch's first criterium of balance.

INVERSION

The chiastic nature of 1 Chr 1–9 is also evident through the inversion that it contains. The ideas and themes that are put forward within the first half are repeated, in reverse order, in the second half. While some of these repeated ideas are very clear – as in B // B^1 "all Israel," or C // C^1 which discusses the two families from which monarchy arose – others are less clear, such as A // A^1 which contains lists of the pre-Israelite and post-monarchic peoples. If, however, the

---

[115] It is the lack of "balance" which argues against Tuell's suggestion of the genealogies as a chiasm centred upon Judah in general and David in particular. Although not impossible, the imbalance presented by the different chiastic levels of 1 Chr 1:1–2:2 (as compared to 1 Chr 5:1–9:44) makes it highly improbable. Tuell, *Chronicles*, 17–18. It is to be noted that in his introduction Tuell includes Simeon (1 Chr 4:24–43) within the chiastic level of the tribe of Judah, while later (page 29–31) Simeon is placed with the other tribes. In either case, Tuell's structure is clearly unbalanced.

[116] Williamson, "Sources." However, see the discussion of his proposal in Kartveit, *Motive*, 36–40.

chiastic nature of the text is recognised, then the criterium of "intensification" can be utilised to investigate the relationship that exists between these texts.[117]

INTENSIFICATION

While each of the individual levels in the structure of 1 Chr 1–9 corresponds in theme and idea to its opposite on the same level, it is not the mere repetition of data which is important, but the observation that the data on the corresponding level in the second half advances, adds to or contrasts with the data in the first half.

Thus, while level D – "tribes of Israel in victory and defeat" – relates several battle accounts in the history of certain tribes, sometimes ending in victory while at other times in defeat and exile, level D^1 reports tribes of Israel in defeat and restoration. Yet, as will be discussed later, level D^1 is itself a chiastic structure focussing not on the armies alone, but on the armies which flank a discussion of a defeat in battle and the raising up of a new leader, Joshua, who knew only ultimate victory. Consequently, while level D relates victory and defeat, level D^1 suggests ultimate victory for tribes of Israel.

At other times the chiastic structure brings together two different aspects of one theme, such as the descendants of Levi and their lands in levels E // E^1.

This brief discussion confirms that the structur of 1 Chr 1–9 meets the three criteria established by Welch for the identification of a text as a chiasmus. In the remainder of this work, the implications of this observation will be examined to determine the purpose of the Chronicler's genealogies.

THE CENTRAL THEME OF 1 CHRONICLES 1–9

It will be noticed that while Knoppers proposes treating Levi as a single unit, I suggest the separation of the cultic officials and the cultic land from 1 Chr 6:33–38 [6:48–53].[118] These two elements of cultic personal and cultic lands, however, clearly complement one another, a complement also indicated within the narrative. By separating these and placing them on a different and supporting level, it becomes clear that the proper cultic duties (level F), performed by the proper cultic officials (level F^1), is the central theme of the genealogies. This further enables one to see that it is the cult in particular, rather than just the tribe of Levi, that is the theme around which all else in the genealogies is organised.

The significance of this observation of the overall structure and the central theme of the genealogies cannot be overestimated.

---

[117] The relationship between A // A^1 is discussed in chapters 11 and 12.
[118] Knoppers, *1 Chronicles 1–9*, 261.

If the genealogies are presented in a chiasmus, then it seems less likely they are primarily the result of a process of textual additions and emendations. As a result, Noth's statement regarding the disorder of the genealogies should be rejected.[119]

It is observed first of all that the structure proposed is neither "disorder" nor "confusion." They are instead a carefully constructed and balanced text which builds to its climax with additional supporting data, expressing ideas significant to the author. The negative assessment of the structure of the text as expressed by Noth and others has arisen not through any fault in the text, but through the failure of modern readers, to fully appreciate and recognise the structure.

Second, while Noth may be correct in his assumption that textual additions and rearrangement only bring "great disorder and confusion,"[120] having established that the text is both ordered and structured, the possibility of later major additions and rearrangements can be disallowed.

This observation of a chiastic structuring in the genealogies is also significant, because it identifies the central theme for the Chronicler. Radday observed that, rarely are readers informed by the authors of the biblical books about their precise purpose in writing.[121] The recognition of this chiastic structure enables the identification of that primary theme. In the following chapters this will be examined more closely, but it is here noted that this theme pivots around the cultic personnel in their duties (level F) and the descendants of Aaron as the ultimate leaders in the cultic community (level F^1). Although it is clear that the Chronicler addresses many themes and ideas not only in the genealogies but the work as a whole,[122] what this structure indicates is of the greatest significance to the Chronicler in his work is: the authorised cultic personnel performing the authorised cultic functions in the authorised cultic place. It is my contention that for the Chronicler all else is secondary to, and supportive of, this overarching theme.

---

[119] Noth, *Chronicler's History*, 36.
[120] Noth, *Chronicler's History*, 36.
[121] Radday, "Chiasmus." 51.
[122] See especially Sara Japhet, *The Ideology of the Book of Chronicles and Its Place in Biblical Thought* (BEATAJ 9; Frankfurt am Main: Verlag Peter Lang, 1997).

Procedure

In the chapters which follow, these two hypotheses will be put to the test to determine if the proposed chiastic structure is justified and if the primary focus of the genealogies is the centrality of the cultic place and personnel. To accomplish this, each level of the proposed structure will be investigated individually to determine its nature and function as a smaller component within the larger chiastic structure. Components sharing the same chiastic level will be compared to discover whether the phenomenon of intensification is present. Furthermore, each section will be investigated to determine what it adds to the overall meaning of the genealogy and to its central purpose.

Since it is being proposed that the central concern of the Chronicler's genealogies is the cultic officials and the cultic place, these central levels will be investigated first to better understand why the cult should be singled out as the focus of the genealogies. This will be followed by investigations of each succeeding level, so that the order followed will be in reverse alphabetic sequence from levels $F // F^1$ to levels $A // A^1$.

As the form and content of each individual level is different, each level will not be treated identically but will be investigated according to its content and the issues which that content raises.

Finally, a summary of the overall findings will be collated to confirm that the hypotheses advanced by this thesis have been proven, and then conclusions regarding the purpose of the genealogies within the context of postexilic Yehud will be put forward.

CHAPTER 2
F: 1 CHRONICLES 6:48–49
THE CULTIC PERSONNEL IN THEIR DUTIES

INTRODUCTION

As was indicated in the previous chapter, the central section of the Chronicler's genealogies pivot around the identification of the cultic functions and the cultic personnel. This indicates what was of greatest importance to the Chronicler in the presentation of his material and sets the primary theme for the genealogies and, as will be shown, for the Chronicler's work as a whole.

In chapters 2–3 we will investigate the content of this central section, 1 Chr 6:33–38 [6:48–53]. This will require us to set the limits of the section and so decide whether these verses belong together in the Chronicler's discussion. This will be followed by discussion of the Chronicler's view of the contrasting roles of the Levites and the sons of Aaron within the cult. The role of Moses as the giver of the cultic laws will be examined, followed by a comparison of the person and roles of Moses and the Chronicler's other great cultic innovator, David.

THE LIMITS OF THE SECTION

The first task is to establish the boundaries of this section. As proposed, this central level is made up of two distinct parts:[1]

1 Chr 6:33–34 [48–49]: The cultic personnel in their duties.
1 Chr 6:35–38 [50–53]: The cultic leaders.

There is some question as to whether this section begins with 1 Chr 6:33 or 6:34 [6:48 or 6:49]. Although BHS places a paragraph division between 1 Chr 6:32 and 6:33 [6:47 and 6:48], this is not followed by all translations or commentators.[2]

---

[1] Pratt also observes this two-fold division, but he overlooks the presence of the Levites in 1 Chr 6:33 [6:48] and suggests that this records only "Priestly Responsibilities." *Chronicles*, 69.

[2] English translations which place a paragraph division between 1 Chr 6:32 and 6:33 [6:47 and 6:48] are: NIV, NCV, NWT, JB, NAB; so also Curtis, Rothstein & Hänel,

The primary observation which links 1 Chr 6:33 [6:48] directly to what precedes is that 1 Chr 6:33 [6:48] follows a discussion of the musicians, their genealogy and duties (6:16–32 [6:31–47]), and begins by mentioning "their brothers the Levites." This phrase appears to link what is being said in 6:33 [6:48] to the previous discussion by indicating that while some of the sons of Levi (as indicated in 6:16–32 [6:31–47]), were made responsible for the musical functions of the tabernacle and then the temple, the Levites not so assigned performed the "duties of the Tabernacle."[3] Thus the NIV reads, "their fellow Levites were assigned to the *other* duties" (italics mine), indicating that these Levites performed the duties that the musicians did not.[4] This would be consistent with the distinction of duties found in various recordings of "priests, Levites, singers, gatekeepers" and would distinguish between the activity of the "Levites" (1 Chr 6:1–15 [6:16–30]) and that of the singers (1 Chr 6:16–32 [6:31–47]).[5]

It should also be noted that reading 1 Chr 6:33 [6:48] with what precedes it leaves the sons of Aaron and their duties alone as the central theme and focus of the genealogies and forces the Levites into a totally subordinate and supportive role. Alternatively, reading 1 Chr 6:33 [6:48] with 1 Chr 6:34 [6:49] provides a contrast between the duties of the Levites on the one hand and the duties of the

---

Rudolph, Myers, Williamson, Ackroyd, Japhet, De Vries, Braun, Allen, Johnstone, Hill, Thompson, and Pratt (it must be noted that Hill and Thompson's commentaries are based upon the NIV text), while those who place the paragraph division after 1 Chr 6:33 [6:48] are: AV, RSV, Goodspeed, NASB, NKJV, NEB, GNB, NRSV, JPS, and also in the works of Selman, Tuell, Oeming, Knoppers.

[3] Rothstein recognizes the difficulty of this verse and its relation to what precedes. He states that although "Im gegenwärtigen Zusammenhang scheint sich ואחיהם auf die zunächst vorhergenannten Personen zu beziehen," the presence of "Levites" causes a problem. He says, "was soll dann die Beifügung von הלויים bedeuten, da ja die vorhergennannten Sänger doch auch als Leviten angesehen werden." He suggests that this problem can be resolved by seeing 1 Chr 6:16–32 [6:31–47] as a later insertion, with the *ursprünglich* which the Chronicler used having 1 Chr 6:33 [6:48] following on directly from 1 Chr 6:15 [6:30]. J. Wilhelm Rothstein and D. Johannes Hänel, *Das erste Buch der Chronik übersetzt und erklärt* (Leipzig: Deichertsche Verlagsbuchhandlung, 1927), 120. Rothstein's suggestion, however, would not resolve the difficulty, since 1 Chr 6:16–30 [6:1–15] is itself a genealogical list of the descendants of Levi, which would make the presence of ואחיהם in 1 Chr 6:33 [6:48] unnecessary, for all of Levi would already be brothers/relatives. Rudolph rejects Rothstein's view, saying, "hinter 1–15 hatte der Chr. gar keinen Grund, vom Dienst der Leviten zu reden," *Chronikbücher*, 60 note 1.

[4] So also Roddy L. Braun, *1 Chronicles* (WBC 14; Waco: Word, 1986), 95; Jacob M. Myers, *I Chronicles* (AB 12; Garden City: Doubleday, 1965), 47. It must be observed that although the NIV reads "other," it attaches 1 Chr 6:33 [6:48] to the verse that follows rather than to the verses that precede. "Other," however, is not found in the text, so NRSV.

[5] See further the discussion of these lists of cultic duties in Chapter 4.

priests on the other.⁶ This contrast, however, is not simply between the functions that each group performs but extends to the terminology that is used to describe the two groups and their duties.

First, although the phrase אֲחִיךָ/אֲחֵיהֶם (their/your brothers) is used throughout the genealogies to describe persons within a clan or group, and thus to join "brothers" to a group that has recently been discussed,⁷ this is not the only way it is so used. These terms are also used three times in Numbers 8:26; 18:2, 6, and in 2 Chr 29:34 to distinguish the priests from the Levites. However, in these instances this was not simply a differentiation of persons or groups, but also one of function. In Num 18:2 the Levites were said to שׁרת (assist) the priests In Num 18:6 the function of the Levites is to עֲבֹדָה (serve). The same word is used in 1 Chr 6:33 [6:48] to describe the function of the Levites, a function which is contrasted to that of the priests in the recitation of priestly duties in 1 Chr 6:34 [6:49].

Second, the Levites are נְתוּנִים (assigned), to their duties.⁸ This reflects the terminology used in other texts where the Levites are shown to be subordinate to the priests.⁹ In Num 3:9; 8:19 and 18:6 the Levites are "given" to Aaron, while in Num 8:16 they are "given" to Yahweh.¹⁰ Although given to Yahweh, Yahweh then gives the Levites as a "gift" to the priests (Num 18:6), while the priesthood itself is a "gift" for the sons of Aaron (Num 18:7). This distinction in the book of Numbers indicates that the priests not only have a higher status but that the Levites are, in some sense, their servants or slaves. The term is further related to the הַנְּתִינִים (temple servants), a lower ranked group of those who performed temple duties.¹¹

---

⁶ A similar pattern is observed in 1 Chr 23, where, in a clan list of the Levites, the duties of the sons of Aaron (1 Chr 23:13) are included alongside the duties of the "Levites" (1 Chr 23:28–31), and the Levites are contrasted to the sons of Aaron by being called, אֲחֵיהֶם, "their brothers."

⁷ 1 Chronicles 5:7, 13; 6:24, 29 [6:39, 44]; 7:5, 35; 9:6, 9, 13, 25.

⁸ Using the Qal passive participle of נתן.

⁹ "The more menial status of these Levites is indicated by the participle 'appointed' . . . with the overtone 'as assistants'," William Johnstone, *1 and 2 Chronicles Volume 1: 1 Chronicles 1–2 Chronicles 9: Israel's Place Among the Nations* (JSOTSup 253; Sheffield: Sheffield Academic Press, 1997), 92. The subordination of Levites to priests in Chronicles is, however, challenged by Knoppers in, Gary N. Knoppers, "Hierodules, Priests, or Janitors? The Levites in Chronicles and the History of the Israelite Priesthood," *JBL* 118 (1999): 49–72.

¹⁰ In each instance the Qal passive participle of נתן is used.

¹¹ "There could also be some allusion to the low order of Temple servants known as Nethinim . . . Their tasks were probably among the most menial . . . the author here *[Num 3:9]* and in Num 18:6 may be thinking of the Levites as Nethinim to Aaron," Philip J.

Third, the term used to describe the work of the Levites is עֲבֹדָה (service). This term is often used in connection with the Levites to denote their actions in relation to the tabernacle/tent of meeting,[12] actions which are under the directions of the priests (Num 7:8). In these instances, while the Levites do the work, the priests are responsible and have overall charge of the precincts (Num 3:32, 38; 4:28, 33).

It is recognised that at times עֲבֹדָה occurs in respect to the duties of the priests, while on other occasions it is used with respect to the combined duties of Levites and priests.[13] In his study of 1 Chr 23:28–32, Knoppers points out that although the Chronicler utilises the terminology of his older sources, he does not necessarily use the terms in an identical manner.[14] While this use of עֲבֹדָה in reference to the priests may be a case in point, it is significant that here, in what is proposed as part of the central passage in Chronicles, the term עֲבֹדָה is used only of the Levites in a clear echo of the terminology of Numbers, a work which contains a distinct demarcation between the duties and status of priests and Levites.

Fourth, the term used for מִשְׁכָּן (tabernacle) is often used in the book of Numbers in connection with the Levites to refer to either their responsibilities for the care of the tabernacle or their duties within the tabernacle.[15] These same sources also stated that the priests have overall control of the tabernacle as well as

---

Budd, *Numbers* (WBC 4; Waco: Word, 1984), 34. Wellhausen suggested that the Levites were turned into Nethinim to the priests, *Prolegomena*, 148. Johnstone, however, disputes this, Johnstone, *Chronicles: Volume 1*, 92. This term only occurs in postexilic literature and indicates a group other than "Levites, singers, gatekeepers" in Ezra 2:70 // Neh 7:72 [7:73]. See further, Baruch A. Levine, "The Netinim," *JBL* 82 (1963): 207–212; Joel Weinberg, *The Citizen-Temple Community* (JSOTSup 151; trans. David L. Smith-Christopher; Sheffield: Sheffield Academic Press, 1992), 75–91.

[12] Numbers 7:5; 8:11, 19, 22, 24, 26; 18:6, 21, 23, cf. 1 Chr 23:24, 28, 32; 25:6; Neh 10:33 [10:32]. Individually it is used to refer to the Gershonites (Num 4:28), and the Merarites (Num 4:33). In Num 3:7, 8 the phrase used is לַעֲבֹד אֶת־עֲבֹדַת הַמִּשְׁכָּן, while in 1 Chr 6:33 [6:48] it is עֲבוֹדַת מִשְׁכָּן. The similar outlook of Numbers and Chronicles at this point is clear. Haran states that עֲבֹדָה is a technical term in P, meaning the "dismantling and reassembling of the tabernacle at the camping sites," Menahem Haran, *Temples and Temple-Service in Ancient Israel: An Inquiry into Biblical Cult Phenomena and the Historical Setting of the Priestly School* (Winona Lake: Eisenbrauns, 1985), 61.

[13] For priests alone see 1 Chr 9:13; 2 Chr 8:14; 35:2; for instances where it is used of priests and Levites together see 1 Chr 28:13, 21; 2 Chr 31:2; 35:10.

[14] Knoppers, "Hierodules," 55–58. Knoppers suggests that the Chronicler, instead of pursuing a pro-Levitical or pro-priestly agenda, seeks to elevate the Levites, while not erasing the distinctions that should exist between priest and Levite.

[15] Numbers 1:50–53; 3–4; 10; 31:30, 47; 1 Chr 6:17, 33 [6:32, 48]; 23:26.

the workers within it.[16] Further, when the duties and responsibilities of priest and Levite with regard to the tabernacle were determined in Numbers, no legislation for "singers" is given. If the Chronicler is here contrasting duties in the tabernacle under the influence of Numbers, then the reference to "their brothers the Levites" would be in contrast to priests rather than to another, not yet legislated, group.

Fifth, the duties and families of the musicians as described in 1 Chr 6:31–47 [6:16–32] are said to be the result of the actions of David (1 Chr 6:16 [6:31]). This cannot be said to be true for the standard duties of the Levites. From the Chronicler's perspective, the duties of the Levites, like those of the priests, had their origins in the commands of Moses, not David.[17] That he is, in 1 Chr 6:33–34 [6:48–49], contrasting the roles of Levites and sons of Aaron indicates that the Mosaic rather than Davidic legislation is in view. This may suggest the Chronicler is seeking to distinguish between the activities and status of Moses and those of David. While acknowledging that both are significant and had made valuable and lasting contributions to the cult, the actions of Moses take precedence over those of David.

Sixth, the Chronicler has already merged discussion of the sons of Aaron alongside that of the Levites (1 Chronicle 5:27–6:15 [6:1–30]), but here a distinction between the groups is indicated.[18] It is not unreasonable then to assume that here also that distinctions in the tasks of the two groups is being indicated.

Seventh, although as noted above, reading 1 Chr 6:33 [6:48] with what precedes has the advantage of elevating the sons of Aaron to an even more prominent place within the postexilic society, this is not consistent with the remainder of the Chronicler's work. While it is true that throughout Chronicles the Levites are assigned a lower status than the priests/sons of Aaron, they maintain an elevated position within the cult. This elevated position is also present in the portrayal of preexilic society and government in Chronicles.

The cumulative affect of these points indicate that it is more probable that the Chronicler was seeking to contrast Levitical and priestly duties in 1 Chr 6:33–34 [6:48–49] than that he was simply describing musical and non-musical (i.e. "other") duties performed by the Levites.[19] Therefore, it is preferable to read 1 Chr 6:48 [6:33] as the beginning of 1 Chr 6:33–39 [6:48–53] than as the conclusion to 1 Chr 6:16–33 [6:31–48].

---

[16] Numbers 4:16–20, 27, 33.

[17] 1 Chronicles 6:34 [6:49]; 15:15; 2 Chr 8:13; 23:18; 24:6, 9; 30:16; 35:12.

[18] See the discussion of this level of the Chronicler's structure.

[19] Although it is recognised that this is a possibility and that even if this were the case, the centrality of the functions of the Levites and the sons of Aaron for the Chronicler would not necessarily be altered.

THE CONTRASTING FUNCTIONS OF LEVITES AND SONS OF AARON

It has been observed in 1 Chr 6:33 [6:48] that the Chronicler presents a view of the Levites which is consistent with that presented in the book of Numbers. In Numbers, although the are Levites cultic officials with cultic responsibilities, they are subordinate to the priests and under the direction and control of the priests. The boundary between priest and Levite is clearly defined, and the Levites are not permitted to exercise priestly prerogatives.[20]

First Chronicles 6:34 [6:49] continues this consistency of portrayal when it discusses the duties of the sons of Aaron.[21] The sons of Aaron offer "burnt offerings" and "incense" as well as doing the work of "the most holy place" and "making atonement."[22]

Although present in both the Deuteronomistic History and some prophets, the direct connection between the priests and the burnt offering (עֹלָה) is most prominent in Leviticus.[23] It is only in the priestly writings and Chronicles, however, that the term "sons of Aaron" and the burnt offering are connected.[24] Although elsewhere in the Hebrew Bible individuals other than priests or sons of Aaron present burnt offerings, the priestly writings insist that it is the priests/sons of Aaron alone who are authorised to make such an offering. The Chronicler shares this outlook in respect to proper cultic functioning. At no point do the priestly writings or Chronicles suggest that Levites were authorised to present עֹלָה.

---

[20] This is made expressly plain in Num 16, where the Levite Korah sought to gain the prerogatives of the priesthood for the Levites.

[21] It is to be noted that "priests" are not mentioned as such in the genealogies until 1 Chr 9:2, a section which recounts the (re)settlement of Jerusalem.

[22] Contrary to the suggestions of Myers, this passage is not presented to "confirm further the position and duties of the Zadokites," *I Chronicles*, 47. So also J. Barton Payne, "1, 2 Chronicles," in *The Expositor's Bible Commentary Volume 4* (ed. Frank E. Gaebelein; Grand Rapids: Zondervan, 1988), 354. The focus is on the "sons of Aaron," and it is Aaron rather than Zadok who is prominent.

[23] In the Deuteronomistic History the priests offer burnt offerings only in 1 Sam 2:28; 2 Kgs 16:15 (although they are made on the "high places"), while in the prophets the priests presenting burnt offerings occurs only in Jer 33:18; Ezek 43:24, 27; 46:2. In the Torah, this action occurs in Lev 1:9, 13, 17; 4:7, 10, 25, 30, 34; 5:10; 6:3, 5 [6:10,12]; 7:8; 12:6, 8; 14:13, 19, 20, 31; 15:15, 30; Num 6:11, 16. In postexilic literature, 2 Chr 23:18; 29:21, 24, 34; 30:15; 31:2; 35:14; Ezra 3:2.

[24] Leviticus 3:5; 6:2, 18 [6:9, 25]; 8:18; 9:2, 7, 12, 22; 10:19; 16:3, 9; 1 Chr 6:34 [6:49]; 2 Chr 29:21; 35:14.

Likewise the offering of incense (קְטֹרֶת) is a priestly prerogative.[25] In Num 16, when Korah and his followers sought to gain priestly privileges and status, it was through the offering of incense that Yahweh's choice of the sons of Aaron was confirmed. The account in Numbers makes it clear that this incident is the proof that, "no-one except a descendant (son) of Aaron should come to burn incense before the Lord, or he would become like Korah and his followers." (Num 16:40).

This insistence has its corollary in 2 Chr 26:16–20, where King Uzziah offered incense and was struck with leprosy. Here as well, the priests said to Uzziah, "It is not right for you, Uzziah, to burn incense to the Lord. That is for the priests, the descendants (sons) of Aaron, who have been consecrated to burn incense."[26]

In discussing the offering of incense and the offering of the burnt offering, it is not just the offering that the Chronicler indicates is important. Both offerings are to be upon the appropriate altar (מִזְבֵּחַ). This indicates that it is not simply the action that is important to proper cultic functioning, but also the place where that act occurs. This insistence upon the correct place is consistent with the commands of Deut 12 and 16 regarding the one designated place of worship within the territory that Yahweh will give to the people.[27] The mention of an altar of incense in Chronicles also links the book to Exodus.[28] By so doing it shows that the cultic

---

[25] Deuteronomy 33:10, however, indicates that it is the prerogative of the Levites as a tribe. First Samuel 2:28 indicates that the family of Eli had been chosen to "go up to my altar, to burn incense."

[26] It could be objected that Hezekiah, while addressing the Levites, stated that the Levites as a tribe had been chosen by Yahweh "to burn incense" (2 Chr 29:11). While it is correct that Hezekiah directly addressed those he termed "Levites" (2 Chr 29:5), the group that he addressed contained both priests and Levites (2 Chr 29:4), while the purification of the temple was conducted by the priests and the Levites (2 Chr 29:15–16). It is probable then that "Levite" could be used collectively for any grouping of the descendants of Levi, whether made up of Levites alone or a mixture of Levites and sons of Aaron; so also, Sara Japhet, *I & II Chronicles* (OTL; Louisville: Westminster/John Knox Press, 1993), 917; Williamson, *Chronicles*, 353. Rudolph suggests that the use of "Levite" alone "verrät eben nur wieder einmal, wie sehr das Herz des Chr. für sie schlägt," *Chronikbücher*, 293.

[27] So also Deut 17:8, 10; 18:6; 26:2. The centralization of cultic worship is presented as one of the central tasks of the "reforming" kings, Hezekiah (2 Kgs 18:4, 22) and Josiah (2 Kgs 23:8–20). The failure of the postexilic Jerusalem community to assist the Elephantine community in their request for help in rebuilding their own temple may be an indication that the centralization of worship was also a significant issue for the postexilic Jerusalem community.

[28] The altar of incense appears in Exod 30:1, 7, 9, 27; 31:8; 35:15; 37:25; 40:5; Lev 4:7; 1 Chr 6:34 [6:49]; 28:18; 2 Chr 26:16, 19. It is also called the "golden altar" in Exod 39:38; 40:5, 26; Num 4:11; 2 Chr 4:19 // 1 Kgs 7:48.

functions being described are those prescribed at the origins of Israel's cult and that the cultic service described is a continuation of that original cultic service.[29]

Thus, as Friedman says, "the way to communicate with this God is through the formal, ordered structures that he has provided as the only channels to him.... It is through prescribed sacrifices at prescribed times, performed by a prescribed priesthood in a prescribed manner."[30]

THE CENTRALITY OF CULTIC FUNCTIONS

Central to the Chronicler's conception of true worship is the prescribed place of that worship, with each group relegated to its own sphere of operation. Thus, the locale of the work of the sons of Aaron and the Levites is different. While the Levites perform their functions within the tabernacle, (1 Chr 6:33 [6:48]), the sons of Aaron work within the "Most Holy Place" (Lev 16:2; 1 Chr 6:34 [6:49]). This area is located only within the tabernacle and the temple, and access is restricted to the sons of Aaron.[31] In this way the Chronicler acknowledges the difference not only in function between the two groups, but also in the arena where those functions take place. While the Levites operate within the tabernacle, most probably meaning the entire sacred area, the sons of Aaron alone are permitted in the Most Holy Place.

This helps to explain the presence of the two phrases "tabernacle, the house of God" (מִשְׁכַּן בֵּית הָאֱלֹהִים; 1 Chr 6:33 [6:48]), and "Most Holy Place" (קֹדֶשׁ הַקֳּדָשִׁים; 1 Chr 6:34 [6:49]).

Of these, the phrase "tabernacle, the house of God" (מִשְׁכַּן בֵּית הָאֱלֹהִים) is important, since by joining them, the Chronicler indicates a continuity of worship

---

[29] On the theme of continuity of cultic service, see John Van Seters, "The Chronicler's Account of Solomon's Temple Building: A Continuity Theme," in *The Chronicler as Historian* (ed. M. Patrick Graham, et al.*Journal for the Study of the Old Testament Supplement 238*; Sheffield: Sheffield Academic Press, 1997).

[30] Richard Elliott Friedman, *Who Wrote the Bible?* (New York: HarperSanFrancisco, 1997), 192.

[31] The phrase קֹדֶשׁ הַקֳּדָשִׁים refers to the "Most Holy Place" (Exod 26:33, 34; 1 Kgs 6:16; 7:50; 8:6; 1 Chr 6:34 [6:49]; 2 Chr 3:8, 10; 4:22; 5:7; Ezek 41:4). It is also used for offerings or food (Num 18:9, 10; Ezra 2:63 // Neh 7:65; Ezek 42:13) and for the articles in the tent (Num 4:4, 19). In the plural it refers to the food to be eaten or to gifts (Lev 21:22; 2 Chr 31:14; Ezek 44:13). The phrase קֹדֶשׁ קֳדָשִׁים is used in Exodus to refer to the tabernacle and its contents (Exod 29:37; 30:10, 29, 36; 40:10), while in Leviticus and Numbers it is used to refer to the offerings that are made (Lev 2:3, 10; 6:10, 18, 22; 7:1, 6; 10:12, 17; 14:13; 24:9; 27:28; Num 18:9). In Ezekiel it is used to refer to the new temple area (43:12), the sanctuary as a whole (45:3), and the land of the sons of Zadok (48:12).

between the Mosaic legislation and the Chronicler's own day. "House of God" does not occur in Leviticus or Numbers, and only rarely in the Deuteronomistic History and the prophets.[32] It primarily occurs in the postexilic literature of Chronicles, Ezra and Nehemiah.[33] Likewise, the phrase "house of Yahweh" does not occur in Leviticus or Numbers. It occurs regularly in the prophets, especially Jeremiah, although rarely in the Deuteronomistic History prior to the account of the building of the temple in 1 Kings.[34]

Similarly, the term מִשְׁכָּן, in the sense of Yahweh's dwelling place or "Tabernacle," occurs primarily in Exodus and Numbers.[35] In Exodus and Numbers the tabernacle was set up in the middle of the camp as the focal point of all cultic activities, and the Levites were set aside, under the direction of the sons of Aaron, for its care and transport. A simple reading of the Pentateuch and the Deuteronomistic History suggests that the Tabernacle was replaced by the temple, for in the early history where there is a מִשְׁכָּן, there is no בַּיִת, and in the later account where there is a בַּיִת, there is no מִשְׁכָּן.

Only two parts of the Hebrew Bible appear to draw these two ideas together to indicate that the tabernacle of the Mosaic legislation fulfils the same function and has the same authority as the temple. The first is Psalms, which identifies the house/temple with the Tabernacle (26:8; 74:7). Most important, however, is Ps 84:2–5 [84:1–4], which first speaks of Yahweh's Tabernacle and then of his house, which contains the altar.[36]

---

[32] It also occurs in the Bethel narrative (Gen 28:17, 22). Interestingly, it never occurs in either Samuel or Kings.

[33] The Chronicler is not consistent in how he uses the phrase "house of Yahweh" from either Samuel or Kings. At times he renders the phrase "house of Yahweh" and at other times "house of God." Even in his new material, the Chronicler uses both phrases. His preference is for "house of Yahweh." Nehemiah contains the phrase "house of Yahweh" only once (Neh 10:36) but "house of God" nineteen times. Likewise, Ezra prefers "house of God" (15 times), to "house of Yahweh" (eight times).

[34] Exodus 23:19; 34:26; Deut 23:19 [23:18]; Josh 6:24. It is interesting that each of these verses deals with what should or should not be brought into the House of Yahweh as a gift. For discussion of the tabernacle as a treasury for the spoils of Yahweh's victories, see, Myung Soo Suh, *The Tabernacle in the Narrative History of Israel from the Exodus to the Conquest* (New York: Peter Lang, 2003).

[35] It also occurs 4 times in Leviticus, twice in Joshua and once in 2 Sam 7:6. Of the prophets, only Ezek 37:27 mentions God as "tabernacling" among the people, and that in the context of a return from exile, a restored Davidic monarch and an everlasting covenant. The term does not occur at all in Deuteronomy, which speaks instead of "the place which Yahweh chooses." Nor does it appear in Kings or Judges.

[36] See Friedman's suggestion that the "Tabernacle" was located within the temple under the wings of the Cherub's. Friedman, *Who Wrote*, 174–187, and especially the illustrations and discussion of the Tabernacle's dimensions on pages 178–182.

The second portion of the Hebrew Bible which seeks to identify the Tabernacle with the house/temple is Chronicles. Although 1 Chr 17:5 and its parallel in 2 Sam 7:6 both mention "house" and "tabernacle," they are not in these verses being identified as the same place, but are instead being contrasted to one another: Yahweh has not dwelt in a house, but in a tent/tabernacle.

1 and 2 Chronicles uses מִשְׁכָּן to indicate the tent structure referred to in the Pentateuch. It is said to be the structure made by Moses (1 Chr 21:29), which the Levites carried as part of their duties (1 Chr 23:26). It is also located in Gibeon (1 Chr 16:39; 21:29; 2 Chr 1:5). What is significant about these references is that at the tabernacle there is a Zadokite priest who officiates, and one of his primary duties is "to present burnt offerings to the Lord on the altar of burnt offering" (1 Chr 16:40). Thus it is observed that the family of Zadok (1 Chr 6:38 [6:53]) officiates at both the tabernacle and the later temple, and the same functions are performed in both places, including that of music and the duties of the gatekeepers. Furthermore, it is to this tabernacle, with its altar of burnt offering, that David desired to visit to enquire of Yahweh (1 Chr 21:29–30). Solomon did visit this tabernacle, with its altar, to enquire of Yahweh (2 Chr 1:5), and it was here that Solomon had his vision of Yahweh (2 Chr 1:7–12).

However, it is in 1 Chr 6:33 [6:48] that the house of God and the tabernacle are identified as the same place and so fulfil the same function. This also suggests that these are alternate names for the locale where the Levites ministered.[37] Furthermore, in 1 Chr 6:16–17 [6:31–32], the "house of Yahweh," "tabernacle" and "tent of meeting" are all said to be one place, where the ark rested and the musicians ministered. It is further suggested that all these became incorporated into the "house of Yahweh" built by Solomon.[38]

The "tent of meeting" is also an expression prominent in the Pentateuch. Although it can refer to a tent that Moses pitched outside the camp (Exod 33:7), it was generally used as an alternative name for the tabernacle. Chronicles also identifies the "tent of meeting" with the "house of God" (1 Chr 23:28, 32), as well as indicating that the original "tent of meeting" was brought into the "house of Yahweh" (2 Chr 5:5).

Another term used to refer to the tabernacle in the priestly material is the אֹהֶל הָעֵדֻת (tent of the testimony). This phrase is only used in Num 9:15; 17:22–23 [17:7–8]; 18:2 and 2 Chr 24:6.

---

[37] That it is Psalms and Chronicles alone which link the tabernacle and the temple together as one unit may give support to the idea that Chronicles is the production of a Levitical singer.

[38] The terminology for the "house of Yahweh" appears to be flexible. On the one hand it is the tent that David built for the ark, and later it is the temple that Solomon built. It is probable that the Chronicler believed that any location which housed the ark was "the house of Yahweh."

Deuteronomy uses different terminology, regularly referring to "the place that Yahweh will choose" to designate the central location of cultic worship.[39] In 1 Kgs 9:3 the temple is "consecrated." The Chronicler alters this and presents Yahweh as saying, "I have heard your prayer and have chosen this place for myself as a temple for sacrifices" (2 Chr 7:12). This indicates a deliberate alteration by the Chronicler to conform to the terminology and expectations of Deuteronomy.[40]

Each of these observations indicate that the Chronicler sought to combine all of the terminology he found in his sources into his text as synonyms for the temple of Yahweh in Jerusalem, even if these terms originally referred to different things. In so doing he seeks to illustrate a continuity in the worship of the people from the beginning of Israel's history until his own day. He thereby indicates that the wide variety of sources he possessed, although using varying terms, speak of the same reality, even if that reality changes from a tent or an undesignated place, into a fully developed and constructed building centuries later.

This observation strongly suggests that the Chronicler was not an innovator, but a synthesiser. The Chronicler appears to have recognised the need for all of the cultic life of the postexilic community to be in conformity with the Torah. It was to be neither new nor innovative, and certainly not deviating from it. Instead the cultic worship of the community was to be consistent with the tradition that handed down by the founder, Moses, with certain allowances for changing circumstances to be brought in by prophets or kings, particularly David.[41]

ATONEMENT: THE PURPOSE OF THE CULT

The genealogies indicate that the priests were to do their work at the altars of incense and burnt offering and within the most holy place. The purpose of this, however, was "to make atonement for Israel" (1 Chr 6:34 [6:49]).[42]

Although a thorough study of "atonement" is beyond the scope of this work, as making atonement is indicated to be the primary purpose of the sons of Aaron, some understanding of this task is necessary.

---

[39] Deuteronomy 12:5, 11, 14, 18, 21, 26; 14:23, 24, 25; 15:20; 16:2, 6, 7, 11, 15, 16; 17:8, 10; 18:6; 26:2; 31:11. The phrase is also used in Josh 9:27 and Neh 1:9.

[40] First Kings 9:3 uses the hif'il of קדש.

[41] See below for further discussion.

[42] "The term *to make an atonement* is used here to indicate the priestly ministry in general," Curtis and Madsen, *Chronicles*, 136. Hill states that atonement is "the goal of the priestly sacrificial material," Andrew E. Hill, *1 & 2 Chronicles* (NIVApp; Grand Rapids: Zondervan, 2003), 138.

It has been suggested that the basic idea behind atonement, כָּפַר, is to cover, ransom, or wipe away.[43]

On the basis of the use of כָּפַר in the Qal stem in Gen 6:14, where Noah is told כָּפַר (to coat) the ark with pitch, it has been suggested that the essential meaning is "to cover."[44]

Although stating that the root כפר in Gen 6:14 comes from a different root than those occurrences which suggest "atonement," Maass points out that Gen 6:14 "has precise equivalents in Akk. . . . *kapāru* II 'to coat with asphalt'," which is used in the Epic of Gilgamesh, "upon which Gen 6:14 is in some way dependent."[45] Averbeck notes, however, that while the Akkadian base stem (where the root *kpr* means "to rub or wipe on") is closer in meaning to the Hebrew Qal stem, the Hebrew Piel stem, in which the majority of occurrences of כָּפַר in the Hebrew Bible appear, is closer in meaning to the Akkadian D stem, which "always means wipe off, wipe away."[46] While this does not demand that the Hebrew Piel of כפר must also mean "wipe away," it does broaden the possible meanings of the verb

The idea of "ransom" for atonement finds strong support in the use of the root in Exod 30:11–16. At the census, each person is to כִּפֶּר (ransom) his life through the giving of כֶּסֶף הַכִּפֻּרִים (atonement money) which will לְכַפֵּר (atone) for their lives. Likewise, in Num 35:31–33, the people are commanded not to accept a כֹּפֶר (ransom) for a murderer because "bloodshed pollutes the land,"

---

[43] Richard E. Averbeck, "כפר," in *New International Dictionary of Old Testament Theology and Exegesis, Volume 2* (ed. Willem A. VanGemeren; Grand Rapids: Zondervan, 1997), 691; F. Maass, "כפר *kpr* pi. to atone," in *Theological Lexicon of the Old Testament* (ed. Ernst Jenni and Claus Westermann; Peabody: Hendrickson, 1997), 625

[44] Hill, *Chronicles*, 138; J. A. Thompson, *1, 2 Chronicles* (NAC 9; Nashville: Broadman & Holman, 1994), 88. Hill, however, appears to be guided in his definition by later, Christian, interpretation, for he says, "the sacrificial offerings were *symbolic* of atonement since 'it is impossible for the blood of bulls and goats to take away sin' (Heb. 10:4)" (italics mine), *Chronicles*, 138–139. First it must be said that Leviticus makes plain that the atonement was real rather than symbolic. The person was atoned for, which made their appearance before God and their ability to remain and participate in the community possible. Second, the Hebrew word used for "forgiven" in the atonement ceremonies of Lev 4–5 is סָלַח which "in all instances . . . is an act of pardon by God alone," J. P. J. Olivier, "סלח," in *New International Dictionary of Old Testament Theology and Exegesis Volume 3* (ed. Willem A. VanGemeren; Grand Rapids: Zondervan, 1997), 260. These are no mere symbolism, but indicate the reality of people's lives as they responded not only to ritual impurity but also to acts which violated the commandments of Yahweh.

[45] Maass, "כפר," 626.

[46] Averbeck, "כפר," 692.

which prevents atonement, יְכֻפַּר (Pual) from being made.⁴⁷ This suggests that a link of some kind exists between "atonement" and "ransom," with the sacrifice being some form of payment for the release of the one who brings it.

This, however, does not explain the many instances of כִּפֶּר which apply, not to people, but to objects. The altar (Exod 29:36–37; Lev 8:15; 16:18, 33; Ezek 43:20, 26), a house cleansed of mildew (Lev 14:53), the Most Holy Place (Lev 16:16, 33), the Tent of Meeting (Lev 16:20, 33), and Ezekiel's temple (Ezek 45:20), all need to be "atoned."

There are also instances in which atonement is made not because the actions of an individual have been contrary to the commandments, but because the issue is one of ritual impurity. A woman who has give birth (Lev 12:7–8), a person with a cured skin disease (Lev 14:1–32), and a person who is cured of a discharge (Lev 15:30) are each given "atonement" through the cultic ritual.

Further, the Levites, as part of their preparation for service in the Tabernacle, "purified" themselves (Num 8:7, 21). This included sprinkling, washing, shaving, and offerings. None of this, however, was in response to sinful actions on the part of the Levites, but was to טהר (make them ceremonially clean; Num 8:6). Yet the entire process, including sacrifice, was "to make atonement for the Levites" (Num 8:12), even though no violation of the commandment is indicated. What is accomplished through this is the consecration of the Levites, the removal of ritual impurity, moving them from the unclean to the clean so that they might serve Yahweh in the Tabernacle.

This suggests that atonement does not deal with sinful actions as much as it does with the consequences of ritual impurity, whether that ritual impurity is caused by violation of the commands or by reasons of health and normal bodily occurrences. Each of these situations result in the inability of the individual, who is "impure" or "unclean" as the result of either their behaviour or their physical circumstances, to approach Yahweh in worship. Atonement is the goal of the process by which a person who is "unclean" can make the transition to being "clean."

The Day of Atonement further relates "atonement" with "cleansing" (Lev 16:19, 30). As Wenham states. "cleanness is the normal condition of most things and persons. Sanctification can elevate the clean into the holy, while pollution degrades the clean into the unclean. The unclean and the holy are two states which must never come into contact with each other."⁴⁸

It is, however, through the act of atonement that the uncleanness of the individual is addressed, their uncleanness brought into a state of cleanness, thus

---

⁴⁷ Averbeck, "כפר," 693

⁴⁸ Gordon J. Wenham, *The Book of Leviticus* (NICOT; Grand Rapids: Eerdmans, 1979), 19–20.

giving the individual the capacity to approach the holy.[49] This is confirmed by the repeated commands for the people to be holy because Yahweh is, himself, holy.[50]

Nor is it necessary for there to be sacrifice for atonement to be achieved. Leviticus 16:10 indicates that the scapegoat makes atonement for the people, not through being killed, but through symbolically carrying the sins of the people into the desert, thus leaving the people "clean" or "atoned."

This suggests strongly that כפר (Piel) has the same meaning as the root *kpr* in Akkadian D stem, "to wipe away." It appears that in atonement, uncleanness is "wiped away" so that the individual or the object which is atoned for is ritually "clean" and therefore may either approach Yahweh or, in the case of objects such as the altar or tabernacle, might exist in the presence of Yahweh.

The Day of Atonement deals with the "uncleanness and rebellion of the Israelites" (Lev 16:16). Because Yahweh dwells in the Tabernacle, it must be atoned for, that is, cleansed of all impurity so that what is unclean does not intrude upon the dwelling of Yahweh, who is holy. The wiping away of ritual impurity for the altar is also important for, if the altar were "unclean," it could not be used to present offerings acceptable to Yahweh. Its ritual cleansing makes the cultic sacrifices both possible and acceptable.

A corollary is found in 2 Chr 29:15–19, where the temple and its precincts, including the altar, had to be purified before sacrifice and atonement could be offered for Israel (2 Chr 29:20–24). Before the Temple was purified, the priests and Levites had to purify themselves (2 Chr 29:3–5; cf. Num 8:5–22). If they had remained impure, then their presence and actions could not have moved the temple from uncleanness to cleanness to holiness, and cultic worship could not have been properly performed.

Again, the making of atonement was the duty of priests alone, with the priestly writings specifically indicating that it belonged to Aaron and his descendants (Exod 30:10; Lev 16:2–34; Num 8:19, 21). In Num 16:46–47, when the people faced the wrath of Yahweh, it was Aaron who ran and made atonement. This duty was to be hereditary, and so passed on to the son of the priest (Lev 16:32–34). As Aaron was the only one officially authorised to make atonement, and the duty was to fall to his son, the priestly writings indicate, and 1 Chr 6:34 [6:49] affirms, that this is a task reserved for the "sons of Aaron" alone.

First Chronicles 6:34 [6:49] further indicates that the atonement the sons of Aaron achieved was "for Israel." Atonement for Israel is a theme that occurs not only in the priestly writings (Lev 16:34; Num 15:25; 25:13), but also in Deut 21:8; Neh 10:33; Ezek 45:17. That the priestly writings and Chronicles alone

---

[49] For a detailed study of purification in the Hebrew Bible, see N. Kiuchi, *The Purification Offering in the Priestly Literature: Its Meaning and Function* (JSOTSup 56; Sheffield: JSOT Press, 1987).

[50] Leviticus 11:44–45; 19:2; 20:7, 26.

reserved this duty for the sons of Aaron further shows the influence of the priestly material on the Chronicler's thought.[51]

Johnstone, however, sees a difficulty in the application of atonement in the Chronicler's day.[52] He views the essential problem in the history of Israel as one of מַעַל (unfaithfulness) which he defines as, "not only to deprive God of what is rightfully his; it is also to misapply what has thus been wrongfully gained to one's own profit."[53]

He thus particularly applies מַעַל (unfaithfulness)" to the failure of Israel in regards to tithes, offerings, and the required gifts for the support of the cult.[54] He further suggests that the settlements of the Levites in טִירָה (dwellings) using a word the Chronicler did not find in his source and which is used "typically in connection with nomadic populations," indicates that:

> the Chronicler stresses that the Levites remain as pastors of flocks with grazing grounds . . . in the midst of the tribes settled in their agricultural lands and are, therefore, dependent like the other landless ones on the tithes . . . As such, the Levites would become immediately aware of מעל, any shortfall in the payment of the sacred dues, on the part of Israel.[55]

In the instance of deliberate unfaithfulness in rendering such dues to Yahweh or appropriating these dues for oneself, such as that of Achan in Josh 7, the only recourse to the community, "is stoning to death by the whole community of the culprit, his family and all living creatures within his household and the burning of the corpses."[56]

Using Lev 4:1–5:13 as his starting point, Johnstone proposes that atonement was only applicable to the actions of an individual and only for inadvertent, rather than deliberate, actions.[57] He contends that the failure of Israel to render to

---

[51] Deuteronomy 21:5 indicates that the atonement made in Deut 21:8 is the task of a priest who is a son of Levi, while Ezekiel states that these are the sons of Zadok, (Ezek 40:46; 43:19; 44:15). The Chronicler, or his sources, incorporated Zadok into the sons of Aaron (1 Chr 5:27–41; 6:35–38 [6:1–15, 50–53]), thus giving/maintaining the right of sacrifice among the sons of Aaron.

[52] See Johnstone, *Chronicles and Exodus*, especially chapter 4, pages 90–114. Chapter 4 was previously published as William Johnstone, "Guilt and Atonement: The Theme of 1 and 2 Chronicles," in *A Word in Season: Essays in Honour of William McKane* (ed. James D. Martin and Philip R. Davies *Journal for the Study of the Old Testament Supplement 42*; Sheffield: JSOT Press, 1986).

[53] Johnstone, *Chronicles and Exodus*, 97.
[54] Johnstone, *Chronicles and Exodus*, 100.
[55] Johnstone, *Chronicles and Exodus*, 109.
[56] Johnstone, *Chronicles and Exodus*, 98.
[57] Johnstone, *Chronicles and Exodus*, 104.

Yahweh what was his, particularly in the cult through sacrifices and tithes, was a corporate rather than an individual act and was deliberate rather than inadvertent.[58] As such, atonement is not possible and the only remedy for Israel is exile. Even though Israel had long since returned to the land by the Chronicler's time, they were still experiencing a theological exile, while awaiting the expectation of Yahweh's gracious action on their behalf at some future point.[59] In the meantime, in the restored Jerusalem temple cult not only are there priests who serve at the altar (1 Chr 9:10–13), but there are also Levites who are in charge of the treasuries, to ensure the faithfulness of Israel in rendering to Yahweh his due so that the people do not fall again into מַעַל (1 Chr 9:26–32).[60]

Although properly emphasizing the central place of the priests and Levites within the postexilic community, Johnstone makes two fundamental errors.

First, he assumes that atonement is only applicable when an individual sins but not the community as a whole. However, Lev 4:13 refers to sin by the community as a whole and gives the proper community response to this sin (cf. Num 15:22–26). As a result of cultic activity Lev 4:20 specifically says "in this way the priest will make atonement for them, and they will be forgiven."

Second, while it is clear that unintentional sin is the primary focus of the commands of Lev 4:1–5:13, they are not the only actions for which atonement is allowed.[61]

Leviticus 5:1 indicates that failing to speak up to give evidence in a judicial case not only brings guilt, but can also be atoned through confession and paying the appropriate penalty (Lev 5:5–6). Leviticus 6:1–3 mentions various property crimes, none of which could be unintentional (deceive, cheat, lie, swear falsely), but all of which could be atoned and the individual who perpetrated them forgiven (Lev 6:7). A man who has sexual intercourse with his slave girl, who is promised in marriage to another man, may also, through the appropriate sacrifice, have his guilt atoned and be forgiven (Lev 19:20–22). The day of Atonement addresses the sins of the entire community, but unintentionality is not one of the prerequisites for these sins "whatever their sins have been" (Lev 16:16) to be atoned for (Lev 16:17). Finally, all the sins of the community are to be repeated over the head of the scapegoat, not just the unintentional ones, which implies that even intentional sins can be atoned for (Lev 16:20–22). It is also clear that some sins cannot be atoned for, and the penalty must be paid by the perpetrators (Lev

---

[58] Johnstone, *Chronicles and Exodus*, 104.
[59] Johnstone, *Chronicles and Exodus*, 106.
[60] Johnstone, *Chronicles and Exodus*, 113.
[61] Unintentional sin is mentioned in Lev 4:13, 22, 27; 5:15, 18; Num 15:22–31; Ezek 45:19–20. There is, however, no mention of atonement for the unintentional manslaughter of another person. Instead, the perpetrator is given safety in one of the cities of refuge (Num 35; Deut 4:41–43; 19:1–7; Josh 20:1–5).

20). These, however, are limited in number and centre on the taking of life, sexual sin or religious unfaithfulness.

Consequently, because Johnstone is inaccurate in his suggestion that only unintentional sin by the individual can be atoned, his conclusion that the postexilic community could only anticipate a future atonement, while doing the best they could in the present, is suspect. It is instead more probable that the Chronicler envisioned a community which lived in accordance to the ideals and commands of the priestly writings. A community where atonement was not simply a future possibility, but was an ongoing daily reality through the work of the sons of Aaron at the altar and in the Most Holy Place.

THE PLACE OF MOSES

The final statement in 1 Chr 6:34 [6:49] says that everything that was done was done "in accordance with all that Moses the servant of God had commanded."

A simple reading of Chronicles may give the impression that the figure of Moses is not significant for the Chronicler. This prompted De Vries to state, "it seems remarkable that the other great literary corpus from postexilic Judaism, the book of Chronicles, seems to make relatively little of Moses while strongly promoting David as a cult founder alongside Moses."[62]

"Moses" only occurs twenty-one times in the text of Chronicles which is, understandably, far fewer than in the books of Exodus to Joshua, where he is a prominent figure.[63] However, in comparison with the other writings of the Hebrew Bible, Chronicles has many references to the figure of Moses. Judges, Samuel and Kings refer to Moses a total of seventeen times,[64] while the prophets refer to him on only seven occasions.[65] The postexilic historiographical works of Ezra and Nehemiah refer to Moses nine times,[66] and the Psalms also on nine occasions. This indicates that, in comparison with most of the collections in the Hebrew Bible, Moses is a more significant figure for the Chronicler.

The importance of Moses is indicated by the titles that the Chronicler uses for him.

---

[62] Simon J. De Vries, "Moses and David as Cult Founders in Chronicles," *JBL* 107 (1988): 619–639, 619.

[63] "Moses" occurs in: Exodus 291X; Leviticus 86X; Numbers 233X; Deuteronomy 39X; Joshua 58X.

[64] Judges 4X; Samuel 3X; Kings 10X.

[65] Isaiah 2X; Jeremiah 1X; Daniel 2X; Micah 1X; Malachi 1X.

[66] Ezra 2X; Nehemiah 7X.

In 1 Chr 6:34 [6:49] Moses is called עֶבֶד הָאֱלֹהִים (the servant of God). This phrase occurs only four times, and only in late biblical texts, and on every occasion it refers to Moses.[67]

Likewise the phrase עֶבֶד־יהוה (servant of Yahweh) is used 23 times in the Hebrew Bible, twice each for David (but only in the Psalms) and Joshua, once for the anonymous servant in Isaiah, and eighteen times for Moses.[68] It is used twice by the Chronicler (2 Chr 1:3; 24:6), and he never uses the phrase to refer to any individual other than Moses. This is not to deny that Yahweh is said to refer to individuals as "my servant," or that others refer to specific persons as "your (i.e. Yahweh's) servant," but Moses is declared by a narrator to be a "servant of Yahweh" in eighteen of twenty occurrences of the term in narrative.[69]

Although the much more general phrase אִישׁ הָאֱלֹהִים (man of God), is used in the Deuteronomistic History, especially in Judges to Kings, to refer to those exercising a prophetic ministry, it is also used of Moses.[70] The phrase is used to refer to prophets in Chronicles, Ezra, Nehemiah, and here again Moses is a prominent figure.[71]

---

[67] 1 Chronicles 6:34 [6:49]; 2 Chr 24:9; Neh 10:29; Dan 9:11.

[68] עֶבֶד־יהוה, refers to Joshua in Josh 24:29; Judg 2:8; to David in Ps 18:1; 36:1; to Isaiah's anonymous servant in Isa 42:19. Moses is called the עֶבֶד־יהוה in Deut 34:5; Josh 1:1, 13, 15; 8:31, 33; 11:12; 12:6 (2X); 13:8; 14:7; 18:7; 22:2, 4, 5; 2 Kgs 18:12; 2 Chr 1:3; 24:6. The phrase is also used in the plural, "servants of Yahweh" in 2 Kgs 9:7; 10:23; Ps 113:1; 134:1; 135:1; Isa 54:17.

[69] Yahweh refers to individuals as "my servant." Abraham (Gen 26:24); Moses (Num 12:7, 8); David (2 Sam 3:18; 7:5, 8; 1 Chr 17:4, 7; Ezek 34:23); Job (Job 1:8; 2:3; 42:7); Isaiah (Isa 20:3); Nebuchadnezzar (Jer 25:9; 43:10); Zerubbabel (Hag 2:23). Yahweh also refers to Israel/Jacob (Isa 44:2; Jer 30:10; 46:28; Ezek 28:25) and an anonymous person (Isa 42:19) as "my servant." In the context of prayer individuals may refer to another as "your (i.e. Yahweh's) servant." Most often this is used by the petitioner to refer to him/herself. It is, however, also used to refer to David (1 Kgs 3:6; 8:24–26; 2 Chr 6:15–17; Ps 132:10) and Moses (1 Kgs 8:53; Neh 1:7, 8; 9:14). Apart from Ps 132:10, all of the "David" references are placed in the mouth of Solomon.

[70] In the Deuteronomistic History "man of God," אִישׁ הָאֱלֹהִים, is used to refer to Samuel (1 Sam 9:6–10); Shemaiah (1 Kgs 12:22); Elijah (1 Kgs 17:18–24; 20:28; 2 Kgs 1:9–13); Elisha (2 Kgs 4–8; 13:19); and several unnamed prophets (Judg 13:6–8; 1 Sam 2:27; 1 Kgs 13; 23:16–17). It is also used to refer to Moses (Deut 33:1; Josh 14:6). The only time the phrase is used in the Prophets is Jer 35:4, in reference to Igdaliah. In the Deuteronomistic History, "man of God" never refers to David.

[71] Moses (1 Chr 23:14; 2 Chr 30:16; Ezra 3:2); Shemaiah (2 Chr 11:2); David (2 Chr 8:14; Neh 12:24, 36); and an anonymous prophet (2 Chr 25:7–9). Moses is also called a "man of God" in Ps 90:1. That David is classed as a "man of God" alongside Moses and other prophets is significant for understanding the Chronicler's view of David.

The Chronicler's use of all three phrases, "servant of Yahweh," "servant of God," and "man of God" to refer to Moses, is an indication of the esteem in which Moses is held by the Chronicler.

This esteem is not, however, for Moses' actions in the exodus. The exodus itself is rarely mentioned in Chronicles, and Moses is only mentioned in connection with it on one occasion.[72] Even then (2 Chr 5:10), Moses is not the one who led the people out of Egypt, he is shown to be the lawgiver, the one who deposited the law tablets into the ark of the covenant. It is in this latter capacity of "lawgiver" that Moses is esteemed in the Chronicler's work.

Of the twenty-one times Moses is mentioned in Chronicles, five of the occurrences place him in a genealogy,[73] five as a giver of laws and decrees,[74] two as the builder of the tabernacle,[75] two as commanding a tax for the maintenance of the tabernacle,[76] and seven in relation to the functioning of the cult.[77] What is significant is that of the twenty-one occurrences of Moses in Chronicles, only four of them occur in the Chronicler's source in 1 and 2 Kings, and each of these refer to Moses simply as a giver of law, not as an establisher of the cult.[78]

The importance that the Chronicler placed upon Moses' relation to the cult is indicated by the high proportion of insertions by the Chronicler into his source material, focussing upon Moses as a cult founder, be that in ritual, location or maintenance (eleven of sixteen non-genealogical references). It is this area, rather than Moses as deliverer, that receives the Chronicler's attention.

This is further highlighted by noting the Moses passages in 1 and 2 Kings that the Chronicler omitted. Second Kings 18:1–12 recounts the rise of Hezekiah and the fall of Samaria. Of this passage, the Chronicler only included 2 Kgs 18:1, 3, which tell of Hezekiah's ascension to the throne and how he "did what was right in the eyes of Yahweh." Omitted, however, are three references to Moses (2 Kgs 18:4, 6, 12).

---

[72] The exodus is mentioned in 1 Chr 17:5, 21; 2 Chr 5:10; 6:5; 7:22. Moses is connected with the exodus in 2 Chr 5:10 in a passage the Chronicler found in his source.

[73] 1 Chronicles 5:29 [6:3]; 23:13, 14, 15; 26:24.

[74] 1 Chronicles 22:13; 2 Chr 5:10; 25:4; 33:8; 34:14. To these may be added 1 Chr 16:40; 2 Chr 31:3 which, although not mentioning Moses by name, do indicate that the regulations are from the Torah, which in other parts is shown to be that of Moses.

[75] 1 Chronicles 21:29; 2 Chr 1:3.

[76] 2 Chronicles 24:6, 9.

[77] 1 Chronicles 6:34 [6:49]; 15:15; 2 Chr 8:13; 23:18; 30:16; 35:6, 12.

[78] 1 Chronicles 22:13 // 1 Kgs 2:3 (although not a direct quote); 2 Chr 5:10 // 1 Kgs 8:9; 2 Chr 25:4 // 2 Kgs 14:6; 2 Chr 33:8 // 2 Kgs 21:8. Second Chronicles 34:14 is an insertion into the Chronicler's source which provides an introduction to the account of the finding of the book of the Law (2 Chr 34:15 // 2 Kgs 22:8).

First, the Chronicler omits reference to the worship of the bronze serpent (2 Kgs 18:4), since he would not want the founder of the cult to be associated either with the production of images or with their worship. By omitting this verse, the Chronicler keeps Moses' reputation pure.

It was also natural to omit 2 Kgs 18:12 which gives a theological explanation for the fall of Samaria, for the Chronicler omitted the majority of references to the northern kingdom.[79]

> This happened because they had not obeyed the LORD their God, but had violated his covenant—all that Moses the servant of the LORD commanded. They neither listened to the commands nor carried them out.

The behaviour of the north is in direct contrast to the actions of Hezekiah in 2 Kgs 18:6, another Moses passage omitted by the Chronicler:

> He held fast to the LORD and did not cease to follow him; he kept the commands the LORD had given Moses.

While it may appear puzzling that the Chronicler would omit such a glowing reference regarding obedience to Moses, what he includes in its place (2 Chr 29:3–31:21), is an account of what obedience to Moses involves. Hezekiah gathers the priests and Levites and encourages them to purify the temple (2 Chr 29:3–19), followed by sacrifice and burnt offerings by the priests to "atone for all Israel" (cf. 1 Chr 6:34 [6:49]), accompanied by the musicians (2 Chr 29:25–26, 30, cf. 1 Chr 6:16–32 [6:31–47]), with the Levites assisting the priests (2 Chr 29:32–35, cf. 1 Chr 6:33 [6:48]). This was followed by the Passover ceremony (2 Chr 30), and the people contributing to the worship, and thus to the support of the priests, so that the proper cultic functions could continue (2 Chr 31).

None of this is found in 2 Kings. All of these actions are a substitute for the statements in 2 Kgs 18:4–6 that Hezekiah removed the high places, trusted in Yahweh, and obeyed the commands of Moses. This is suggests that the Chronicler was signifying that obedience to the commands of Moses demands the proper relationship of the people to the cult, its sacrifices and officials.

The Chronicler further emphasised this point when he omitted another Moses reference. Second Kings 23:25 says:

> Neither before nor after Josiah was there a king like him who turned to the LORD as he did—with all his heart and with all his soul and with all his strength, in accordance with all the Law of Moses.

---

[79] For the Chronicler's attitude toward the north, see Roddy L. Braun, "A Reconsideration of the Chronicler's Attitude toward the North," *JBL* 96 (1977): 59–62; Japhet, *Ideology*, p 308–334.

While the Chronicler omits reference to Josiah's obedience to Moses' commands, he includes a fuller description of Josiah's Passover ceremony (2 Chr 35:2–17). Again, obedience to Moses is described rather than stated.[80]

This is also shown by one of the Chronicler's inclusions of Moses (2 Chr 34:14), which, unlike the text of 2 Kgs 22:8 // 2 Chr 34:15, specifically calls the book of the Law, "the book of the Law of Yahweh that had been given through Moses." Josiah makes a covenant "to follow Yahweh and keep his commands, regulations and decrees with all his heart and all his soul, and to obey the words of the covenant written in this book" (2 Chr 34:31). This is followed by the Chronicler's elaboration of Josiah's celebration of the Passover.

What this indicates is that, for the Chronicler, obedience to Yahweh is to be exhibited by obedience to the commands of Yahweh given through Moses, and will be displayed through the cultic worship. It is the exhibition of obedience, particularly as displayed in the cult, that is of importance to the Chronicler.

Although the Chronicler is very clear that Moses' teachings and commands, as well as the cultic worship he founded, remains the standard for temple worship in his day, the status of the person of Moses does not carry on beyond Moses. That is, his descendants do not retain the status that Moses had.

This is highlighted by the Chronicler's use of 1 Kgs 8, which contains Solomon's prayer of dedication when the temple is completed and is repeated almost in its entirety in 2 Chr 6.

First Kings 8:53, which describes Moses as Yahweh's spokesman is replaced by a quotation from Ps 132:1, 8–10, which speaks of a cultic object (i.e. the ark), and the cultic officials (the priests). In the Chronicler's retelling of the event, it is the cultic officials who now take the place of Moses as the spokespersons of Yahweh.

First Kings 8:56 is part of the larger section of 8:54b–61, which is replaced by 2 Chr 7:1b–3. First Kings 8:56 speaks of how all of Yahweh's promises spoken through Moses have come to pass, while 1 Kgs 8:57 is a prayer that Yahweh's presence would remain with the people in the present as it had been in the past. Second Chronicles 7:1b–3, however, contains an account of fire coming from heaven and consuming the sacrifices, the Glory of Yahweh filling the house, the priests being unable to fulfil their duties because of the glory of Yahweh and

---

[80] It is uncertain, however, why the Chronicler did not explicitly state that these actions were in obedience to Moses, or why he omitted the name "Moses." It is clear that conformity to what Moses legislated is in view, even if Moses himself is not mentioned. This purpose of the Chronicler becomes more obvious when one examines the text in a work such as John C. Endres, William. R. Millar, and John Barclay Burns, *Chronicles and Its Synoptic Parallels in Samuel, Kings, and Related Biblical Texts* (Collegeville: The Liturgical Press, 1998), which presents the works of Kings and Chronicles in their synoptic relationships.

concludes (2 Chr 7:3), with the people prostrate before Yahweh in worship. Although this is a near repetition of 2 Chr 5:11–14//1 Kgs 8:10–11, what is important for the Chronicler's view of Moses is that these events are patterned on Exod 40:34–35, where the cloud descends upon the Tent of Meeting, the glory of Yahweh fills the tabernacle, and Moses is not able to enter into the tabernacle. In Exodus, Moses is unable to enter the tent, but in Chronicles the priests are unable to enter the temple. What is evident by this, and by the Chronicler's repetition of the one event, is that the priests (the sons of Aaron) replace Moses and are now the religious leaders of the community.

This is highlighted in the appearances of Moses in Chronicles. While in a list of the sons of Aaron (1 Chr 5:27–41 [6:1–15]), it is natural that the sons of Moses would not be listed, 1 Chr 23:13–17 contrasts the place of the sons of Aaron and the sons of Moses. Consistent with 1 Chr 6:34 [6:49], the sons of Aaron perform cultic duties. The sons of Moses, however, are "counted as part of the tribe of Levi" (1 Chr 23:14).[81] This is made clear in the list of duties in 1 Chr 26:24–28, where Moses' descendants were given responsibility for the treasuries alongside the descendants of the other branches of the sons of Levi (1 Chr 26:29–32). As such, the sons of Moses have not retained the status of their ancestor as the religious leaders of the community. This position has been passed on to the sons of Aaron.

What this indicates is that, for the Chronicler, Moses' importance is as lawgiver and cult founder. Nothing else is as important as these two aspects of Moses' life. This then may also explain why there are no references which connect Moses and the exodus, except 2 Chr 5:10, which has Moses putting the tablets of the law into the ark. Here again, it is the law, rather than the exodus, which is important.

PRESENTATION OF MOSES AND DAVID

As previously mentioned, the Chronicler's introduction of Moses as cult founder in 1 Chr 6:34 [6:49] is contrasted with the role of David in establishing and ordering certain aspects of the cult (1 Chr 6:16–17 [6:31–32]).

---

[81] Although not too much should be made of the use of בדל (separated), in relation to the sons of Aaron (1 Chr 23:13), it may be significant that of the three sons of Levi and the four sons of Kohath, only one of the sons of Amram was בדל (separated), and Moses was not a part of this group being קרא (called) among the remainder of Levi. Not only were the sons of Aaron separated, but so also were the Gadites, who defected to David (1 Chr 12:9 [12:8]), the musicians (1 Chr 25:1), and the mercenaries (2 Chr 25:10).

Both Moses and David are presented in Chronicles as heavily engaged in the setting up of the cult.[82] It is clear that the Chronicler sought to pattern David upon Moses, just as he patterned the transition of power from David to Solomon upon the transition of power from Moses to Joshua.[83]

It is, however, stretching the comparison to suggest that David and Moses are both "cult founders." While the Chronicler's presentation of David and Moses both indicate a strong emphasis upon the cult, there is a clear distinction in the realm of their respective activities.

Although both Moses and David establish a cultic place (1 Chr 6:16, 34 [6:31, 49]), Moses' realm of activity is presented in terms of the cultic rules of sacrifice and atonement, of *how* the cultic activities were to be performed (1 Chr 6:34 [6:49]; 2 Chr 8:13; 23:18; 30:16; 35:6, 12). Moses is also presented as the one who indicates *who* is to perform these cultic tasks (1 Chr 15:15). This is presented in Chronicles as the cultic norm from which the cultic officials should not deviate. It is in fact deviation from the cultic regulations established by Moses that David blames for his failure to bring the ark into Jerusalem on his first attempt (1 Chr 15:13–14).[84]

David is presented, not as one who establishes either cultic rules of sacrifice, nor as the one who determines which group(s) shall perform the cultic rites. David is instead an organiser of the cultic officials within the existing cultic structure. David is not the one determining who the priests are; instead he organises the priests into divisions to provide for the efficient operations of the priesthood (1 Chr 24:1–19). He does the same for Levites (1 Chr 24:20–31) musicians (1 Chr 25) gatekeepers (1 Chr 26:1–19) treasurers and other cultic officials (1 Chr 26:20–32).[85]

---

[82] For David and Moses as "cult founders," see De Vries, "Moses and David."

[83] For the Chronicler's patterning the transition from David to Solomon upon the transition of Moses to Joshua, see: H. G. M. Williamson, "The Ascension of Solomon in the Book of Chronicles," *VT* 26 (1976): 351–361; Roddy L. Braun, "Solomon, the Chosen Temple Builder: The Significance of 1 Chronicles 22, 28, and 29 for the Theology of Chronicles," *JBL* 95 (1976): 581–590; Dillard, "Chronicler's Solomon."

[84] It is also the charge that Abijah uses to condemn Jeroboam and Israel in 2 Chr 13:10–12. Because Judah has the sons of Aaron and the Levites, as well as the proper cultic offerings, "God is with us."

[85] This is also the picture of David presented in Ezra 3:10; 8:20; Neh 12:24, 36, 45. David's organizational abilities are also extended to the army and tribal officers (1 Chr 27). Williamson suggests that most of 1 Chr 23–27 is late additions, with only 1 Chr 23:6b–13a, 15–24; 25:1–6; 26:1–3, 9–11, 19; 26:20–32 as original to the Chronicler's work. It will be observed, however, that this still leaves David as an organizer of pre-existing cultic personnel. H. G. M. Williamson, "The Origins of the Twenty-Four Priestly Courses: A Study of 1 Chronicles 23–27," in *Studies in Persian Period History and Historiography* FAT 38; Tübingen: Mohr Siebeck, 2004).

In all of this, however, David does not go outside the restrictions that the regulations of Moses have already laid down for the cult. The only modification that David makes to a command of Moses is contained in 1 Chr 23:24–27, and it deals with the beginning age of service of the Levites, reducing the starting age to twenty from 25 (Num 8:24).[86]

This latter modification by David highlights the Chronicler's presentation of David's reorganization of the cultic personnel due to changing circumstances. Moses' work assignments envisioned a mobile cultic site, which would require workers to physically transport the cultic site from place to place (Num 4), including the ark (1 Chr 15:15).[87] With the establishment of a permanent cultic site, these workers would no longer be required in the same capacity as previously. The Chronicler then presents David as reorganizing the cultic officials to express the new reality of a fixed, rather than portable, cultic site. Consequently, positions are said to be created which received no mention in the organization of the cult by Moses: musicians, gatekeepers, and treasurers.

What is important is that while the Chronicler allows for David's reorganization of the cultic officials, he does not permit David to bring in new cultic officials (i.e. non-Levites), nor does he allow David to blur the distinction of task between the Levites and the sons of Aaron.[88] Neither does he allow David

---

[86] There is some confusion over the starting age of the Levites. Numbers 8:24 indicates twenty-five years of age, while Num 4:3, 23, 30, 35, 39, 43, 47; 1 Chr 23:3 indicate that the age was thirty. A starting age of twenty is indicated in 1 Chr 23:24, 27; 2 Chr 31:17; Ezra 3:8. Gray suggests "the simplest way of accounting for the differences would be to assume that they correspond to actual differences in the age of service at the different periods to which the several references belong", *A Critical and Exegetical Commentary on Numbers* (ICC; Edinburgh: T&T Clark, 1903), 32.

[87] Japhet points out that although 1 Chr 15:15 states that the ark was to be carried "with poles on their shoulders, as Moses had commanded," nowhere in the Pentateuch is this command present. It is instead inferred through the observation that poles were made for the ark and fitted into rings on its sides (Exod 25:12–15), a detailed description of preparing the tabernacles for transportation is given in Num 4:4–15, and Num 7:9 states that the sons of Kohath were to carry the "holy things" on their shoulders, *Ideology*, 242. That the interpretive processes had developed to the point of utilizing various texts to formulate a combined "this is written" statement is an indication of the growing importance of the Torah in the postexilic community.

[88] The Chronicler does allow at times for Levites to perform priestly duties, when there were not enough priests to adequately perform certain tasks (2 Chr 29:34). While this may have been viewed as a temporary expedient until the shortage of priests was addressed, with the expectation that when the crisis was past the Mosaic regulations would again have precedence, 2 Chr 35:11 makes plain that what was temporary (by virtue of it occurring once), can become the norm.

to implement changes to the duties of the sons of Aaron in regard to sacrifice and atonement.[89]

While the Chronicler presents later kings and leaders as being obedient to the cultic organization of David (2 Chr 8:14–15; 23:18; 29:25; 35:15), he also presents David as being obedient to the cultic commands of Moses (1 Chr 15:2; 16:39–40). While Japhet is correct when she states, "David and Moses have their own well-defined, separate spheres of authority in the book of Chronicles,"[90] and is essentially correct when she says that the three sources of authority in Chronicles are Moses, David and the present king,[91] it is also true that while the present king is shown to be obedient to Moses and David, David is said to be obedient to Moses. Just as the present king's obedience to the commands of David indicate his submission to David and the superiority of David over the present king, so also does David's submission to the commands of Moses indicate David's submission to Moses, and the superiority of Moses over David.

This is further exhibited when it is observed that on five occasions David's authority to implement organizational change is the result, not of David's actions alone, but that of David and another person(s).

- First Chronicles 9:22 claims that the gatekeepers are "assigned to their positions of trust by David and Samuel the seer."
- First Chronicles 25:1 shows that the musicians were reorganised through the actions of "David, together with the commanders of the army."
- Second Chronicles 29:25 says that Hezekiah "stationed the Levites in the temple of the Lord with cymbals, harps and lyres in the way prescribed by David and Gad the king's seer and Nathan the prophet."
- Second Chronicles 35:4 indicates that the instructions for divisions into which priest and Levite should be divided come from "David king of Israel and his son Solomon."
- Second Chronicles 35:15 states that "the musicians, the descendants of Asaph, were in the places prescribed by David, Asaph, Heman and Jeduthun the King's seer."

First Chronicles 9:22; 2 Chr 29:25, 35:15 specifically show that David's innovations were not the unilateral decisions of a king, but were the actions of a king working in harmony with, and perhaps in response to, the word of Yahweh's prophets. Second Chronicles 29:25 concludes that David's actions were, "commanded by the Lord through his prophets." First Chronicles 25:1 states that the ministry of Asaph, Heman and Jeduthun was that of "prophesying," while 1

---

[89] "Chr preserves the traditional order, 'priests and Levites' and never challenges the rights of the 'sons of Aaron' to officiate at the sacrificial ritual," De Vries, "Moses and David," 638.

[90] Japhet, *Ideology*, 237–238.

[91] Japhet, *Ideology*, 235.

Chr 25:2 indicates that Asaph "prophesied under the king's supervision" and 1 Chr 25:3 that "Jeduthun prophesied using the harp." It must also be noted that it was a prophet who prevented David from personally building the temple (1 Chr 17:3–15).

This indicates another level of authority in Chronicles in addition to those proposed by Japhet. Moses is the authority that all obey. There are also prophets who speak the word of Yahweh into a given situation. Finally, there are kings, with David being the greatest, whom other kings are to obey, who also act in obedience to the words of the prophets. David is shown to be acting in obedience to both Moses and the prophets, subservient to them and therefore of a lesser status to prophets in general and Moses in particular, in relation to cultic matters.

What remains clear throughout Chronicles, irrespective of the actions of kings or prophets, is that the priests/sons of Aaron are always the only group authorised to present offerings on the altar and that through their work atonement is made for Israel.[92] Likewise, the Levites assist the priests in the work and have the responsibility for the music, gate keeping, treasuries and other non-priestly duties.[93]

What is significant for the Chronicler's presentation is that throughout Chronicles it is only as the nation operates in the Mosaic pattern expressed in 1 Chr 6:34–35 [6:48–49] that the nation is blessed by Yahweh, and it is when the nation departs from this pattern that it comes under judgment.[94] The great times of national renewal under Jehoiada, Hezekiah and Josiah are those times when the priests and Levites are restored to their positions in the temple and the proper cultic activities, with their focus on sacrifice by the priests accompanied by music performed by the Levites (2 Chr 23:18–19; 29:20–31:1; 35:1–19). This is the pattern that Solomon also followed at the dedication of the temple (2 Chr 5:11–14; 7:1–7).

This indicates that for the Chronicler, as expressed in his genealogy and confirmed in his narrative, what was vital for the ongoing success of the restored community was the prescribed cultic officials performing the prescribed cultic functions in the prescribed cultic place.

---

[92] Priests as sons of Aaron: 2 Chr 13:9–10; 26:18; 31:19. Priests presenting offerings on the altar: 1 Chr 23:13; 2 Chr 23:18; 29:21–24; 35:14. Priests as providing atonement: 1 Chr 6:34 [6:49]; 2 Chr 29:24.

[93] 1 Chronicles 23:24–32; 2 Chr 13:10; 23:18–19; 29:20–25; 30:15–16; 35:10–15.

[94] This is made clear in Hezekiah's speech in 2 Chr 29:3–11.

THE FUTURE OF MOSES AND DAVID

While it is certain that the Chronicler presents the law of Moses as the ultimate law to which all must conform, while allowing the possibility of modifications as the need arises, he indicates that the commands of David also have a continuing validity. Later kings are judged not only for their implementation of the commands of Moses, but also for their implementation of the commands of David.

This is not to say, however, that the Chronicler anticipated a future, restored Davidic kingdom with a Davidide reigning on the throne of Judah or Israel.

Just as it was observed that although the laws of Moses are valid even if the family of Moses does not have the same status as Moses once had, so it is also with David.[95] Although this will be addressed more fully in discussion on the tribe of Judah, I will anticipate that discussion by stating that the Chronicler, although insisting that the cultic organization of David was still the norm for his postexilic society, had no expectation of a restored Davidic monarchy. In the Chronicler's view, the period of David had passed, never to be repeated, while the period of Cyrus had arrived.

CONCLUSION

This section has investigated the first part of the central section of the Chronicler's genealogies. It has been observed that there were Levites who operate at the central cultic site whose tasks are distinct from the sons of Aaron. While the Levites discharge general duties, the sons of Aaron alone perform those rituals that culminate in atonement for the community. The Chronicler insists that this division of personnel and duties is in accordance with the command of Moses himself, and while the duties of the Levitical personnel can be altered due to changing circumstances, the distinction between sons of Aaron and Levites must be maintained.

---

[95] De Vries, "Moses and David." 637.

CHAPTER 3
F1: 1 CHRONICLES 6:35–38 [6:50–53]
THE CULTIC LEADERS

THE PLACE OF THE PASSAGE IN THE GENEALOGIES

First Chronicles 6:35–38 [6:50–53] presents a twelve generation linear genealogy from Aaron to Ahimaaz. The list begins by stating that the following persons are the בְּנֵי אַהֲרֹן (sons of Aaron). This links the names in the list with the statement in 1 Chr 6:34 [6:49] that אַהֲרֹן וּבָנָיו (Aaron and his sons) were the individuals responsible for performing the cultic rituals of sacrifice and making atonement.

The contents of this list are similar to a portion of the list contained in 1 Chr 5:27–41 [6:1–15]. First Chronicles 5:29–34 [6:3–8], contains each of the names found in 1 Chr 6:35–38 [6:50–53], and in the same order. There are, however, four significant differences.

First, 1 Chr 5:29–34 [6:3–8], uses the term הוֹלִיד (became the father of), to indicate the relationship between the persons named, while 1 Chr 6:35–38 [6:50–53] uses בְּנוֹ (his son).

Second, while the names located in 1 Chr 6:35–38 [6:50–53] do occur in the same order as in 1 Chr 5:29–34 [6:3–8], 1 Chr 5:29–34 [6:3–8] records each of the four sons of Aaron before following the line of the third listed son, Eleazar. First Chronicles 6:35–38 [6:50–53] does not contain the names of the three other sons of Aaron: Nadab, Abihu, and Ithamar.

Third, the list in 1 Chr 5:29–34 [6:3–8] is not designed to be a list of the sons of Aaron. It is instead a part of the larger list of the sons of Levi (1 Chr 5:27 [6:1]). In this list, Levi's sons are listed first, followed by his grandchildren through Kohath, his great-grandchildren through Amram,[1] and his great-great-

---

[1] Miriam, who is elsewhere called the sister of Aaron and Moses (Exod 15:20; Num 26:59), is in 1 Chr 5:29 [6:3] the "son," בֵּן, of Amram. This is not unusual in the genealogies. Cf. 1 Chr 3:19; 7:30 where Shelomith and Serah are listed as "sons," although in both cases they are also called "their sister," אֲחוֹתָם, which is the same phrase used of Miriam in Num 26:59. "Son," בֵּן, may also mean the more general "offspring."

grandchildren through Aaron, before finally following the line of Eleazar. The different starting ancestor speaks of the differing functions of the two lists.[2]

Fourth, the two lists are not of similar length. Just as the list in 1 Chr 5:27–41 [6:1–15] begins with Levi and not Aaron, so also it extends much further than the list contained in 1 Chr 6:35–38 [6:50–53]. The list in 1 Chr 5:27–41 [6:1–15] claims to reach down to the exile of Jerusalem at the hand of the Babylonian king, Nebuchadnezzar. The list in 1 Chr 6:35–38 [6:50–53] reaches only until the time of David or Solomon.[3]

Consequently, even if one list did form the basis for the other, in their current location in the text and in their current form, the two lists are performing clearly different functions.[4]

THE LIST OF THE SONS OF AARON

The list in 1 Chr 6:35–38 [6:50–53] indicates that it contains the "sons of Aaron." The phrase בְּנֵי אַהֲרֹן (sons of Aaron) occurs forty-nine times in the Hebrew Bible.[5] On almost every occasion it refers to a group who are involved in the cultic service of the tabernacle/temple rather than a simple list of biological offspring of Aaron. The duties of the sons of Aaron presented in 1 Chr 6:34 [6:49] are also highlighted in the narrative of Chronicles. The sons of Aaron are

---

[2] Wilson commented that genealogies which function in different spheres, while they may be similar, will be structured differently, and will contain different information, dependent upon the different purposes for which they were formulated. Wilson, *Genealogy*, 37–45.

[3] Even this point is uncertain. While a Zadok is recorded in the reign of Solomon taking over the office of priest from Abiathar (1 Kgs 2:35), there is no mention of a son of Zadok named Ahimaaz in the period of Solomon. An Ahimaaz son of Zadok does appear in the reign of David (2 Sam 15:27, 36; 18:19, 22, 27), while a (different?) Ahimaaz marries a daughter of Solomon (1 Kgs 4:15). There is nothing in the text to indicate that these references are to the same individual.

[4] The list in 1 Chr 5:27–45 [6:1–15], will be discussed in chapter 4. The debate regarding which list was the source for the other has been long. For those who favour 1 Chr 6:35–38 [6:50–53] as the source for 1 Chr 5:27–41 [6:1–15], see Noth, *Chronicler's History*, 39–40; Braun, *1 Chronicles*; 81. For those who hold to the priority of 1 Chr 5:27–41 [6:1–15], see Williamson, *Chronicles*, 71; Thompson, *Chronicles*, 89; Gary N. Knoppers, "The Relationship of the Priestly Genealogies to the History of the High Priesthood in Jerusalem," in *Judah and the Judeans in the Neo-Babylonian Period* (ed. Oded Lipschits and Joseph Blenkinsopp; Winona Lake: Eisenbrauns, 2003); 116–122; Ralph W. Klein, *1 Chronicles* (Minneapolis: Fortress Press, 2006), 176.

[5] Exodus 2x; Leviticus 22x; Numbers 3x; Joshua 4x (only in the distribution of towns); 1 Chronicles 10x; 2 Chronicles 7x; Nehemiah 1x.

the true priests who offer burnt offerings and incense (2 Chr 13:10–11). The sons of Aaron present burnt offerings, sprinkle the blood of the sacrifice on the altar and make atonement for the people (2 Chr 29:21–22), and make sacrifices (2 Chr 35:14). The duties of the sons of Aaron presented in the genealogies are consistent with the portrayal of the duties of the sons of Aaron in the remainder of the work.

> But Aaron and his descendants were the ones who presented offerings on the altar of burnt offering and on the altar of incense in connection with all that was done in the Most Holy Place, making atonement for Israel, in accordance with all that Moses the servant of God had commanded. (1 Chr 6:34 [6:49]).

The portrayal of the "sons of Aaron" as cultic functionaries in the genealogies and narrative sections of Chronicles is also consistent with the portrayal of their duties in Leviticus. They are the ones who sprinkle the blood (Lev 1:5, 11; 3:2, 8, 13), prepare the wood and fire on the altar (Lev 1:7), arrange the sacrifice on the wood (Lev 1:8; 3:5), burn the memorial portion of the grain offering on the altar (Lev 2:2; 6:7 [6:14]), and on certain occasions bring the blood of the sacrifice to Aaron who sprinkles the blood (Lev 9:9, 12, 18).[6] That the Chronicler's vision of the sons of Aaron is close to that of the priestly literature indicates not only the normative nature of the priestly literature in the Chronicler's thought, but also that the priestly literature, even if now incorporated into a larger work, is seen as the standard for the cultic life of the community.

This listing of the sons of Aaron also indicates that there are no alternatives to the Aaronite priesthood. The Levites have their duties within the tabernacle/house of God, which are for them alone, and likewise the sons of Aaron have their duties and responsibilities which are for this group alone. The Chronicler is here allowing for no variation, nor is he allowing for any outside intruders into the authorised cultic celebrants.

Through the inclusion of a list of Aaron's sons, the Chronicler builds into his chiastic structure the element of "intensification" spoken of by Welch.[7] The

---

[6] While in Lev 9:9, 12, 18 it is the sons of Aaron who pass the blood to the officiating priest so that the blood can be sprinkled on the altar, in 2 Chr 30:16 it is affirmed, and in 2 Chr 35:11 it is implied, that it is the Levites who pass the blood to the priests so that it can be sprinkled. While the Chronicler seeks to portray the temple worship in continuity with that of the tabernacle, he does not demand exact conformity, and allows for deviation from the priestly norm in special circumstances.

[7] Intensification occurs in a chiasm through "building to a climax at the center as well as by strengthening each element individually upon its chiastic repetition," Welch, "Introduction." 10. That the Chronicler here repeats information solely for the sons of Aaron, and not for the Levites as a whole as found in level F, may be further evidence of the centrality of the function of the sons of Aaron in respect to atonement.

Chronicler has stated his primary point, the distinct duties of Levites and the sons of Aaron in the tabernacle/house of God, and he intensifies this through giving a listing of the ongoing identity of these "sons of Aaron." There can therefore be no misunderstandings regarding which group has the right and responsibility of sacrifice and atonement.

Since he has made clear the identity of the "sons of Aaron" who perform the sacrificial and atonement responsibilities, it is not necessary to further explain who the "Levites" are who perform the other duties. In 1 Chr 5:27–6:32 [6:1–47] the Chronicler had already identified varying groups who were classified as "sons of Levi" or Levites. Through singling out one of these previously mentioned groups as "sons of Aaron" to perform sacrifice, he automatically indicates what the duties and responsibilities of the other Levites are. Specifically, everything not done by the sons of Aaron is the responsibility of these other groups. As such, the emphasis in this list is not on the genealogy, but on the "son" who carries out the task assigned to the group.

INTERPRETATIONS OF THE LIST OF THE SONS OF AARON

A HIGH PRIEST LIST

There are various alternative understandings of this list of the sons of Aaron. One suggestion is that this is a list of those who held the position of "High Priest."[8]

It must be observed at the outset that nowhere in this list, nor in the list of 1 Chr 5:27–41 [6:1–15], is it suggested that these individuals held the position of "High Priest."[9] The term כֹּהֵן (priest) is not mentioned in the genealogies until 1 Chr 9:2, although the verb כהן (to serve as priest) occurs in 1 Chr 5:36 [6:10]. This occurrence does not demand that a person served in the capacity of "High Priest," for the verb is normally used to indicate the work of serving as a priest in general.[10] כהן sometimes refers to a son succeeding his father into the position of

---

[8] This has been stated by many authors, e.g. Leslie C. Allen, *1, 2 Chronicles* (Waco: Word, 1987), 63; Braun, *1 Chronicles*, 95.

[9] The list in 1 Chr 5:27–41 [6:1–15] will be investigated in Chapter 4.

[10] Although often used in the infinitive with the meaning "to serve as priest" (Exod 28:1, 3, 4; 29:1, 44; 30:30; 31:10; 35:19; 39:41; Lev 7:35; 16:32; Num 3:3; 2 Chr 11:14; Ezek 44:13; Hos 4:6), it is sometimes used in the plural for many persons serving as priests (Exod 28: 41; 40:15; 1 Chr 24:2).

High Priest (Lev 16:32; Deut 10:6),[11] and once to a person being rejected from what may be assumed to be a high priestly position (Hos 4:6).[12]

The function of this list of the sons of Aaron is dictated not by the position that Aaron himself held as הַכֹּהֵן הַגָּדוֹל (the great priest; Lev 21:10),[13] but by the duties and tasks that the sons of Aaron as a group were to perform as specified in 1 Chr 6:34 [6:49].[14] This list in 1 Chr 6:35–38 [6:50–53] indicates who these sons of Aaron are who were to perform these stated duties.

THE LEGITIMIZATION OF ZADOK

Some writers have suggested that the purpose of this list is the need to legitimise Zadok and his descendants as the lawful high priests in the postexilic community. This need is said to develop because of the Deuteronomistic History's statement that Zadok replaced Abiathar as priest (1 Kgs 2:35).[15]

The Need for Legitimization

In the Deuteronomistic History Zadok is presented as an equal priest alongside Abiathar (2 Sam 20:25), or Ahimelech (2 Sam 8:17), during the reign of David. During Absalom's rebellion, when David fled from Jerusalem, it is Zadok who appears to have the custodianship of the ark of the covenant (2 Sam 15:24),

---

[11] Leviticus 16:32 does not say that this is a succession to the position of "high priest" (NIV), but to one of succeeding his father. However, as all the "sons of Aaron" operated as priests, the succession here is reasonably to that of "head of the priests." This is further highlighted by the observation that the commands of Lev 16:2–25 are directed to Aaron, and Lev 16:32 addresses the issue of the succession to the duties that Aaron performed on the day of atonement. Deuteronomy 10:6 does not state that Eleazar succeeded his father as High Priest, but only as "priest." The context, however, makes it clear that Eleazar had assumed the position of "head of the priests" in place of his father, consistent with the commands of Lev 16:32. These are the only passages which speak of the hereditary succession of the high priesthood.

[12] Although not accepted by all scholars, some do suggest that this is a reference to a high priestly position. "While no special title is given, it is clear that Hosea is speaking of a high priest or chief priest at a central shrine," Francis I. Andersen and David Noel Freedman, *Hosea* (AB 24; Garden City: Doubleday, 1980), 353. Although the NIV makes this plural ("I reject you as priests"), the Hebrew here is singular (so NRSV).

[13] Ezra 7:5, however, refers to Aaron as הַכֹּהֵן הָרֹאשׁ (the head priest). These are the only places where either term is applied to Aaron.

[14] So also Knoppers, "Relationship." 113.

[15] "Diese Priesterschaft, die Bene Sadok, erheben den Anspruch, die rechtmäßigen Erben Aharons zu sein, und das konnte nur durch eine feste Genealogie bewiesen werden," Rothstein and Hänel, *Chronik*, 112. Payne agrees, saying that this list "confirms that the Zadokite priests, alone among the Levitical divisions in David's day, had the authority to make a sacrificial atonement," "Chronicles," 354.

although both Zadok and Abiathar escort the ark back into Jerusalem (2 Sam 15:29). In the political instability which occurred toward the end of David's life, when rival claimants for the throne arose, Abiathar supported Adonijah, who was next in line for the throne (1 Kgs 1:5–7), while Zadok supported Solomon (1 Kgs 1:32–45).

As a result of Solomon's ascendancy, Abiathar was dismissed from his position as priest and replaced by Zadok (1 Kgs 2:35). This is presented in the Deuteronomistic History as fulfilment of a prophetic message to the family of Eli (1 Sam 2:27–36; 1 Kgs 2:26–27). Following this, Zadok disappears from the written record apart from a list of Solomon's officials in which he and Abiathar are both priests and one of Zadok's sons appears as priest (1 Kgs 4:2, 4).

The means whereby Zadok comes to the prominent priestly position, and the story generated which justifies that ascendancy, has raised questions regarding the legitimacy of Zadok as a priest. These questions would also have been present when the story was proclaimed, and the story would have acted to counter questions of Zadok's legitimacy and his right to replace an established priesthood. Once established in his position, and with the story accepted, his legitimacy would not be again questioned until an alternative means of legitimization arose in the community which would challenge the previously accepted story.

The story presented in 1 Sam 2:27–36 and said to be fulfilled in 1 Kgs 2:26–27 is shaped so as to present Zadok, his ascendancy and his heirs in the best possible light. Corrupt priests, who did not treat the people's sacrifices according to the tradition (1 Sam 2:12–17), whose behaviour was morally questionable (1 Sam 2:22), and who refused to listen to their father when rebuked (1 Sam 2:23–25), were justly and properly condemned by a man of God. This condemnation resulted in that priestly family losing its right to dominate the priestly service (1 Sam 2:31–33).[16] Yahweh promised instead that a "faithful priest" (1 Sam 2:35) would be raised up to minister before Yahweh's "anointed."[17] He would occupy

---

[16] That opportunity to serve in a priestly capacity was still a possibility is indicated in 1 Sam 2:36.

[17] The contrived nature of this prophecy is obvious from the term "my anointed." This phrase is used to refer to the king, yet at the time of Eli, no king had yet been anointed for a priest to stand before, cf. 1 Sam 2:10. Saul (1 Sam 9:16; 10;1; 12:3, 5; 15:1, 17; 24:6, 10; 26:9, 11, 16, 23; 2 Sam 1:14, 16), David (1 Sam 16:3, 6, 12, 13; 2 Sam 2:4, 7; 3:39; 5:3, 17; 12:7; 19:21; 22:51; 23:1; 1 Chr 29:22), Jehu (1 Kgs 19:16; 2 Kgs 9:3, 6, 12; 2 Chr 22:7), Hazael of Damascus (1 Kgs 19:15) and the unnamed king of Lamentations 4:20, probably Zedekiah, are all said to be the "Lord's anointed," or simply the "anointed" king of the people. Other kings were said to be anointed, but none were anointed explicitly at Yahweh's command, Absalom (2 Sam 19:10), Solomon (1 Kgs 1:34, 39, 45; 5:1; 1 Chr 29:22); Joash (2 Kgs 11:12; 2 Chr 23:11), Josiah (2 Kgs 23:30).

the priesthood in perpetuity. As a product of its own time, the story of the rise of Zadok prompts little comment. It is a piece of political propaganda used to justify the replacement of one priesthood by a new one.[18] It is only in the light of later cultic developments, particularly the emphasis in the priestly literature upon the "sons of Aaron," that the legitimacy of Zadok might be questioned.

The Background in Ezekiel

Apart from the historiographical books of the Hebrew Bible, Zadok appears only in Ezekiel.[19] Although the portrayal of Zadok in Ezekiel is often said to present the demotion of unfaithful priests to the status of Levites and to justify the claim to the exclusive rights to the altar by the Zadokites in Ezekiel's idealised temple, this is uncertain.[20] Although this is not the place to fully investigate Ezekiel's view of the Zadokites, certain points are clear (see Figure 3.1).

Figure 3.1: Ezekiel and the Zadokites

Ezek	כֹּהֵן	שֹׁמְרֵי מִשְׁמֶרֶת	צָדוֹק	קרב	שרת
40:45	לַכֹּהֲנִים	שֹׁמְרֵי מִשְׁמֶרֶת הַבַּיִת			
40:46	לַכֹּהֲנִים	שֹׁמְרֵי מִשְׁמֶרֶת הַמִּזְבֵּחַ	בְנֵי־צָדוֹק	הַקְּרֵבִים	לְשָׁרְתוֹ
43:19	הַכֹּהֲנִים הַלְוִיִּם		צָדוֹק מִזֶּרַע	הַקְּרֵבִים	לְשָׁרְתֵנִי
44:15	הַכֹּהֲנִים הַלְוִיִּם	שָׁמְרוּ אֶת־מִשְׁמֶרֶת מִקְדָּשִׁי	בְנֵי צָדוֹק	יִקְרְבוּ לְהַקְרִיב	לְשָׁרְתֵנִי
44:16		וְשָׁמְרוּ אֶת־מִשְׁמַרְתִּי		יִקְרְבוּ	לְשָׁרְתֵנִי
48:11	לַכֹּהֲנִים	שָׁמְרוּ מִשְׁמַרְתִּי	צָדוֹק מִבְּנֵי		

First, Ezekiel clearly makes a distinction between the בְּנֵי צָדוֹק (sons of Zadok) and the Levites.[21] Although the sons of Zadok are both כֹּהֲנִים (priests)[22]

---

[18] For an evaluation of the entire account of David as "propaganda," see Baruch Halpern, *David's Secret Demons: Messiah, Murderer, Traitor, King* (Grand Rapids: Eerdmans, 2001).

[19] Ezekiel 40:46; 43:19; 44:15; 48:11. Although the originality of Ezek 40–48 to the work of Ezekiel has been questioned, what is not in question is the emphasis placed in this section on the prominence of Zadok.

[20] For challenges to this view see, Raymond Abba, "Priests and Levites in Ezekiel," *VT* 28 (1978): 1–9; Rodney K. Duke, "Punishment or Restoration? Another Look at the Levites of Ezekiel 44.6–16," *JSOT* 40 (1988): 61–81; Daniel I. Block, *The Book of Ezekiel Chapters 25–48* (NICOT; Grand Rapids: Eerdmans, 1998), 616–637.

[21] Ezekiel 40:46; 44:15; 48:11. In Ezek 43:19 they are called זֶרַע צָדוֹק (seed of Zadok).

[22] Ezekiel 40:45–46; 43:19; 44:15; 48:11.

and הַלְוִיִּם (Levites)[23] nowhere does Ezekiel identify them with Aaron, who is never mentioned in Ezekiel.[24] This indicates that while the Zadokites are Levites, they are different and distinct to other groups of Levites. It must be noticed, however, that, unlike the priestly literature, this distinction is not based on their ancestry, either from Aaron who is not mentioned or from Zadok who is, but on account of the faithfulness of the sons of Zadok to Yahweh (as opposed to the faithfulness of Zadok himself) when the other Levites followed idols along with the rest of Israel.

Second, the duties of the sons of Zadok are within the realm of the cult. They are to be the guards, (שֹׁמְרֵי מִשְׁמֶרֶת),[25] of the house (הַבַּיִת), altar (הַמִּזְבֵּחַ),[26] and the sanctuary (מִקְדָּשִׁי).[27] As such, the duties of the sons of Zadok are consistent with the duties given to Aaron in the priestly literature (Num 18:5), and the limitations placed by Ezekiel on the non-Zadokite Levites in prohibiting them from approaching the altar are consistent with the limitations on the non-Aaronite Levites (Num 18:3).

The sons of Zadok are more than guards, however, for they alone are able to draw near (קרב) to Yahweh, his table and sanctuary, and they alone serve (שרת) Yahweh in this manner. Again, this is consistent with the portrayal of the sons of Aaron in the priestly material, for only Aaron and his sons could draw near to Yahweh and his sanctuary (Num 3:10, 38; 18:7), and only Aaron and his sons could serve before Yahweh (Exod 28:35, 43; 29:30; 30:20; 35:19; 39:1, 26, 41). Levites, however, served Aaron and his sons (Num 3:6; 18:2), or at the tabernacle (Num 1:50; 8:26; cf. Ezek 45:5).[28]

---

[23] Ezekiel 43:19; 44:15. In Ezek 40:46 they are said to be "from the sons of Levi," מִבְּנֵי לֵוִי.

[24] In the Prophets, only Mic 6:4 mentions Aaron, and then not in his capacity as priest, but as a deliverer alongside Moses and Miriam.

[25] "The priests here are not primarily functionaries in the cult, but defenders of the sanctity of temple space and altar," Block, *Ezekiel 25–48*, 537. The phrase is used in respect to being a guard in 2 Kgs 11:5–7; 1 Chr 12:30 [12:29]; Neh 12:45. The phrase is also used with respect to a person's obedience, or otherwise, to a command or an agreement, Gen 26:5; Lev 8:35; 18:30; 22:9; Josh 22:3; 1 Kgs 2:3.

[26] Ezekiel 40:45–46. Block persuasively argues that instead of two different classes of priests, a lower group with responsibility for the house and a higher group with responsibility for the altar, that both are the responsibility of the sons of Zadok, Block, *Ezekiel 25–48*, 535–539.

[27] Ezekiel 40:45–46; 44:15. The combination of מִשְׁמֶרֶת and שמר also occurs in 44:16; 48:11.

[28] This right is said to belong to the Levites in Deut 10:8; 18:5, 7; 21:5 and Jer 33:21, 22.

The priestly literature, however, ascribes the place of priority to the Aaronites, and the role and functions ascribed to the Zadokites in Ezekiel are performed by the Aaronites in the priestly literature. Although the exact process is uncertain, it is clear that the claimed priority of the Zadokites in Ezekiel becomes the established priority of the Aaronites in the priestly literature, and it is the established priority of the Aaronites that forms the basis for the Chronicler's genealogies of the sons of Aaron.[29]

It also appears from these differences between the priestly literature and Ezekiel that different views existed in the exilic and postexilic eras as to what constituted a person's right to serve as a legitimate priest. The Ezekiel tradition, or that of his later editors, indicated that legitimacy came from descent from Zadok. The priestly tradition insisted on descent from Aaron. The genealogies of the early postexilic period, however, did not refer to either of these persons as the means of legitimisation. Instead, reference to descent from Aaron or Zadok in the ancestry of those who claimed to be priests only appears in the later literature of the postexilic era.

The Genealogical Evidence

As stated above, there is no genealogy from the early postexilic period which connects any priest to either Zadok or Aaron. There is reference to Joshua the son of Jehozadak (Hag 1:1, 12, 14; 2:2, 4; Zech 6:11),[30] as high priest during the construction of the second temple, but no reference to Joshua being a descendant of either Aaron or Zadok. Even those who were excluded from the priesthood (Ezra 2:59–63), were not excluded because they could not trace their ancestry to either Zadok or Aaron, but because "they could not show that their families were descended from Israel" (Ezra 2:59b).[31]

In the lists of those who returned, the legitimate priestly families were Jedaiah (through Jeshua), Immer, Pashhur, and Harim (Ezra 2:36–39; Neh 7:39–42).[32] None of these families were said to be connected to either Zadok or Aaron.

---

[29] It is to be noted that in both the priestly literature and in Ezekiel the Levites exist as a lower level of cultic official.

[30] Referred to as Jeshua son of Jozadak in Ezra 3:8; 5:2; 10:18; Neh 12:26.

[31] Knoppers says that "given the paucity of thorough genealogical information about priests . . . some of the priests who considered themselves to be of excellent pedigree may have had difficulty substantiating their claims," "Relationship," 109. This, however, appears to suggest that these returning priests had to prove their priestly status. This is not, however, what is stated. What is stated is that they had to prove that they were descended from Israel. The text suggests that their claim to priestly status would have been acceptable if they could have proven their ethnic descent from Israel.

[32] While it is uncertain when and in what circumstances these lists originated, that they were used by Nehemiah in his attempt to repopulate Jerusalem indicates a date at

Likewise, in the list of those who had married foreign women in the time of Ezra (Ezra 10:18–22), the priestly families were, again, Jeshua son of Jozadak, Immer, Harim, and Pashhur.[33] Again, there is no attempt to trace the heritage of the priestly families back to either Aaron or Zadok.

It appears from this that in the early postexilic period, leading at least to the time of Ezra and Nehemiah, Zadokite or Aaronite ancestry was not considered to be so important that it had to be demonstrated in genealogical form as a means of legitimisation. This does not mean that such descent could not have been assumed. What it does mean is that it was not yet felt important enough to establish one's right to the priesthood by means of a genealogical connection to either Zadok or Aaron. It is only in the period of Ezra/Nehemiah that longer genealogical lists begin to appear which connected individuals to either of these priestly ancestors.[34]

Nehemiah 11 reproduces a list of those who volunteered, or were volunteered, to dwell in Jerusalem after the building of the walls. A similar list is produced in 1 Chr 9:10–13, where it is presented as those who resettled in Jerusalem.[35] The heads of the leading priestly families are presented in Figure 3.2.[36]

---

least prior to Nehemiah. For a discussion of the compositional history of Ezra 2, see H. G. M. Williamson, "The Composition of Ezra 1–6," in *Studies in Persian Period History and Historiography* FAT 38; Tübingen: Mohr Siebeck, 2004), 245–250; David J. A. Clines, *Ezra, Nehemiah, Esther* (NCB; Grand Rapids: Eerdmans, 1984), 43–45. A far more extensive list of "heads of the priestly families" is given from the days of Joiakim. This list includes the family of Harim (Neh 12:15) and two families of Jedaiah (Neh 12:19, 21). There is no record here of Immer or Pashhur.

[33] The change in order from the list of Ezra 3:36–39 (Jedaiah, Immer, Pashhur, Harim) to Ezra 10:18–22 (Jeshua, Immer, Harim, Pashhur) may suggest, but certainly does not demand, a lessening status, influence, or numbers in the family of Pashhur in relation to that of Harim. Jeremiah 20:1 speaks of a Pashhur son of Immer, the priest, while Jer 21:1 speaks of Pashhur son of Malkijah, although this verse does not identify him as a priest. It is possible that the postexilic priestly families of Pashhur and Immer trace their origins to these individuals. Harim is not known outside of Ezra and Nehemiah.

[34] This is not to suggest that such lists did not exist prior to this period. Ezra 2:62–63 makes it clear that family records of some type were kept to prove membership in Israel. The extent and fullness of these particular lists are unknown.

[35] The relationship between the two lists will be investigated in chapter 13.

[36] The place of Jedaiah, Jehoiarib, Jakin in 1 Chr 9:10 // Neh 11:10 is uncertain. Neh 11:10 makes Jedaiah the son of Jehoiarib, while 1 Chr 24:7, 17 makes each the head of one of the priestly courses, as also is Immer (1 Chr 24:14b), Malkijah (1 Chr 24:9), and Jeshua (1 Chr 24:11).

Several things are of interest here. First, the family of Harim is not mentioned. Whether this is an accidental or deliberate omission is uncertain.[37]

Second, that Pashhur son of Malkijah is a contemporary of the prophet Jeremiah (Jer 21:1; 38:1), and therefore also of Seraiah the high priest, is an indication that the list of the family of Jeshua is not complete.[38] Telescoping is a common feature of genealogies, and indicates that the narrator of the genealogy is primarily interested in establishing the relationship between the last person named and a significant ancestor who heads the list.

Third, the family of Immer presents two, different, genealogical lines, which suggests that although the two lists are related, they record different genealogical segments.[39]

Fourth, in the family of Jeshua, one of the names in 1 Chronicles is Azariah, while in Neh 11 it is Seraiah. This may not be significant, for Azariah (עֲזַרְיָה) is similar to Seraiah (שְׂרָיָה).[40]

---

[37] "As there is no apparent reason for this, it is probable that we should again reckon with its loss at some stage in the transmission of the text," H. G. M. Williamson, *Ezra, Nehemiah* (WBC 16; Waco: Word, 1985), 351. Clines suggests that the differences in totals of priests given in Neh 11:10–14 (1,192) and 1 Chr 9:13 (1,760) may result from the omission of Harim in Nehemiah, although Harim is also not mentioned by name in 1 Chr 9, *Ezra, Nehemiah, Esther*, 215.

[38] Wilson states, "because people who use genealogies tend to cite only the portion of a genealogy that is relevant to the situation at hand, certain unessential names may temporarily be omitted from the recital," *Genealogy*, 32–33.

[39] Mishillemith and Meshillemoth are variants of the same name, with either the compilers or a later copyist confusing the י or ו.

[40] As the text stands however, this list ends at the exile with the death of Azariah/Seraiah (cf. 2 Kgs 25:18). To extend the list into the postexilic period, Rudolph suggests reading Jakin, יָכִין, in Neh 11:10 as "son of," בֶּן, thus giving a reading of "Jedaiah the son of Joiarib, the son of Seraiah," *Chronikbücher*, 84. Even this emendation need not be necessary if it is suggested that "son" was omitted between Joiarib and Jakin, as well as between Jakin and Seraiah. 1 Chronicles 9:11 does not contain "son" at all, even though one instance does occur in Neh 11:10, "Jedaiah the son of Joiarib." A similar phenomena occurs in 1 Chr 1:1–4, 24–27, where descendants are listed without any relationship markers. This would give the proposed reading of, "Jedaiah the son of Joiarib the son of Jakin the son of Seraiah" Wilson's observation, "without this expression of the kinship relationship, the names simply constitute a list and are not a genealogy," is applicable here, *Genealogy*, 10. Without express relationships being stated, the relationship, if any, between the names is uncertain. Because the relationship is known in the lists of 1 Chr 1:1–4 through the book of Genesis, these can be supplied by the reader. It is possible that the Chronicler omitted the relational terminology in 1 Chr 9:10–11 on the assumption it also would be known to the readers. At the time of writing perhaps it was. In our present time period, we can only make an educated guess.

It would be easy for a scribe to combine עׂ, to read שׂ, or vice versa, thus bringing the variation in the names.[41]

Figure 3.2: Priestly Families in 1 Chronicles 9 // Nehemiah 11

Family of Jeshua		Family of Pashhur		Family of Immer	
1 Chr 9:11	Neh 11:11	1 Chr 9:12a	Neh 11:12	1 Chr 9:12b	Neh 11:13
Ahitub	Ahitub				
Meraioth	Meraioth				
Zadok	Zadok				
Meshullam	Meshullam				
Hilkiah	Hilkiah	Malkijah	Malkijah		
Azariah	Seraiah	Pashhur	Pashhur	Immer	Immer
			Zechariah	Meshillemith	Meshillemoth
			Amzi	Meshullam	
Jakin	Jakin		Pelaliah	Jahzerah	Ahzai
Jehoiarib	Joiarib	Jeroham	Jeroham	Adiel	Azarel
Jedaiah	Jedaiah	Adaiah	Adaiah	Maasai	Amashsai

What is significant in these lists is that here, for the first time in postexilic literature, there is mention of a Zadok. What is more, this is a Zadok who is the stated ancestor of a person who is recorded to have been the high priest.[42] Significantly, however, this Zadok is not the more ancient Davidic Zadok, but a more recent person bearing that name. Neither is he the lineage founder, and therefore he is not the most prominent ancestor. What this indicates is that while Zadokite descent is being acknowledged genealogically, Zadokite descent is not suggested to be normative for priestly legitimisation for if it was, Zadok would have headed the list.

By contrast, Ezra 8:2–14 purports to list those who accompanied Ezra from Babylon to Jerusalem. Among this group were priests who, although not giving complete genealogies, claimed to be descendants of Phinehas or Ithamar (Ezra 8:2). This appears to be a claim to a direct descent from Aaron, although Aaron

---

[41] Knoppers, *1 Chronicles 1–9*, 496. Knoppers also notes the similar phenomena in Ezra 2:2 (Seraiah), and Neh 7:7 (Azariah). Japhet, however, following the genealogy contained in 1 Chr 5:27–41 [6:1–15] suggests reading "'Azariah' and 'Seraiah' as two consecutive names in the official priestly genealogy," *Chronicles*, 211.

[42] Hilkiah in 2 Kgs 22:4, 8; 23:4; 2 Chr 34:9.

himself is not mentioned. By mentioning the descendant of Aaron through whom they claimed to be priests, they were aligning themselves with the sons of Aaron. Furthermore, these individuals staked a claim to priesthood on a more ancient family relationship than did those who placed Zadok into their lineage. This is evidence that the claimed superiority of the Zadokites in Ezekiel was not only in conflict with that of the Aaronites, but was already being superseded by the claims of the sons of Aaron.[43]

What this indicates is that at approximately the time of Ezra and Nehemiah there is a diminishing significance in Zadokite descent, and an increasing emphasis upon being a part of the "sons of Aaron." This too, is in keeping with the emphasis of the priestly literature which was also becoming normative in the period following Ezra.

Ezra's Genealogy

The postexilic historiographic works (Chronicles, Ezra, Nehemiah) contain five genealogies of varying length which connect an individual to Zadok, Aaron or both.[44] 1 Chr 9:10–11 // Neh 11:10–11 has already examined and it was observed that these are the first genealogies which reach back to a person named Zadok. As yet, however, the genealogies do not reach back to the person of Aaron. The first extant genealogies to reach back to Aaron from the postexilic era are found in Ezra 7:1–5 and 1 Chr 5:27–41 [6:1–15]. The exact relationship between these two genealogies is debated. Some hold that the list in Ezra 7 is dependent upon that in 1 Chr 6,[45] while others hold that the list in 1 Chr 6 is dependent upon that in Ezra 7.[46]

Other authors suggest that both lists draw from a separate, independent source,[47] while Noth dismisses it as a secondary insertion.[48]

The issue of priority is not significant to our purposes. What is of importance is that these are the first lists in the postexilic period to speak of descent from

---

[43] The genealogy of Ezra (Ezra 7:1–5) is not included at this point for, as Williamson explains, it is probably the work of the editor of the work rather than being an original part of the Ezra Memoir, *Ezra, Nehemiah*, 91.

[44] See Figure 3.3, where these are presented from the shortest to the longest.

[45] Jacob M. Myers, *Ezra Nehemiah* (AB 14; Doubleday: Garden City, 1965), 60; Clines, *Ezra, Nehemiah, Esther*, 99; Noth, *Chronicler's History*, 62–63; W. Boyd Barrick, "Genealogical Notes on the 'House of David' and the 'House of Zadok,'" *JSOT* 96 (2001): 29–58, 44.

[46] Braun, *1 Chronicles*, 85; Rudolph, *Chronikbücher*, 53. So also Johnson on "the supposition that the shorter of the two is prior," *Purpose*, 40.

[47] Williamson, *Ezra, Nehemiah*, 91. Knoppers, "Relationship," 111–112.

[48] Noth, *Chronicler's History*, 62–63. It is to be noted that Noth allows for this as either the work of the Chronicler or a later redactor.

Aaron as either the means of legitimising one in the priestly office, or the means by which the sons of Aaron were connected to the Levites. What is important is that while both lists record the order: "Azariah, Amariah, Ahitub, Zadok, Shallum" (levels 18–20, 22–23),[49] the Chronicler's list includes the names "Amariah, Ahitub, Zadok, Ahimaaz, Azariah, Johanan" (levels 12–17).

It has been suggested that this group of names was lost from the Ezra list through homoioteleuton, with a scribe jumping from Amariah I to Amariah II thus omitting the intervening names.[50] This, however, is not reasonable, for if this were to happen, the Ezra list should not contain Azariah (G18), but should jump from Meraioth to Amariah II.[51] That it does not, is an indication that these names were either deliberately omitted by the author of Ezra, or deliberately inserted by the Chronicler.

The question must be asked as to which author would have the greater motive for either inclusion or omission. It could be argued that the author of Ezra sought to omit the family of Zadok I, who, according to the Deuteronomistic History was not an Elide, and therefore possibly not an Aaronite either. If this were the case, then this only explains Ahitub, Zadok, Ahimaaz and Azariah. It does not explain the omission of Amariah and Johanan. These names do not occur in relation to Zadok in either 2 Samuel or 1 Kings, and there would therefore be no reason to exclude them because of association with Zadok.

There is, however, good reason for the Chronicler to include these names, particularly that of Zadok. This reason is not in regard to the legitimising of Zadok, which by the Chronicler's time had become a moot point because of the normative nature of the priestly literature and its insistence on descent from Aaron, but simply because Zadok was the priest in the time of David.

It is well established in the Deuteronomistic History that Zadok and Abiathar were co-priests under David.[52] It is also established that Solomon replaced Abiathar with Zadok (1 Kgs 2:35), and perhaps that one of Zadok's sons acted as the leading priest.[53]

---

[49] This appears differently in the lists in 1 Chr 9:10–11; Neh 11:10–11 (levels 20–23), as Ahitub, Meraioth, Zadok, Meshullam.

[50] G12, 19. Knoppers, *1 Chronicles 1–9*, 409.

[51] The omission of Meraioth at G21, and the inclusion of Meraioth at G11, as Knoppers states "is a problem for any theory" regarding the origins of these lists, "Relationship," 122.

[52] 2 Samuel 8:17; 15:24–29, 35; 17:15; 19:11; 20:25; 1 Kgs 4:4.

[53] This is often stated on the basis of 1 Kgs 4:2, but the text itself does not say this. In this list of officials, Azariah son of Zadok, Zadok, Abiathar, Zabud son of Nathan are all called "priests" (1 Kgs 4:2, 4, 5).

Figure 3.3: Priestly Genealogies in Chronicles; Ezra; Nehemiah

	1 Chr 9:10–11	Nehemiah 11:10–11	Ezra 7:1–5	1 Chr 6:45–48 [6:50–53]	1 Chr 5:27–41 [6:1–15]
1					Levi
2					Kohath
3					Amram
4			Aaron	Aaron	Aaron
5			Eleazar	Eleazar	Eleazar
6			Phinehas	Phinehas	Phinehas
7			Abishua	Abishua	Abishua
8			Bukki	Bukki	Bukki
9			Uzzi	Uzzi	Uzzi
10			Zerahiah	Zerahiah	Zerahiah
11			Meraioth	Meraioth	Meraioth
12				Amariah	Amariah
13				Ahitub	Ahitub
14				Zadok	Zadok
15				Ahimaaz	Ahimaaz
16					Azariah
17					Johanan
18			Azariah		Azariah
19			Amariah		Amariah
20	Ahitub	Ahitub	Ahitub		Ahitub
21	Meraioth	Meraioth			
22	Zadok	Zadok	Zadok		Zadok
23	Meshullam	Meshullam	Shallum		Shallum
24	Hilkiah	Hilkiah	Hilkiah		Hilkiah
25	Azariah		Azariah		Azariah
26		Seraiah	Seraiah		Seraiah
27					Jehozadak
28			Ezra		

In 1 Chr 6:16 [6:31] the Chronicler indicates the actions of David in establishing the music within the "house of the Lord." Later, David's actions regarding the divisions of priests, singers, gatekeepers and Levites are also recorded (1 Chr 23–26). It would therefore appear to be natural that the Chronicler would also desire to include the priest and his known family members who were also active in the time of David and whose family was known to continue at least into the reign of Solomon.

Furthermore, when the Chronicler's attention to David's two priests is noted, Abiathar all but disappears in Chronicles as compared to the Deuteronomistic History, while Zadok, although also not occurring as frequently as in the

Deuteronomistic History, is not only prominent in Chronicles, but gains a status that he does not have in the Deuteronomistic History. In the Deuteronomistic History, Abiathar is mentioned twenty-six times.[54] In Chronicles he is mentioned on only four occasions, and in two of these only as the father of Ahimelech.[55] Abiathar is still a priest (1 Chr 15:11), but he appears to be sidelined by making him a counsellor (1 Chr 27:34). In this passage the normal designation "the priest" is absent.

Zadok appears twenty-four times in the Deuteronomistic History,[56] but only sixteen times in Chronicles: six times in the genealogies and ten times in the narrative.[57] While Abiathar appears to be removed from his position as priest relatively early, Zadok continues as priest throughout the reign of David.[58] When the divisions of the priests and Levites are decided, it is Zadok who is first mentioned after David as being a witness.[59] Zadok is said to be the leader of the house of Aaron (1 Chr 27:17), and it is Zadok who is anointed to be priest when Solomon is anointed to be king (1 Chr 29:22). This anointing of Zadok to be priest has been inserted by the Chronicler into his source, in a clear echo of the priestly material and indicates Zadok to be the Chief/Head priest.[60]

Even the manner in which Zadok assumes the position of High Priest is presented by the Chronicler in such a way as to make Zadok appear in a better light. In Kings, Zadok assumed the position of High Priest during the political turmoil surrounding Adonijah's two attempts to lay claim to the throne. The first attempt occurred when Adonijah had himself declared king with the full support of Joab and Abiathar (1 Kgs 1:5–9, 41–53). The second attempt came through his attempt to acquire Abishag as his wife (1 Kgs 2:13–22). These actions resulted in the deaths of Adonijah and Joab, the banishment of Abiathar (1 Kgs 2:23–35), and Zadok acquiring Abiathar's position (1 Kgs 2:26–27, 35). Unlike the portrayal in Kings, in Chronicles Zadok, like Solomon, assumes his position peacefully during the lifetime of David and with what appears to be the full assent of the people.[61]

---

[54] Seventeen times in 1 and 2 Samuel, nine times in 1 Kings.

[55] 1 Chronicles 18:16; 24:6. In 1 Chr 18:16, many manuscripts read "Abimelech."

[56] Thirteen times in 2 Samuel, eleven times in 1 Kings.

[57] However, in 2 Chr 27:1 if the mother of Jotham, Jerusha daughter of Zadok, is considered to be of the family of Zadok the priest, then there are seventeen references to Zadok in Chronicles, with eleven being in the narrative.

[58] The list of officers in 1 Chr 18:16, while still retaining Zadok as priest, has Abiathar replaced by his son Ahimelech/Abimelech.

[59] Ahimelech is also mentioned on each occasion, but always after Zadok.

[60] Leviticus 4:3, 5, 16; 6:22; 16:32; 21:10; Num 35:25.

[61] This may be inferred from the manner in which Solomon is said to ascend the throne in 1 Chr 29:22b–24 with not only the people, but the officers, mighty men "as well

Consequently, with the Chronicler's focus upon Zadok in the lifetime of David, it is reasonable that the Chronicler would seek to ensure Zadok's genealogical inclusion within the sons of Aaron and the sons of Levi during the lifetime of David, and therefore that the Chronicler added the names of Zadok and his recorded relatives within the list that he found in Ezra 7:1–5.

As such, Zadok is included in the genealogies not to legitimise him as a son of Aaron, for this was easily accomplished in 1 Chr 27:17 which indicates that Zadok is over the Aaronites. Zadok was included in the lists of the sons of Aaron simply because he was David's priest, and the Chronicler gives him the status, that of a son of Aaron, which was expected of a priest.

Why Legitimise Zadok?

The question remains as to why it is so often stated that Zadok is included in the genealogical lists of 1 Chr 6 in order to legitimise his position as a descendant of Aaron. Again, on the basis of the prophecy against the house of Eli and its fulfilment (1 Sam 2:27–36; 1 Kgs 2:26–27), it has been assumed that Zadok was of no blood relation to Eli, and that he was therefore not a legitimate Aaronite priest.[62] There are indications in the text, however, that this assertion is not correct, that instead of being a non Elide, Zadok was in fact a descendant of Eli, and relative of Abiathar.

This being the case, it would appear that Zadok has required legitimisation as an Aaronite because he has fallen victim to his own propaganda. As has been stated, 1 Sam 2:27–35 presents a prophecy against the house of Eli which indicates that although Yahweh had chosen Eli's house in Egypt (2:27), to serve as priests forever (2:30), this was now coming to an end (2:31–33). First Kings 2:26–27 claims to present the fulfilment of this prophecy when Solomon banishes Abiathar to Anathoth as punishment for his part in Adonijah's attempt to gain the throne, and Zadok was made priest in his place (1 Kgs 2:35).

A simple reading of these incidents would suggest that Zadok has no blood relationship to Eli or Abiathar, and that an entirely new priestly line has now been instituted. If Eli's house had been chosen in Egypt (1 Sam 2:27), and to a later audience it is clear from the priestly literature that this priestly line should be that of Aaron, then it follows that Zadok cannot be an Aaronite. As such Zadok, in order to be seen by later persons as a legitimate High Priest, needed to be incorporated into the family of Aaron and is consequently legitimised through his inclusion into Aaron's genealogy.

---

as all of King David's sons" pledging their submission to Solomon. As Zadok gained his position at the same moment, the Chronicler is probably seeking to indicate that he received the same support and acclamation.

[62] Wellhausen, *Prolegomena*, 126.

The one difficulty with this scenario is the statement in 2 Sam 8:17 that Zadok was the son of Ahitub. This appears to connect Zadok with the family of Eli, as illustrated in Figure 3.4.

These relationships are established in 1 and 2 Samuel as follows:
- Eli father of Phinehas and Hophni: 1 Sam 1:3
- Phinehas father of Ichabod: 1 Sam 4:19–22
- Ahitub the brother of Ichabod, and Ahijah the son of Ahitub: 1 Sam 14:3
- Ahimelech son of Ahitub: 1 Sam 22:9, 11
- Abiathar son of Ahimelech: 1 Sam 22:20; 30:7
- Jonathan son of Abiathar: 2 Sam 15:27; 1 Kgs 1:42.
- Ahimelech son of Abiathar: 2 Sam 8:17[63]
- Zadok son of Ahitub: 2 Sam 8:17
- Ahimaaz son of Zadok: 2 Sam 18:19–27
- Azariah son of Zadok: 1 Kgs 4:2

It is properly reasoned that if these relationships be correct, then Zadok is a descendant of Eli, contrary to the prophecy and its declared fulfilment. Consequently, to maintain the statements in the prophecy, the relationship indicated in the text must be invalidated. This is done either through the suggestion of a textual emendation, to make 2 Sam 8:17 read, "Zadok and Abiathar the son of Ahimelech son of Ahitub,"[64] or through suggesting that two different persons named Ahitub are intended.[65]

---

[63] This reading has been questioned and the order often changed to read, "Abiathar the son of Ahimelech," cf. 1 Sam 22:20, Henry Preserved Smith, *A Critical and Exegetical Commentary on the Books of Samuel* (ICC; Edinburgh: T&T Clark, 1899), 309. So also John Mauchline, *1 and 2 Samuel* (NCB; London: Oliphants, 1971), 237. Although possible, it is also unnecessary, for there is no reason why Abiathar could not have named his son after his own father. So too C. F. Keil, *The Books of the Chronicles* (K&D 3; trans. Andrew Harper; Grand Rapids: Eerdmans, 1976), 114. If the order of these names had been altered from "Abiathar the son of Ahimelech" to "Ahimelech the son of Abiathar," this change must have occurred early, as this is the order attested in 1 Chr 18:16; 24:6.

[64] H. W. Hertzberg, *I & II Samuel* (OTL; trans. John Bowden; London: SCM Press, 1964), 293–294; Saul Olyan, "Zadok's Origins and the Tribal Politics of David," *JBL* 101 (1982): 177–193, 177. This suggestion apparently first came from Wellhausen but was rejected as early as Smith, *Samuel*, 309. Cross also rejects this on text critical grounds, *Canaanite Myth and Hebrew Epic: Essays in the History of the Religion of Israel* (Cambridge: Harvard University Press, 1973), 212–214.

[65] Curtis and Madsen, *Chronicles*, 128; Cross, *Canaanite Myth*, 214; Arnold A. Anderson, *2 Samuel* (WBC 11; Dallas: Word, 1989), 137.

Figure 3.4: The Family of Eli

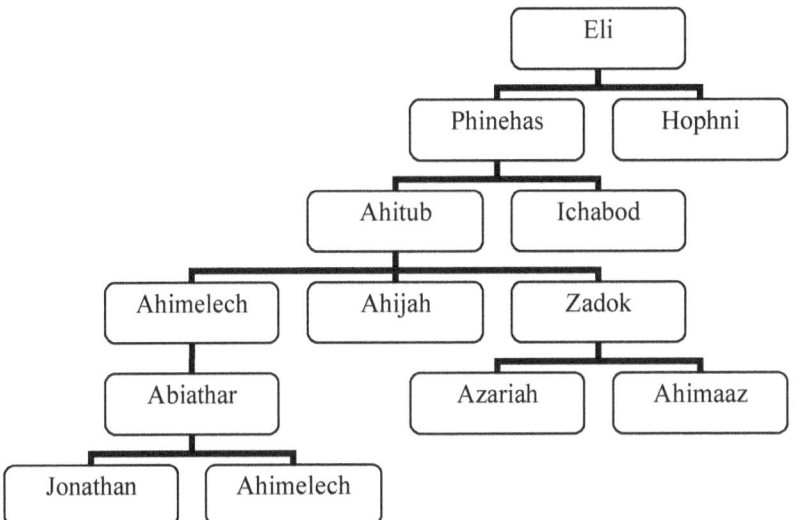

Although the latter suggestion has some merit, both are unnecessary because both fail to recognise the propagandistic nature of the text. The text of Samuel and Kings functions to legitimise the removal of an old, established priestly family, that of Abiathar, and the establishment of a new priestly family, that of Zadok. That this is done for political purposes is evident in the text of Kings, where the political reason is given. However, just as David required religious justification for his rise to the throne (1 Sam 15), so also Zadok required the same to explain his rise to the high priesthood.

The "prophecy" and its "fulfilment" give Zadok legitimacy because his rise to the high priesthood is sanctioned through a word of Yahweh. As such, his relationship to the house of Eli is substantially hidden, although it does appear once (2 Sam 8:17).[66] There is, in fact, no other reason to hide the identity of his father except to hide his relationship with the house of Eli.[67]

---

[66] What this indicates is that a member of the house of Eli was prominent in the fall of the house of Eli, as well as being the replacement for the house of Eli. It must be noted that in recent history, King George V began his reign as head of the house of Saxe-Coburg-Gotha, but due to political considerations during World War I, ended that house and began the house of Windsor. He was, nonetheless, the same king, with the same ancestry.

[67] It has been suggested that Zadok's ancestry was hidden because he was a Jebusite priest in Jerusalem prior to David's conquest of the city, Christian E. Hauer, "Who Was

It may be objected, on the basis of 1 Chr 24:3, that Zadok did not belong to the same immediate family as Abiathar:

> With the help of Zadok a descendant of Eleazar and Ahimelech a descendant of Ithamar, David separated them into divisions for their appointed order of ministering.

Ahimelech, the son of Abiathar (1 Chr 24:6), is said to have descended from Ithamar, while Zadok descended from Eleazar. This, however, does not disprove that a closer family relationship existed. Wilson says:

> Nowhere in our study of genealogical function did we see genealogies created or preserved only for historiographic purposes. Rather, we saw that oral genealogies usually have some sociological function in the life of the society that uses them. Even when genealogies are recited as part of a lineage history, they are likely to reflect domestic, political, or religious relationships existing in the present rather than in the past. The purpose of the recital is not to provide the sort of accurate historical account that is the goal of the modern historian but to legitimize contemporary lineage configurations.[68]

Just as the account of the prophecy against Eli and its fulfilment were political statements, so also is the declaration that Zadok is descended from Eleazar and Ahimelech from Ithamar.[69] The priestly literature, which was normative for the Chronicler, states that Eleazar is the one who was chosen to wear the sacred clothes and to succeed his father as priest (Num 20:25–28; cf. Lev 16:32). From that point on in Numbers, Eleazar is seen at Moses' side having taken Aaron's position of authority. By aligning Zadok with Eleazar's family, the Chronicler is simply indicating that the family who held the position of high priest in the days of David, is the one which should hold that position.[70]

Zadok?," *JBL* 82 (1963): 89–94; and more recently Deborah W. Rooke, *Zadok's Heirs: The Role and Development of the High Priesthood in Ancient Israel* (Oxford: Oxford University Press, 2000), 68. This has been refuted by Cross, who instead proposes that Zadok was an Aaronite from Hebron, *Canaanite Myth*, 209–215, while Olyan, "Origins," 179–184, rejects both a Jebusite and Hebronite origin for Zadok, suggesting instead that he was an Aaronite from Kabzeel, and son of the high priest Jehoiada (1 Chr 12:27–28), 185–190.

[68] Wilson, *Genealogy*, 54, italics mine.

[69] Laato draws a distinction between what he calls "historical" and "ideological" genealogies, "The Levitical Genealogies in 1 Chronicles 5–6 and the Formation of Levitical Ideology in Post-exilic Judah," *JSOT* 62 (1994): 72–99, 77.

[70] Leviticus 16:32 makes it clear that the succession to the position of High Priest should be from father to son.

Conclusion

In this chapter it has been observed that the list of the sons of Aaron is located to balance and to intensify the Chronicler's previous discussion of the duties of the sons of Aaron, and to clearly specify which group is responsible for these duties. As such, this is not a list of high priests, even if some of these persons may have served in this capacity, but is a list of those who performed the rituals of sacrifice and who made atonement for the people. While, in the Chronicler's view, there were other sons of Aaron who operated within the cultic system and who performed the cultic rites, those persons in this list were included as representatives of this wider group of atonement makers.

Zadok is viewed in the narrative of Chronicles as the most prominent priest, and therefore a descendant of Eleazar, and is portrayed as the anointed priest, the leader of the family of Aaron, and head of the priests.

Zadok was himself incorporated into this list, not to legitimise him as an Aaronite, but because he was the priest in the days of David and possibly while the first temple was being built. As numerous other of David's cultic officials had been included in other lists, the Chronicler felt that it was appropriate to include Zadok as well.

CHAPTER 4
E: 1 CHRONICLES 6:1–47
THE DESCENDANTS OF LEVI

INTRODUCTION

Having observed in levels F and F^1 the focus of the Chronicler upon the cultic officials (the "sons of Aaron" and the "Levites") and their respective duties, levels E and E^1 deal with "Levites," in the wider sense of the term.

Level E records the genealogy or ancestry of those who are affiliated with the sons of Levi, showing either how Levi is represented in the later community through certain lines of his descendants, or how certain individuals traced their ancestry back to Levi. The necessity to show descent from Levi is essential for, as was shown previously, it is only this group who have the right and responsibility to officiate in the cult. This is true for those who act in a priestly capacity (the "sons of Aaron"), as well as those whose task is the "duties of the tabernacle" (the "Levites").

While level E within the chiastic structure identifies the sons of Levi according to their genealogy and families, level E^1 identifies them according to where they live. As will be shown in the following chapter where the Levitical cities will be discussed, people and land are tied inextricably to one another. Level E^1 will emphasise and expand upon the identity of the Levites by identifying the allocation of land to them and their rightful possession of land within Israel. In this chapter we will examine Level E, and will seek to determine its structure, purpose and function within the Chronicler's genealogies.

STRUCTURE

First Chronicles 5:27–6:32 [6:1–47] can be divided into three separate sections: 1 Chr 5:27–41 [6:1–15]; 6:1–15 [6:16–30]; and 6:16–32 [6:31–47]. The first two sections begin with the nearly identical "the sons of Levi: Gershon,

Kohath and Merari."[1] The first section focuses on the line of Kohath through Amram, Aaron and finally Eleazar to the time of the exile. The second section mentions the immediate sons of each of the three sons of Levi, and then follows only one particular line for a number of generations. The third section is distinct, in both form and purpose. While the first two sections present descending genealogies of the "sons of Levi" and give no direct indication of the function of these persons, the third section is clearly marked as "these are the men David put in charge of the music" (1 Chr 6:16 [6:31]. The third section then proceeds to give ascending genealogies from these Davidic appointments back to the tribal or national founder.

The first two sections are said to be records of "the sons of Levi" (1 Chr 5:27; 6:16 [6:1, 16]). The beginning of these lists is consistent with the beginnings of the other genealogical lists which begin with the name of the tribal founder before continuing to record that founder's descendants.[2]

The third section records the ancestry of three individuals whom "David put in charge of the music of the house of the Lord" (1 Chr 6:16 [6:31]). This third set of lists records the ancestry of these three individuals from the time of David to at least Levi and in one case to Israel (1 Chr 6:23, 28, 32 [6:38, 43, 47]).[3] As such, each of the three sections record the ancestry or lineage of individuals for whom descent from Levi is claimed.

Although these lists are separate and distinct, there are several points of connection between them.

First Chronicles 5:27–28; 6:1, 3 [6:1–2, 16, 18] are nearly identical, and both may have their origins in Exod 6:16–18 (Figure 4.1).

---

[1] Although the NIV consistently records the name of Levi's first named son as "Gershon," גֵּרְשׁוֹן, the MT reads גֵּרְשֹׁם in 1 Chr 5:27, 28, 31; 6:13, 32, 41 [6:1, 2, 5, 28, 47, 56]; 15:7. The Chronicler only uses the form גֵּרְשׁוֹן in 1 Chr 5:27 [6:1]; 23:6. גֵּרְשֹׁם is also the name of the son of Moses (1 Chr 23:15, 16; 26:24, cf. Exod 2:22; 18:3; Judg 18:30), and appears to be the Chronicler's preferred spelling for both the name of Levi's son as well as that of Moses' son.

[2] 1 Chronicles 2:3; 4:24; 5:1, 7:1, 6, 13, 14, 20, 30; 8:1. Only the Transjordanian tribes of Gad and half Manasseh (1 Chr 5:11, 24), do not follow this pattern, but rather speak of "chiefs" and "heads of families."

[3] Although Genesis records the name of Isaac's youngest son as "Jacob" (Gen 25:26), which was later changed to Israel (Gen 32:28; 35:10), the Chronicler prefers to use the latter when referring to the person (cf. 1 Chr 1:34; 2:1; 5:1, 3; 6:23 [6:38]; 7:29; 29:10, 18). The only instances of "Jacob" in Chronicles are in a psalm (1 Chr 16:13, 17), and even then these usages are in parallel to "Israel." This preference of the Chronicler is not unusual, as Joshua, Judges, Samuel and Kings each prefer "Israel" to "Jacob," although this may have more to do with "Israel" as the name for the people rather than the name of a person. It is in the prophets and Psalms where "Jacob" is often found as a term referring to the people as a whole.

Figure 4.1: Parallel Texts of the Sons of Levi

1 Chronicles 6:1–2	1 Chronicles 6:16–18	Exodus 6:16–18
The sons of Levi:	The sons of Levi:	These were the names of the sons of Levi according to their records:
Gershon, Kohath and Merari.	Gershon, Kohath and Merari.	Gershon, Kohath and Merari. Levi lived 137 years.
	These are the names of the sons of Gershon: Libni and Shimei. The sons of Kohath: Amram, Izhar, Hebron and Uzziel.	The sons of Gershon, by clans, were Libni and Shimei. The sons of Kohath were Amram, Izhar, Hebron and Uzziel. Kohath lived 133 years.
The sons of Kohath: Amram, Izhar, Hebron and Uzziel.		

There are clear connections between the lists of 1 Chr 6:5–13, 18–23 [6:20–28, 33–38] in the sons of Kohath as well as 1 Chr 6:5–6, 24–28 [6:20–21, 39–43] in the sons of Gershom.[4]

The forms of the first two sections are also similar. They both begin with a segmented genealogy for several generations before focusing on a particular line in a descending linear genealogy.[5] The form of the third section is different. It contains three separate ascending linear genealogies from the person named to the significant ancestor Levi, or Israel through Levi.

It has already been shown in the previous chapter that the first of these three lists, which records the sons of Aaron, contains those individuals who were given the priestly responsibility for presenting sacrifices upon the altar and making atonement for Israel (1 Chr 6:34 [6:49]).

The third section, according to the text itself, are those who are responsible for the music which accompanies the cultic functions, first in the tabernacle/tent of meeting, and then in the temple (1 Chr 6:16–17 [6:31–32]).

The middle portion gives no details of the duties or roles of the individuals named. As those who minister at the altar and those who are responsible for the

---

[4] See further Figure 4.5
[5] The lines of Aaron through Eleazar (1 Chr 5:29 [6:3]); Gershom through Libni (1 Chr 6:5–6 [6:20–21]); Kohath through Amminadab (1 Chr 6:7–13 [6:22–28]) and Merari through Mahli (1 Chr 6:14–15 [6:29–30]).

music are named elsewhere, it is probable that this group does not have these responsibilities. It perhaps may be assumed, on the basis of the other two portions and the statement in 1 Chr 6:33 [6:48], that these individuals were "assigned to the duties of the tabernacle, the house of God." If we needed to give a name to this group, "Levites" would appear to be the best choice, as will be explained in the following section.

This would give an order "sons of Aaron, Levites, musicians," or, based upon other lists of cultic officials found in the Hebrew Bible, "priests, Levites, singers."

THE ORDER OF LISTING

The previous conclusion is justified by the observation that this order of presentation (priests, Levites, singers) is not only found in this section of Chronicles, but is also found in other portions of the postexilic literature.[6]

An analysis of the occurrences of the various terms and their order of presentation indicates that during the postexilic era standard format for the presentation of the groups within society developed, and that this standard format was followed by the Chronicler in his genealogical presentation in 1 Chr 6.

CLARIFYING NOTES FOR FIGURE 4.9

Certain clarifications need to be made regarding the chart prior to the examination of the data.

- This chart does not list those occurrences where only "priest and Levite" are mentioned.
- This chart does not list random occurrences in the narrative, but only those instances where families/groups as a whole, rather than an individual, are recorded.
- "Judah and Benjamin" (1 Chr 9:3), includes also Ephraim and Manasseh.
- The listing under "Israel" in Ezra 2:1–58 // Neh 7:7–70 is divided into lists of people (Ezra 2:2b–20 // Neh 7:7b–25), and towns (Ezra 2:21–35 // Neh 7:26–38).
- In some groups, the duties of the singers/musicians are included among the listing of the "Levites" (2 Chr 8:14; Neh 11:15–18; 12:8–9, 24). In the chart for Neh 11:4–19; 12:1–9; and 12:12–25, because the text indicates that a only a portion of those named as Levites were responsible for or participated in the music, both Levites and singers are indicated on the chart. While these

---

[6] Figure 4.9 details where these various groups and others occur. This is placed at the end of this chapter.

three passages do not mention singers as a separate group, it should be noticed that those who perform musical duties are listed after "Levites" generally.
- At times, Levites who are called a descendant of Asaph (1 Chr 9:15, but cf. Neh 11:17), are not said to have had musical duties, and therefore are not classified as "singers" in the chart but only as Levites.
- In Neh 10:1–27, it is assumed that Nehemiah, as governor, acts on behalf of all the people, while the leaders act on behalf of their respective groups.

Nehemiah 11:3 contains the "descendants of Solomon's servants," which does not appear in 1 Chr 9:2. Although 1 Chr 23 gives a list of the "Levites" prior to discussion of the priests (1 Chr 24), this has not been included as part of the pattern for 1 Chr 24–27. This is because: A) the "sons of Aaron" are included in the list of 1 Chr 23, and therefore 1 Chr 23 is not strictly "Levites" as distinct from priests, but is a combination of all Levites. B) The duties of the "sons of Aaron" (1 Chr 23:13), are listed as are the duties of the "sons of Levi" (1 Chr 23:28–31), which themselves overlap with the duties

- of the singers and gatekeepers (1 Chr 9:28–32). C) Most of the Kohathites and Merarites (1 Chr 23:12–23), are repeated in either 1 Chr 24:20–30 or 1 Chr 26:20–32 and many of the Gershonites (1 Chr 23:8), are repeated in 1 Chr 26:21–22. D) It appears that 1 Chr 23 is a list of all the available Levitical clans, out of which the various cultic duties were allocated. This allocation is recorded in 1 Chr 24–26, beginning with the "sons of Aaron" (i.e. "the priests").[7]

OBSERVATIONS ON THE DATA

- Of the twenty-three occasions where Israel/Judah/Benjamin occur, seventeen times Israel/Judah/Benjamin occur in the first position,[8] followed by the cultic officials. On the other six occasions, Israel/Judah/Benjamin occur last.[9]
- Of the seventeen occasions in which Israel/Judah/Benjamin occur in the first position, priests occur in the second position on sixteen occasions.[10]

---

[7] It is to be noticed that the list of 1 Chr 23 presents no connection at all with the singers and only a tenuous connection with the gatekeepers. The list of singers in 1 Chr 25 only mentions the descendants of Asaph, Heman and Jeduthun, not their ancestors, and therefore not their means of connection to Levi, although this may have been assumed on the basis of the data in 1 Chr 6. The list of gatekeepers mentions one group as being members of the "sons of Asaph" (1 Chr 26:1), which only connects them to the singers, and another family as being descendants of Merari (1 Chr 26:10).

[8] In the case of Judah and Benjamin, the first two positions. For the purpose of these observations, they will be counted as sharing the first position, as this will aid the perception of the relative places of the cultic officials.

[9] In Neh 11:3–4, Israel occurs first while Judah/Benjamin occurs last.

- On each of the six occasions where Israel/Judah/Benjamin occur in the last position, priests occur in the first position.
- Of the thirteen occasions where Israel/Judah/Benjamin do not occur, on nine occasions priests appear in the first position, once in the second position, twice in the last position, and once they do not occur.[11] Priests and Levites occur together in thirty of thirty-one occasions, and in twenty-eight of these thirty occasions priests precede Levites. Both of the occasions in which this order does not occur are in Nehemiah.[12]
- Singers are never given priority over priests, and on only one occasion priority over Levites.[13] This one occasion occurs in Nehemiah where gatekeepers have priority over singers and Levites, and singers have priority over Levites. On this occasion, priests are not mentioned.
- Of the ten occurrences of either "temple servants" or "descendants of the servants of Solomon," these groups are always placed after priests, Levites, singers, gatekeepers.[14]
- Descendants of the servants of Solomon occur on only four occasions, and only in conjunction with, and following, the temple servants.[15]
- The singers (or reference to musicians) occur with references to gatekeepers on fifteen occasions. Gatekeepers appear without singers/musicians only in 1 Chr 9:3–17; 2 Chr 8:14, while singers/musicians occur without gatekeepers in 1 Chr 5:27–6:32[6:1–47]; Neh 12:1–9.
- Chronicles (twice), and Ezra (five times), only list the singers prior to the gatekeepers.
- Nehemiah appears to be less certain in the issue of priority of singers and gatekeepers as on four occasions it lists the gatekeepers before the singers,

---

[10] Only Neh 10:39 does not follow this pattern. But even here, this is because of the verse's context, where the actions of the people and the Levites on behalf of the priests, gatekeepers and singers are recorded.

[11] They occur in the second position in Neh 8:13; last in Neh 9:38; 13:5, and do not occur at all in Neh 7:1.

[12] Nehemiah 10:39; 13:5.

[13] Nehemiah 7:1.

[14] Although singers and gatekeepers do not occur on three of these occasions: 1 Chr 9:2; Neh 11:3–4, 20–21.

[15] It is uncertain if the reference in Ezra 7:24 is to the descendants of Solomon's servants as they are simply called, "other workers at this house of God." Their position in this list, and the pattern observed elsewhere, is suggestive that this group is intended. Weinberg states, "it can perhaps be assumed that the $n^e t\hat{\imath}n\hat{\imath}m$ and 'sons of the slaves of Solomon' are on the lowest level of the socio-professional pyramid of the postexilic community," *Citizen-Temple*, 80. He further points out that in the Talmud a "child of a whore [comes before] a *nātîn*," (page 77).

while on four occasions it lists the singers before the gatekeepers. On one occasion it mentions singers without mentioning gatekeepers.
- Of the fourteen times that priests, Levites, singers, gatekeepers occur together:
  - Nine times they appear in this order.
  - Once, although in the order priests, Levites, singers, gatekeepers, the "people" occur between Levites and singers (Ezra 2:70).[16]
  - Twice in the order: priests, Levites, gatekeepers, singers.
  - Once in the order: Levites, priests, gatekeepers, singers.
  - Once in the order: Levites, singers, gatekeepers, priests. Each of these previous three points occur only in Nehemiah.
- Of the five occasions where "family heads" or "leaders" occur, three times the order is "priest, Levite, family head"; one time "family head, priest, Levite" and one time "family head, Levite, priest." These latter two are found only in Nehemiah.
- Chronicles and Ezra only have the order: "Israel/Judah/Benjamin, priests . . . " or the order "priests, Levites . . . Israel/Judah/family heads or leaders."
- Nehemiah, although more susceptible to variation in order than either Chronicles or Ezra, retains the essential order except in four verses, Neh 7:1; 9:38; 10:40 [10:39]; 13:5.[17] This can be better visualised in Figure 4.2.[18]
- Although many texts indicate that the musicians were Levites,[19] it is Nehemiah who specifically locates the musical duties within the Levitical group.[20]

---

[16] This is not apparent in the NIV, which reads, "The priests, the Levites, the singers, the gatekeepers and the temple servants settled in their own towns, along with some of the other people, and the rest of the Israelites settled in their towns" The MT reads:
וַיֵּשְׁבוּ הַכֹּהֲנִים וְהַלְוִיִּם וּמִן־הָעָם וְהַמְשֹׁרְרִים וְהַשּׁוֹעֲרִים וְהַנְּתִינִים בְּעָרֵיהֶם וְכָל־יִשְׂרָאֵל בְּעָרֵיהֶם:
cf. the NRSV, JPS, "The priests, the Levites, and some of the people . . ." Interestingly, the parallel text in Neh 7:72 [7:73] reads: וַיֵּשְׁבוּ הַכֹּהֲנִים וְהַלְוִיִּם וְהַשּׁוֹעֲרִים וְהַמְשֹׁרְרִים וּמִן־הָעָם וְהַנְּתִינִים וְכָל־יִשְׂרָאֵל. Here again the NIV alters the order to, "the priests, the Levites, the gatekeepers, the singers and the temple servants, along with certain of the people." In both cases, the NIV repositions "the people" to a place after the cultic officials and workers contrary to the text.

[17] The only other major variation is that on four occasions singers precede gatekeepers (7:7–60; 11:4–19; 12:12–25; 13:5), and on four occasions gatekeepers precede singers (7:1, 72 [7:73]; 10:28, 39).

[18] That Nehemiah is more likely than either Chronicles or Ezra to modify the order need not demand that Nehemiah was written while the determining of the order was still in a state of flux while Ezra was written later, after the order of recording had solidified. It is possible that the differences are a reflection in the different origins of the texts. Ezra and Chronicles from a more cultic viewpoint and Nehemiah from a secular governmental perspective. Even with these different perspectives, the general order remains similar.

Figure 4.2: The Order of Listing in Nehemiah

Reference								
7:7–60	I	P	L	S	G		TS	SS
11:4–19	J/B	P	L	S	G			
11:3–4	I	P	L				TS	SS	J/B
11:20–21	I	P	L				TS	
10:1–27	I	P	L			Pl		
8:13	FH	P	L					
12:12–25		P	L	S	G			
12:1–9		P	L	S				
10:34		P	L			FH		
10:28	I	P	L	G	S		TS	
7:73		P	L	G	S	Pl	TS	I
10:39	I	L	P	G	S			
9:38	FH	L	P					
13:5		L	S	G	P			
7:1		G	S	L				

J/B: Judah/Benjamin   I: Israel   FH: Family Head
P: Priests   L: Levites   S: Singers
G: Gatekeepers   Pl: People   TS: Temple Servants
SS: Solomon's Servants

What this appears to indicate is that during the postexilic period a general pattern developed for referring to those who made up the second temple community. This pattern clearly distinguished between lay and clergy (with the lay members normally having the priority).[21] It also distinguished between

---

[19] 1 Chronicles 9:33; 2 Chr 5:12; 7:6; 34:12; 35:15; Neh 11:22; 12:27.

[20] Nehemiah 11:15–18; 12:8–9, 24

[21] This appears to change by the Talmudic period, where "ten hereditary castes came up out of Babylon—priests, Levites, Israelites, ones who were dedicated, proselytes, freedmen, $n^e tînîm$, enslaved and foundlings," as quoted in Weinberg, *Citizen-Temple*, 77. Here, neither singers nor gatekeepers is mentioned. This may be because, after the destruction of the temple, these cultic positions were no longer necessary. What is

members of the clergy on the basis of their function, giving higher status to the priests over the Levites and expressing the relative status of the various cultic groups according to the viewpoint of the particular author or time period.[22]

That this form had become, or was in the process of becoming, the standard is indicated by Neh 12:12–26, which states that the data it contains comes from different sources or time periods.[23] Even though reputably coming from a variety of times and sources, they are still presented in the growing standard form of "priests, Levites, singers, gatekeepers."[24] This indicates that within the postexilic period there developed a standard format for the presentation of member groups within the society. This would result in the nearly automatic use of this style when reports are made. This is further substantiated, if Williamson's observation regarding the development of the lists in Ezra 2 // Neh 7 is correct. He says regarding the form of these lists, "the list has the appearance of being well ordered . . . Closer inspection reveals, however, that this order has probably been imposed upon originally diverse material."[25]

If this order has been "imposed" as Williamson suggests, then it is probable that this imposition followed a recognizable and socially accepted norm.

The implications of these observations for the order presented in 1 Chr 6 are clear.

First Chronicles 5:27–41 [6:1–15] is a list of the "sons of Aaron," that is, the "priests."

First Chronicles 6:16–32 [6:31–47] is a list of the musicians, or the "singers."[26]

It is therefore reasonable to conclude on the basis of the standard of reporting cultic officials, that 1 Chr 6:1–15 [6:16–30] is a list of the "Levites," giving the

---

significant, however, is the priority of the priests, and that "Israelites" have been removed to a middle position, unlike in the lists of Chronicles, Ezra, and Nehemiah (except Ezra 2:70 // Neh 7:72 [7:73]).

[22] It is possible that Nehemiah gives greater status to the gatekeepers because of their position in enforcing Sabbath day restrictions on trade (Neh 13:22).

[23] The days of Joiakim (Neh 12:12); days of Darius (Neh 12:22); days of Johanan (Neh 12:23); days of Joiakim and Nehemiah (Neh 12:26).

[24] For discussion on the source, history and content of these lists in Nehemiah, see, Williamson, *Ezra, Nehemiah*, 358–362; Clines, *Ezra, Nehemiah, Esther*, 223–228.

[25] Williamson, *Ezra, Nehemiah*, 28.

[26] Although the verb is translated as both "singer" and "musician," the one Hebrew word שִׁיר is used to refer to both. The exact translation depends upon the context. The verb שִׁיר can refer to "singing a song" (1 Chr 16:9, 23; 2 Chr 20:21), singers (1 Chr 15:19, 27; 2 Chr 5:13; 23:13), choirs (1 Chr 15:27; Neh 12:42), or musicians (1 Kgs 10:12; 2 Chr 5:12; 9:11). At times the noun שִׁיר refers to songs (1 Chr 13:8; 16:42; 2 Chr 23:18) while at others the שִׁיר plays a musical instrument (1 Chr 15:16; 25:6, 7; 2 Chr 5:13; 7:6; 34:12).

order in this portion of 1 Chronicles, Priests, Levites, singers.[27] This group of Levites, together with the singers, make up the wider group termed "Levites" indicated in 1 Chr 6:33[6:48] who perform those duties in the tabernacle/house of God that are not performed by the sons of Aaron/priests mentioned in 1 Chr 6:34 [6:49].[28] As such, these three genealogical listings record those cultic officials who are responsible for all the cultic activities that are carried on in the tabernacle/house of God.[29]

FORM OF THE LISTS

The form of the various lists in this section normally do not present any difficulties, particularly in the lists of the sons of Aaron and the singers. They both contain primarily either ascending or descending lists of father and son. The list of the sons of Aaron uses הוֹלִיד (became the father of) to designate the father to son relationship, while the list of singers uses בֶּן (the son of) to show the son to father relationship. Both forms are common in the Chronicler's genealogies.

The Levite list uses another common term for expressing relationship, בְּנוֹ (his son).[30] The usage of this term presents difficulties in the understanding of the list of Levites. The question lies in who is indicated by the phrase "his son." In the phrase: "PN1, PN2 his son, PN3 his son, PN4 his son," are each of the persons (PN2, PN3, PN4), the "son" of the previously named person, or is it possible that each of these can be the "son" of PN1? The answer to this question is vital in understanding this list of the sons of Levi.

---

[27] That the gatekeepers are not here represented, even though the narrative suggests that they, like the musicians, were instituted by David's command (1 Chr 15:18; 16:38; 23:5; 26:1, 12, 19), should not automatically be taken as evidence that the post of gatekeeper was a later development, or that the gatekeepers represent a demoted group of Levites, as suggested by Dan Olson, "What Got the Gatekeepers into Trouble?" *JSOT* 30 (2005): 223–242. For the place of the gatekeepers see especially John Wesley Wright, "Guarding the Gates: 1 Chronicles 26:1–19 and the Roles of the Gatekeepers in Chronicles," *JSOT* 48 (1990): 69–81; Gary N. Knoppers, *1 Chronicles 10–29* (AB 12A; New York: Doubleday, 2004), 860–873.

[28] Knoppers, however, suggests that 1 Chr 6:1–32 [6:16–47] deals with the singers alone and that the placement of the genealogies of the sons of Aaron and the singers "tie the priests and singers together," *1 Chronicles 1–9*, 428.

[29] This may in fact suggest the reason why the gatekeepers are not listed, as their activities do not *directly* relate to the cult, but primarily to the protection of the cultic area from ritual contamination.

[30] See also 1 Chr 3:10–17; 4:25–26; 5:4–6; 6:35–38 [6:50–53]; 7:20–21; 25–27; 8:33 // 9:43. It is also found in 1 Chr 26:25.

As mentioned previously, the term בֵּן (son) can refer to either a biological offspring, or a successor to an office. בְּנוֹ can be used similarly, as observed in 1 Chr 3:16 where the relationship of Zedekiah to a previously named person is said to be בְּנוֹ (his son).[31]

The relevant question in this list, however, is whose "son" is Zedekiah.[32] First Chronicles 3:16 reads: וּבְנֵי יְהוֹיָקִים יְכָנְיָה בְנוֹ צִדְקִיָּה בְנוֹ.

The list suggests that both named persons are the "sons" of Jehoiakim because of the use of the plural construct וּבְנֵי (sons of). Yet, the list is then presented in the same form "X בְּנוֹ," "Y בְּנוֹ" as is found in 1 Chr 6:5–15 [6:20–30] and elsewhere. In the list of Jehoiachin's sons (1 Chr 3:17–18), no son named "Zedekiah" is indicated, suggesting that the Zedekiah of 1 Chr 3:16, along with Jehoiachin, is the son of Jehoiakim. If both listed names are the "sons" of the primary person, then בְּנוֹ can be used to express not only a linear genealogy, but a horizontal list of "sons" of the same father.

It is this observation that presents difficulties for understanding the lists of the sons of Levi in 1 Chr 6:1–15 [6:16–30]. Are these a listing of successive generations of father and son, a father with many sons, or some combination of fathers and multiple sons followed by a list of the sons of the first named group? Although this is a difficult question to answer, the text gives some indications.[33]

First, the descendants of Gershom and Merari (1 Chr 6:5–6, 14–15 [6:20–21, 29–30]), are of approximately the same length. From Gershom to Jeatherai is eight generations while the genealogy from Mahli to Asaiah is seven generations.

The list from Kohath to Abijah, however, is not only much longer, but also broken. From Kohath to Shaul (1 Chr 6:7–9 [6:22–24]), are eleven generations. After a break, either one, two or three persons named Elkanah are mentioned. The list then continues for another eight generations to Abijah. If this second list of the sons of Elkanah is a reference to the Elkanah of 6:8 [6:23], then the entire genealogy is fourteen generations long, while if it refers to the second Elkanah (6:10 [6:25]), then the entire genealogy is nineteen to twenty-one generations,

---

[31] Not translated in NIV, cf. NRSV and JPS.

[32] Whether two different Zedekiah's are intended, one being a son of Jehoiachin or Jehoiakim and the other the king, son of Josiah, so Williamson, *Chronicles*, 56–57; the Chronicler (or a "glossator") made an error, Curtis and Madsen, *Chronicles*, 100–101; or we suggest that the confusion came when the Chronicler read "his brother," אָחִיו for "the brother of his father," אֲחִי אָבִיו, cf. LXX of 2 Chr 36, Rudolph, *Chronikbücher*, 28–29, is not at issue here. The issue is the use of the term and the relationship it suggests to another person.

[33] See the discussion in Japhet, *Chronicles*, 153–155. She suggests that the list underwent three literary stages: 1) three genealogies tracing the traditional forefathers to eight generations. 2) The genealogy of Samuel the prophet was added to the list. 3) The transition to the head singers in the following passage.

depending on whether the third Elkanah ([6:11 [6:26]), is the son of Amasai or the son of the Elkanah II. In either scenario, the number of generations is out of proportion with the other two lists of Levites.[34]

How is this list to be understood? Other texts give certain clues. (Figure 4.3).

As can be observed, the correspondences between the two lists are suggestive of a direct or indirect influence of one upon the other. Even the one set of names that have the main divergence, Tohu/Nahath, share two of the same letters, albeit transposed, which could have occurred as the result of transcriptional errors.[35]

Another indication of the original form of part of this list is found in Exod 6:24: "The sons of Korah were Assir, Elkanah and Abiasaph." First Chronicles 6:7-8 [6:22-23] reads, "The descendants of Kohath: Amminadab his son, Korah his son, Assir his son, Elkanah his son, Ebiasaph his son." What this indicates is that a horizontal relationship (the three sons of the one person Korah), was understood as a linear relationship of successive fathers and sons.[36]

Figure 4.3: The Family of Samuel

1 Sam 1:1; 8:2		1 Chr 6: 11–12 [26–27]	
Zuph	צוּף	Zophai	צוֹפַי
Tohu	תֹּחוּ	Nahath	נַחַת
Elihu	אֱלִיהוּא	Eliab	אֱלִיאָב
Jeroham	יְרֹחָם	Jeroham	יְרֹחָם
Elkanah	אֶלְקָנָה	Elkanah	אֶלְקָנָה
Samuel	שְׁמוּאֵל	Samuel	שְׁמוּאֵל
Joel / Abijah	אֲבִיָּה יוֹאֵל	Abijah[37]	אֲבִיָּה

First Chronicles 6:8 [6:23] continues with "Assir his son." If the above list of names is a horizontal, rather than linear, genealogy, then it is legitimate to identify this Assir with Assir the son of Korah, and to suggest that the following four names "Tahath his son, Uriel his son, Uzziah his son and Shaul his son" (1 Chr 6:9 [6:24]), are the descendants of Assir, son of Korah. It is uncertain as to whether this should be viewed as a linear or segmented genealogy, i.e. whether it represents successive generations of Assir's family, or the four sons of Assir. In view of the segmented genealogy for Korah, it is probable that a horizontal

---

[34] Although the list of thirteen names from Kohath to Zadok, at the time of David (1 Chr 5:28-35 [6:2-8]) is similar, albeit still shorter.

[35] The relation of Samuel, an Ephraimite (1 Sam 1:1), to a list of the sons of Levi will be discussed at a later point.

[36] Cf. the discussion and the chart in Johnson, *Purpose*, 71–72.

[37] Joel does not appear in the MT of 1 Chr 6:18 [6:33], and is inserted into the NIV on the basis of 1 Chr 6:18 [6:33]. The LXX reads "the second," שֵׁנִי as a proper name: Σανι.

genealogy of Assir was reflected in an early form of this list. Whether the Chronicler's source presented a linear or segmented genealogy is uncertain.

First Chronicles 6:10 [6:25] presents two sons of Elkanah (Amasai and Ahimoth).

This Elkanah is probably the Elkanah son of Korah.

First Chronicles 6:11 [6:26] is difficult. BHS reads: אֶלְקָנָה בְּנוֹ אֶלְקָנָה צוֹפַי בְּנוֹ וְנַחַת בְּנוֹ. Rudolph suggests following the LXX here and deleting the second "Elkanah." Furthermore, he suggests that ו (and) has been omitted before the first Elkanah.[38] He concludes that Elkanah is the brother of both Amasai and Ahimoth, which would be following the same pattern of having a horizontal rather than linear genealogy as was suggested for both Korah and Assir.

The remainder of the list, which parallels 1 Sam 1:1; 8:2, could be the descendants of any of the sons of Elkanah son of Korah presented in linear form, although on the basis of the recurrence of "Elkanah" as Samuel's father, it may be presumed that the descent of Elkanah son of Elkanah is given.

If we were to follow only the linear relationships, ignoring the horizontal, this would give a genealogy of: Kohath – Amminadab – Korah – Elkanah – Elkanah – Zophai – Nahath – Eliab – Jeroham – Elkanah – Samuel – Joel. Although this twelve generation genealogy is longer than the eight and seven generations of Gershom and Merari, it is consistent with the list of the sons of Aaron.[39] It is probable then that the Chronicler, or the compiler of his source, understood what was at one time a segmented genealogy as a linear genealogy and supplied the relationship term בְּנוֹ (his son).[40]

SAMUEL AS LEVITE

The attachment of the genealogy of Samuel to a Levitical list is difficult. Nowhere in the book of Samuel is it suggested that Samuel was of Levitical descent, instead indicating that his father was "from the hill country of Ephraim" and an "Ephraimite" (1 Sam 1:1). It must be admitted, however, that such a connection is not impossible. The list of Levitical cities indicates that some cities were given from "the hill country of Ephraim" (1 Chr 6:52 [6:67]; Josh 21:20–

---

[38] Rudolph, *Chronikbücher*, 54. The LXX here reads: Ελκανα υἱὸς αὐτοῦ Σουφι υἱὸς αὐτοῦ καὶ Νααθ υἱὸς αὐτοῦ.

[39] Or an eleven generation genealogy if Elkanah of 1 Chr 6:11 [6:26] is identified with Elkanah son of Korah, rather than himself being the son of Elkanah and brother of both Amasai and Ahimoth.

[40] Johnson, *Purpose*, 71–72.

21). That these cities were given to the "Kohathites," the family that Samuel is attached to, enhances this possibility.[41]

The suggestion of Curtis and others that Samuel, "is made a Levite by the Chronicler according to the notions of his own times respecting Samuel's service at the sanctuary,"[42] does not fully explain the text. Although Samuel did perform Levitical functions, such as guarding the ark (1 Sam 3:3), he also performed the priestly functions of sacrifice (1 Sam 7:7–10), which the Chronicler allowed for only the sons of Aaron (1 Chr 6:34 [6:49]). It would therefore be unusual for the Chronicler to attach Samuel to the Levites because of his priestly functions. It must also be observed that, in Chronicles, Samuel performed no Levitical or priestly duties. In Chronicles Samuel is a prophet or seer (1 Chr 9:22; 11:13; 26:28; 29:29; 2 Chr 35:18). He assigned the gatekeepers to their positions (1 Chr 9:22), dedicated material goods taken in warfare to Yahweh (1 Chr 26:28),[43] and wrote written records (1 Chr 29:29).

It is perhaps better to see this list not as the attachment of Samuel to a Kohathite family, but given for the purpose of showing that his sons, Joel and Abijah, were legitimately entitled to be "Levites." This is highlighted in 1 Chr 6:18 [6:33] where Heman, the son of Joel, is the head musician appointed by David. If we follow Johnson's dictum that a genealogy points to the importance of the last named person and seeks to connect him to "a worthy family or individual in the past,"[44] this latter genealogy seeks to justify Heman's place as a musician in the cultic structure. That Samuel performed certain priestly functions is irrelevant. In certain respects, Samuel's presence is not important except as the ancestor of one of the cultic musicians appointed by David. What is important in the ancestry of the singers is that Heman could trace his ancestry to Kohath, and therefore Heman could, legitimately, serve as a musician in the cult. Likewise, in

---

[41] "Elkanah and his son Samuel were Levites living among the Ephraimites," Pratt, *Chronicles*, 84. See also Williamson who suggests that it is possible to understand "Ephraimite" as "a resident of Ephraim," *Chronicles*, 72.

[42] Curtis and Madsen, *Chronicles*, 132. Laato also suggests that "Later religious ideology, which stated expressly that only those who belonged to the tribe of Levi could perform cultic functions, and the perception that Samuel's genealogy contravened this regulation, may have led to the forging of genealogical links to 'legitimate' Samuel posthumously," Laato, "Levitical Genealogies," 80.

[43] This conclusion is validated when it is noted that the other persons who dedicate material goods are Saul, Abner and Joab. The first was a king, the latter two were leaders of the army. First Chronicles 26:26 also mentions materials dedicated by the commanders of thousands and commanders of hundreds and by the other army commanders," while 1 Chr 26:27 mentions "plunder taken in battle."

[44] Johnson, *Purpose*, 79.

the list of Levites, what is important is not Samuel, but the status of Joel and Abijah as Levites.

THE RELATIONSHIP BETWEEN THE LISTS OF LEVITES AND SINGERS

Although it has been suggested that the lists of Levites and the list of singers present individuals or groups who perform two separate tasks in the cult, there is significant overlap in the genealogies presented for both the Kohathites (1 Chr 6:7–13 [6:22–28]; 6:18–23 [6:33–38]), and the Gershomites (1 Chr 6:5–6 [6:20–21]; 6:24–28 [6:39–43]). The lists of Merarite Levites and singers do not correspond except in respect to Mahli son of Merari (1 Chr 6:14–15 [6:29–30]; 6:29–32 [6:44–47]).[45]

THE GERSHOMITE LISTS

A comparison chart of the Gershomite Levites and singers follows (Figure 4.4).[46] The correspondences between the two lists are obvious.

Of the eight names in the list of Levites, four appear in the list of singers in the same order. Two others appear with slight variation of spelling which may be accounted for through scribal activity. One name does not relate at all to the corresponding name in the other list, while one name does not appear.[47]

---

[45] It is probable that in 1 Chr 6:32 [6:47] a horizontal lineage was read vertically. Mahli and Mushi are both said to be the sons of Merari (1 Chr 6:4 [6:19]; cf. Exod 6:19; Num 3:20). This connection may have been confused by the Chronicler or his sources which led to Mahli being a grandson of Merari, rather than his son, and Mahli being the son of Mushi rather than his brother.

[46] It is to be noted that the Chronicler here assumes that the origins of the cultic musicians date to the period of David. For the Chronicler, this is not a matter for debate or discussion, but simply reflects the received and accepted tradition of the community. For the historical issues in regard to the origins of the cultic musicians, see Gerhard von Rad, *Das Geschichtsbild des chronistischen Werkes* (Stuttgart: Kohlhammer, 1930), 98–115; Hartmut Gese, "Zur Geschichte der Kultsänger am zweiten Tempel," in *Vom Sinai zum Zion: Alttestamentliche Beiträge zur biblischen Theologie* (*Beiträge zur evangelischen Theologie 64*; München: Chr. Kaiser, 1974).

[47] Although the LXX gives little assistance in regards the relationship of the two lists, or the variations contained therein, it is interesting to note the variations in spellings for some of the names. What is of particular interest is that both read גֵרְשׁוֹם as Γεδσων, which indicates that they not only both read the ר as a ד, but they also both reverted to the name in Exodus, גֵּרְשׁוֹן, for their translation. Γεδσων is the more common rendering of גֵרְשׁוֹן

100   THE CHRONICLER'S GENEALOGIES

Figure 4.4: The Gershomite lists

1 Chr 6:5–6			1 Chr 6:24–28	
LXX	MT	MT		LXX
		לֵוִי		Λευι
Γεδσων	גֵּרְשׁוֹם	גֵּרְשֹׁם		Γεδσων
Λοβενι	לִבְנִי			
Ιεεθ	יַחַת	יַחַת		Ηχα
		שִׁמְעִי		Σεμει
Ζεμμα	זִמָּה	זִמָּה		Ζαμμα
Ιωαχ	יוֹאָח	אֵיתָן		Αιθαν
Αδδι[48]	עִדּוֹ	עֲדָיָה		Αδια
Ζαρα	זֶרַח	זֶרַח		Ζαραι
Ιεθρι	יְאָתְרַי	אֶתְנִי		Αθανι
		מַלְכִּיָּה		Μελχια
		בַּעֲשֵׂיָה		Μαασια
		מִיכָאֵל		Μιχαηλ
		שִׁמְעָא		Σαμαα
		בֶּרֶכְיָהוּ		Βαραχια
		אָסָף		Ασαφ

What is of interest is that while the list of Levites contains the name of one of Gershom's sons, Libni, which is not in the list of singers, the list of singers contains the name of Gershom's other son, Shimei, which does not appear in the list of Levites. While this may suggest either some confusion in the transmission of the list, or that the lists were formulated out of different circumstances and for different reasons, both lists clearly indicate that the persons named in the lists trace their ancestry to Gershom, son of Levi.

The singer list also extends several generations beyond that of the Levite list. This, coupled with the different lists for the Merarites in regards the Levites and

---

throughout Exodus and Numbers. Whether this is evidence of an intentional preference for the reading in Exodus or the existence of a different Hebrew text is uncertain.

[48] The LXX suggests that the translator had עדי in his *Vorlage* in 1 Chr 6:6 [6:21], which is a minor corruption from עדיה.

the singers indicates that, for the Chronicler, while the singers are related to the Levites and were taken from the Levites at some point, their duties, functions and personnel are distinct to that of the Levites.

This is consistent with the command of David as recorded in 1 Chr 15:16 where

> "David told the leaders of the Levites to appoint their brothers as singers to sing joyful songs, accompanied by musical instruments: lyres, harps and cymbals."

This is further explained in 1 Chr 25:1 when

> "David, together with the commanders of the army, set apart some of the sons of Asaph, Heman and Jeduthun for the ministry of prophesying, accompanied by harps, lyres and cymbals."

The key term in 1 Chr 25:1 is וַיַּבְדֵּל, from the root בדל (to separate, distinguish between). It is the term that is used to indicate the separation of the sons of Aaron from the Levites for the task of making sacrifice (1 Chr 23:13), and indicates that the smaller group has been taken from the larger group to perform a specific function.[49]

This has several results.

First, it indicates the unity of the tribe of Levi. While different groups may be set apart from others within the tribe to perform different functions, the essential unity of, and perhaps equality within, the tribe is asserted.[50] This is clear from 1 Chr 23 where a list of the Levitical clans includes the sons of Aaron who are "set apart" for a particular task (1 Chr 23:13), yet they remain part of the tribe of Levi. The sons of Aaron are neither excised from Levi nor distinct from Levi except in their function within the cult. The same is also true for the singers who are listed in 1 Chr 6, and by extension also for the gatekeepers whose Levitical status is later asserted (1 Chr 9:17–27).

---

[49] It is also used to speak of Levi's being separated from Israel for its cultic duties (Num 8:14; 16:9; Deut 10:8), and Israel being separated from the nations (Lev 20:24, 26; cf. Ezra 9:1; 10:11; Neh 9:2; 10:19 [10:18]; 13:3 for postexilic actions of separation). It is used throughout P's creation account in Gen 1:4, 6, 7, 14, 18, to indicate separation between light/darkness, water/water, day/night. The word is also used to speak of the distinguishing between clean and unclean (Lev 10:10; 11:47; 20:25), and the setting apart of cities of refuge (Deut 4:41; 19:2, 7).

[50] So Knoppers, "the writers tie the priests and singers together. Both groups ultimately share the same Levitical pedigree . . . all descend from one progenitor: Levi. . . a basic kinship is maintained between the Levites who serve as priests and the Levites who serve as singers," *1 Chronicles 1–9*, 428.

The second observation is that "Levites," when not referring to the tribe, can refer to that group of Levites who have duties and functions within the cult that are not included under the terms "priest, singer, gatekeeper." "Levite" then can have two separate meanings. It can refer to either a group who performs a specific function or to all or some of the groups which together make up the tribe.

This may help to explain such passages as 2 Chr 29:4–14 where Hezekiah gathered the "priests and the Levites" (2 Chr 29:4), but addressed the assembled group as "Levites" (2 Chr 29:5). Further, although the "Levites" went to work (2 Chr 29:12), some of these Levites included descendants of the singers (2 Chr 29:13b–14). Consequently, any group may still be addressed as "Levites" when speaking to or of them as part of the greater tribal structure. However, it is when they are addressed in relation to their task within the cult (priest, Levite, singer, gatekeeper) that the specific title will be used. Therefore, again in Hezekiah's reform, although the Levites did the work, the "priests" went into the sanctuary to purify it (2 Chr 29:16), while the "Levites," which also included the singers, removed the material to the Kidron Valley (2 Chr 29:16). Also, it is the Levites who reported that "we have purified the entire temple" (2 Chr 29:18), even though those who held the specific function of priest were involved. This observation makes unnecessary Welch's assertion that the original form of 2 Chr 29 was one that exalted the Levites and that a pro-priestly redactor later modified the text to establish the place of the priests.[51]

THE KOHATHITE LISTS

Although the Gershomite lists may be easily accounted for, this is not so with the two Kohathite lists (Figure 4.5). Of the twenty names in the MT of 1 Chr 6:5–14 [6:20–29], eleven are identical to those found in 1 Chr 6:18–23 [6:33–38], five are similar with the differences being possibly accounted for through scribal changes,[52] two are clearly different, two are not recounted, and one may be

---

[51] Welch, *Work*, 103–105. Welch rightly points out the anomaly found in 2 Chr 29:11 where Hezekiah tells the "Levites" that they have been chosen "to stand before him and serve him, to minister before him and to burn incense." He questions how Hezekiah could say such things to Levites, and concludes that the Chronicler proposed the equality of priest and Levite as described in Deuteronomy. This is, however, unnecessary, for if Levites as a group are being addressed, rather than Levite as a function, then these tasks are those which Levites (in their varying roles) perform.

[52] Αχιμωθ / אֲחִימוֹת in 1 Chr 6:10 [6:25] and its parallel Μεθ / מַחַת in 1 Chr 6:20 [6:35] presents some difficulties. Apart from the initial א, the two names share the same consonants ח מ ת, although the מ and ח are in a different order in the two words. It is possible that a transposition of these two letters led to מחת being written as חמת. The insertion of a beginning א and the inclusion of vowel letters would lead to אחימות. Although it is possible that the reverse process occurred, this would have been easier if the

related, but would have undergone a series of textual changes.[53] If we allow, as suggested by Rudolph and others, that Joel was omitted from the MT of 1 Chr 6:12–13 [6:27–28], then this presents twelve identical names out of twenty-two.[54] Furthermore, the identical or similar names are in the same order in the two lists.

All of these observations indicate a literary relationship between the two lists, but not necessarily a direct literary link. The differences in the two lists speak against the suggestion that one list is the direct source of the other.[55] Neither is the solution to the differences to be found in the suggestion that 1 Chr 6:18–42 [6:33–47] is a later insertion, for if it had been, then it is more probable that the redactor would have adhered more closely than is the case to the previous list.[56]

It is more probable to conclude that both lists were dependent upon a common source, which was utilised by the producer(s) of these lists for differing purposes. It is clear from the extent of the lists that the first Kohathite list seeks to establish Joel and Abijah as Levites, while the second list seeks to establish Heman, not as a Levite, but as head of the singers.

---

vowel letters were not present. However, the LXX of 1 Chr 6:20 [6:35] suggests that the text before the translator read מת, which could be a corruption of אחי מת; "the brother of the dead" (cf. Deut 25:6) or "his brother is dead (cf. Gen 42:38; 44:20). In a list of "sons of" it would be natural for a copyist to omit "brother of."

[53] תוֹחַ in 1 Chr 6:19 [6:34] is clearly related to תֹהוּ in 1 Sam 1:1. The only difference is the transposition of one letter which leads to a difference in pronunciation, and either of these may represent the original form of the name. נַחַת in 1 Chr 6:11 [6:26], which contains two of the same letters as each of the other alternatives, may have been the result of תחו read as תחן and then transposed into נחת. This is, of course, speculation, but it does account for both the similarities and the differences in the names. It must be observed, however, that such changes in names, although possible, are unlikely to have occurred through oral recitation, where the names, and their pronunciation, would be more accurately remembered. It is more probable that these changes occurred once the genealogies were committed to writing and passed on in written form.

[54] Rudolph, *Chronikbücher*, 54. If this did occur, then the name of Joel must have been lost prior to the LXX translation which reads "the second," שֵׁנִי as a proper name, Σανι. JPS, however, reads this as a proper name, "Vashni."

[55] Contra Curtis who says, "the latter genealogies [i.e. the list of singers] are probably dependent upon the former [i.e. the list of Levites]," *Chronicles*, 134. Williamson agrees when he states, "this is clearly the same list as in vv. 22–27," *Chronicles*, 73. Braun, however, disagrees with this conclusion stating, "the variations are more complex than that, and reflect differing perceptions, ages and conditions of Israel's Levitical families," *1 Chronicles*, 92.

[56] Rudolph indicates that although 1 Chr 6:18–32 [6:33–47] is completely consistent with the Chronicler's thoughts of the singers as Levites, he says, "Trotzdem kann das Stück nicht von ihm stammen," *Chronikbücher*, 58. Von Rad agrees when he indicates that the genealogy of the singers is secondary, *Geschichtsbild*, 102–103.

Figure 4.5: The Kohathite Lists

1 Chr 6:7=14 [22–29]		1 Chr 6:18–23 [33–38]		1 Sam 1:1
LXX	MT	MT	LXX	
		יִשְׂרָאֵל	Ισραηλ	
		לֵוִי	Λευι	
Κααθ	קְהָת	קְהָת	Κααθ	
Αμιναδαβ	עַמִּינָדָב	יִצְהָר	Ισσααρ	
Κορε	קֹרַח	קֹרַח	Κορε	
Ασιρ	אַסִּיר			
Ελκανα	אֶלְקָנָה			
Αβιασαφ	אֶבְיָסָף	אֶבְיָסָף	Αβιασαφ	
Ασιρ	אַסִּיר	אַסִּיר	Ασιρ	
Θααθ	תַּחַת	תַּחַת	Θααθ	
Ουριηλ	אוּרִיאֵל	צְפַנְיָה	Σαφανια	
Οζια	עֻזִּיָּה	עֲזַרְיָה	Αζαρια	
Σαουλ	שָׁאוּל	יוֹאֵל	Ιωηλ	
Ελκανα	אֶלְקָנָה	אֶלְקָנָה	Ελκανα	
Αμασι	עֲמָשָׂי	עֲמָשַׂי	Αμασιου	
Αχιμωθ	אֲחִימוֹת	מַחַת	Μεθ	
Ελκανα	אֶלְקָנָה	אֶלְקָנָה	Ελκανα	
Σουφι	צוֹפַי	צִיף	Σουφ	צוּף
Νααθ	נַחַת	תּוֹחַ	Θιε	תֹּחוּ
Ελιαβ	אֱלִיאָב	אֱלִיאֵל	Ελιηλ	אֱלִיהוּא
Ιδαερ	יְרֹחָם	יְרֹחָם	Ηδαδ	יְרֹחָם
Ιδαερ	אֶלְקָנָה	אֶלְקָנָה	Ελκανα	אֶלְקָנָה
Σαμουηλ	שְׁמוּאֵל	שְׁמוּאֵל	Σαμουηλ	
Σανι	אֲבִיָּה	יוֹאֵל	Ιωηλ	
		הֵימָן	Αιμαν	

This difference in purpose may therefore explain why the Levite list extends only to Kohath in the past (the connection of Kohath to the sons of Levi being supplied by the Chronicler from Exod 6:16–24). The Kohathite singer list extends, however, not to the clan leader, Kohath, but to the national founder, Israel. Each of the other two singer lists also reach back, not to its respective clan founders, but to Levi (1 Chr 6:28, 32 [6:43, 47]). This indicates that one of the original purposes of these lists of singers was not to establish their places within their clans, but within Levi itself.[57]

This conclusion is strengthened when it is observed that, like the Kohathite singers, the Gershomite and Merarite singers also extend beyond the final named person in the previous Levitical lists. The Gershomite list extends an additional six generations, and the Merarite list an additional five generations. The Levite lists are structured to display the place of a particular clan or portion of a clan, while the singer lists are structured to present the place of a particular family (Heman, Asaph, Ethan). This difference in function probably influenced their difference in form (ascending rather than descending), their different length, and also their choice of relating themselves not to a clan founder but to either Israel or Levi.[58]

These different functions may also account for the inclusion or exclusion of names, as well as the presence of different names. Thus אוּרִיאֵל (Uriel) in the Levite list (1 Chr 6:9 [6:24]), may have had a significance for the founder of that list that was held by צְפַנְיָה (Zephaniah) in the compiling of the singer list (1 Chr 6:21 [6:36]).

AMMINADAB: THE SON OF KOHATH?

This observation may also help to account for the statement in 1 Chr 6:7 [6:22] that Amminadab is the son of Kohath. Every other listing of Kohath's sons indicates that he had four: Amram, Izhar, Hebron, and Uzziel (Exod 6:18; Num 3:19, 27; 1 Chr 5:28; 6:3 [6:2, 18]; 23:12). Other lists indicate that Korah's father was Izhar (Exod 6:21; Num 16:1; 1 Chr 6:22–23 [6:37–38]).

The Hebrew Bible only mentions two persons named Amminadab: Amminadab, the father of Nahshon who was leader of the tribe of Judah (Num 1:7; 2:3; 7:12, 17; 10:14),[59] and an Amminadab who was a Levite in the time of David from the clan of Uzziel (1 Chr 15:10–11).

It would appear as if Amminadab has been substituted for Izhar in 1 Chr 6:7 [6:22]. Although Rothstein suggests a series of scribal errors to account for the loss of Izhar and the appearance of Amminadab, this is probably not necessary.[60]

---

[57] A similar situation may be envisioned in the list of Ezra's ancestry (Ezra 7:1–5), where Ezra's legitimacy for his task as a reformer, and perhaps as a new lawgiver, is traced directly to his relationship to Aaron the high priest.

[58] "The lineage genealogy must also alter its form in order to continue to reflect the lineage structure in various contexts. This fact may cause several conflicting genealogies to exist at the same time, but each one can be considered accurate in its own context," Wilson, *Genealogy*, 46–47.

[59] Cf. the genealogies in Ruth 4:19, 20; 1 Chr 2:10; Matt 1:4; Luke 3:32–33.

[60] Rothstein suggests that a copyist mistakenly began to write the name of Kohath's firstborn, Amram, עַמ, realised his mistake and simply joined the appropriate "Izhar," יִצְהָר,

Two possibilities present themselves.

First, that there was an otherwise unknown Amminadab who was a significant person in the family or clan history and was "promoted" to the place of "son" of Kohath and the founder of the clan list that follows. Wilson discusses a similar phenomenon in an Arabian family in the context of the changes in genealogical relationships occurring over a fifty year period.[61] Significantly, Wilson indicates that in this family three persons had been elevated to a higher genealogical level to more prominent positions (making these persons "brothers" of the one who in the earlier tradition had been their "father"), while previously unknown persons were included in another portion of the genealogy with the result that twelve "brothers" were divided off into two, distinct, and politically distant, groups. It is possible that a similar phenomena occurred which influenced the production of the source of our text as well.

The second possibility is that one of the two known persons named Amminadab was inserted for reasons now unknown, but can be surmised. Amminadab in 1 Chr 15:10–11 is the head of the clan of Uzziel, fourth son of Kohath. What is interesting in the list of the "sons of Kohath" (1 Chr 15:5–10), is that while a clan leader for each of Kohath, Merari and Gershom is given (1 Chr 15:5–7), clan leaders for Elizaphan, Hebron and Uzziel are also given (1 Chr 15:8–10).[62] Hebron and Uzziel are both sons of Kohath (Exod 6:18; Num 3:19; 1 Chr 5:28; 6:3 [6:2, 18]; 23:12), while an Elzaphan is recorded elsewhere as the son of Uzziel (Exod 6:22; Lev 10:4), and Elizaphan was himself the leader of Uzziel (Num 3:30).[63] First Chronicles 15:5–10 therefore presents the same type of elevation in genealogical position that Wilson illustrated.[64] This passage presents two sons and one grandson of Uzziel being elevated to equal clan status with Uzziel and his brothers.

---

to what he had written. The text would then read עמיצהר. He suggests that a later copyist, under the influence of Exod 6:23 changed this to Amminidab, עמינדב, *Chronik*, 114–115; cf. Rudolph, *Chronikbücher*, 54 who also suggests the possible influence of 1 Chr 15:10. Rothstein points out that although the LXX[a] reads here "αμιναδαβ υιος αυτου ισσααρ ουις αυτου," and that this has probably been inserted on the basis of 1 Chr 6:23 [6:38]. He maintains that LXX[b] = MT represents the earlier text.

[61] Wilson, *Genealogy*, 48–54, and especially the charts on page 49–50.

[62] Cf. 2 Chr 29:12–14 where clan leaders from Kohath, Merari, Gershom, Elizaphan, Asaph, Heman and Jeduthun are presented as heading the cleansing of the temple under Hezekiah.

[63] The difference in the names is only the absence of a *yod*, י: אֱלִיצָפָן / אֶלְצָפָן.

[64] Wilson, *Genealogy*, 48–54. A similar example can be found in Ezra 8:18–19 where a Mahli is made a son of Levi (rather than a son of Merari, son of Levi), and his descendants are placed on equal terms with descendants of Merari.

Wilson's study indicates that genealogical presentation was dependent upon the social, political and religious relationships present when these genealogies were constructed and that those relationships were reflected in the genealogies. It is therefore not impossible, for reasons which cannot now be ascertained, that Amminadab, the leader of the clan of Uzziel, was "elevated" to a position as a son of Kohath and inserted into a genealogy as the father of the Korahites. These same leaders were the persons who were responsible for carrying the ark (1 Chr 15:11–15), as well as for appointing those who were to become the heads of the musical guilds (1 Chr 15:16–18). Either of these could have been of such significance to a later genealogist as to demand the incorporation of Amminadab the leader of Uzziel as a father of Korah and son of Kohath.

Likewise, it is possible that Amminadab, the father of Elisheba who was married to Aaron (Exod 6:23), was incorporated into the genealogy of Kohath, as a son of Kohath, because of that marriage. Amminadab possibly could not be put on an equal footing with Kohath who was more closely related to the twelve Patriarchs than Amminadab was, but could be placed on the same level as Kohath's sons. It is possible that this could be realised because, through marriage, they were now considered "brothers." It is significant also that Judah, which was led by Nahshon son of Amminadab (and possibly by Amminadab himself at one stage), was the tribe that supplied cities to the sons of Aaron (Josh 21:9–19).[65]

That the "sons of Aaron" could also be viewed as "Judahites" through the daughter of Amminadab, speaks of the closeness of these two groups, and gives credence to the possibility that the Amminadab of 1 Chr 6:7 [6:22] is Amminadab father of Nahshon, leader of the tribe of Judah. His incorporation would have been influenced through his position in Judah, the joining of the clans together through marriage, and the giving of cities to the sons of Aaron.

1 CHRONICLES 5:27–41 [6:1–15]: A HIGH PRIEST LIST?

It was stated previously that the lists of the sons of Aaron (1 Chr 5:27–41; 6:35–38 [6:1–5, 50–53]), were not lists of High Priests, but instead represented those who fulfilled the duties at the altar in regard to sacrifice and atonement for Israel. While it is true that a high/chief priest would be counted among their number, the duties at the altar were not restricted to this high/chief priest.[66]

---

[65] Of the thirteen towns supplied to the sons of Aaron, nine came from Judah/Simeon and four from Benjamin. However, because all of the territory of Simeon was excised from Judah (Josh 19:2–9), it could be concluded that Judah contributed the nine towns themselves.

[66] The terminology used to designate the High/Chief Priest is not consistent. The most common term "the great priest," הַכֹּהֵן הַגָּדוֹל, is used in Lev 21:10; Num 35:25, 28

Although this list is often called a "High Priest List," several observations have already been made which speak against 1 Chr 5:27–41 [6:1–15] being seen as a list of High/Chief priests.[67] First, the text itself initially claims to be a list of the sons of Levi, which is narrowed down to a list of the sons of Aaron (1 Chr 5:27–29 [6:1–3]). In the entire list no person is called a chief/high priest, and only one person (Azariah in 1 Chr 5:36 [6:10]), is said to have served in a priestly capacity. Even here, Azariah is not said to have served as a high/chief priest.

Second, the pattern which lists cultic officials is that of "priests, Levites, singers." If this pattern is being followed here, then this is simply a list of those who were eligible to serve in a priestly capacity rather than a list of those who served as "high/chief priest." This does not deny the possibility that some of these persons served as high/chief priest, but neither does it demand that all of them did so.

Third, it is obvious that some of these persons did not serve in a priestly, let alone high/chief priestly capacity. Even if we were to assume the formation of the priesthood in the time of Moses, then it is clear that those persons listed prior to Aaron (Levi, Kohath, Amram) as well as their sons other than Aaron, could not have served in a high priestly position that did not exist.[68] Likewise, according to

---

(x2); Josh 20:6; 2 Kgs 12:11; 22:4, 8; 23:4; 2 Chr 34:9; Neh 3:1, 20; 13:28; Hag 1:1, 12, 14; 2:2, 4; Zech 3:1, 8; 6:11. The other common phrase is some combination of ראש and כֹּהֵן. הַכֹּהֵן הָרֹאשׁ, is used in 2 Chr 31:10; Ezra 7:5. כֹּהֵן הָרֹאשׁ, in 2 Kgs 25:18; 2 Chr 19:11; 24:11; 26:20; Jer 52:24. הַכֹּהֵן רֹאשׁ is used in 1 Chr 27:5. Knoppers suggests reading הַכֹּהֵן הָרֹאשׁ here in line with the LXX reading ὁ ἱερεὺς ὁ ἄρχων, Knoppers, *1 Chronicles 10–29*, 892, 895. This Jehoiada is also called the "leader of the family of Aaron" (1 Chr 12:26–27), a position later assumed by Zadok (1 Chr 27:17). Olyon contends that Zadok is the son of this Jehoiada, and assumed leadership of the clan of Aaron on his father's death. He further asserts that Benaiah, the son of Jehoiada (1 Chr 11:22, 24; 18:17; 27:5, 34), who eventually assisted Solomon in his claim to the throne (1 Kgs 1–2; 4:4) was Zadok's brother, Olyan, "Origins," 185. If 1 Chronicles accurately reflects the political realities, this suggests that it was not simply the priesthood or the army that sided with Solomon, but two key officials within the priesthood or army, who as brothers, worked together to mutually support and promote one another's position.

[67] Wellhausen both assumed that this was a list of the High Priests and then condemned the list's historicity by showing that it was not a list of high priests, *Prolegomena*, 221–222. It is clear that his faulty initial assumption led to his conclusion. Others who assume that this is a High Priest List are, Braun, *1 Chronicles*, 83; Curtis and Madsen, *Chronicles*, 128; Hill, *Chronicles*, 134; Japhet, *Chronicles*, 146; Keil, *Chronicles*, 112; Klein, *1 Chronicles*, 177–181; Rudolph, *Chronikbücher*, 51–53; Williamson, *Chronicles*, 70. Knoppers, however, prefers to refer to it as a "priestly heritage," *1 Chronicles 1–9*, 400, see further Knoppers, "Relationship," 112–116.

[68] However, Exod 19:22, 24 suggests that prior to the law and the Aaronite priesthood there were "priests" within the community.

2 Kgs 25:18 and Jer 52:24, the final high priest was Seraiah, who was executed after the destruction of Jerusalem and the temple by the Babylonians. As such, Jehozadak, son of Seraiah, could not have served as high priest in Jerusalem, although he could have served as a priest prior to being taken captive into Babylon (1 Chr 5:41[6:15]).

Finally, although the Hebrew Bible does indicate that some of these named persons did serve as the high/chief priest, there are others who are called high/chief priest in the narratives who are not recorded in this list. Figure 4.6 lists those who are called either "high priest" or "chief priest" in the Hebrew Bible.

Figure 4.6: Persons Given the Title "High/Chief Priest"

Term	High Priest	King	Reference
הַכֹּהֵן הָרֹאשׁ	Aaron	--	Ezra 7:5
הַכֹּהֵן רֹאשׁ	Jehoiada	David	1 Chr 27:5
כֹּהֵן הָרֹאשׁ	Amariah	Jehoshaphat	2 Chr 19:11
הַכֹּהֵן הַגָּדוֹל	Jehoiada	Joash	2 Kgs 12:11 [12:10]
כֹּהֵן הָרֹאשׁ			2 Chr 24:11
כֹּהֵן הָרֹאשׁ	Azariah	Uzziah	2 Chr 26:20
הכהן הראש	Azariah	Hezekiah	2 Chr 31:10
הַכֹּהֵן הַגָּדוֹל	Hilkiah	Josiah	2 Kgs 22:4, 8; 23:4; 2 Chr 34:9
כֹּהֵן הָרֹאשׁ	Seraiah	Zedekiah	2 Kgs 25:18; Jer 52:24
הַכֹּהֵן הַגָּדוֹל	Joshua	--	Hag 1:1, 12, 14; 2:2, 4; Zech 3:1, 8; 6:11
הַכֹּהֵן הַגָּדוֹל	Eliashib	--	Neh 3:1, 20
הַכֹּהֵן הַגָּדוֹל	Joiada	--	Neh 13:28

The relationship of this data to the list of the sons of Aaron in 1 Chr 6 can be better appreciated if the above table is combined with the list of the sons of Aaron (Figure 4.7).[69]

Because the Chronicler's list ends with the exile, it is understandable that the postexilic high priests Joshua, Eliashib and Joiada are not listed by the Chronicler.

---

[69] And see the chart in Klein, *1 Chronicles*, 178. Note, however, that in Klein's chart, Ahimaaz (column F), should be positioned in column G. And Amariah (column A), should be positioned under "omitted priests."

The omission of both high priests named Jehoiada is difficult to understand, however, if this is a list of high priests. Perhaps the first Jehoiada was a minor figure and therefore his name was omitted through the telescoping of the genealogy. There is, however, no reasonable explanation for the omission of the second named Jehoiada who is prominent in both the Kings and Chronicles accounts.[70]

Figure 4.7: The Sons of Aaron

Term	1 Chr 6	Other High Priests	King	Reference
הַכֹּהֵן הָרֹאשׁ	Aaron			Ezra 7:5
הַכֹּהֵן	Eleazar			Num 26:3, 63; 27:2; 31:12; 32:2
	Phinehas			Judges 20:28
	Abishua			
	Bukki			
	Uzzi			
	Zerahiah			
	Meraioth			
	Amariah			
	Ahitub			
הַכֹּהֵן רֹאשׁ		Jehoiada	David	1 Chr 27:5
הַכֹּהֵן	Zadok		David/ Solomon	1 Kgs 2:35
	Ahimaaz			

---

[70] Wilson gives seven reasons for "telescoping," or the loss of a name from a genealogy: 1) The lineage segment may be destroyed. 2) No children are produced and the line dies out. 3) Individuals or groups migrate to another lineage. 4) Unimportant names may be forgotten. 5) Names may be deliberately suppressed. 6) The name no longer has a function within the lineage. 7) Two persons sharing the same name are merged into one person. *Genealogy*, 33–34. Of these possible reasons, only #6 is reasonable in regards the first Jehoiada. This is particularly so if Olyan is correct in asserting that this Jehoiada was Zadok's father, "Origins," 185. In regards the second Jehoiada, however, no reason can justify the omission of the great reforming High Priest from a list of High Priests. See, however, the discussion earlier regarding Zadok's genealogical ties to the family of Eli. Katzenstein suggests that this list, instead of being a list of all the high priests, was a list of Zadokite high priests. He further suggests that Jehoiada was not a Zadokite but owed his position as high priest to his being the son in law of King Jehoram (2 Chr 22:11). Because he was not a Zadokite, his name was omitted from the list. H. J. Katzenstein, "Some Remarks on the Lists of the Chief Priests of the Temple of Solomon," *JBL* 81 (1962): 377–389, 379–380.

Term	1 Chr 6	Other High Priests	King	Reference
הַכֹּהֵן	Azariah		Solomon	1 Kgs 4:2
	Johanan			
	Azariah			
כֹּהֵן הָרֹאשׁ	Amariah[71]		Jehoshaphat	2 Chr 19:11
הַכֹּהֵן הַגָּדוֹל		Jehoiada	Joash	2 Kgs 12:11 [12:10]
כֹּהֵן הָרֹאשׁ				2 Chr 24:11
כֹּהֵן הָרֹאשׁ		Azariah	Uzziah	2 Chr 26:20
הַכֹּהֵן		Uriah	Ahaz	2 Kgs 16:10–16
כֹּהֵן הָרֹאשׁ		Azariah	Hezekiah	2 Chr 31:10
	Ahitub			
	Zadok			
	Shallum			
הַכֹּהֵן הַגָּדוֹל	Hilkiah		Josiah	2 Kgs 22:4, 8; 23:4; 2 Chr 34:9
	Azariah			
כֹּהֵן הָרֹאשׁ	Seraiah		Zedekiah	2 Kgs 25:18; Jer 52:24
	Jehozadak			
הַכֹּהֵן הַגָּדוֹל	Joshua		--	Hag 1:1, 12, 14; 2:2, 4; Zech 3:1, 8; 6:11
הַכֹּהֵן הַגָּדוֹל	Eliashib		--	Neh 3:1, 20
הַכֹּהֵן הַגָּדוֹל	Joiada		--	Neh 12:28

While it is clear that this list is not a complete genealogy, and that some telescoping must have occurred, telescoping does not adequately explain the omission of the majority of high priests of whom we do know, and the inclusion of "high priests" not recorded elsewhere.[72]

Hilkiah and Seraiah are names well attested in the accounts of the reforms of Josiah and the fall of Jerusalem under Zedekiah, and are among the last recorded

---

[71] Japhet does not identify Amariah, the priest in the time of Jehoshaphat, with the Amariah in this portion of the list, *Chronicles*, 150, so also Klein, *1 Chronicles*, 178.

[72] That telescoping has occurred is evident when it is recognized that the genealogy from the time of Solomon to that of the exile, from Ahimaaz to Seraiah (i.e. from the building of the temple to its destruction) is approximately 368 years which, which requires almost thirty-seven years of service per high priest.

preexilic high priests. As such, their inclusion in a list of the sons of Aaron is understandable, as would their inclusion in a list of high priests.[73]

Ezra 7:5 is the only instance of Aaron being specifically called the "high priest," however his portrayal in the priestly literature as the lineage founder for all subsequent priests, be they high priests or other priests, compels his presence in this list.

What this indicates is, of the eleven persons specifically named as high/chief priests in the Hebrew Bible, only four of them are recorded in the list of the sons of Aaron in 1 Chr 5:27–41 [6:1–15], while three of the postexilic high priests are not listed.[74] Further, four other persons, one of whom is a prominent reformer, are omitted from the genealogy. This indicates that, of the twenty-two possible high priests from Aaron to Seraiah which are presented in the list, only four of them are called high/chief priest and seven persons elsewhere so called are not in the list of twenty-two.

The situation is further complicated when it is recognised that both Jehoiada and Hilkiah are not only called the high priest, but also by the shortened form הַכֹּהֵן (the priest).[75] If this situation applies to other prominent priestly officials, this indicates that Eleazar (Num 26:3, 63; 27:2; 31:12; 32:2; 34:17; Josh 14:1), Zadok (1 Kgs 2:35), and Azariah (1 Kgs 4:2), each of whom is listed in 1 Chr 5:27–41 [6:1–15], were also considered to function as high/chief priests.[76] It may also be assumed that Phinehas (Judg 20:28), rose to the position of high/chief

---

[73] As stated previously, it is also possible that Seraiah and Azariah are the same person. See, however, Katzenstein who disputes this, suggesting that Azariah preceded Seraiah as the High Priest at the time of the exile of Jehoiachin, Katzenstein, "Chief Priests," 383.

[74] Klein, who reconstructs his list differently, has only three "high priests" in the list of the sons of Aaron, *1 Chronicles*, 178.

[75] For Jehoiada: 2 Kgs 11:9, 10, 15; 12:2, 7, 9; 2 Chr 22:11; 23:8, 9, 14; 24:2, 20, 25. For Hilkiah: 2 Kgs 22:10, 12, 14;; 23:24; 2 Chr 34:14, 18. If "Eliashib the priest" in Neh 13:4 is also to be understood as Eliashib the high priest (cf. Neh 13:28), this is another example. This identification is rejected by Williamson, *Ezra, Nehemiah*, 386; Myers, *Ezra Nehemiah*, 214; F. Charles Fensham, *The Books of Ezra and Nehemiah* (NICOT; Grand Rapids: Eerdmans, 1982), 260. It is, however, affirmed by Loring W. Batten, *A Critical and Exegetical Commentary on The Books of Ezra and Nehemiah* (ICC; Edinburgh: T&T Clark, 1913), 288; Derek Kidner, *Ezra and Nehemiah* (TOTC; Leicester: Inter-Varsity Press, 1979), 129.

[76] This distinction between "the priest" as an alternative title for "chief/high priest" may help to explain the list of Solomon's officials in 1 Kgs 4:1–6. This list indicates four persons who are called "priests" (Azariah, Zadok, Abiathar, Zabud). Only one of them, Azariah, is called הַכֹּהֵן. The other three are given the title כֹּהֵן.

priest on the death of his father. This brings the recognition of an additional four persons in the list, bringing the total to eight of the twenty-two.[77]

This, however, also raises other problems, for in the book of Samuel, Eli (1 Sam 1:9; 2:11), Ahijah (1 Sam 14:3, 19, 36), Ahimelech (1 Sam 21:1–9; 22:11), and Abiathar (1 Sam 23:9; 30:7), all are said to be הַכֹּהֵן (the priest) and clearly act in the capacity of the leading priest at the shrine or for the king. None of these four appear in the Chronicler's list.[78]

Attention could also be brought to Pashhur הַכֹּהֵן (the priest; Jer 20:1), who is the "chief officer" at the house of God, and Zephaniah (Jer 21:1; 29:25–29; 37:3), who is "appointed priest in place of Jehoiada to be in charge of the house of the Lord." If these are a reference to "high priest," then it indicates that there are two or perhaps three additional chief/high priests (Pashhur, Jehoiada who was exiled and Zephaniah who replaced him) who are not in the Chronicler's list.[79]

Finally, 2 Kgs 16:10–16 mentions Uriah who was the priest during the reign of Ahaz and who, following the orders of Ahaz, constructed a new altar to replace

---

[77] It must be noticed, however, that Ithamar (Num 4:28, 33; 7:8), and Jonathan (Judg 18:6, 18, 20, 24, 27), are both called "the priest." It is clear that Ithamar was not considered to be a high/chief priest, although Jonathan was the priest in charge of a shrine and may therefore have been thought of as a "chief/head priest" in that location. Mattan, "the priest" of Baal (2 Kgs 11:18), must also have acted in a high priestly capacity at that particular shrine. This is probably also true of Amaziah the priest in Amos 7:10. Others are called "the priest" without any leading role being indicated: Ezekiel (Ezek 1:3), Shelemiah (Neh 13:13), Ezra (Ezra 7:11; 10:10, 16; Neh 8:2, 9; 12:26), and Meremoth (Ezra 8:33). Koch, however, suggests that Meremoth "the priest" was the high priest upon Ezra's arrival in Jerusalem, Klaus Koch, "Ezra and Meremoth: Remarks on the History of the High Priesthood," in *Sha'arei Talmon: Studies in the Bible, Qumran, and the Ancient Near East Presented to Shemaryahu Talmon* (ed. Michael Fishbane and Emmanuel Tov; Winona Lake: Eisenbrauns, 1992), 110. Koch further suggests that Ezra removed Meremoth from his position for not being descended from Aaron. Even so, Meremoth remained active in the postexilic community. Cf. Ezra 2:61–63 where "Hakkoz" is exiled from the priesthood and Neh 3:4, 21 where Meremoth son of Uriah son of Hakkoz is one of the builders of the wall, but no longer a priest, Koch, "Ezra and Meremoth," 108–109.

[78] See, however, 2 Esdras 1:1–3 which includes Ahijah, Phinehas and Eli as ancestors of Zadok. This is clearly an insertion into the list of Ezra 7:1–5 and appears to be an attempt by a later author to include other, known, high priests. If this is the case, then this later author assumed that Ezra's list, and perhaps also the Chronicler's, was a list of high priests.

[79] Jeremiah 52:24, however, says that Seraiah was the chief priest and Zephaniah was the priest next in rank. Both were executed by the Babylonians. It is not impossible, however, that Zephaniah was "demoted" and Seraiah "promoted" during the varying political struggles in Zedekiah's reign. Zephaniah is condemned for failing to silence Jeremiah. Thus, if there was a change in the high priesthood, Zephaniah's support for (or at least his lack of action against) Jeremiah may have been a mitigating factor.

the altar of Yahweh in the temple. Although Uriah acted in the capacity of high/chief priest, he is not in the Chronicler's list. It has been suggested that Uriah was omitted because of his actions with the alternate altar,[80] but the vision of Ezek 8–11 is no less condemning of the leadership of the temple during the reign of Zedekiah, which would indicate the failure of Seraiah in his duties as high priest. Yet, Seraiah is named in the list in spite of the failure and compromise of the period he oversaw.

Although it has been observed that there are a number of correspondences between the high/chief priests in the narrative and the names in the Chronicler's list, there are enough divergences and unexplainable omissions to warrant the conclusion that this is not a list of high/chief priests.

It is better to view this list in the same manner in which the list of Levites and singers was viewed, with the focus on the last named person in the list. This person, Jehozadak, is mentioned only here in 1 Chr 5:40–41 [6:14–15] and in Hag 1:1, 12, 14; 2:2, 4; Zech 6:11. In Haggai and Zechariah he is only mentioned in association with Joshua, the high priest at the time of the construction of the second temple.

It is therefore probable that this list of the sons of Aaron in 1 Chr 6 is designed to present a link between the pre and postexilic periods, and to establish through the last named, Jehozadak, a link between the pre and postexilic sons of Aaron or priests. By establishing Jehozadak's credentials as a son of Aaron, this automatically establishes Joshua and his descendants' credentials and their right to officiate as priests in the postexilic community (cf. Neh 12:10–11).[81] This also explains the presence of Seraiah in this list, for Seraiah was, according to the Deuteronomistic History, a legitimate high priest. By genealogically connecting Jehozadak to Seraiah, the postexilic high priests who trace their ancestry to Jehozadak are legitimised as sons of Aaron through the Chronicler's connection of Jehozadak with Seraiah. Consequently, just as Asaph, Heman and Jeduthun were the primary focus in the genealogy of the singers, so also Jehozadak, and not the

---

[80] Braun, *1 Chronicles*, 86. See also Wilson's fifth reason for the omission of names in a genealogy, note 70, above. Katzenstein suggests that Uriah was omitted because he was "a non-Zadokite," "Chief Priests," 382.

[81] So also Japhet, *Chronicles*, 152. It must be noticed, however, that Ezra, about whom a claim to priestly status is made, does not trace his lineage through Jehozadak, but only through Seraiah (Ezra 7:1). Although the exact reason is not known, it is possible that Ezra was considered to be a part of a different branch of the family that did not trace itself through Jehozadak. It is also possible that the link between Seraiah and Jehozadak (only found here in 1 Chr 5:40–41 [6:14–15]), was an artificial construct of the early postexilic period devised to justify the position of Joshua as high priest of the second temple.

others who are named, is the primary focus of the Chronicler's list of the sons of Aaron.[82]

THE STRUCTURE OF THE LIST OF THE SONS OF AARON

Knoppers, although rejecting the list of the sons of Aaron as a high priest list,[83] sees in it instead an attempt to highlight the person and place of Zadok through a chiastic structure.[84] This is unlikely for several reasons.

First, to gain his chiasm, Knoppers must omit the first named person "Levi" as well as most of his sons and grandchildren. It must be recognised that, if the "descendants" of Levi are in view, this cannot be restricted to only those who would later be sons of Aaron, for all of Levi's descendants would include his three sons (Gershon, Kohath, Merari), the four sons of Kohath (Amram, Izhar, Hebron, Uzziel), the three "sons" of Amram (Aaron, Moses, Miriam), as well as the four sons of Aaron (Nadab, Abihu, Eleazar, Ithamar).[85] Knoppers claims that

---

[82] This could also answer Knopper's valid question, "if the author was concerned to support the cause of the Levitical musicians, why stop with David? Why not continue the lineage to the singers living during the author's own time?," "Greek Historiography and the Chronicler's History: A Reexamination," *JBL* 122 (2003): 627–650, 645. Just as Jehozadak provided the link between the pre and postexilic sons of Aaron, so also did Heman, Asaph and Ethan/Jeduthun provide the link between the pre and postexilic cultic musicians. No intermediate names would be required, because that one link name from the preexilic period (Jehozadak, Heman, Asaph, Ethan/Jeduthun), would be all that is necessary to establish the legitimacy of the person in the postexilic period. This is a somewhat different scenario than presented previously, when an *external* clan seeks to incorporate itself into an *existing* genealogy. In the latter case, those who seek to link themselves to the existing genealogy must establish the relationship between themselves and the lineage ancestor. When, as here, a person in the present is already known or believed to be genealogically linked to an ancestor, all that is required is to show that ancestor's link to the legitimising genealogy.

[83] Knoppers, "Relationship," 112–116; Knoppers, *1 Chronicles 1–9*, 412–415.

[84] Knoppers, "Relationship," 124–126, and especially the chart on page 125, and his discussion in Knoppers, *1 Chronicles 1–9*, 410–412.

[85] In the case of Miriam, "son" is here used in the more general meaning of "descendant." Changes in relationships, and perhaps gender, do occur in the Chronicler's genealogies. Cf. 1 Chr 1:36 where, Timna the wife of Eliphaz (Gen 36:12) becomes his "son." Another example is found in 1 Chr 7:15, where Zelophehad may be considered as a second sister to Makir instead of the father of five daughters (Num 26:33). Curtis proposes changing "the second" to "his brother," Curtis and Madsen, *Chronicles*, 152, and the proposed reconstruction of the original text in Rudolph, *Chronikbücher*, 69–70. In the case of Timna, Wilson proposes that the Chronicler "has apparently extracted the names from Gen. 36:11–12 and omitted notes on the kinship relations between the persons named. Again the reader would be expected to supply the missing information on the basis of his

the Chronicler sought only to focus on Levi's descendants "from Kohath to Jehozadaq," with Zadok in the centre. However, even this claim would omit the other descendants of Kohath, Amram and Aaron respectively. His suggested chiastic structure then would not be obvious in the text but could only be recognised through the excision of between eight and eleven names.

Second, he states that in this structure "twelve generations of priests precede him [i.e. Zadok] . . . and twelve generations of priests succeed him."[86] This is, however, inaccurate as neither Kohath nor Amram were priests and it is unknown if Jehozadaq was able to serve in the capacity of priest, being exiled instead to Babylon. If this were an attempt to show Zadok as the focus of the priesthood, then the names of other "sons of Aaron" rather than "sons of Levi" should be inserted. Further, Nadab, Abihu and Ithamar were all "priests," but Knoppers does not include them among the priests leading up to Zadok.

Third, although Knoppers claims that this is a chiastic structure, it fails to meet the criteria of a chiasm as set forward by Welch.[87] Although there is "balance" (if certain names are excised), there is no inversion, no repetition, no intensification. The varying levels do not build upon one another, nor do they lead to an understandable climax in the centre. They are, in effect, a mere list of names. Even the two historical notes are not on the same level in the chiasm, and therefore do not intensify one another. Although Knoppers' insights into the priestly genealogy are helpful, it is doubtful if his conclusion that they are presented chiastically is valid.[88]

A more valid conclusion is that the genealogy of the sons of Aaron divides history into two epochs. From the exodus to the building of the temple, and from the building of the temple to the exile.[89] At least as early as Wellhausen it has been observed that the genealogy of the sons of Aaron has been structured according to a particular view of history.[90] He observed that there are twelve

---

(sic) knowledge of the complete genealogy," *Genealogy*, 180. This, however, is the problem. If the person only knows the genealogy recited, and not the narrative or another genealogy which explains it, then relationships and even "gender" can become lost, confused, or changed over time. Wilson gives an example where an individual was considered to be the son of a prominent person, the wife of that person, or identical to that person but with an alternate name, *Genealogy*, 29.

[86] Knoppers, "Relationship," 124.

[87] Welch, "Introduction," 10.

[88] If a chiasm was to be observed, it would probably start with Aaron rather than Kohath. This would make the centre point Azariah, the first priest in the temple of Solomon.

[89] Knoppers suggests instead that Zadok appears as the halfway point between the ancestral age represented by Levi and the exile represented by Jehozadak, Knoppers, "Relationship," 124.

[90] Wellhausen, *Prolegomena*, 221–222. Also Japhet, *Chronicles*, 150.

generations of forty years listed from the Exodus to the building of the temple (Aaron to Ahimaaz), and a further eleven generations from the building of the temple to the exile (Azariah to Jehozadak).[91] Keil notes that this allocation of forty years to a generation lies behind the statement of 1 Kgs 6:1 regarding the building of the temple, "in the four hundred and eightieth year after the Israelites had come out of Egypt."[92] Wellhausen viewed this structure as artificial, and therefore unhistorical,[93] and Keil notes that the average of thirty-nine and one quarter years per, "generation is high, but allows for the possibility of omissions in the list."[94]

If the Chronicler was claiming that what he was presenting was an unbroken list of fathers and sons, then the concerns raised by Wellhausen and others would be valid. Wilson's study has, however, shown that genealogies are rarely complete. He observes that, "normally the maximal lineage genealogy does not exceed a depth of ten to fourteen generations, with the average maximum depth being twelve generations."[95]

It would appear then that the Chronicler utilised a source that was itself limited by the strictures inherent in oral genealogies, and modified it according to

---

[91] It is on the basis of this scheme that Wellhausen suggested, followed by many others, that the historical note on Azariah serving in Solomon's temple should be moved from Azariah II to Azariah I (1 Chr 5:35–36 [6:9–10]), Wellhausen, *Prolegomena*, 222. It is also to be noted that in the Chronicler's genealogies, Ahimaaz is cited as the father of Azariah even though 1 Kgs 4:2 and 2 Sam 15:27, 36; 18:19–29 indicate that both are sons of Zadok.

[92] Keil, *Chronicles*, 113; also Williamson, *Chronicles*, 70.

[93] However, see Wilson's comment, "even though oral genealogies are not created or preserved for strictly historiographic purposes, the genealogies that are accepted by a society are nevertheless considered to be accurate statements of past domestic, political, and religious relationships. . . Only the fact that genealogies are considered to be accurate historical records permits them to be used as charters. It should also be noted that oral genealogies may in fact contain a great deal of accurate information. . . they can therefore provide the modern historian with helpful insights into the social perspectives of these people. . . They are not usually invented by their users. . . the question of genealogical accuracy must be raised and answered in connection with each individual case. No generalizations on this question can be made with respect to the genre of genealogy as a whole," *Genealogy*, 54–55.

[94] See his full discussion in Keil, *Chronicles*, 112–121. In his allowance for omissions, or names dropping out through varying reasons (i.e. "telescoping"), Keil anticipated some of the conclusions of later anthropological studies of genealogies in tribal traditions.

[95] Wilson, *Genealogy*, 21.

his own historical scheme.[96] This would not make the Chronicler's list "unhistorical" as history was understood in his own time period. It would mean that the historical presentation of the Chronicler in this list is shaped by those factors which influence oral genealogies and was further guided by the purposes for which the Chronicler shaped his written genealogy.

THE PURPOSE OF THE LISTS OF THE SONS OF LEVI

Although not clearly stated within the text, the observations of Wellhausen, Keil and others on 1 Chr 5:27–41 [6:1–15] do present a valuable insight into the Chronicler's structure and therefore his purpose in presenting the lists of the sons of Aaron, Levites, and singers.

The historical notes also highlight this focus on the temple, its service, and being exiled from it. First Chronicles 5:36 [6:10] points out that a descendant of Aaron served in the temple while 1 Chr 5:41 [6:15] indicates that another descendant of Aaron was exiled, and therefore unable to serve in the temple.

While 1 Chr 6:33–38 [6:48–53], points out that the proper place for the sons of Aaron and the Levites is within the tabernacle/house of God doing the ministry assigned to them, the genealogies and the narrative make it clear that exile and destruction, resulting in the temple service not being performed, comes as the result of unfaithfulness. The primary terms used to express this unfaithfulness are the verb מָעַל and the noun מַעַל.[97] These terms are always used in Chronicles in respect to unfaithfulness to Yahweh, and always result in judgement of some kind (Figure 4.8)[98]

---

[96] Cf. the discussion in Johnstone where he refers to *midrash Exodus Rabbah*, which states that "royalty would last for them only until the end of thirty generations." The text indicates that Solomon is the middle point of this, with fifteen generations from Abraham to Solomon. Johnstone suggests that the end point is not the exile, but Josiah, for there are fifteen generations from Rehoboam to Josiah, *Chronicles and Exodus*, 124. Another genealogical scheme is found in Matt 1:2–17, which divides history into three epochs, each fourteen generations long: Abraham to David; David to the exile; and the exile to Jesus.

[97] The verb מָעַל occurs in 1 Chr 2:7; 5:25; 10:13; 2 Chr 12:2; 26:16, 18; 28:19, 22; 29:6; 30:7; 36:14. The noun מַעַל occurs in 1 Chr 9:1; 10:13; 2 Chr 28:19; 29:19; 33:19; 36:14. They occur together on three occasions, 1 Chr 10:13; 2 Chr 28:19; 36:14. Significantly, the first and last of these resulted in the destruction of a reigning monarchy and the transference of monarchy to another.

[98] Notice that although Ahaz is mentioned more often than any other person or group, the results of his unfaithfulness are mentioned only once (2 Chr 28:17–18). When

Figure 4:8: מָעַל/מַעַל in Chronicles

Text	Term(s)	Actor	Result
1 Chr 2:7	מָעַל	Achar/Achan	trouble for Israel[99]
1 Chr 5:25	מָעַל	Transjordanian Tribes	exile
1 Chr 9:1	מַעַל	Judah	exile
1 Chr 10:13	מָעַל־מַעַל	Saul	death
2 Chr 12:2	מָעַל	Rehoboam / Israel	defeat in battle
2 Chr 26:16	מָעַל	Uzziah	leprosy
2 Chr 26:18	מָעַל	Uzziah	leprosy
2 Chr 28:19	מָעַל־מַעַל	Ahaz	defeated, humbled
2 Chr 28:22	מָעַל	Ahaz	
2 Chr 29:6	מָעַל	Ancestors	defeat and exile
2 Chr 29:19	מַעַל	Ahaz	
2 Chr 30:7	מָעַל	Fathers/brothers	object of horror
2 Chr 33:19	מַעַל	Manasseh	exile
2 Chr 36:14	מָעַל־מַעַל	Leaders/priests	exile

Johnstone defines מָעַל/מַעַל as the, "failure to accord God what is his due. . . The duty owed to God is, in particular, exclusive obedience and utter reliance . . ., the ancestral faith of Israel being sometimes stated as the ground for such trust. . . מעל is evidenced in turning to other gods."[100]

Johnstone further indicates that the references to unfaithfulness (מָעַל/מַעַל) in Chronicles, indicates that the actions of the people from the beginning of settlement until the end, both east and west of the Jordan were corrupted by this "unfaithfulness" (מָעַל/מַעַל).[101]

This is true not only in the narrative, but in the genealogies as well (1 Chr 2:7; 5:25; 9:1). Unfaithfulness (מָעַל/מַעַל) brought an end to the kingdoms of Saul (1 Chr 10:13), and David (2 Chr 36:14). It brought exile for people (1 Chr 5:25;

Hezekiah later recounts this time, he places the guilt not upon Ahaz, but upon "our fathers" (2 Chr 29:6).

[99] In Josh 7 this trouble is recounted as defeat in battle and, ultimately, the death of Achan and his family.

[100] Johnstone, *Chronicles and Exodus*, 98.

[101] Johnstone, *Chronicles and Exodus*, 106.

9:1; 2 Chr 29:6), for kings (2 Chr 33:19), and for leaders and priests (2 Chr 36:14).

The Chronicler, however, also extends hope to people who are suffering the consequences of מַעַל/מָעַל. Although 1 Chr 9:1b speaks of Judah being taken captive to Babylon for their unfaithfulness, (מָעַל) 1 Chr 9:2 has them returning to the land and resettling in their towns. Second Chronicles 33:19 speaks of the unfaithfulness of Manasseh (which is more fully described in 2 Chr 33:2–9), and which resulted in his captivity "to Babylon" (2 Chr 33:11). Second Chronicles 33:12–13, however, speaks of his humility before Yahweh and his "seeking" Yahweh.[102] The result of these actions on the part of Manasseh was restoration to Jerusalem and his kingdom" (2 Chr 33:13).

What is significant in both instances is the place of the cult upon restoration to the land. First Chronicles 9:2 indicates that among the first to return were the "priests, Levites and temple servants" while 1 Chr 9:10–34 discusses the presence of priests, Levites, gatekeepers, and singers as well as the varying duties performed by the gatekeepers. This indicates that restoration to the land was accompanied by restoration of the cult, with the proper cultic officials performing their duties as prescribed (1 Chr 9:22 emphasises the role of David and Samuel in establishing some of the cultic positions and duties).

Likewise, upon his return from Babylon, Manasseh removed the idols and restored the altar of Yahweh and its proper sacrifices (2 Chr 33:15–16).

Hezekiah also, in response to Yahweh's judgement in exiling some of the people due to their unfaithfulness (2 Chr 29:6–9), had the temple purified (2 Chr 29:10–17), restored the proper cultic officials to their places (2 Chr 29:18–30), and re-instituted the sacrifices (2 Chr 29:32–36), and the feasts of Yahweh (2 Chr 30; 31:3). This resulted in the destruction of the idols and high places (2 Chr 30:14; 31:1), and the proper provision for the cultic officials by the king and the people (2 Chr 31:2–21). These actions of Hezekiah were in accordance with the commands of David (2 Chr 29:25–27), and the commands of God (2 Chr 31:21).

Importantly for the Chronicler's scheme, Hezekiah indicates that although there had been unfaithfulness (2 Chr 30:7), if the people submit to Yahweh, come to his sanctuary, serve Yahweh, and return to Yahweh, then those who are in exile will be able to return to the land (2 Chr 30:8–9).

Each of these three examples indicate that, although there are severe consequences for unfaithfulness (מַעַל/מָעַל) there is also hope if the people return to Yahweh. Central to this returning to Yahweh, however, is the place of the cult. The mere formality of cultic worship is not here in view. For both the people of

---

[102] Cf. Yahweh's response to the prayer of Solomon in 2 Chr 7:14, which is an addition to that found in the Chronicler's source in 1 Kgs 9:3–9.

Judah and king Manasseh the reestablishment of cultic worship occurred after restoration, and therefore is not the cause of restoration to the land. The key attitudes of the people which brought restoration are seeking, humbling, and praying (2 Chr 33:12–13). It is this attitude which resulted in restoration to the land and which, according to Hezekiah, will result in the restoration of those then in exile (2 Chr 30:8–9). Restoration, however, also enabled the one restored to recognise Yahweh (2 Chr 33:13), which led to the restoration of cultic worship (2 Chr 33:15–16).

Johnstone highlights this connection between unfaithfulness, its consequences, and the place of the cult.[103] He notes that in 1 Chr 5:25 the Transjordanian tribes are unfaithful and as a consequence are taken into exile by the Assyrians. This is said to be the result of God's "stirring up the spirit of Pul king of Assyria" (1 Chr 5:26). Immediately following this action is the Chronicler's discussion of the priests, Levites and singers.

Although Johnstone seeks to show that through the exile of Jehozadak the priests were also contaminated with unfaithfulness (מָעַל/מַעַל)[104] it is better to view the location of the priests, Levites and singers within the genealogies as representing part of the solution to the מַעַל just mentioned for the Transjordanian tribes. As occurred with Hezekiah (2 Chr 29–31), the postexilic community (1 Chr 9), and Manasseh (2 Chr 33:15–16), the visible sign of a change in attitude (a turning from unfaithfulness (מָעַל/מַעַל) back to Yahweh) was a restored and fully functioning cult. This is represented in the genealogies as priests, Levites and singers (1 Chr 5:27–6:32 [6:1–47]), being established in their positions as well as to their functions of service within the temple, the service of the altar and atonement (1 Chr 6:33–34 [6:48–49]).

These elements: unfaithfulness → exile → cultic officials → cultic action → atonement → restoration,[105] are presented in the narrative as the solution to a current crisis. Because the genealogies are not restricted to one time and place, but through their arrangement cover large tracts of time, this format is presented in the genealogies as the solution to every crisis.[106] They are presented not only as the solution to the particular incident of the Transjordanian tribes, but are depicted as the solution to each incident with which the Chronicler's readers are confronted.

---

[103] Johnstone, *Chronicles and Exodus*, 110–111.
[104] Johnstone, *Chronicles and Exodus*, 110. He also points out that the list of the sons of Aaron has its "false starts," those who were unfaithful and suffered for it, in Nadab and Abihu (cf. Lev 10:1–3).
[105] Although not always in this order.
[106] Jabez, who inflicted pain upon his mother in childbirth, had the consequences of his actions reversed as he "cried out to the God of Israel," 1 Chr 4:9–10.

This is particularly important in a postexilic society which had no indigenous king. The major reforms in the narrative of Chronicles were led by kings, while the postexilic community had no indigenous king to lead such a reform. First Chronicles 6, as also 1 Chr 9, does not allocate a position for kings or political leaders in reforms, returns, reinstitution of the cult, or atonement. What is presented on the one hand are the people and their actions, and on the other, the presence and activity of the proper cultic officials performing the proper cultic functions in the proper cultic place.

Conclusion

This investigation into the three sets of lists of the sons of Levi has shown that they are presented according to the common format of the postexilic period: priests, Levites, and singers. These three groups make up the three primary functionaries at the tabernacle/house of God, and these three groups are essential for the proper cultic functions that occur at the house of God.

These lists of three types of functionaries, each descended from Levi, leads into the discussion of the cultic duties in 1 Chr 6:33-34 [6:48-49]. They also flow from the previous discussion of the Transjordanian tribes in 1 Chr 5, and appear as the solution to the problems which befell the Transjordanian tribes, and by extension, the problems which have befallen the entire people. This is the case whether the problems have impacted upon an individual tribe or group of tribes, persons, kings, priests or officials.

The central problem which afflicts the people is unfaithfulness to Yahweh. This unfaithfulness has impacted upon all and has resulted in death, defeat and exile. The Chronicler, however, extends hope to the people. This hope is bound up in two things. First, hope is bound up in a change of attitude to Yahweh as expressed in humility, turning to Yahweh, prayer, and seeking Yahweh. Second, hope is bound up in the functions of the cult. Cultic action is not presented as a substitute for this change of attitude, but is instead a part of that change. When individuals or the people as a whole turn back to Yahweh, Yahweh hears and restores these individuals to the land. Upon restoration, individuals or groups ensure that the cult is also fully restored and functioning. A changed attitude may bring restoration, but the cult, with its proper officials, place and service, is essential for atonement. And atonement is the primary purpose of the cult.

Figure 4.9: The Order of Listing in the Postexilic Community

	1 Chr 6:1-47	1 Chr 9:2	1 Chr 9:3-21	1 Chr 13:2	1 Chr 23:2	1 Chr 24-27	2 Chr 8:14	2 Chr 35:11-15	2 Chr 35:18	Ezra 1:5	Ezra 2:1-58	Ezra 2:70	Ezra 3:12	Ezra 6:16	Ezra 7:7	Ezra 7:13	Ezra 7:24	Ezra 8:29	Ezra 9:1	Ezra 10:5	Ezra 10:18-43
Israel		1		—		6			4		1	7		—	—	—			—	3	5
Judah			1						3	1											
Benjamin			2							2											
Priests	1	2	3	2	2	1	1	1	1	3	2	1	1	2	2	2	1	1	2	1	1
Levites	2	3	4	3	3	2	2	2	2	4	3	2	2	3	3	3	2	2	3	2	2
Singers	3					3		3			4	4			4		3				3
Gatekeepers			5			4	3	4			5	5			5		4				4
Temple Servants		4									6	6			6		5				
Descendants of Solomon's servants											7						6				
The "people"/ the "remainder"												3		4							
Treasurers						5															
Family Heads/ Leaders													3					3			

Figure 4.9 Continued

	Neh 7:1	Neh 7:7-60	Neh 7:73	Neh 8:13	Neh 9:38	Neh 10:1-27	Neh 10:28	Neh 10:34	Neh 10:39	Neh 11:3-4a	Neh 11:4b-19	Neh 11:20-21	Neh 12:1-9	Neh 12:12-25	Neh 13:5
Israel		—	7			—	—		—	—		—	—		
Judah										6	1				
Benjamin										7	2				
Priests	3	2	1	2	3	2	2	1	3	2	3	2	1	1	4
Levites	2	3	2	3	2	3	3	2	2	3	4	3	2	2	1
Singers		4	4				5		5		5		3	3	2
Gatekeepers	1	5	3				4		4		6			4	3
Temple Servants		6	6				6			4		4			
Descendants of Solomon's servants		7								5					
The "people"			5			4									
the "remainder"															
Treasurers								3							
Family Heads/Leaders				1										1	

CHAPTER 5
E1: 1 CHRONICLES 6:54–81
THE DESCENDANTS OF LEVI IN THEIR LAND

INTRODUCTION

Complementing the discussion of Level E which presented genealogies of the sons of Levi, 1 Chr 6:39–66 [6:54–81] presents the dwelling places of these sons of Levi. The passage begins with a general introduction (1 Chr 6:39a [6:54a]), followed by a list of thirteen towns allocated to the sons of Aaron from the tribes of Judah, Simeon and Benjamin (6:39b–45 [6:55b–60]).[1] This is followed by a general summary which indicates which particular tribes donated towns to which particular Levitical clan (6:46–50 [6:61–65]). The non-Aaronite Kohathites received towns from the tribe of Manasseh (6:46 [6:61]),[2] the clan of Gershon from the tribes of Issachar, Asher, Naphtali and Transjordanian Manasseh (6:47 [6:62]), the clan of Merari from the tribes of Reuben, Gad, and Zebulun (6:48 [6:63]). This is followed by a general summary which indicates that Israel as a whole gave the Levitical clans towns and pasturelands (6:49 [6:64]). The contribution from Judah, Simeon and Benjamin is again mentioned, without indicating which group received towns from these tribes (6:50 [6:65]). This is followed by three detailed lists which give the names of the towns, the tribes which gave these specific towns, and which Levitical clan received these towns. First Kohath (6:51–55 [6:66–70]), then Gershon (6:56–61 [6:71–76]), and finally Merari (6:62–66 [6:77–81]), are listed. This is the same order in which the

---

[1] That this allocation was also from Simeon is only made known in 1 Chr 6:50 [6:65]. First Chronicles 6:39b–45 [6:55b–60] only mentions Judah and Benjamin.

[2] This verse is clearly corrupt. The MT reads קְהָת הַנּוֹתָרִים מִמִּשְׁפְּחַת הַמַּטֶּה מִמַּחֲצִית מַטֵּה חֲצִי מְנַשֶּׁה וּלִבְנֵי: "from the family of the tribe from the half tribe half Manasseh." The parallel passage in Josh 21:5 reads, "and to the remaining sons of Kohath, from the family of the tribe of Ephraim, and from the tribe of Dan, and from the half tribe of Manasseh." The NIV seeks to smooth over this textual problem, translating the passage, "The rest of Kohath's descendants were allotted ten towns from the clans of half the tribe of Manasseh." The NRSV, however, acknowledges the problem without explanation, "To the rest of the Kohathites were given by lot out of the family of the tribe, out of the half-tribe, the half of Manasseh, ten towns," so also JPS.

genealogies of the families of the cultic musicians are listed in 1 Chr 6:18–32 [6:33–47], but different to the order found in the list of the sons of Levi (1 Chr 6:1–15 [6:16–30]), where the order "Gershon, Kohath, Merari" is maintained.

Klein states that there are six "introductory questions [which] face any interpreter of the cities of the priests and Levites" in 1 Chr 6:39–66 [6:54–81]:[3]

1) What is the relationship of the list of the cities of the priests and Levites in this chapter to the same list in Josh 21:1–40?
2) Were the cities of refuge always a part of this list?
3) When is the list to be dated and on what basis?
4) Is the list historical, fictional, or utopian?
5) How might this list have arisen?
6) What is the function of the list in 1 Chr 6?

Although questions 2 through 5 are vital for our understanding of the history and development of the Levites, as well as the place of the Levites within the societies of preexilic Judah or Israel, a detailed investigation into these issues is outside the parameters of this study.[4]

---

[3] Klein, *1 Chronicles*, 183.

[4] Wellhausen rejected any historical elements to either of the lists contained in 1 Chr 6 or Josh 21 and suggested that they were "utopian" in outlook. He did acknowledge that "apart from the historical fiction, the other claims that are made for the endowment of the clergy are, however exorbitant, nevertheless practicable and seriously meant," *Prolegomena*, 164 and his fuller discussion in pages 159–167. Haran, in a series of studies, although conceding the utopian nature of some of the material, did recognize within the lists some historical features: the distribution of the towns throughout Israel rather than in a central district (as in Ezekiel), or around the temple (as in Numbers with the encampment around the Tabernacle); these towns were not former cultic sites, and therefore must have been towns in which Levites actually lived; the towns are not within the "ideal boundaries of the land of promise," "Studies in the Account of the Levitical Cities: I. Preliminary Considerations," *JBL* 80 (1961): 45–54; "Studies in the Account of the Levitical Cities: II. Utopia and Historical Reality," *JBL* 80 (1961): 156–165. (These are reprinted and slightly revised in his *Temples*, 112–131). He concludes by saying that "this fact can be explained only on the assumption that in the account of the cities P was bound to a certain historical reality," "Levitical Cities: II," 163. Haran, however, did not date the origins of the scheme of Levitical towns. On the basis of 1 Chr 26:30–32, Mazar seeks to date the origins of the list to either the co-regency of Solomon with David or Solomon's sole reign. This passage indicates that David placed some Hebronites into Transjordan with responsibility for "every matter pertaining to God and for the affairs of the king." The city into which they are placed is "Jazer" which is recorded as one of the Levitical towns donated by the tribe of Gad (Josh 21:39), and this act of David is therefore proposed as the foundation of the setting aside of towns for David's public servants, "The Cities of the Priests and the Levites," in *Congress Volume* (*Supplements to Vetus Testamentum VII*; Leiden: Brill, 1960), 198–199, also Myers, *1 Chronicles*, 48. Mazar is followed here by Kallai, who also suggests that over time the towns changed, which accounts for the differences between the

lists of 1 Chr 6 and Josh 21. He further suggests the possibility that more than 48 towns were used in this manner, but due to the enforced limit of "48" brought in through the legislation of Num 35:7, only a portion of this fuller number were recorded, "The System of Levitic Cities and Cities of Refuge: A Historical-Geographical Study in Biblical Historiography," in *Biblical Historiography and Historical Geography: Collection of Studies* (*Beiträge zur Erforschung des Alten Testaments und des antiken Judentums 44*; Frankfurt am Main: Peter Lang, 1998), 38–39. Hauer generally agrees with a Davidic dating, and sees the establishment of the Levitical towns as an act of David to place loyal public servants within his territories for the purpose of control and taxation, "David and the Levites," *JSOT* 23 (1982): 33–54, 48. See further Fried, who suggests that the "law of God and the Law of the King," indicates the imposition of the instructions of the king who is seen as the earthly representative of the deity, *The Priest and the Great King: Temple-Palace Relations in the Persian Empire* (Winona Lake: Eisenbrauns, 2004), 213–221. Boling sees "precedent for this system in early Israel" in "Egypt's late Bronze Age administration" of Canaan and suggests that Solomon, instead of devising the system of Levitical towns, simply manipulated a system that had already been in place, "Levitical Cities: Archaeology and Texts," in *Biblical and Related Studies Presented to Samuel Iwry* (ed. Ann Kort and Scott Morschauser; Winona Lake: Eisenbrauns, 1985), 28. Consistent with Kallai's suggestion of a fluid and changing list, Miller suggests that after the division of the kingdom, Rehoboam built new cities and placed the Levites who came from Israel into them to help bolster his position and to prevent further rebellion (2 Chr 11:5–17), "Rehoboam's Cities of Defense and the Levitical City List," in *Archaeology and Biblical Interpretation: Essays in Memory of D. Glenn Rose* (ed. Leo G. Perdue, et al.; Atlanta: John Knox, 1987), 279. De Vaux suggests that because there are no Levitical towns surrounding either Jerusalem or Bethel, that the origins of these lists date to a time after the division of the kingdom and the establishment of the cult at Bethel by Jeroboam. No Levitical towns were needed in these vicinities because they were served by central cult sites, *Ancient Israel: Its Life and Institutions* (trans. John McHugh; London: Darton, Longman & Todd, 1961), 367. Although Rudolph holds to a preexilic origin for the list of Levitical towns, he places the list's origins not at the beginning of the monarchy, but at the time of Josiah's reform. Rudolph stated, "es ist eine einleuchtende Vermutung, daß das nachexilische theoretische Schema der Levitenstädte schwerlich ohne einen gewissen Anthalt in konkreten vorexilischen Verhältnissen sein wird," *Chronikbücher*, 64. Although not stated, it is probable that Rudolph assumed that the list reflected the location of the cultic sites that were destroyed during the centralization of worship at the Jerusalem temple, and that the cultic officials continued to reside in these towns. Although 2 Kgs 23:8–9 indicates that Josiah brought the cultic officials into Jerusalem, it is unclear whether these persons were expected to dwell in Jerusalem, or simply to work there, while returning to their own homes if/when they were not rostered to officiate in the temple. Ben Zvi, however, places the origins of the lists into the postexilic period, and suggests that they were compiled on the basis of the list of tribal boundaries (Josh 13:15–19:51). As such they reflect "a glimpse into the world of claims, disappointments and hopes of the post-monarchic period," and contain no historical data from the preexilic period, "The List of the Levitical Cities," *JSOT* 54 (1992): 77–106, 105.

Oeming summarises the problems of the varying viewpoints as well as the historical uncertainties regarding the Levitical town list:

> However—we hardly have solid reason for a sure historic judgment. We could always form endless chains with more unknowns: If the list is integral [to the text] and if it mirrors an historical reality, then the late Solomonic period is in consideration. If the list is integral [to the text], but however not an historic reality, but represents a program, then the Josianic or even the Persian time comes into consideration. If the list is not integral [to the text], but grew in several layers, then. . . . About these things we know little, but we could write much, because sufficient area remains for presumptions and fantasies. Without new sources however this index of the historic Levitical cities remains an unsolved riddle.[5]

Klein's first question is important because it touches upon the Chronicler's sources and his use of these sources.[6] If the Chronicler utilised a known source, then we are in a better position to understand his style and purposes in writing through the comparison of his work with that source. Additions, alterations, and deletions to a known source become significant because they may help to highlight a purpose, bias or viewpoint of the Chronicler which give clues as to his meaning. However, if the Chronicler did not utilise a known source, but instead developed the content of the Levitical town list himself,[7] then different questions would need to be addressed in respect to the text:
1) Why was this list developed?
2) What is the significance of the order in which the data is recorded?
3) Why were these particular towns included?

---

[5] "Jedoch—wir haben kaum festen Grund für ein sicheres historisches Urteil. Wir können immer nur Kettenschlüsse mit mehreren Unbekannten bilden: Wenn die Liste einheitlich ist und wenn sie eine historische Realität spiegeln soll, dann kommt nur die späte Salomozeit in Betracht. Wenn die Liste einheitlich ist, sie aber nicht eine historische Realität, sondern ein Programm darstellt, dann kommen die josianische und sogar die persische Zeit in Betracht. Wenn die Liste nicht einheitlich ist, sondern in mehreren Schichte gewachsen, dann . . . Wovon wir wenig wissen, darüber können wir viel schreiben, weil für Vermutungen und Phantasien genügend Raum bleibt. Ohne neue Quellen aber bleibt dies Verzeichnis der Levitenstädte historisch ein ungelöstes Rätsel," Oeming, *Das wahre Israel*, 154–155. I would like to take this opportunity to thank Manfred Oeming for meeting with me and discussing my work at the *Society of Biblical Literature* Annual Meeting in Atlanta, Georgia in 2003. I would also like to thank him for the gift of his, now, out of print book.

[6] In what follows, certain issues in relation to Klein's second and third questions are also addressed.

[7] See discussion on Auld, below.

4) Where did the Chronicler, writing in the postexilic period, find the town names recorded in his list?
5) What was the status of these towns in the postexilic period?
6) Was this list a postexilic Levitical claim to these towns, or a reflection of where Levites then lived?
7) Was the entire list original with the Chronicler, or were other portions added at a later date?

THE RELATION OF 1 CHRONICLES 39–66 [6:54–81] TO JOSHUA 21

Joshua 21 contains a list which is similar to, yet contains a number of differences from, the list in 1 Chr 6. The similarities and differences in the lists will be addressed in detail later, but two of the most obvious differences are the context in which the lists are placed, and the order in which the lists are recorded.

The lists appear in different literary contexts. In Josh 21 the list appears in the context of the demand for settlements by the Levitical clans in fulfilment of the command of Moses (Josh 21:2), and as a consequence puts their actual settlement by the Levitical clans into the future from the perspective of the text. First Chronicles 6, however, relates not what will be, but what has been. These lists are מוֹשְׁבוֹתָם (their dwelling places) not where they will be at some future point, but where they were or are.[8] Further, Josh 21:43–45 indicates that the Levitical towns were part of the historical promises of Yahweh to the people for land, and that with their allocation all of the promises of Yahweh have been fulfilled. As such, the Levites living within their cities are seen to be a sign that Yahweh has kept his promises, blessed his people, and settled them in their own land.

In regards to the structure of the lists, Josh 21 and 1 Chr 6:39–66 [6:54–81] are very similar, but not identical. Joshua, after an introduction relating the command to give settlements to the Levitical clans (Josh 21:1–3), begins its list with a summary of the number of towns for each clan and from which tribe (Josh 21:4–8), before giving details regarding the specific towns given (Josh 21:9–42). These clans are recorded in the order: Aaron, Kohath, Gershon, Merari. Chronicles, however, has a different structure. After an introduction (1 Chr 6:39a

---

[8] The NIV translates the phrase, "these were the locations of their settlements," however, Braun notes that this could also be translated "these are their dwelling places," Braun, *1 Chronicles*, 95, so also JPS. Although the difference may appear slight from our perspective, it may in fact be significant from the Chronicler's viewpoint. By suggesting that these "are" rather than "were" the settlements of the Levitical clans, he is indicating a present claim to land which is consistent with his views elsewhere in the genealogies that only Israel possesses land. Here it goes beyond that, however, to indicate that this possession is in the here and now, not in the dim past.

[6:54a]), the Chronicler lists the Aaronite settlements (1 Chr 6:39b–45 [6:54b–60]). This is followed by the summary of the number of towns for each clan and from which tribe (1 Chr 6:46–50 [6:61–65]). Finally, the Chronicler concludes with the list of towns for Kohath, Gershon and Merari (1 Chr 6:51–66 [6:66–81]).

The list in Josh 21 is the longer and more detailed of the two, containing details of forty-eight settlements allocated to the Levitical clans while the list of 1 Chr 6 contains details of only forty-two settlements.[9]

There are minor differences in the spelling of some of the names which could easily be attributed to scribal variations, but there are also major differences between the lists in that some names which occur in Josh 21 do not occur in 1 Chr 6, being represented by completely different names. In spite of the appearances of different names in the two lists however, on only one occasion are the names that are common in the lists in a different order in the two lists.[10]

Although it has been generally held that the similarities between the two lists are to be explained by suggesting that the list of Levitical towns in Josh 21 was the source for the list in 1 Chr 6, this view has recently been challenged.[11]

In a series of articles, A. Graeme Auld has suggested that instead of Josh 21 being the source for 1 Chr 6, the reverse is true.[12] Auld's thesis is that 1 Chr

---

[9] The LXX of 1 Chr 6 has references to forty-three settlements, containing one name not found in the MT tradition of 1 Chr 6. Further, it must be recognised that although Josh 21 records forty-eight towns, a portion of this list is built on the reconstruction of the MT text of Josh 21:36–37 on the basis of LXX Josh 21 and 1 Chr 6.

[10] In Josh 21:17–18 the order for the settlements from Benjamin is "Gibeon, Geba, Anathoth, Almon" while in 1 Chr 6:45 [6:60] the order "—, Geba Alemeth, Anathoth," with Gibeon being absent from the Chronicler's list, and only a spelling variation the difference in "Alemeth" עלמת and "Almon" עלמון. Kalimi sees the reversal of Almon/Alemeth and Anathoth as examples of "chiasmus between parallel texts," which is not an uncommon phenomena in Chronicles, *Reshaping*, 254 and his wider discussion chapter 11, pages 215–274.

[11] Among others, the priority of Josh 21 (or its underlying source) is maintained by: Curtis and Madsen, *Chronicles*, 137; De Vries, *Chronicles*, 65; Japhet, *Chronicles*, 147; Knoppers, *1 Chronicles 1–9*, 443–446. Braun has suggested the possibility that instead of the Chronicler utilizing Josh 21, they both made use of a common source, *1 Chronicles*, 98, so also Mazar, "Cities," 196. This suggestion, however, is not new. Keil and Delitzsch, in their commentary on Joshua, suggested, "the author of the Chronicles has inserted an ancient document that was altogether independent of the book [i.e. Joshua] before us," *Joshua* (K&D 2; trans. James Martin; Grand Rapids: Eerdmans, 1976), 212, note 1.

[12] A. Graeme Auld, "Cities of Refuge in Israelite Tradition," *JSOT* 10 (1978): 26–40; "Textual and Literary Studies in the Book of Joshua," *ZAW* 90 (1978): 412–417; "The 'Levitical Cities': Texts and History," *ZAW* 91 (1979): 194–206; "The Cities in Joshua 21: The Contribution of Textual Criticism," *Textus* XV (1990): 141–152. These have been

6:39–66 [6:54–81] is not "a rearranged abridgement (subsequently damaged by several losses) of Josh 21:1–42,"[13] but is instead the document from which Josh 21 gleaned and expanded the Levitical city allotments. Auld indicates that the contents of the Chronicler's list is the result of growth over time in the following stages:[14]

- An initial list of Aaronite cities in "Judah," the land rather than the tribe.
- A summary of allotment of cities by three clans is added. The inclusion of "Benjamin" (1 Chr 6:45 [6:60]), turns the Aaronite list into cities from the "tribe" of Judah instead of from the "land" of Judah.
- A "pedantic note" (1 Chr 6:50 [6:65]), regarding the source of Aaronite cities using a different word for "tribe"
- A list of Levitic towns.
- The addition of totals.

He suggests that the author of Joshua then took the list contained in First Chronicles, and through rearranging the material "logically," filling out the list to equal forty-eight towns, and placing the list in a narrative framework to give it meaning in the context of Joshua, reshaped and expanded the list into the current text of Josh 21.[15]

He concludes that, "the Chronicler's text is something of a 'collage' fashioned only gradually; that in Joshua we see the logical rearrangement of this source material and its expansion in narrative form."[16]

Auld's essential arguments revolve around three, basic, observations:

1) The list in 1 Chr 6 is shorter than the list in Josh 21, and, working on the principle that the shortest text is the more original, 1 Chr 6 is the earlier text.
2) The list in 1 Chr 6 is more disordered and therefore more "natural" than that in Josh 21. Consequently, the author of Joshua developed, refined and ordered the list that he found in 1 Chr 6.
3) The MT of 1 Chr 6 is closer to the LXX of Josh 21 than it is to the MT of Josh 21. The LXX of Josh 21 therefore represents an intermediate stage between the text of MT 1 Chr 6 and that of MT Josh 21.

These presuppositions will be treated in order.

---

reprinted in *Joshua Retold: Synoptic Perspectives* (Edinburgh: T&T Clark, 1998). All page references are to the reprinted articles in this latter work.

[13] Auld, *Joshua Retold*, 27.
[14] Auld, *Joshua Retold*, 27–28.
[15] Auld, *Joshua Retold*, 28.
[16] Auld, *Joshua Retold*, 31.

1 CHRONICLES 6 IS SHORTER THAN THE LIST IN JOSHUA 21

One of Auld's underlying presuppositions is that the shorter text is always to be preferred as reflecting the original, while the longer text reflects the consequences of later additions.[17] As such, 1 Chr 6:39–66 [6:54–81] is earlier because it is shorter than Josh 21. Further, because Josh 21 LXX is shorter than Josh 21 MT, it also reflects an earlier text which has been expanded in later Hebrew editions of Josh 21.

Although the principle behind this presupposition is valid in certain circumstances, it cannot be considered to be a hard and fast rule. There are issues in the Chronicler's work which indicate that this passage is an exception to this principle.

First, this principle is not applicable here because it fails to recognise the Chronicler's practice when he utilises his sources. As will be observed through investigation of the Chronicler's use of Genesis in 1 Chr 1,[18] the Chronicler regularly abbreviated his sources, deleting material unnecessary to or inconsistent with his purpose. On Auld's theory, the longer genealogical lists in Genesis would have to be later than, and expansions of, the genealogical lists contained in 1 Chr 1, a position not maintained by anyone (to the best of my knowledge) and which is at total variance to any theory of Pentateuchal development. In his comments on the comparative details between the texts of Josh 21 and 1 Chr 6, Auld states:

> In the matter of the introductory and concluding formulae in both texts it may be sufficient to recall J. P. Ross's *reductio ad absurdum:* were Joshua deemed prior, 'we should have to suppose that the general tendency of texts to grow and accrete had here been reversed; that the compiler of Ch had such an objection to the term 'Levites' that he removed it from all the introductions—although this whole major section of his work is devoted to their cities and genealogies; and that, for obscure reasons, he had set his face against concluding formulae (except in the case of the Aaronites)'.[19]

However, as has been noted, this reductionism is exactly what the Chronicler did in 1 Chr 1. In his use of Genesis in 1 Chr 1, the Chronicler deleted all reference to all possession of land or language on the part of all other parties but Israel (and the dead kings of Edom). He deleted the precise kinship relationships

---

[17] Auld, *Joshua Retold*, 29, 31. In response to Contese's objections to Auld's thesis, Auld indicates that Contese's weakness is in trying to show "that the longer text is prior to the shorter," (page 52).

[18] This issue is addressed later in Excursus 3.

[19] Auld, *Joshua Retold*, 29.

within two lists of names.[20] He further deleted the possibility that Israel was descended from any person or family other than Abraham. The Chronicler also rearranged the order of some of the lists.[21] Throughout the genealogies, he avoids all reference to the conquest, even though he mentions Joshua the conqueror (1 Chr 7:27), and in place of the conquest suggests that Israel had always been in the land. Furthermore, in the remainder of his work, the Chronicler omits the succession narrative giving an impression, refuted by the Deuteronomistic History, that the transition from David to Solomon was smooth, uncomplicated, totally accepted, and one in which nobody died. The Chronicler purges Solomon of sin and of blame for the division of the kingdom. He further omits almost all of the story of northern Israel, transforms Manasseh into a model of repentance and Josiah into a man who ignored Yahweh and suffered the consequences.

The Chronicler therefore was not averse to deleting from, adding to, or altering his sources in order to tell his own story.[22] Consequently, in this particular case, the length of the text cannot be used as a guide to determine which text is original.

Second, Auld's presupposition fails because it does not take into account the possibility of loss from a text, and assumes that all differences are the result of growth. As one example, in MT Josh 21:21 and 1 Chr 6:52 [6:67] the Hebrew text contains the phrase בְּהַר אֶפְרַיִם (in the hill country of Ephraim). This phrase, however, is not reflected in LXX Josh 21:21. On the basis of Auld's thesis, LXX Josh 21:21 reflects the original text, and the Hebrew texts of both Josh 21 and 1 Chr 6 would have received the identical textual expansion, and this prior to the LXX of 1 Chronicles which contains the phrase ὄρει Εφραιμ, unless it is also assumed that a later scribe inserted this expansion into LXX 1 Chr 6 as a result of a later expanded Hebrew text.[23] It is easier here to assume that the LXX

---

[20] Genesis 5:1–32; 11:10–27.

[21] In 1 Chr 1, the descendants of Hagar (1 Chr 1:29–31), are placed before the descendants of Keturah (1 Chr 1:32–33), even though in Genesis, the descendants of Keturah (Gen 25:1–4) are located before the descendants of Hagar (Gen 25:13–16).

[22] In speaking of the Chronicler's use of Samuel and Kings, Kalimi states that these works "served him [the Chronicler] as raw materials for manipulation as he saw fit: he adapted, supplemented, and omitted from them according to his own ideological-theological outlook, applying his literary and historiographical methods, as well as his linguistic and stylistic tastes," *An Ancient Israelite Historian: Studies in the Chronicler, His Time, Place and Writing* (SSN 46; Assen: Konninklijke Van Gorcum, 2005), 25.

[23] On several occasions Auld indicates that this phrase represents an expansion in the MT traditions, *Joshua Retold*, 42, 47. However, he fails to address how it could have expanded in both traditions in an identical manner.

translators of Josh 21 or a later scribe omitted this phrase either accidentally or deliberately.[24]

Third, this presupposition fails because it does not allow for the harmonizing influence of versions upon one another which would allow an older text to be influenced by a newer.[25] LXX Josh 21:9 and MT 1 Chr 6:50 both contain the phrase "and from the tribe of the sons of Benjamin." This phrase is not found in either MT Josh 21:9 or LXX 1 Chr 6:50. This leads to several possibilities. That the phrase is not in LXX 1 Chr 6 may indicate its absence in the original of MT 1 Chr 6. Its absence in MT Josh 21:9 may indicate that it was either omitted from that text in the copying process, or that it was added to the LXX of Josh 21. It is possible then that this phrase was added to the LXX of Josh 21:9, perhaps under the influence of Josh 21:4 where Benjamin is mentioned, and this influenced later copying of MT 1 Chr 6:50 into which it was incorporated some time after the LXX translation of that passage where the phrase does not occur.[26] A similar phenomenon of harmonization is found in the Gospel texts of the New Testament. However, such a phenomenon does not speak to which of the texts is the more original, but only to later scribal practices.[27]

When these three considerations are taken into account (the Chronicler's practice, scribal omissions from a text, harmonization) the length of the text is not a valid criterium by which to determine which document was the original, and which document is secondary.

---

[24] Margolis does indicate one Palestinian recension which contains this phrase, but not after "Shechem" as in the Hebrew tradition and the LXX of 1 Chr 6, but after the complete phrase "Shechem and the pasturelands which were with it *in the hill country of Ephraim,*" *The Book of Joshua in Greek: Part V: Joshua 19:39–24:33* (Philadelphia: Annenberg Research Institute, 1992), 407.

[25] For a discussion of harmonization in the Bible, see Emmanuel Tov, "The Nature and Background of Harmonizations in Biblical Manuscripts," *JSOT* 31 (1985): 3–29; Tomotoshi Sugimoto, "The Chronicler's Techniques in Quoting Samuel-Kings," *AJBI* 16 (1990): 30–70, esp. 44–46.

[26] Braun allows that "the two texts have continued to influence each other throughout various stages of their development," *1 Chronicles*, 98.

[27] It must be noted that Auld does allow for some cross influence. He suggests that Josh 21:11–12 // 1 Chr 6:40–41 [6:55–56] was not original to the Chronicler's text. It was first formulated in Joshua and was later incorporated into the Chronicler's already existent work, *Joshua Retold*, 30–31.

1 CHRONICLES 6 IS MORE DISORDERED AND "NATURAL" THAN JOSHUA 21

Auld contends that Josh 21 is the "*logical* rearrangement" of the material found in the Levitical town list in 1 Chr 6.[28] Because of this, Auld suggests that Chronicles is the older list which was adapted and ordered by the author of Joshua.

The order of Josh 21 in respect to 1 Chr 6 can be observed in Figure 5.1.[29] This chart illustrates that, in relation to Josh 21, the Aaronite summary is absent from 1 Chr 6, and the Aaronite allocation has been placed prior to the summary statements for the other Levitical clans.

Figure 5.1: The Order of Joshua 21 // 1 Chronicles 6 Compared

Joshua 21	Action in Text	1 Chronicles 6
1–3	Introduction	54a
4	Aaronite Summary	
5	Kohathite Summary	61
6	Gershonite Summary	62
7	Merarite Summary	63
8	Clan summary conclusion	64
9–19	Aaronite Allocation	54b–60, 65
20–26	Kohathite Allocation	66–70
27–33	Gershonite Allocation	71–76
34–40	Merarite Allocation	77–81
41–42	Concluding Summary	
43–45	Conclusion	

The Josh 21 order, however, deals with each of the four clans in a consistent pattern. Each is listed in terms of their clan summary prior to the listing of the clans in respect to their town allocations. First Chronicles 6 contains a different

---

[28] Auld, *Joshua Retold*, 28. Italics his. Rothstein had previously made the observation that, "the Chronicler's order is more natural than that of Joshua 21," *Chronik*, 127, so also Johann Goettsberger, *Die Bücher der Chronik oder Paralipomenon* (Bonn: Peter Hanstein, 1939), 75.

[29] A good verse by verse presentation of order, omissions, and deletions is found in Endres, Millar, and Burns, *Synoptic Parallels*, 31–34. For a comparison of the Hebrew text see, Abba Bendavid, *Parallels in the Bible* (Jerusalem: Carta, 1972), 24–25.

introduction, most probably because of its different literary context, and lacks both the concluding summary to the lists as well as the conclusion to the entire episode.

It is clear that the presentation of material in Josh 21 is more orderly and consistent than that found in 1 Chronicles. While Auld questions why the orderliness of Josh 21 should automatically make it prior to the text of 1 Chr 6,[30] it is also valid to question why the differently ordered text of 1 Chr 6 should make it prior.

The orderliness of Josh 21 in relation to 1 Chr 6 is, however, not simply to be found in the overall structure. The presentation of the town allocations follows a much more consistent pattern in Josh 21. The basic pattern which Josh 21 follows is:

1) "To the clan name."
2) "From the tribe name."
3) "Town name."
4) "and its pasturelands."
5) Steps 3 and 4 are repeated for each town given from a tribe.
6) "Tribal summary."
7) Steps 2–6 are repeated for each tribe who gives to the clan.
8) "All the towns for clan name were X towns and their pasturelands."

The Josh 21 list concludes with an overall summary in the same format as step 8 (Josh 21:41).

The list in 1 Chr 6, however, does not contain some of this data. First Chronicles 6 regularly lacks reference to "pasturelands" (step 4), all of the "tribal summaries" (step 6), and all but one of the "clan summaries" (step 8, that of the Aaronites). It must be recognised, however, that even with these omissions, the presentation found in 1 Chr 6 still follows a basic order. Steps 1, 2, 3, 5, 7 are consistently present, and step 4 is regular, but not consistent.

What sets Josh 21 apart from 1 Chr 6 is the fullness of its presentation as well as the consistent presence of its component parts. Josh 21 does not omit any step, at any time, while 1 Chr 6 appears happy to omit those steps which do not deal directly with the town allocation to the Levitical clans. The Chronicler appears to be more interested in mentioning clan, tribe and town than any of the other information.

How can these observations be judged? What is it about "order" that would automatically make the text of Joshua late. What is it about "disorder" that automatically makes the text of 1 Chr 6 early?

Perhaps a way forward can be found through examining similar passages elsewhere in the Hebrew Bible. The Hebrew Bible presents at least seven

---

[30] Auld, *Joshua Retold*, 28.

accounts where consistent patterns of repetition occur.[31] Each of these, although generally different in content and function in relation to Josh 21 // 1 Chr 6, show the same propensity to stylised forms, patterns, and repetition, to that found in Josh 21 and to a lesser extent in 1 Chr 6.

Numbers 7 is particularly instructive as it is the one passage which in many ways parallels Josh 21. Numbers 7:1–2 presents a narrative introduction to the giving of the gift of oxen and carts by the tribes to the Levitical clans for the work that they had been set aside to do (Num 7:3–9).[32] Following the recording of this gift is a second introduction to the giving of offerings for the dedication of the altar (Num 7:10–11). After this introduction, Num 7:12–83 records these further gifts given by each of the twelve tribes. The gifts are identical in their content, and the narrative pattern of the gift is:

1) "On the X day"
2) "Tribal leader name"
3) "Leader of the tribe of tribal name"
4) "Brought his offering"
5) (Description of the offering)[33]
6) "This was the offering of tribal leader"

This cycle is followed by a summary statement which indicates the total gifts given for the work of the tabernacle (Num 7:84–88). Finally, the passage as a whole concludes with Moses and Yahweh speaking to one another within the Tent of Meeting (Num 7:89).[34]

---

[31] The first creation account (Gen 1:1–2:3); the genealogy from Adam to Noah (Gen 5:1–32); the genealogy from Shem to Tera (Gen 11:10–26); the first census (Num 1:20–42); the arrangement of the tribes around the tabernacle (Num 2:1–34); the catalogue of gifts for the tabernacle (Num 7:1–89); the second census (Num 26:1–65).

[32] Although the passage mentions the four Levitical clans found in Josh 21 (sons of Aaron, Kohath, Gershon, Merari), the sons of Kohath in Numbers do not receive any of the oxen or carts donated because their task is to "carry on their shoulders the holy things, for which they were responsible" (Num 7:9). The sons of Aaron also do not receive oxen or carts, but the other clans are "under the direction of Ithamar son of Aaron the priest" (Num 7:8).

[33] "Except for minor verbal variations, the description of each tribal leader's gift is identical," Timothy R. Ashley, *The Book of Numbers* (NICOT; Grand Rapids: Eerdmans, 1993), 162. The Good News Bible deals with this section by first listing the leaders, and then providing only one list of items given, thus avoiding the "wearisome repetitions," Gray, *Numbers*, 74.

[34] Levine suggests that "Numbers 7 is a highly instructive source of information about the accounting methods employed by the priests of biblical temples and by representatives of other agencies operating within biblical society over an extended period of time," *Numbers 1–20* (AB 4; New York: Doubleday, 1993), 259, and his fuller discussion in pages 259–266. See also his "tabular chart" of Num 7 on page 260. He

This treatment of tribal gifts to the Levitical clans and the tabernacle in Num 7 is therefore similarly structured to that of Josh 21, with introduction, gift giving recorded repetitively, summaries and conclusion. Both passages are shown as the gifts of the full complement of twelve tribes, with Judah being recorded as the first giver in both instances, contrary to the normal listing of the tribes which records Reuben in the first position. Both lists have an equality of giving by the tribes.[35] Both conclude with a statement about Yahweh and his relationship to the people. Numbers 7:89 concludes with Yahweh present in the tent of meeting conversing with Moses. Joshua 21:43–45 concludes with the observation that Yahweh had fulfilled his promises, given the people rest, and delivered Israel's enemies over to them. Furthermore, Num 7 and each of the passages previously identified,[36] are part of the priestly material.[37]

It is also probable that both Num 7 and Josh 21 fulfilled the same function within their own contexts. In response to the question as to why the author of Numbers included such repetitive detail when a summary would suffice, Ashley states:

> The answer must surely be that the author wanted the cumulative effect that results from a reading of the account of twelve identical offerings. By repetition the author showed that each tribe had an equal stake in the support of the sacrificial ministry of the tabernacle. No tribe had a monopoly on the responsibility for support and no tribe was unnecessary. That the support came

---

observes that "in cuneiform tablets we often find lines for columns actually incised on the clay, with headings that provide various kinds of information" (page 261 and the chart on page 265). He suggests that this pattern also lies behind Josh 12:19–24; 15:32; Ezra 1:9–11; 8:35, and that when it appears within cultic texts (Num 28:11; 29:13, 17), "it is reasonable to assume that priestly scribes employed an accounting method essentially identical to that used in other administrative agencies of biblical Israel," (page 263). He concludes that this type of "accounting" source document lay behind the fuller, written records within the Hebrew Bible. This observation opens up the possibility that the list in Josh 21 // 1 Chr 6 was also originally written in this "tabular" format, and that the origins of Josh 21 // 1 Chr 6 lie within some administrative document.

[35] Although in Josh 21, Judah and Simeon together give nine towns while Naphtali gives only three. Each of the other tribes give four towns.

[36] See note 31, above.

[37] Gray assigns Num 7 to P^s, which he suggests is part of the later expansion of the original priestly material, *Numbers*, xxxviii. Cf. Campbell and O'Brien, who identify it as a supplement to the priestly material, *Sources of the Pentateuch: Texts, Introductions, Annotations* (Minneapolis: Fortress Press, 1993), 74–77.

from the tribes themselves rather than from the priests or Levites is also significant.[38]

Such a conclusion also sits well with any evaluation of the lists in Josh 21. It is therefore probable that Josh 21, the list of tribal towns given to the Levites, and Num 7, the list of tribal gifts for the tabernacle, were formulated by persons from a similar background and to fulfil a similar purpose.[39]

These observations, however, cannot address the issue of which text is prior, particularly when it is recognised that the proposed dates for the authorship of Chronicles overlap with the proposed dates of the priestly school and their revisers.[40] What they do indicate is that in the postexilic period there was a tendency to methodical repetition in the formulation of some narratives and lists, and that this tendency is most evidenced within the priestly school. It is therefore not impossible that a priestly writer formulated the list in Josh 21, following a pattern of order which is reflected in other priestly literature, and that a later author, for reasons of his own, brought some disorder into the list.

What this does indicate is that the issue of "order" as a criterium for dating a document is subjective. While it is true that some authors or schools may have preferred order and repetition, it must also be acknowledged that not every author was so inclined. Auld's demand therefore that the author of Joshua brought the

---

[38] Ashley, *Numbers*, 164. Cf. Wenham's comment, "to emphasize as strongly as possible that every tribe had an equal stake in the worship of God, and that each was fully committed to the support of the tabernacle and its priesthood," *Numbers* (TOTC; Leicester: Inter-Varsity Press, 1981), 93

[39] Driver identified Josh 21:1–42 as being part of the Priestly material, *An Introduction to the Literature of the Old Testament* (Edinburgh: T&T Clark, 1892), 105. Although Joshua is considered to be a part of the Deuteronomistic History, it is not impossible that sources that originated within a priestly setting were incorporated into this work. Noth suggests that Josh 13–22 is not part of the Deuteronomist's original work, but is a later interpolation. However, "the language and attitude of this section are very akin" to the Deuteronomist, and must have been added shortly after the completion of Joshua, Martin Noth, *The Deuteronomistic History* (JSOTSup 15; trans. Jane Doull and John Barton; Sheffield: JSOT Press, 1981), 40. He further states that Josh 21:1–42 and 22:7–34 "are even later interpolations" (page 117 note 18). Noth also rejects Josh 21 as being part of "an independent P-narrative" or belonging to "the basic P material" (page 118). Noth does, however, indicate that Josh 21 has clear connections with what he terms "genuine indications of P" in Josh 14:1; 19:51a (page 113). This would allow the material to have a priestly origin, without being part of P. This is not to suggest that Josh 21 is part of P, but only that it had its origins in its present form in a priestly setting, and was perhaps part of a later priestly redaction of Joshua.

[40] This is true whether one concludes that the genealogies are integral to Chronicles or are a later addition to the work.

disorderly content of 1 Chr 6 into some form of order is an unprovable hypothesis. It is equally possible to argue that the author of 1 Chr 6 brought a different order to the orderly text of Josh 21, based upon a different criteria for ordering.[41]

MT 1 CHRONICLES 6 IS CLOSER TO THE LXX JOSHUA 21 THAN TO MT JOSHUA 21.

Auld's third presupposition is that LXX Josh 21 is an intermediate step between MT 1 Chr 6 and MT Josh 21. Auld insists that LXX Josh 21 "is witness to a Hebrew tradition preferable in many respects to the that of the Masoretic text. At several points in Josh 21 it is shorter than or different from the MT; and in almost every one of these details it is closer to the source in Chronicles."[42]

The question here is whether Auld's claim is provable. One difficulty is that there are different ways of viewing the evidence.

Scenario 1

First, under Auld's thesis, 1 Chr 6 is the source of the original text of Josh 21 utilised by the translators of LXX Josh 21. This Hebrew text of Josh 21 was later modified and shaped into what is now MT Josh 21. This can be illustrated as follows:

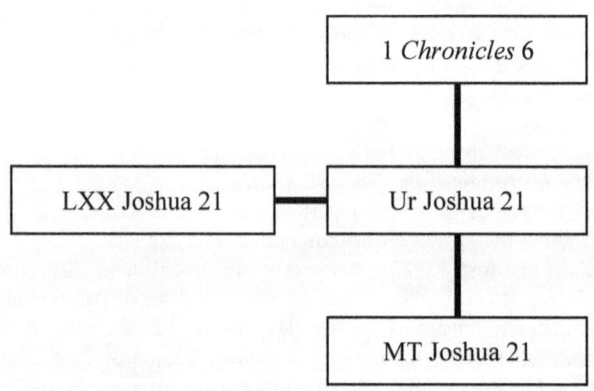

---

[41] Whether one assumes that the books of Ezra and Nehemiah were the work of one author, or were the product of a series of revisional steps, there are clear evidences of disorder within these texts. Therefore, it cannot be demanded that an author will automatically be orderly, nor can it be demanded that a later redactor will bring order to a disorderly text. It is just as possible that a later editor will bring some form of disorder. The question must be asked, however, as to whether the text is "disordered" or simply "differently ordered" in line with the thoughts and purposes of the author.

[42] Auld, *Joshua Retold*, 31.

If this contention is correct, then one would expect to find agreements between 1 Chr 6 and LXX Josh 21 against MT Josh 21 and agreements between LXX Josh 21 and MT Josh 21 against 1 Chr 6 because of their use of a common source. However, although not impossible, one would not expect to find agreements between MT Josh 21 and 1 Chr 6 against LXX Josh 21, for *Ur* Josh 21 reflects the intermediate step between 1 Chr 6 and MT Josh 21.[43]

Scenario 2

A second possibility is that 1 Chr 6 utilised MT Josh 21, which was itself a revision of an *Ur Joshua*, utilised by LXX Josh 21. If this was the case then it would be expected that 1 Chr 6 would agree with MT Josh 21 against any deviance in LXX Josh 21, and LXX Josh 21 to agree with MT Josh 21 against 1 Chr 6 because of changes made by the Chronicler. It would not be expected that LXX Josh 21 would agree with 1 Chr 6 against MT Josh 21 because of the additional steps that exist between 1 Chr 6 and LXX Josh 21.

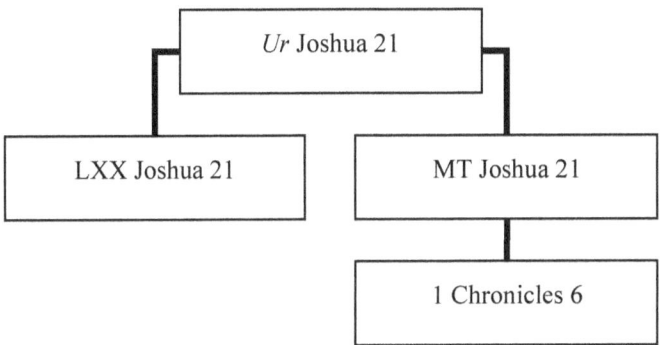

Scenario 3

A third possibility is that both 1 Chr 6 and LXX Josh 21 utilised MT Josh 21. In this scenario one would expect to find agreements between MT and LXX Josh 21 against 1 Chr 6, agreements between MT Josh 21 and 1 Chr 6 against LXX Josh 21. One would not, however, expect to find agreements between LXX Josh 21 and 1 Chr 6 against MT Josh 21, because both had utilised MT Josh 21 as its source, and would not be expected to deviate in an identical manner.

---

[43] Such agreements would be possible if it is assumed that LXX Josh 21 deviated from *Ur* Josh 21, while *Ur* Josh 21 remained faithful to its source, and that MT Josh 21 remained close to its source.

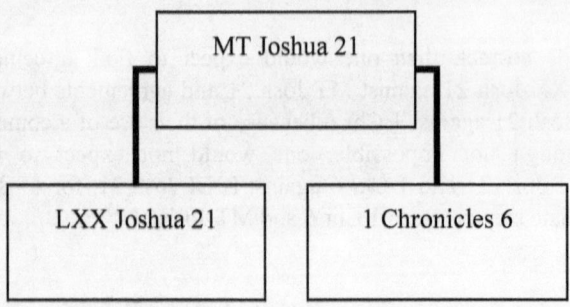

Scenario 4

There is, however, a fourth possible scenario. If 1 Chr 6 utilised an earlier version of Josh 21 than is now represented in the Masoretic tradition, then the possibilities expand. Under this scenario, agreements between MT Josh 21 and 1 Chr 6 against LXX Josh 21 would not be unexpected, because either LXX Josh 21 or Josh 21 (revised) may have made modifications to their *Vorlage*. One would also expect LXX Josh 21 to agree with MT Josh 21 against 1 Chr 6 because of the editing processes of the Chronicler. One would also expect there to be agreements between LXX Josh 21 and 1 Chr 6 against MT Josh 21 because of the editing processes of the final redactor of MT Josh 21. In other words, in this scenario, any agreement between any two of the traditions against the third is easily explained.

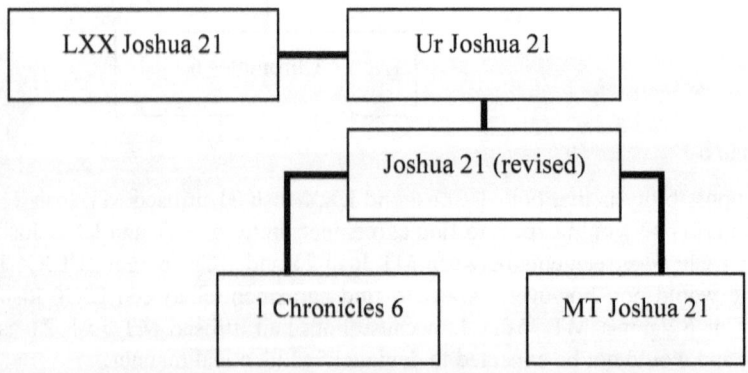

The four scenarios and their options are presented in Figure 5.2. In the following, we will investigate the texts to see which of these scenarios is most in agreement with the evidence.

Figure 5.2: The Four Scenarios of Textual Relationship of Joshua 21 // 1 Chronicles 6

Scenario:	1	2	3	4
MT Josh 21 // LXX Josh 21 against 1 Chr 6	yes	yes	yes	yes
MT Josh 21 // 1 Chr 6 against LXX Josh 21	no	yes	yes	yes
LXX Josh 21 // 1 Chr 6 against MT Josh 21	yes	no	no	yes

Figure 5.3 presents those occasions when LXX Josh 21 agrees with 1 Chr 6 against MT Josh 21.[44] These occurrences relate to those times when LXX Josh 21 and 1 Chr 6 contain text not contained in MT Josh 21 or to those instances where they jointly do not contain text that is contained within MT Josh 21. Of these 18, twelve are pluses for LXX Josh 21 // 1 Chr 6 against MT Josh 21. Six of these twelve are the conjunction "and." Of the remaining six, one is a reference to "the sons of Benjamin," one is a reference to the "lot," two are geographical descriptions, one is the presence of a different word. The most difficult is the minus of two complete verses in MT Josh 21:36–37.[45]

Of the six MT Josh 21 pluses, two are references to "pasturelands," one inclusion each of "lot," "first," "priest," "these." None of these MT Josh 21 pluses can be viewed as major or overly significant.

One aspect not examined closely by Auld, is the closeness of MT Josh 21 // MT 1 Chr 6 as opposed to LXX Josh 21 (Figure 5.4). Although few in number, some of these differences are significant for the evidence they present against Auld's presupposition that LXX Josh 21 is a middle text between MT Josh 21 and MT 1 Chr 6.

---

[44] In the following three charts we will not be addressing directly the issues of town name. This will be dealt with separately, below.

[45] "The best MT witnesses show an ancient loss of vv. 36–37 through haplography triggered by the repetition of 'four cities.' The loss was restored in some Hebrew witnesses by taking part of the corresponding text from Chronicles. This is evidenced by the absence of the tag line 'city of refuge for the killer,' the elimination of which is characteristic of the Chronicles parallel. Verse 36 has been restored on the basis of OG and 1 Chron. 6:63 [78E]," Richard D. Nelson, *Joshua* (OTL; Louisville: John Knox Press, 1997), 236; cf. Trent C. Butler, *Joshua* (WBC 7; Waco: Word, 1983), 222; cf. Marten H. Woudstra, *The Book of Joshua* (NICOT; Grand Rapids: Eerdmans, 1981), 313, note 1. Auld never discusses these verses in the broader context of the agreement of 1 Chr 6 with LXX Josh 21 as opposed to MT Josh 21. He only discusses them in relation to the cities of refuge, and treats these verses as if original, rather than restored, to MT Josh 21, *Joshua Retold*, 32, 38, 39.

Figure 5.3: LXX Joshua 21 = MT 1 Chronicles 6 Against MT Joshua 21

LXX Joshua 21 // MT 1 Chronicles 6		MT Joshua 21
21:6 // 6:47 [62]	omits[46]	"the lot"
21:7 // 6:48 [63]	"the lot"	omits
21:8 // 6:49 [64]	omits	"these" cities
21:9 // 6:50 [65]	"tribe of the sons of Benjamin"	omits
21:10 // 6:39 [54]	omits	"first"
21:13 // 6:42 [57]	omits	"priest"
21:16 // 6:44 [59]	"and"	omits
21:19 // 6:45 [60]	omits	"and its pasturelands"
21:20 // 6:51 [66]	"boundaries"	"lots"
21:24 // 6:54 [69]	"and"	omits
21:30 // 6:59 [74]	"and"	omits
21:31 // 6:60 [75]	"and"	omits
21:33 // 6:61 [76]	omits	"city and its pasturelands"[47]
21:36–37 // 6:63–64 [78–79]	Two complete verses	omits
21:36 // 6:63 [78]	[Bezer] "in the desert"	omits
21:36 // 6:63 [78]	"across the Jordan from Jericho, the east side of the Jordan"[48]	omits
21:37 // 6:64 [79]	"and"	omits
21:39 // 6:66 [81]	"and"	omits

Each of these examples present problems for Auld's thesis. If LXX Josh 21 is the middle text, then it is to be expected that LXX Josh 21 should either agree with 1 Chr 6 (with the conclusion that MT Josh 21 deviated from the original as reflected in LXX Josh 21) or it should agree with MT Josh 21 (with the conclusion that LXX Josh 21 reflects a difference in the *Ur* Josh 21 text which developed into MT Josh 21). That both Hebrew texts deviate from LXX Josh 21 in an identical manner indicates that at these particular points, the two Masoretic Text traditions are closer to one another than to LXX Josh 21. This indicates that

---

[46] "Omits" should not be taken to mean that the author has "left out" something that his source contained. In this part of the study, "omits" is the equivalent of "does not contain."

[47] Joshua 21:33 is unrepresented in 1 Chr 6.

[48] The LXX of Josh 21:36 reads the direction "east" מִזְרָח, (1 Chr 6:63 [6:78]) as the name of a city Μισωρ.

in these instances, LXX Josh 21 does not reflect a middle position, contrary to Auld.

Figure 5.4: MT Joshua 21 = MT 1 Chronicles 6 Against LXX Joshua 21

MT Joshua 21 // MT 1 Chronicles 6		LXX Joshua 21
21:6 // 6:47 [62]	"family"	omits
21:9 // 6:50 [65]	"these" cities	omits
21:12 // 6:40 [55]	omits	"Joshua" gave to the "sons" of Caleb
21:21 // 6:52 [67]	omits	"the things before it"
21:21 // 6:52 [67]	"hill country of Ephraim"	omits
21:22 // 6:53 [68]	omits	"upper" Beth Horon
21:27 // 6:56 [71]	"families"	omits
21:34 // 6:62 [77]	"tribe" of Zebulun	omits
21:34 // 6:61 [76]	omits	"and"
21:36 // 6:63 [78]	omits	"city of refuge for the slayer"

When MT and LXX Josh 21 are compared to MT 1 Chr 6, the closeness of the two Joshua texts can be seen (Figure 5.5).

These examples consist primarily of data found in the summary material that is not contained within 1 Chr 6, references to "pasturelands," and "city of refuge for the slayer." Interestingly, on the two occasions where 1 Chr 6 mentions a city of refuge (1 Chr 6:42, 52 [6:57, 67]), the Chronicler puts these into the plural, making all the Kohathite towns (Aaronite and the "rest" of the Kohathites), into cities of refuge. This is a clear deviation from both MT and LXX Josh 21 where only five or six of the listed towns are cities of refuge.[49]

There is, however, one more piece of evidence that must be considered in seeking to determine which text is prior, and that is the names of the towns in the lists themselves. An investigation of these indicates that MT Josh 21 is considerably closer to 1 Chr 6 than to LXX Josh 21.[50]

---

[49] MT Josh 21 only lists five cities of refuge (Josh 21:13, 21, 27, 32, 38). Although recording the sixth city name, Bezer (Josh 21:36), MT Josh 21, unlike LXX Josh 21, does not refer to this as a "city of refuge."

[50] This comparison is based upon the LXX^B, as used by Auld. LXX^A is much closer to the MT of Josh 21 than is LXX^B.

Figure 5.5: Joshua 21 MT = Joshua 21 LXX Against 1 Chronicles 6 MT

Joshua 21 MT // Joshua 21 LXX		1 Chronicles 6	
21:5	"Ephraim"	omits	6:46 [61]
21:5	"Dan"	omits	6:46 [61]
21:5	"half" tribe of Manasseh	omits	6:46 [61]
21:8	"just as Yahweh/the Lord commanded by the hand of Moses"	omits	6:49 [64]
21:8	"by lot"	omits	6:49 [64]
21:9	omits	"by lot"	6:50 [65]
21:11	"Kiriath Arba, he was the father of Anak" [51]	omits	6:40 [55]
21:11	"hill country" of Judah	"land" of Judah	6:40 [55]
21:12	"as his possession"	omits	6:41 [55]
21:13	"city" of refuge	"cities" of refuge	6:42 [57]
21:13	"for the slayer"	omits	6:42 [57]
21:13	"and its pasturelands"	omits	6:42 [57]
21:14	"and its pasturelands"	omits	6:42 [57]
21:16	"Juttah and its pasturelands"[52]	omits	6:44 [59]
21:16	"nine cities from these two tribes"	omits	6:44 [59]
21:17	"Gibeon and its pasturelands"	omits	6:45 [60]
21:18	"four cities"	omits	6:45 [60]
21:19	the cities of "the sons of Aaron the priest"	"their" cities	6:45 [60]
21:20	"the remaining Levites from the sons of Kohath"	omits	6:51 [66]
21:21	"city" of refuge	"cities" of refuge	6:52 [67]
21:21	"for the slayer"	omits	6:52 [67]
21:22	"four cities"	omits	6:53 [68]
21:24	"four cities"	omits	6:54 [69]
21:25	"two cities"	omits	6:55 [70]
21:26	"all these ten cities and their pasturelands"	omits	6:55 [70]
21:27	"the Levites from the half tribe" of Manasseh	omits	6:56 [71]
21:27	"city of refuge for the slayer"[53]	omits	6:56 [71]

---

[51] The LXX of Josh 21:11 reads "the mother city of Anak," rather than the "father of Anak."
[52] Joshua LXX reads Τανυ.
[53] Joshua LXX reads "cities," which occurs in 1 Chr 6:42, 52 [6:57, 67].

Joshua 21 MT // Joshua 21 LXX		1 Chronicles 6	
21:27	"two cities"	omits	6:56 [71]
21:31	"four cities"	omits	6:60 [75]
21:32	"city of refuge for the slayer"	omits	6:61 [76]
21:32	"three cities"	omits	6:61 [76]
21:34	"families"	omits	6:62 [76]
21:34	"Levites"	omits	6:62 [76]
21:37	"four cities"	omits	6:64 [79]
21:38	"city of refuge for the slayer"	omits	6:65 [80]
21:39	"all four cities"	omits	6:66 [81]

As observed in Figure 5.7,[54] there are numerous similarities in the names of towns between the two lists. Of the forty-two names recorded in 1 Chr 6, 27 appear in MT Josh 21 in an identical form (with allowances for plené spelling and one instance of letter transposition).[55] Eight of the names are similar enough in form to conclude that the differences are due to scribal practices, or perhaps minor changes in the town names over time. There are only seven town names in which there is no correlation between the two lists.

It is these seven city names that present the greatest challenge to the consensus view that 1 Chr 6 borrowed directly from Josh 21. If, however, that view is correct, then it demands that either the Chronicler or a later copyist copied his source incorrectly in these seven instances or that the Chronicler or an editor "updated" the name to a more recent, well known location. Another possibility is that the Joshua text itself was altered in the copying process after it was utilised as a source by Chronicles.[56]

However, there are also problems in this list of town names for Auld's view that LXX Josh 21 represents an intermediate text between 1 Chr 6 and MT Josh 21. Of the forty-eight names in the Josh 21 lists, on twenty-five occasions the town names are identical, while on thirteen occasions they are similar, that is there are minor differences in the names. However, they are similar enough for the process by which the text was corrupted or misread to be identified. Further, on ten occasions the town names in the two Joshua lists are clearly different and

---

[54] Because of its size, this is located at the end of this chapter.

[55] It must be recognized that this figure may be slightly distorted through the absence of Josh 21:36–37 in the major Hebrew manuscripts. However, as the LXX of these verses is also similar in its listing of city names, there is a good probability that the reconstruction is valid in these points.

[56] This latter may receive some support in that in LXX Josh 21, three of these seven are clearly different than in MT Josh 21. However, that none of these three agree with 1 Chr 6, could demand at least two changes in Josh 21, the first to a Hebrew text reflected in the LXX, and the second to the current MT of Josh 21.

do not give the appearance of being a textual corruption. While these differences are not, in themselves, significant in light of other variations between the MT and LXX of Josh 21, what is important to notice is that on none of these ten occasions does LXX Josh 21 agree with 1 Chr 6 (Figure 5.6). Furthermore, on two of these occasions MT Josh 21 does agree with 1 Chr 6 against LXX Josh 21, on three occasions MT Josh 21 is similar to 1 Chr 6, on three occasions MT Josh 21 is different to 1 Chr 6, while on two occasions the town name is absent in 1 Chr 6. Thus, of these ten occurrences of difference between MT and LXX Josh 21, on five of the eight where a town name occurs in 1 Chr, MT Josh 21 is closer to 1 Chr 6 than to LXX Josh 21. This is the opposite of what Auld's thesis demands.

The data from LXX 1 Chr 6 are not helpful to Auld's thesis either. Of the forty-two names in MT 1 Chr 6, thirty-one are identical to LXX 1 Chr 6, six are similar, while only five are different. LXX 1 Chr 6 also contains one name not found in MT 1 Chr 6.[57] However, on none of these five occasions where MT and LXX 1 Chr 6 deviate from one another does LXX Josh 21 agree with LXX 1 Chr 6 against MT 1 Chr 6. LXX 1 Chr 6 therefore gives no evidence that an earlier form of MT 1 Chr 6 was closer to LXX Josh 21.

What this survey indicates is that none of the first three proposed scenarios are capable of dealing with all of the evidence. There are agreements between two texts against the third which are not consistent with the textual relationships implied within that scenario. To account for these deviations, one must propose later cross influence of one text upon the other in the copying process. However, it would be anticipated that cross influence would bring greater harmonisation to the texts than what they now exhibit.

Because of these issues, some scholars have suggested that the Chronicler and MT Joshua utilised a common source (scenario 4).[58] What this survey has observed is that the proposition of a common source has the advantage of satisfactorily addressing each of the three types of relationship observations. This suggestion also has the advantage of explaining the common shape, order, and details, as well as explaining those instances where the respective authors of Joshua and Chronicles copied the one list differently, although it does not explain why the different authors did so. It also helps to explain those instances where, when the town names are different in the Hebrew tradition, the LXX of one list never agrees with the MT of the other list. If the Chronicler and MT Joshua had copied from the same Joshua text, and either had later been corrupted, it would be

---

[57] Ατταν (1 Chr 6:44 [6:59]).

[58] The list in 1 Chr 6 "agrees on the whole with the register in Josh. xxi., if we except different forms of some names of cities, and many corruptions of the text, but differing in many ways from it in form; whence we gather that it is not derived from the book of Joshua, but from some other ancient authority," Keil, *Chronicles*, 127. See also, Braun, *1 Chronicles*, 98; Mazar, "Cities," 196.

reasonable to assume that the LXX of either list may reflect the pre-corrupted text and thus be closer to the Hebrew in the other list. This, however, is not the case, which helps to support the theory of a common source which was itself a revision of that used by LXX Joshua.

Figure 5.6: Different Town Names in the Levitical Town Lists

Josh 21 MT	Josh 21 LXX	Josh 21 Verse	1 Chr 6 Verse	1 Chr 6 MT	1 Chr 6 LXX
יתר	Αιλωμ	14	42	יתר	Σελνα
חלן	Γελλα	15	43	חילז	Ιεθθαρ
עין	Αοα	16	44	עשן	Ασαν
יטה	Τανυ	16	44	----	Ατταν
גבע	Γαθεθ	17	45	גבע	Γαβεε
גת רמון	Ιεβαθα	25	55	בלעם	Ιεβλααμ
קרתן	Θεμμων	32	61	קריתים	Καριαθαιμ
יקנעם	Μααν	34	62	רמונו	Ρεμμων
קרתה	Καδης	34	62	תבור	Θαχχια
נהלל	Σελλα	35	---	----	

Furthermore, positing a revised form of the *Ur* Joshua (Joshua (revised)) as the source for 1 Chr 6 and MT Josh 21, helps to explain those instances where MT Josh 21 and 1 Chr 6 agree against LXX Josh 21, for if each of the three texts has utilised the same source, then much greater correspondence would be anticipated.

Finally, the suggestion of the use of "Joshua (revised)" by 1 Chronicles and MT Josh 21 also explains those instances in the town lists where LXX and MT Josh 21 as well as 1 Chr 6 are not in agreement on the town names. It would appear as if a number of changes in the town list occurred between *Ur* Joshua and Joshua (revised). Therefore, LXX Josh 21 utilised one list of names (that of *Ur* Joshua) while 1 Chr 6 and MT Josh 21 utilised a slightly different list of town names (that of Joshua (revised)).[59]

This survey indicates that, contrary to Auld, 1 Chr 6 is not the source of Josh 21, but was instead based upon an earlier edition of Josh 21 than is available in

---

[59] It is also possible that the list used by MT Josh 21 was also slightly different to that used by the Chronicler in 1 Chr 6.

our current text. This source text contained all of the data currently contained within 1 Chr 6, although it appears as if the Chronicler rearranged the text in accordance with his own purposes. This is evidenced by LXX Josh 21 which reflects the order of *Ur* Joshua and MT Josh 21 which retains the order of "Joshua (revised)." This indicates also that the town list in 1 Chr 6 was not incorporated into the text in stages, as suggested by Auld, but was brought into 1 Chronicles intact, albeit edited.

Auld's three presuppositions that: the shorter text is the original, the more orderly text is the later, and that 1 Chr 6 was the source of Josh 21 have each shown to be inadequate to explain the interrelationships of these texts. In regard to his first two presuppositions, equally plausible alternatives were put forward. In regard to the third, it was demonstrated that the data does not support this view, and in fact suggests an alternative relationship between the texts.

TEXTUAL EVIDENCE FOR THE PRIORITY OF JOSHUA 21

In support of his view that Joshua utilised 1 Chr 6, Auld says that the author of Joshua placed, "the setting of the whole in a narrative framework which explained the editor's intentions."[60]

In other words, Auld contends that the author of Joshua shaped his source to fit his narrative. This implies as well that what the author of Joshua found in 1 Chr 6 was a list that was shaped to suit its function within 1 Chr 6. Furthermore, it indicates that these two purposes were different.

There are two observations which speak against Auld's view, and which indicate instead the priority of Josh 21 over 1 Chr 6.[61] The first is the repetition of the phrase, נָתְנוּ (they gave; 1 Chr 6:41, 42 [6:56, 57]), or וַיִּתְּנוּ (and they gave; 1 Chr 6:40, 49, 50, 52 [6:55, 64, 65, 67]). Within the context of 1 Chr 6, the "giving" of towns to the Levitical clans is out of character with the list itself. In the introduction to the list in 1 Chr 6:39 [6:54], these towns are said to be the places where the Levitical clans dwelled (מוֹשְׁבוֹתָם). Although these towns were allocated by the lot (הַגּוֹרָל) the introduction to the Chronicler's town list nowhere indicates that these towns originated from within the tribes, nor that it was the tribes themselves who gave these towns to the Levitical clans. Unlike Josh 21, the text of 1 Chr 6 gives no reason why these towns should be "given."

Further, the act of "giving" does not fit the narrative context of 1 Chr 6. The town list in 1 Chr 6 occurs within the context of dwelling, not gaining. Yet the list indicates that the towns were given. This is evidence that the Chronicler utilised the list as represented in Josh 21, where the command of Yahweh to give is

---

[60] Auld, *Joshua Retold*, 28.

[61] Priority in the sense of its overall textual history extending back to the proposed *Ur* Joshua.

contained (Josh 21:1–3). While the Chronicler omitted references to Yahweh's command to give, he retained the references to the giving of towns themselves. If the list were to have its origins within 1 Chr 6, as contended by Auld, then reference to the tribes "giving" towns would be unexpected. These are said to be towns where the Levites had their settlements (מוֹשְׁבוֹתָם). What would be expected is a reference to the Levites יָשַׁב (dwelling) in towns in the varying tribes, rather than the tribes נָתַן (giving) towns to the Levites.

The Chronicler's indication that these are the towns where the Levites lived, is consistent with other statements in the genealogies. Often in the genealogies the Chronicler emphasises where the people lived (יָשְׁבוּ). Judah (1 Chr 2:55; 4:23); Simeon (1 Chr 4:28, 41, 43); Reuben (1 Chr 5:8–10); Gad (1 Chr 5:11, 16, 22); Manasseh (1 Chr 5:23); Joseph (1 Chr 7:29); Benjamin (1 Chr 8:6, 13, 28, 29, 32); and those who returned from exile (1 Chr 9:2, 3, 16, 34), each dwelled in particular towns and regions. Like Levi, Simeon and Ephraim have their מוֹשָׁב (settlements; 1 Chr 4:33; 7:28). In light of the Chronicler's emphasis on where the tribes dwelt, it is understandable that he would alter a list whose emphasis was upon the "giving" of land, into one whose emphasis was "dwelling" in land.

However, within the context of Josh 21, these references to the giving of towns are perfectly reasonable. The Levites came to Joshua saying, "Yahweh had commanded through Moses that you give us towns" (Josh 21:2). As a consequence, "the Israelites gave the Levites the following towns" (Josh 21:3). The following list of towns then repeats which towns were "given" by the various tribes (Josh 21:8, 9, 11, 12, 13, 21). The list concludes with a summary that "Yahweh gave Israel all the land he had sworn" (Josh 21:43), as well as "rest" (Josh 21:44). Josh 21 then is a statement about giving by the command of Yahweh as Yahweh also gave according to his own promises. As such, the terminology of "giving" fits the context of Josh 21 better than it does the context of 1 Chr 6, thus indicating the priority of Josh 21.

The second piece of evidence which suggests the priority of Josh 21 over 1 Chr 6 is 1 Chr 6:50 [6:65]. In 1 Chr 6 this verse appears after the allocation to the sons of Aaron (1 Chr 6:42–45 [6:57–60]), and the summary of giving to the non-Aaronite Levitical clans (1 Chr 6:46–49 [6:61–64]). The statement of 1 Chr 6:50 [6:65] itself implies that a list of these towns should follow. What in fact follows is a list of the towns allocated to the remaining Kohathite clans.[62]

---

[62] The NIV recognises this problem when it translates the phrase, "from the tribes of Judah, Simeon and Benjamin they allotted the *previously* named towns" (italics mine).

The related phrase is also found in Josh 21:9.[63] In Josh 21:9 it introduces, as the wording suggests, a list of the towns allocated to the sons of Aaron from Judah, Simeon and Benjamin.[64] It is clear that Josh 21:9 // 1 Chr 6:50 [6:65] is within its proper context within Josh 21, as an introduction to allocated towns (cf. Josh 21:20, 27, 34). However, it is also apparent that it has been dislocated from its proper context within 1 Chr 6, appearing several verses after it would be expected.

The best explanation for this observation is that this dislocation would have occurred when the Chronicler rearranged the list he found in Josh 21, listing the towns of the sons of Aaron first (Josh 21:10–19), and then the summary statements (Josh 21:4–8). It appears that the Chronicler attached Josh 21:9 to the preceding summary statements rather than as the introduction to the allocation of towns to the sons of Aaron, thus placing 1 Chr 6:50 [6:65] out of its context.[65]

Auld suggests that 1 Chr 6:50 [6:65] is a "pedantic note . ... setting straight the record as to which tribes had allocated cities to the Aaronites,"[66] which was added after the list of other tribal allocations had been included to the original, shorter, list in 1 Chr 6. What Auld fails to explain is why this "pedantic note" was placed in a position within the text so that it does not explain what he suggests it was designed to explain. It is reasonable as an explanation only prior to the list of Aaronite towns, not after.

Both of these textual issues, the to the "giving" of towns, as well as the position of 1 Chr 6:50 [6:65] within the Chronicler's text give evidence that the Chronicler utilised a forerunner of Josh 21 in the formation of his list, and therefore the source behind Josh 21 is prior to 1 Chr 6.

---

[63] There are differences in the text which are not significant for our purposes. First Chronicles 6 contains reference to "the lot" and "and from the tribe of the sons of Benjamin," which are not contained in MT Josh 21, but are in LXX Josh 21.

[64] The NIV here translates the virtually identical phrase, "from the tribes of Judah and Simeon they allotted the *following* towns by name" (italics mine). Cf. 1 Chr 6:50 [6:65]) above, note 62.

[65] "That he should have transcribed and left Jos. 21^9 ... where it did not harmonise with the text is not strange. He is guilty elsewhere of similar infelicities," Curtis and Madsen, *Chronicles*, 137.

[66] Auld, *Joshua Retold*, 27.

THE FUNCTION OF THE LIST IN 1 CHRONICLES 6

Having addressed Klein's first question, it is now necessary to address his last, namely "what is the function of the list in 1 Chr 6?" The primary answer must lie with the importance of the land within the genealogies as well as the wider narrative.[67]

The first observation to be made is that the genealogies are not unique in ascribing towns, dwelling places or land to the Levitical clans. Nor are the genealogies unique in suggesting that these towns were scattered throughout Israel as a whole. First Chronicles 13:1–3 indicates that not only did the Levites dwell within towns, but that these towns were scattered throughout Israel. Second Chronicles 11:13–14 states that the Levites, who dwelt in Israel in the days of Rehoboam, abandoned "their pasturelands and property" because of the religious policies of Jeroboam, and came to live instead in Judah and Jerusalem. Second Chronicles 31:19 has the sons of Aaron "who lived on the farm lands around their towns or in any other towns" being catered for by the distribution of cultic gifts. Ezra 2:70 // Neh 7:73 records that the priests, Levites, singers, gatekeepers, and temple servants "settled in their own towns." This is consistent with the Chronicler's emphasis upon land throughout the genealogies.

Much of Judah's list contains details of towns and territories controlled by the tribe (1 Chr 2:50b–55; 4:9–10, 21–23). The lists of Simeon and the Transjordanian tribes consist of settlements (1 Chr 4:28–33; 5:8b–9, 16, 23), or expansion of territory (1 Chr 4:41–43; 5:10, 18–22). Levi has its allotted settlements (1 Chr 6:39–66 [6:54–81]. Manasseh and Ephraim have their lands and settlements (1 Chr 7:28–29). Benjamin's second listing centres on land, particularly land in the vicinity of Jerusalem (1 Chr 8:6, 13, 28, 29, 32), and the people, either as original settlers or returnees, live in אֲחֻזָּה (their possessions)[68] or in Jerusalem (1 Chr 9:2–3).[69]

Furthermore, the genealogies indicate that loss of land is the result of unfaithfulness (מַעַל) to Yahweh, with the implication that the continuing possession of land is the result of continuing faithfulness to Yahweh. גָּלָה, in the sense of "exile" is only used seven times in Chronicles, six of which are in the genealogies (1 Chr 5:6, 26, 5:41 [6:15]; 8:6, 7; 9:1). The only non-genealogical use is 2 Chr 36:20, but four of these references to exile are directly or indirectly related to unfaithfulness (מַעַל). The Transjordanian tribes lose their land and are

---

[67] For an examination of the larger question of "land" within the genealogies, see, Kartveit, *Motive*.

[68] In Chronicles only in 1 Chr 7:28 (Ephraim and Manasseh) and 9:2.

[69] Regarding the issue of whether this refers to "settlers" or "resettlers," see the discussion in chapter 13.

exiled because of unfaithfulness (1 Chr 5:6, 25–26), as were the people as a whole (1 Chr 9:1b; 2 Chr 36:20).[70]

The Chronicler's narrative also mentions the connection between unfaithfulness and the loss of land or exile. Solomon's prayer (2 Chr 6:36–39), as well as Hezekiah's speech to the Levites (2 Chr 29:6–9), connects unfaithfulness with captivity, and by implication, faithfulness with the continued possession of land. Yahweh's response to Solomon indicates that the people can only continue to live in the land if they continue to be faithful, while unfaithfulness will result in Yahweh "uprooting Israel from my land" (2 Chr 7:19–20).

In 2 Chr 33:1–11, Manasseh was taken captive as a result of his unfaithfulness and was restored to his kingdom by the favour of Yahweh only when he repented, humbled himself and prayed (2 Chr 33:12–13; cf. 2 Chr 7:14). In the context of the genealogies, the return of the people to their towns (1 Chr 9:2), is to be understood as an act of Yahweh on behalf of his people when they humbled themselves and prayed.

Likewise in warfare, the people were victorious in their conflict when they "cried out to Yahweh" (1 Chr 5:20; 2 Chr 14:11–15; 20:1–30), and were faithful to him, a faithfulness that exhibited itself in the proper cultic personnel and rites (2 Chr 13:10–12). However, when the people were unfaithful, they were defeated in battle (2 Chr 12:1–5), even by a smaller and weaker force (2 Chr 24:23–24).

It is in this context of faithfulness/possession or unfaithfulness/exile that the list of Levitical towns is to be understood. That the Levitical clans possessed towns and dwelt within them is to be understood as a sign of Yahweh's blessing and restoration. This is to be contrasted with the previous mention of "exile" in relation to Jehozadak (1 Chr 5:42 [6:15]), in Level E. While the sons of Aaron may have been exiled, they now have dwellings within Israel. This connection between exile and dwellings may further explain why the Chronicler brought the list of the towns of the sons of Aaron forward to a position prior to the summary statements. As the "exile" had been explicitly mentioned in relation to the sons of Aaron, and not to the other Levitical clans, so also must a mention of the "dwelling places" be explicitly made to the sons of Aaron. If the Chronicler had allowed the reference to the towns of the sons of Aaron to remain in its Josh 21 position, the dwellings could be taken to refer to all of the Levitical clans, and possibly bring the legitimacy of the sons of Aaron, who had been exiled, into question. By drawing attention to the current dwelling places of the sons of Aaron, the Chronicler is indicating that those actions which caused the exile of the sons of Aaron have been atoned for, and as such the sons of Aaron have been restored not only to their lands, but also to their position within the cult. The sons

---

[70] This leaves the implication that the sons of Aaron (1 Chr 5:41 [6:15]), and the descendants of Ehud (1 Chr 8:6–7), were also exiled because of their "unfaithfulness."

of Aaron still retain the duty of offering sacrifice and making atonement for the people.

In 2 Chr 36:14 the Chronicler makes explicit reference to the unfaithfulness of the priests and people, but not to any unfaithfulness on the part of the Levites. If therefore the priests were "unfaithful," then the priests must also respond to Yahweh as did Manasseh, in humility and prayer, to be restored. By expressly mentioning the dwellings of the sons of Aaron, the Chronicler is stating that the causes of the exile of the sons of Aaron have been effectively dealt with, they have been forgiven, and the sons of Aaron have been restored, not only to their land but to their position. This is also the case with Manasseh, who was returned to his throne (2 Chr 33:13). This indicates that the sons of Aaron are no longer in exile, and thus "unfaithful," but are instead dwelling back in the land in their towns, and are now considered to be "faithful."[71]

The probability of this suggestion is enhanced when it is recognised that the phrase, וְאֵלֶּה מוֹשְׁבוֹתָם לְטִירוֹתָם (these are the locations of their settlements) are the Chronicler's words, and are found in neither MT or LXX Josh 21. That this phrase speaks primarily to the sons of Aaron, and not just to the Levites as a whole, is further strengthened by the position of this phrase immediately after the list of the "sons of Aaron" (1 Chr 6:35–38 [6:50–53]).

Thus, in order, the Chronicler mentions the duties of the sons of Aaron (1 Chr 6:34 [6:49]), the identity of the sons of Aaron (1 Chr 6:35–38 [6:50–53]), and the dwelling places of the sons of Aaron (1 Chr 6:39–45 [6:54–60]). The concluding summary statement "these towns ... were thirteen in all" (1 Chr 6:45 [6:60]), only appears in Chronicles in relation to the sons of Aaron. The other lists of towns for the Levitical clans do not contain this summary, unlike Josh 21.

If the sons of Aaron and the remainder of the Levites are portrayed in the genealogies as dwelling in the land and occupying their own towns, this is an indication that they are all now "faithful." This automatically leads to the question, "how will the people continue to dwell in the land?" The answer to that question is also provided in 1 Chr 6, and enhanced by the Chronicler's rearrangement of the his source material.

Remaining in the land ("these are their dwellings"), depends upon having the proper cultic officials ("the sons of Aaron"), performing the proper cultic functions ("the sons of Aaron presented burnt offerings"), in the proper cultic place ("altar of burnt offering," "the Most Holy Place"). Allied with this requirement is the presence of the Levites as assistants to the sons of Aaron, some of whom deal

---

[71] Curtis notes that the Chronicler "wishing to separate the account of the priestly cities form that of the Levites ... transposed the verses," *Chronicles*, 137. He, however, does not indicate why the Chronicler would wish to bring this separation.

with the "duties of the tabernacle, the house of God," and others who are concerned with the cultic music.[72]

As this proper order of the officials, duties and place can only continue if the people themselves are faithful in their service to the cult, a proper functioning cult becomes the visible sign of the ongoing faithfulness of the people to Yahweh. In 2 Chr 31:4 Hezekiah ordered the people to "give the portion due to the priests and Levites so that they could devote themselves to the law of Yahweh." As the people responded in obedience, the cultic officials "had enough to eat and plenty to spare" and were able to continue with their cultic activities (2 Chr 31:10). Compare this to Neh 13:10–14 where, when the people ceased to be faithful to the cult, the cultic officials were forced to abandon their duties to provide for themselves. When Nehemiah corrected this situation, he asked God to remember what "I have so faithfully done for the house of my God and its services" (Neh 13:14). Nehemiah associated what he had "faithfully done" (חֲסָדַי; NIV) for Yahweh or his "good deeds" (NRSV), with the provision of goods for the support of the cultic officials in their task.

The Chronicler also portrays times of renewal after unfaithfulness by the gathering of the Levites. Although Saul died for his unfaithfulness (1 Chr 10:13), and for neglecting the ark (1 Chr 13:3), when David sought a cultic renewal, he first gathered the Levites from their towns (1 Chr 13:2). It is inferred that the Levites were not present, because in Saul's unfaithfulness, they were scattered to fend for themselves. Jehoiada, before he could overthrow Athaliah, install Joash and restore the worship, first had to gather the Levites and the heads of Israelite families (2 Chr 23:2). Hezekiah first gathered the priests and Levites when he wanted to restore and purify the temple which had been abandoned by the unfaithfulness of Ahaz (2 Chr 29:4–7). That the cultic officials had to be gathered together to bring about renewal and restoration suggests that the cult had been neglected during the unfaithfulness of the preceding generation, and with it the required support for the cultic officials.

It therefore appears that the presence of the cultic officials is intrinsically tied to the faithfulness of the people in their cultic worship. When the people are faithful, the cultic officials are present, and society is properly ordered under Yahweh's blessing. When the people are unfaithful, the cultic officials disperse, the cultic duties cannot be performed, and the people are sent into exile.[73]

---

[72] Although Japhet says that 1 Chr 6:35–38 [6:50–53] "serve(s) to introduce the list of Levitical cities," it is clear that their presence is much more significant and speaks to the restoration and continued presence of the people in the land, *Chronicles*, 159. Cf. Braun, *1 Chronicles*, 94.

[73] See Johnstone, "Guilt and Atonement," and especially pages 128–129.

In answer to Klein's sixth question,[74] "what is the function of the list in 1 Chronicles 6?," the answer appears clear. First, the list of Levitical towns is presented to show that the people are back in the land, they and their priests have been restored and forgiven by Yahweh. The proper cultic officials, the sons of Aaron, Levites and musicians are present. That these groups are present is an indication that the now returned people are living in "faithfulness" to Yahweh, and are properly observing the cultic rituals. Second, the list of Levitical towns is a reminder of the consequences of unfaithfulness. Just as in Level E there has been a reference to exile, with the implication of "unfaithfulness," the spectre of exile hangs over the returned people. Although it is not anticipated, expected or deserved (for the people are currently faithful), "unfaithfulness" and exile are an ever present danger. The change in fortunes as depicted for the Transjordanian tribes where they quickly went from victory (1 Chr 5:18–22), to defeat and exile (1 Chr 5:25–26), was an ongoing warning to the people to remain faithful. Third, the list shows the legitimacy of the postexilic sons of Aaron. Although the sons of Aaron had been exiled for their own unfaithfulness (1 Chr 5:42 [6:15]; 2 Chr 36:14), Yahweh had restored them to their dwellings as well as to their position in the cult, offering sacrifice in the Most Holy Place and making atonement for the people. This group has not been replaced, but maintained its function in Yahweh's cult. Fourth, this list also shows the necessity for the ongoing presence and activity of the other three Levitical clans. They also dwell in their towns, and they also have their proper duty, function and purpose within the cult. Some remain as assistants to the sons of Aaron, while some are musicians. All, however, are vital, and the presence of all are reflective of the ongoing faithfulness of the people. As such, all are deserving the support of the people in material goods,[75] while a failure to provide such support, which would force the Levitical clans to provide for themselves, would be a sign of the unfaithfulness of the people, and would return the shadow of exile over the people.

Finally, the position of the cultic officials (1 Chr 5:27–6:32 [6:1–47]) and the Levitical lands (1 Chr 6:40–66 [6:55–81]), surrounding the cultic place and functions, shows the centrality of the cult to the restored community. They are a sign of restoration, as well as the means of maintaining possession of the land.

---

[74] Klein, *1 Chronicles*, 183.

[75] In respect to the gifts in Number 7, Ashley says, "By repetition the author showed that each tribe had an equal stake in the support of the sacrificial ministry of the tabernacle. No tribe had a monopoly on the responsibility for support and no tribe was unnecessary," *Numbers*, 164.

Figure 5.7: Towns Named in the Different Levitical Towns Lists

Josh 21 MT	Josh 21 LXX	Verse Josh 21	Verse 1 Chr 6	1 Chr 6 MT	1 Chr 6 LXX	MT =Same	MT ≈Similar	MT ≠Different	Josh 21 LXX=MT	Josh 21 LXX≈MT	Josh 21 LXX≠MT	1 Chr 6 LXX=MT	1 Chr 6 LXX≈MT	1 Chr 6 LXX≠MT
חברון	Χεβρων	13	42	חברון	Χεβρων	X			X			X		
לבנה	Λεμνα	13	42	לבנה	Λοβνα	X			X			X		
יתר	Αιλωμ	14	42	יתר	Σελνα	X					X			X
אשתמע	Τεμα	14	42	אשתמע	Εσθαμω	X					X	X		
חלן	Γελλα	15	43	חילן	Ιεθθαρ		X				X	X		
דבר	Δαβιρ	15	43	דבר	Δαβιρ	X			X			X		
עין	Ασα	16	44	עשן	Ασαν		X				X	X		
יטה	Τανυ	16	44	---	Ατταν	-	-	-	X					X
בית שמש	Βαιθσαμυς	16	44	בית שמש	Βασαμυς	X			X			X		
גבעון	Γαβαων	17	---	---	---	-	-	-	X			-	-	-
גבע	Γαθεθ	17	45	גבע	Γαβεε	X					X	X		
ענתות	Αναθωθ	18	45	עלמת	Γαλεμεθ		X				X	X		
עלמון	Γαμαλα	18	45	עלמת	Αγχωχ	X					X			X

| | | Verse | | MT | | | Josh 21 | | | 1 Chr 6 | | |
Josh 21 MT	Josh 21 LXX	Josh 21	1 Chr 6	1 Chr 6 MT	1 Chr 6 LXX	= Same	≈ Similar	≠ Different	LXX = MT	LXX ≈ MT	LXX ≠ MT	LXX = MT	LXX ≈ MT	LXX ≠ MT
שכם	Συχεμ	21	52	שׁכם	Συχεμ	X			X			X		
גזר	Γαζαρα	21	52	גזר	Γαζερ	X			X			X		
קבצים	Καβσαϊμ	22	53	יקמעם	Ιεκμααμ			X	X			X		
בית חורן	Βαιθωρον	22	53	בית חורן	Βαιθωρον	X			X			X		
אלתקא	Ελκωθαιμ	23	---	---	----	-	-	-	X			-	-	-
גבתון	Γεθεδαν	23	---	---	----	-	-	-	X			-	-	-
אילון	Αιλων	24	54	אלון	Εγλαμ	X			X			X		X
גת-רמון	Γεθερεμμων	24	54	גת רמון	Γεθρεμμων	X			X			X		
תענך	Ταναχ	25	55	ענר	Αναρ		X		X			X		
יבלעם	Ιεβαθα	25	55	בלעם	Ιεβλααμ			X			X		X	
גולן בבשן	Γαυλων ἐν τῇ Βασανιτιδι	27	56	גלון בבשן	Γωλων ἐκ Βασαν	X			X			X		
בעשתרה	Βοσοραν	27	56	עשתרות	Ασηρωθ		X			X		X		

Figure 5.7 Continued

Josh 21 MT	Josh 21 LXX	Verse Josh 21	Verse 1 Chr 6	1 Chr 6 MT	1 Chr 6 LXX	MT = Same	MT ≈ Similar	MT ≠ Different	Josh 21 LXX = MT	Josh 21 LXX ≈ MT	Josh 21 LXX ≠ MT	1 Chr 6 LXX = MT	1 Chr 6 LXX ≈ MT	1 Chr 6 LXX ≠ MT
חברון	Χεβρων	13	42	חברון	Χεβρων	X			X			X		
לבנה	Λεμνα	13	42	לבנה	Λοβνα	X				X		X		
יתר	Αιλομ	14	42	יתר	Σελνα	X					X			X
אשתמע	Τεμα	14	42	אשתמע	Εσθαμω	X			X			X		
חלן	Γελλα	15	43	חילן	Ιεθθαρ		X		X					X
דבר	Δαβιρ	15	43	דביר	Δαβιρ	X			X			X		
עין	Ασα	16	44	עשן	Ασαν		X				X	X		
יטה	Τανυ	16	44	---	Ατταν		-	-			X		-	X
בית שמש	Βαιθσαμυς	16	44	בית שמש	Βασαμυς	X			X					X
גבעון	Γαβαων	17	---	---	----		-	-	X			-	-	-
גבע	Γαθεθ	17	45	גבע	Γαβεε	X			X			X		
ענתות	Αναθωθ	18	45	עלמת	Γαλεμεθ		X		X			X		
עלמן	Γαμαλα	18	45	ענתות	Αγχωχ	X			X				X	
שכם	Συχεμ	21	52	שכם	Συχεμ	X			X			X		

Josh 21 MT	Josh 21 LXX	Verse Josh 21	Verse 1 Chr 6	1 Chr 6 MT	1 Chr 6 LXX	MT = Same	MT ≈ Similar	MT ≠ Different	Josh 21 LXX = MT	Josh 21 LXX ≈ MT	Josh 21 LXX ≠ MT	1 Chr 6 LXX = MT	1 Chr 6 LXX ≈ MT	1 Chr 6 LXX ≠ MT
גזר	Γαζαρα	21	52	גזר	Γαζερ	X			X			X		
קבצים	Καβσαϊμ	22	53	יקמעם	Ιεκμααμ			X	X			X		
בית חורן	Βαιθωρων	22	53	בית חורון	Βαιθωρων	X			X			X		
אלקתא	Ελκωθαιμ	23	--	---	---	-	-	-	X			-	-	-
גבתון	Γεθεδαν	23	--	---	---	-	-	-	X			-	-	-
איל	Αιλων	24	54	אלון	Εγλαμ	X			X					X
גת רמון	Γεθερεμμον	24	54	גת רמון	Γεθερεμμον	X			X			X		
תענך	Ταναχ	25	55	ענר	Αναρ		X		X				X	
גת בא	Ιεβαθα	25	55	בלעם	Ιεβλααμ			X			X			
גולן בבשן	Γαυλων εν τη Βασανιτιδι	27	56	גלון בבשן	Γωλαν εκ Βασαν	X			X			X		
בעשתרה	Βοσοραν	27	56	עשתרות	Ασηρωθ		X		X			X		

CONCLUSION

In this chapter, 1 Chr 6:39–66 [6:54–81] has been examined. Through investigating the proposals by Auld that 1 Chr 6 was the source of Josh 21, and that 1 Chr 6 developed in a series of stages, it has been concluded instead that both 1 Chr 6 and MT Josh 21 utilised a common source, which was itself a revision of the *Ur* Joshua utilised by LXX Josh 21.

It was further concluded that 1 Chr 6 was brought into its present context and rearranged by the Chronicler as part of his process of emphasising the necessity for the ongoing support of the cult and its officials. A properly functioning cult, with the prescribed cultic personnel performing the prescribed cultic functions in the prescribed cultic place are the visible sign of the faithfulness of all the people. As the people continue to support the cult and its officials, the ongoing presence of the people in the land is also assured. If the people abandon the required support of the cult and its officials, this is a sign that the people have become unfaithful, and is also an assurance that exile will follow.

Finally, the presence of the people in the land was an assurance that the sons of Aaron, the Levites, and the people as a whole have been forgiven by Yahweh for their previous unfaithfulness, an unfaithfulness that led them into exile. Yahweh's restoration of the people to the land, like his restoration of repentant Manasseh to his kingdom, was an act of mercy in response to their humility and prayer. However, this restoration is never unconditional, but is ongoing only on the condition that the people maintain their faithfulness to Yahweh, as expressed by their support of the cult.

CHAPTER 6
D: 1 CHRONICLES 4:24–5:26
TRIBES OF ISRAEL IN VICTORY AND DEFEAT

Although presented as a chiasm, the Chronicler's genealogies (1 Chr 1–9) can be divided into three main sections: First Chronicles 1 presents the genealogy of the nations using material taken almost exclusively from the genealogies located in Genesis. First Chronicles 2–8 presents the genealogy of Israel as represented in the traditional twelve tribes.[1] First Chronicles 9 presents an idealistic view of Jerusalem as occupied by all the tribes of Israel along with the properly instituted cultic officials.

First Chronicles 2:3–8:39 divides into five sections, with the major listings at the beginning (Judah, 1 Chr 2:1–4:23), middle (Levi, 1 Chr 5:27–6:66 [6:1–81]), and end (Benjamin, 1 Chr 8:1–40), of this section.

Between the genealogies of Judah and Levi lie details regarding Simeon and the Transjordanian tribes (Reuben, Gad, and one-half Manasseh), while between Levi and the major listing of Benjamin lie details of what were the northern tribes of Israel (Issachar, Benjamin,[2] Dan[?], Naphtali, Manasseh, Ephraim, Asher).

Although Pratt refers to these latter two groupings as the "tribes easily forgotten," and "other tribes easily forgotten,"[3] their presence should not be taken as an afterthought, nor to ensure that the memory of these tribes was retained.

---

[1] Zebulun is not recorded in this section outside of the initial list of Israel's sons (1 Chr 2:1–2). Dan may have been listed cryptically as Ir or "the city" in 1 Chr 7:12. However, the traditional number of tribes as "twelve" is still maintained through the double mention of Manasseh (one in Transjordan, the other in Cisjordan), and the inclusion of Levi which, because of its cultic function, did not receive an inheritance within the land. The genealogy of Benjamin is also recorded twice (1 Chr 7:6–12; 8:1–40). That the Chronicler was seeking to give the impression that all of the traditional tribes were included is evident in 1 Chr 2:1–2 "these were the sons of Israel," and 1 Chr 9:1a "all Israel was listed in the genealogies." These statements represent Levels B and B^1 in the Chronicler's chiasm, and act as the beginning and the end of the Chronicler's discussion of tribal Israel. See further Chapter 10.

[2] The presence of Benjamin here is a matter of contention. Curtis suggests that it should refer to Zebulun, *Chronicles*, 145–149. Regarding this suggestion Williamson says, "the textual emendations proposed are too violent to inspire confidence," *Chronicles*, 77. Further, because Benjamin was nominally allied to, or incorporated into, Judah, to label 1 Chr 7 as "the northern tribes of Israel" should not therefore be seen as a reference to what became Israel after the break up of David/Solomon's kingdom.

[3] Pratt, *Chronicles*, 75–82, 86–90.

The placing of these two lists of tribes on the same chiastic level indicates that their listing is in accordance with a plan of presentation which seeks to highlight the Chronicler's purposes. Being on the same chiastic level also suggests that the two sections should complement one another and that Level D^1 should advance the discussion in Level D.

In this chapter we will review the tribal listings of Simeon and the Transjordanian tribes (1 Chr 4:24–5:26), examining their form and content in order to understand their function within the work of the Chronicler. In the following chapter, Level D^1 (1 Chr 7) will be investigated to understand how it builds upon and advances the arguments found in Level D.

THE STRUCTURE OF THE LISTS

This section can be subdivided into two sub-sections: First Chronicles 4:24–43 (the account of Simeon) and 1 Chr 5:1–26 (the account of the Transjordanian tribes: Reuben, Gad, and one-half Manasseh). This division is based upon three observations. The first is geographical. Simeon is located west of the Jordan River, within the territorial boundaries of the tribe of Judah (Josh 19:1–9), while the Transjordanian tribes are located east of the Jordan, with each having its own, distinct, territory. The second observation is that Simeon is dealt with separately, while Reuben, Gad and one-half Manasseh are, in two sections, treated as one unit. First Chronicles 5:18 discusses the joint conduct of the three tribes in warfare, and 1 Chr 5:25–26 discusses their joint unfaithfulness and exile. The third observation is that both sections conclude with the phrase עַד הַיּוֹם הַזֶּה (until this day; 1 Chr 4:43; 5:26).[4] This suggests that this phrase is acting as a conclusion to the two sections. The discussion of each of the four tribes is presented in a similar, although not identical, shape (Figure 6.1).

While each tribal list in this section shares certain similarities with the others, the details they contain are not in the same order nor is as much emphasis laid upon each of the elements in the differing lists. Thus Reuben has the reference to "genealogical records" prior to the list of settlements, while Simeon places the settlements first. Gad has two lists of settlements, one on either side of the list of descendants. Manasseh has only settlements and clan leaders, but no list of descendants.

---

[4] See note 12, below.

Figure 6.1: Order of Presentation in the Simeonite and Transjordan Lists

	Simeon 1 Chr 4	Reuben 1 Chr 5	Gad 1 Chr 5	½ Manasseh 1 Chr 5
descendants	24–26	1a, 3–6	12–15	
relation to Judah	27	1b–2		
settlements	28–33a	7b–9	11, 16	23
genealogical record	33b–37	7a	17	24
expansion of land	38–43	10, 18–22	18–22	18–22

Simeon and Reuben share the most in common. They are the only lists in this group that indicate descendants, settlements and genealogical records, and that speak of an independent expansion of land (1 Chr 5:18–22 speaks of a joint effort of the Transjordanian tribes). Neither Gad nor Manasseh is recorded in relation to Judah, and neither records any direct descendants of the tribal founder.[5] Gad has a list of "chiefs" and their relatives, while Manasseh has only later "heads of families" (1 Chr 5:11–15, 24).[6]

---

[5] Interestingly, both Jer 49:1 and the Mesha inscription refer to "Gad" as a region distinct from Israel. Although the Jeremiah passage dates after the fall of Israel, the Mesha inscription's reference to Gad may indiate that the king of Israel's control over the Transjordan was insecure enough to allow the people their own identity. Second Kings 10:33 is the only reference after Joshua to "Gad" in the Deuteronomistic History and, as in 1 Chr 5, only in its relationship with Reuben and Manasseh. Ezekiel 48:27–28, however, sees a place for Gad in the future community, while Ezek 48:34 mentions the gate of Gad in the restored city.

[6] The reason for this lack of a list of descendants is uncertain. The Chronicler appears to have some knowledge of the material found in Numbers, in which there is a listing of the descendants of Manasseh (Num 26:29–34). This may not have been mentioned at this point, because the Chronicler was also to record Manasseh in 1 Chr 7:14–19. So Curtis and Madsen, *Chronicles*, 124. Yet even this latter passage only connects with Num 26 in mention of Makir, the father of Gilead (1 Chr 7:14; Num 26:29), which itself is east of the Jordan. Williamson suggests that Manasseh is not original to 1 Chr 5 at this point, because: (1) the reference to Manasseh after the editorial mention of two and one-half tribes is "awkward"; (2) v. 25–26 are only "an expansion" of v. 22; (3) the Chronicler does not normally give much attention to the northern tribes; and (4) the military census data

The details of these four tribes, their expansions and exiles, are also intertwined with the details of various domestic and foreign kings. David (1 Chr 4:31), Hezekiah (1 Chr 4:41), Saul (1 Chr 5:10), Jotham and Rehoboam (1 Chr 5:17), and Tiglath Pileser (1 Chr 5:6, 26), are all mentioned within the context of the possession, expansion or loss of land and territory. What is interesting is the observation that no Israelite king is mentioned as being actively involved in assisting the tribe(s) to expand their territory. Territorial expansion is only ever accomplished by the actions of the tribe(s) itself/themselves. For Simeon, the independent expansion of territory is related to the time of Hezekiah (1 Chr 4:41), Reuben's expansion to the time of Saul (1 Chr 5:10), while Gad's chiefs and territories are related to the days of Jotham of Judah and Jeroboam of Israel (1 Chr 5:17).[7] The joint conquest recorded in 1 Chr 5:18–22, however, is not related to the reign of any particular king.

"would be more at home" in 7:14–19, *Chronicles*, 66–67. These objections are not necessary. 1) While it is true that one would expect treatment of Manasseh after the mention of Gad and prior to the record of the Hagrite war, the inclusion of the Manasseh data after the Hagrite war allows the Chronicler to lead from the victory of the Transjordanian tribes, to their unfaithfulness and exile. 2); 5:25–26 are not merely an "expansion" of 5:22, but an amplification and extension of it. While 5:22 mentions that the Transjordanian tribes occupied the land "until the exile," it gives no causes for exile, who exiled the people, where the people were exiled to, or what is the current status of those who were exiled. These are all clarified in 1 Chr 5:25–26. 3) While the Chronicler does not give as much attention to the northern tribes, it is also true that they are expressly mentioned as being present at the inauguration of David, and during the reforms of Hezekiah and Josiah. In other words, the Chronicler mentions the other tribes as necessary for his purposes. 4) The account of Manasseh only describes the warriors (see below), but unlike the lists in 1 Chr 7 and 1 Chr 5:18, does not give totals for either clans nor tribes.

[7] Why or how Jotham and Jeroboam would cooperate in a census over land which was, nominally at least, under the control of the latter is uncertain. Further, it is clear from 2 Kgs 15:32 that Jotham did not begin his reign until after the death of Jeroboam. This prompts Wellhausen to say, "Jotham and Jeroboam . . . make so impossible a synchronism that the partisans of Chronicles will have it that none is intended," *Prolegomena*, 213. Several possibilities present themselves: (1) this census refers to the period of co-regency of Jotham and Azariah/Uzziah mentioned in 2 Kgs 15:5; (2) a joint census was not intended, only that the census took place during the reigns of both kings, irrespective of who actually organised it. For a comparison of the various dates proposed for the reigns of the Kings of Judah and Israel, see Andrew E. Hill and John H. Walton, *A Survey of the Old Testament* (Grand Rapids: Zondervan, 2000), 232–233 and the references cited there; (3) it is clear that during the reigns of Omri and Ahab, Israel was dominant over Judah. This is evident by the quick submission of Jehoshaphat to Ahab's request for a joint expedition against Aram (1 Kgs 22:1–5), and by the intermarriage between the two royal houses on terms that favoured Israel rather than Judah (2 Kgs 8:26). It does appear that after Ahab's death, Jehoshaphat felt able to reject a request from Ahab's son Ahaziah (1 Kgs 22:49). 1

Simeon records settlement areas by occupied towns (1 Chr 4:28–33),[8] while the Transjordanian tribes are listed by geographical regions (1 Chr 5:8b–9, 11, 16, 23).[9]

All of these suggest that in tribal reports, although certain material was expected, there was no standard form to be followed in reporting or recording this information. These variations suggest that the Chronicler was following various independent sources available to him rather than creating the lists, for if he was the originator of the lists a greater standardization would be expected.[10] However, the Chronicler does not appear to have slavishly followed his sources. He feels free to add theologically motivated editorial comments (1 Chr 5:18–22, 25–26), as well as historically motivated editorial comments (1 Chr 4:27; 5:1–2).[11]

Both lists (Simeon and Transjordan), end in the same manner, recording the present status "to this day" of the tribe(s) in question (1 Chr 4:41, 43; 5:26).[12]

Chr 5:17 may then refer to a later period when Israel was again dominant, and able to enforce a joint census over both kingdoms.

[8] See Figure 6.2. The Simeonite list has many similarities with the settlement list in Josh 19, although the lists are not exact. Joshua 15 indicates the tribal allotment for Judah, out of which the allotment for Simeon was derived.

[9] The tribal areas indicated in 1 Chr 5 are not identical with the tribal allotment in Josh 13. As Figure 6.3 shows, there is conflict over the rights to Bashan and Aroer in the various texts. These could reflect different claims to land at different times. It is probable that the borders were flexible, with shifting "control" by different clans dependent upon the social, political, economic, and military situation at any one time. The Mesha inscription mentions Baal Meon, Sharon, Nebo, Aroer as towns conquered and (re)built by the king of Moab. For an English translation of the Mesha inscription, see, William W. Hallo and K. Lawson Younger, *The Context of Scripture Volume 2: Monumental Inscriptions from the Biblical World* (COS; Leiden: Brill, 2003), 137–138.

[10] Cf. the standard reports in Num 1:20–42; 7:12–83; 26:5–62.

[11] "History" in the sense of finding causes in the past in order to explain the experiences of the present.

[12] עַד הַיּוֹם הַזֶּה occurs seventy-six times in the Hebrew Bible and frequently in contexts which speak of the past cause of a present reality. It is used to refer to naming or changing the name of a city/town (Gen 26:33; Josh 5:9), destruction of enemy armies (Deut 11:4; 1 Chr 4:41), the reason behind cultural customs (Gen 32:33 [32:32]; Jer 35:14), the presence of a monument (1 Sam 6:18). It also appears to be used in reference not to what is the reality in the writer's present, but to the time period which was being written about. First Kings 8:8 speaks of the poles being present in the temple "to this day." If Kings is an exilic document this must refer to the time in which the writer is referring. If, however, Kings underwent a number of redactional stages, this phrase could be from a preexilic redaction (when the poles were present) which was not adjusted in the exilic final edition. See further Jeffrey C. Geoghegan, ""Until This Day" and the Preexilic Redaction of the Deuteronomistic History," *JBL* 122 (2003): 201–227. This phrase was unaltered by the Chronicler in his usage in 2 Chr 5:9. This could be simply because his source

When it is observed that the probable source of 1 Chr 5:26 is 2 Kgs 17:6; 18:11, neither of which contains the phrase, "to this day," it becomes apparent that this phrase must be an editorial comment by the Chronicler and, as they are the only occurrences of the phrase in the genealogies, must be an attempt to contrast the differing "present day" of the two groups.[13]

Figure 6.2: The Cities of the Tribe of Simeon

City	1 Chr	Josh	Josh
Beersheba	4:28	19:2	15:28
Sheba		19:2	
Moladah	4:28	19:2	15:26
Hazar Shual	4:28	19:3	15:28
Bilhah	4:29	19:3 (Balah)	15:29 (Baalah)
Ezem	4:29	19:3	15:29
Tolad	4:29	19:4 (Eltolad)	15:30 (Eltolad)
Bethuel	4:30	19:4 (Bethul)	
Hormah	4:30	19:4	15:30
Ziklag	4:30	19:5	15:31
Beth Marcaboth	4:31	19:5	
Hazar Susim	4:31	19:5 (Hazar-susah)	
Beth-lebaoth		19:6	15:32 (Lebaoth)
Beth Biri	4:31		
Shaaraim	4:31	19:6 (Sharuhen)	15:36
Etam	4:32		
Ain	4:32	19:7	15:32
Rimmon	4:32	19:7	15:32
Ether		19:7	15:42
Token	4:32		
Ashan	4:32	19:7	15:42
Baalath	4:33	19:8 (Baalath-beer)	15:29 (Baalah)

---

contained the phrase, or it could be part of the Chronicler's purpose to show the continuity of the second temple with the first. For the Chronicler's concern regarding the continuity of the temple vessels see Van Seters, "Solomon's Temple Building."

[13] The phrase is located in 2 Kgs 17:23. The significance of this phrase, along with alternative understandings, will be investigated below.

Figure 6.3: The Transjordanian Tribal Allotments

City/Region	Reuben	Gad	Manasseh	Josh 13
Aroer	1 Chr 5:8 Josh 13:16	Num 33:34		Josh 13:9
Baal Hermon Senir Mount Hermon			1 Chr 5:23	Josh 13:11
Baal Meon	1 Chr 5:8 Josh 13:17 Num 32:38			
Bashan		1 Chr 5:16	1 Chr 5:23 Josh 13:30–31	Josh 13:11
Gilead	1 Chr 5:9	1 Chr 5:16 Josh 13:25	Josh 13:31 Num 32:39	Josh 13:11
Nebo	1 Chr 5:8 Num 32:38			
Salecah		1 Chr 5:16		Josh 13:11
Sharon[14]		1 Chr 5:16		

SOURCES

Determining which source(s) the Chronicler utilised in his presentation is difficult. It has already been suggested, above, that the Chronicler may have had access to independent sources which indicated territorial expansion as well as tribal and clan leaders. The text also has certain affinities with other portions of the Hebrew Bible (Figure 6.4).

As observed in Figure 6.4,[15] the genealogy of Reuben (1 Chr 5:3) is nearly identical to that found in Gen 46:8b–9 except for:

---

[14] The Mesha inscription mentions Aroer, Baal Meon, Nebo, Sharon. That Sharon is mentioned indicates that the reference in 1 Chr 5:16 is not "Sharon" west of the Jordan, but to another location of the same name east of the Jordan.

[15] In Figure 6.4, words or phrases that are underlined indicate that they are either in a different location in relation to 1 Chr 5:3, or that they substitute an alternative term than

Figure 6.4: The Source of 1 Chronicles 5:3

בְּנֵי רְאוּבֵן בְּכוֹר יִשְׂרָאֵל חֲנוֹךְ וּפַלּוּא חֶצְרוֹן וְכַרְמִי	1 Chr 5:3
בְּנֵי רְאוּבֵן בְּכֹר יִשְׂרָאֵל חֲנוֹךְ וּפַלּוּא חֶצְרוֹן וְכַרְמִי	Exod 6:14
בְּכֹר יַעֲקֹב רְאוּבֵן	Gen 46:8–9
וּבְנֵי רְאוּבֵן חֲנוֹךְ וּפַלּוּא וְחֶצְרוֹן וְכַרְמִי	
רְאוּבֵן בְּכוֹר יִשְׂרָאֵל	Num 26:5–6
בְּנֵי רְאוּבֵן חֲנוֹךְ ~~מִשְׁפַּחַת הַחֲנֹכִי~~	
~~לְפַלּוּא מִשְׁפַּחַת הַפַּלֻּאִי~~	
~~לְחֶצְרֹן מִשְׁפַּחַת הַחֶצְרוֹנִי~~	
לְכַרְמִי ~~מִשְׁפַּחַת הַכַּרְמִי~~	

- the absence of the conjunction ו prior to the third son Hezron.
- the substitution of "Israel" for "Jacob."[16]
- The phrase: "the firstborn of Israel" placed after the name "Reuben" instead of prior to it.

Numbers 26:5–6 also contains many similarities. This passage contains the phrase "Reuben, the firstborn of Israel"[17] as well as a list of each of the sons.

---

found in 1 Chr 5:3. Words or phrases that are stricken indicate words or phrases that do not occur in 1 Chr 5:3. Plené or defective spellings are not considered significant in this comparison.

[16] "Jacob" only occur in Samuel and Kings in 1 Sam 12:8; 2 Sam 23;1; 1 Kgs 18:31; 2 Kgs 13:23; 17:34. None of these passages are cited by the Chronicler. "Israel' occurs fourteen times in the genealogical section (1 Chr 1:34, 43; 2:1, 7; 4:10; 5:1 [x2], 3, 17, 26; 6:23, 34, 49 [6:38, 49, 64]; 7:29; 9:1 [x2], 2. Of these 1 Chr 1:34; 2:1; 5:1, 3; 6:23 [6:38]; 7:29 "Jacob" would be more natural than "Israel" as it either refers to the son of Isaac or the father of one of the tribal founders. "Most of the instances are in stereotyped formulae which use the name Jacob elsewhere in the Bible," Williamson, *Israel*, 62. It is possible to conclude from this that the Chronicler had a preference for "Israel" over "Jacob." Williamson further notes that "Jacob" only occurs in 1 Chr 16:13, 17, quoting from Ps 105 and in parallel in both instances with "Israel," although in 1 Chr 16:13 // Ps 105:6, the Psalm has "Abraham"

[17] This, however, is different for the full phrase is "Reuben, the firstborn of Israel: the sons of Reuben" whereas 1 Chr reads "the sons of Reuben the firstborn of Israel"

These, however, are not in the same form as in either Gen 46 or 1 Chr 5. Numbers 26 lists the descendants of Reuben by their מִשְׁפַּחַת ("clans," a phrase found in Exod 6:14b, but not in Gen 46 or 1 Chr 5).

An even closer verbal connection is found with Exod 6:14b, which contains the identical phrase as Chronicles, in the identical order, with no alteration in the order of "firstborn of Israel" and no absence of the conjunction וְ. It is therefore probable that Exod 6:14 was the Chronicler's source for the sons of Reuben.

Simeon, however, contains differences with all the other lists of Simeonite clans.[18] The Genesis and Exodus lists are identical to one another, but contain one extra person (Ohad) and two different names (Yacin for Yarib and Tsohar for Zerah), than what is found in the list in Chronicles. The Numbers list only differs from the Chronicler's list in the name Yacin. The list of Simeonite towns is also very similar to that located in Josh 19.[19]

Figure 6.5: The Clans of Simeon

1 Chr 4:24	Gen 46:10	Exod 6:15	Num 26:12–13
נְמוּאֵל	יְמוּאֵל	יְמוּאֵל	נְמוּאֵל
יָמִין	יָמִין	יָמִין	יָמִין
	אֹהַד	אֹהַד	
יָרִיב	יָכִין	יָכִין	יָכִין
זֶרַח	צֹחַר	צֹחַר	זֶרַח
שָׁאוּל	שָׁאוּל	שָׁאוּל	שָׁאוּל

The genealogies of Gad and Manasseh bear no resemblance to the lists of Gen 46:16 or Num 26:15–18, 29–34,[20] even though it is clear from 1 Chr 1 that the Chronicler had access to the text of Genesis and utilised it with reasonable care.[21] The end of the Manasseh list (1 Chr 5:25–26), which refers to the exile of the Transjordanian tribes, bears several verbal similarities with 2 Kgs 15:19;

---

[18] See Figure 6.5.
[19] See Figure 6.1.
[20] Recognising of course that no genealogy of Manasseh would be included in Gen 46 as it is specifically the sons of Jacob who migrated to Egypt. Manasseh and Ephraim are recorded with Joseph in Gen 46:19–20. Genesis 50:23 does recount that Manasseh had a son "Makir" who also had children prior to Joseph's death, but the names of these children are not recorded in this text.
[21] Genesis 46:16 and Num 26:15–18 do maintain some similarities, agreeing in six of the seven sons/clans of Gad. On the relation of 1 Chr 1 to Genesis, see Excursus 3.

17:6–8, 23; 18:11, although the differences in wording would suggest a knowledge of the topic rather than direct dependence at this point.[22]

Beyond these small, and often variant, readings, much of the content of these texts has no parallel within Biblical material and, unless it is suggested that all of the non-parallel material is the Chronicler's own composition, must have been based upon some other source(s), whether that source(s) was directly quoted or simply formed the basis for the Chronicler's material.

Some of these sources appear to be יחש (1 Chr 4:33; 5:17)[23] or תולדות (1 Chr 5:7),[24] (genealogical records)[25] and appear to be the record of leaders of the clans (1 Chr 4:34–37; 5:4–6, 7b–8, 12–14), and possibly dwelling places for these clans (1 Chr 4:28–33a; 5:8b–9, 16).

Similar is the list of בֵּת אָב (heads of families; 1 Chr 5:24),[26] which lists leaders and possibly dwelling places (1 Chr 5:23), although in this instance the list of dwelling places may be from a separate source for the dwellings and leaders are not linked as tightly as they are in Reuben (1 Chr 5:7–9), or Gad (1 Chr 5:11–16).[27] The בֵּת אָב are, however, often recounted with military musters,

---

[22] See further Robert K. McIver and Marie Carroll, "Experiments to Develop Criteria for Determining the Existence of Written Sources, and Their Potential Implications for the Synoptic Problem," *JBL* 121 (2002): 667–687, especially pages 668–673 for discussion on the criteria for determining that an author had a source available to him while he wrote as opposed to a knowledge of the source. What is significant is that while the Deuteronomist refers to Israel (as distinct from Judah) going into exile in his text, the Chronicler only refers to the Transjordanian tribes as going into exile. As such "Israel" west of the Jordan is never directly said to have been exiled in the genealogies. Exile only occurs to Reuben, Transjordan, Judah and Levi (1 Chr 5:6, 26; 5:42 [6:15]; 9:1).

[23] Used in 1 Chr 1–9 in 4:33; 5:1, 7, 17; 7:5, 7, 9, 40; 9:1, 22, in the genealogies of Simeon, Reuben, Gad, Issachar, Benjamin, Asher, "all Israel," gatekeepers.

[24] Used in 1 Chr 1–9 in 1:29; 5:7; 7:2, 4, 9; 8:28; 9:9, 34, in the genealogies of Ishmael, Reuben, Issachar, Benjamin (on three occasions), gatekeepers.

[25] Both terms are translated as "genealogical records" in the NIV and NRSV.

[26] First Chronicles 5:15, 24; 7:2, 7, 9, 11, 40; 8:6, 10, 13, 28; 9:9, 13, 33, 34, the genealogies of Gad, Manasseh, Issachar, Benjamin, Asher, priests, musicians, gatekeepers. It is worth noting that the lists for Judah, although extensive, never once use these terms. These terms imply written records for official functions. Perhaps this term was used for these tribes because of the lack of living personnel (except for Benjamin and Levi), in these other tribes whom could be cited, or perhaps Israel utilised a different system than Judah did owing to its greater tribal diversity. For discussion of this term see Weinberg, *Citizen-Temple*, 49–61.

[27] In other uses of בֵּת אָב in the genealogies, only rarely (5:15; 8:6) is it used in the context of dwelling places. Although it is used in context with both יחש and תולדות, these normally appear to be muster lists rather than settlement lists. This may further suggest that the Manasseh "genealogy" is a composite from various sources according to the

and it is possible therefore that the list of "heads of families" for Manasseh was associated with the muster recorded in 1 Chr 5:18.[28]

Some of the material appears to be the Chronicler's own interpretive work, either of an historical (1 Chr 4:27b; 5:1b–2), or of a theological nature (1 Chr 5:20, 25–26).[29] That the Chronicler felt free to adapt or paraphrase his sources (1 Chr 5:25–26), or to ignore material that his sources contained (the omission of the sons of Gad), or to give his own interpretations to events or circumstances, indicates that the Chronicler was not a slave to his sources. Nor was he trying to include all the available data, for there is much that the source material available to us contains which was omitted by the Chronicler. It is probable then that the Chronicler included only what was necessary to make his particular point. Consequently, absence of, or differences in, material must not automatically be taken to indicate textual corruption or the work of a later editor. The text needs to be investigated first to determine if it provides a coherent meaning within the context of the genealogies and of the work as a whole.

In summary, it appears that the Chronicler utilised various types of written sources in forming his account of Simeon and the Transjordanian tribes. Among these are works that now appear in the canonical Hebrew Bible as well as other sources now lost. The Chronicler may also have "filled out" his accounts with "educated guesses" based upon what appeared in other sources. Finally, these

---

Chronicler's purpose of dealing with all of the Transjordanian tribes, even though he has little substantial information about some of them.

[28] See the muster totals in 1 Chr 7:2, 4, 7, 9, 11, 40 where in each case the clan total is linked with the "heads of families" or simply "heads."

[29] First Chronicles 5:1b appears to rely on the wording of Gen 49:4 regarding the "defiling" of Jacob's bed even though the incident is reported in Gen 35:22 without comment. First Chronicles 5:2 *may* be an interpretation of Gen 48:5, 14 regarding the "adoption" of Manasseh and Ephraim by Jacob, because of the "double portion" that a firstborn child was to receive, Deut 21:17, Japhet, *Chronicles*, 133. If this is the case, then a careful reading of Deuteronomy should in fact reverse Jacob's decision, for Reuben was Jacob's firstborn from the "unloved wife," the sign of his "father's strength" (cf. Gen 49:3) and as such Jacob's actions were unlawful (Deut 21:16). That the assigning of the rights of the firstborn to another was legitimate in the Chronicler's sight is evidenced by 1 Chr 26:10. Exactly why this is so, and how it could be justified in light of the other writings is not sure. Japhet, however, disputes that Shimri was given the rights of firstborn, only that he was made the "chief." However, she further says that as the lists in 1 Chr 26 are a "metaphorical abstraction of the ordering of the father's houses," and she concludes that the Hosah clan simply gave way to the Shimri clan, *Chronicles*, 457–458. Genesis 48:14, 19 appears to indicate that pre-eminence in a family or clan was not dependent upon birth order although Joseph's response to Jacob's elevating the youngest over the eldest (Gen 48:17–18), was such that this was far from normal, or even "proper."

sources were shaped and presented in a way which was consistent with the Chronicler's purposes.

THE BATTLE ACCOUNTS

This section of the genealogies contains five battle accounts:[30]
- Simeon against the Hamites and Meunites in the days of Hezekiah (1 Chr 4:41).
- Part of Simeon against the hill country of Seir (1 Chr 4:42–43).
- Reuben against the Hagrites in the days of Saul (1 Chr 5:10).
- Reuben, Gad, and Manasseh against the Hagrite alliance (1 Chr 5:18–22).
- Assyria against the Transjordanian tribes (1 Chr 5:26).

These battle accounts are associated with an expanding tribal or clan population (1 Chr 4:38),[31] the need to gain land for flocks (1 Chr 4:40; 5:9), and with the occupation of the land conquered (1 Chr 4:41, 43; 5:10, 22). Gaining the possessions of the conquered, apart from land, does not appear to be a primary motive of the battle accounts, although it is sometimes the consequence of the battle (1 Chr 5:21). Battles often result in the destruction (1 Chr 4:41, 43), or near destruction (1 Chr 5:21b–22), of the defeated people and this itself is tied to the ability to possess the land of the defeated peoples (cf. 1 Chr 4:41 "they destroyed ... and settled"; 1 Chr 4:43 "they killed ... and lived"; 1 Chr 5:21a–22 "they took captive ... others fell slain ... they occupied").

What is significant in this section is that battles occur for only two reasons, 1) to gain land because of an increase in flocks and/or families; 2) at the instigation or with the assistance of Yahweh (1 Chr 5:20, 26).[32] The first is clearly the

---

[30] On the battle accounts in Chronicles, see John W. Wright, "The Fight for Peace: Narrative and History in the Battle Accounts in Chronicles," in *The Chronicler as Historian* (ed. M. Patrick Graham, et al.*Journal for the Study of the Old Testament Supplement 238*; Sheffield: Sheffield Academic Press, 1997).

[31] The reference to "their families increased greatly" (1 Chr 4:38), is not to be seen as contradicting the statement of 1 Chr 4:27, "his brothers did not have many children; so their entire clan did not become as numerous as the people of Judah." First Chronicles 4:27 is speaking of Simeon in comparison to Judah, while 1 Chr 4:38 is speaking of Simeonite clans in relation to themselves.

[32] The role of Yahweh in the Hagrite confederation battle is, however, debatable. Yahweh is said to intervene in the conflict rather than to instigate it (contra 1 Chr 5:26). However, even if Yahweh did not instigate the conflict, neither did he "sit on the sidelines" but became an active participant in the conflict, unlike in the wars of Simeon and that of Reuben against the Hagrites. It is possible that this section is simply an expansion of the account of 1 Chr 5:10. This may be inferred because the enemy, and the

sociological justification of the battle, while the latter is the theological interpretation of the results of the battle.[33] Although three of the battles are given sociological justification due to the numerical growth of the clans, two give contrasting theological reasons. The Transjordanian tribes are said to suffer defeat or victory dependent upon their response to Yahweh. In the Hagrite war (1 Chr 5:18–22), they are aided by Yahweh because they cried out to Yahweh, prayed and trusted. They are later defeated, and exiled, by Assyria because they were "unfaithful" to Yahweh and "prostituted themselves" to other deities (1 Chr 5:25–26).

In his recounting of the Transjordanian victory (1 Chr 5:18–22), the Chronicler uses three words which are rare in the rest of his work:

- בטח (trust) used only here and in 2 Chr 32:10.
- עתר (pray) used only here and in the context of Manasseh's prayer when taken captive to Babylon (2 Chr 33:13, 19).
- זעק (cry out) used only when the individual or group was under threat: Jehoshaphat in battle (2 Chr 18:31),[34] and when under threat from Moab and Ammon (2 Chr 20:9), and also Hezekiah and Isaiah when Jerusalem was threatened by Assyria (2 Chr 32:20). That this term is only used in Chronicles when the individual or group is under threat suggests that the battle was going against the Transjordanian tribes (note the phrase "they

---

results, are the same. However, the account in 1 Chr 5:18–22 implies a much more extensive conflict than that envisioned in 1 Chr 5:10. Both sides have increased in their number of allies. Reuben is joined by Gad and Manasseh. The Hagrites are joined by Jetur, Naphish and Nodab. The extent of victory appears to be greater, applying only here in the battle accounts to possessions, not just land. It is possible that this account reflects the on-going tribal conflicts in the Transjordanian region, Braun, *1 Chronicles*, 77. Braun, like Williamson, considers that this section "probably results from later editorial work."

[33] Wright suggests that the Chronicler's battle accounts are a gauge by which to judge the relationship of the regime to the ideal. Those far from the ideal of a faithful Davidic king, temple, and proper cult personnel lose battles, while those close to that ideal are victorious. He indicates that the Simeonite victory reflects the Chronicler's view of Hezekiah while the exile of the Transjordanian tribes reflects their apostasy. His analysis, however, fails to deal with the Reubenite victory in the days of Saul in which there was neither Davidic king nor temple. Wright, "Fight for peace," 151–158.

[34] The word is only used in Kings in 1 Kgs 22:32, again in the case of Jehoshaphat. The Chronicler, however, makes one significant alteration through the addition of the phrase "and Yahweh helped him; God lured them away from him." For the Chronicler, Jehoshaphat's "crying out" was a plea to Yahweh for help, which Yahweh answered. For the Deuteronomist, Jehoshaphat's cry could have been one of fear or panic, and it was the fear that made his pursuers recognise that this was not the king of Israel and so they left him. The Chronicler transforms Jehoshaphat into a man who turns to Yahweh, and is aided by Yahweh.

cried out to him *during the battle*" (בַּמִּלְחָמָה)) and it was only because of their cry for help that they gained a victory.[35]

The Chronicler's use of all three terms in one context must indicate the theological significance of these three acts. Victory in war and the gaining or ongoing possession of land only occur when a trusting people cry out to Yahweh who will then answer their cry. The fact that the only other occurrences of any of these words in his work resulted in the deliverance of the king, city, or nation indicates that, for the Chronicler, these three actions are indispensable to maintain possession of the land. What is equally significant is that in none of these instances is cultic ritual indicated as a factor in the deliverance.

This is shown also in the accounts of Jehoshaphat and Manasseh. Although Jehoshaphat's prayer was "before Yahweh" (2 Chr 20:3, 13, 18), and Yahweh's answer resulted in the cultic officials leading in praise (2 Chr 20:19), the sacrificial ritual was no where invoked. Even upon his victory, Jehoshaphat entered the temple with music (harps, lutes, trumpets), but no sacrifice is recorded (2 Chr 20:28). Manasseh was recorded as offering sacrifices after his return to Jerusalem (2 Chr 33:16), but the sacrifice itself was not an ingredient in either his prayer or his restoration.[36]

In the account of the exile of the Transjordanian tribes, the Chronicler again uses two words which are significant words in the remainder of his account.

- זנה (to be faithless) only in 1 Chr 5:25 and 2 Chr 21:11, 13 regarding the actions of Jehoram. Jehoram was "faithless" זנה, to Yahweh by presenting himself to other deities which resulted in rebellion by subject nations (2 Chr 21:8–10), attack by foreign nations (2 Chr 21:16–17), disease (2 Chr 21:18), dishonour and death (2 Chr 21:19–20).
- מַעַל (unfaithfulness) only speaks of the unfaithfulness of individuals to Yahweh, and in Chronicles it always ends in disaster. Achar and Saul are killed (1 Chr 2:7; 10:13), while Uzziah gets leprosy (2 Chr 26:16–18). Rehoboam and Ahaz's kingdoms are invaded and defeated (2 Chr 12:2; 28:19–22), Manasseh is deported to Babylon (2 Chr 33:19), while the leaders, priests and people are exiled (1 Chr 9:1; 2 Chr 36:14).[37]

Both terms indicate the response of individuals or groups to Yahweh. The contexts in which they occur also clearly indicate the negative consequences of

---

[35] Further terms used elsewhere in Chronicles are צעק (2 Chr 13:14), and קרא (2 Chr 14:11). Each of these events involved a person or group "crying out" for aid in the face of threats or from within a battle.

[36] This is consistent with Solomon's prayer in 2 Chr 6 which shows that the solution to every crisis is prayer towards the temple and confessing the name of Yahweh. This results in Yahweh "hearing from heaven," forgiving, and possibly restoring.

[37] The term is also used in 2 Chr 29:6; 30:7 in reflections on the actions of past generations.

these actions. That they are used here in one context, when they are not used in the same context elsewhere in his work,[38] indicates that the Chronicler was here using the example of the Transjordanian tribes for everything else that would happen in his later work. The response to Yahweh, either positive or negative, was to be the determining factor in either the people's prosperity and retention of land or of their poverty and exile.[39]

That the Chronicler places these incidents at the end of the Transjordanian section may indicate that he sought to imply that the land settlements recorded to that point also followed the same pattern. Thus when Simeon gained land, it was the result of faithfulness to Yahweh, even if that faithfulness is not explicitly spelt out.[40] Likewise, Reuben's initial victory over the Hagrites and dwelling in their land is also the result of faithfulness to Yahweh, for if they had been unfaithful they would have suffered defeat.[41]

This positioning of the data for Simeon and the Transjordanian tribes lead into the central theme of the Chronicler's genealogies: the place, position, and

---

[38] With the exception of "prayer" and "unfaithful" in regard to Manasseh (2 Chr 33:18–19).

[39] "As throughout Chr's history, however, one thing remains constant: victory in battle still follows faithfulness to Yahweh; defeat follows unfaithfulness," Wright, "Fight for peace," 165.

[40] Heard, *Echoes*, 3.1.3 and Wright, "Fight for Peace," 153, both indicate that Jabez' acquisition of land was the only acquisition based on peaceful means, i.e. prayer alone (1 Chr 4:9–10). Simeon used violence (Heard refers to Simeon's violence in Gen 49:5 as showing this tendency although he ignores Levi who is also mentioned and was "given" land in Josh 21 // 1 Chr 6), while Reuben/Manasseh use violence and prayer. Interestingly he omits "Reuben alone" on the assumption that this is the same event, and does not mention Gad at all, preferring the connection between Manasseh and Joseph who succeeds because of God's help (Gen 49:24–25). Although Heard attempts an intertextual reading, his selectivity should prompt caution in his conclusions.

[41] The significance of placing this incident with the Reubenites in the reign of Saul is uncertain. Saul lost his life for his unfaithfulness (1 Chr 10:13), but certain aspects of his reign indicate faithfulness to Yahweh. That Saul was able to dedicate to Yahweh plunder taken in battle (1 Chr 26:27–28), is an indication that Saul had been victorious in battle, and therefore he had been faithful. This indicates that Wright is incorrect when he states the necessity of a "Davidic king" for peace and prosperity. What this indicates is that a "faithful king" is required, and such a king Saul must have been at that time in the Chronicler's view, for his people gained a victory in battle. The exact relation of Saul's faithfulness to his people's victory in battle, presumably without him as it is a tribal rather than national conflict, is not clear. Elsewhere in Chronicles, the Chronicler holds the faithfulness or otherwise of the king to be the indicator of the faithfulness or otherwise of the people as a whole, and an indication of what the ultimate consequence for the people would be.

function of the Levites and sons of Aaron. The link between the accounts of the Transjordanian tribes and Levi is the phrase "to this day."

"TO THIS DAY" AND THE CHRONICLER'S PLAN

Both the Simeonite and Transjordanian sections conclude with the phrase "to this day." This phrase is located after the recounting of victory (1 Chr 4:41, 43), or defeat (1 Chr 5:26), and helps to establish the current situation of the tribe(s) as a consequence of the named victory or defeat.

The Chronicler uses the relative sizes of the armies of Simeon and the Transjordanian tribes to make a significant point. Simeon conquered and held "the hill country of Seir" (1 Chr 4:42), with only 500 men. By contrast the Transjordanian army numbered 44,760 (1 Chr 5:18), when it defeated the Hagrite alliance.[42] This, however, should not be taken to imply that it was the size of the army that enabled victory, for the Transjordanian tribes took 100,000 captives (1 Chr 5:21), and killed many others (1 Chr 5:22).[43] In both conflicts, victory was achieved against overwhelming odds. Victory in such situations is only possible through the actions of God (1 Chr 5:20), in response to the faithfulness of the people. Therefore, land is neither retained nor lost due to the size of the army but through the actions of God in response to the faithfulness or otherwise of the people. Simeon with its small numbers live in Seir "to this day" while the Transjordanian tribes, in spite of their large numbers who are "brave warriors, famous men, heads of families" (1 Chr 5:24), were later defeated and exiled "to this day" (1 Chr 5:26b).

---

[42] It is uncertain as to whether these incidents are a postexilic claim to land. Transjordan lay outside the province of Yehud, although it is possible that some (re)settlers had moved into what had been the traditional tribal territory of Simeon. It is possible that the Chronicler looked upon the lack of settlements within Transjordan by those associated with his community as evidence of the ongoing exile, "to this day," of these tribes. In the same way, it is possible that he saw the (re)settlers within traditional Simeon as confirmation of their, and Yahweh's, ongoing faithfulness.

[43] The precise understanding of the numbers in the Hebrew Bible has long challenged commentators. See: Alan R. Millard, "Large Numbers in the Assyrian Royal Inscriptions," in *Ah, Assyria . . . Studies in Assyrian History and Ancient Near Eastern Historiography Presented to Hayim Tadmor* (ed. Mordechi Cogan and Israel Eph'al; Jerusalem: Magnes Press, 1991); Ralph W. Klein, "How Many in a Thousand?," in *The Chronicler as Historian* (ed. M. Patrick Graham, et al.*Journal for the Study of the Old Testament Supplement 238*; Sheffield: Sheffield Academic Press, 1997); J. W. Wenham, "Large Numbers in the Old Testament," *TynBul* 17 (1967): 19–53.

This indicates that the phrase "to this day" is used by the Chronicler to emphasise his message to his readers. Japhet disagrees. Although noting that "to this day" is only found in the non-synoptic material in 1 Chr 4:42–43; 5:26, she nevertheless concludes, "the reference 'to this day' here is also derived from the Chronicler's source material; the vantage point of the narrative would be some period in the First Commonwealth."[44]

As such, she sees the phrase as having no special significance for the Chronicler.[45] Curtis regards "to this day" of 5:26 as a misunderstanding of "and the cities of the Medes" in the parallel text in 2 Kings,[46] while Johnstone suggests that the "to this day" of 1 Chr 4:43 indicates that the Simeonites, although dispossessed by David, have outlived the Davidic monarchy.[47] He, however, wants to define "this day" as the "time of the dawning of the eschatological return."[48] For Johnstone "this day" is not the Chronicler's present, but all the time since the return to Jerusalem authorised by Cyrus.

In the context of a relatively small population,[49] dominated by an imperial power and having been in recent history under threat from other potential imperial powers (Egypt and Greece), as well as the perception by some in the community that their neighbours were threats to their continued existence (as evidenced in the response of Ezra and Nehemiah to "foreigners"), the Chronicler is here emphasizing that the only way to gain or retain land is ongoing faithfulness to Yahweh, while any deviance from this faithfulness will result in disaster or exile.

It has been stated, above, that the Simeonites and Reubenites gain victory in battle and increase their landholdings without any reference to the cult, its officials or sacrifices. Likewise, the three Transjordanian tribes of Reuben, Gad and one-half Manasseh have a victory over their enemies when they cry out to Yahweh. Jehoshaphat's prayer also led to victory, without resort to the cult or its officials, although the prayer was made within the temple and cultic officials were present (2 Chr 20:13–14, 19).

This victory and gaining of land, however, is to be contrasted with the place of the Transjordanian tribes after their unfaithfulness and exile. Immediately after relating that the Transjordanian tribes are still in exile "to this day" (1 Chr 5:26),

---

[44] Japhet, *Chronicles*, 126. As mentioned above, this phrase is not found in 2 Kgs 17:6; 18:11.
[45] So also Braun, *1 Chronicles*, 68.
[46] Curtis and Madsen, *Chronicles*, 126.
[47] Johnstone, *Chronicles: Volume 1*, 69.
[48] Johnstone, *Chronicles: Volume 1*, 81.
[49] For a discussion of the population of postexilic Yehud, see Charles E. Carter, *The Emergence of Yehud in the Persian Period: A Social and Demographic Study* (JSOTSup 294; Sheffield: Sheffield Academic Press, 1999), 172–213.

the Chronicler begins his account of the "sons of Levi" (1 Chr 5:27 [6:1]), a group who were to be active in the temple, and specifically the sons of Aaron who were to make "atonement" for all Israel. The linking of these two concepts, "unfaithfulness" and "atonement" is not accidental, but appears to be a deliberate action by the Chronicler in indicating that the solution to unfaithfulness, and its consequences, is the cult, its sacrifices and atonement.

If this conclusion is correct, then this indicates that the genealogies were not produced merely, or even primarily, to present the community's past,[50] or to legitimate its present leaders.[51] Neither is their order of presentation to be reduced to matters of geography,[52] or the status of the various tribes within the post-exilic community.[53] They were instead produced and shaped, in part at least, to present a theology of land retention to the Chronicler's generation when either external threats or internal unfaithfulness appeared to challenge the community's perception of their hold on the land.[54] It is apparent from the Chronicler's presentation, that land retention or loss "to this day" is connected to the faithfulness or unfaithfulness of the people.

Johnstone, however, looks beyond the report of the Transjordanian exile to what he sees as the Chronicler's ultimate solution to the people's failure to be faithful when he points out that immediately after the מַעַל (unfaithfulness), and exile of the Transjordanian tribes the Chronicler presents the full compliment of Levi: priests, Levites, and singers (1 Chr 5:27–6:32 [6:1–47]), working in the tabernacle to present "atonement."[55]

This pattern appears to be followed also in:

- First Chronicles 9:1–21 where, after the unfaithfulness of Judah and its exile, the community appears in Jerusalem with the full complement of cultic officials, including the gatekeepers.
- First Chronicles 10:13–14 where, after Saul's death due to his unfaithfulness, David becomes king, brings the ark to Jerusalem (1 Chr 13, 15–16), prepares to build the temple (1 Chr 22, 28), and organises the cultic officials (1 Chr 23–26).

---

[50] Contra Selman, Martin J. Selman, *1 Chronicles* (TOTC; Leicester: Inter-Varsity Press, 1994), 85–89.

[51] Williamson, *Chronicles*, 39.

[52] So Johnstone, Johnstone, *Chronicles: Volume 1*, 70, and contra Braun who states, "the order here seems to be in part one of preeminence, in part geographical, in part unknown," *1 Chronicles*, 10.

[53] Jonathan E. Dyck, *The Theocratic Ideology of the Chronicler* (Leiden: Brill, 1998), p. 128–129.

[54] This was clearly part of the intention of the authors of Ezra and Nehemiah resulting from the issue of foreign wives (Ezra 9:13–15; Neh 13:25–27).

[55] Johnstone, *Chronicles and Exodus*, 110.

- First Chronicles 21, where David, after he recognised his sin before Yahweh by counting his available fighting men, built an altar and offered sacrifices (1 Chr 21:26, 28). Yahweh saw the actions of David within a cultic context and ended the plague.[56]
- Second Chronicles 29, where after the results of Ahaz' unfaithfulness, Hezekiah purified the temple and "brought in the priests and the Levites" (1 Chr 29:3), to oversee the work before the Passover could be celebrated (1 Chr 30).
- Second Chronicles 33, where, after his return from Babylon, Manasseh rebuilds the altar of Yahweh and presents sacrifices (1 Chr 33:16).
- Second Chronicles 34, where, after Amon's unfaithfulness, Josiah gives money to the high priest, which has been collected by Levites and doorkeepers, for the restoration of the temple under the supervision of the Levites (2 Chr 35: 9–13). Only after this is the Passover celebrated (2 Chr 35).
- The book ends on the same note. After the unfaithfulness of the people (2 Chr 36:14), they were exiled, yet an opportunity to return and "build a temple" for Yahweh (2 Chr 36:23), is given.[57]

What these suggest is that just as unfaithfulness brings judgement, and judgment brings exile; so also do humility and prayer bring return and restoration Return and restoration then lead to the individual or nation having the right attitude and action towards the cult, its observances and sacrifices.[58] That the

---

[56] That the Chronicler recognised the technical incorrectness of David's actions is clear. He brings the reader's attention to the fact that the tabernacle was elsewhere, but David was unable to go to it to offer sacrifice for atonement in the authorised manner (1 Chr 21:29–30). The Chronicler makes clear as well, that in these extraordinary circumstances, Yahweh accepted what was not strictly lawful. This principle is also confirmed by the actions of Hezekiah (2 Chr 30:17–20), when many who were not ritually clean were still able to partake of the Passover because they "set their hearts on seeking Yahweh, even if they are not clean according to the rules of the sanctuary" (2 Chr 30:19).

[57] Although the decree of Cyrus does not mention it, the list of returnees implies that temple officials were integral to this reconstruction (Ezra 2:36–58). The return under Ezra is much more explicit (Ezra 7:13, 24), in listing the proper cultic officials who, as soon as they arrive in Jerusalem "sacrificed burnt offerings" (Ezra 8:35). It must also be noted that not every act of unfaithfulness is (or even could be), atoned for, for the Transjordanian tribes remain in exile, without priest, Levite, or atonement. However, the structure of the genealogies is such that, if those in exile were to humble themselves and pray, restoration and return from exile would follow.

[58] If this observation is correct, then it may also explain the purpose of the conclusion to the Chronicler's work (2 Chr 36:22–23). Although Williamson dismisses this as a later addition to Chronicles for liturgical purposes, the giving of hope, or to guide the reader to where the next stage of the nation's story could be found in the book of Ezra, *Chronicles*,

Transjordanian tribes were still in exile "to this day" is an indication that the prayer and humility required for restoration had not been achieved. That the text follows with the ministry of the Levites and the sons of Aaron is an indication that when/if the Transjordanian tribes do humble themselves and pray, then atonement is available through the cult, and restoration will be accomplished.

Atonement is thus only necessary when a person, clan, tribe or people have been "unfaithful." This may further explain why Simeon and the Transjordanian tribes were victorious in their early wars without reference to the cult. Being dwellers in the land, rather than exiles from it, they were not "unfaithful," but "faithful." Their victories in battle and the expansion of their territories being signs of that faithfulness. If they were faithful, they did not require the atonement that the cult provided. It is only through acts of unfaithfulness that atonement becomes a necessity.

This may also indicate why the Chronicler was compelled to present his data in the order in which he did. In 1 Chr 4:24–5:22, all of the victories are recorded first. Although exile is mentioned (1 Chr 5:6, 22b), the reasons for this exile are only presented at the end (1 Chr 5:25–26). Acts of "unfaithfulness" therefore only entered the picture at the end of the account, and resulted in an immediate defeat and exile. This order of presentation is important. Although it would have been possible for the Chronicler to mention the unfaithfulness of the Reubenites in relation to their exile (1 Chr 5:6), this would have placed acts of "unfaithfulness"

419, this judgment is too harsh. This passage is consistent with the Chronicler's understanding that unfaithfulness, judgment, and restoration must be followed by proper attention to the cult through which atonement is found. The first three elements are contained in the Chronicler's work: unfaithfulness (2 Chr 36:11–14), judgement (2 Chr 36:16–21), and restoration, with the implication from the Chronicler's writing that this was in response to the turning of the people to Yahweh in humility and prayer (2 Chr 36:22–23). It is perhaps better to see this quotation from Ezra 1:1–3 as a call for the postexilic Yehudite community to give proper attention to the temple, its cult and officials. Having been the recipients of Yahweh's mercy through now being enabled to dwell in the land, they must now "go up" to the temple, not to build it as Cyrus' decree in Ezra 1:3 proclaims, but to worship at it, to receive atonement, and to support the temple personnel through their offerings. That lack of support was, at times, a threat to the ongoing viability of the temple in Jerusalem is clear from Neh 13:10; Mal 3:8–10. It is possible that the Chronicler's conclusion is partly aimed at addressing this issue. Kalimi's suggestion that the ending is "to be seen as a practical 'Zionistic' encouragement of the Chronicler for immigration . . . from the existing Jewish communities in Babylon and Egypt" back to Yehud is also attractive, *Ancient Israelite Historian*, 153. It would, however, demand further reinterpretation of the work, for Chronicles would no longer be written for the community in Yehud, or perhaps even by a scribe within postexilic Yehud, but for, and perhaps by, a scribe within the exilic community who is encouraging a return to Yehud by those who are yet in "exile."

among the Transjordanian tribes prior to their victory over the Hagrite coalition. In the Chronicler's scheme, this would be an impossibility. Acts of unfaithfulness bring judgement. It would therefore have been impossible for the Chronicler to present unfaithfulness and exile prior to presenting Yahweh's giving of victory over the Hagrite coalition.

Although the Chronicler does present a person who committed acts of unfaithfulness later being blessed by Yahweh, these accounts always respond to the unfaithfulness with an act of judgment, and precede the blessing with an act of humility. In 2 Chr 12 Rehoboam is established as king, strays from Yahweh, and is defeated in battle by Shishak. He later hears a prophetic word (2 Chr 12:5), humbles himself and is not destroyed. The result is that he is allowed to remain in the land, although having to serve a foreign king (2 Chr 12:7–8, 12).

This indicates that there must be humility, prayer, or response to a prophetic word before there can be restoration and the receipt of blessings from Yahweh. If the Chronicler had mentioned the unfaithfulness of the Transjordanian tribes at an earlier point, he either could not have included their victory over the Hagrite coalition or he would have needed to introduce an act of humility, prayer or a prophetic word to which they responded. By presenting the material as he does, he leaves the Transjordanian tribes as faultless prior to their final unfaithfulness and exile, and with their ongoing exile opens the way for the introduction of his central themes of Levi, the sons of Aaron, and the cult.[59]

This mitigates against a mere geographical understanding for the representation of the tribes, for this arrangement would suggest that the Chronicler deliberately placed the Transjordanian material after that of Simeon, and the account of the Transjordanian unfaithfulness at the very end, in order to lead from a series of consequences of faithfulness as exhibited in the increase of numbers and the gaining of land to the consequences of the unfaithfulness of the Transjordanian generation which was exiled, to the remedy for unfaithfulness in the cultic system.

"Atonement," that is the performance of cultic rituals, should not be viewed as a substitute for faithfulness but as the solution to unfaithfulness leading to a renewed faithfulness, and for this the descendants of Levi played an essential role. This passage does present a more complex view than that suggested by Johnstone. The cult alone is inadequate without the proper response of the people to Yahweh in humility and trust. It is evident that while the people continue to live in "unfaithfulness," atonement will be impossible. It is the humbling of one's self (cf. Rehoboam, Manasseh) in prayer which leads to restoration, not the sacrifice as such. Yet the properly instituted cult should become a priority within

---

[59] It could also be surmised that the "crying out" in battle was the act of humility and repentance in the face of certain defeat.

the community that has truly been humbled and cried out to Yahweh. It is important to notice here that Rehoboam, unlike Manasseh, is not recorded as responding to Yahweh through the cult after he humbled himself. The last words about Rehoboam are "he did evil because he had not set his heart on seeking Yahweh" (2 Chr 12:14). This is, perhaps, an oblique reference to the fact that after receiving Yahweh's mercy Rehoboam did not respond to Yahweh through the cult and overlooked the need for atonement. This is in contrast to the actions of David and Manasseh.

By concluding 1 Chr 5 with the Transjordanian tribes in exile, the Chronicler is able to move uninterruptedly into an important part of the solution to the problem, which is the authorised cultic officials, working in the authorised cultic place, performing the authorised cultic duties.

Conclusion

In this section it has been observed that the Chronicler has shaped his presentation of four of the tribes (Simeon, Reuben, Gad, Manasseh) to express his theology of faithfulness to Yahweh. Those who through trust cry out to Yahweh in prayer are heard and Yahweh responds through enabling that group to expand their holdings of land and to retain those holdings. Those who turn from Yahweh in unfaithfulness, even if previously aided by Yahweh, will be turned out of their land by the actions of Yahweh. For those exiled there remains hope for atonement through the properly constituted cult in Jerusalem, and with atonement the restoration of land. Vital to all of this is the place of the cult. Although the cult is no automatic cure-all for the unfaithfulness of the nation, those who have been unfaithful and set themselves to return to Yahweh, will give evidence of that in their faithfulness to the cult, and in the cult, those who return to Yahweh in humility, will find atonement.

CHAPTER 7
D1: 1 CHRONICLES 7:1–40
TRIBES OF ISRAEL IN DEFEAT AND RESTORATION

INTRODUCTION

If, as has been proposed, the Chronicler's genealogies are presented in a chiastic pattern with the priests and Levites acting in accordance to their appointed function in the centre of the restored people (1 Chr 6:33–38 [6:48–53]), this indicates that the material presented in 1 Chr 7:1–40 is placed in the text so as to parallel the material in 1 Chr 4:24–5:26.

As was indicated in the previous chapter, 1 Chr 4:24–5:26 deals primarily with the gaining, losing, and retention of land. Land was gained and wars won when the people were faithful to Yahweh. Land and wars were lost when the people were unfaithful to Yahweh. Faithfulness to Yahweh resulted in gaining captives, land, towns, and material possessions. Unfaithfulness to Yahweh resulted in the loss of everything that had been gained as well as becoming the captive of another people and undergoing exile to a foreign land "to this day." Continuing faithfulness to Yahweh resulted in the continued presence of the people in the land "to this day."

STRUCTURE AND CONTENT OF 1 CHRONICLES 7

First Chronicles 7, like 1 Chr 4:24–5:26, contains a primarily military theme. Three tribes are listed in what appears to be a military muster list with totals of available fighting men. These lists contain no reference to land or possessions (Issachar: 1 Chr 7:1–5; Benjamin: 1 Chr 7:6–12; Asher: 1 Chr 7:30–40).

The genealogy of Naphtali, and possibly that of Dan, is placed prior to that of Manasseh (1 Chr 7:12b–13), and after the military muster lists of Issachar and Benjamin. For this (or these) tribe(s) there are no narratives, no successes or failures. Their existence is mentioned, but nothing more.

The descendants of Manasseh and Ephraim are recorded (1 Chr 7:14–27), but there is no reference to a military muster. These lists are followed by a list of towns and settlements (1 Chr 7:28–29). The list of Ephraim contains the interesting and puzzling account of the deaths of Ezer and Elead who were killed in a raid upon the Gittites (1 Chr 7:21–22). After their death, the beginning of the genealogy of Joshua son of Nun is presented.[1] What is significant, is the observation that the land and settlements of Ephraim and Manasseh are only recorded after the deaths of Ezer and Elead and after the recorded birth of Joshua son of Nun.[2] Like the genealogies as a whole, this section may also be portrayed in a chiastic manner.

Figure 7.1: The Chiastic Structure of 1 Chronicles 7

A   Tribes of Israel mustered for battle (1 Chr 7:1–12)
  B   The people of Yahweh in their generations (1 Chr 7:13–21a)
    C   Retribution upon the wicked (1 Chr 7:21b)
      D   Restoration of family (1 Chr 7:22–23)
      D^1 Building of towns (1 Chr 7:24)
    C^1 Provision of a godly warrior (1 Chr 7:25–27)
  B^1 The people of Yahweh in their land (1 Chr 7:28–29)
A^1 Tribes of Israel mustered for battle (1 Chr 7:30–40)

This structure indicates that the central focus of the Chronicler here is not upon armies, land or retribution. The central focus of the Chronicler here is the restoration of families and the building of towns. If this analysis is correct, then this structure suggests several things in regard to the Chronicler's purposes in this section. First, this structure suggests that the possession of powerful armies, of themselves, is not a guarantee of success on the battlefield. For this reason large armies are not at the centre of the community, but on the periphery. This was also seen in 1 Chr 5:20 where, in spite of their 44,760 men (1 Chr 5:18), the Transjordanian tribes were being defeated in battle until they cried out to Yahweh for help. Only then were they able to defeat their enemies and gain the land and possessions of their enemies. Further, the terms used to describe the heads of the Manassite family; "brave warriors, famous men, and heads of their families" (1 Chr 5:24), indicate that the quality of the warrior is of no value in the face of unfaithfulness within the community (1 Chr 5:25). Unfaithfulness brings defeat, irrespective of the size of the army, while faithfulness brings victory.[3] This is born out in 1 Chr 4:27 where the Chronicler indicates that the Simeonites "did not become as numerous as the people of Judah" yet were able to defeat their

---

[1] Here alone in the Hebrew Bible "Non," נון, rather than the more regularly observed "Nun," נון.

[2] First Chronicles 7:24 does mention the towns built by Sheerah prior to the recorded birth of Joshua, however, this is also after the deaths of Ezer and Elead.

[3] Wright, "Fight for peace," 165.

enemies (1 Chr 4:39, 41, 42), and remain in their conquests "until this day" (1 Chr 4:43).[4]

Second, the people of Yahweh and their land cannot be separated, for the people are still listed in their generations alongside their land (B // B[1]). Even though some of the people may be in exile from their land, it is their land nonetheless. First Chronicles 9:2 indicates this when it says that the people resettled "on their own property in their own towns." This suggests that, for the Chronicler, the land was theirs even while in exile.[5]

Third, wicked behaviour is judged, while right behaviour brings blessings of land. The former is clearly indicated in the text. Ezer and Elead went on a raiding party to steal other people's cattle and suffered death as a result. As such, they received what their actions deserved. The blessings of right behaviour, however, are only hinted at in the text through the mention of Joshua, the Israelite leader of the conquest. This is the only reference to Joshua in Chronicles, and like Moses, he is a minor character in the Chronicler's story. The reference to Joshua here is probably meant as a foil to the account of Ezer and Elead. Joshua was the man, chosen by Yahweh, who led the people into the land, conquered it and divided it among the people of Yahweh. The book of Joshua presents him as almost faultless, the exception being the account of the Gibeonite deception in Josh 9 where the people "did not enquire of Yahweh" (Josh 9:14).[6]

Fourth, suffering is followed by restoration of family and lands. It is uncertain here if the Chronicler is intending to show that the "mourning" of

---

[4] This theme of victory in the face of overwhelming odds also occurs in 2 Chr 13:2b–18; 14:8–15; 20:1–30; 32:1–23. In each instance, crying out to Yahweh or prayer to Yahweh by the people is central to the victory.

[5] I appreciate the difficulties which arise through the use of the word "exile," however for our purposes here it refers to those members of the Israelite tribes and their descendants who had been deported from their land, from the time of the Babylonian conquest until the time of Cyrus' decree. On the methodological, historical and interpretational issues which arise through the use of "exile" see the various studies in Lester L. Grabbe, ed., *Leading Captivity Captive: 'The Exile' as History and Ideology* (*Journal for the Study of the Old Testament Supplement 278*; Sheffield: Sheffield Academic Press, 1998).

[6] The word used in Josh 9:14 is שאל. The Chronicler uses this word to speak of Saul's consultation with a medium (1 Chr 10:13), David's inquiring of God (1 Chr 14:10, 14), and Solomon's request for wisdom rather than wealth and fame (2 Chr 1:7, 11). A more common word by the Chronicler for asking, seeking or inquiring of someone is דרש. It is clear that, for the Chronicler, seeking Yahweh is a major theme and the failure to "seek Yahweh" brings destruction (1 Chr 10:14; 15:13; 2 Chr 25:15), see especially Rodney K. Duke, *The Persuasive Appeal of the Chronicler: A Rhetorical Analysis* (JSOTSup 88; Sheffield: Almond Press, 1990); Christopher Begg, "'Seeking Yahweh' and the Purpose of Chronicles," *LS* 9 (1982): 128–141.

Ephraim is connected to the behaviour of his sons or simply over their deaths. It is evident that that this "mourning" brought about the restoration. אבל (mourn) is used only twice in Chronicles. Here in 1 Chr 7:22 and in 2 Chr 35:24 where "all Judah and Jerusalem mourned for Josiah." The latter mourning did not bring with it restoration, for what follows is the destruction of the nation. However, in Isaiah 19:8 the Egyptians אבל (mourn) with the ultimate consequence of blessing upon Egypt. The Egyptians will speak the language of Canaan and swear allegiance to Yahweh (Isa 19:18), while an altar to Yahweh with appropriate worship (Isa 19:19–21) will be built. Finally, Egypt, along with Assyria and Israel, will be the people and inheritance of Yahweh (Isa 19:24–25). Isaiah 61:1–3 also speaks of mourning as one of the causes or prerequisites of a reversal of fortune. It is possible, but uncertain, therefore that the Chronicler had this idea of mourning over evil (both the actions of Ephraim's sons and the consequences of their actions) which brought about the reversal.[7]

Furthermore, if this analysis of the Chronicler's presentation in this chapter is correct, this indicates that the order of tribal presentation is based not on Num 26 or any other list,[8] or upon geographical positioning.[9] The order of the material, and the material itself, are shaped in such a manner as supports the Chronicler's theme and purpose of "seeking Yahweh."

---

[7] See further Anthony Oliver, "אבל," in *New International Dictionary of Old Testament Theology and Exegesis: Volume 1* (ed. Willem A. VanGemeren; Grand Rapids: Zondervan, 1997), 243–248; G. Johannes Botterweck and Helmer Ringgren, *Theological Dictionary of the Old Testament* (TDOT; trans. John T. Willis; vol. 1; Grand Rapids: Eerdmans, 1974), 44–48. Furthermore, although the origins of the account of the deaths of Ephraim's sons is unknown, it has certain parallels with the report of Joseph's death to Jacob in Gen 37:34–35. In both the person mourns. The mourning is for "many days" (this phrase is connected with mourning in only these two accounts), and the comforters are relatives, in Genesis "sons and daughters" (the sons being the brothers of Joseph), while in Chronicles the comforters are Ephraim's "brothers." For an alternate view see Rudolt-E. Hoffmann, "Eine Parallele zur Rahmenerzählung des Buches Hiob in I Chr 7:20–29," *ZAW* 92 (1980): 120–132, with a rejoinder by Rudolph, "Lesefrüchte," *ZAW* 93 (1981): 291–292.

[8] Contra Noth, *Chronicler's History*, 36–42. This also renders unnecessary Noth's hypothesis of massive disruption and dislocation within the text or corruption of the text. Also, this conclusion is opposed to Williamson who states, "no particular significance appears to attach to the internal order of the chapter, which may have been dictated by the order of the Chronicler's extra-biblical source," Williamson, *Chronicles*, 76.

[9] Contra Japhet, *Chronicles*, 9.

THE ARMIES OF YAHWEH

As stated above, it has been suggested that the lists for Issachar, Benjamin and Asher reflect military muster lists which the Chronicler has incorporated into his genealogical data.[10] The lists share certain characteristics:
- Each list begins with the tribal founder and his immediate offspring.[11]
- Issachar and Benjamin follow through the descendants of one or more offspring,[12] giving numerical totals for each clan. Issachar follows the sons of Tola and Uzzi through Izrahiah,[13] while Benjamin follows Bela, Beker, and Jediael through Bilhan.

---

[10] Johnson, *Purpose*, 60–68.

[11] The list for Asher in 1 Chr 7:30–31a is identical to that found in Gen 46:17 with the exception of a conjunction ו and a plené spelling for "their sister" אֲחוֹתָם. Numbers 26:44–47 contains all of these names except the second "Ishvah." Serah, instead of being the sister of the brothers is identified as the daughter of Asher and is placed after the sons of Beriah instead of with her four brothers as in Genesis and Chronicles. The list for Issachar has two variations from both Gen 46:13 and Num 26:23–24. Chronicles reads the second son as פוּאָה while both Genesis and Numbers have פֻּוָה. The third son is יָשִׁיב, while in Numbers it is יָשׁוּב and in Genesis יוֹב. ו and י are commonly confused in the Chronicler's lists, and the LXX of Gen 46:13 reads Ιασουβ, suggesting a textual corruption in the Hebrew tradition at this point. The list for Benjamin is more difficult as only two of the names of Benjamin's immediate offspring, and none of his later descendants, are known from other sources. Benjamin's firstborn "Bela" is common to the lists in Num 26:38; Gen 46:21; 1 Chr 8:1. Beker occurs in Gen 46:21 (where the LXX reads Χοβωρ, either a transposition of the first two letters or reflecting a common misreading of ב and כ), in second place between Bela and Ashbel. (For another instance of the LXX transposing letters in a name see 1 Chr 7:37 were the LXX reads Σοβαλ for בֶּצֶר). However, in 1 Chr 8:1 Bela is the firstborn and Ashbel the second in a numbered list. It is possible, however, that "Beker" is a misreading of "firstborn," as they share the same spelling בכר. If a following conjunction ו was misread as the possessive pronoun of a preceding noun, or vice versa, then "his firstborn" and "Beker and" could easily become confused. See further the discussion in Excursus 2.

[12] Curtis suggests that the Benjamin list originally appeared in the text as a Zebulun list but through a series of misunderstanding and corruptions was transformed, *Chronicles*, 145–149. This, he suggests, accounts for the appearance of two separate Benjamin lists, and the absence of Zebulun. He further suggests that Dan should appear in 1 Chr 7:12, thus accounting for the full complement of tribes. I follow the majority of commentators in rejecting this hypothesis in regards to Zebulun.

[13] That the Issachar lists indicate totals for Tola as well as for his grandson Izrahiah suggests that these numbers, if genuine, reflect different censuses at different historical periods. 7:2 states that the census of Tola's descendants was "during the reign of David" leading Hill to conclude that the origins of this part of the list was David's census (2 Sam 24), *Chronicles*, 150.

- Issachar and Asher conclude with totals for the entire group, unlike Benjamin, whose numberings are only based on the clan, with no tribal total given.

The lists also contain similar military terms and terminology.

- ראש בֵּית אָב (heads of families). This phrase and its variations occur in military contexts in 1 Chr 5:24 (X2); 7:2, 7, 9, 40. Outside of Chronicles it occurs in a military context in Num 1:4, 7:2. Although the phrase is not used exclusively in military contexts,[14] when it does appear in military contexts it gives the suggestion that the "heads of families" were also the leaders of the army. The phrase ראש אָב occurs in a military context also in 1 Chr 7:11; 26:26; 27:1.[15] These last two occurrences suggest that in the Chronicler's understanding, the "heads of families" were considered to be, in David's time, "the commanders of thousands, and commanders of hundreds."[16] This leads Johnson to conclude, "in Chronicles, and especially in the genealogies, the 'heads of fathers' houses' are given one main characteristic: they are military commanders."[17]

- גִּבּוֹרֵי חַיִל (fighting men; 1 Chr 5:24; 7:2, 5, 7, 9, 11, 40; 8:40).[18] "This combination can mean someone who is exceptionally strong and/or valiant . . . someone who is exceptionally capable and or/ industrious . . . or someone who is wealthy . . . sometimes one who possesses a large amount of land."[19]

Like "heads of families" the phrase does not demand a military connotation unless the context determines it, thus Boaz (Ruth 2:1), Kish (1 Sam 9:1), and

---

[14] The phrase ראש בֵּית אָב, and its variations, also occurs in: Exod 6:14; Num 17:18; 25:15; Josh 22:14; 1 Chr 5:15; 9:9, 13; 23:24; 24:4; Ezra 10:16.

[15] It also occurs in 1 Chr 9:9, which appears to be a mixture of the two: רָאשֵׁי אָבוֹת לְבֵית אֲבֹתֵיהֶם. So also 1 Chr 23:24, which reverses this order: לְבֵית אֲבֹתֵיהֶם רָאשֵׁי הָאָבוֹת.

[16] Cf. 2 Chr 26:12, where the "heads of families" are "over the fighting men." There is probably little difference in meaning and function between the "head of the fathers" and the "head of the house of the fathers." Both groups are seen to be leaders, officials, decision makers and, when necessary, leaders of the army. It is probable that the simple use of "chief," ראש, in 1 Chr 7:3 for the sons of Izrahiah also reflects this usage, for 1 Chr 7:4 goes on to speak of the number of men "ready for battle."

[17] Johnson, *Purpose*, 63.

[18] The phrase is also used of individuals, rather than just groups: Gideon (Judg 6:12); Jephthah (Judg 11:1); David (1 Sam 16:18); Naaman (2 Kgs 5:1); Zadok (1 Chr 12:28); Eliada of Benjamin (2 Chr 17:17). The phrase is found 41X in the Hebrew Bible, 25 of them in Chronicles.

[19] Robin Wakely, "גבר," in *New International Dictionary of Old Testament Theology and Exegesis: Volume 1* (ed. Willem A. VanGemeren; Grand Rapids: Zondervan, 1997), 810.

Jeroboam (1 Kgs 11:28), were each a "man of standing," and priests, gatekeepers, and others could be "able men" (1 Chr 9:13; 26:6, 31; Neh 11:14). The phrase can also be used to indicate those who are wealthy (2 Kgs 15:20).[20] In military contexts, the "fighting men" are differentiated from the "heads of families" and "chiefs" (1 Chr 7:11; 2 Chr 26:12), and in certain contexts are differentiated from the regular army (Josh 8:3; 10:7).[21] The phrase is also used to signify David's "mighty men" (1 Chr 11:26).[22] This may suggest that, for the Chronicler, all of those listed in the muster lists were the equivalent of David's "mighty men," and were equally capable of great military accomplishments.

- צְבָא מִלְחָמָה (men ready for battle; 1 Chr 7:4, 11, 40; 12:34, 37, 38 [12:33, 36, 37]).[23]

---

[20] Japhet suggests that the meaning has less to do with military matters and refers more to "men of property," *Chronicles*, 140. Braun prefers "valiant men" but admits that the phrase "regularly ha[s] military associations," *1 Chronicles*, 70, 78. Eising rejects the idea of wealth or property holders as the primary meaning of חַיִל for "it would be hard to characterize the 30,000 men led by Joshua against Ai (Josh. 8:3) . . . as wealthy property owners," in G. Johannes Botterweck and Helmer Ringgren, *Theological Dictionary of the Old Testament* (TDOT; trans. David E. Green; vol. 4; Grand Rapids: Eerdmans, 1980), 351; see further Robin Wakely, "חיל," in *New International Dictionary of Old Testament Theology and Exegesis: Volume 2* (ed. Willem A. VanGemeren; Grand Rapids: Zondervan, 1997), 119–120.

[21] That the "fighting men" may have been considered separately from the "regular army" may suggest that when the Transjordanian tribes crossed the Jordan river to assist in the conquest of the land (Josh 1:12–15), that not all the able bodied men were required to go, but only those designated as "fighting men." Even if the numbers given are discounted, the 40,000 of Josh 4:13 who crossed to aid in the battle is about one third of those available according to the census in Num 26: Reuben: 43,730; Gad: 40,500; Manasseh: 52,700 (Num 26:7, 18, 34). Allowing for one-half of Manasseh to settle on the east side of the Jordan, this would give an available figure (based upon the figures in Num 26) of 110,580. Even if the figures in Numbers simply represent the relative sizes of the tribes at some point in history (cf. 44,760 of 1 Chr 5:18 at the time of the Hagrite war, and the 120,000 of 1 Chr 12:37 in the time of David), this disparity may suggest the various authors' view that the Transjordanian wives and children were not left defenceless during the period of the conquest, but had the "militia" available for protection, see further Woudstra, *Joshua*, 93; Donald H. Madvig, "Joshua," in *The Expositor's Bible Commentary Volume 3* (ed. Frank E. Gaebelein; Grand Rapids: Zondervan, 1992), 258. Hess, however, states that these reflect simply "40 armed groups." Richard S. Hess, *Joshua* (TOTC; Leicester: Inter-Varsity Press, 1996), 113.

[22] However, the more common designation is simply הַגִּבֹּרִים (1 Chr 11:11, 12, 24; 28:1).

[23] The phrase, or variations of it, occurs only also in Num 31:14, 21; 32:27; Josh 4:13; Isa 13:4.

- בְּרוּרִים (choice men; 1 Chr 7:40). The more common meaning of ברר is "pure, clean and therefore comes to mean something that is choice, special."[24] It is sometimes used of being chosen for a task (1 Chr 9:22; 16:41). Goliath's challenge to Israel to "choose a man to fight" indicates that being "chosen" can refer to combat (1 Sam 17:8).[25] The idea here seems to be that these warriors were chosen to their position on the basis of their ability or conduct, rather than on their family ties or wealth. Yet they were still "heads." This raises the question as to whether they were appointed to their position as "heads" on the basis of their fighting skills. They are also called "chief of the princes." Did their fighting skills distinguish them from all others, leading to their superiority among their brothers? This is probably the only word that separates the descriptions of the three tribes.[26]

- גְּדוּד (raider; 1 Chr 7:4).[27] "Its basic meaning is a group or band of military personal *(sic)*, and it most often refers to small parties of loosely organized

---

[24] Richard E. Averbeck, "ברר," in *New International Dictionary of Old Testament Theology and Exegesis, Volume 1* (ed. Willem A. VanGemeren; Grand Rapids: Zondervan, 1997), 773.

[25] BHS suggests that this should read בחר, cf. Smith, *Samuel*, 155.

[26] It must be noted that these statements, and the muster total given for Asher in 1 Chr 7:40, appear differently to those of either Issachar or Benjamin. For Issachar and Benjamin subtotals are given for particular clans while listing only two generations, while for Asher, only one total is given after as many as seven generations. This may suggest that 1 Chr 7:40 was not originally part of the genealogy listed in 1 Chr 7:30–39. It is possible that the Chronicler had a genealogical list for Asher and a military muster total for Asher and combined the two in this chapter to express his theological and ideological purposes. It is also possible that Asher composed their census differently to the others. If the census was not "national" but "regional," each tribe may have been free to report it as they chose. Although Williamson and Hill seek to see in the lower totals for Asher (26,000), especially in relation to the totals in Numbers (41,500 in Num 1:40–41; 53,400 in Num 26:47) evidence for the misfortunes of Asher, the observation of Curtis that "the census here, however, is evidently confined to the clan of Heber" and therefore reflects not the entire tribe, but only a portion of one of the four clans, must be kept in mind. Curtis and Madsen, *Chronicles*, 156. Cf. Williamson, *Chronicles*, 82. Hill, *Chronicles*, 155. It must also be recognised that the 40,000 Asherites who came to make David king (1 Chr 12:36), represents a higher figure than any tribe except Zebulun and the combined Transjordanian tribes.

[27] BHS suggests amending גְּדוּדֵי to גִּבּוֹרֵי on the basis of the LXX reading ἰσχυροί. This is followed by the NIV "men ready for battle," NRSV "fighting force." This, I believe, is unnecessary and may have been influenced by a hesitation to ascribe to Issachar the task of being part of "raiding parties," particularly in the context of 1 Chr 7:21 where Ezer and Elead were killed during a raid on the men of Gath.

raiders . . . The goal of these groups was usually not conquest . . . but pillaging and robbery . . . [or] troops for hire."[28]

The Hebrew Bible normally uses this term pejoratively of those who attack Israel or Judah (Gen 49:19; 1 Sam 30:8, 15; 2 Kgs 5:2; 6:23; 13:20–21), hired mercenaries (2 Chr 25:9–13), or bandits (Hos 6:9; 7:1). David himself, however, had his raiding bands (2 Sam 3:22; 1 Chr 12:18), and it appears that they could be incorporated into the regular army (2 Chr 26:11). The word occurs only here in the genealogies, so may indicate that this group of Issachar were special bands, for special services, or perhaps even that they hired themselves out for wars with other nations. Their traditional geographical location in the centre of the northern kingdom of Israel, being the buffer zone that the other tribes would bring against enemies, may speak against the impracticality of the former while giving allowance for the latter.

Census data are recorded in the Hebrew Bible on a number of occasions. Some are said to be for building public works (2 Chr 2:17–18),[29] while others are connected to the raising of funds for the central sanctuary (Exod 30:12; 2 Kgs 12:4).[30] Other censuses were conducted to organise the tabernacle personnel (Num 4:2, 21, 29). The recording of names in genealogies, which is possibly the official form of the census, is mentioned in 1 Chr 4:41; 5:17; 7:2. However, Num 1, 26 and 2 Sam 24 indicate that one of the primary reasons for performing a census was to determine the numbers available for military service.

That 2 Sam 24 was an enrollment of "fighting men" is indicated by David's sending Joab and the commanders of the army to perform the task, and that the total is of those who are "able-bodied (חיל) men who could handle a sword" (2 Sam 24:9).[31] The censuses in Num 1 and 26 are specifically stated to be of those

---

[28] Tremper Longman, "גדד," in *New International Dictionary of Old Testament Theology and Exegesis: Volume 1* (ed. Willem A. VanGemeren; Grand Rapids: Zondervan, 1997), 821.

[29] The source of this passage is 1 Kgs 5:13–16 which makes no mention of a census. However, 1 Chr 22:2 speaks of David assembling the "aliens living in Israel" whom he made into stonecutters. It is possible that the Chronicler viewed this assembling as a census by David, as opposed to the counting of the army in 1 Chr 21, and that Solomon's census here is yet another assembling of the aliens in order to assign them to further duties in the temple preparation.

[30] "Another counting, and quite possibly a periodic counting given the continuing needs of the Tabernacle, may be in view" John I. Durham, *Exodus* (WBC 3; Waco: Word, 1987), 402.

[31] So the NIV. The text simply says העם "the people," so NRSV. See also 2 Sam 24:3 where the NIV translates the same phrase as "troops." In the report of Joab (2 Sam 24:9) "the people" again appears in the text, yet the NIV translates as "fighting men." The translation of "fighting men" or "troops" throughout is no doubt determined by the work of

who "are able to serve in the army."[32] The census in Num 26 is particularly instructive because it is listed by tribal founder and tribal clans followed by the tribal total. This format is similar to that found in 1 Chr 7.[33]

On the evidence available, the data contained in 1 Chr 7 regarding Issachar, Benjamin and Asher do suggest that some form of military muster list(s) was/were utilised by the Chronicler.[34] They are likely to have been shaped by him in accordance with his purposes, yet as Braun states:

> The data ... are couched in the terminology of the military census list ... and suggests that it too had its origin in ... a military enrollment. Since there is no ostensible reason for the invention of such material, it should be assumed to rest upon ancient records.[35]

THE PEOPLE OF YAHWEH IN THEIR GENERATIONS AND IN THEIR LAND

The second level of the Chronicler's chiastic structure deals with the people of Yahweh in their generations and in their land. The generations of the people of Yahweh are contained in 1 Chr 7:13–21a,[36] while the land is contained in 1 Chr 7:28–29. This placing of people and land on the same chiastic level is also seen in the accounts of the Levites and their land, Levels E // E¹. The three tribes that are clearly included here are Naphtali, Manasseh, and Ephraim.

Joab and army commanders and by the observation that those counted were labelled "swordsmen," שֹׁלֵף חֶרֶב.

[32] Numbers 1:3, 20, 22, 24, 26, 28, 30, 32, 34, 36, 38, 40, 42, 45; 26:2.

[33] What is also instructive is that the military census contained in Num 26 is interrupted by the recounting of the rebellion of Korah, Dathan and Abiram (Num 26:8–11), as also are the lists in 1 Chr 5 with accounts of wars, victories and spoils of war (1 Chr 5:10, 18–22). Johnson points to the Safaitic inscriptions, dated to the first centuries B.C.E. and C.E., which contain, along with strictly genealogical data, accounts of wars, watering rights, and times of mourning, *Purpose*, 60–62. Consequently, narrative data cannot be rejected as being genuine to a list for it is apparent that in certain circumstances narrative material may be incorporated into a genealogical list in accordance with both the purpose of the list and the relevance of the narrative.

[34] These "lists themselves were organised in a genealogical form," Johnson, *Purpose*, 66.

[35] Braun, *1 Chronicles*, 119.

[36] Or, if Dan is postulated, 7:12b–21a. The issue of Dan's inclusion will be discussed below, the exact details of which tribes are included in this section is not as important as the observation that the people of Yahweh cannot be considered separately from their land.

NAPHTALI

As can be observed below, the Naphtalite genealogy is almost exactly as it occurs in Gen 46:24–25a. The only differences are in the use of vowel letters which are a common occurrence in Chronicles when compared to its sources. This has resulted, in the Massoretic tradition, of a variation in the pronunciation of Jahziel/Jahzel and Shillem/Shallum.

1 Chr 7:13 בְּנֵי בִלְהָה בְּנֵי נפתלי יחציאל וגוני ויצר ושלום
Gen 46:24–25 וּבְנֵי נַפְתָּלִי יַחְצְאֵל וְגוּנִי וְיֵצֶר וְשִׁלֵּם אֵלֶּה בְּנֵי בִלְהָה

The genealogy of Naphtali contains no additional information beyond what is contained in the source, and omits the detail that Bilhah was Laban's gift to his daughter Rachel contained in Gen 46:25, and the details of Rachel giving Bilhah to Jacob as a wife in order to raise a family (Gen 30:1–8). Bilhah, however, is the only wife of Jacob mentioned in the Chronicler's genealogies. The sisters Rachel and Leah are omitted as also is Jacob's other concubine Zilpah.

MANASSEH

Ephraim and Manasseh, unlike the twelve sons of Jacob, do not have any of their descendants recorded in Gen 46.[37] In that chapter they are simply the sons of Joseph (Gen 46:20). The only record of their descendants is in the list contained in Num 26:29–34 (Manasseh), and Num 26:35–37a (Ephraim). The list contained in 1 Chr 7:14–19 bears little relation to that in Num 26. The list in Num 26 mentions seven different clans, yet five clans are said to be the "sons" of Gilead,[38] who himself is the son of Makir.[39]

---

[37] Cf. the LXX of Gen 46:20b which reads "And there were sons born to Manasses, which the Syrian concubine bore to him, even Machir. And Machir begot Galaad. And the sons of Ephraim, the brother of Manasses; Sutalaam, and Taam. And the Sons of Sutalaam; Edom." This passage is important in that it indicates the mother of Makir was Syrian, as also in the LXX of 1 Chr 7:14 (only in 1 Kgs 11:1 is there another reference to a Συρα mentioned in the LXX). It is also probable that the LXX Σουταλααμ of Gen 46:20 is to be considered equivalent with Σωθαλαθ in 1 Chr 7:20, although the names listed in Gen 46:20 Σουταλααμ Τααμ Εδωμ are more closely related to Num 26:39–40: Σουθαλα Ταναχ Εδεν. It would appear then that the addition to the LXX of Gen 46:20 is a mixture based upon both the text of Numbers and that of 1 Chr 7:14.

[38] These same five clans (with Iezer becoming Abiezer) are also found in Josh 17:2.

[39] A constant claim throughout the Hebrew Bible is the association of Makir as the father of Gilead. Sometimes this is in the sense of a biological father (Num 26:29; 27:1; 36:1; Josh 17:3; 1 Chr 2:21, 23; 7:14, 17) while in other occurrences it is in the sense of a person or clan who controlled a territory (Num 32:39; Deut 3:15; Josh 13:31; 17:1).

In 1 Chr 7:14, Asriel is a "son" of Manasseh while in Num 26:31 he is a great grandson.[40] Zelophehad, who in Num 26:33 is a male with five daughters, in 1 Chr 7:15 becomes a female who is either a sister or wife of Makir.[41] Abiezer/Iezer, a son of Gilead in Numbers becomes a nephew, the son of his sister Hammoleketh, while Mahlah, daughter of Zelophehad and grandson of Hepher becomes a son of Hammoleketh.[42]

As Wilson has noted, genealogies do not necessarily reflect actual descendants but present day tribal relationships.[43] As such, this genealogy, with its variations reflects either a different time period, and the relationships that it brings, or else is serving a different function within the same time period as the other Manassite genealogies.

One thing that this genealogy does indicate is the existence of inter tribal marriage, for descendants of Manasseh married descendants of Benjamin (1 Chr 7:15).[44] Further, it indicates the existence of 'interracial' marriage, for Manasseh

---

[40] BHS suggests deleting Asriel on the basis of dittography: אשר ילדה "whom she bore" was repeated as אשריאל. This suggestion is simply to remove the genealogical difficulty, and has no textual basis. LXX has Ασεριηλ.

[41] The interpretation of Zelophehad's place is complicated. Braun points out that in Num 27:1 Zelophehad is a male, "ruling out the idea . . . that this individual might be considered a second wife or sister of Machir," *1 Chronicles*, 110. While this might be true historically, it is not necessarily true genealogically, for relationships, and genders, do change, cf. 1 Chr 1:36 where Timna, Esau's son's concubine, becomes one of Esau's grandsons. (The NIV masks this through reading "'by Timna: Amalek"). BHS here proposes that instead of אחתו "his sister" the reading should be אחתם "their sister." Note that the following word begins with a מ, and perhaps this was omitted and the ו inserted. The LXX has "his sister," but if the text had been "their sister" it would refer to the sister of Shuppim and Huppim, who are brothers in the tribe of Benjamin. Maacah then would be their sister whom Makir marries, and Makir is reported to have taken a second sister "Zelophehad" as well. This would also explain how the text could suggest that Makir had both a sister (1 Chr 7:15) and a wife (1 Chr 7:16) named Maacah.

[42] Although some of these instances may be examples of fluidity, some of these observations work on the very dubious method of assuming that every name located in a genealogy can refer to only one person, and that names did not repeat among the family.

[43] Wilson, *Genealogy*, 54. He states that at times changes in the genealogical relationships occur "if a segment attains more political power or more social status than its coordinate segments, its founding ancestor may move to a higher position in the lineage genealogy in order to indicate the segment's superiority to its former equals," (page 31). The elevation of Judah at the expense of Reuben in the Chronicler's genealogies is a case in point.

[44] Cf. 1 Chr 2:21-23 which indicates that a daughter of Makir also married into the Calebite clan of Judah. One very significant inter tribal marriage is reflected in Exod 6:23 where Aaron marries a daughter of Amminadab and sister of Nahshon. See further the discussion in Chapter 4, "Amminadab: The Son of Kohath?."

had an "Aramean concubine" (1 Chr 7:14). For both Ezra (Ezra 9–10), and Nehemiah (Neh 13:1–5, 23–28), this situation brought potential disaster upon the people. The Chronicler's stance, however, is less certain.

One important observation, however, is that in this genealogy there is no mention of land or armies. What is significant here is people: fathers, mothers, sisters, children. It is the human relationships which exist between Yahweh's people which are being described.

EPHRAIM

The Ephraimite list (1 Chr 7:20–29), is complex, and raises numerous questions.[45]

- What is the relationship between the beginning of this list (Shuthelah, Bered, Tahath) and that of Num 26:35 (Shuthelah, Beker, Tahan)? Do these reflect variations upon the same names,[46] which would indicate that this part of the list had been a horizontal genealogy of brothers which was read as a vertical genealogy of father/son?
- Is the list of 1 Chr 7:20–21a, a chiasm, and does this suggest that these were originally two separate lists, each indicating the sons of Ephraim in Num 26 as a long list of fathers/sons?[47]
- What is the relation of the first part of the list (1 Chr 7:20–21a), and the latter part (1 Chr 7:25–27)?
- Is the list in 1 Chr 7:25 a corruption of the list of Num 26?[48]
- Is Beriah, the son born to Ephraim connected to the Beriah of 1 Chr 8:12–13).[49]
- Is Sheerah the daughter of Beriah or the daughter of Ephraim?[50]

---

[45] See: Gerson Galil, "The Chronicler's Genealogy of Ephraim," *BN* 56 (1991): 11–14; Nadav Na'aman, "Sources and Redaction in the Chronicler's Genealogies of Asher and Ephraim," *JSOT* 49 (1991): 99–111.

[46] Myers, *I Chronicles*, 55. Williamson, *Chronicles*, 80.

[47] Na'aman, "Sources," 109. However, it must be noted that to do this, he must postulate that Bered and Zabad are both corruptions of Beker.

[48] Na'aman, "Sources," 109. Curtis feels similarly, but while Na'aman suggests that Resheph and Telah were shaped out of a corruption of Shuthelah, Curtis simply suggests that Telah is an abbreviation for Shuthelah, *Chronicles*, 154.

[49] Japhet, *Chronicles*, 182. If so, then is the Chronicler also indicating that the failure of Beriah's older brothers, has now become Beriah of Benjamin's success? But if this is the case, by what means did Beriah change family tribal affiliations? Why also was this not declared directly under Ephraim's line, to show the recovery from sin and the gaining of land? Wright suggests that the victory of Benjaminite Beriah in 1 Chr 8:13 "closes the event narrated" in 1 Chr 7:23, "Fight for peace," 156.

- Whose son is Rephah? Is he the son of Beriah, Ephraim, or Shuthelah (or one of his brothers if the vertical list of 1 Chr 7:20–21a should be read as a horizontal list of Ephraim's sons). The pronouns are ambiguous.
- On what basis is Nun declared to be the son of Elishama (1 Chr 7:26b), when no other source so indicates this connection.[51]
- Who are Ezer and Elead, and what relation are they to Ephraim?

The text as it stands indicates that both Ezer and Elead are the sons of Ephraim, son of Joseph. This, however, presents a number of difficulties:

- Because other sources indicate that Ephraim was born in Egypt (Gen 41:50–52), what were his sons doing in Canaan on a raid to steal cattle? Did the men of Gath raid from Canaan to Egypt?[52]
- Did Ezer and Elead raid from Egypt to Canaan?[53]
- Is the Ephraim recorded here a later descendant of the patriarch who shares the same name?[54]
- Is it possible that "Ephraim" here refers to the tribe as a whole?[55]

---

[50] While Sheerah as the daughter of Beriah would make the most sense as Beriah is the nearest referent to the term "his daughter," the Chronicler frequently places daughters at the end of a list, after all the sons are mentioned, even if the sons are younger than the daughter (cf. 1 Chr 5:29 [6:3]), "the children of Amram: Aaron, Moses, Miriam").

[51] Elishama son of Ammihud is regularly declared to be the leader of Ephraim during the exodus period (Num 1:10; 2:18; 7:48, 53; 10:22). Joshua is from the tribe of Ephraim (Num 13:8, 16). There is, however, no textual connection between Joshua and Elishama other than this, although it cannot be ruled out.

[52] Payne, "Chronicles," 358. Although not impossible, it seems unlikely that Gathite raiders would travel so far through inhospitable territory with other forces in the way in order to attack Egypt (cf. Exod 13:17), and the fortifications along the *Via Maris*, cf. Durham, *Exodus*, 185. Williamson rejects the idea of a raid on Goshen by the men of Gath, saying that it stretches "credulity to breaking point," *Chronicles*, 81.

[53] This is mentioned as a view of the "older commentators" by Curtis, without specifying which persons, *Chronicles*, 153. Although mentioned by Rudolph as a possibility, he rejects it asking "how a little Israelite group, in order to plunder livestock, could advance through the isthmus-desert, the Negeb, to Philistine Gath, which is almost as far as Jerusalem," *Chronikbücher*, 73. The idea that Ephraimites raided Canaan from Egypt has recently been restated by, Winfried Corduan, *I & II Chronicles* (Nashville: Holman Reference, 2004), 60.

[54] Keil, *Chronicles*, 141; Hill, *Chronicles*, 154. Braun's suggestion is similar. He suggests that this incident refers to a later time and involves a clan associated with Ephraim, *1 Chronicles*, 115, Curtis and Madsen, *Chronicles*, 154.

[55] "The father Ephraim, who mourned his sons, is the tribe Ephraim," Rudolph, *Chronikbücher*, 73. This option is to be rejected for Ephraim "went in to his wife," which

- Is this simply an anachronistic reference to Ephraim because of their importance in later history?[56]

The text as it stands clearly identifies the patriarch Ephraim with Ephraim, father of Ezer and Elead (1 Chr 7:20, 22), and also clearly places them in Canaan rather than Egypt.[57] The text further indicates that "his brothers" were also in Canaan, for they came to comfort him.[58]

There is no consensus among scholars on how to respond to each of these questions. The only consensus appears to be that this account is made up of divergent lists which the Chronicler has shaped according to a scheme of his own.

The more accepted understanding is that this passage is derived from three primary sources: the genealogy of Joshua (1 Chr 7:20–21a, 25–27),[59] the account of Ezer and Elead (1 Chr 7:21b–24), and the list of dwelling places (1 Chr 7:28–29).[60]

If this is accepted, then it must be concluded that the account of Ezer and Elead was deliberately placed within the Joshua genealogy in such a manner as to break that genealogy into two separate parts which the Chronicler no longer intended to be read as a continuous list, and that this insertion itself must be of significance for the structure of the passage as a whole.[61]

---

clearly indicates an individual, rather than the tribe as a whole, Williamson, *Chronicles*, 81; Keil, *Chronicles*, 141.

[56] Myers, *I Chronicles*, 55.

[57] As Selman notes, the phrase *"went down . . .* is inappropriate for a journey from Egypt to Canaan and the building of the two *Beth Horons* (v. 24) is a natural activity for a clan already resident in the area," *1 Chronicles*, 116.

[58] Although Ephraim only had one brother, the term can also be used to indicate wider family members, cousins, uncles, etc. It should not, however, be taken to mean his descendants (NIV is vague here when it says "his relatives," which can also refer to descendants). As such, the text states that Ephraim's extended family, not simply his own offspring, dwelt in the land of Canaan.

[59] If this is to be understood as a linear genealogy of Joshua, then other problems arise. Particularly important is the question as to why there are as many as seventeen generations from Ephraim to Joshua (eleven if the list of 7:20 is determined to have originally been a segmented genealogy read linearly) while the genealogies of the majority of those of the exodus generation list from three to five generations from the patriarch to the exodus participant. See further Gary A. Rendsburg, "The Internal Consistency and Historical Reliability of the Biblical Genealogies," *VT* 40 (1990): 185–206.

[60] Williamson, *Chronicles*, 80; Rudolph, *Chronikbücher*, 71–73. This is rejected by Na'aman who insists that the passage was built up from the core material concerning the birth of Beriah and the building activity of Sheerah, to which were added the Ephraimite genealogies, the genealogy of Joshua, and the settlements of Joseph, "Sources," 105–109.

[61] For the purposes then of understanding the Chronicler's themes and purposes, this also renders unnecessary the prehistory and development of these lists, and by what

If we ignore the divisions in the text based upon tribe (i.e. Issachar, Benjamin, Naphtali, Manasseh, Ephraim, Asher) and instead observe the thematic similarities that link the tribal accounts together, this confirms our previous observation that 1 Chr 7:20–21a is to be connected to the genealogies of Naphtali and Manasseh on the basis of a common theme (the people of Yahweh in their generations) just as 1 Chr 7:1–12, although detailing two separate tribes, was thematically related through the focus on the armies of Yahweh.

This also confirms our previous conclusions that, just as 1 Chr 7:30–40 are presented on the same level as 1 Chr 7:1–12 as representing the armies of Yahweh, so also is the account of the "lands and settlements" (1 Chr 7:28–29), to be viewed on the same level as 1 Chr 7:13–21a. While 1 Chr 7:13–21a presents the people of Yahweh in their generations, 1 Chr 7:28–29 present the people of Yahweh in their land. We have seen this juxtapositioning of land and people on the same level in chiastic structures in 1 Chr 6. First Chronicles 5:27–6:32 [6:1–47] presents the cultic servants of Yahweh in their generations while 1 Chr 6:39–66 [6:54–81] presents the cultic servants of Yahweh in their land. This pattern is repeated here.

THE LAND

First Chronicles 7:28–29 presents a list of territories that are the possessions of "the sons of Joseph."[62] Two of the towns (Naaran and Ayyah; 1 Chr 7:28), only occur here in the Hebrew Bible. Of the other three, Bethel and Gezer are presented in Josh 16:1–3 as the eastern and western most settlements respectively of the Joseph tribes.[63] Shechem is in "the hill country of Ephraim" (Josh 20:7),

---

process they came into the Chronicler's possession. What is significant here is what the Chronicler does with his sources, rather than the origins and function of the source. The historical reconstruction of the sources is of course of great importance for the understanding of the development and history of ancient Israel.

[62] Only here in the genealogies is the relationship between Joseph and Ephraim/Manasseh clarified. In the list of Israel's sons (1 Chr 2:1–2), neither Ephraim or Manasseh is listed, only Joseph. For the Chronicler's readers this clarification was not necessary, for their written records and their ancient traditions would have provided them with the knowledge of the relationship of Ephraim and Manasseh to Joseph, and thus to Israel.

[63] However, Josh 18:22 indicates that Bethel was a Benjaminite town and Neh 11:31 records it as a town to which Benjaminites returned. Judges 1:22–23 indicates that "the house of Joseph" conquered Bethel while Judg 4:5 says that its was "in the hill country of Ephraim. Judges 20:18; 21:2 indicates that Bethel was the town to which Israel went to enquire of Yahweh in their fight with Benjamin. It is unlikely that they would have gone to a Benjaminite shrine to enquire about fighting Benjamin. Bethel was also the place of the royal shrine of the northern kingdom (Amos 7:10–13; 1 Kgs 12:29). All of this suggests

and was a city of refuge. Each of the towns recorded in 1 Chr 7:29 were located in a Manassite enclave in the tribal land of Issachar and Asher (Josh 17:11), which, however, Manasseh never fully occupied (Josh 17:12).

What these two verses represent is the totality of Ephraimite and western Manassite territory. Not only is their main territory included (represented by Bethel to Gezer), but so is the small enclave within the territory of Issachar and Asher. As such, these two verses represent the entire land, just as the genealogies of 1 Chr 7:13–20a represent the entire people.[64]

RETRIBUTION UPON THE WICKED AND THE PROVISION OF A GODLY WARRIOR

THE DEATHS OF EZER AND ELEAD

The third layer in the Chronicler's chiastic structure contrasts Ezer and Elead with Joshua through the use of narrative and genealogy respectively. As previously stated the Ezer and Elead narrative raises numerous historical and source critical questions.[65]

---

that Bethel, even if given to Benjamin, was occupied by Ephraim and only occupied by Benjamin after the fall of the northern kingdom when they expanded into the former northern kingdom. Gezer was a Canaanite stronghold (Josh 16:10; Judg 1:29), which only fell under Israelite control in the reign of Solomon (1 Kgs 9:15–17), when conquered by Egypt and given to Solomon's wife as a wedding gift.

[64] It is possible that the Chronicler presented the order of the tribes in 1 Chr 7 in order to indicate this totality of the land for the entire people, for the Manassite enclave was located in Issachar and Asher, which are also the first and last tribes recorded in this chapter. However, even if the Chronicler's presentation had been influenced in this way, it is uncertain this would have been recognised by his readers as the passage is obscure.

[65] Not least of which is the attitude of the Chronicler to the conquest of Canaan under Joshua. The text, as it stands, indicates clearly that Israel's tribes were always in the land, and does not make any allowance for a period in Egypt or for a conquest. This prompts Japhet to conclude that the Chronicler's account "and that of the Pentateuch are thus mutually exclusive and, understood on their own terms, virtually irreconcilable," "Conquest and Settlement in Chronicles," *JBL* 98 (1979): 205–218, 214. She further (page 215), makes the point that, in the Chronicler's account, as it stands, "Joshua did not conquer the land, he was simply there." Galil rejects this conclusion, indicating that the Chronicler "intended to point out that there is no contradiction between [Ephraim's genealogy] and the traditions of the Pentateuch and the Former Prophets" and that the Chronicler "was probably [trying] to point out the importance of Joshua," "Ephraim," 13. Galil's conclusions are difficult, for why would the Chronicler, in an attempt to deny contradictions, introduce contradictions? Furthermore, if he wanted to "point out the importance of Joshua" through his family connections, why would he (artificially?) ally

202   THE CHRONICLER'S GENEALOGIES

As recorded in the text, Ezer and Elead, sons of Ephraim, "go down"[66] to Gath to seize the livestock of the people of Gath.[67] The native born men of Gath kill them which leads to a period of mourning by their father Ephraim,[68] after which he goes in to his wife and fathers a son who is named in recognition of the time of misfortune. The text then records the actions of Sheerah who built two towns.[69]

It is probable that Ezer and Elead's raid, and its consequences, should be viewed in light of the Chronicler's other statements about success and failure in warfare elsewhere in his genealogies. Success is seen as the result of crying out to Yahweh (1 Chr 5:20), while failure is the consequence of unfaithfulness to Yahweh (1 Chr 5:25-26). Those who gain land and remain in the land are seen as the faithful (1 Chr 4:38-43), while those who lose land and go into exile are considered to be the unfaithful (1 Chr 5:25-26; 9:1b). Further, those who are רַע (wicked; 1 Chr 2:3) are put to death, while those who are מֹעֵל (unfaithful; 1 Chr 2:7), bring trouble to the community.

As such, Ezer and Elead's deaths are to be viewed as the result of their own unfaithfulness, which suggests that their attempt to steal the cattle belonging to

---

him to Elishama son of Ammihud, who was among the people who grumbled in the wilderness, refused to obey God and take the land, and died in the wilderness as a result? If the greatness of Joshua is to be indicated, then it would more easily have been indicated through Joshua's conquests (as in 1 Chr 4:24–5:22). Japhet's view is, however, also overstated. Although the Chronicler does not mention the conquest under Joshua as such, Yahweh's deliverance of Israel from Egypt, which implies captivity in Egypt and the gaining by some means the land of Canaan, is often spoken of (1 Chr 17:5, 21; 2 Chr 5:10; 6:5; 7:22).

[66] The use of ירד "go down" indicates that this was a raid by Ephraimites upon Gath as the idea of "going down" is more appropriate in speaking of going from the hills where Ephraim lived down onto the plains where Gath was located. See note 57, above.

[67] Williamson suggests that this refers to Gittaim rather than Philistine Gath because of Gittaim's closer proximity to Ephraimite territory, *Chronicles*, 81. Myers indicates that Gath is twenty-five miles further south, too far for a raiding party, *I Chronicles*, 55.

[68] The emphasis in the text on the הַנּוֹלָדִים בָּאָרֶץ (native born) men of Gath is puzzling. It may have been included in the source, but the more significant question is why was it included in the genealogies? Is it simply a faithful recording of the source, or is it for polemical purposes in the Chronicler's own period. Is it a plea for, and a warning regarding, maintaining the rights to land of those "born in the land" as well as for those of non Yehudites which may have been under threat from those who labelled themselves "returnees" from exile?

[69] These are the only towns to be founded by a woman in the genealogies. This prompts Curtis to regard this verse as "suspicious," *Chronicles*, 154. In the following section I will argue that the period from Ephraim's mourning until the building activities of Sheerah constitute the final level and the focus of this section of the text.

the men of Gath was an act of unfaithfulness.[70] It is also possible that their deaths were viewed as the result of previous unfaithfulness, and that this incident provided the divine opportunity to execute judgement.[71]

THE GENEALOGY OF JOSHUA

As previously mentioned, the Joshua genealogy appears to be artificially constructed, and artificially intruded upon by the Ezer and Elead narrative. The Joshua genealogy itself, however, presents difficulties. Not least among these are the observations that the Biblical text nowhere associates Nun to Elishama son of Ammihud,[72] and the number of generations recorded in the genealogy is inconsistent with all other genealogies that record data from the Patriarchs to the Exodus.[73] As a result, it may be safer to conclude that the Joshua genealogy is

---

[70] It is, however, uncertain as to exactly why this should be so considered. The gaining of livestock as a consequence of warfare is seen as a result of Yahweh's blessing (1 Chr 5:21–22). The primary difference in the two accounts appears to be that for Ezer and Elead the goal was the acquisition of cattle alone, while in the Hagrite war the goal was acquisition of land. It is uncertain, however, why the acquisition of land through conflict would be blessed, while the acquisition of cattle would not be. Furthermore, it is uncertain why "raiders" are spoken of in a muster list (1 Chr 7:4), while Ezer and Elead, as persons involved in a raiding party, are condemned.

[71] Although it is often indicated that the Chronicler holds to a doctrine of "immediate retribution" this should be understood to refer to the lifetime of the guilty rather than "instantaneous," see further Raymond B. Dillard, "Reward and Punishment in Chronicles: The Theology of Immediate Retribution," *WTJ* 46 (1984): 164–172; Brian E. Kelly, *Retribution and Eschatology in Chronicles* (JSOTSup 211; Sheffield: Sheffield Academic Press, 1996); W. F. Stinespring, "Eschatology in Chronicles," *JBL* 80 (1961): 209–219; H. G. M. Williamson, "Eschatology in Chronicles," in *Studies in Persian Period History and Historiography* FAT; Tübingen: Mohr Siebeck, 2004).

[72] It must be kept in mind, however, that there is also nothing in the Biblical text to exclude such an association, as no ancestor beyond Nun is ever mentioned, except for the Patriarch Ephraim.

[73] However, if the proposals of various scholars are accepted, and we assume that Shuthelah to Shuthelah (1 Chr 7:20–21a), is simply a double repetition of a single horizontal list of Ephraim's sons read vertically, and that Resheph, Telah, Tahan and Ladan (1 Chr 7:25–26a), reflect a corruption of this same list, then this would present us with the following:

Ephraim → Ladan → Ammihud → Elishama → Nun → Joshua

Ladan is selected as the ancestor simply because the text, as is, records him as the father of Ammihud. If this is a horizontal list read vertically, then any of the three recorded sons of Ephraim could be the direct ancestor of Joshua. This also assumes that Rephah (7:25), is the son of Beriah. However, this reconstruction presents only six generations from Patriarch to Exodus, which is much more consistent with the other data. Rendsburg

present not for its details, but for the most significant person in that genealogy, the last named Joshua.

While the conquest of Canaan under Joshua is not expressly stated in Chronicles, the Chronicler's use of the book of Joshua as a source for the land holdings of the Levites and Simeonites indicates his, and possibly the community's, acquaintance with the accounts contained in that work and the role of Joshua in the initial gaining of Canaan. Furthermore, the Chronicler's patterning of the relationship of David and Solomon after that of Moses and Joshua indicates the high esteem in which he held Joshua, as the one who completed Moses' task, just as Solomon completed David's task.[74]

Although absolute certainty is not possible, it is probable that the Chronicler, in structuring his account, presents the genealogy of Joshua, and all that the person of Joshua represented to the people in respect to land acquisition, as the foil to Ezer and Elead. Ezer and Elead are symbols of unfaithfulness, and the consequences of that unfaithfulness. Joshua, however, is a symbol of the exact opposite: faithfulness and the blessings of Yahweh that flow from faithfulness.[75] As a result, the Chronicler did not need to detail the activities of Joshua, the mention of his name sufficed to prove his point, as his name was associated with all the good that Yahweh had done for the people.[76]

What is significant in the Chronicler's structure, however, is the place of the defeat of Ezer and Elead and the victories of Joshua. These are not located at the centre of his structure, but on a lower level. As such, the gaining of land and

---

points out that "all the characters whose lives are depicted in Exodus through Joshua as being coeval with those of Moses and Aaron, and for whom we have genealogies, are three, four, five, or six generations removed from their tribal fathers," "Internal Consistency," 189. He further (page 194–195), discusses the problem of the Joshua genealogy, and offers his own reconstruction.

[74] On this see, Braun, "Solomon, the Chosen"; "Roddy L. Braun, "Solomonic Apologetic in Chronicles," *JBL* 92 (1973): 503–516; Dillard, "Chronicler's Solomon"; Raymond B. Dillard, "The Literary Structure of the Chronicler's Solomon Narrative," *JSOT* 30 (1984): 85–93; Williamson, "Ascension."

[75] The account of Josh 1 is instructive in this regard. Upon the death of Moses, Joshua is appointed to replace him and to lead the people to possess all the land that Yahweh has given to them. The only requirement is that Joshua "obey all the law my servant Moses gave you . . . meditate on it day and night . . . then you will be prosperous and successful" (Josh 1:6–8). Joshua's obedience to Yahweh's commands brought about the success that he experienced. That Yahweh is said to have fulfilled all of his promises (Josh 21:43–45), is a sign that Joshua and the people were faithful to Yahweh.

[76] This is similar to the result if someone (in an American context), simply mentioned the name George Washington. All that Washington did would not need to be recounted, for the name itself is adequate to bring it to mind, and the name itself is sufficient to prove the point.

victory in battle, is not to be seen as the primary purpose of this passage, nor the primary goal of the Chronicler's work, but should be understood instead as flowing from and associated with the Chronicler's purpose.

RESTORATION AND REBUILDING

The central point in the chiastic structure of 1 Chr 7 is 1 Chr 7:22–23 and its parallel in 1 Chr 7:24. The former details Ephraim's mourning as a result of the deaths of his sons, the comfort he received from his family, and the birth of a new son. The latter records the building of cities.[77]

For the Chronicler, positive building activities, like victory in battle and the gaining of land, were a sign of Yahweh's blessing upon those who were faithful to him. Consequently, throughout the narrative of Chronicles, only those kings who were faithful to Yahweh are recorded as having positive building activities.[78] If any king is recorded as abandoning Yahweh, and not humbling himself and turning back to Yahweh, then no further building activities are recorded for that king.[79] However, if a king goes astray from Yahweh and later returns to Yahweh, then that king is recorded as having further positive building activities, but only after his return to Yahweh.[80] Likewise, if a king who is judged by the Chronicler as "evil" returns to Yahweh, then that king is recorded with positive building activities, but only after their return to Yahweh.[81]

---

[77] Uzzen Sheerah is only mentioned here in the Hebrew Bible and "has not been identified with any certainty," Williamson, *Chronicles*, 82. Beth Horon is mentioned thirteen times in the Hebrew Bible: Upper Beth Horon (Josh 16:5; 1 Chr 7:24; 2 Chr 8:5); Lower Beth Horon (Josh 16:3; 18:13; 1 Kgs 9:17; 1 Chr 7:24; 2 Chr 8:5); not specified (Josh 10:10–11; 18:14; 21:22; 1 Sam 13:18; 1 Chr 6:53 [6:68]; 2 Chr 25:13). Second Chronicles 8:5 indicates that Solomon built both locations, but this could indicate that he "rebuilt" them (so NIV), as he also did Gezer after it had been destroyed (1 Kgs 9:17).

[78] See Figure 7.2. By "positive building activities" I mean the construction of buildings, towns, facilities, and military structures. Kings and queens who are regarded as "evil" by the Chronicler did make, עשה, items, but these are always considered as negative items. Jeroboam made goat and calf idols (2 Chr 11:15; 13:8); Maacah made an Asherah pole (2 Chr 15:16); Jehoram made high places (2 Chr 21:11); Ahaz made idols, altars and high places (2 Chr 28:2, 24–25); and Manasseh made Asherah poles and a carved image (2 Chr 33:3). The term בנה is only used for the production of negative items in the case of Manasseh, who built high places and altars (2 Chr 33:3–5).

[79] i.e. Asa, Jehoshaphat, Uzziah.

[80] i.e. David, Rehoboam, Hezekiah.

[81] i.e. Manasseh.

The key term in the attitude of the king which brings positive building activities is "humble."[82] This term is seen to be the key element in the Chronicler's insertion into Yahweh's speech to Solomon contained in 2 Chr 7:13–15.[83]

It is possible that the Chronicler is using the term אבל (mourn) in 1 Chr 7:22 as indicating mourning over the sin/unfaithfulness of Ephraim's sons rather than just their deaths.[84] This mourning is then to be seen as akin to humility, which the Chronicler will later detail as one of the requirements for restoration, with the signs of that restoration being evidenced in positive building projects.[85] As a consequence of the mourning of Ephraim, there is restoration of people (the son Beriah), and the restoration of land (through the building projects of Sheerah). It is this concept which is the Chronicler's goal in this passage. There is here the ongoing recognition that unfaithfulness results in death, judgment and exile. There is also the ongoing hope that humility, crying out to Yahweh, and, here specifically, mourning before Yahweh results in restoration. The restoration of the family that was lost in unfaithfulness, as well as the restoration of land.

---

[82] Rehoboam and the people (2 Chr 12:6–7, 12); Hezekiah (2 Chr 32:26); Manasseh (2 Chr 33:12); Josiah (2 Chr 34:27).

[83] So also Josiah "humbled himself" (2 Chr 34:27), unlike Amon (2 Chr 33:23), and Zedekiah (2 Chr 36:12). Josiah's early death (2 Chr 35:20–24), in spite of his humbling himself before Yahweh may have caused difficulties for the Chronicler. This may have helped lead him to a reinterpretation of the death of Josiah through the possible treachery of Pharaoh (2 Kgs 23:29), into an act of judgment upon Josiah for his own failure to respond to the words of Yahweh.

[84] Cf. Isa 19:8 and its consequences of blessing with Egypt speaking the language of Canaan and swearing allegiance to Yahweh (Isa 19:18), an altar to Yahweh with appropriate worship (Isa 19:19–21), and Egypt, along with Assyria and Israel, being the people and inheritance of Yahweh (Isa 19:24–25).

[85] This presents an interpretative problem. First, if this view that positive building projects are a sign of Yahweh's blessing upon the faithful is the Chronicler's own idea, then at this point of his account his readers/hearers would not be able to comprehend his meaning, unless the reading of the text was accompanied by explanation (cf. Neh 8:7–8), cf Ehud Ben Zvi, "Observations on Ancient Modes of Reading of Chronicles and Their Implications, with an Illustration of Their Explanatory Power for the Study of the Account of Amaziah (2 Chronicles 25)," in *History, Literature and Theology in the Book of Chronicles* (London: Equinox, 2006), 44–45. Second, if this view was the Chronicler's view alone, and there was no accompanying explanation, then this conclusion in regards to the text of 1 Chr 7:22–24 could not be gained unless there was later reflection on the text by the readers/hearers, or until there was at least a second reading of the text. Third, if this view regarding positive building projects was a more widely shared belief, then it is possible that the Chronicler's readers/hearers would have understood his purpose at the first reading, and in light of Ephraim's mourning, they may have even expected it.

CONCLUDING OBSERVATIONS

This study highlights several significant concepts for the Chronicler. First, in Chronicles people and land are linked and are inseparable. This has already been observed in the structure of this passage as a whole, with the people of Yahweh in their generations on the same structural level as the people of Yahweh in their land. This is also evident in the structure of 1 Chr 6, where the Levites in their generations are set along side the Levites in their land. Furthermore, 1 Chr 4:24–5:26 indicates that when the people of Yahweh are blessed by Yahweh, they dwell in the land that Yahweh gives to them. However, in this section, mourning (i.e. humility, seeking Yahweh) results in both descendants and land.

Second, the greatest requirement in the Chronicler's view is neither great armies, nor great military leaders, but humility, mourning and faithfulness before Yahweh. Nothing else can restore the people to the purposes that Yahweh has for them. This is shown elsewhere by the Chronicler through his use of "seeking" Yahweh.

Third, "retribution" should not be thought of simply in negative terms of judgement. It implies that people receive what their actions (good or evil), deserve. If those actions are evil, then evil comes upon a person. If those actions are good, then good also comes. Furthermore, when humility before Yahweh occurs, blessing automatically follows.

Fourth because 1 Chr 7 is not the centre of the Chronicler's genealogies, this motif of "mourning" must not be seen in isolation from that central message. Mourning before Yahweh and seeking Yahweh must be seen in the context of that centre, which is the proper cultic officials, performing the proper cultic duties, in the proper cultic place (1 Chr 6:33–38 [6:48–53]). Mourning before Yahweh and seeking Yahweh finds its fulfilment in the cult and atonement.

Fifth, this passage acts as a counter to the conclusion of 1 Chr 4:24–5:26, which is on the same structural level. While that passage spoke of the blessings that come from faithfulness to Yahweh, it concluded with the Transjordanian tribes in exile for unfaithfulness. This section indicates that exile (which is the ultimate judgement of Yahweh for unfaithfulness), while it may be a present reality, does not need to be on ongoing state. If humility before Yahweh, mourning, and seeking Yahweh becomes the present state of those in exile, then they also have the possibility of restoration of both family and land, and consequently a place within the restored Yehudite society. This, then, becomes reflective of the Chronicler's "all Israel" ideology. All Israel are in the restored community (1 Chr 9:2–3), because they may all be in that community if the proper requirements are met.[86]

It is instantly conceded that the proposed chiastic structure, and its understanding, is the weakest to be presented in respect the Chronicler's genealogies. As such, on its own, it is the most difficult to recognise or defend. However, once the overall chiastic structure of the Chronicler's genealogies is accepted, and 1 Chr 7 is seen within the context of the genealogies as a whole, it will be recognised that this understanding of 1 Chr 7 fits easily within the structure and purpose of the Chronicler's genealogical section.

---

[86] This is further indicated in the Chronicler's narrative where, during the reigns of various Judean kings, residents from Israel come to join in the worship of Yahweh (2 Chr 11:13–17; 30:11, 18).

EXCURSUS 1: THE PLACE OF DAN

If the above conclusions regarding the structure and purpose of 1 Chr 7 are correct, then it follows that the appearance, or non-appearance, of the tribe of Dan in the Chronicler's genealogies is of no great significance in the Chronicler's overall scheme. The presence of Dan and the listing of his descendants in the structural level in which it would be expected to occur would be consistent with this interpretation of that level as being "the people of Yahweh in their generations." Dan's absence does not detract from that interpretation. It is clear that the Chronicler was not seeking to enumerate every tribe, or every part of every tribe. He was clearly selective in his material. However, in terms of the development and history of the text of Chronicles, this is an important question, for it seeks to understand if there has been some corruption in the text at this point.

It must be stated at the outset that no proposed solution to the place of Dan in the text is without its problems. It is possible that textual corruption may have been incorporated into the text through various means. A very common type of textual corruption in the Chronicler's genealogies has been the result of the fact that much of this text is simply names, rather than narrative. The continuous listing of names provides far less control in the copying process than does narrative because in narrative the word being copied must make some sense in relation to the words copied around it. With names there is no such control. A name is more isolated from its context than are narrative words, allowing for greater variations and misunderstandings. Thus, with names, it is far easier to discover different spellings, transpositions of letters, and other variations than narrative would allow, for while the name exists, it supplies no meaning of itself.

Not only does this allow for the corruption of names, but it also allows for the copyist to interpret his text so as to make sense of it from his own perspective. The very process of interpretation, however, carries the real possibility that corruptions will be introduced into the text as the copyist seeks to "make sense" of his text. It is also possible that the copyist's own biases may be introduced into a text.[87]

---

[87] In this regard it may be suggested that a copyist substituted "Ir/City," עיר, for "Dan" because of his dislike for Dan as a centre of idolatry. It is also to be noticed that Dan is omitted from 1 Chr 6:46 [6:61] in the list of cities given to the Levites. If this then did occur, then the copyist's bias had corrupted the text, and in the case of 1 Chr 7:12 opened the way for more corruptions. It must be stated, however, that an anti-Dan bias is not detected throughout the text of Chronicles, for Dan still appears in the list of tribes (1 Chr 2:1–2) as well as in the list of those who came to David (1 Chr 12:35). Dan was included in the invitation of Hezekiah to the Passover (2 Chr 30:1–5). As such, if there was an "anti-Dan" bias on the part of a copyist, he was inconsistent in applying it, or more than

The differing viewpoints, and their justifications, are summed up by Japhet and Williamson.[88] Japhet, who supports reading "Dan" in 1 Chr 7:12, gives the following reasons:
- Hushim is the name of Dan's only son in Gen. 46:23.
- LXX reads υἱος αὐτου, (his son) for the MT's בְּנֵי (sons of).
- Shuppim and Huppim are clearly out of place in the Benjaminite list, which covers the three sons of Benjamin, their genealogy and their fighting men. Therefore Shuppim and Huppim are a gloss to 7:12 in order to "finish out" Benjamin and was "the first of a series of scribal errors."
- "Ir" is a secondary correction for "Dan."
- First Chronicles 7:13 is a "literal reproduction" of Gen 46:24," and therefore reference to Dan (Gen 46:23), would be expected.
- The phrase "sons (plural) of Bilhah" "clearly implies" that Dan as well as Naphtali was originally included.[89]

Williamson represents the alternative view, that Dan was omitted from the text.
- He suggests "Ir" is the "Iri" of 1 Chr 7:7.
- "Hushim" is also to be found in 1 Chr 8:8, eleven in the Benjaminite genealogy which makes its appearance in 7:12 as part of Benjamin appropriate.[90]

---

one copyist was involved in the process. See further H. G. M. Williamson, "A Note on 1 Chronicles VII 12," *VT* 23 (1973): 375–379, 379 where he discusses Bacher, who originally made this proposal. See also the discussion in Mark W. Bartusch, *Understanding Dan: An Exegetical Study of a Biblical City, Tribe and Ancestor* (JSOTSup 379; London: Sheffield Academic Press, 2003), especially chapter 5.

[88] Japhet, *Chronicles*, 174; Williamson, "Note."

[89] Myers suggests that the presence of both "Hushim" and "Bilhah" allows for the possibility that Dan was omitted, *1 Chronicles*, 54. However, that the plural "sons" is often used in the Chronicler's genealogies when only one descendant is listed. Therefore, having "sons of Bilhah" of itself does not demand the presence of more than one son. As the text stands, if we did not have the text of Genesis available to us as providing an indication of the wives of Jacob and the relationships of his sons to one another, there would be nothing to suggest that Bilhah was a wife of Jacob in 1 Chr 7:13. It would in fact be a more probable assumption that she was the wife of Naphtali and the mother of the Jahziel, Guni, Jezer, and Shallum, see Braun, *1 Chronicles*, 109. As such, the presence of "the sons of Bilhah" only implies the presence of Dan because we know from other sources the relationship of Dan, Naphtali and Bilhah. Keil rejects the notion that Dan was originally in the text because of the lack of the conjunction ו prior to "sons of Naphtali." He insists that, as in Gen 46:24, the ו joins both Dan and Naphtali together as sons of Bilhah, and that its absence indicates that Naphtali alone is intended, *Chronicles*, 134–135.

- He associates Shuphan and Huphan with Muppim and Huppin (Gen 46:21), and Shephuphan, Huphan (Num 26:39), as well as Ard and Addar (1 Chr 8:3; Num 26:40).[91]
- As such, 1 Chr 7:12 is simply a corrupted continuation of the Benjaminite list of 1 Chr 7:6–11, "added without connection to what precedes."[92]

It is certain from the Chronicler's use of Genesis in 1 Chr 1 that the Chronicler had the text of Genesis available to him while he wrote his work.[93] This increases the possibility that Genesis was a potential source for each of his genealogies, whether he used them in full or not. The texts of Genesis and Chronicles referring to the offspring of Dan and Naphtali are given in Figure E1.1.

Figure E1.1: The Offspring of Dan and Naphtali

1 Chr 7:12	וְשֻׁפִּם וְחֻפִּם בְּנֵי עִיר חֻשִׁם בְּנֵי אַחֵר:
Gen 46:23	וּבְנֵי־דָן חֻשִׁים:
1 Chr 7:13a	בְּנֵי נַפְתָּלִי יַחֲצִיאֵל וְגוּנִי וְיֵצֶר וְשַׁלּוּם
Gen 46:24	וּבְנֵי נַפְתָּלִי יַחְצְאֵל וְגוּנִי וְיֵצֶר וְשִׁלֵּם
1 Chr 7:13b	בְּנֵי בִלְהָה
Gen 46:25	אֵלֶּה בְּנֵי בִלְהָה

As can be seen, there are significant correspondences between these two passages, but also a number of differences. In 1 Chr 7:12, "Shuppim and Huppim" and "the sons of Aher" are included; "Ir" stands in the place of "Dan" while in 1 Chr 7:13 "these" is omitted. There are also variations in the spellings of some of the names. The direct correspondences, however, increase the probability that Gen 46 was the source for 1 Chr 7:12–13. This probability is furthered by the observation that Num 26:42 records the son of Dan as שׁוּחָם (Shuham) a simple transposition of the letters of this name when compared to both Genesis and Chronicles.[94]

---

[90] Although he does not address the fact that in the Benjaminite list, Hushim is female, the divorced wife of Shaharaim and mother of his children.

[91] Payne indicates that Aher (7:12) is a shortened form of Aharah (1 Chr 8:1) or Aharam (Num 26:38), both of which are located in Benjaminite genealogies, "Chronicles," 358.

[92] Williamson, "Note," 378.

[93] This will be established in Excursus 3.

[94] The LXX reads Σαμι (Num 26:42: [26:46 LXX]) and Ασομ (Gen 46:23).

The substitution of Ir for Dan may be accounted for by an anti-Dan bias, but it is also possible that it is simply an oblique reference to the founding of northern Dan, as opposed to allotted Dan.[95]

BHS proposes that instead of reading בְּנֵי אַחֵר (sons of Aher) we read instead בְּנוֹ אֶחָד (his son, one).[96] The misreading of ד and ר, as well as ו and י is a common occurrence in the Chronicler's genealogies. This phrase "his son, one," would be an addition to the Chronicler's source, but it would be consistent with his presentation of Issachar and Benjamin who have the total number of their offspring listed in certain places (1 Chr 7:1, 3, 7).[97]

The process of textual corruption may have been as follows:
1) Substitution of Ir for Dan by a later copyist, *or* if Ir was originally in the text as an alternative for Dan, a misunderstanding of the significance of Ir in the genealogy by succeeding copyists.
2) Because of the loss of the word "Dan," the control that Dan brought to the interpretation of "his son, one" was also lost, which allowed for the copying/interpreting error of "the sons of Aher."
3) The insertion of "Shuppites and Huppites" on the basis of either their connection to Benjamin,[98] or through their marrying into the tribe of Manasseh (1 Chr 7:15).

While all of this is conjectural, and not accepted by many commentators, it accounts for the text as it is, and demands the least amount of scribal error, bias, or emendation on our part.

---

[95] Cf. Judg 18; Josh 19:40–48. This emendation does not require the misreading of the text. Williamson rejects Klostermann's proposed orthographic confusion, Williamson, "Note," 379.

[96] Rudolph, the BHS editor for Chronicles, followed here the suggestion of Klostermann, *Chronikbücher*, 66. Against the similar view of Bertheau see the discussion in Keil, *Chronicles*, 135 note1.

[97] While this point is acknowledged by Williamson, he indicates that this suggests instead that a numeral could not be located here because "in the case of cardinal numbers this is usually again in the context of a census list," Williamson, "Note," 378. However, it must be noted that numbers are also used in non-census lists: cf. 1 Chr 2:3, 4, 6; 3:4, 8, 22, 23, 24.

[98] In Num 26:39 represented by Shephupham and Hupham. Genesis 46:21 also contains the similar Muppim and Huppim. Their presence prompts Williamson to call these a "Benjaminite fragment," Williamson, "Note," 379.

Figure 7.2: Building Texts

King	Term	Building Texts	Building Project	Change in Attitude To Yahweh	Result
David	בנה	1 Chr 11:8; 14:1	terraces, walls, palace	1 Chr 21: Counts people	1 Chr 21:8-13: plague
	בנה	1 Chr 21:26	altar		
Solomon	בנה	2 Chr 8:1-6	Temple, palace, villages, store cities, cities for chariots and horses		
Rehoboam	בנה	2 Chr 11:5-10	towns for defence	2 Chr 12:1: abandoned law of Yahweh	2 Chr 12:6: Humbled self
Asa	עשה	2 Chr 12:10	bronze shields		
	בנה	2 Chr 14:6-7	fortified cities	2 Chr 16:7: reliance on foreign power	2 Chr 16:9: war
Jehoshaphat	בנה	2 Chr 16:6	Geba, Mizpah		
	בנה	2 Chr 17:12	forts, store cities		
	עשה	2 Chr 20:36	ships	2 Chr 20:35: Ahaziah "wickedness"	2 Chr 20:37: ships destroyed
Uzziah	בנה	2 Chr 26:2, 6, 9, 10	Elath, towns in Ashdod & Philistine territory, towers, cisterns		
	עשה	2 Chr 26:15	machines for war	2 Chr 26:16: in pride offered incense	2 Chr 26:19: Leprosy

Figure 7.2 Continued

King	Term	Building Texts	Building Project	Change in Attitude To Yahweh	Result
Jotham	בנה	2 Chr 27:3-4	upper gate of temple, wall, towns, forts, towers		
Hezekiah	בנה	2 Chr 32:5	wall, towers, terraces	2 Chr 32:25: pride	2 Chr 32:26: repentance
	עשׂה	2 Chr 32:5	weapons, shields		
	עשׂה	2 Chr 32:27, 29	treasuries, villages		
Manasseh	בנה	2 Chr 33:3-5	high places, altars	2 Chr 33:12-13: humbled, prayer	2 Chr 33:13b: restored
	עשׂה	2 Chr 33:3, 7	Asherah poles, carved image		
	בנה	2 Chr 34:14-16	outer wall, altar of Yahweh		

CHAPTER 8
C: 1 CHRONICLES 2:3–4:23
JUDAH: THE TRIBE OF KING DAVID

INTRODUCTION

The genealogy of the tribe of Judah is at once the longest and most convoluted of any of the genealogies within 1 Chr 1–9. Furthermore, its character, layout, and style is decidedly different to what is found in many of the other tribal lists. These differences are due to the purposes for which the various lists were developed.

As stated in Chapter 1, Wilson indicates that genealogies have three major spheres of operation: politico-jural, religious, and domestic.[1]

> Lineages function domestically by expressing social relationships between persons within the lineage, as well as by expressing the relationships of individuals to lineage groups and the relationships of lineage groups to each other. These social relationships in turn govern social conduct.[2]

Wilson goes on to say, "genealogies that function in the domestic sphere are usually segmented, for their purpose is to justify the social relations existing between lineage members."[3]

The various components of the Judahite list give the appearance of having been formulated in the domestic sphere, which accounts for the differences that exist between the Judahite list and many of the other lists of the sons of Israel. The different nature of the Judahite list, and consequently its different purpose, is observed when it is compared with the contents of the other tribal lists. These differences are certainly due to the different purposes for which these lists originated.

The accounts of Simeon and the Transjordanian tribes (1 Chr 4:24–5:26), as well as Issachar, Benjamin and Asher (1 Chr 7), are examples of the politico-jural genealogy. They refer to the "heads of families" and the military leaders around

---

[1] Wilson, *Genealogy*, 38–45.
[2] Wilson, *Genealogy*, 38.
[3] Wilson, *Genealogy*, 40.

whom the society is organised in times of conflict. Unlike these tribes, Judah contains no military muster lists. Additionally, no census totals are listed, and Judah contains no descriptions of the military prowess of the people as are mentioned for Simeon (1 Chr 7:40; cf. 5:18, 24). Further, accounts of the expansion of land holdings through military means or even the occurrence of military conflict within its own territory are absent, although Judah does relate the loss of land in Transjordanian Manasseh which was controlled by a member of Judah (1 Chr 2:22–23). Judah is reported as having numerous towns, but the text suggests that these towns have always been their possession, rather than becoming their possession through conflict and struggle (1 Chr 4:41; 5:10, 22), or, as with Levi, through being given to them by other tribes (1 Chr 6:39–66 [6:54–81]).

Levi is an example of a genealogy which operates within the religious sphere, for Levi's genealogy focuses upon cultic officials and their duties. Judah's genealogy is not, however, focussed upon any one aspect of Judah. Although the monarchy is given prominence through the genealogy of David, the Davidic genealogy does not dominate the Judahite list, as the cultic officials dominate the list of Levi. Although, like Levi, the genealogy of Judah contains some, extended linear genealogies,[4] Judah's genealogy also contains numerous segmented genealogies as well as some segments which do not appear to present any connection to other segments or to the tribe of Judah as a whole.

The closest comparison within the genealogical section to Judah's genealogy is that of Manasseh, Ephraim (1 Chr 7:14–29), and Benjamin (1 Chr 8).[5] Like Ephraim and Manasseh, the Judahite genealogy is primarily made up of segmented genealogies, and contains accounts of marriages, conceptions, births, deaths, as well as the significance of the names of certain children. Like Ephraim, Manasseh, and Benjamin, Judah mentions not only the names of males, but those of wives, sisters, and daughters. Each of these speaks of domestic relationships, rather than political or cultic ones.

While the genealogies of Levi give the appearance of arising from within the cult, and those of the Transjordanian tribes, as well as Simeon, Issachar, Benjamin,[6] and Asher give the appearance of originating within the context of the tribe's wars and warriors, those of Judah, Manasseh, Ephraim, and Benjamin give the impression of arising within the daily activities of a tribe, clan, or family. They belong within the settled, daily lives of people in their relationships with one another and with the communities and clans surrounding them.

---

[4] The genealogy of Ram (1 Chr 2:10–17); David's descendants who reigned as king (1 Chr 3:10–16); and the descendants of Sheshan (1 Chr 2:35–41).

[5] This is the second Benjaminite list, and will be discussed in greater detail in Chapter 9.

[6] This is in reference to the first Benjaminite genealogy in 1 Chr 7:6–12.

Content of the Judahite Genealogy

As mentioned, the genealogy of Judah is the most convoluted of any of the Chronicler's genealogies. It begins with a list of the sons and grandsons of Judah (1 Chr 2:3–6), followed by a narrative account relating to one of the sons of Carmi, without, however, stating where or how Carmi connects with Judah (1 Chr 2:7). First Chronicles 2:8 follows with the son of Ethan, who himself is said to be a grandson of Judah through Zerah (1 Chr 2:6), which gives the impression that somehow Carmi and his family are also connected to Judah through Zerah.[7]

First Chronicles 2:9 acts as an introduction to the remainder of 1 Chr 2 through mention of Judah's grandson Hezron and three of his sons, Jerahmeel, Ram and Caleb.[8] Following this is a linear genealogy of the descendants of Ram leading to David and his siblings (1 Chr 2:10–17),[9] a segmented genealogy of Caleb (1 Chr 2:18–24), and a segmented genealogy of Jerahmeel (1 Chr 2:25–33). A linear genealogy of Sheshan follows a brief introduction to the circumstances behind the genealogy (1 Chr 2:34–41). It is possible that this Sheshan is meant to be understood as the Sheshan of 1 Chr 2:31. That the Sheshan of 2:34 is said to have no sons, and the Sheshan of 2:31 is the father of Ahlai, should not be seen to contradict this possible connection, as the linear genealogy that arose through the marriage of Sheshan's daughter to Sheshan's Egyptian servant Jarha (1 Chr 2:34–41), is still considered to be that of Sheshan's descendants. It is therefore possible that Ahlai in 2:31 was understood by the Chronicler as a "son" of Sheshan through one of his other daughters.

Following the list of Sheshan is another list of the sons of Caleb, although containing different names to those previously mentioned (1 Chr 2:42–50a; cf. 2:18). That the same Caleb is intended is indicated through the clear identification of him as "brother of Jerahmeel" (1 Chr 2:42). Another group of the sons of Caleb through his wife Ephrathah is then recounted (1 Chr 2:50b–55; cf. 2:19–20).

First Chronicles 3 is concerned with the descendants of David, and can be divided into four sections. David's sons born in Hebron (1 Chr 3:1–4a), his sons born in Jerusalem (1 Chr 3:4b–9), his descendants who were kings of Judah (1 Chr 3:10–16), and his descendants during and after the exile (1 Chr 3:17–24).

---

[7] Joshua 7:1 indicates that Achan/Achar is the "son of Carmi, son of Zabdi [LXX: Zimri], son of Zerah."

[8] "Caleb" is here written as כְּלוּבָי, which most authorities take to be a variant of כָּלֵב. Hezron is said to have another son, Segub, through a different wife (1 Chr 2:21).

[9] Only here in 1 Chr 2:16–17 are Zeruiah and Abigail said to be David's sisters, and the sons of Zeruiah (Abishai, Joab and Asahel), and the son of Abigail (Amasa), shown to be David's nephews. Abigail and Zeruiah are said to be sisters in 2 Sam 17:25, and daughters of Nahash.

First Chronicles 4 commences with a short genealogy of the "sons" of Judah, without, however, providing any other relationship terms (1 Chr 4:1). This is followed by a further genealogy of Hur (1 Chr 4:2–4; cf. 2:50b), and a genealogy of Asshur, who is also a son of Ephrathah (1 Chr 4:5–8; cf. 2:24). The short narrative account of Jabez follows without indicating how he is connected to Judah (1 Chr 4:9–10), although that he has some connection with the town of the same name cannot be dismissed out of hand (1 Chr 2:55).

Following the account of Jabez, 1 Chr 4:11–20 contains a number of smaller genealogies, whose connections to Judah are not indicated by the Chronicler, although these lists do contain a reference to "Caleb son of Jephunneh" (1 Chr 4:15), who is called a Judahite in other texts (Num 13:6; 34:19; Josh 14:6; 15:13). The Judahite genealogy closes with a list of the sons of Shelah, son of Judah (1 Chr 4:21–23).

On first impressions, it would appear as if the Judahite genealogy consists of two lists of the "sons of Judah" (1 Chr 2:3; 4:1), flanking a centre section of the sons of David. If this is correct, then it may be that the Chronicler is seeking to portray the tribe of Judah as a chiasm centred on David and his descendants. Although it has been suggested that the Chronicler is seeking to focus attention upon the Davidic monarchy,[10] and to suggest that the Davidic monarchy retains a certain significance within the postexilic community, I will argue, below, that this is not the case. Instead, it will be demonstrated that David and his family, although having been important in the past, are now on the periphery of Judahite political aspirations.

FAMILIAL TERMINOLOGY IN THE JUDAHITE GENEALOGY

As mentioned above, the Judahite genealogy contains the names, not just of the males in the tribe or clan, but also of some females.[11] Wives are mentioned by name in 1 Chr 2:18, 24, 26, 29; 3:1–3; 4:5, 18.[12] Wives are mentioned without being named, in 1 Chr 2:21, 35; 4:18, 19.[13] Concubines are mentioned by name

---

[10] Knoppers, *1 Chronicles 1–9*, 332–336.

[11] For a fuller discussion of the place of women in the Chronicler's genealogies, see Antje Labahn and Ehud Ben Zvi, "Observations on Women in the Genealogies of 1 Chronicles 1–9," *Bib* 84 (2003): 457–478.

[12] If "Bathshua" is considered to be the name of Judah's wife, instead of an indication that she is the "daughter of Shua" (1 Chr 2:3; cf. Gen 38:2), then this would be another instance. Tamar, however, is not called Judah's "wife," but his "daughter-in-law," כַּלָּה.

[13] Of the sixteen occurrences of "wife," אִשָּׁה, in the genealogies of the sons of Israel, nine occur in Judah. See Figure 8.1 for the appearances of familial terms in the genealogies.

(1 Chr 2:46, 48), and generally (1 Chr 3:9).[14] Daughters also are named regularly in the Judahite genealogies (1 Chr 2:49; 3:2, 5; 4:18), while at other times their presence is simply acknowledged (1 Chr 2:3, 21, 34, 35).[15] Further, sisters within the Judahite tribe are often named by the Chronicler (1 Chr 2:16; 3:9, 19; 4:3, 19).[16] The only occurrences of the term אֵם (mother) in the genealogies are found in the Judahite lists in 1 Chr 2:26; 4:9.[17] Judah's כַּלָּה (daughter-in-law) Tamar is mentioned (1 Chr 2:4), which is the only occurrence of this term within Chronicles.

Figure 8.1: Familial Terms in the Genealogies of the Sons of Israel

	אָב	אָח	אָחוֹת	אֵם	אִשָּׁה	בְּכֹר	בֵּן	בַּת	ילד	פִּלֶגֶשׁ
Judah	31	4	5	2	9	10	93	8	51	3
Simeon	1	1					22	1		
Reuben	1	2				3	15			
Gad	2						11	1		
Manasseh	3						1			
Levi	1	3				1	116		21	
Issachar	2	1			1		5			
Benjamin	3						8			
Naphtali							2			
Manasseh	1	1	2		2		8	1	4	1
Ephraim	1	1			1		19	9	2	
Asher	2	1	2				10		1	
Benjamin	5	3			3	3	23	1	14	

The observation that, when these feminine relationship terms do occur elsewhere in the genealogies, they primarily occur in the accounts of Ephraim and Manasseh, is an indication that the genealogical information contained within Judah, Ephraim and Manasseh arose within a similar context. This context is clearly not military or cultic, but appears to be within the family structure of these tribes.

---

[14] The only other occurrence of a "concubine," פִּלֶגֶשׁ, in the sons of Israel is in 1 Chr 7:14, with no name given.

[15] Daughters, בַּת, are also mentioned in 1 Chr 4:27; 7:15, without indicating a name, and in 7:24 with a name given. In 1 Chr 5:16; 7:28, 29; 8:12, the term is used to indicate "villages" surrounding a main population centre.

[16] אָחוֹת, also occurs in 1 Chr 7:15, 18, 30, 32. On each occurrence the sister is named.

[17] This is confused somewhat in the NIV where "mother" is also used in 1 Chr 2:17, 46, 49 to translate the Hebrew ילד, "to give birth." The NRSV has in each case "bore," rather than "mother."

While the term בֵּן (son) is a common term within the genealogies,[18] אָח (brothers) are referred to in the Judahite genealogy on only four occasions, either in reference to a physical brother (1 Chr 2:32, 42; 4:11), or in the perhaps wider sense of "relative" (1 Chr 4:9).

Although the familial term בְּכֹר (firstborn) occurs often in Chronicles,[19] it is to be noticed that of the twenty-six occurrences of בְּכֹר within Chronicles, seventeen are in the genealogies, and ten of these are within the Judahite genealogy.

LEADERS OF JUDAHITE COMMUNITIES

Although the Judahite genealogy utilises a number of familial terms, on only one occasion does it use the term אָב (father) to describe the relationship of one person to another (1 Chr 2:17). Although reference to a physical father occurs on occasion in the genealogies as a whole,[20] the primary use of אָב (father) in the Judahite genealogy is to describe the relationship of an individual to a town.[21] Figure 8.2 presents each of the towns in the Judahite genealogy which have a אָב (father) and where those towns occur in other locations within the Hebrew Bible.[22]

As can be observed, of the twenty-four localities which are listed as having a "father," sixteen of these appear as towns within other sections of the Hebrew Bible. This lends substance to the proposition that the remaining eight occurrences also refer to towns.

It will be further noticed that some towns have more than one "father." Bethlehem (Salma: 1 Chr 2:51; Hur: 1 Chr 4:4), Gedor (Penuel: 1 Chr 4:4; Jered 1 Chr 4:18), and Etam (Jezreel, Ishma, Idbash: 1 Chr 4:3),[23] each has more than one "father," or leader presented.

---

[18] In 1 Chr 1–9, "son," בֵּן, occurs 435 times out of a total 606 times within Chronicles as a whole. It occurs 94 times within the Judahite genealogy.

[19] 1 Chronicles 1:13, 29; 2:3, 13, 25[x2], 27, 42, 50; 3:1, 15; 4:4; 5:1[x2], 3; 6:13 [6:28]; 8:1, 30, 39; 9:5, 31, 36; 26:2, 4, 10; 2 Chr 21:3

[20] 1 Chronicles 5:1, 25; 6:4 [6:19]; 7:22; 9:19. The NIV often translates ילד, "to give birth," as "the father of." See also note 17, above.

[21] The other common use of "father" in the genealogies is in variations of the phrase "house/head of the father(s)"; 1 Chr 4:38; 5:13, 15, 24; 7:2, 4, 7, 9, 11, 40; 8:6, 10, 13, 28; 9:9, 13, 19, 33, 34. It is noteworthy, that the term does not occur in either Judah, Ephraim, or Cisjordan Manasseh. Nor does it occur in Levi, which is not a military but a religious list. On this term, see further Weinberg, *Citizen-Temple*, 49–61.

[22] The genealogies record a person as "father" of a town also in 1 Chr 7:14, 31; 8:29.

[23] This identification is made by rejecting the BHS emendation of "father," אָב, to "sons" on the basis of the LXX υιοι, and instead recognizing each of the following persons

Figure 8.2: אָב as Town Leader in the Genealogies

Town	1 Chr	Josh	Judg	Sam
Beth Gader	2:51			
Beth Recab	2:55			
Beth Zur	2:45	15:58		
Bethlehem	2:51; 4:4	19:15	12:8, 10; 17:7–9	1S 17:12; 2S 23:14–16
Eshtemoa	4:17, 19	15:50; 21:14		1S 30:28
Eshton	4:11, 12			
Etam	4:3		15:8, 11	
Gedor	4:4, 18	15:58		
Ge Harashim	4:14			
Gibea גִּבְעוֹן	2:49 גִּבְעָא	15:57; 18:28; 24:33	19:12–20:43	1S 10:5, 26; 13:15–16; 2S 21:26
Gilead	2:21, 23	12:2–5; 17:1–6	10:3–18; 11:1–29; 12:4–7	1S 13:7; 2S 2:9
Hebron/ Kiriath Arba	2:42	10:3; 5; 11:21	1:10, 20	1S 30:31; 2S 2:1–4
Hushah	4:4			
Ir Nahash	4:12			
Jorkeam	2:44			
Keilah	4:19	15:44		1S 23:1–13
Kiriath Jearim	2:50, 52	9:17; 15:9, 60; 18:14	18:12	1S 6:21; 7:1–2
Lecah	4:21			
Macbenah	2:49			
Madmannah	2:49	15:31		
Mareshah	4:21	15:44		
Soco שׂוֹכֹה	4:18 שׂוֹכוֹ	15:35, 48		1S 17:1
Tekoa	2:24; 4:5			2S 14:2–9
Zanoah	4:18	15:34, 56		
Ziph	2:42	15:24, 55		1S 23:14–15, 24; 26:2

This suggests that some of these lists may date to different time periods, which are reflected in the different town leadership.

However, the example of Etam suggests that a town may have more than one "father" at any one time. That these individuals are considered to be the fathers of

---

as "father" or leader, of Etam. Klein assumes that the "father" of Etam has been lost, *1 Chronicles*, 130.

towns, as opposed to the "heads of father's houses," a phrase often used to indicate leaders in the military census lists, is a further example of the proposition that the Judahite lists arose from within the social context of the daily affairs of the people, rather than from within a military or cultic context.

DOMESTIC TERMINOLOGY IN THE JUDAHITE GENEALOGY

As indicated above, Wilson states that genealogies operate within the politico-jural, religious, and domestic spheres.[24] First Chronicles 6, the sons of Levi and the cultic officials, is one illustration of a genealogy operating within the cultic sphere. The muster lists of 1 Chr 7 are examples of genealogies operating in the political sphere. Many of the Judahite lists give evidence of originating within the domestic sphere. This has already been partly noticed with the varying uses of familial terms. The domestic operations of the Judahite genealogies, apart from the Davidic list, may also be observed in the types of data contained within it. Within the Judahite genealogy are a number of terms and incidents which are indicative of the reality of life and its struggles.

Within the Chronicler's genealogies of the sons of Israel, only in the Judahite genealogies are people said to "die" (מוּת; 1 Chr 2:3, 19, 30, 32), or "suffer death" (מָוֶת; 1 Chr 2:24). Although it is a genealogy, and the focus of a genealogy is progeny, two persons are said to have been "childless" (1 Chr 2:30, 32), while a third is said to have had no sons (1 Chr 2:34). The common term "to give birth" (יָלַד) most often occurs in the genealogies within the Judahite lists.[25] Judah alone mentions the reality that childbirth is a painful, even dangerous, event (1 Chr 4:9).

Three times in the Judahite genealogy are persons said to have "taken" (לָקַח) a wife (1 Chr 2:19, 21; 4:18).[26] In one of these instances (1 Chr 2:24, cf. 2:19), a person is said to have "taken" a woman who had already been the wife of his own father, while in a separate incident (1 Chr 2:4), a man has children by his daughter-in-law. These two incidents give the suggestion that the social context within which such information was formulated and retained looked upon these relationships as contrary to normal practice, and therefore the details behind these relationships demanded retention and transmission.

Further, the Judahite genealogy mentions various crafts and guilds that were active within the community. There are references to scribes (1 Chr 2:55),

---

[24] See note 1, above.

[25] "To give birth," יָלַד, occurs in the Judahite genealogy fifty-one times. This compares to Levi (twenty-one times), Manasseh (four times), Ephraim (twice), Asher (once), Benjamin ([1 Chr 8] fourteen times).

[26] Only elsewhere in the genealogies in the context of marriage in 1 Chr 7:15. In the Hebrew Bible לָקַח, is often used to indicate marriage, cf. Deut 20:7; 22:13, 14.

craftsmen (1 Chr 4:13), linen workers (1 Chr 4:21), and potters (1 Chr 4:23). Again, these references are an indication that the various genealogies contained within the Judahite genealogy had their origins within the day-to-day workings of the clans in community.

RETRIBUTION IN THE JUDAHITE GENEALOGY

The Judahite genealogy also contains references to occasions when "wickedness" of some sort arose within the community which brought with it negative consequences for the individual or the community. Er "was wicked in the eyes of Yahweh" (רַע בְּעֵינֵי יְהוָה) resulting in Yahweh putting Er to death (וַיְמִתֵהוּ; 1 Chr 2:3). Achar, "brought trouble on Israel by violating the ban," (עוֹכֵר יִשְׂרָאֵל אֲשֶׁר מָעַל בַּחֵרֶם; 1 Chr 2:7). Although the genealogy itself does not indicate the precise consequences,[27] the term "brought trouble" (עוֹכֵר) indicates that the consequences were negative, and impacted upon the entire community.[28] First Chronicles 2:22–23 relates that while Segub "controlled twenty-three towns in Gilead," sixty towns were captured by Geshur and Aram. This indicates that although the tribe of Judah had increased their town holdings through intermarriage with another tribe, even more towns were lost than gained. As was observed in the incidents of the Transjordanian tribes, in the Chronicler's scheme, loss of land is always the end result of unfaithfulness to Yahweh on the part of individuals or society. The implication here is that these towns were also lost as the result of unfaithfulness of some kind, perhaps the unfaithfulness which the Chronicler will mention in 1 Chr 5:25. First Chronicles 3:17 mentions the captivity of Jehoiachin, a captivity which the Chronicler will later make plain is the result of the unfaithfulness of kings, priests, leaders and the people as a whole (1 Chr 9:1; 2 Chr 36:11–14). However, the incidents of unfaithfulness by the people are not limited to simply the ones specified.

The Chronicler was certainly familiar with the traditions contained in the writings he used as his sources. Although not all of the Chronicler's readers may have been familiar with the content of these other sources, those readers who were familiar with these other traditions would possibly link the name listed in the genealogy with the incident recorded in these writings. This being the case, his readers would recognise that Onan was also put to death for defying Yahweh (1 Chr 2:3; cf. Gen 38:8–10). The mention of Bathshua (1 Chr 3:5), would bring to mind David's adultery and his murder of Uriah (2 Sam 11). Mention of

---

[27] Cf. Josh 7:24–26 where the consequences for Achar (Achan in Joshua), are explained.

[28] Joshua 7:1 indicates that as a result of Achan's actions, the entire community were considered to be "unfaithful," while Josh 7:3–5 indicates that the people were defeated in battle with the loss of thirty-six soldiers.

David's daughter Tamar would suggest the account of Amnon's rape of his own sister (2 Sam 13). The names of David's sons Absalom and Adonijah speak of murder, rebellion, and political intrigue (2 Sam 13–18; 1 Kgs 1–2). The mention of Solomon may recall his unfaithfulness, while many of the kings of Judah were shown in the Deuteronomistic History to be not fully faithful to Yahweh, with the nation suffering the consequences.

In the Judahite genealogy, as in the rest of the work, the Chronicler makes clear his understanding of retribution: that a person or community receives the consequences of their actions, whether those actions be good or evil. As with Simeon and the Transjordanian tribes, faithfulness to Yahweh brings land and settlement "to this day," while unfaithfulness brings exile from land "to this day."

FOREIGN ELEMENTS IN THE JUDAHITE GENEALOGY

Interestingly, the Judahite genealogy also contains a number of references to "foreigners," that is, to those who were not descended from Israel, and who were incorporated into Judah through marriage. Unlike his references to the actions of Er or Achar, the incorporation of non-Israelite elements are included without any comment by the Chronicler, either positive or negative. Bathshua is a Canaanite (1 Chr 2:3), while an Ishmaelite marries a sister of David (1 Chr 2:17).[29] Sheshan marries his daughter to his Egyptian servant (1 Chr 2:34), and Mered marries the daughter of Pharaoh (1 Chr 4:17–18). David also marries the daughter of a foreign king (1 Chr 3:2). No other Israelite tribe is explicitly said to intermarry with non-Israelite elements, but likewise, the Chronicler does not here condemn the practice.

Knoppers states, "if the genealogist found the mixed marriages highly objectionable or reprehensible, he could have criticised them,"[30] and again, "given the propensity of the Chronicler to interject criticisms when it suits him, the absence of such criticisms vis-à-vis mixed marriages is important."[31]

The Chronicler, however, goes beyond simply mentioning without comment that Judahites married non-Israelites. He indicates that he considered the tribes, clans, and families, who in certain traditions in the Hebrew Bible are said to be external to Israel, to be fully a part of Judah. First Samuel 27:10 speaks about the "Negev of Judah, the Negev of Jerahmeel, and the Negev of the Kenites," as if

---

[29] Second Samuel 17:25 says that Jether is an "Israelite." The NRSV, under the influence of 1 Chr 2:17, reads "Ishmaelite" in 2 Sam 17:25, as is indicated in the footnote to this verse. There is a minor spelling variation in the names. First Chronicles 2:17 reads: יֶתֶר while 2 Sam 17:25 reads יִתְרָא.

[30] Gary N. Knoppers, "Intermarriage, Social Complexity, and Ethnic Diversity in the Genealogy of Judah," *JBL* 120 (2001): 15–30, 19.

[31] Knoppers, "Intermarriage," 20.

these represent the territory of three distinct and separate clans. First Samuel 30:29 speaks of the "towns of the Jerahmeelites and the Kenites."

The most striking of these are the Kenites (קֵינִי; 1 Chr 2:55). According to other traditions, this group are said to be the family of Moses' father-in-law (Judg 1:16), and were considered as a group distinct from the Israelites (1 Sam 15:6), with land and settlements of their own (Gen 15:19; Num 24:21–22; 1 Sam 27:10; 30:29). In 1 Chr 2:55, this group is still recognised as "Kenites," with the implication that they retained their historical distinctiveness, yet they are also classified as part of "the sons of Salma" (1 Chr 2:54). In Chronicles, it appears that the Kenites are considered to be Judahites.[32]

Jerahmeel, who is listed as the firstborn son of Hezron (1 Chr 2:9, 25), is not recorded as a clan outside of 1 Chronicles and 1 Samuel.[33] However, upon analogy with the Kenites (1 Sam 27:10; 30:29), it is probable that they also constituted a clan which was separate to, but a neighbour with, Judah.[34] It would appear from David's actions in 1 Sam 27:8–11 and 30:26–31, that David was on good terms with this group and wandered freely within their territory, and perhaps even offered them "protection" through the presence of his men. This suggests that either Judah had a good relationship with these groups prior to David, which he maintained, or that David nurtured good relations with them while he was on the run from King Saul.

Like the Kenites, the Jerahmeelites are not mentioned after David becomes king, which may suggest that their incorporation into Judah was affected by David's rise to the monarchy. This also indicates, however, that their becoming "Judahite" was on the basis of factors other than physical descent. The Chronicler, however, appears unconcerned by, or perhaps unaware of, these issues, and merely presents these groups as part of Judah.

Another group which appears to have been incorporated into Judah is Kenaz (1 Chr 4:13, 15). In the Joshua tradition, the location of Kenizzite settlements is given as within the Negev (Josh 15:19), which is consistent with this group being portrayed elsewhere as a clan of Edom (Gen 36:11, 15, 42; 1 Chr 1:36, 53). Caleb is called a קְנִזִּי (Kenizzite; Num 32:12; Josh 14:6, 14), yet the Kenizzites were, like the Kenites, considered by some traditions to be separate to Israel (Gen

---

[32] It is also possible that the Kenites were simply considered to be under the control of Salma rather than a part of Judah. Even if this be the case, this situation would also be unique within the genealogies, and would place the Kenites in a position held by no other group.

[33] 1 Samuel 27:10; 30:29; 1 Chr 2:9, 25, 26, 27, 33, 42. A Jerahmeel is recorded in 1 Chr 24:29 as a Levite in the clan of Merari, while Jer 36:26 records a Jerahmeel as an otherwise unknown son of King Jehoiakim of Judah.

[34] Knoppers suggests, on the basis of the Jerahmeelites possessing towns, that they were a semi-nomadic group, Knoppers, "Intermarriage," 25.

15:19).³⁵ However, the portrayal of Kenaz in 1 Chr 4:13–15 is consistent with other portions of the Hebrew Bible which declare that Kenaz was a brother of Caleb, who was himself a full member of the tribe of Judah (Josh 15:17; Judg 1:13; 3:9, 11). Although this may appear to make Caleb's lineage suspect, he is always called "the son of Jephunneh,"³⁶ and his legitimacy within Judah is clearly maintained in P and Joshua.³⁷

There appear to be additional clan links between Judah and Edom/Seir. Onam (1 Chr 1:40; 2:26, 28), Shobal (1 Chr 1:38; 2:50, 52; 4:1, 2), Shammah/Shammai (1 Chr 1:37; 2:28), Ezer (1 Chr 1:42; 4:4), appear in the genealogies of both groups, which may reflect the incorporation of one group into another.

Two important caveats are required, however, before any of these groups can be clearly identified as "foreign" elements which have been incorporated into Judah. First, that more than one clan may share the same or similar clan name cannot be discounted. If this is the case, then the suggested incorporation of groups into Judah may be more apparent than real. Second, one must never think that incorporation is merely a "one way street," that is, with all the incorporation of clans being on the part of Judah. In the Judahite genealogy it is noted that Hezron married into Manasseh, and that his offspring controlled towns within Manasseh (1 Chr 2:21–22). Jair, son of Segub, son of Hezron could therefore be included in the genealogies of both Judah and Manasseh (cf. Num 32:41; Deut 3:14; 1 Kgs 4:13). In one sense, part of Judah could be seen to be incorporated into Manasseh, but likewise, part of Manasseh is portrayed by the Chronicler as being incorporated into Judah.³⁸

It therefore becomes possible that the links exhibited between Judah and other clans may be based upon marriages or other formal agreements, and that both groups could then feel free to incorporate the other into their own genealogy. In the case of a marriage, the offspring of such marriages could identify themselves with either or both clans.³⁹ As mentioned, the Judahite genealogy specifies that a son of a Judahite father became a leader within Manasseh. Judah claimed him as their own, but that he controlled Manassite towns may suggest

---

³⁵ Here as well, prior to their incorporation into Esau/Edom.
³⁶ Numbers 13:6; 14:6, 30, 38; 26:65; 32:12; 34:19; Deut 1:36; Josh 14:6, 13, 14; 15:13; 21:12
³⁷ Numbers 13:6; 34:19; Josh 14:6; 15:13.
³⁸ A similar example has already been discussed, whereby Aaron married into a Judahite family, with the result that descendants of Aaron have their territory primarily within Judah (Exod 6:23; Josh 21:9–19). As such, these towns are both Aaronite and Judahite.
³⁹ This still continues today. By means of a personal example, my brother identifies more with the "Arnold" clan of our mother, while I identify more with the "Sparks" clan of our father. We belong to both, but have a closer affinity with one.

that Segub identified, and was accepted as one of their own, by Manasseh. In our current state of knowledge, however, it is impossible to determine the direction in which some of these incorporations of "foreign" elements occurred, and what they signify in respect to the social structures of ancient Israelite/Judahite society.

One example of this may be found in 1 Chr 2:6, which mentions four descendants of Zerah (Ethan, Heman, Calcol, Darda). In 1 Kgs 4:31, Ethan is said to be an "Ezrahite," while the other three are "sons of Mahol." De Vaux sees in the name "Mahol" a reference to choristers, and suggests that the earliest choristers in the temple were non-Israelites.[40] Knoppers, however, suggests that these names may reflect the claims of different clans to the cultic musicians (cf. 1 Chr 6:18, 29 [6:33, 44]):

> it is possible that members of two different tribes claimed Heman and Ethan among their ancestors. The appearance of these well-known names in two different lineages may reflect competing ancestral claims. Such a phenomenon in the composition of genealogies is also attested in ancient Greece.[41]

It is uncertain the exact method by which these tribes, clans, or families, who are elsewhere external to Judah were counted as part of Judah. What is clear is that those who, in certain contexts, are considered to be external to Judah are, in the Judahite genealogy of 1 Chr 2–4, considered to be a part of Judah.[42] What is also important is the observation that the Chronicler nowhere condemns the incorporation of these persons or clans within Judah. They are said to exist in, and belong to, Judah.

UNDERSTANDING THE STRUCTURE OF THE JUDAHITE GENEALOGY

Two basic methods have been used in seeking to understand the Judahite genealogy. It has been suggested that the Judahite genealogy is the product of random textual growth, or, it is a deliberately formed chiastic structure focusing upon the family of David.

---

[40] de Vaux, *Ancient Israel*, 382; cf. Simon J. De Vries, *1 Kings* (WBC 12; Waco: Word, 1985), 74.

[41] Knoppers, *1 Chronicles 1–9*, 303.

[42] Knoppers suggests that some of these groups may have "become part of mainstream Judah," while others "are not integrated completely by means of clear lineage connections," Knoppers, "Intermarriage," 27. In this latter group he places the "Jephunnite Calebites," in spite of their clear Judahite identity within the priestly and Deuteronomistic literature which the Chronicler drew upon for much of his narrative, and some of his genealogical, material (Num 13:6; 34:19; Josh 14:6; 15:13).

RANDOM TEXTUAL GROWTH

In line with his suggestion that the Chronicler's genealogies have been expanded upon from a basic core, which was itself based upon Num 26,[43] Martin Noth has suggested that the Judahite portion of this "core" consisted only of 1 Chr 2:3–5, 9–15.[44] Everything else was a later addition.[45] However, even within this minor section of core material, Noth suggests that some parts, such as 1 Chr 2:3b, may be a later addition,[46] and, in reference to 1 Chr 2:9, he states that there "there has clearly been some later interference here."[47]

Noth's judgements are, however, guided by his principle that the Chronicler could only have utilised materials from the Pentateuch. He has no objections to the material in 1 Chr 1 being original as it is taken from Genesis,[48] but rejects as secondary almost all that is in the remainder of the genealogies that cannot be traced in some form to the Pentateuch.[49]

Even if it be granted that there were no other sources upon which the Chronicler could draw for the content of the genealogical section, it does not automatically follow that what cannot be located within the Pentateuch is a secondary addition. There is nothing within the genealogies themselves which would prevent them from being the creation of the Chronicler (if it is assumed that he had no other sources).

The substance of Noth's argument appears to arise from his presuppositions that; first the Chronicler was only a manipulator of sources, rather than an author; second, that the Chronicler only had the Pentateuch and the Deuteronomistic

---

[43] Noth, *Chronicler's History*, 37. In the same work, Noth had previously stated, "It stands out in even bolder relief, therefore, that secondary material has grown up round the work of Chr. in *the introductory genealogical section in 1 Chron. 1–9*. In the form in which it has come down to us the condition of this section is one of unusually great disorder and confusion, but for this . . . Chr. cannot be held responsible. Here again it is innumerable genealogies and lists which have been subsequently added in to Chr.'s work," 36. Italics his.

[44] Noth, *Chronicler's History*, 38.

[45] "It is hardly to be expected that anything which follows in 2.18–4.23 is to be attributed to the basic core which can be traced back to Chr," Noth, *Chronicler's History*, 39. Wellhausen also considered much of the Judahite list to be later additions, Wellhausen, *Prolegomena*, 215–218.

[46] Noth, *Chronicler's History*, 151 note 24.

[47] Noth, *Chronicler's History*, 151 note 26.

[48] Noth, *Chronicler's History*, 36.

[49] "In 1 Chron. 2ff., accordingly, Chr. continues to follow his procedure in 1 Chron. 1 of extracting from the Pentateuch all kinds of lists for his genealogical introduction," Noth, *Chronicler's History*, 38.

History and no other sources available; and third, that the Chronicler could not adapt his sources or create new material to present his own story.

Rudolph likewise sees in the Judahite genealogy a basic core around which has grown supplemental material.[50] He suggests that the first form of the text consisted of 1 Chr 2:3–9, 25–33, 10–17, 42–50aα. This was supplemented by 1 Chr 2:21, 34–41, 18f, 50aβ–55. A third stage came when 1 Chr 3:1–4:23 was inserted, and the final form of the text was reached with the transposition of 1 Chr 2:18 to its current place, the secondary addition of 1 Chr 2:20 and the inclusion of 1 Chr 2:24. Like Noth, Rudolph rejects the possibility that these were the Chronicler's own additions, although he does allow for the use of sources by whoever included them into the text.

It is difficult to challenge the conclusions of Noth or Rudolph in text critical terms alone. The biggest challenge to Noth and Rudolph comes when the Judahite genealogy as a whole is investigated, and it is observed that there is a discernable chiastic structure within the Judahite genealogy. This being the case, this indicates that the contents are not the product of haphazard, later additions to a genealogical core, as suggested by both Noth and Rudolph, but are the result of the deliberate planning and structuring of the content of the text by the Chronicler.

A CHIASTIC STRUCTURE

Two different, and somewhat contradictory, chiastic structures have been observed within the Judahite genealogy. The simplest of these is put forward by Knoppers.[51]

a   The Descendants of Judah (1 Chr 2:3–55)
 b   The Descendants of David (1 Chr 3)
a¹ The Descendants of Judah (1 Chr 4:1–23)

Knoppers sees the two lists of the descendants of Judah (1 Chr 2, 4), as being similarly structured.[52] Both lists begin with the phrase בְּנֵי יְהוּדָה (the sons of Judah; 1 Chr 2:3; 4:1), and both lists end with a list of professionals (1 Chr 2:55; 4:21–23). He also sees correspondence between the opening and closing of the genealogy with reference to the person of Shelah (1 Chr 2:3; 4:21–23). He suggests that Shelah forms an *inclusio* surrounding the other descendants of

---

[50] Rudolph, *Chronikbücher*, 13.
[51] Knoppers, *1 Chronicles 1–9*, 356. So also Goettsberger, *Chronik*, 37; Japhet, *Chronicles*, 68. Cf. the slightly different scheme of Johnstone, *Chronicles: Volume 1*, 42–48.
[52] Knoppers, *1 Chronicles 1–9*, 354.

Judah.[53] He further observes that while the presentation within 1 Chr 2 is ascending (sons of Judah, Ashhur, sons of Hur, Haroeh) the presentation in 1 Chr 4 is descending (Reaiah, sons of Hur, Ashhur, Shelah).[54] He concludes by suggesting that the relationship between 1 Chr 2 and 4 is such that it "creates ties between the two sections surrounding the Davidic genealogy,"[55] which, "calls attention to the intervening genealogy – the descendants of David. David is firmly related to one of Judah's major families and his descendants occupy a privileged place within the tribe as a whole."[56]

While attractive due to its simplicity,[57] Knoppers' suggestion is not without its problems. First, while the lists in 1 Chr 2 and 4 begin with "the sons of Judah," the lists themselves present differing data. First Chronicles 2:3–4 is a segmented genealogy which presents data sourced from Gen 38:2–7. It is a mixture of a genealogy taken from a narrative as well as some narrative comments in respect to the persons named. In 1 Chr 2:3–8, the relationships between the persons are clearly declared, with the exception of Carmi. First Chronicles 4:1 is different. Although 4:1 begins with, "the sons of Judah," and, if read in isolation would give the appearance of being a segmented genealogy, it is in reality a linear genealogy recorded as a segmented genealogy. The order "Perez, Hezron, Carmi, Hur, Shobal" follows the order contained in 1 Chr 2:4, 5, 7, 19, 50.[58] It would appear then that "son" is here used with the wider meaning of "descendant," and that the Chronicler has omitted the relationship terms under the assumption that his readers would be acquainted with them and supply these terms themselves.[59] It would appear that 1 Chr 4:1 is a recapitulation of 1 Chr 2, rather than a parallel to it, and seeks to bring the reader back to the person from whom the Chronicler

---

[53] Knoppers, *1 Chronicles 1–9*, 354. So also Williamson, *Chronicles*, 49. On the necessary precautions that must be taken prior to claiming that a passage is an *inclusio*, see Chris Wyckoff, "Have We Come Full Circle Yet? Closure, Psycholinguistics, and Problems of Recognition with the *Inclusio*," *JSOT* 30 (2006): 475–505.

[54] Knoppers, *1 Chronicles 1–9*, 355. Knoppers also sees a potential inversing when the presentation of the "sons of Kenaz" (1 Chr 4:13), are concluded with "Kenaz" (1 Chr 4:15), 356.

[55] Knoppers, *1 Chronicles 1–9*, 355.

[56] Knoppers, *1 Chronicles 1–9*, 356.

[57] "Simplicity" is not to be confused with being "simplistic."

[58] Many suggest reading "Caleb" for "Carmi: Curtis and Madsen, *Chronicles*, 104; Japhet, *Chronicles*, 106; Knoppers, *1 Chronicles 1–9*, 337; Klein, *1 Chronicles*, 124. This is rejected by Williamson, *Chronicles*, 59, who suggests that there may have been confusion here on account of the sons of Reuben, "Hezron, Carmi" (Gen 46:9; 1 Chr 5:3).

[59] The Chronicler follows a similar pattern in 1 Chr 1:1–4, 24–27 where he simply supplies the names from the longer lists contained in Gen 5, 11. This pattern may be evidence, contra Williamson, that 1 Chr 4:1 is the Chronicler's own composition, "Sources," 111.

had just digressed, i.e. Shobal (1 Chr 2:50, 52; 4:2). If 4:1 is a recapitulation, then it follows that the Chronicler views his material in 1 Chr 4 as leading on from 1 Chr 2, and continuing the story he had begun, before his digression on the descendants of David in 1 Chr 3.[60]

Second, while Knoppers maintains that both 1 Chr 2 and 4 end with a "list of professionals," closer examination indicates that this is not completely accurate. While it is true that 1 Chr 4:21–23 contains two professions (linen workers, potters), 1 Chr 2:54–55 contains only one (scribes). These do not constitute a "list," but rather a passing reference in the context of the discussion of clans, families, and towns. Professions are also mentioned in 1 Chr 4:14 (craftsmen). It is probable that the sources available to the Chronicler, arising from within the social context of Judah, at times made references to professions.

Third, Knoppers' suggestion the Judahite genealogy is a chiasm centering upon David are open to an alternative interpretation. Knoppers bases his conclusion on the observations that:

1) First Chronicles 2:3 acts as an *inclusio* with 1 Chr 4:21–23 because of the mention of Shelah, son of Judah.
2) First Chronicles 2 presents data in an ascending manner (from Shelah up to Haroeh) while 1 Chr 4 presents data in a descending manner (from Reaiah down to Shelah).

If Knoppers' two observations were combined, however, together they would present the possibility that all of 1 Chr 2 is "ascending," from Shelah to Haroeh, and all of 1 Chr 4 is descending, from Reaiah to Shelah.[61] It would therefore be possible to conclude that the entire genealogy is constructed chiastically, rather than simply the three main chapters.

This leads to the suggestion of Williamson, which has been followed by others, that in the Judahite genealogy the Chronicler has adapted his sources into a chiasm in such a way as to focus upon David, not as the centre, but as the base and foundation of the chiasm.[62]

---

[60] First Chronicles 4:1 is an "editorial note to remind the reader where he was . . . before the interruption," Williamson, "Sources," 111. Williamson elsewhere refers to this as an occurrence of "repetitive resumption," "Origins," 138. For a discussion of 'repetitive resumption,' see Shemaryahu Talmon, "Ezra and Nehemiah (Books and Men)," in *The Interpreter's Dictionary of the Bible* (*Supplementary Volume;* ed. George A. Buttrick; Nashville: Abingdon, 1976), 322.

[61] Haroeh, הָרֹאֶה, (1 Chr 2:52), is considered to be a corruption of Reaiah, רְאָיָה, (1 Chr 4:2), Knoppers, *1 Chronicles 1–9*, 301. Williamson points out that "Haroeh" (the "seer"), is not a personal name, *Chronicles*, 55.

[62] Williamson, "Sources." He is followed in his analysis by Selman, *1 Chronicles*, 94; Thompson, *Chronicles*, 60; Hill, *Chronicles*, 77; McKenzie, *Chronicles*, 68; Klein, *1 Chronicles*, 87. Williamson's observations of a chiasm were foreshadowed by Curtis and

Williamson begins his analysis of the Judahite genealogy by determining the sources upon which the Chronicler drew for his presentation. He sees the overall genealogy as being comprised of four sources:[63]
1) Earlier biblical texts or their equivalents: 1 Chr 2:3–8, 10–17, 20; 3:1–16
2) First Chronicles 2:25–33, 42–50a. He states that this is a single unit on the basis of the opening and closing statements, "the sons of Jerahmeel."
3) A source which has become disjointed, and was added by the Chronicler:
   a) First Chronicles 2:50b–52; 4:2–4: "the sons of Hur."
   b) First Chronicles 2:24; 4:5–7: Ashhur, "the father of Tekoa"
   c) First Chronicles 2:18, 19 which are an introduction to 2:24. Together these were the original introduction to 2:50b.
   d) The Chronicler inserted 1 Chr 2:20, the descendants of Hur, who was the craftsman employed to construct the tabernacle (Exod 31:2).
   e) The Chronicler inserted 1 Chr 2:21–23 at this location from an unknown source, for it presents details of Hezron prior to the Chronicler's relation of Hezron's death (1 Chr 2:24).

Miscellaneous data from unknown sources: 1 Chr 2:21–23, 34–41, 53–55; 3:17–24; 4:1, 8–23. What links 1 Chr 2:24 and 2:50b together is that both persons are called the sons of Ephrath/Ephrathah and Caleb. On the basis of Williamson's analysis, it is probable that the original source was: 1 Chr 2:18, 19, 24; 4:5–7; 2:50b–52; 4:2–4. This would then relate the births of the two sons of Caleb and Ephrath/Ephrathah (Hur and Ashhur), followed by their progeny, in reverse order (Ashhur and Hur). This reversal is a common occurrence within the sources utilised by the Chronicler, and repeated by him in his work.[64]

Williamson suggests that the only part of the Judahite genealogy that is the Chronicler's own construction is 1 Chr 2:9, which "introduces the following substantial section," where the Chronicler ties together biblical genealogical data (the sons of Ram), with two separate and distinct genealogies, those of the sons of Caleb and the sons of Jerahmeel.[65]

Madsen, *Chronicles*, 82. Braun rejects Williamson's analysis, saying that it "may also be more apparent to some students than to others, who may view it as at best accidental," *1 Chronicles*, 28. It must be recognised, however, that "accidental" chiasms with the length and complexity of Williamson's proposal are unlikely.

[63] Williamson, "Sources," 107–111. See Figure 8.3.

[64] This is seen in 1 Chronicles 1:4, where the order of the sons of Noah is "Shem, Ham, Japheth, while the order of discussion of the sons' descendants is Japheth (1 Chr 1:5–7), Ham (1 Chr 1:8–16), and Shem (1 Chr 1:17–23). This follows the order that the Chronicler found in his source in Gen 10:1–29).

[65] Williamson, "Sources," 112. David's father and some of his brothers are indicated in 1 Sam 16:5–13. It is uncertain where the names of David's other brothers originated, nor why David is listed as the seventh son when 1 Sam 16:10–11 indicates that David was

Figure 8.3: The Chronicler's Sources for the Judahite Genealogy

Chronicler	Biblical Texts	1st Complete Unit	2nd Complete Unit	Miscellaneous Data
	2:3–8			
2:9				
	2:10–17			
			2:18–19	
	2:20			
				2:21–23
			2:24	
		2:25–33		
				2:34–41
		2:42–50a		
			2:50b–52	
				2:53–55
	3:1–16			
				3:17–24
				4:1
			4:2–4	
			4:5–7	
				4:8–23

He then suggests that 1 Chr 2:3; 4:21–23 were included as an *inclusio* to the sons of Judah, while 1 Chr 2:4–8; 4:1–20 provide data on Perez. Williamson concludes that these, coupled with the insertion of the Davidic data in 1 Chr 3, present a chiastic structure. (Figure 8.4)[66]

Williamson interprets this structure in two, different, ways. First, he sees the Judahite genealogy as one, large, chiastic structure, with the focus upon the sons of Hezron (1 Chr 2:9–3:24).[67] He states, "this draws attention to the centrality of

---

the eighth. The lineage from Perez, through Ram and then to David is found in Ruth 4:18–22. There is debate as to whether the Chronicler utilised Ruth, Pratt, *Chronicles*, 71; Ruth utilised Chronicles, Rudolph, *Chronikbücher*, 16; or both go back to an original, common source, Myers, *I Chronicles*, 13–14; Thompson, *Chronicles*, 61.

[66] Williamson, "Sources," 113–114; *Chronicles*, 49.
[67] Williamson, "Sources," 114.

David's family in the tribe, just as the section we have been mainly concerned with here emphasises its prominence."[68]

Figure 8.4: Williamson's Structure of the Judahite Genealogy

a   descendants of Judah: Shelah: 2:3
    b   descendants of Perez: 2:4–8
       c   descendants of Ram (as far as David): 2:10–17
          d   descendants of Caleb: 2:18–24
             e   descendants of Jerahmeel: 2:25–33
             e^1 supplementary material on Jerahmeel: 2:34–41
          d^1 supplementary material on Caleb 2:42–55
       c^1 supplementary material on Ram (David's descendants): 3:1–24
    b^1 supplementary material on Perez: 4:1–20
a^1 supplementary material on Shelah: 4:21–23

Second, he concludes that the chiastic structuring of the middle section concerning the descendants of Ram (levels C to C^1), with David and his family at the base, is an attempt by the Chronicler to emphasise the position of David and his descendants within the tribe of Judah, and this is fully in line with his interests later on in the work.[69]

Williamson's work, although rightly drawing attention to the sources that the Chronicler utilised, as well as the observation that the Chronicler himself was responsible for the arrangement of the material, has several shortcomings. First, he fails to recognise that the Chronicler, by placing the Davidic genealogy in 1 Chr 3:1–24 has divided previously joined supplementary Calebite material (1 Chr 2:42–55; 4:2–8). Williamson's proposed chiastic structure does not allow for this division, and it appears to be out of place within Williamson's thesis.

Second, his suggestion that there are in fact two different structures in this section is not consistent with his analysis. Williamson's analysis of the Judahite genealogy has Shelah as its base, and Jerahmeel as its focal point. In this structure, David and his descendants are neither the focus, nor the base, of this proposed chiasm but only a supporting element within the larger structure. Williamson's attempt to: a) have a structure which focuses upon the central element of David as a son of Hezron by conflating levels c through e, or b) to only take account of levels c through c^1 to suggest that David and his family are the foundational basis of the structure, overlooks the completeness of the structure that he has identified. It is a violation of the chiastic structure to ignore the ongoing chiasm as evidenced in levels d and e, thus conflating levels c

---

[68] Williamson, "Sources," 114.
[69] Williamson, "Sources," 114.

through e. Using the same methodology, one could conflate levels d and e to focus upon Caleb, or levels b through e, in order to focus upon Perez. It is also a violation of the chiastic structure to ignore the beginning of the chiasm, levels a and b, to place level c as the base.[70] Again, utilising the same methodology, one could ignore levels a through c to propose the descendants of Caleb as the base.

Third, it appears as if Williamson's primary concern is to present the structure of the Judahite genealogy as focussing upon David. If Williamson's analysis is correct, then it is apparent that the focus of the chiasm is upon Jerahmeel rather than David or his family.

Both Williamson and Knoppers appear to be swayed in their positions by the statement in 1 Chr 5:2 that "Judah was the strongest of his brothers and a ruler came from him" as to the primacy of Judah in the genealogies as a whole, and the primacy of David within the Judahite genealogy.[71]

Notwithstanding the difficulty presented by the presence of additional "sons of Caleb" in 1 Chr 4:2–8, subsumed by Williamson under the broader phrase "supplementary material on Perez," it is clear that Williamson is correct in his identification of a chiastic structure within the Judahite genealogy.[72] This being the case, however, it follows that neither Williamson's nor Knoppers' conclusion that the Judahite genealogy centres upon David can be correct, for the centre of the chiasm represents the chiasm's focus and climax,[73] and that centre is Jerahmeel. If David and his descendants are not the focus of the genealogy of Judah, a conclusion that the chiastic structure compels us to make, then this forces us to reassess the Chronicler's purpose in relating this genealogy.

---

[70] Both of these options are well presented graphically in Selman, *1 Chronicles*, 94.

[71] Gary N. Knoppers, *"Great Among His Brothers," but Who is He? Heterogeneity in the Composition of Judah* (2000) [cited August 21, 2006]; available from www.purl.org/jhs, 1.2; Williamson, *Chronicles*, 63.

[72] That an additional element, or level, is supplied in the chiastic structure should not be taken as an argument against Williamson's overall structure. Although the "perfect chiasm" is one that is well structured, with balanced ascending and descending elements, "such perfection however will not emerge everywhere. Not infrequently, we shall find the sequence to be ABC – D – $B^1C^1A^1$ or even less ordered and more scrambled, particularly when the number of members is large," Radday, "Chiasmus," 52, and the varying examples given throughout Radday's article.

[73] Welch, "Introduction," 10.

THE JUDAHITE GENEALOGY AS PRESENTING ALTERNATIVE PATHS

Two observations made by Williamson and Knoppers do, however, point to an alternative understanding of the Judahite genealogy. Although, on the basis of Williamson's more thorough analysis, Knoppers' proposed simple chiastic structure is to be rejected, Knoppers is correct in drawing attention to the opening verse of 1 Chr 4, which parallels 1 Chr 2:3 in presenting a list of the "sons of Judah."[74] This list in 1 Chr 4:1, which draws names from throughout 1 Chr 2, acts as a reminder to data which the Chronicler had previously related, and appears to be an attempt to refocus the reader's attention upon this previous data from which point the Chronicler will continue his account. Williamson refers to this as "a clear editorial note to remind the reader where he was, so to speak, before the interruption" brought about by the insertion of the Davidic material.[75]

He goes on to say,"the names mentioned quickly trace the line again (father to son) from Judah to Shobal, the father of Reaiah, and hence to the very point at which the interruption had occurred."[76]

Talmon refers to this authorial method as "repetitive resumption,"[77] and says:

> These seem to mark the insertion of a self-contained unit into a given context. This technique is characterised by the partial repetition after the insert of the verse which closed the preceding part of the comprehensive unit, generally with some textual variation.[78]

This authorial style is also utilised in 1 Chr 5:1–3 where, after an initial mention of "the sons of Reuben the firstborn of Israel" (1 Chr 5:1a), the Chronicler digresses on the reason why the firstborn Reuben is not mentioned first in the genealogy of the sons of Israel. In this digression he mentions that, as a result of Reuben's actions the birthright now belonged to Joseph (1 Chr 5:1b), although Judah was the strongest (1 Chr 5:2).[79] In 1 Chr 5:3 the Chronicler

---

[74] Knoppers, *1 Chronicles 1–9*, 354.
[75] Williamson, "Sources," 111.
[76] Williamson, "Sources," 111.
[77] Talmon, "Ezra and Nehemiah," 322.
[78] Talmon, "Ezra and Nehemiah," 322. Talmon sees these in Ezra 4:4–5, 24b; 6:16b, 22b; 2:1b, 70; Neh 7:4–5; 11:1, and suggests that the intervening passages were sources which were inserted into the narrative, while the "repetitive resumption" helps to identify where the author's material is taken up again after the digression. Repetitive resumption is also used in the New Testament writings of Paul: Ephesians 3:1; 4:1.
[79] Japhet says that 1 Chr 5:1–2 "comprise one of the most distinct examples of Midrash in Chronicles," *Chronicles*, 131.

resumes where he had been prior to his digression with the phrase, "the sons of Reuben the firstborn of Israel."

That the Chronicler here utilised a "repetitive resumption" in 1 Chr 4:1 indicates several things. First, it indicates that David and his line were not his primary thought or purpose in the Judahite genealogy. David and his line are, in fact, a digression from the overall thought of the Chronicler. Although David's genealogy is a part of the Chronicler's chiasm, it is neither the purpose nor the focus of that chiasm. This has already been illustrated by Williamson, although the significance of this was not recognised by him. The focus of the Judahite genealogy is in fact Jerahmeel. This would suggest that neither monarchy, nor a return to monarchy, is the purpose of the Chronicler in the Judahite genealogy generally, and in the inclusion of the Davidic line in particular.

Second, this use of repetitive resumption indicates that the ultimate purpose or thought of the Chronicler is to be found within 1 Chr 4, which continues the Chronicler's initial thoughts in 1 Chr 2.

After the repetitive resumption found in 1 Chr 4:1, 1 Chr 4:2–8 continues in a similar pattern to the material contained in 1 Chr 2. First Chronicles 4:2–8 contains mention of wives (1 Chr 4:4, 5–6), sisters (1 Chr 4:3), births (1 Chr 4:6), and leaders of communities (1 Chr 4:3, 4, 5). The same type of data are also contained within 1 Chr 4:11–23.

What marks a turning point in the Judahite genealogy (overlooking for the moment the Davidic genealogy), is the narrative regarding Jabez (1 Chr 4:9–10). In the Judahite genealogy there are seven narratives:

- Er, son of Judah (1 Chr 2:3)
- Achar (1 Chr 2:7)
- The wives of Caleb (1 Chr 2:18–19)
- Segub, son of Hezron (1 Chr 2:21–23)
- The death of Hezron (1 Chr 2:24)
- Sheshan (1 Chr 2:34–35)
- Jabez (1 Chr 4:9–10)

Each of the first six narratives relate aspects of life which are negative and disruptive within the life of a community. These narratives contain portraits of death (1 Chr 2:3, 19, 24, cf. 2:30, 32), wickedness (1 Chr 2:3), unfaithfulness, with its resulting "trouble" for Israel (1 Chr 2:7), loss of land (1 Chr 2:23), having no sons (1 Chr 2:34; cf. 2:30, 32), and marrying the wife/widow of one's father (1 Chr 2:24).[80]

---

[80] There is general agreement that the phrase בְּכָלֵב אֶפְרָתָה "in Caleb Ephrathah" should be read as בָּא כָלֵב אֶפְרָתָה "Caleb went in to Ephrath," following the LXX ἦλθεν Χαλεβ εἰς Εφραθα, Rudolph, Chronikbücher, 16; Japhet, Chronicles, 81; Knoppers, 1 Chronicles 1–9, 299; Klein, 1 Chronicles, 84, notes 25, 26. Some scholars further propose amending וְאֵשֶׁת חֶצְרוֹן אֲבִיָּה "and the wife of Hezron was Abijah," to וְאֵשֶׁת חֶצְרוֹן אֲבִיהוּ

The account of Jabez also begins with the relation of certain negative aspects of life. Jabez' mother relates his name to the fact that "I gave birth to him in pain" (יְלִדְתִּי בְּעֹצֶב; 1 Chr 4:9), which is a clear echo of Gen 3:16, "in pain you will give birth to children" (בְּעֶצֶב תֵּלְדִי).[81] This passage ends, however, with answered prayer. For Jabez, while there is a negative beginning, there is a positive outcome. This is in clear contrast to the narratives of Er and Achar which begin the opening part of the Chronicler's Judahite genealogy. While the narratives of Er and Achar begin negatively and end in death or trouble, the Jabez narrative begins with pain and ends with answered prayer. While there is a reversal in the narrative of Segub, it is a reversal that goes from positive to negative. The narrative of Segub begins positively with the birth of Segub, but ends negatively with the loss of towns.

What is further to be noted is that in the material following the Jabez narrative (1 Chr 4:11–23), there is no more mention of death, suffering, wickedness or loss of land, while there are a number of references to these following the accounts of Er and Achar (1 Chr 2:8–55). This gives the impression that the Chronicler is presenting, through the Jabez narrative, an alternative path in life and community relationships. The first path is that of Er and Achar, which the Chronicler indicates brings numerous negative results for the people and the

---

"the wife of Hezron his father," thus indicating that Caleb's wife Ephrathah (cf. 1 Chr 2:19), had previously been the wife of his father Hezron. Curtis suggests that "the taking of a father's wife was asserting claim to the father's possessions," *Chronicles*, 92, cf. Goettsberger, *Chronik*, 40; Rudolph, *Chronikbücher*, 16; Japhet, *Chronicles*, 81–82. This proposal is rejected by Klein because: 1) there is no versional support, and, 2) it makes Caleb marry his father's wife, *1 Chronicles*, p 84, note 27. This latter, of course, may be the entire point of its inclusion. Williamson suggests that the phrase "the wife of Hezron was Abijah" is simply a "misplaced gloss" on 1 Chr 2:21, Williamson, *Chronicles*, 53–54, although Japhet rejects this by saying that there is no reason for a gloss in this place, Japhet, *Chronicles*, 82. One important observation is that the proposed emendation would make the form of the text nearly identical with 1 Chr 2:21 which relates a similar situation:
1 Chronicles 2:21   וְאַחַר בָּא חֶצְרוֹן אֶל־בַּת־מָכִיר אֲבִי גִלְעָד
1 Chronicles 2:24   וְאַחַר מוֹת־חֶצְרוֹן בָּא כָלֵב אֶפְרָתָה וְאֵשֶׁת חֶצְרוֹן אֲבִיָּהוּ

It will be observed that the order of presentation in these two verses is the same: 1) "after," 2) person X "went in to," 3) person Y, 4) the relation of person Y to person Z. The alteration from אֲבִיָּהוּ "his father," to אֲבִיָּה "Abijah," could easily have been made to avoid the possibility that a man married his father's wife (an act which is in contravention of Lev 18:8, 20:11; Deut 22:30; 27:20; cf. in the New Testament 1 Cor 5:1), especially in the light of 1 Chr 5:1 and the reason which was given explaining why Reuben was no longer listed first in the genealogies of the sons of Israel.

[81] Kalimi, *Reshaping*, 252; Pechawer, *Jabez*, 55; Heard, *Echoes*, 2.7; Kalimi sees the phrase in 1 Chr 4:9 as a chiasmus in relation to the phrase in Gen 3:16. Both Pechawer and Heard are writing in direct response to Wilkinson, *Prayer*.

community. The second is the path of Jabez which leads to answered prayer, and Jabez being "more honoured" than his brothers (1 Chr 4:9).[82]

It has already been noted that it was when the Transjordanian tribes cried out to Yahweh (1 Chr 5:20), that they were victorious in battle and gained land.[83] Answered prayer is seen not simply as a sign of Yahweh's favour, but is an indication that the individual(s) who have sought Yahweh in prayer have either turned from "unfaithfulness" (cf. Manasseh, 2 Chr 33:12–13), or are living in "faithfulness" to Yahweh (cf. Jehoshaphat; 2 Chr 19:4–7; 20:6–17).[84]

This presentation of Jabez as "honoured," and therefore "faithful," is in clear contrast to Er, who was "wicked in the eyes of Yahweh" (רַע בְּעֵינֵי יְהוָה; 1 Chr 2:3), and Achar who committed "unfaithfulness" (מָעַל; 1 Chr 2:7).

That Jabez' honour is related to his answered prayer, and thus to his faithfulness, is made clear when the structure of the entire narrative is observed, (Figure 8.5). Although this structure is not properly chiastic, the overall structure is one of repetition and comlementarity so often present in chiasms.

It can be observed that Jabez' honour was related to God's providing the things for which he had asked God. There are also two speeches, introduced by קרא (called): that of Jabez' mother when she named Jabez, and Jabez' calling (קרא) on Yahweh as the counterpoint to his mother's calling.[85] Both of these

---

[82] Although the NIV, NASB, NKJV, RSV have here "more honourable," it is to be noted that the nifal participle of כבד always has the meaning of "honoured, esteemed, noble, great." In its only other occurrences in Chronicles (1 Chr 11:21, 25), it carries the meaning of "more honoured," so here NRSV, JPS. See also Heard, *Echoes*, 2.1.

[83] See Chapter 6. Heard notes that the Chronicler does not indicate who the "brothers" are that Jabez is more honoured than. He suggests that this refers to the, later, accounts of Simeon, Reuben, and the Transjordanian tribes. He suggests that, unlike Simeon and Reuben who acquired land through conflict alone (1 Chr 4:38–43; 5:10), or the Transjordanian tribes who acquired land through conflict and prayer (1 Chr 5:18–22), Jabez was more "honoured" because he gained land through prayer alone. He suggests that Jabez's honour came "because he sought a non-violent means of attaining land," or, because of "Jabez's receipt of more land without the necessity of wresting it violently from others," Heard, *Echoes*, 3.1.3. Klein responds, saying, "while the proposed theological message is very attractive . . . the somewhat forced interpretation of עצבי as referring to nonviolence make this proposal somewhat unlikely," *1 Chronicles*, 133.

[84] It is to be noted that "Yahweh," יהוה, rarely occurs in the genealogies (1 Chr 2:3; 5:41; 6:16–17 [6:15, 31–32]; 9:19, 20, 23). Jabez prays to "the God of Israel," while the Transjordanian tribes pray "to God."

[85] It is often suggested that in giving him the name "Jabez," his mother had placed a curse, a bad omen, or a negative wish upon him. Typical is the statement of Allen who says, "in popular thinking so negative a name, which commemorated the hard time his mother had in giving birth to him, made Jabez a born loser. Dogged with such an unlucky name, how could he ever succeed in life?," and again, "his name created an emotional

speeches are concerned with "pain" (עצב). For Jabez' mother this was the pain of childbirth, while for Jabez it is the "pain" of not having enough land for his flocks. Finally, the content of Jabez' prayer expressed the desire for Yahweh's blessing/presence, which would be indicated through the provision of larger boundaries/pastures.

The Chronicler's presentation in 1 Chr 2, 4 is indicative of the theology reflected in the narrative of the work. In the remainder of the work, the Chronicler indicates that מַעַל (unfaithfulness) or רַע (acts of wickedness) consistently led to negative consequences (or retribution) upon the people.[86]

This is displayed in 1 Chr 2, which contains incidents of death, childlessness, unlawful relationships, and loss of land. Second Chronicles 7:14 presents the solution to the negative consequences of רַע (wickedness). Part of this solution is the turning from רַע (wickedness) while another is prayer. It is the attitudes and actions found in 2 Chr 7:14 which leads to a reversal of the negative consequences of רַע. This is illustrated in 1 Chr 4 where, after Jabez' prayer and

---

hang-up, stopping him from leading a full life," *Chronicles*, 47–48. Even though the letters are transposed עצב/יעבץ, thus indicating that the name is not to be identified with the meaning "pain," Japhet says, "this discrepancy, between the actual pronunciation of the name and its assumed root, is the implicit but probably the strongest illustration of the premise of the story: the potent force of the name! The fear of the potentially harmful effects of a 'wrong' name is such that two precautions are taken to forestall its action: first, an intentional mis-pronunciation . . . as if to fool the messengers of fate, and second . . . an urgent plea to God to avert the name's inherent dangers," *Chronicles*, 109, and similarly also Curtis and Madsen, *Chronicles*, 107; Hill, *Chronicles*, 95; Keil, *Chronicles*, 88; Klein, *1 Chronicles*, 132–133; Knoppers, *1 Chronicles 1–9*, 346; Myers, *1 Chronicles*, 28; Rudolph, *Chronikbücher*, 33. Braun, however, rejects this connection, stating that "the play on words . . . is popular rather than scientific," *1 Chronicles*, 56, and the discussion in Pechawer, *Jabez*, 19–24. This identification, although appealing, is unsatisfactory. In response to Japhet, if Jabez' mother sought to "fool the messengers of fate" with an "intentional mis-pronunciation," why would she give him this name at all? Why not give Jabez an alternative name that was so different, that "fate" would have no reason to harm him. Furthermore, it is to be noted that names of children are often reflective, not of the hope of the parent(s) for the child's future, but of a circumstance that attended the child's birth. Thus Samuel (1 Sam 1:20); Ichabod (1 Sam 4:21); Ben-Oni/Benjamin (Gen 35:18); and, in fact, the names of the other sons of Jacob (Gen 29:32, 33, 34, 35; 30:6, 7, 11, 13, 18, 20, 24), reflect something of the circumstances of their births, rather than an omen, or a wish, for them. The same is true of Ishmael (Gen 16:11, 15); Isaac (Gen 21:3); Esau and Jacob (Gen 25:25–26).

[86] Other than Er in 1 Chr 2:3, and the "ancestors" in 2 Chr 29:6, only kings are said to do "wickedness," רַע: Rehoboam (2 Chr 12:14), Jehoram (2 Chr 21:6), Ahaziah (2 Chr 22:4), Manasseh (2 Chr 33:2, 6, 9), Amon (2 Chr 33:22), Jehoiakim (2 Chr 36:5), Jehoiachin (2 Chr 36:9), Zedekiah (2 Chr 36:12).

God's positive response, none of the negative aspects of life contained in 1 Chr 2 are present within the community.

Figure 8.5: The Structure of the Jabez Narrative

a   And Jabez (יַעְבֵּץ) was honoured more than his brothers
  b   and his mother called (קרא) his name "Jabez" saying,
    c   "I gave birth in pain" (בְּעֹצֶב)
  b¹   And Jabez called (קרא) on the God of Israel saying,
    d   If only you would surely bless me
      e   and make my boundaries great
    d¹   And your hand would be with me
      e¹   and would provide pasture[87]
    c¹   so that pain (עָצְבִּי) will not exist for me
a¹   And God brought in what he had asked

It would appear then that 1 Chr 2 and 4 present a linear flow of theological thought which is reflective of the Chronicler's understanding of history.[88]

---

[87] Repointing BHS "from evil," מֵרָעָה, as מִרְעֶה, "pasture," Pechawer, *Jabez*, 51–54; Heard, *Echoes*, 2.10–11. This was, however, proposed at least as early as Curtis and Madsen, *Chronicles*, 108. This reading has several advantages. First, it makes this request parallel to the request to "make my boundaries great." Second, the identical pointing to read "pastureland" is used in relation to Simeon in 1 Chr 4:39, 40, 41. In the sense of land acquisition, which the greater boundaries imply, it is clear that Jabez would require not just "land," but pasture for his flocks, which is also the context of the appearance of the term in the Simeonite list. Pechawer points out that praying for "pasturelands" was not considered to be a selfish prayer, for the provision of "pasturelands" was one of the duties of Hammurapi, acting as agent for the deity, Pechawer, *Jabez*, 72; cf. Hallo and Younger, *Context: Vol 2*, 257, 336. Third, this helps to make sense of the phrase, וְעָשִׂיתָ מֵּרָעָה. Pechawer points out that the word עשה, "occurs over 2,600 times in the Old Testament and never with the sense proposed by our English translations." Furthermore, עשה "can carry the idea of 'provide'" (cf. Judg 21:7, 16; 2 Sam 15:1; Ezek 43:25; 45:22, 23, 24), which is consistent with the idea of Jabez requesting that God provide "pasturelands" *Jabez*, 63. Heard further states that "the translation 'keep me from harm' requires assigning the construction עשה ("to make, do") + מן the sense 'to keep [someone/something] away from [the noun to which מן is affixed],' or the sense 'to turn [the noun to which the מן is affixed] away from [someone/something].' However, none of the other biblical instances of עשה + מן exhibit any such sense," Heard, *Echoes*, 2.9, and especially his note 17.

[88] If it is correct that 1 Chronicles 2–4 presents a linear flow within its theological argument, then the conclusion cannot be avoided that narrative can be expressed within a chiastic arrangement. This, however, is to be expected, as the chiastic shape of of the flood narrative indicates.

This begins with the wickedness/unfaithfulness of the people which leads to negative consequences, however, if the people turn to Yahweh in prayer, then these negative consequences are reversed.

If, 1 Chr 2 and 4 present a linear flow of thought, what is the purpose of 1 Chr 3? Although it would be easy to suggest on the basis of the preceding that the Davidic genealogy is a later insertion which divided the Chronicler's thought, a more suitable alternative explanation could be advanced. Just as the Chronicler utilised repetitive resumption in 1 Chr 4:1 to bring his reader's attention back to his previous place in 1 Chr 2:55, so also has he used key names in 1 Chr 3 in order to link the Davidic genealogy to 1 Chr 2:3–4.

The two names which link the Davidic genealogy to the list of the sons of Judah are בַּת־שׁוּעַ (Bath-shua; 1 Chr 2:3; 3:5), and תָּמָר (Tamar; 1 Chr 2:4; 3:9). Although it is has been suggested that בַּת־שׁוּעַ is a simple scribal error for בַּת־שֶׁבַע (Bathsheba)[89] Japhet hints at an alternative. She says:

> These could reflect alternative spellings or an adaptation of the original 'Bathsheba' to the name of Judah's first wife, following a general inclination to parallelism between David's household and that of Judah; note that both Bathshua and Tamar are explicitly mentioned in Judah's biography.[90]

If, as Japhet suggests, this is a deliberate action of the Chronicler, then it is probable in light of the repetitive resumption utilised in 1 Chr 4:1, that 1 Chr 3, the Davidic genealogy, is to be seen as the continuation of the narrative begun with the "sons of Judah" in 1 Chr 2:3–4. This being the case, through the Jabez narrative and the Davidic genealogy, the Chronicler is offering two alternative solutions to the problems of wickedness and unfaithfulness. The first is the path of monarchy, as reflected in the Davidic genealogy, while the second alternative is prayer and faithfulness, as reflected in Jabez.

It has already been noted that, in 1 Chr 4:11–23 following on from Jabez, the Chronicler presents nothing of the negative aspects of life (death, loss of land, childlessness, improper relationships). The Davidic genealogy of 1 Chr 3 explicitly mentions only one negative aspect. In 1 Chr 3:17, Jehoiachin is called אַסִּר (the captive).[91] If our analysis is correct, this suggests that the Chronicler proposes that the end result of monarchy is only exile. As such monarchy, even

---

[89] Curtis says that this is the result of "a phonetic variation arising from the similar sound of ב bh and ו w," *Chronicles*, 99. The LXX reads here Βηροαβεε, which is also the rendering for the town name "Beersheba."

[90] Japhet, *Chronicles*, 96.

[91] Or, אַסִּיר. Only here in 1 Chr 3:17; Isa 10:4; 24:22; 42:7 with the meaning "captive." It also appears as a name in Exod 6:24; 1 Chr 6:7, 8, 22 [6:22, 23, 37]. The AV understood it as a name in 1 Chr 3:17.

Davidic monarchy, is not the solution to the problem of wickedness or unfaithfulness.[92] Furthermore, not only is exile the only possible outcome of the monarchy, but the Chronicler does not present any of Jehoiachin's descendants returning from exile. Unlike in 1 Chr 9:1–2 where some "Israelites, priests, Levites and temple servants" as well as "those from Judah, from Benjamin, and from Ephraim and Manasseh" resettled in their towns and in Jerusalem, the Chronicler presents no Davidide as returning from exile.

It may be objected that some of the Chronicler's readers would know that some Davidides, such as Zerubbabel, had returned (Ezra 2:2; 3:2, 8; Hag 1:1, 12; Zech 4:6–10). While this is granted, it must also be acknowledged that these readers would also know the story of the kings, the account of David and Bathsheba, the rape of Tamar and its aftermath. That a small number had returned from exile would be more than counterbalanced with the understanding of the problems that had accompanied the monarchy. Many of the kings in these other sources are presented as examples of the unfaithfulness which led, ultimately, to the retribution of the exile. It must be further noted that while the Chronicler mentions the ongoing descendants of David during the exilic and postexilic period, he omits any reference to any Davidide returning to the land. In the Chronicler's presentation, the Davidides remain in exile. This bolsters the conclusion that, for the Chronicler, the monarchy is a dead end.

By contrast, the only person about whom anything is known in the genealogies that follow the narrative of Jabez, is Caleb, son of Jephunneh (1 Chr 4:15), who elsewhere is held up as a model of faithfulness to Yahweh (Num 32:12; Deut 1:36; Josh 14:6–10). In the two alternatives provided by the Chronicler, it is clear that the way of monarchy is portrayed as leading to unfaithfulness and exile, while the way of prayer leads to faithfulness and the retention, or in Caleb's case, the gaining of land.[93]

---

[92] This is probably opposite to the view of the author of Judges, cf. Judg 17:6; 18:1; 19:1; 21:25.

[93] See Figure 8.6.

Figure 8.6: The Alternate Paths of the Judahite Genealogy

	1 Chr 3	1 Chr 2	1 Chr 4
		• Sons of Judah	
		• Bathshua	
		• Tamar	
Repetitive Resumption	• Bathshua • Tamar		• Sons of Judah
Persons and their actions	• Solomon – Zedekiah: Assumed knowledge of the history of the Kings	• Judah: Inappropriate sexual relationship • Er: Wicked • Achar: Violated ban • Caleb: Questionable Marriage	• Jabez: prayer
Results	• Exile • No descendant returning from exile	• Troubling Israel • Loss of towns • Childlessness • Death	• Answered prayer • Reversal of Fortune • Honour • gaining of land • Caleb: example of faithfulness

THE FOCUS ON JERAHMEEL

As was observed in Williamson's chiastic structure, although he himself did not appreciate the implications of this observation, David and his line are not the central focus of the chiasm. The central focus of the chiasm is Jerahmeel. The question which must be asked, however, is, "why Jerahmeel?" Although there is no definitive answer to this question, it is possible to propose a purpose for

Jerahmeel at the centre of the Judahite list based upon the Chronicler's own political, social, and economic circumstances. It is certain that the production and dissemination of literary texts in ancient societies was an undertaking that could only be made by certain persons or groups, and only in specific political, social, or religious contexts. Although it is uncertain how many people in Yehud would have had rudimentary literacy skills which would be suitable for minor commercial, building, and other needs, the skills required to produce a major literary work such as Chronicles would require considerable training on behalf of the scribe who produced it, and would also require considerable financial backing to support the scribe while he produced it. In the case of Chronicles, which appears to have made use of other written sources, access to these sources would also be needed. Such access to official records, be they within temple or government archives, would suggest that the sponsor(s) of the literary work would be in a position of some power and prestige so as to overcome any potential barriers that may arise to such access.

Such a sponsor may arise from within the cult, a rich or prominent family, or from within government circles. It is reasonable to surmise that neither the cultic nor governmental leaders would have a vested interest in promoting a return to Davidic rule. Such a return, if successful, would diminish their own power and prestige, while a failed attempt to return to Davidic rule would result in their deaths or, at the least, loss of power and prestige at the hands of the Persians. Rich and prominent families would probably support the return of a Davidic king only if they themselves were of the Davidic family and would be in a position to benefit from such a return through increased wealth or societal status. As the sponsors of the work, the cultic or government officials, as well as the rich, would have nothing to gain through the promotion of the Davidic monarchy.

The answer to the question "why is Jerahmeel central," may hinge upon another question: "Who benefits through the placing of Jerahmeel in the central position?" The answer may be "the descendants of Jerahmeel." One of the longest linear genealogies in Chronicles is that of Sheshan (1 Chr 2:34–41). Extending thirteen generations, it exceeds in length all other linear genealogies save David and the cultic officials. Regarding linear genealogies, Wilson says:

> linear genealogies may play an important role in the political sphere, for by means of such genealogies claims to inherited offices can be justified, and the authority of incumbents can be assured. For this reason, holders of important political offices frequently maintain long linear genealogies linking them to the first persons to occupy the offices, and in this way they justify their own right to power.[94]

---

[94] Wilson, *Genealogy*, 41.

It is therefore possible that Jerahmeel is in the centre of the Judahite genealogy because one of the major sponsors of the work was a prominent government official, and the Chronicler rewarded his sponsorship by placing the sponsor's genealogy in the central position, and by so doing justifying the sponsor's position in postexilic Yehud.

Who that person might be is uncertain. The final name in the genealogy of Sheshan is Elishama, and although this name appears within certain works of the Hebrew Bible, no one in the postexilic period canonical tradition is identified as having this name. Although a number of seals have been found with the name "Elishama,"[95] and although most appear to be dated to the seventh to sixth centuries B.C.E., it is not impossible that prominent persons in the late postexilic period also bore this name.

Whether or not Jerahmeel is in the centre because of the sponsorship by a postexilic leader of the Chronicler's work, Jerahemeel in the centre is an attempt by the Chronicler to encourage the people to look to other than David for their political authority and hope. David is thus de-centred. This being the case, then although the people may have had a hope of a restored Davidic monarchy, the Chronicler himself did not share it, and instead actively discouraged it.[96] Furthermore, by centring Judah on a government official, the Chronicler may be indicating that legitimate political power lay, not with the Davidic king, but with the Persians as represented by their local officials.

---

[95] David J. A. Clines, ed., *The Dictionary of Classical Hebrew* (vol. 1; Sheffield: Sheffield Academic Press, 1993), 293.

[96] Although a full exploration of the Chronicler's Davidic hope is outside the scope of this study, it appears as if the overall structure of the Chronicler's work speaks against his having such a hope. Just as king Saul is removed from the kingship because of his unfaithfulness and replaced by David (1 Chr 10:13–14), who plans and provides for the building of the house of Yahweh (1 Chr 28–29), so also the Davidic monarchy is removed from the kingship due to wickedness (2 Chr 36:11–13), and replaced by Cyrus who authorises the building of the house of Yahweh (2 Chr 36:23). That the list of Davidides extends beyond the exile (1 Chr 3:17–24), does not speak of the possibility of a restored Davidic monarchy any more than the ongoing presence of Saulides (1 Chr 8:33–38), is suggestive of a hope of a restored Saulide dynasty. For issues regarding temple building in the Ancient Near East, see Victor (Avigdor) Hurowitz, *I Have Built You an Exalted House: Temple Building in the Bible in Light of Mesopotamian and Northwest Semitic Writings* (JSOTSup 115; Sheffield: Sheffield Academic Press, 1992).

JUDAH: FIRST AMONG HIS BROTHERS

This recognition that David is not the focus of the Judahite genealogy also forces a re-evaluation of the Chronicler's reasons for placing Judah at the beginning of the genealogies of the sons of Israel. First Chronicles 5:1-3 indicates the Chronicler's view that Reuben, as the firstborn, should have been the first tribe listed in the genealogies.[97] However, because of Reuben's actions, the rights of the firstborn "were given to the sons of Joseph."[98] Joseph, however, is also not listed first, with his two sons only being recorded in 1 Chr 7:14-29. The Chronicler is adamant that Judah, although the strongest, did not inherit this birthright which "belonged to Joseph."[99] Although not receiving the birthright, and thus not having the right to be listed first, Judah is the first tribe recorded.[100] It would appear then that the Chronicler's order in the genealogies is based on

---

[97] Of the fourteen lists of the sons of Israel in the Pentateuch, eleven have Reuben listed first. In six of these, Reuben is specifically called the "firstborn," בְּכוֹר, of Jacob (Gen 35:23; 46:8; 49:3; Exod 6:14; Num 1:20; 26:5). For a study of the "firstborn" in Genesis, see Roger Syren, *The Forsaken First-Born: A Study of a Recurrent Motif in the Patriarchal Narratives* (JSOTSup 133; Sheffield: JSOT Press, 1993), and especially 130–135. On the place of Reuben as the firstborn, see Frank M. Cross, "Reuben, First-Born of Jacob," *ZAW* 100 (sup; 1988): 46–65.

[98] For a reconstruction of the interpretive processes by which the birthright was transferred to Joseph, see Knoppers, *1 Chronicles 1–9*, 382–384, and the discussion in Williamson, *Israel*, 89–96. There are two possible understandings of the phrase, וְלֹא לְהִתְיַחֵשׂ לַבְּכֹרָה (1 Chr 5:1). Japhet says that it refers "to Joseph, who 'could not be registered as the oldest son,' although the status of first-born was in fact conferred on him," *Chronicles*, 133, so also Klein, *1 Chronicles*, 155 note 5. Knoppers, although acknowledging that "the antecedent to 'he' is unclear," concludes, "contextually, however, the subj. should be Reuben, because the next verse concludes that 'the birthright belonged to Joseph,'" *1 Chronicles 1–9*, 377. Curtis' suggestion that this refers to Joseph, but that Reuben retained the right to be listed first in the tribal registers (as throughout the Pentateuch), fails to recognise that this statement is a product of an ongoing interpretive process, and also that Reuben is himself not listed first in the Chronicler's genealogies, *Chronicles*, 119.

[99] Rudolph disagrees. He amends the text by adding לֹא לוֹ prior to לְיוֹסֵף, and translating the verse, "denn Juda wurde der mächtigste unter seinen Brüdern, und aus ihm ging ein Führer hervor, so daß ihm nicht Josef das Erstgeburtsrecht zustand," *Chronikbücher*, 42. Rudolph goes on to suggest that because David became the leader, נָגִיד, "Deshalb, das ist logisch der einzig mögliche Schluß, stand das Erstgeburtsrecht Juda zu, und deshalb setze der Chr. Juda an den Anfang," *Chronikbücher*, 43.

[100] Syren does note that, in the Joseph narrative, it is Judah who supplants Reuben in both relation to their father Jacob, as well as to Joseph (Gen 43:3–10; 44:16, 18–34), *Forsaken First-Born*, 132.

neither birth order nor birthright, but upon which tribe held political power within the community. Judah is listed first because David and his descendants maintained political power over either the entire people or a significant minority of the tribes.

It will be observed that in the structure of the genealogies, Judah is on the same chiastic level as Benjamin (1 Chr 8), which itself has a lengthy genealogy of King Saul (1 Chr 8:29–38). Saul, like David, had at one time held legitimate political power over the people. In this structure, Judah and Benjamin, the two tribes which provided legitimate royal lines, are presented first and last. It would appear then that the Chronicler sought to frame his discussion of the descendants of Israel with the two tribes which had held legitimate royal power within Israel.[101]

The recognition that the placement of both Judah and Benjamin is based upon their having held legitimate political power is important. It has been suggested that the placement of the tribes has been determined by geographic factors, or because Judah, Levi, and Benjamin were the primary tribes within the postexilic community.[102] The placement of these tribes on the basis of preexilic political power indicates something of the Chronicler's views of political authority in his own time period. That David/Judah and Saul/Benjamin held political power at some time in the past is acknowledged by the Chronicler. However, placing both Judah and Benjamin at a lower level within the overall genealogical list is an indication that the power which these tribes had held through their respective kings, does not continue to carry significance in the community of the Chronicler's day. Just as David is not at the centre of the Judahite list, and therefore the Chronicler is not advocating a return to the Davidic monarchy, so also Judah and Benjamin are not at the centre of the Chronicler's genealogical structure. It would appear that the Chronicler is not advocating a return to any indigenous monarchy within the postexilic community of Yehud.

What is at the centre of the genealogy is the cult. If the fundamental problem which faced the community was unfaithfulness and its consequences, and the fundamental solution to this problem was the authorised cultic officials performing the authorised cultic functions in the authorised cultic place, then this leaves neither room, nor reason, for an indigenous monarchy.

Furthermore, while it is recognised that "Judah was the strongest" (1 Chr 5:2), this does not mean that Judah retains its pre-eminent place within the

---

[101] It is clear from the Deuteronomistic History that members of other tribes held political power in northern Israel. The Chronicler, however, views these other rulers as both illegitimate and in rebellion against Yahweh and his cult (2 Chr 13:4–12).

[102] Williamson, *Chronicles*, 38–40, 46–47.

restored community.[103] Pre-eminence belongs to the cult, for it is only the true worship of Yahweh, not the power of monarchy, that can maintain the presence and prosperity of the people within the land.

CONCLUDING OBSERVATIONS

In this chapter it has been observed that the Chronicler presented the Judahite genealogy in such a way as to present two separate paths by which the people could find the solution to the negative consequences of evil and unfaithfulness. The Chronicler has acknowledged that the problem of evil and unfaithfulness existed, and that the consequences of evil and unfaithfulness are death, trouble, childlessness, inappropriate sexual behaviour, and loss of land.

He proposes two different solutions to this problem. The first is the way of monarchy, as exhibited in David. This path, however, is shown to lead to unfaithfulness, and ultimately, to exile. The other path is typified by Jabez. It is a path of prayer, and leads to blessing and the elimination of the negative consequences of unfaithfulness. As such, the Chronicler does not advocate a return to monarchy, either Davidic or Saulide, but a continued focus upon the centrality of Yahweh through the maintenance of the cult.

---

[103] In 1 Chr 9:6 Judah had 690 people living in Jerusalem, while Benjamin had 956 (1 Chr 9:9).

CHAPTER 9
C1: 1 CHRONICLES 8:1–40
BENJAMIN: THE TRIBE OF KING SAUL

INTRODUCTION

The final genealogy of the "sons of Israel" to be investigated is that of Benjamin. Although there has already been one listing of Benjamin (1 Chr 7:6–12a), the content and purposes of these two lists are different.

First Chronicles 7:6–12a is contained within the context of the tribes of Israel prepared for war (1 Chr 7:1–40). In 1 Chr 7, Benjamin does not stand alone, but is presented as simply one part within a greater whole. The genealogy of Benjamin, along with Issachar and Asher, consists of muster lists of "fighting men." They form part of the outside level of a structure which progresses through the generations and lands of the people, retribution upon the wicked and the provision of a godly leader, to the restoration of family and the building of new towns.[1] In 1 Chr 7, Benjamin is not the focus, but is simply one of the supporting elements within the Chronicler's overall structure and purpose. First Chronicles 7 has already been shown to be the counterpart to 1 Chr 4:24–5:26, which also focussed upon the military activities of the people, their victories and defeats, their acquisition and loss of land.

First Chronicles 8:1–40 is different. Each part of this chapter contains those who are shown to be a part of Benjamin, or who have been claimed to have a share within Benjamin. This is made clear by both the opening phrase וּבְנְיָמִן הוֹלִיד (and Benjamin bore …) and the final phrase כָּל־אֵלֶּה מִבְּנֵי בִנְיָמִן (all these were the sons of Benjamin). These act as inclusive statements, indicating that each individual named between them is to be counted as within Benjamin. As such, the presentation of Benjamin in this chapter is not of a small part within a greater whole. In 1 Chr 8 Benjamin is the whole, the subject of the entire list.

First Chronicles 8:1–40, the tribe of Benjamin, is presented on the same chiastic level as 1 Chr 2:3–4:23, the tribe of Judah, and shares a number of the characteristics found within the description of Judah which will be addressed

---

[1] See Chapter 7.

below. First Chronicles 8:29–40 also presents an extended genealogy of the royal line of Saul, who came from Benjamin, just as 1 Chr 3:1–24 presents an extended genealogy of the royal line of David, who came from Judah. The similarities that exist between the Judahite and Benjaminite genealogies are best observed when the same categories are utilised to describe the contents of Benjamin as were utilised to describe the contents of Judah.

CONTENT OF THE BENJAMINITE GENEALOGY

First Chronicles 8 is made up of four separate lists.[2] First Chronicles 8:1–7 begins with the presentation of five sons of Benjamin in a numbered list, which is then traced through the firstborn of these sons, Bela.[3] This list concludes with the deportation of the people of Geba to Manahath by Gera, descendant of Ehud.

This is followed by a list which gives the descendants of Shahariam (1 Chr 8:8–28), who is elsewhere unattested and whose connection to the tribe of Benjamin as a whole, and to the preceding names, is not specified. This list opens with mention of Shahariam's divorce from two of his wives and his sons through a third wife, and continues with his descendants through one of his sons from one of his earlier marriages. This section concludes with the statement that these individuals lived in Jerusalem.

---

[2] The relationship between the Benjaminite list of 1 Chr 8 and other Benjaminite lists is discussed in Excursus 2.

[3] Baker suggests reading the conjunction ו in וַאֲבִיהוּד, "as explicative. . . It appears likely that there would be an epithet with Gera's name in this verse since there is another Gera, son of Bela, in the same list . . . This *wāw* would explain that the first mentioned is 'Gera, *that is,* the father of Ehud,'" "Further Examples of the *Waw Explicativum,*" *VT* 30 (1980): 129–136, 133. This is followed by Klein, *1 Chronicles*, 242 note 4, and Williamson, *Chronicles*, 83. As will be seen in Figure E2.5, I understand Abihud, אֲבִיהוּד, (1 Chr 8:3), as אֲבִי אֵהוּד, "the father of Ehud," and Abishua, אֲבִישׁוּעַ, (1 Chr 8:4), as "the father of Shua," אֲבִי שׁוּעַ, cf Curtis and Madsen, *Chronicles*, 158. Shua appears as a proper name in Gen 38:2; 1 Chr 7:32, while Ehud, son of Gera, is one of the heroes of the judges period and a Benjaminite (Judg 3:12–30). The text would then be read, "Gera the father of Ehud the father of Shua, Naaman, Ahoah." This reading has the advantage of preventing Bela from having two sons with the name Gera. While the reading "the father of Ehud" is accepted by many commentators, the reading "the father of Shua" is not. Cf. Braun, *1 Chronicles*, 120; Japhet, *Chronicles*, 191; Klein, *1 Chronicles*, 242; Knoppers, *1 Chronicles 1–9*, 474; Rudolph, *Chronikbücher*, 76; Williamson, *Chronicles*, 83.

The third list (1 Chr 8:29–32), also does not indicate how those listed are connected to Benjamin genealogically.[4] The connection that is established between the second and third lists is that these latter individuals are said to make their dwelling in Jerusalem with אֲחֵיהֶם (their brothers; 1 Chr 8:32, cf. 1 Chr 8:28), who are to be identified with as those contained in the preceding list and who also lived in Jerusalem.

The final list is the sons of Ner, which is traced through Saul and his sons (1 Chr 8:33–40). This genealogy is twelve generations long and, if no names have been omitted, would indicate that there were those who traced their descent from Saul until almost the end of the kingdom of Judah. If there had been telescoping, then the list of Saul's descendants could extend into and beyond the exile. It appears that this list has been joined to the preceding list because of the presence in both of "Kish," the father of Saul (1 Sam 9:1).[5]

FAMILIAL TERMINOLOGY

Like Judah, this Benjaminite list contains several familial terms. בֵּן (son) occurs 23 times in 1 Chr 8. אָח (brother) occurs in 1 Chr 8:32, 39 in its wider meaning of "relative." There are also references to אִשָּׁה (wife; 1 Chr 8:8, 9, 29), and, as in the Judahite list, each of these wives are named. Unlike the Judahite list, there are no references to sisters, daughters,[6] or concubines.

LEADERS

As in the Judahite list, Benjamin also refers to its community leaders. Some of these are the רָאשֵׁי אָבוֹת (heads of clans or households; 1 Chr 8:6, 10, 28), while some appear to be leaders, אָב (father) of a town (1 Chr 8:13, 29).

DOMESTIC TERMINOLOGY

Unlike the Judahite list, there are no references in Benjamin to death. Neither are there narratives indicating marriage, or the "taking" of a wife. What is striking

---

[4] The MT of 1 Chr 8:29 does not list the name of the "father of Gibeon." On the basis of the parallel list in 1 Chr 9:35, most commentators supply the name "Jeiel." This name is only attested in Chronicles and Ezra.

[5] This list is not reconcilable with the genealogy of Saul presented in 1 Sam 9:1; 14:50–51. In Samuel, Saul is the son of Kish, son of Abiel, אֲבִיאֵל, and Kish and Ner are brothers. In Chronicles, Kish is the son of Ner. Ner does not appear in the MT of 1 Chr 8:30, but is supplied in the NIV on the basis of 1 Chr 9:36. It is possible that יְעִיאֵל, Jeiel, is a corruption of אֲבִיאֵל, Abiel.

[6] The only use of "daughter," בַּת, is in 1 Chr 8:12, which refers to smaller settlements surrounding a larger one, a usage found also in 1 Chr 2:23: 5:16; 7:28, 29.

in the Benjaminite list is the reference to divorce, or the "sending away" of wives (1 Chr 8:8), which is the only occurrence of divorce within Chronicles.[7] Like Judah, there is narrative reference to the birth of children (1 Chr 8:8), and the repeated emphasis on a person as the בְּכֹר (firstborn; 1 Chr 8:1, 30, 39).[8] This list contains references to towns which were inhabited (1 Chr 8:6, 13, 28, 29, 32), and towns which were built (1 Chr 8:12).

Unlike the Judahite list, there are several references to wars and warfare within Benjaminite territory.[9] The occupants of one town are deported (1 Chr 8:6), while another town is conquered (1 Chr 8:13). Although not a major focus, the Benjaminite list also includes an account of one family who are "brave warriors" and who could handle the bow (1 Chr 8:40). Their recorded numbers, 150, are small in relation to other muster lists, and in particular the first list of Benjamin (1 Chr 7:6–12a), which counts 59,434 warriors.

RETRIBUTION

The Benjaminite list contains accounts of victory and defeat, of city building and exile. It has already been shown that victory or defeat in battle are reflections of whether a person or society and their actions are approved or disapproved by Yahweh. Those whose lives are reflective of unfaithfulness are defeated in battle and/or put to death, while those who are faithful are victorious in battle. As this is clearly the viewpoint of the Chronicler, and is probably shared by his community, then the deportation of the people of Geba to Manahath (1 Chr 8:6, 7), would be understood as retribution upon the people of Geba for some, unspecified, action.[10] Furthermore, the conquest of Gath (1 Chr 8:13; cf. 7:21),

---

[7] For the use of שלח as "divorce," see Deut 22:19, 29; 24:1, 3, 4; Jer 3:1. Divorce is also not found within the Deuteronomistic History.

[8] The term occurs ten times in the Judahite lists (1 Chr 2:3, 13, 25 [x2], 27, 42, 50; 3:1,15; 4:4).

[9] There is a reference in the Judahite list to warfare in Judahite controlled towns in the Transjordan (1 Chr 2:23).

[10] First Chronicles 8:6–7 is confusing. Although most translations render the Hiphil, וַיַּגְלוּם, in 1 Chr 8:6, as a passive, "they were deported," it is better to understand this as the active, "they deported them," so also Knoppers, *1 Chronicles 1–9*, 476. This would suggest that the leaders of the community deported the members of their own community to a different one. Klein, however, suggests that "'They' may be a circumlocution for the passive," Klein, *1 Chronicles*, 248, note 16. Williamson suggests the possibility that it was the native men of Geba who were deported to make way for the Benjaminites, Williamson, *Chronicles*, 83. The active sense is also present in 1 Chr 8:7 where the Hiphil, הֶגְלָם, is often translated "he deported them." The NRSV suggests that 1 Chr 8:7, reflects a proper name, "Heglam," which is also reflected in the LXX rendering ιγλααμ, although this is rejected by most commentators, cf. Williamson, *Chronicles*, 84. Since "exile," גלה, is

would also be understood as reflecting the result of Yahweh's presence and blessing upon those who were faithful to Yahweh.

This is highlighted when 1 Chr 8:13 is compared to 1 Chr 7:21. In the latter passage, Ezer and Elead are killed when they raided Gath in an attempt to steal cattle. Their deaths are shown to be the result of their actions. Their actions were to be considered as "unfaithfulness," and their deaths the natural consequence of that unfaithfulness. Contrary to these negative circumstances, Beriah and Shema are able to bring about a complete conquest of Gath. That Beriah and Shema were victorious in battle is to be taken as a sign of their faithfulness.

That these two accounts are meant to be read together is demonstrated through the presence of the name Beriah. In 1 Chr 7:23, Beriah is the son born to Ephraim after the death of Ezer and Elead, and his name is reflective of Ephraim's misfortune. As was observed, the mourning of Ephraim also marked the turning point in the account of Ephraim, and led to the building of cities (1 Chr 7:24). In Chronicles, positive building projects are only performed by those who are faithful to Yahweh, and only during their times of faithfulness.[11] In 1 Chr 7:22–24, Ephraim's mourning led to Yahweh's restoration, which led to the birth of another son (Beriah), and the building of towns. In 1 Chr 8:13, the conquest of Gath by a Beriah is also contained within the context of the building of towns (1 Chr 8:12). These accounts in 1 Chr 8 of either exile or building projects, clearly indicate that, for the Chronicler, retribution was active within Benjamin, whether it be upon righteous or unrighteous actions.

FOREIGN ELEMENTS

Like the Judahite list, there are also foreign elements within the Benjaminite list. As certain Judahites had lived within Moab (1 Chr 4:22), so also certain Benjaminites lived within Moab and had sons there (1 Chr 8:8). It is uncertain whether or not Hodesh, wife of Shaharaim (1 Chr 8:9), was herself a Moabite, or whether she only gave birth to her children while she lived in Moab. If she was a Moabite, this would indicate the inclusion of foreign elements within Benjamin, just as foreign elements had been included within Judah, and this also without negative comment from the Chronicler.

---

considered to be negative and a sign of God's judgment, the actual circumstances are not as great in importance as the theological concept that the word conveys: people were exiled, therefore people had been unfaithful to Yahweh. Geba was considered a Benjaminite town (Josh 18:24; 1 Kgs 15:22), and was allocated to the sons of Aaron as one of their cities (Josh 21:17; 1 Chr 6:45 [6:60]). In the postexilic era it was still considered to be Benjaminite, although the people from Geba lived in many other locations (Neh 11:31).

[11] See Figure 7.2, "Building Texts."

As was observed in discussion of the foreign elements in Judah, the fact that clans, families, or individuals may have had historical origins outside of the individual Israelite tribe is not important for the Chronicler. What is of importance is not their past connection with foreign elements, but their present genealogical connection with the pertinent Israelite tribe. The Chronicler's viewpoint is therefore more inclusive of the foreigner than either Ezra or Nehemiah. These latter sought to exclude all traces of the foreign, while the Chronicler appears to accept those who demonstrate any trace of the Israelite.

OBSERVATIONS ON THE CONTENT OF THE BENJAMINITE GENEALOGY

As observed, there are a number of similarities between the Judahite and Benjaminite lists. It is therefore probable that portions of the Benjaminite lists, like those of Judah, had their origins within the domestic life of Benjamin. The differences which exist between the two lists (lack of some relationship terms and references to death in Benjamin; no mention of divorce, warriors or warfare in Judah) may simply be the result of the greater quantity of material contained within the Judahite list and the differences that existed within the communities.

Another important similarity between the Judahite and Benjaminite lists is the long genealogies given for the two royal lines, David and Saul (1 Chr 3:1–24; 8:33–40). An interesting observation which may impact on the Chronicler's understanding of the *present* status of the Davidic and Saulide lines, is that although David was said to have reigned (1 Chr 3:4), neither David, Saul, or any of their descendants is called "king" within the genealogies.[12] Although it is uncertain, this may have to do with the Chronicler's understanding of the *present* place of the these two persons within postexilic Yehud. While both are acknowledged in the genealogies as significant person's in Israel and/or Judah's *past*, this acknowledgement is not to be equated with a desire to restore either monarchic line to power in Yehud's *present*. While the existence of descendants of either person into the postexilic era is acknowledged, descendants of neither person is recorded as being present within the postexilic Yehudite community. This indicates that the Chronicler possessed neither a desire nor expectation that these persons would take up the royal duties and functions which their exalted ancestors had possessed.

This confirms the earlier observation that the Chronicler sees no place for a restored indigenous monarchy. The inclusion of Saul's genealogy would emphasise this point. Both David and Saul are presented as minor, yet important,

---

[12] David is frequently called "king" in Chronicles (1 Chr 15:29; 17:16;18:10, 11, 14; 21:24; 27:24, 31; 29:24; 2 Chr 8:11; 23:9; 29:27; 30:26; 35:3, 4), while Saul is called "king" only in 1 Chr 11:2.

BENJAMIN: THE TRIBE OF KING SAUL 257

elements within the Chronicler's chiastic structure. Neither Saul nor David is given the title "king" in the genealogies. Although both have lineages that extend far beyond the time in which either had descendants who reigned, in neither the Judahite nor the Benjaminite genealogies is the line of the king (David or Saul) the central point of the chiastic structuring of those lists. Instead they are placed in an inferior, subordinate, position.[13] In Judah, this subordinate position is to the sons of Jerahmeel, while in Benjamin it is to those who "dwelt in Jerusalem." In the genealogies, the Chronicler treats the lineage of Saul and David in the same manner. It is therefore necessary that the conclusions that are made in regard one lineage, are also applied to the other.

If it is insisted that David's genealogy speaks of the desire for a restored Davidic monarchy in the postexilic period, then the question, "what to do with Saul" naturally arises. A restored Davidic monarchy cannot be insisted upon on the basis of the Chronicler's genealogies, without also allowing for the restoration of the Saulide line. The listing of Saul's lineage therefore acts as a foil to those who may have been longing for a restored Davidic throne. Both had been legitimate kings. The lines of both were removed from their positions of power because of unfaithfulness. Both lines had neglected the cult (1 Chr 13:3; 2 Chr 29:6–7). The kingdoms of both men were given to another (1 Chr 10:13–14; 2 Chr 36:20–23). Just as there would be no expectation of a restored Saulide monarchy, Saul's presence would suggest that neither should there be an expectation or a demand for a restored Davidic monarchy. The presence of Saul therefore acts as a deterrent to any Davidic expectation which may have been present within Yehud in the Chronicler's day.

THE STRUCTURE OF THE BENJAMINITE GENEALOGY

Although there are a number of similarities between the Judahite and Benjaminite lists, a significant difference does exist between them. As was noted in the previous chapter, the account of Jabez marks a turning point within the Judahite genealogy. Before the account of Jabez there are details of evil, unfaithfulness, retribution, loss of land, and death. After the account of Jabez, these events and actions are no longer recorded. What occurs instead is answered prayer, blessing, and the mention of Caleb, who is presented in the Pentateuch and the Deuteronomistic History as an example of faithfulness to, and trust in, Yahweh.

The Benjaminite genealogy has no such figure around whom the account pivots. What Benjamin does present, and which is totally absent in the Judahite

---

[13] See "The Structure of the Benjaminite Genealogy," below, and Figure 9.1.

account, is the phrase, יָשְׁבוּ בִירוּשָׁלָם (they lived in Jerusalem; 1 Chr 8:28, 32).[14] This phrase appears at the centre of a very loose organising structure within the chapter (Figure 9.1).

The following analysis should not be taken as a proper chiasm, although it is presented in that format. It is, at best, a loose organisation of material around a focal point. It does, however, appear to perform the same type of function, in that it focuses the reader's attention upon a central point, that is, "they lived in Jerusalem." Further it functions well as part of the overall chiastic structure of the Chronicler's genealogies,

Figure 9.1: The Structure of the Benjaminite Genealogy

a   Benjamin: 1 Chr 8:1a
   b   a numbered list of sons: 1 Chr 8:1b–2
     c   descendants of Bela: 1 Chr 8:3–7
       d   those who lived in Jerusalem: 1 Chr 8:8–28
       d^1 those who lived in Jerusalem: 1 Chr 8:29–32
     c^1 descendants of Ner: 1 Chr 8:33–38
   b^1 a numbered list of sons: 1 Chr 8:8:39–40a
a^1 Benjamin: 1 Chr 8:40b

THE SIGNIFICANCE OF THE BENJAMINITE STRUCTURE

Here, as with the Judahite list, it is apparent that the focal point of the text is not upon the royal line. The line of Saul (technically that of Ner), like the line of David in 1 Chr 3, is merely part of the supporting structure. In the case of Saul, the genealogy of Saul directs attention to the central place of Jerusalem.

In the genealogies of the sons of Israel (1 Chr 2–8), Jerusalem only occurs twice in Judah (1 Chr 3:4, 5), twice in Benjamin (1 Chr 8:28, 32), and three times in Levi (1 Chr 5:36, 41; 6:17 [6:10, 15, 32]). While one of the references in the Levitical list refers to the exile of Jerusalem (1 Chr 5:41 [6:15]), the other two occurrences are to the temple of Yahweh in Jerusalem. The only other references to Jerusalem in the genealogies, occur in 1 Chr 9:3, 34, in both cases with the verb יָשַׁב (to dwell). As will be observed later in the discussion on 1 Chr 9,[15] after the exile (1 Chr 9:1a), there is a return to the land (1 Chr 9:1b–2). Following this is an introduction to a list of those who "dwell in Jerusalem" (1 Chr 9:3). This

---

[14] This phrase only occurs in 1 Chr 8:28, 32; 9:34, 38; Neh 11:3. The variation, וּבִירוּשָׁלַם יָשְׁבוּ, occurs in 1 Chr 9:3; Neh 11:4. It is to be noted that David reigned in Jerusalem, מָלַךְ בִּירוּשָׁלָם, (1 Chr 3:4), had sons there (1 Chr 3:5), and Solomon built the temple in Jerusalem (1 Chr 5:36; 6:17 [6:10, 32]), but no group, other than Benjamin, is said to have lived in Jerusalem prior to the postexilic era.

[15] See Chapter 13.

list, which consists of representatives of the people and the Levites in their varying duties, closes with the statement "they lived in Jerusalem" (1 Chr 9:34).

The use of this phrase in 1 Chr 9 suggests that being able to dwell in Jerusalem is the consequence of returning to the land, and that the focus of Jerusalem is the temple, as represented by the full complement of cultic personnel, each of whom is actively engaged in their assigned work (1 Chr 9:10–33). Similarly, the central significance of Jerusalem in the Levitical lists, which focus attention upon the cultic personnel and their duties (1 Chr 6:33–38 [6:48–53]), is the presence of the temple for Yahweh that Solomon built. Both references to the temple in Jerusalem in 1 Chr 6 point to individuals serving within the temple.[16] Like 1 Chr 9, the Levitical lists point to the significance of Jerusalem as the place where Yahweh's temple is, and Yahweh's appointed personnel operate.

This understanding of Jerusalem in the genealogies as the place where people dwell, and the place where Yahweh's appointed cultic personnel perform their assigned tasks, suggests the purpose of the centrality of "they lived in Jerusalem" in the Benjaminite list. It was noticed that the pivotal point in the Judahite genealogy was the account of Jabez. In the Judahite account, Jabez prayed to Yahweh, and Yahweh answered, with the result that nothing negative was again recorded for the community. In the same way, in the Benjaminite list, the focus upon dwelling in Jerusalem is seen to be the pivotal point for what life should be like within the postexilic community, if the people desire that community to continue. To dwell in Jerusalem speaks not simply of a location, but of an ideology which has Yahweh's temple and its personnel as the focus of life. This is the emphasis of the genealogies as a whole, with the central, pivoting point being the authorised cultic officials performing their assigned duties in the authorised cultic place (1 Chr 6:33–38 [6:48–53]). To maintain that focus is to ensure continued life and prosperity. To turn from that focus is to invite a return to exile. Upon their return from exile, people returned to Jerusalem (1 Chr 9:3). The way to stave off another exile, is also to maintain Jerusalem, and all that it stands for, as central to the life of the community. This idea may lie in part behind the Chronicler's final word, וְיָעַל (let them go up; 2 Chr 26:23). Having been offered the opportunity to rebuild a temple, and to live again in Jerusalem, the people have the obligation to make Jerusalem and all that it signifies into the ideological centre of the nation, the focus of their lives.

This is consistent with 2 Chr 6:6. Here, after reinforcing Yahweh's choice of Jerusalem, the Chronicler presents Solomon's prayer which is focussed not on Jerusalem but upon the centrality, function and purpose of Yahweh's temple which is in Jerusalem (2 Chr 6:7–39). Jerusalem is therefore important, not in and of

---

[16] First Chronicles 5:36 [6:10] speaks of Johanan who served as a priest within the temple, while 1 Chr 6:17 [6:32] has the cultic musicians ministering first at the tabernacle prior to the building of the temple, and, by extension, at the temple after it was built.

itself, but for what it contains, and what it symbolises. It is this symbolic aspect of Jerusalem which the Chronicler places at the centre of the Benjaminite genealogy.

As was mentioned above, including the Saulide list may be a foil to any Davidic aspirations among the people. By giving long lists of the descendants of both Saul and David, the Chronicler is indicating that while both lines may have continued, the Davidides have no more rightful claim to throne than the Saulides, who, along with the Davidides, continued as a clan long after their ancestors were deposed. What this further indicates is that prosperity and security, that is, growth, the retention of land and the prevention of another exile, depend not on a monarchy, be it Davidic or Saulide, but on the proper attention to the cult in Jerusalem. Dependence upon kings in the past had only led to unfaithfulness to Yahweh and exile. Only proper attention to the cult in Jerusalem could ensure that the people continued to remain in the land.

The presence of Saul in the Benjaminite list should not, however, be understood merely in relation to David. The proximity of the Saulide list to the mention of Jerusalem is also significant and may indicate that no group, or family, is to be considered irredeemable or is to be excluded from the community. The one condition of this, however, is that they must approach Yahweh in his temple. Just as those who rejected Yahweh were exiled from the land, so also those who seek a return to the land must return to Yahweh. Further, if part of the Chronicler's purpose is to encourage a return to Jerusalem and to the cult of Yahweh which is contained within it, then the Chronicler must also present the certainty that those who do return will be accepted into the cultic community of Jerusalem. Placing Saul's family in close proximity to Jerusalem is suggestive that all who return to Yahweh will be accepted, irrespective of the past failures of the individuals or clans.

This understanding of the acceptance of the one who is unfaithful to Yahweh, and yet repents of that unfaithfulness, is part of the intent of Solomon's prayer (2 Chr 6:22, 24, 29, 32, 34, 38), and is illustrated by the account of Manasseh (2 Chr 33:12–13). Saul and his family, and by extension all of the people, could therefore be accepted back into the community if they were to follow that pattern. That acceptance, however, is dependent upon a return to Yahweh and his cult, and is symbolised by a renewed focus on Jerusalem.

It must further be recognised that Saul is not presented as the worst king. Although Saul's unfaithfulness is given as the reason for his death and the kingdom being transferred to David (1 Chr 10:13–14), the Chronicler also suggests Saul's faithfulness to Yahweh at certain points during his life when he reports that "some of the plunder taken in battle" and dedicated to Yahweh (1 Chr 26:27), came from the hand of Saul (1 Chr 26:28). That Saul was victorious in battle suggests that, at one time, Saul had been faithful, although he later abandoned that faithfulness. The Chronicler then presents Saul as simply one of many kings who went from faithfulness to unfaithfulness, some of whom returned to Yahweh and were blessed (2 Chr 12:6–7; 19:2–4; 32:25–29). What is significant is that those who had been unfaithful to Yahweh could return to Yahweh and be blessed. This would be an encouragement for the people of postexilic Yehud to maintain their focus upon Jerusalem as the centre of the Yahwistic cult, the temple, and the cultic personnel. It would also be a means of encouraging new "returnees," those who continued to migrate from other provinces of the Persian Empire into Yehud. These new persons also are to be accepted into the community, if they also make Yahweh, his cult and his city, the focus of their lives.

Concluding Observations on Benjamin

The first and last of the genealogies of the sons of Israel were tribes out of which royal dynasties arose; Saul from Benjamin, and David from Judah. In neither genealogy, however, is the royal dynasty the focus, and in neither is a return to an indigenous monarchy envisioned. In both Judah and Benjamin, the solution to the problems of unfaithfulness were not to be found in the monarchy. As the Chronicler will make clear in the remainder of his work, many of the acts of unfaithfulness, and their resulting consequences, came from within the royal lines, beginning with Saul and ending with Zedekiah in the line of David. Each of the unfaithful kings received what their actions warranted, and the people suffered for these actions along with their rulers.

In both the Judahite and Benjaminite genealogies, the royal families are not the focus, but simply part of the greater structure, and help point to the greater purpose the Chronicler has in his writing. In Judah, this purpose was the necessity for prayer to Yahweh, which resulted in Yahweh's answer, and the removal of the negative consequences which unfaithfulness would bring. In Benjamin, the central focus is upon "those who dwelt in Jerusalem." This has been shown, on the basis of 1 Chr 9, to include not just the individuals who lived there, but the entire cult, from the temple, to its personnel and their functions. Just as the central point of the genealogies as a whole is the authorised cultic personnel offering the authorised cultic sacrifices in the authorised cultic place, so the Benjaminite genealogy focuses the attention upon Jerusalem, the city in which the authorised cultic place is located.

EXCURSUS 2: THE CONFLICTING GENEALOGIES OF THE SONS OF BENJAMIN

One of the difficulties which faces the interpreter of the Benjaminite genealogies is the differences that exist between the list of the sons of Benjamin in 1 Chr 8 and the other occurrences of the lists of Benjamin's sons elsewhere in the Hebrew Bible.[17] These are illustrated in the diagrams at the end of this chapter.

On the following page, in Figure E.2.1 it can be observed that there are numerous differences and similarities in the genealogies given. The order of the names has been adjusted in their presentation, with those showing the greatest similarity across the lists displayed first.

First, it is observed that Bela is listed first in each of the genealogies of Benjamin, while in 1 Chr 8:1 Bela is specifically called the "firstborn." This is the only time he is called בְּכֹר (firstborn) and it is possible that the name בֶּכֶר (Beker) had been at times confused for the genealogical term בְּכֹר (firstborn).[18] Only in the names Bela and Beker does 1 Chr 7 agree with any other listing of Benjamin

Second, Ashbel, Naaman, and Ard/Addar appear in all of the Benjamin lists except 1 Chr 7,[19] although the genealogical relationship is not the same in each. Ashbel is always listed after Bela, or Beker if present, and is always a direct son of Benjamin. Naaman is a son in Gen 46 (MT), grandson through Bela in Gen 46 (LXX), grandson (through Bela) in Num 26, and great-great grandson in 1 Chr 8 (through Bela, Gera, Ehud and Shua). The position of Ard/Addar is also fluid in the lists. In Gen 46 (MT) he is a son, Gen 46 (LXX) he is a great-grandson through Gera and Bela. In Num 26 and 1 Chr 8 he is a grandson through Bela, The fluidity of the positions of Ard and Naaman may reflect ongoing political or social instability within the community which developed these particular lists.[20]

Third, there are five names which are common to two lists: Beker (Gen 46; 1 Chr 7); Huphim/Hupham (Gen 46; Num 26); Gera and Ahi/Ahoah (Gen 46; 1 Chr 8);[21] Shephupham/Shephuphan (Num 26; 1 Chr 8).

---

[17] Lists of the sons of Benjamin appear in Gen 46:21; Num 26:38–41; 1 Chr 7:6–11; 8:1–7.

[18] In Gen 46:21 (LXX), the name is read as Chobar, Χοβωρ. This appears to be the result of a transposition of the letters ב and כ in either the text before the translator, or in his reading of it.

[19] LXX Num 26:44 also reads Αδαρ. This identification is fairly certain.

[20] See further the discussion in, Wilson, *Genealogy*, 46–55.

[21] The identification of Ahi and Ahoah is tentative.

Fourth, there are ten names that cannot be correlated to other names within the lists.[22]

Due to the large number of differences, it is impossible to reconcile the data in these four lists. This is, however, one of the common difficulties with ancient written and oral genealogies. Before these genealogies are dismissed as unhistorical, it is best to recall Wilson's observations regarding the functions of genealogies in society, and to remember that different functions demand a different genealogy, because these different functions reflect different social realities.[23] Wilson also observed that genealogies changed over time to reflect the changes in these social, political, and religious realities.[24]

That the four lists developed at different times, and for different purposes, is therefore probable. First Chronicles 7 is clearly a muster list, and was developed for militaristic/political purposes. Although the original functions of the other lists cannot be determined from this historical distance, the fluidity that is expressed within them, not only in the names that they present or omit, but also the fluid relative relationship between some names and others, indicates that they probably arose in different social or political circumstances.

As Wilson points out, however, the differences that the different genealogies contain are not to be thought of as in conflict, for they each rightly reflect the historical social reality at the given point in time at which they were formulated.[25] Wilson further indicates that it is probable that even if conflicting genealogies arose within the same historical context, that the society in which they were formulated would not view them as in conflict, but would recognise that the differences which they project are reflections of the different social, political or religious contexts which brought the differing genealogies into existence. He

---

[22] This is not including the list in 1 Chr 7 which has a Benjamin and an Ehud as sons of Jediael. These have not been included because it is clear from 1 Chr 7 that these individuals are not to be considered as direct "sons" of Benjamin. They are the leaders, "heads of families" who are in charge of the mustered fighting men. It is possible that Ahiram/Aharah, אֲחִירָם/אַחְרַח, reflect the same person/clan, or even Ahiram/Huram, חוּרָם/אֲחִירָם. Care, however, must be taken in seeking to identify names, or to reconstruct the text based upon similarities of names. The works of Hogg and Marquart contain numerous of these attempts, and lead to less than satisfactory results, Hope W. Hogg, "The Genealogy of Benjamin: A Criticism of 1 Chronicles VIII," *JQR* 11 (1898): 102–114; J. Marquart, "The Genealogies of Benjamin," *JQR* 14 (1902): 343–351.

[23] Wilson, *Genealogy*, 37–45.

[24] Wilson, *Genealogy*, 46–54.

[25] See Wilson's fuller discussion on fluidity, Wilson, *Genealogy*, 27–36, and also his description of the changing relationships of the Humr people as reflected in their changing genealogical relationships, 48–54.

says, "this fact may cause several conflicting genealogies to exist at the same time, but each one can be considered accurate in its own context."[26]

Figure E2.1: Variations in Names in the Benjamin Traditions

Genesis 46:21 (MT)	Numbers 26:38-41	1 Chronicles 7:6-11	1 Chronicles 8:1-7
Appearing in Four Traditions			
בֶּלַע	בֶּלַע	בֶּלַע	בֶּלַע
Appearing in Three Traditions			
אַשְׁבֵּל	אַשְׁבֵּל		אַשְׁבֵּל
נַעֲמָן	נַעֲמָן		נַעֲמָן
אַרְדְּ	אַרְדְּ		אַדָּר
Appearing in Two Traditions			
בֶּכֶר		בֶּכֶר	
חֻפִּים	חוּפָם		
גֵּרָא			גֵּרָא
אֵחִי			אֲחוֹחַ[27]
	שְׁפוּפָם		שְׁפוּפָן
Appearing in One Tradition			
רֹאשׁ	אֲחִירָם	יְדִיעֲאֵל[28]	אֲחְרַח
מֻפִּים			נוֹחָה
			רָפָא
			אֲבִי אֵחוּד
			אֲבִי שׁוּעַ
			חוּרָם

The difficulty that modern historians face in reconstructing the history of Benjamin is not because of the lists themselves, but because of a lack of understanding of the historical circumstances which gave rise to these lists. Even though the lists of Benjaminites in Genesis and Numbers appear in an historio-

---

[26] Wilson, *Genealogy*, 47.
[27] This is a tentative identification on the basis of LXX: Αχια
[28] Jediael, third son of Benjamin, is a name which only appears in Chronicles; 1 Chr 7:6, 10–11; 11:45; 12:20; 26:2.

graphic context, it is certain that they did not originate within that historiography, but were incorporated into their current textual location. As such, the original historical context within which the written lists of Benjaminites arose has been lost, and with it has been lost the social, political and religious context in which the lists were created, and their true meaning in that original context.

Figure E2.2: Genesis 46:21 (MT)

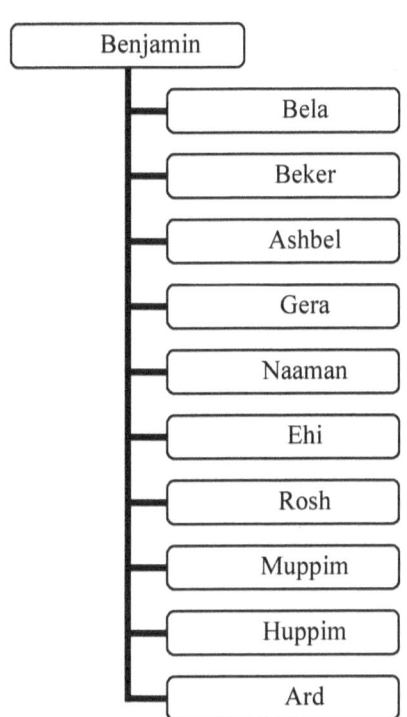

Figure E2.3: Genesis 46:21 (LXX)[1]

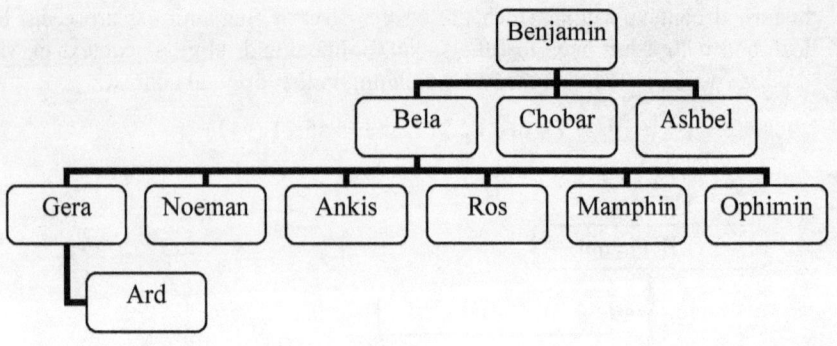

Figure E2.4: Numbers 26:38–41

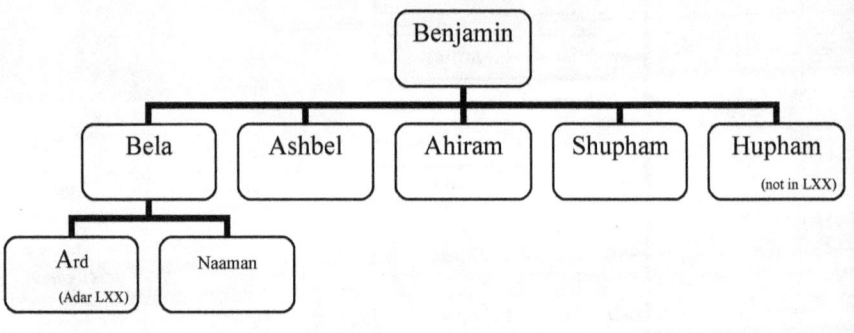

---

[1] The LXX of Gen 46:21 is listed primarily because it presents different relationships between the persons than are indicated in MT Gen 46. The basis for the names are essentially the same, and certain portions of the LXX list are not consistent with the other lists.

Figure E2.5: 1 Chronicles 7:6–11

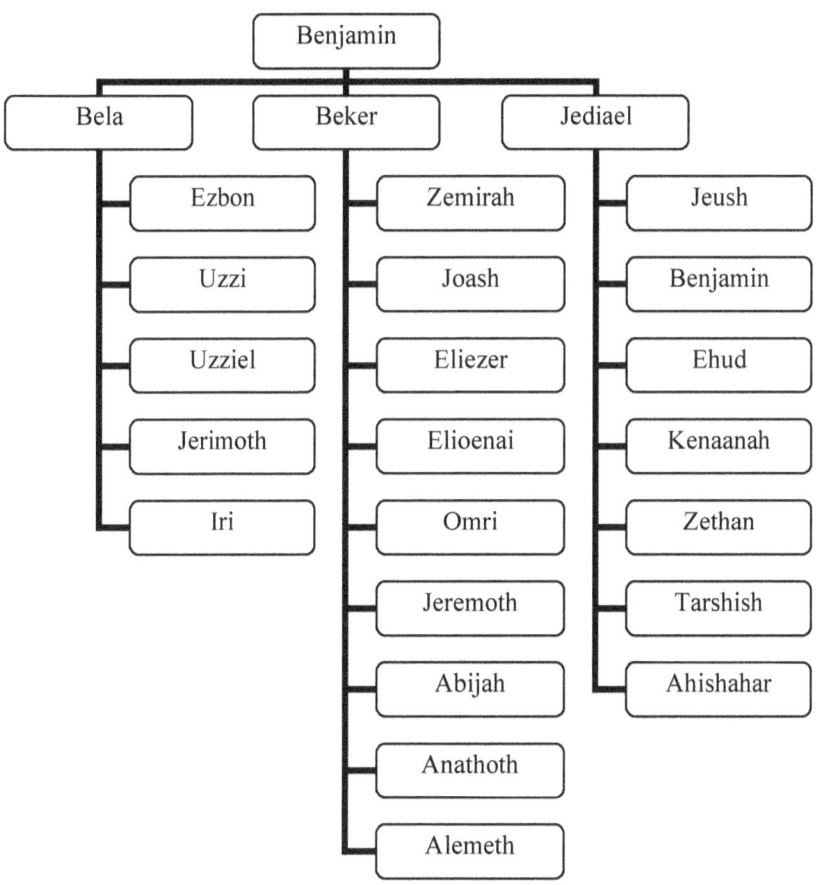

Figure E2.6: 1 Chronicles 8:1–7

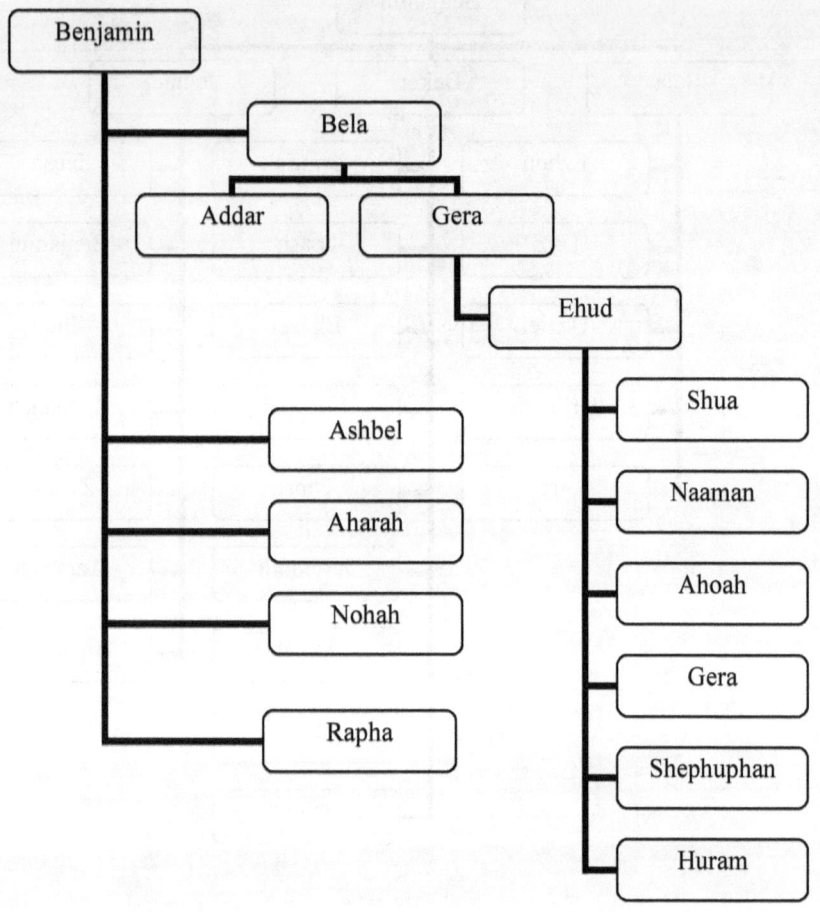

CHAPTER 10
B AND B1: 1 CHRONICLES 2:1–2; 9:1A
"ALL ISRAEL"

INTRODUCTION

As has long been noted, 1 Chr 2:1–2 and 9:1a provide the introduction and conclusion to the Chronicler's lists of the sons of Israel.[1] In respect of 1 Chr 9:1a, Rothstein says: "The name 'Israel,' reminds one greatly of 2:1, where the various genealogies are preceded by a specified list of the sons of Israel."[2]

These two texts, 1 Chr 2:1–2; 9:1a, appear on the same chiastic level in the Chronicler's structure, and as such these two texts complement one another. Just as 1 Chr 2:1–2 introduces the tribal lists by giving a complete list of the traditional twelve tribes,[3] 1 Chr 9:1a concludes the tribal lists with the statement, "all Israel was listed in the genealogies." It would appear then that the Chronicler

---

[1] "In balance with 1 Chr. 2:1–2 the Chronicler closed his focus on the breadth of God's people with a brief summation," Pratt, *Chronicles*, 92, cf. Selman, *1 Chronicles*, 122.

[2] "Der Name 'Israel' erinnert dann sehr lebhaft an 2, 1, wo die Reihe der Genealogien der Stämme durch die Aufzählung der 'Söhne Israels' eingeleitet wird," Rothstein and Hänel, *Chronik*, 169. Speaking in respect to 1 Chr 9:1a, Johnstone says that it "picks up 'these are the descendants of Israel' in 1 Chron. 2.1 and acts as the concluding formula for all the intervening material," *Chronicles: Volume 1*, 118. Hill states that 1 Chr 9:1a "has its parallel in the introduction to the genealogical prologue listing the twelve sons of Israel," *Chronicles*, 171; cf. Klein, *1 Chronicles*, 265. Braun sees 1 Chr 9:1 as "the conclusion of the lists of Chapters 1–8, but does round off the listings begun by 2:1," *1 Chronicles*, 138. Williamson suggests that it is a "summarising conclusion" to 1 Chr 2–8, *Chronicles*, 86, so also Japhet, *Chronicles*, 206; De Vries, *Chronicles*, 85.

[3] With Joseph being represented by himself, rather than being represented by his two sons, Ephraim and Manasseh. In the tribal lists of Genesis and Exodus, Joseph is always listed, while Numbers always lists Ephraim and Manasseh. First Chronicles 2–8 maintains this distinction. First Chronicles 2:2 mentions "Joseph," although it is Ephraim and Manasseh who are listed within the genealogies themselves (1 Chr 5:23–24; 7:14–29). It is to be noted that, although the tribal lists are introduced with all of Israel's sons, not every son is located within the tribal lists.

equated "the sons of Israel" with "all Israel." The importance of this phrase and its identification with the entire family of Israel will be investigated below.

The two texts do, however, present certain difficulties which must first be investigated. The first issue is whether or not 1 Chr 9:1a should be read as part of 1 Chr 9:1b, or whether it represents, as suggested here, a separate level within the Chronicler's structure. Second, the ordering of the sons of Israel in 1 Chr 2:1–2 is unique within the Hebrew Bible. The question must be asked as to whether any special significance is to be understood by this ordering. A third question is, what is meant by the phrase "all Israel?" The final question which is of concern here is, what is meant by "the book of the kings of Israel (and Judah?)?" When were "all Israel" listed in such a work? Is this to be understood as an individual historical source, or a general reference to a variety of sources?

THE TEXT OF 1 CHRONICLES 9:1A

The Hebrew text of 1 Chr 9:1 reads; וְכָל־יִשְׂרָאֵל הִתְיַחְשׂוּ וְהִנָּם כְּתוּבִים עַל־סֵפֶר מַלְכֵי יִשְׂרָאֵל וִיהוּדָה הָגְלוּ לְבָבֶל בְּמַעֲלָם. The first issue arises through the phrase; סֵפֶר מַלְכֵי יִשְׂרָאֵל וִיהוּדָה הָגְלוּ. The verb הָגְלוּ (they were exiled) is in the plural, and would suggest that the reference is to both Israel and Judah, as also would the plural pronominal suffix on בְּמַעֲלָם (their unfaithfulness).[4] This, however, is not the problem that it may appear to be. It will be observed that the verb הִתְיַחְשׂוּ (they were listed in the genealogies) is also in the plural with a singular subject "Israel." Furthermore, the particle וְהִנָּם, has the same plural pronominal suffix as "their unfaithfulness," yet also refers back to the singular noun "Israel." The Hebrew Bible often mixes singular and plurals when referring to people(s).

A greater problem is the construct סֵפֶר מַלְכֵי (the book of the kings of . . .) which demands a phrase in the absolute, and would suggest that the reference is at least Israel, while the use of the conjunction ו (and) before Judah would suggest that Israel and Judah must be read together. Taken together, this suggests that "the book of the kings of Israel and Judah" is being cited. This reading, however, would leave הָגְלוּ (they were exiled) without a subject. However, one would expect at least one subject, and perhaps two, to the verb הָגְלוּ (they were exiled).

What 1 Chr 9:1 contains, then, is an instance of a verb, הָגְלוּ, as well as a construct chain, סֵפֶר מַלְכֵי, both requiring at least part, or preferably all, of the intervening phrase יִשְׂרָאֵל וִיהוּדָה (Israel and Judah) as part of its own grammatical construction. It is reasonable to conclude that the one phrase, יִשְׂרָאֵל וִיהוּדָה,

---

[4] Knoppers, *1 Chronicles 1–9*, 479.

should not be connected to both grammatical constructions, and yet this is what the text appears to require.

Several solutions have been proposed. Keil has argued strongly for reading the text, "the book of the kings of Israel. And Judah was exiled."[5] This is the way in which the phrase is often translated in English versions, and is given support by the presence of the *athnach* in BHS under יִשְׂרָאֵל, which connects "Israel" with the book of the kings, and "Judah" with those who are exiled.[6] Keil says that "Israel" in 1 Chr 9:1 and 9:2 is used in an identical manner to denote the covenant people as a whole, while "Judah" refers to only one portion of it. He indicates that just as that part of Israel which resided in the Transjordan had gone into exile (1 Chr 5:6, 22, 26), so here in 1 Chr 9:1b it is that part of Israel made up of Judah who are exiled. What he fails to address is the place of the conjunction ו (and) which suggests that "and Judah" should be read with the preceding "Israel." Nor does he address why, if it is Judah that is exiled in 1 Chr 9:1b, it is Israel, cultic officials, Judah, Benjamin, Ephraim and Manasseh who live on their properties and in Jerusalem after the exile (1 Chr 9:2–3).[7] Further, in the list "Israel, priests, Levites, temple servants," "Israel" is used to denote, not the people as a whole, but the people as distinct from the cultic officials, while "all Israel" in 1 Chr 9:1a refers to the people as a whole, including Levi.[8] As such, contrary to Keil's suggestion, the two uses of "Israel" in 1 Chr 9:1, 2 are not identical.

Some scholars suggest the inadequacy of the text as it stands to answer all of the concerns raised, and insist that a word or words have been omitted from the text due to haplography. The most common suggestion is that וִיהוּדָה (and Judah) has been omitted, and that the text originally read, "the book of the kings of Israel and Judah. And Judah was exiled . . . ."[9] This resolves the concerns raised in regard to the conjunction ו.

A similar proposal is that of Braun.[10] He also suggests that there has been haplography, but instead of reinserting the phrase וִיהוּדָה (and Judah) he suggests that the longer phrase יִשְׂרָאֵל וִיהוּדָה (Israel and Judah) has been omitted. This would make the text read, "the kings of Israel and Judah. And Israel and Judah were exiled . . . ." This suggestion has the advantage of answering all of the concerns previously raised, including the presence of plural verbs and pronominal

---

[5] Keil, *Chronicles*, 152–153. So also Rothstein and Hänel, *Chronik*, 169; Klein, *1 Chronicles*, p 259, Note 1.

[6] It is so translated in the NASB, NIV, NRSV, JPS, GNB, NCV.

[7] This is working on the assumption that 1 Chr 9:2 is speaking of a "return" from exile and a "resettlement" of territory. This issue will be addressed in Chapter 13.

[8] See Figure 4.2.

[9] Rudolph, *Chronikbücher*, 82; Knoppers, *1 Chronicles 1–9*, 480. Rothstein and Hänel, *Chronik*, 170, allows this as a possibility, although preferring the text as it stands.

[10] Braun, *1 Chronicles*, 129, 130 note 1.a–a.

suffixes, which, however, may be subject to other explanations. It does, however, make Israel a captive in Babylon, a fate suggested by neither the Deuteronomistic History nor by the Chronicler himself. This is not an impossible obstacle to overcome. In 2 Chr 33:11, Manasseh is taken captive by the king of Assyria to Babylon.[11] If it is inferred that "Babylon" here is simply a euphemism for captivity of any sort by any power, then the Chronicler would be correct in saying that Israel was taken captive to Babylon. Furthermore, in 2 Chr 30:1–11, portions of the former Israel were present during Hezekiah's Passover, while in 2 Chr 34:9, "the entire remnant of Israel," contributed to the restoration of the temple. It is probable then that, in the Chronicler's eyes, "Israel" was still in their land up until the exile of Judah, and therefore Israel could also be taken as prisoners into Babylon.

A final proposal to this problem which neither splits "Israel" from "Judah" nor emends the text is that of Goettsberger. He suggests, "there, just as at the beginning of verse 1, so also in verse 2 'Israel' is in the minds of the people, so it is plain that 'Judah' is not the subject of verse 1c."[12]

Here, Goettsberger is suggesting that the subject of "they went into exile" is neither "Judah," nor "Israel and Judah," but "all Israel," which appears at the beginning of 1 Chr 9:1.[13] Although attractive, if "Israel" were the subject of both verbs, הִתְיַחְשׂוּ and הָגְלוּ, a conjunctive *waw* would be expected with הָגְלוּ in order to link the two thoughts together.[14]

Scholars have often turned for help in resolving this issue to the book title, "the book of the kings of Israel." It has been pointed out that although a "book of the kings" is often cited as a source for the Chronicler's work, the more common name for this work is either "the book of the kings of Judah and Israel" (2 Chr

---

[11] For a discussion of the historical circumstances that may lay behind this narrative, see Williamson, *Chronicles*, 391–393; Jacob M. Myers, *II Chronicles* (AB 13; Garden City: Doubleday, 1965), 197–199.

[12] "Da, wie am Anfang von V. 1, so auch V. 2 'Israel' im Sinne des Gesamtvolkes gemeint ist, ist 'Juda' nicht als Subjekt zu V. 1c zu ziehen," Goettsberger, *Chronik*, 88.

[13] Goettsberger, *Chronik*, 88–89. Johnstone mentions this in "Guilt and Atonement," 138 note 25, although he does not mention this in his commentary on these verses, *Chronicles: Volume 1*, 118–119, and it is unknown if he had changed his opinion. See also Selman, *1 Chronicles*, 122. Knoppers suggests this as a possibility, but prefers the presence of an haplography, Knoppers, *1 Chronicles 1–9*, 480. Although not the same, the AV is similar, translating, "kings of Israel and Judah, *who* were carried away to Babylon." This makes the phrase "Israel and Judah" serve as both part of the book title and the subject of the verb. Myers translates, "when they were exiled," *I Chronicles*, 59, but this implies a registration at the point of exile, and by those who exiled them. This is how the LXX understands the phrase, μετὰ τῶν ἀποικισθέντων εἰς Βαβυλῶνα ἐν ταῖς ἀνομίαις αὐτῶν.

[14] Bruce K. Waltke and M. O'Connor, *An Introduction to Biblical Hebrew Syntax* (Winona Lake: Eisenbrauns, 1990), 32.3d.

16:11; 25:26; 28:26; 32:32),[15] or "the book of the kings of Israel and Judah" (2 Chr 27:7; 35:27; 36:8).[16] This would suggest that the full book title is evident here in 1 Chr 9:1a, and that haplography has taken place.[17] However, the phrase does appear simply as "the book of the kings of Israel" (2 Chr 20:34),[18] or "the annals of the kings of Israel" (1 Chr 33:18).[19] As such, the book title cannot be used to give a definitive answer to this problem, although it does suggest the strong probability that the full title "the book of the kings of Israel and Judah" is to be understood here. If this is the case, then this would indicate that haplography, either of the phrase "and Judah," or "Israel and Judah," has taken place. It is my conclusion that haplography provides the best solution to the problems raised.

THE BOOK OF THE KINGS OF ISRAEL AND JUDAH

The above conclusion raises the question of what is meant by "the book of the kings of Israel and Judah?" The Chronicler refers to numerous written sources in his work.[20] The titles given to some of these works give the appearance that they were official documents produced by the state: the book of the kings of Israel and Judah (1 Chr 9:1; 2 Chr 27:7; 35:27; 36:8); the book of the kings of Judah and Israel (2 Chr 16:11; 25:26; 28:26; 32:32); the day book of King David (1 Chr 27:24), the book of the kings of Israel (2 Chr 20:34); the words of the kings of Israel (2 Chr 33:18). Other works are said to be the result of the writing activities of prophets: Samuel (1 Chr 29:29), Gad (1 Chr 29:29), Nathan (1 Chr 29:29; 2 Chr 9:29), Ahijah (2 Chr 9:29), Iddo the Seer (2 Chr 9:29; 12:15; 13:22), Shemaiah (2 Chr12:15); Jehu son of Hanani (2 Chr 20:34), Isaiah (2 Chr 26:22; 32:32), and Hozai (2 Chr 33:19),[21] are all said to have left written sources which the Chronicler utilised, and to which he referred his readers for more information in respect to the account he has related.

---

[15] סֵפֶר מַלְכֵי־יְהוּדָה וְיִשְׂרָאֵל. Second Chronicles 16:11 is slightly different, סֵפֶר הַמְּלָכִים וְיִשְׂרָאֵל לִיהוּדָה.
[16] סֵפֶר מַלְכֵי־יִשְׂרָאֵל וִיהוּדָה. This is also the reading in 1 Chr 9:1.
[17] Japhet, *Chronicles*, 206.
[18] סֵפֶר מַלְכֵי יִשְׂרָאֵל.
[19] דִּבְרֵי מַלְכֵי יִשְׂרָאֵל.
[20] See Figure 10.1.
[21] The LXX here reads τῶν ὁρώντων, "the seers," which suggests הַחֹזִים rather than חוֹזָי should be read here.

Figure 10.1: Book of the Kings

1 Chr	Title	1 Kgs	Title
9:1	סֵפֶר מַלְכֵי יִשְׂרָאֵל וִיהוּדָה		
27:24	דִּבְרֵי הַיָּמִים לַמֶּלֶךְ דָּוִיד בְּמִסְפָּר		
29:29	דִּבְרֵי שְׁמוּאֵל הָרֹאֶה		
29:29	דִּבְרֵי נָתָן הַנָּבִיא		
29:29	דִּבְרֵי גָּד הַחֹזֶה		
2 Chr			
9:29	דִּבְרֵי נָתָן הַנָּבִיא	11:41	סֵפֶר דִּבְרֵי שְׁלֹמֹה
9:29	וְעַל־נְבוּאַת אֲחִיָּה הַשִּׁילוֹנִי		
9:29	וּבַחֲזוֹת יֶעְדּוֹ הַחֹזֶה		
12:15	בְּדִבְרֵי שְׁמַעְיָה הַנָּבִיא	14:29	סֵפֶר דִּבְרֵי הַיָּמִים לְמַלְכֵי יְהוּדָה
12:15	וְעִדּוֹ הַחֹזֶה		
13:22	בְּמִדְרַשׁ הַנָּבִיא עִדּוֹ	15:7	סֵפֶר דִּבְרֵי הַיָּמִים לְמַלְכֵי יְהוּדָה
16:11	סֵפֶר הַמְּלָכִים לִיהוּדָה וְיִשְׂרָאֵל	15:23	סֵפֶר דִּבְרֵי הַיָּמִים לְמַלְכֵי יְהוּדָה
20:34	בְּדִבְרֵי יֵהוּא בֶן־חֲנָנִי	22:46	סֵפֶר דִּבְרֵי הַיָּמִים לְמַלְכֵי יְהוּדָה
20:34	סֵפֶר מַלְכֵי יִשְׂרָאֵל		
		2 Kgs	
--		8:23	סֵפֶר דִּבְרֵי הַיָּמִים לְמַלְכֵי יְהוּדָה
24:27	מִדְרַשׁ סֵפֶר הַמְּלָכִים	12:20	סֵפֶר דִּבְרֵי הַיָּמִים לְמַלְכֵי יְהוּדָה
25:26	סֵפֶר מַלְכֵי־יְהוּדָה וְיִשְׂרָאֵל	14:18	סֵפֶר דִּבְרֵי הַיָּמִים לְמַלְכֵי יְהוּדָה
26:22	יְשַׁעְיָהוּ בֶן־אָמוֹץ הַנָּבִיא	15:6	סֵפֶר דִּבְרֵי הַיָּמִים לְמַלְכֵי יְהוּדָה
27:7	סֵפֶר מַלְכֵי־יִשְׂרָאֵל וִיהוּדָה	15:36	סֵפֶר דִּבְרֵי הַיָּמִים לְמַלְכֵי יְהוּדָה
28:26	סֵפֶר מַלְכֵי־יְהוּדָה וְיִשְׂרָאֵל	16:19	סֵפֶר דִּבְרֵי הַיָּמִים לְמַלְכֵי יְהוּדָה
32:32	בַּחֲזוֹן יְשַׁעְיָהוּ בֶן־אָמוֹץ הַנָּבִיא		
32:32	סֵפֶר מַלְכֵי־יְהוּדָה וְיִשְׂרָאֵל	20:20	סֵפֶר דִּבְרֵי הַיָּמִים לְמַלְכֵי יְהוּדָה
33:18	דִּבְרֵי מַלְכֵי יִשְׂרָאֵל	21:17	סֵפֶר דִּבְרֵי הַיָּמִים לְמַלְכֵי יְהוּדָה
33:19	דִּבְרֵי חוֹזָי		
--		21:25	סֵפֶר דִּבְרֵי הַיָּמִים לְמַלְכֵי יְהוּדָה
35:27	סֵפֶר מַלְכֵי־יִשְׂרָאֵל וִיהוּדָה	23:28	סֵפֶר דִּבְרֵי הַיָּמִים לְמַלְכֵי יְהוּדָה
36:8	סֵפֶר מַלְכֵי יִשְׂרָאֵל וִיהוּדָה	24:5	סֵפֶר דִּבְרֵי הַיָּמִים לְמַלְכֵי יְהוּדָה

Two sources are said to be a midrash, (מִדְרָשׁ). One was written by Iddo (2 Chr 13:22), and the other a midrash on the "book of the kings" (2 Chr 24:27).

There have been several ways in which this evidence has been assessed. Curtis concludes that the different works entitled "the book of the kings" are simply variations on the title of one and the same work.[22] Further, working from

---

[22] Curtis and Madsen, *Chronicles*, 22.

the observation that both the works of Jehu (2 Chr 20:34), and the prophet Isaiah (2 Chr 32:32), are said to be incorporated into the book of the kings, he suggests that these "prophetic" works are sections within this book of the kings, and that the prophetic names act like "catchwords in the book of Kings" to that particular section of the larger work.[23] He, therefore, concludes that the Chronicler only had access to two sources for his writing. The first is the canonical writings, the second is "this Midrashic Book of Israel."[24]

Torrey is more sceptical about the availability of additional sources to the Chronicler. Although acknowledging that the Chronicler had access to the canonical works, he rejects the possibility that the Chronicler had any other sources.[25] He observes that in the material unique to the Chronicler, "the material which has come to us only through the books of Chronicles is perfectly homogeneous."[26]

And again, "the language, style, and tendency, throughout these long and important chapters and sections, *are those of the Chronicler himself and of no one else.*"[27]

He, therefore, questions the possibility that, "Samuel, Nathan, Gad, Ahijah, Iddo, Shemaiah, Jehu, Isaiah and the authors of the other 'sources,' used all exactly the same language and style, and wrote with the selfsame tendency."[28]

As a result, he concludes that the Chronicler's references to "sources" were "partly literary adornment, but partly also [to give] an apologetic advantage . . . against the rivals of the Jews."[29]

Williamson has proposed a third alternative which avoids the postulation of the existence of an alternative history of Israel and Judah to the canonical Samuel/Kings, while also seeking to avoid the scepticism of Torrey about the possibility that other sources were available to the Chronicler.[30]

---

[23] Curtis and Madsen, *Chronicles*, 23.

[24] Curtis and Madsen, *Chronicles*, 24. Keil is similar in that he says that the Chronicler utilised a larger source made up of a wide variety of materials. He suggests, however, that the Chronicler possessed a combined copy of "the book of the kings of Israel and Judah," while the Deuteronomist had available the separate editions. He suggests however, that both authors extracted the material that was consistent with their own purposes, which accounts for both the similarities and differences in the two works, *Chronicles*, 31.

[25] Charles C. Torrey, *Ezra Studies* (New York: KTAV Publishing House, 1970), 227–231.

[26] Torrey, *Ezra*, 229.

[27] Torrey, *Ezra*, 229–230. Italics his.

[28] Torrey, *Ezra*, 229.

[29] Torrey, *Ezra*, 231.

[30] Williamson, *Chronicles*, 17–21.

Williamson points out that with only two exceptions (1 Chr 29:29; 2 Chr 35:26–27), every source citation by the Chronicler is in the identical position of the source citations in Kings.[31] He further points out that the source citations found in 2 Chr 16:11; 20:34; and 25:26 do not occur at the end of the reign of the particular king in Kings, and yet they appear in the identical location in Chronicles as they do in Kings, suggesting that the Chronicler was following the text of Kings rather than another source. Also, even though the Chronicler reports numerous sources available for the reign of Solomon (2 Chr 9:29), his report of Solomon's reign comes entirely from Kings, with no additions from these alleged sources.[32]

Finally, Williamson's observation that, apart from the reference to David, the Chronicler does not insert any source citations into his text that do not have a corresponding citation in Kings is evidence that the Chronicler was not inserting his source citations for mere apologetic or literary reasons. It can be observed that most of the prophets cited are either mentioned within the Deuteronomistic History or in postexilic writings,[33] and that when they are recorded in Chronicles it is in regard to a king who received a generally good assessment from the Chronicler.[34] These facts indicate something of the Chronicler's viewpoint that positive responses to the word of Yahweh through prophets is a requirement to turn a king or society from evil to good, as well as to enable that king or society to continue to do what is right in the eyes of Yahweh.

Williamson's study has, in one sense, confirmed Torrey's position that the references to sources were "partly literary adornment, but partly also [to give] an apologetic advantage."[35] This apologetic advantage, however, was not against the

---

[31] Williamson, *Chronicles*, 18. First Chronicles 29:29 in regard to David has no corresponding entry in Samuel/Kings, while the reference to Josiah in 2 Chr 35:26–27 is in a different location than in Kings.

[32] Williamson, *Chronicles*, 18.

[33] Gad (1 Sam 22:5; 2 Sam 24:11–19), Nathan (2 Sam 7, 12; 1 Kgs 1), Ahijah (1 Kgs 11:29–30; 12:15; 14:2–6, 18), Iddo (Ezra 5:1; Zech 1:1, 7), Shemaiah (1 Kgs 12:22), Jehu (1 Kgs 16:1, 7, 12). Samuel and Isaiah are known as prominent persons in the works that carry their names, but Isaiah is also a prominent character in 2 Kgs 19–20.

[34] "It is, furthermore, of interest to observe that he only ever uses this particular formula of kings whom, either in part or in whole, he judges favourably; they are never used in the case of wholly bad kings," Williamson, *Chronicles*, 19. This is true even though Rehoboam is said to have "done evil" in the eyes of Yahweh (2 Chr 12:1, 14). Nevertheless, when challenged by the prophet over his behaviour he and the people humbled themselves and were not destroyed by Yahweh (2 Chr 12:5–7). Likewise Uzziah was a king who "did right in the eyes of Yahweh" (2 Chr 26:4), and although afflicted with leprosy for his cultic violation (2 Chr 26:16–20), had a positive assessment during his reign.

[35] Torrey, *Ezra*, 231.

"enemies of the Jews," but was in the furtherance of the Chronicler's own purpose in writing his work for his own people, for when the Chronicler cites sources he is often speaking of the necessity and benefits of responding positively to the prophetic message, so that positive benefits might flow to the community.

The one reference which fits neither of these categories is 1 Chr 9:1, for neither a specific king nor a prophet is cited in this text. First Chronicles 9:1 appears as a summary statement for the lists contained in 1 Chr 2–8, and seeks to indicate that all of those who could be identified with Israel (i.e. the sons of Israel (1 Chr 2:1–2)), had had their relationship to Israel recorded. It is clear, however, that the lists of 1 Chr 2–8 contain only a portion of the descendants of the sons of Israel mentioned in 1 Chr 2:1–2, while none of Zebulon's descendants are listed at all in 1 Chr 2–8. Is the Chronicler suggesting that these are only an extract from a larger source termed "the book of the kings of Israel and Judah?" This is unlikely. It has already been shown that when the Chronicler gives a source citation he is merely adapting a citation found in 1 and 2 Kings. What, then, is this "book of the kings of Israel and Judah" cited here?

It is probable that the Chronicler had in mind both the prophetic and the royal aspects that his other citations contain. First Chronicles 9:1 speaks of an הִתְיַחְשׂוּ (enrollment) and implies an official registration of the people. Second Chronicles 12:15 indicates that the words of Iddo the seer were in regard to a לְהִתְיַחֵשׂ (genealogical enrollment).[36] This same root, יחשׂ, is used in 1 Chr 9:1 and often in the genealogies to speak of the enrollment of the people.[37] What is important about this is that the term is used in respect to the enrollment for warfare (1 Chr 5:1, 7; 7:5, 7, 9, 40), is connected with warfare (1 Chr 4:33; cf. 4:41), or is for enrollment into cultic service (1 Chr 9:22; 2 Chr 31:16–19). In each of these instances, the enrollment would indicate that the needs of the state, either military or religious, were invoked to demand of the people that they be enrolled. This is illustrated in 1 Chr 5:17, which indicates that the "enrollment" was undertaken during the reigns of Jotham of Judah and Jeroboam II of Israel. Furthermore, the assignment of the people into divisions for cultic (1 Chr 23–26) or military service (1 Chr 27) was in response to the demands of David the king.

Since several kings are mentioned in respect to enrollments (1 Chr 4:41; 5:10, 17; 2 Chr 12:15), the Chronicler probably considered any enrollment to be at the command of a king. It is for this reason that the Chronicler could say that "all Israel was enrolled in the book of the kings." Enrollments were only performed at the insistence of kings (cf. 1 Chr 21), and for the purposes

---

[36] Japhet, *Chronicles*, 682.

[37] יחשׂ is used in the genealogies in 1 Chr 4:33; 5:1,7, 17; 7:5, 7, 9, 40; 9:1, 22. It is used elsewhere only in postexilic literature: 2 Chr 12:15; 31:16, 17, 18, 19; Ezra 2:62; 8:1, 3; Neh 7:5 [x2], 64.

established by kings (1 Chr 23–27; 2 Chr 2:17–18). If Israel had been enrolled, then it would, of necessity, have been on the orders of a king and the totals would have been listed in the official records of the kings.[38] It is uncertain whether the Chronicler had a particular king in mind, or if he simply assumed that the muster lists that he had incorporated into his genealogies had originally been part of the royal records. Since he refers to a number of kings, prophets, and writings, it is more likely that the Chronicler assumed that his sources came from the royal records.

Although speculative, because prophets were, at times, said to be involved in the enrollment process (2 Chr 12:15), it may be reasonable to conclude that the Chronicler had also the prophetic aspect in mind. That Iddo was involved in recording genealogies indicates that, at times, a census was consistent with Yahweh's plan for the king, and that such an enrollment should be recorded in respect to that king's reign. This is illustrated by David's census (1 Chr 21). This census was objectionable to Yahweh, who sent his prophet to condemn it (1 Chr 21:7–13). Consequently, the results of this census were not recorded (2 Chr 27:24). However, that at times a prophet was involved in recording genealogies which were allegedly incorporated into the royal archives is an indication that such a census was not always objectionable to Yahweh. It is therefore reasonable to conclude that when the Chronicler said that "all Israel" was recorded in the genealogies that he has in mind an official census which was sanctioned by Yahweh and recorded by one of his prophets.

ALL ISRAEL

The question must now be asked, "what is meant by the phrase 'all Israel'?" The phrase כָּל־יִשְׂרָאֵל (all Israel) appears 153 times in the Hebrew Bible, and forty-six times in Chronicles alone. In Chronicles, כָּל־יִשְׂרָאֵל appears another twenty-seven times with some variations,[39] for a total of seventy-three occurrences. Nineteen of these seventy-three occurrences are identical to the Chronicler's source in

---

[38] That 1 Chr 27:24 specifically says that the totals from David's census were not entered into the official records confirms this.

[39] All the "men" of Israel (1 Chr 10:7; 16:3; 5:3), "elders" (1 Chr 11:3; 2 Chr 5:4); "assembly" (קָהָל; 1 Chr 13:2; 2 Chr 6:3 [x2], 12, 13); "land" (1 Chr 13:2; 2 Chr 34:7); "chosen" (1 Chr 19:10); "boundaries" (1 Chr 21:12); "leaders" (1 Chr 22:17; 23:2; 28:1); "assembly" (עֵדָה; 2 Chr 5:6); "tribes" (2 Chr 6:5; 11:16; 12:13; 33:7); "your people" (2 Chr 6:29); "sons" (2 Chr 7:3; 31:1); "remainder" (2 Chr 34:9); "kings" (2 Chr 35:18); "Judah and Israel" (2 Chr 35:18).

Samuel/Kings, (Figure 10.2).[40] This continues a pattern of how the Chronicler often remains close to his sources without variation. Although beneficial once the Chronicler's overall understanding of the phrase "all Israel" has been analysed, it is possible that these nineteen are included under the influence of the source rather than the Chronicler's own understanding of the term.

Figure 10.2: "All Israel"—Identical to the Chronicler's Source

1 Chr 11:3	כָּל־זִקְנֵי יִשְׂרָאֵל	2 Sam 5:3	כָּל־זִקְנֵי יִשְׂרָאֵל
1 Chr 18:14	כָּל־יִשְׂרָאֵל	2 Sam 8:15	כָּל־יִשְׂרָאֵל
1 Chr 19:10	מִכָּל־בָּחוּר בְּיִשְׂרָאֵל	2 Sam 10:9	מִכֹּל בְּחוּרֵי בְיִשְׂרָאֵל
1 Chr 19:17	כָּל־יִשְׂרָאֵל	2 Sam 10:17	כָּל־יִשְׂרָאֵל
2 Chr 5:3	כָּל־אִישׁ יִשְׂרָאֵל	1 Kgs 8:2	כָּל־אִישׁ יִשְׂרָאֵל
2 Chr 5:4	כֹּל זִקְנֵי יִשְׂרָאֵל	1 Kgs 8:3	כֹּל זִקְנֵי יִשְׂרָאֵל
2 Chr 5:6	וְכָל־עֲדַת יִשְׂרָאֵל	1 Kgs 8:5	וְכָל־עֲדַת יִשְׂרָאֵל
2 Chr 6:3	כָּל־קְהַל יִשְׂרָאֵל	1 Kgs 8:14	כָּל־קְהַל יִשְׂרָאֵל
2 Chr 6:3	וְכָל־קְהַל יִשְׂרָאֵל	1 Kgs 8:14	וְכָל־קְהַל יִשְׂרָא
2 Chr 6:5	מִכֹּל שִׁבְטֵי יִשְׂרָאֵל	1 Kgs 8:16	מִכֹּל שִׁבְטֵי יִשְׂרָאֵל
2 Chr 6:12	כָּל־קְהַל יִשְׂרָאֵל	1 Kgs 8:22	כָּל־קְהַל יִשְׂרָאֵל
2 Chr 6:29	וּלְכֹל עַמְּךָ יִשְׂרָאֵל	1 Kgs 8:38	לְכֹל עַמְּךָ יִשְׂרָאֵל
2 Chr 7:8	וְכָל־יִשְׂרָאֵל	1 Kgs 8:65	וְכָל־יִשְׂרָאֵל
2 Chr 9:30	כָּל־יִשְׂרָאֵל	1 Kgs 11:42	כָּל־יִשְׂרָאֵל
2 Chr 10:1	כָּל־יִשְׂרָאֵל	1 Kgs 12:1	כָּל־יִשְׂרָאֵל
2 Chr 10:16	וְכָל־יִשְׂרָאֵל	1 Kgs 12:16	כָּל־יִשְׂרָאֵל
2 Chr 12:13	מִכֹּל שִׁבְטֵי יִשְׂרָאֵל	1 Kgs 14:21	מִכֹּל שִׁבְטֵי יִשְׂרָאֵל
2 Chr 18:16	כָּל־יִשְׂרָאֵל	1 Kgs 22:17	כָּל־יִשְׂרָאֵל
2 Chr 33:7	מִכֹּל שִׁבְטֵי יִשְׂרָאֵל	2 Kgs 21:7	מִכֹּל שִׁבְטֵי יִשְׂרָאֵל

Thirty-seven of the seventy-three occurrences are unique to the Chronicler (Figure 10.3). These normally appear in passages unique to the Chronicler, although they sometimes appear as additions which he embeds within his source material. As part of his own material, these additions are very important to gaining an understanding of what the Chronicler meant by the phrase, "all Israel." What is particularly noticeable is that these occurrences revolve around three basic themes: people, land and "northern" Israel as distinct from Judah. "Israel" is used in reference to the people as a group of twelve tribes (1 Chr 9:1; 11:10; 13:2; 15:3; 2 Chr 7:3, 6; 11:16; 29:24 [x2]; 35:3), or to representative groups from the twelve tribes (1 Chr 22:17; 23:2; 28:1; 28:8; 2 Chr 1:2 [x2]; 6:13).

---

[40] There are a further fifty-six instances where the Chronicler does not include "all Israel," or a variation of it, which he found in his source.

Figure 10.3: "All Israel"—the Chronicler's Unique and Added Material

Reference	Hebrew	Category
1 Chr 9:1	וְכָל־יִשְׂרָאֵל	unique material
1 Chr 11:10	כָּל־יִשְׂרָאֵל	added to source
1 Chr 12:39	כָּל־יִשְׂרָאֵל	unique material
1 Chr 13:2	לְכֹל קְהַל יִשְׂרָאֵל	unique material
1 Chr 13:2	בְּכֹל אַרְצוֹת יִשְׂרָאֵל	unique material
1 Chr 15:3	כָּל־יִשְׂרָאֵל	unique material
1 Chr 22:17	לְכָל־שָׂרֵי יִשְׂרָאֵל	unique material
1 Chr 23:2	כָּל־שָׂרֵי יִשְׂרָאֵל	unique material
1 Chr 28:1	כָּל־שָׂרֵי יִשְׂרָאֵל	unique material
1 Chr 28:4	כָּל־יִשְׂרָאֵל	unique material
1 Chr 28:8	כָּל־יִשְׂרָאֵל	unique material
1 Chr 29:21	לְכָל־יִשְׂרָאֵל	unique material
1 Chr 29:23	כָּל־יִשְׂרָאֵל	unique material
1 Chr 29:25	כָּל־יִשְׂרָאֵל	unique material
1 Chr 29:26	כָּל־יִשְׂרָאֵל	unique material
2 Chr 1:2	לְכָל־יִשְׂרָאֵל	added to source
2 Chr 1:2	לְכָל־יִשְׂרָאֵל	added to source
2 Chr 6:13	כָּל־קְהַל יִשְׂרָאֵל	added to source
2 Chr 7:3	וְכֹל בְּנֵי יִשְׂרָאֵל	added to source
2 Chr 7:6	וְכָל־יִשְׂרָאֵל	added to source
2 Chr 11:13	בְּכָל־יִשְׂרָאֵל	unique material
2 Chr 11:16	מִכֹּל שִׁבְטֵי יִשְׂרָאֵל	unique material
2 Chr 12:1	וְכָל־יִשְׂרָאֵל	added to source
2 Chr 13:4	וְכָל־יִשְׂרָאֵל	unique material
2 Chr 13:15	וְכָל־יִשְׂרָאֵל	unique material
2 Chr 24:5	מִכָּל־יִשְׂרָאֵל	added to source
2 Chr 28:23	וּלְכָל־יִשְׂרָאֵל	unique material
2 Chr 29:24	כָּל־יִשְׂרָאֵל	unique material
2 Chr 29:24	לְכָל־יִשְׂרָאֵל	unique material
2 Chr 30:1	כָּל־יִשְׂרָאֵל	unique material
2 Chr 30:5	בְּכָל־יִשְׂרָאֵל	unique material
2 Chr 30:6	בְּכָל־יִשְׂרָאֵל	unique material
2 Chr 31:1	כָּל־יִשְׂרָאֵל	unique material
2 Chr 31:1	כָּל־בְּנֵי יִשְׂרָאֵל	unique material
2 Chr 34:9	וּמִכֹּל שְׁאֵרִית יִשְׂרָאֵל	added to source
2 Chr 35:3	לְכָל־יִשְׂרָאֵל	unique material
2 Chr 35:18	וְכָל־יְהוּדָה וְיִשְׂרָאֵל	added to source

The references to the land are either to "all Israel" as a geographic region (1 Chr 13:2; 2 Chr 11:13; 24:5; 30:5), or to an "all Israel" which was ruled by the king (1 Chr 12:39 [12:38]; 28:4; 29:26; 2 Chr 12:1; 28:23). There are also some references where it is uncertain whether the land or the people are in view (1 Chr 29:21, 23, 25), and instances where "all Israel" refers to that portion of David and Solomon's kingdom which rebelled against, and separated itself from, Rehoboam (2 Chr 13:4, 5; 30:1, 6; 34:9).

These compare favourably with the instances where the Chronicler is identical to his source. It refers to the land which was ruled by the king (1 Chr 18:14; 2 Chr 9:30), and also to the people made up of the twelve tribes (1 Chr 19:10, 17; 2 Chr 5:3, 6; 6:3 (x2], 12, 29; 7:8; 10:1; 18:16), or representatives from the twelve tribes (1 Chr 11:3; 2 Chr 5:4). Again, there are instances where it is uncertain if the land or the people are in view (2 Chr 6:5; 12:13; 33:7). There are only two instances in the shared material where "all Israel" is used to designate northern Israel (2 Chr 10:16 [x2]), although these occur often in the Chronicler's source. This, however, is not surprising in light of the Chronicler's omission of most of the references to the north found in 1 and 2 Kings.

Seventeen instances present a significant variation to the Chronicler's source (Figure 10.4). Some of these are instances of the Chronicler modifying his source to read "all Israel," while others remove a clarifying word, thus reducing a longer statement in Samuel/Kings to "all Israel" in Chronicles.

Here, again, there is the emphasis on the people (1 Chr 10:7; 11:1, 4; 13:5, 6, 8; 15:28; 16:3; 2 Chr 10:3),[41] the land, whether ruled by the king (1 Chr 14:8), or as a geographical entity (1 Chr 21:12), and the distinctions between Judah and "northern" Israel (1 Chr 21:5; 2 Chr 10:16; 35:18).[42]

Again, there are certain instances where it is unclear whether the land or the people are in view (1 Chr 17:6; 21:4).[43]

There are five further occasions where the Chronicler modified the phrase "All Israel" which he found in his source (Figure 10.5)

Here again, the essential meaning has not been altered.

---

[41] Although the changes the Chronicler made from his source in 1 Chr 11:4 // 2 Sam 5:6; 1 Chr 13:5 // 2 Sam 6:1 have a theological significance, they are not significant for the Chronicler's understanding of the term "all Israel." In 1 Chr 11:4 it is now "all Israel," rather than just David and his men, who capture Jerusalem, showing that Jerusalem is the centre for all the people, and not just Judah. In 1 Chr 13:5 the Chronicler shows that it is "all Israel" and not just David's picked men who bring the ark of Yahweh up to Jerusalem. This shows that just as Jerusalem belongs to all the people, so also is it the centre of cultic life for all the people. There is, however, no difference to the Chronicler's understanding of what "all Israel" is, only what it does, or should do.

[42] Although 2 Chr 10:16 may appear ambiguous, 2 Chr 10:17 makes it clear that it refers to that part of Solomon's kingdom which was outside of Judah. Second Chronicles 35:18 utilised 2 Kgs 23:22, which was making a clear distinction between Israel and Judah. Second Chronicles 35:18 appears to blur that distinction.

[43] This is more clear in the Chronicler's sources where the "people/sons of Israel" are clearly identified (2 Sam 7:7; 24:4).

Figure 10.4: "All Israel"—Modified from the Chronicler's Source

1 Chr 10:7	כָּל־אִישׁ יִשְׂרָאֵל	1 Sam 31:7	אַנְשֵׁי־יִשְׂרָאֵל
1 Chr 11:1	כָּל־יִשְׂרָאֵל	2 Sam 5:1	כָּל־שִׁבְטֵי יִשְׂרָאֵל
1 Chr 11:4	וְכָל־יִשְׂרָאֵ	2 Sam 5:6	וַאֲנָשָׁיו
1 Chr 13:5	כָּל־יִשְׂרָאֵל	2 Sam 6:1	כָּל־בָּחוּר בְּיִשְׂרָאֵל
1 Chr 13:6	וְכָל־יִשְׂרָאֵל	2 Sam 6:2	וְכָל־הָעָם
1 Chr 13:8	וְכָל־יִשְׂרָאֵל	2 Sam 6:5	וְכָל־בֵּית יִשְׂרָאֵל
1 Chr 14:8	כָּל־יִשְׂרָאֵל	2 Sam 5:17	עַל־יִשְׂרָאֵל
1 Chr 15:28	וְכָל־יִשְׂרָאֵל	2 Sam 6:15	וְכָל־בֵּית יִשְׂרָאֵל
1 Chr 16:3	לְכָל־אִישׁ יִשְׂרָאֵל	2 Sam 6:19	לְכָל־הֲמוֹן יִשְׂרָאֵל
1 Chr 17:6	בְּכָל־יִשְׂרָאֵל	2 Sam 7:7	בְּכָל־בְּנֵי יִשְׂרָאֵל
1 Chr 21:4	בְּכָל־יִשְׂרָאֵל	2 Sam 24:4	הָעָם אֶת־יִשְׂרָאֵל
1 Chr 21:5	כָּל־יִשְׂרָאֵל	2 Sam 24:9	יִשְׂרָאֵל
1 Chr 21:12	בְּכָל־גְּבוּל יִשְׂרָאֵל	2 Sam 24:13	בְּאַרְצֶךָ
2 Chr 10:3	וְכָל־יִשְׂרָאֵל	1 Kgs 12:3	וְכָל־קְהַל יִשְׂרָאֵל
2 Chr 10:16	כָּל־יִשְׂרָאֵל	1 Kgs 12:16	כָּל־יִשְׂרָאֵל
2 Chr 11:3	כָּל־יִשְׂרָאֵל	1 Kgs 12:23	וְיֶתֶר הָעָם
2 Chr 35:18	וְכָל־מַלְכֵי יִשְׂרָאֵל	2 Kgs 23:22	וְכֹל יְמֵי מַלְכֵי יִשְׂרָאֵל וּמַלְכֵי יְהוּדָה

Of these twenty-two instances of variation, only one stands out as possibly presenting a different view of "Israel" than is presented in Samuel/Kings. Second Chronicles 11:3 reports the word which the prophet Shemaiah was to give, "say to Rehoboam son of Solomon king of Judah and to all Israel in Judah and Benjamin."

Figure 10.5: "All Israel"—Removed by the Chronicler

1 Chr 20:1	אֶת־חֵיל הַצָּבָא	2 Sam 11:1	כָּל־יִשְׂרָאֵל
1 Chr 21:2	יִשְׂרָאֵל	2 Sam 24:2	בְּכָל־שִׁבְטֵי יִשְׂרָאֵל
2 Chr 7:4	וְכָל־הָעָם	1 Kgs 8:62	וְכָל־יִשְׂרָאֵל
2 Chr 7:5	וְכָל־הָעָם	1 Kgs 8:63	וְכָל־בְּנֵי יִשְׂרָאֵל
2 Chr 10:18	בְּנֵי־יִשְׂרָאֵל	1 Kgs 12:18	כָּל־יִשְׂרָאֵל

This is decidedly different than the Chronicler's source, "say to Rehoboam son of Solomon king of Judah, to the whole house of Judah and Benjamin, and to the rest of the people" (1 Kgs 12:23).

The text of Kings speaks of three entities, Judah, Benjamin, and the remainder of the people.[1] Chronicles speaks of only one, "all Israel" which happens to reside in Judah and Benjamin. Von Rad utilises this verse to suggest, "Judah and Benjamin are now the true Israel,"[2] He suggests that as a result of the rebellion of the "Nordreich" against the legitimate rule of the Davidic monarchy (2 Chr 13:5–8), Israel is now constituted only of Judah and Benjamin, and as such, "all Israel" is to be found in these two tribes alone. He points out that the phrase "All Israel" is also used when it is clear that only Judah is indicated (2 Chr 12:1; 24:5; 28:23).

This conclusion has been strongly rejected in recent years. Williamson has demonstrated that the term "Israel" is used to designate both the northern and southern kingdoms.[3] He says, "the Chronicler uses the word Israel eighty times in connection with the divided monarchy, the majority of these references being to the Northern Kingdom. Fifty-one instances are without question so intended."[4]

He goes on to say that of the remainder, "there are eleven cases where there is no reasonable cause for doubt" that Judah is being indicated by the term "Israel."[5] In the context of 2 Chr 11:3, which von Rad utilised as the crux of his argument, Williamson points out that the identical terminology is used of both political entities (Figure 10.6).[6]

Williamson states that by using the term "Israel" to refer to both northern and southern kingdoms, "either party has equal justification in terming itself Israel."[7] Williamson concludes that the Chronicler is not suggesting that "Israel" is now to

---

[1] De Vries says, "among his [Shemaiah's] addressees are 'the rest of the people,' suggesting that others besides Judahites and Benjaminites intended to fight for King Rehoboam," *1 Kings*, 158.

[2] "Juda und Benjamin sind jetzt das wahre Israel," von Rad, *Geschichtsbild*, 31, and his wider discussion of Israel in Chronicles (pages 25–37). He is followed by Rudolph, who states "nach dem Abfall des Nordreichs nur Juda und Benjamin die Träger des alten Würdenamens sind und das wahre Israel darstellen," *Chronikbücher*, 227; so also Myers, *II Chronicles*, 65. Earlier, Keil had stated that the phrase "characterises all who had remained true to the house of David as Israel, i.e. those who walked in the footsteps of their progenitor Israel," Keil, *Chronicles*, 341. Cf. Curtis and Madsen, *Chronicles*, 169, who suggests that "Israel" refers to Judah and "the elements which adhered to the S. kingdom after 722 B.C."

[3] Williamson, *Israel*, 97–110. See also Japhet, *Ideology*, 267–278.

[4] Williamson, *Israel*, 102.

[5] Williamson, *Israel*, 102.

[6] Williamson, *Israel*, 110.

[7] Williamson, *Israel*, 110.

be found only in Judah, but is instead seeking to show the continuity of Judah with the days of the United Monarchy, to show that Judah is a full heir to all that lay in the past. "It is thus evident that his use of Israel . . . is not intended as a political expression, but in the sense of a community that stands in the direct line of the Israel of an earlier generation."[8]

Figure 10.6: Which Kingdom is "All Israel"

	Southern Kingdom	Northern Kingdom
כָּל־יִשְׂרָאֵל	2 Chr 11:3; 12:1	2 Chr 10:16; 11:13
בְּנֵי יִשְׂרָאֵל	2 Chr 10:17	2 Chr 10:18
יִשְׂרָאֵל	2 Chr 12:6	2 Chr 10:16, 19; 11:1

This is the only clear distinction between the usage of the Chronicler and his sources. In 1 and 2 Kings, once the kingdom is divided, Israel refers only to the northern kingdom. Although Yahweh is often called the "God of Israel" even when referred to by Judahites during their worship (2 Kgs 18:5; 19:15, 20; 21:12; 22:15, 18), the people of Judah themselves are never called "Israel." In Chronicles, both Israel and Judah are "Israel." This willingness to describe Judah as Israel probably developed in the postexilic period. In the lists of Ezra and Nehemiah, it is the people of Israel who return (Ezra 2:2; Neh 7:7). When the groups are described, "Israel" heads the list of priests and other cultic officials (Ezra 6:16; 7:7; 9:1; Neh 11:3, 20).[9] Other than this one point, "Israel" and especially "all Israel" are used in the same way in both the Deuteronomistic History and by the Chronicler. Even in Chronicles, however, "Israel" will still refer to either the land or the people. The meaning of the term may have been broadened to include Judah, but it still refers only to people or land, as it does also in Kings.

Consequently, the Chronicler's use of "all Israel" in 1 Chr 9:1 can be understood to mean only the people or the land which they occupied. The context of 1 Chr 9:1 within the Chronicler's genealogies, and as the counterpoint to "the sons of Israel" (1 Chr 2:1–2), indicates that the people are here in view.

---

[8] Williamson, *Israel*, 107.

[9] As such, the Chronicler should not be seen as the one who is seeking to establish an "Israelite" identity among the postexilic people. This had already been established at least as early as Ezra/Nehemiah. The Chronicler is one who identifies with this tradition, and takes it as normative in his society. For the Chronicler, the people of Yehud in the postexilic period are "Israel."

The Order of the Sons of Israel

Although not vital for the understanding of the text, the order of listing of the twelve tribes is a matter of debate. There are seventeen different lists of the sons of Israel recorded in the Hebrew Bible. Four of these occur in Genesis, two in Exodus, seven in Numbers, one in Deuteronomy, two in Ezekiel, and one in 1 Chr 2:1–2.[10] The Ezekiel lists are different in character, and will therefore not be utilised in this discussion.[11]

As observed in Figure 10.7, the organising principle which underlies the listing of the sons of Israel is which sons were born of wives, and which were born of concubines. This is most clearly seen in Numbers where five of the six sons of Leah are almost always mentioned first, followed by the descendants of Rachel: Ephraim, Manasseh, and Benjamin.[12] The sons of the concubines, headed by Dan, are then listed. In Numbers, Gad, who is the first son of Leah's servant Zilpah, is moved up into a position among the six sons of Leah as a replacement for Levi, who in Numbers is listed separately as the cultic tribe. The choice of Gad for this would appear to be governed by his direct connection with Leah.[13]

The four listings in Genesis as well as Exod 1:1–4 also make this distinction between the children of wives and the children of concubines. Although at times the children of concubines are mixed together (Gen 49 and throughout Numbers), and on two occasions the children of wives are mixed together (Num 13; Deut 33), the children of concubines are never mixed together with those of wives.[14]

---

[10] See Figure 10.7. In the chart, the tribes are listed in order of appearance, and only the first initial is used, except for Joseph, where Jo is used. The list in Num 34:19–28 is not included as this is not a list of all tribes, but only of the Cisjordanian tribes and their representatives for allocating land west of the Jordan. Neither is the list in Num 27 included, as it is not a true list of the sons of Israel, but is the division of those tribes who pronounce blessings and curses. Wilson makes the point that only Gen 29:30–30:24; 35:23–26; 46:8–27; 1 Chr 2:1–2 are, technically, genealogies. The other occurrences are lists, rather than genealogies, *Genealogy*, 183–193.

[11] On the tribal lists in Ezekiel, see the fuller discussion in Block, *Ezekiel 25–48*, 719–746.

[12] In this, only Num 13 does not follow the pattern, but even here, the sons of wives precede those of concubines. In this respect, Num 13 is similar to Deut 33, where Zebulun is mentioned after the sons of Rachel, although in Num 13, Zebulun is prior to Manasseh. In Numbers, the sons of Levi, son of Leah, are always listed separately.

[13] See also Gen 46:8–27, which lists the sons of Leah, followed by the sons of her servant Zilpah, with Gad heading the list, prior to the sons of Rachel and her servant Bilhah.

[14] Except for Gad, as previously mentioned, and then only to fill a gap in the marching and camping sequence left by the setting apart of Levi for cultic service.

Wilson says "in the idiom of genealogy, the assigning of the sons to different mothers implies that the sons are not related to each other as equals but are on different status levels."[15]

This differentiation is made clear in the listings not only by the way the tribes are grouped, but also the way they are mixed with or isolated from one another.[16] The tribal list in 1 Chr 2:1–2 is therefore similar, yet different, to the other lists. Like the other lists, the sons of Leah are listed first, and like most of the other lists, Reuben is listed in the primary position.[17]

The list in 1 Chr 2:1–2 ends with three of the sons of concubines, preceded by the two sons of Rachel.[18] Unlike other lists, and unique to the Chronicler, Dan is moved to a position between the sons of Leah and Rachel, but separated from the sons of the other concubines. Wilson states, "the significance of this move is unclear."[19]

In certain respects, this positioning of Dan after the sons of Leah is reminiscent of both Gen 29:6, where Dan, the son of Rachel's servant Bilhah, is born after the first four sons of Leah. The position of Dan in 1 Chr 2:1–2 is more closely associated with Gen 49:16–17, where in the blessing of Jacob, Dan is

---

[15] Wilson, *Genealogy*, 185. He goes on to make the point that "to correctly interpret the significance of these groupings, one must be familiar with the Yahwist's story of Jacob and his wives," 186. This indicates that the true significance of a genealogy is determined by the story that lies behind the genealogy. Without the knowledge of the story, i.e. the social, political, and religious setting which gave rise to the genealogy, the original purpose and function of a genealogy is difficult to determine.

[16] In the allocation list of tribes to pronounce the blessings and curses (Deut 27:12–13), Reuben and Zebulun are included among the sons of the concubines. As Reuben and Zebulun are respectively the oldest and youngest son of Leah, this may only mean that the sons of the concubines have been brought under the umbrella of Leah, and are therefore considered as true and full sons. Driver, however, suggests that Reuben was placed with the sons of the concubines because he forfeited his birthright, while Zebulun, as the youngest, was more easily transferred, *A Critical and Exegetical Commentary on Deuteronomy* (ICC; Edinburgh: T&T Clark, 1902), 298. McConville, however, objects, saying, "if Reuben is displaced from his natural priority because of Gen. 49:3–4, how do Simeon and Levi retain their places in view of the same list of blessing; Gen. 49:5–7?," *Deuteronomy* (Leicester: Inter-Varsity Press, 2002), 390–391. He suggests instead a rough north/south divide (with Gad and Reuben included in the North, although on the east).

[17] The only time Reuben is not so listed is in Numbers in the order of marching and camping. Although Reuben is not called "firstborn" in 1 Chr 2:1–2, this is a common title for him in the Hebrew Bible: Gen 35:23; 46:8; 49:3; Exod 6:14; Num 1:20; 26:5; 1 Chr 5:1, 3. On Reuben as the "firstborn," see Cross, "Reuben."

[18] Here, Joseph and Benjamin, although Joseph will be discussed separately as Ephraim and Manasseh in the lists themselves.

[19] Wilson, *Genealogy*, 189.

listed after the six sons of Leah, as he is in 1 Chr 2:1–2. In Gen 49, however, Dan stands first before all the sons of the concubines, while in 1 Chr 2:1–2, the Chronicler mentions the two sons of Rachel after Dan before going on to mention the three other sons of the concubines. In Gen 49, the sons of Rachel are listed last, as per their birth order in Gen 29–30, 35. Closer still is Gen 35:23–26 which has the identical order of all the tribes, except for the displacement of Dan.[20]

The question arises then as to whether Dan is being elevated to a higher position after Leah and prior to Rachel and the other concubines, or isolated from the concubines, and wedged between the dominant sons of Leah and Rachel. This may simply be a textual rather than an ideological issue, with the Chronicler or a later copyist introducing a variation into his text.

From this distance it is impossible to give a definitive answer. One thing that is clear, is that the order in which the sons of Israel are listed in 1 Chr 2:1–2, is not the order in which they are presented in 1 Chr 2–8. As has been demonstrated in the preceding chapters, the Chronicler's order in his genealogical section has been based upon criteria other than birth order, or whether the son descended from a wife or a concubine.

CONCLUSION

It has been observed that these two passages (1 Chr 2:1–2; 9:1a), parallel and complement one another. First Chronicles 2:1–2 lists the twelve sons of Israel while 1 Chr 9:1a concludes the genealogies of these twelve sons with the inclusive phrase "all Israel." In Chronicles, this phrase has been shown to refer to either all of the people or the land in which they lived. Its use here in parallel with the "sons of Israel" and in the context of a census is an indication that the reference is to all of the people. Although at times "all Israel" can refer to just a few of the tribes, or even to each of the divided kingdoms, its use in 1 Chr 9:1a portrays the Chronicler's ideal view that "all Israel" should be made up of all of the tribes. This is highlighted in 1 Chr 9:3 where, when Israel returns from captivity, Judah and Benjamin are present, but so also are Ephraim and Manasseh.[21] The northern kingdom, although in rebellion against Yahweh and his appointed dynasty (2 Chr 13:4–9), are still called "Israel," and during the cultic renewal instigated by Hezekiah, these groups were invited to join with the "Israel" which was located in Judah in the worship of Yahweh (2 Chr 30:1, 10–11, 18; 31:1). Further, Ephraim and Manasseh contributed to the upkeep of the

---

[20] Japhet, *Chronicles*, 65.
[21] Ephraim and Manasseh are not found in the parallel passage in Neh 11:3–4.

temple during the days of Josiah (2 Chr 34:9), and were among the areas in which Josiah sought to implement worship of Yahweh alone (2 Chr 34:6–7).

Not only do those who are in rebellion against the Davidic king remain a part of Israel, the Chronicler indicates that those who are in exile also remain a part of Israel. They are "your brothers (אֲחֵיכֶם) and children [who] . . . will come back to this land," if the people who are in the land turn back to Yahweh (2 Chr 30:9). In 2 Chr 11:4, Rehoboam was forbidden to attack rebellious Israel because, although in rebellion, they were still "your brothers (אֲחֵיכֶם)," and thus still "Israel." Rebellion and exile do not change a person's status as a member of "all Israel," although it is hoped that those who are in rebellion against Yahweh or exiled from his land would return to him, and consequently return to his land.

What is significant is that when Hezekiah invited those who were in rebellion to Jerusalem, it was not to rejoin a political entity. It was instead to rejoin the religious entity "Israel," and to reacknowledge Yahweh, as represented by his temple, cultic officials, and cultic rites, as the centre of their existence. This is what the Chronicler also does within his genealogies of "all Israel" when he places the cultic place, rites and officials at the centre of his discussion of what constitutes "Israel." The cultic place, rites and officials at the centre of the nation, with the tribes around it and focussed upon it, makes the tribes "the true Israel."[22]

---

[22] "Das wahre Israel." See also Oeming, *Das wahre Israel*, 210. Oeming sees within the genealogies an increasing focussing of attention from the world, to Israel, Jerusalem, and culminating in the restored temple, personnel, and duties in 1 Chr 9.

Figure 10.7: The Recorded Order of the Sons of Israel

Order in list	Gen 29–30, 35	Gen 35:23-26	Gen 46:8-27	Gen 49:1-27	Exodus 1:1-4	Exodus 6:14-26	Num 1:5-15	Num 1:20-42	Num 2:1-34	Num 7:12-83	Num 10:14-28	Num 13:4-15	Num 26:4-51	Deut 33:6-29	1 Chr 2:1-2	Ezek 48:1-29	Ezek 48:30-34
1	R	R	R	R	R	R	R	R	J	J	J	R	R	R	R	D	R
2	S	S	S	S	S	S	S	S	I	I	I	S	S	J	S	A	J
3	L	L	L	L	L	L	J	G	Z	Z	Z	J	G	L	L	N	L
4	J	J	J	J	J		I	J	R	R	R	I	J	B	J	M	Jo
5	D	I	I	Z	I		Z	I	S	S	S	E	I	Jo	I	E	B
6	N	Z	Z	I	Z		E	Z	G	G	G	B	Z	Z	Z	R	D
7	G	Jo	G	D	B		M	E	E	E	E	Z	M	I	D	J	S
8	A	B	A	G	D		B	M	M	M	M	M	E	G	Jo	B	I
9	I	D	Jo	A	N		D	B	B	B	B	D	B	D	B	S	Z
10	Z	N	B	N	G		A	D	D	D	D	A	D	N	N	I	G
11	Jo	G	D	Jo	A		G	A	A	A	A	N	A	A	G	Z	A
12	B	A	N	B	Jo		N	N	N	N	N	G	N		A	G	N

R=Reuben S=Simeon L=Levi J=Judah D=Dan N=Naphtali G=Gad A=Asher I=Issachar Z=Zebulun Jo=Joseph B=Benjamin M=Manasseh E=Ephraim

CHAPTER 11
THE CHRONICLER'S USE OF HIS SOURCES

INTRODUCTION

Before investigating the nature and purpose of 1 Chr 1 within the Chronicler's genealogy, it will be useful to use this text as the foundation of an investigation into how the Chronicler utilised his sources. This investigation into how the Chronicler used his sources may, of itself, provide some insights into the Chronicler's purposes in his inclusion of the data contained in 1 Chr 1 into his work.[1]

McIver and Carroll have recently sought to determine more closely the relationships that exist between the Synoptic Gospels.[2] Their goal was to develop objective criteria by which it may be determined whether or not the author of one work directly copied the work of another author.

In their fifth experiment, which was developed as a consequence of their observations in previous experiments, volunteers were divided into three groups on the basis of arrival time. From a list of eight topics they were each to select any six about which they would be asked to write.

The first group was asked to write up to one page about their first two topics without reference to any sources (i.e. based upon personal knowledge only). They were then asked to write about their second two topics, but were first given "short descriptive notes about each of these" topics which "included a number of specific facts."[3] They were permitted to read these notes as often as they desired, but before writing about their topics they had to return these notes. For the third set of two topics the participants were also given a set of notes but they were allowed to retain these notes while they wrote their paper on those topics. The

---

[1] This is a revised version of a paper presented to the *Society of Biblical Literature* International Conference, Singapore, 2005.

[2] McIver and Carroll, "Experiments." Although their application of their observations to the Synoptic Gospels has recently been challenged, their fundamental observations regarding the relationship of two documents to one another is still valid. See further John C. Poirier, "Memory, Written Sources, and the Synoptic Problem: A Response to Robert K. McIver and Marie Carroll," *JBL* 123 (2004): 315–322.

[3] McIver and Carroll, "Experiments," 668.

other two groups went through the same procedure, but in a different order (see Figure 11.1), to maximise the randomness of the data received.[4]

Figure 11.1: McIver's Group Organisation

Topics	Group1	Group 2	Group 3
1, 2	No Sources	Source Retained	Source Returned
3, 4	Source Returned	No Sources	Source Retained
5, 6	Source Retained	Source Returned	No Sources

When the data was analysed, it was observed that greater access to a written source at the time of writing resulted in a closer relationship to exist between the source and the secondary document. Among their results they observed that a greater access to a source while writing resulted in:[5]

1) A greater number of "common words" appearing in the secondary document in relation to the source than when no source document was provided (5 percent for no sources; 15.3 percent for source returned; 28.4 percent for source retained).

2) A greater number of "words in exact sequence" appearing in the secondary document in relation to the source than when no source document was provided. Although this was as high as fifteen consecutive words for those papers for which the source was returned (the average was less than six), the greatest number of "words in exact sequence" (over forty) occurred in those instances where the source had been retained while the secondary document was being produced (with an average of 12.6 words in exact sequence).[6]

3) A greater number of "common elements," that is ideas and themes, appeared in the secondary document in relation to the source than when no source document was provided.[7]

---

[4] This forced differing of the order becomes significant when it is observed that only "eighteen of forty-three volunteers completed six responses in the experiment, and most of the rest completed four of them," McIver and Carroll, "Experiments," 673.

[5] McIver and Carroll, "Experiments," 673.

[6] McIver and Carroll, "Experiments," 673. For a chart displaying the frequency of words in exact sequence, see their page 679.

[7] There was no significant difference in relation to those who had access to a written document *prior to* writing and *during* writing, although it was much greater than those who were simply writing from personal knowledge. Although not addressing this directly, it is possible that the access to a written source helped to determine the shape and content, if not the exact wording, of the secondary document. See point 4.

4) A greater number of "elements in sequence" appeared in the secondary document in relation to the source than when no source document was provided.

In examining their results they concluded that:

> Any sequence of exactly the same [sixteen] or more words that is not an aphorism, poetry, or words to a song is almost certain to have been copied from a written document.[8]

Although they applied their findings primarily to the Synoptic Gospels in the New Testament, there is also an application to be found in the Hebrew Bible.[9]

Johnstone has pointed out that the book of Chronicles is a work for which at least some of the sources are still available to us and as such, "Chronicles also provides a valuable case study in critical method"[10] as well as "a controllable case study for methodology in Hebrew Bible criticism."[11] Careful study of Chronicles may give an indication of how ancient writers utilised, adjusted, modified and added to their sources to bring about their finished products.[12]

---

[8] McIver and Carroll, "Experiments," 680. The caveats regarding "aphorism, poetry, or words to a song" are based on other aspects of their experiments which are not significant to our purposes here, McIver and Carroll, "Experiments," 674–677. It must be also noted that while the sixteen consecutive words may be utilised to indicate direct copying, the absence of sixteen consecutive words cannot be utilised to suggest that the author did not have access to a particular source. He/she may in fact have only used it as a reference rather than resorting to direct copying. As McIver and Carroll observed, "many of the volunteers who retained the written summary . . . did not produce long sequences of words. But here is the point . . . *only* those who retained the text and could copy from it produced long sequences of words that were exactly the same" (emphasis theirs), McIver and Carroll, "Experiments," 678.

[9] Their application of their conclusions to the Synoptic Gospels has been challenged by Poirier because, unlike in the experiments where a copy was compared directly to its source, in the Synoptic Gospels they are comparing two documents which utilised a common source to one another. Poirier states, "in order to apply their experimental results in a way analogous to their views of Mathew and Luke, they should have compared Matthew-Luke sequential agreements with agreements appearing *between the students participating in the experiment*, rather than with agreements between the students and their source" (emphasis his), Poirier, "Memory," 317. However, it must be noted that Poirier's objections are only valid if it is assumed that Matthew and Luke utilised the same source document. They would not be valid if it is assumed that Matthew utilised Luke or *vice verse*, in which case the observations of McIver and Carroll would be applicable.

[10] Johnstone, *Chronicles and Exodus*, 142.

[11] Johnstone, *Chronicles and Exodus*, 44.

[12] While the findings of McIver and Carroll can be applied to Chronicles, their findings are less applicable to the Pentateuch because the sources of these writings are no

It is in this area where the conclusions of McIver and Carroll may be applied. Through utilising their findings, it may be determined whether or not the Chronicler had the source documents available *while* he wrote his work as opposed to having *access* to the source document prior to his work or even a simple *knowledge* of the topic without reference to documents.

If it is determined that the Chronicler had before him a particular written document while he compiled his work, then this may help to determine the origin of some of the Chronicler's material which, although not a direct quote, has certain affinities with other Biblical material. It may also help in other areas:

1) It may help to understand the Chronicler's (and by extension other ancient writer's), editing style and methodology as he edited, reworked and reshaped a known written source into his final product.

2) It may help to illuminate how an ancient writer incorporated their own viewpoint, not directly reflected in a source, into their final product and which in turn makes the assignment of that portion to a "source" inappropriate as that portion is in fact the work of the "author" rather than of a source.[13]

3) This may help us to re-evaluate those portions of the Chronicler's work for which no source has been identified, but has been assumed to exist. If we can identify the Chronicler's methodology in utilising sources in one area where we can compare his sources to his final work, this can then be applied to those areas where we have no available source to compare with in order to make sounder judgements regarding what the Chronicler has done and why.

For the purposes of this excursus I will be looking specifically at the list of genealogies in 1 Chr 1. This has been selected primarily because it is the one portion of the genealogical section which shows the greatest affinity with another

---

longer available. However it is probable that through a better understanding of how the Chronicler produced his work, a greater appreciation of the methodology of the redactions of P or D, or the earlier works of J and E may be gained.

[13] Lemke is correct, however, when he warns that not all variations between the Chronicler and his sources are the result of the Chronicler's *tendenz* or bias but may in fact be due to changes in the text of the source over time. "The Synoptic Problem in the Chronicler's History," *HTR* 58 (1965): 349–363. I would suggest that Lemke's argument not be utilised to dismiss all of the differences between the Chronicler and his source(s), as being the result of later scribal activity, and also that a careful study of the parallel texts will better aid in understanding (although not resolving), issues in the textual history of different books of the Hebrew Bible. It is also possible that some of the differences exhibited between the MT of Samuel (the object of Lemke's investigation), and the Qumran texts of Samuel may not be due to changes in what became the MT, but attempted harmonisations by a copyist under the influence of Chronicles, a similar phenomenon often observed in the textual traditions of the Synoptic Gospels.

known document in the Hebrew Bible, and is therefore of greatest use in determining the Chronicler's methodology.[14]

Three caveats apply to this examination.
1) Although chronological relationships between documents may be determined from other criteria, the studies of McIver and Carroll cannot be used to determine which document was copied from the other. It can only be used to determine whether copying has occurred.[15]
2) McIver and Carroll also indicate that copying may be from a third document, now lost, rather than being copying by one extant document from another.[16]
3) They also suggest that their results are "accurate for narrative only."[17] However, as they did not directly test in relation to names (for example, a list of Australian Prime Ministers or United States Presidents), the applicability of their findings to genealogies cannot be ruled out. The studies by Wilson and Johnson have indicated that oral, as opposed to written, genealogies are extremely fluid dependent upon the time and purpose of the genealogy's oral recitation. Writing, however, "fixes" a genealogy making it less amenable to change.[18] As such, exact correspondence between two written genealogical documents may still indicate direct copying.

---

[14] Noth states that "no serious objection can be raised against any part of the first chapter" in regards to its originality in the Chronicler's genealogies, *Chronicler's History*, 36.

[15] In this regard it must be noted that although 1 Chr 8:29–38 is almost identical to 1 Chr 9:35–44, it is uncertain in which direction the copying took place. Did a genealogist copy 1 Chr 9:35–44 into his genealogical section (1 Chr 1–9), which he appended to the Chronicler's work or did the Chronicler copy either a source or his own imagination in these two separate locations? Or did a later editor copy 1 Chr 9:35–44 from the Chronicler's genealogical section to show from where Saul, narrated in 1 Chr 10, originated. None of these options can be confirmed based upon McIver and Carroll's methodology.

[16] McIver and Carroll, "Experiments," 682–3. They point out that Matt 22:41–46 // Mark 12:35–37 contain a citation from Ps 110 (LXX). Poirier clearly overlooked this statement in his objections (see note 9, above). It is impossible, however, to determine whether both copied from the Psalm; one copied the Psalm while the other copied from the parallel Gospel account, or if both copied from another source which copied from the Psalm. All that their conclusions can indicate is that copying did occur. Determining who copied from whom must be based upon other criteria.

[17] McIver and Carroll, "Experiments," 679.

[18] "Change may be hindered if the genealogy is recorded in written form. While oral genealogies may be altered without too much difficulty, the alteration of written genealogies is more problematic, for a public record of the genealogy is available for consultation. In addition, the normal process of forgetting . . . has no effect on written

THE CHRONICLER AS COPIER OF HIS SOURCE MATERIAL

The Genealogies contained in 1 Chr 1 have numerous parallels to those contained in the book of Genesis,[19] with most of the genealogies contained in Genesis making an appearance in the Chronicler's opening chapter.[20]

These genealogies include extracts from the "table of nations" (Gen 10), as well as the descendants of Keturah (Gen 25:1–4), Ishmael (Gen 25:13–16), Esau (Gen 36:1–30, 40–43), and the rulers of Edom (Gen 36:31–39).

Four of the genealogies contained in 1 Chr 1 have no direct parallel with material in Genesis: 1 Chr 1:1–3 (Adam to Lamech); 1:24–27 (Shem to Abraham); 1:28 (the descendants of Abraham), and 1:34 (the descendants of Abraham).[21] There is also a considerable amount of data from the genealogical material in Genesis that is not repeated or reflected in 1 Chr 1.[22] In applying the findings of McIver and Carroll to 1 Chronicles, it is observed that there are six passages that meet their criterium of a "sequence of exactly the same 16 or more words" (Figure 11.3):[23]

---

genealogies. Even the most obscure and useless name can be remembered if it is part of a written document," Wilson, *Genealogy*, 47.

[19] See Figure 11.2.

[20] Almost all of the genealogical material contained in Genesis is reflected in 1 Chr 1 except for the genealogy of Cain (Gen 4:17–22), the other descendants of Terah: Nahor (Gen 22:20–24), and Haran through Lot (Gen 19:30–38). The former may be excused because it did not lead into the post flood period. The absence of the genealogy of Lot, and its emphasis on Lot as the ancestor of Ammon and Moab through incestuous relations with his daughters (Gen 19:36–38), is more puzzling, particularly regarding the concerns over intermarriage with the Ammonite and Moabite in Nehemiah's day (Neh 13:1–3), and opposition from a leader of the Ammonites to the reconstruction of the walls (Neh 4:3–8). The Chronicler does recount wars with both Ammon and Moab (1 Chr 18–20, 2 Chr 20). Their absence from 1 Chr 1 could reflect this animosity by denying them any place in the world, although considering the Chronicler's generally open attitude to foreigners in comparison with that of Nehemiah, this is uncertain.

[21] It will be suggested later that 1 Chr 1:1–3, 24–27 are, however, extracted from genealogies within Genesis.

[22] Genesis 10:5, 9–12, 18b–21, 30–32; 25:3b, 5–12, 17–18; 36:1–9, 15–19, 25b, 29b–30, 43b.

[23] For the purpose of this exercise, the conjunction ו, inseparable prepositions, and definite articles are counted with the word they are attached to, not as separate words. Words joined by a *maqqef* are treated as separate words. If a conjunction ו is omitted, the remainder of that word, which is a word in its own right, is used to begin a new sequence, if applicable.

Figure 11.2: Parallel Passages in 1 Chronicles 1 and Genesis

1 Chr	Gen
1:1–3	
1:4–7	10:1b–4
	10:5
1:8–10	10:6–8
	10:9–12
1:11–16	10:13–18a
	10:18b–21
1:17–23	10:22–29
	10:30–32
1:24–27	
1:28	
1:29–31	25:13–16a
	25:3b, 5–12, 16b–18
1:32–33	25:1–3a, 4
1:34	
	36:1–9
1:35–37	36:10–14 (extracts)
	36:15–19
1:38–40	36:20–24a
1:41–42	36:25a, 26–28a
	36:25b
	36:29–30
1:43–51a	36:31–39
1:51b–54	36:40–43a
	36:43b

On this basis alone, it is evident that copying of the Genesis material by the Chronicler took place.[24] This demands, according to the findings of McIver and Carroll, that not only did the Chronicler have access to the text of Genesis as he

---

[24] Although the date of composition of the Pentateuch is part of an ongoing debate, it is generally agreed that it was finalized at least by the time of Ezra in the mid-fifth century B.C.E. Chronicles, however, especially if disassociated from the works of Ezra and Nehemiah, is normally dated into the fourth century, and as late as the Greek period. For discussion of the theory that the Pentateuch was the result of Persian authorization, and the impact this has on the dating of the Pentateuch, see the various articles in James W. Watts, ed., *Persia and Torah: The Theory of Imperial Authorization of the Pentateuch* SBLSymS 17; Atlanta: Society of Biblical Literature, 2001).

was compiling his account, but that he had the text of Genesis before him and copied directly from that text.[25]

Figure 11.3: Sequences of Exactly the Same Sixteen or More Words

Parallel Texts		Consecutive Words
1 Chr 1:11b–13	Gen 10:13–15	19 words
1 Chr 1:13b–16	Gen 10:15–18a	21 words
1 Chr 1:18–22a	Gen 10:24–28a	39 words
1 Chr 1:43b–45	Gen 36:32b–34	18 words
1 Chr 1:47–50a	Gen 36:36–39c	24 words
1 Chr 1:51b–54	Gen 36:40–43a	21 words

Examination of the differences exhibited in these texts further demonstrates the closeness of the texts. In the parallel texts the differences may be reduced to two main types: "differences due to copying" and "differences due to editing."[26] Of these, the most common differences between the texts is a result of the plené spelling of a word[27] or of a misread letter.[28] It is evident that while any of these differences may have entered either text at a date subsequent to their composition, the phenomena of plené spelling or misreading a letter is common enough to suggest that, even if introduced by the Chronicler, they are not significant "errors." If these are disregarded we find the following (Figure 11.4).

Figure 11.4: Sequences of Exactly the Same Sixteen or More Words with Allowances for Plené Spelling and Misreading Letters

Parallel Texts		Consecutive Words
1 Chr 1:5–7	Gen 10:2–4	17 words
1 Chr 1:11–16	Gen 10:13–18a	45 words
1 Chr 1:18–23	Gen 10:24–29	54 words
1 Chr 1:43b–46a	Gen 36:32b–35a	35 words
1 Chr 1:47–50a	Gen 36:36–39c	24 words
1 Chr 1:51b–54	Gen 36:40b–43a	25 words

---

[25] "It is clear that long sequences of [sixteen] or more words belong exclusively to the group that *retained the source and could copy from it*" (emphasis mine), McIver and Carroll, "Experiments," 679.

[26] See Figures 11.7 to 11.16 at the end of this chapter.

[27] Of the twenty occurrences of this, in eighteen of them the Chronicler presents the plené spelling.

[28] ד for ר (2X), ר for ד (2X), י for ו (7X), ו for י (1X).

Some of these can be further expanded and longer strings can be recognised by allowing for other minor variations (Figure 11.5).

Figure 11.5: Sequences of Exactly the Same Sixteen or More Words with Allowances for Minor Variations

Parallel Texts		Consecutive Words	Type of Variation
1 Chr 1:43b–50a	Gen 36:32–39a	60 words	one occurrence (1 Chr 1:46), of transposed letters
1 Chr 1:29–31	Gen 25:13b–16a	19 words	absence of 2 conjunction ו 2 plené spellings
1 Chr 1:8–10	Gen 10:6–8	26 words[29]	different final letter in three names
1 Chr 1:5–7	Gen 10:2–4	20	final ה in one word

What these indicate is that each of the three major genealogical sources in Genesis were available to the Chronicler in compiling his work and that he frequently sought to copy portions of his source directly without any change or variation. In this regard it is important to note that on only two occasions does the Chronicler alter the order in which material occurs in the text of Genesis.[30]

First Chronicles 1 not only has multiple instances of the same words in the same order as Genesis, but the overall order of the genealogical material is also in the same order as found in Genesis This is another indication of the Chronicler's

---

[29] In this section there are two differences due to plené spelling, two conjunction ו omitted (both from Gen 10:6 // 1 Chr 1:8), and three instances where a final ה is substituted with a final א (1 Chr 1:9 // Gen 10:7). There are three other names in this verse that end with an א and it is possible that the changes were made for consistency.

[30] In Gen 25, the descendants of Keturah are listed first and then the order of Ishmael's sons. The Chronicler reverses this, I argue later, because there was no easy way of including the Keturah material without including narrative. The other out of order genealogy is that of the sons of Israel (1 Chr 2:1–2). The original location and source of this is, however, more difficult to determine in that Genesis presents four lists of Jacob/Israel's sons: Gen 29:31–30:23; 35:16–20 (the birth of the sons of Jacob); Gen 35:23–26 (a list of Jacob's twelve sons); Gen 46:8–27 (Jacob, his sons and their sons); Gen 49 (Jacob's blessing of his sons). As demonstrated in Chapter 10, 1 Chr 2:1–2 is closest to Gen 35:23–26.

use of Genesis, not only for the genealogies that he includes but also for the structure of his presentation.[31]

This is significant because it indicates the unlikelihood of the Chronicler's direct use of the J or P sources utilised by the author of Genesis. If the Chronicler had made use of J and P as distinct sources, then to present the same order as found in Genesis, he would have had to have combined his sources in the identical manner as did the author of Genesis.[32] This is particularly noticeable in 1 Chr 1:4–17 which parallels Gen 10:1–23 (Figure 11.6).[33]

That the Chronicler repeats the same alternation from one source to the other, as does Genesis, indicates that the Chronicler was not utilising these sources directly, but was dependent upon the text of Genesis, which had already combined these sources in this particular order.[34]

Although McIver had indicated the possibility that the similarity exhibited between texts may be the result of dependency of two texts on the same source,[35] that the Chronicler follows the Genesis order indicates that he is here dependent not on J or P as was the author of Genesis, but upon Genesis itself.

---

[31] Although Williamson makes a great deal out of the order of the sons of Noah (Shem, Ham, Japeth), which is reversed as the Chronicler deals with the sons in the order Japeth, Ham, Shem, as reflecting "the line that was to lead eventually to Israel," he fails to recognise that the Chronicler here is simply following the order of Genesis. Therefore, there may be no polemical purpose in this order at all, *Israel*, 63. See also Knoppers, *1 Chronicles 1–9*, 247.

[32] The significance of this cannot be overestimated, for the genealogies that the Chronicler omits (Cain, Gen 4:17–22; Lot, Gen 19:30–38; Nahor, Gen 22:20–24), have all been classified as coming from the J source. If the Chronicler utilised P instead of Genesis, then the omission of these genealogies is to be explained on the basis of their absence from his source rather than for any polemical or ideological purposes. Noth states that nothing in 1 Chr 1:1–2:2 is secondary, and that the Chronicler "made use of Gen. 10 in a form in which J and P were already joined," *Chronicler's History*, 52.

[33] This identification of sources as either J or P is based upon Campbell and O'Brien, *Sources*, 27, 97–98.

[34] As such, it is unnecessary to classify the data in 1 Chr 1 as being either P or J (cf. the work of Curtis and Madsen, *Chronicles*, 60), for from the Chronicler's perspective they are neither. They are simply the data which he found in his own source, Genesis. Rothstein and Hänel's suggestion that the Chronicler had the priestly source in his possession because he only utilised the P material and not the J, is rejected by Rudolph, *Chronikbücher*, 9, cf. Noth, *Chronicler's History*, 51–52. It must be noted, however, that Rudolph does this not because of the presence of the former J material in 1 Chr 1, but because he rejects 1 Chr 1:4b–23 (which contains this material), as originally part of the Chronicler's work. He views it as a later intrusion into the linear genealogy from Adam to Abraham, *Chronikbücher*, 6–7. Noth, however, accepts 1 Chr 1 as original to the Chronicler's work, *Chronicler's History*, 36.

[35] McIver and Carroll, "Experiments," 682–683.

Figure 11.6: The Chronicler Following Genesis Rather than J/P

1 Chr		Gen	
P Source	J Source	P Source	J Source
1:4–9		10:1–7	
	1:10–16		10:8–19
-		10:20	
	-		10:21
1:17		10:22–23	
	1:18–23		10:24–30
-		10:31–32	

The implications of this evidence leads to the first observation regarding the Chronicler's methodology:

Observation 1: While compiling his work, the Chronicler had access to Genesis and, at times, directly copied the material contained in Genesis without change or alteration.

THE CHRONICLER AS EDITOR OF HIS SOURCE MATERIAL

If it is recognised that the Chronicler had access to the text of Genesis, which at times he felt free to copy directly, this enables us, on the basis of how he made use of the text of Genesis, to better understand his approach to the text and his use of his sources, in general. In two verses the Chronicler omitted a total of ten occurrences of the direct object marker found in his source.[36] First Chronicles 1:32 is particularly significant. While the Chronicler freely omitted seven words from his source, he did not omit a single name nor did he alter the order in which the names were recorded.[37] On eight other occasions, the Chronicler omitted the word אֵלֶּה(וְ; (and) these).[38]

In this process of editing the Chronicler appears free not just to omit words, but to adjust and modify words and phrases within the source. In 1:32 // Gen 25:3 the Chronicler records וּבְנֵי יָקְשָׁן (and the sons of Jokshan), while the source contains וְיָקְשָׁן יָלַד (and Jokshan became the father of). In 1:51 he modifies וְאֵלֶּה

---

[36] Figure 11.13.

[37] Note, however, that the Chronicler retained the direct object marker throughout 1:10–23 (34 occurrences), and even in 1:32 retained one occurrence of it. Why he failed to retain it in this instance is uncertain.

[38] Figure 11.14. The Chronicler was again not consistent in this, as he retained אֵלֶּה in 1:23, 29, 31, 33, 43, 54.

שֵׁמוֹת (these were the names), in relation to the chiefs of Edom, to וַיִּהְיוּ (and there were; Gen 36:40). Finally, Timna who is Eliphaz's concubine in Gen 36:12 becomes his son in 1 Chr 1:36. However, this occurs through the omission of the explanatory note in Gen 36:12a, which results in a bare list of names in 1 Chr 1:36, all as "sons" of Eliphaz.[39]

None of these alterations are significant nor do they significantly alter the meaning of the text.

What may be significant, however, is the observation that, while the Chronicler feels free to omit certain words or phrases, or rewords a phrase slightly differently, in 1 Chr 1 he rarely adds new words. With the exception of four occurrences of the conjunction וְ,[40] the Chronicler only adds a word or phrase to his Genesis source in 1:32 בְּנֵי (sons of), and in 1:51 וַיָּמָת הֲדָד (and Hadad died), (Figure 11.16). Of these, the first is simply because the focus of the passage has shifted from Abraham to Keturah, and the latter to bring the list into conformity with the recording of other kings who "died," possibly with a polemic regarding land ownership.[41]

Observation 2: In his use of sources the Chronicler chose at times to adhere closely to his source, making only slight modifications through deletions, alterations, and the additions without necessarily changing the meaning or intent of his source.

THE CHRONICLER AS SUMMARISER OF HIS SOURCE MATERIAL

If it is concluded that the Chronicler utilised Genesis as his source, then this also enables us to understand his method in the four passages that have no exact parallel in Genesis. First Chronicles 1:1–3, 24–27, 28, 34 do not, on the surface, appear to reproduce any text from Genesis. Both 1:1–3 and 1:24–27 are a bare list of names running from Adam to Lamech and Shem to Abram (Abraham).[42]

---

[39] Figure 11.16.

[40] 1:35, 36 (2X), 38.

[41] 1:44, 45, 46, 47, 48, 49, 50. For the use of the phrase in the Chronicler's land theology see below.

[42] Unlike, Japhet, *Chronicles*, 56, I feel that 1 Chr 1:4 probably reflects Gen 10:1 rather than Gen 5:32, so also Williamson, *Chronicles*, 42. This is for three reasons: 1) Gen 5:32 connects each of the three sons with Noah by means of the Direct Object Marker אֶת, while neither Gen 10:1 or 1 Chr 1:4 uses this. Although later in Chronicles the Direct Object Marker is omitted on a number of occasions, that there is a parallel text to 1 Chr 1:4 in Gen 10:1, which does not use the Direct Object Marker, suggests that this is the primary source of the phrase; 2) the use of the conjunction וְ before Japhet is identical to Gen 10:1

There are, however, no kinship terms which express the relationships between these individuals. This in itself speaks against these lists being from an independent genealogical source, for a genealogy cannot exist without expressing relationships.[43]

The list of 1 Chr 1:1–3 matches exactly the names (in both spelling and order), of Gen 5:1–32, while that of 1 Chr 1:24–27 is identical to Gen 11:10–32, except 1 Chr 1:27 adds the explanatory note הוּא אַבְרָהָם (that is Abraham).[44] Since it has already been established that the Chronicler had the text of Genesis before him as he wrote, it is probable that in these passages the Chronicler was summarizing portions of his source. In Gen 5 and 11 the genealogical list repeats the formula, "When "A" had lived "X" years he became the father of "B"." After he became the father of "B," "A" lived "Y" years and had other sons and daughters." Genesis 5 alone concludes with, "altogether "A" lived "Z" years."[45] The Chronicler eliminates the formula, while retaining the names from both lists. However, in omitting the formula, he also omits the terms which expressed the kinship relationships between the names. It is possible therefore that the Chronicler assumed his reader's familiarity with the lists contained in his source and, by inference, with the source itself and that his readers would automatically supply the kinship relationships. Otherwise, those relationships would have been specifically related.[46]

---

and unlike Gen 5:32, which has the ו prior to the Direct Object Marker. Simply omitting the Direct Object Marker would not require the retention of the conjunction, particularly as no conjunction had been used in the text of Chronicles up to this point, and 3) the close connection with the following texts regarding the descendants of Shem, Ham and Japhet, as also in Gen 10, more easily places the origins of 1 Chr 1:4 in Gen 10:1. Endres, Millar, and Burns, *Synoptic Parallels*, 4 also indicates that 1 Chr 1:4 originates in Gen 5:32. The LXX, perhaps in order to avoid confusion, specifically indicates the relationships of Noah, Shem, Ham, and Japhet with the inclusion of υιοι Νωε. If, as Williamson suggests, this was omitted through parablepsis, this would further confirm the origins of 1 Chr 1:4 in Gen 10:1 which reads בְּנֵי־נֹחַ.

[43] Wilson, *Genealogy*, 10.

[44] The LXX of Gen 10:24; 11:12, however, includes Cainan as the son of Arphaxad and father of Shelah (cf. Luke 3:35–36). Wenham rejects this as a secondary addition to the text, *Genesis 1–15*, 251. This is evidenced most clearly by the identical numbers given for Kainan and Shelah for their age at the birth of the son, years lived after the birth of the son, and total years lived. (130, 330, 460 respectively).

[45] This is only changed in regard to Enoch, who did not die (Gen 5:24), and the last named persons of the lists, Noah (Gen 5:32), and Terah (Gen 11:26), both of whom are listed with their three offspring.

[46] I disagree with Williamson who states that the Chronicler "gives the direct line of descent only, since of course for him, Noah represented a completely fresh start in

Observation 3: The Chronicler felt the freedom to summarise his source through the elimination of material that was not of significance to his purposes.

The other two passages without any direct parallel to Genesis are 1 Chr 1:28, 34. The first of these (1 Chr 1:28), refers to the two sons of Abraham; Isaac and Ishmael. The only other passages which locate Abraham, Isaac and Ishmael together and refer to both Isaac and Ishmael as "sons" of Abraham are Gen 21:8–11, the account of Isaac's weaning and the sending away of Ishmael, and Gen 25:8–9, the account of Abraham's death and burial. Genesis 25:9 lists the two in the order "Isaac and Ishmael," even though Ishmael was the elder, as also does 1 Chr 1:28. It would appear here, that the Chronicler is making use of Gen 25:9 for his wording and his order.

The second passage without any direct parallel to Genesis is 1 Chr 1:34, the account of Abraham's son Isaac and Isaac's sons Esau and Israel. First Chronicles 1:34 has no parallel in Genesis, for on no occasion are these four persons recorded in the text of Genesis with clear kinship relations between them indicated.[47] For both of these, it is only through knowledge of Genesis as a whole that these statements can be made. This does not demand that the Chronicler used Genesis and merely "summarised" it, for this occurrence could simply reflect the common understanding within the community. However, since the relationship of Ishmael to Abraham and thus to Isaac and his sons, is only recorded in Genesis in the Hebrew Bible, the very source which the Chronicler is clearly using for the construction of the remainder of 1 Chr 1, it is probable that his inclusion of this data is at the very least influenced by its presence in Genesis. That the Chronicler could explicitly state relationships which were only inferred in his source indicates that he did not feel bound to his source, but that he felt some freedom in his use and recounting of past materials even if that material was well known within the community.

The location of 1:28 is probably influenced by the need to recount Ishmael's sons (1 Chr 1:29–31), as also the sons of Isaac occurs immediately prior to the listing of Esau's sons (1 Chr 1:35–37).

---

genealogical terms," *Israel*, 62–63. It is more likely that the Chronicler was simply relating his source in an efficient manner.

[47] Genesis 32:8–11 does contain reference to all four persons. However, although Isaac is "father" and Esau is "brother," Abraham is also called "father," which simply indicates (unless other parts of the account are known), that Isaac and Abraham are equally ancestors, but the relationship between these two is uncertain, neither is their precise relationship to Jacob given. Joshua 24:3–4 reflects the relationships between the four, but uses the term נתן to describe their relationship, which is also used to describe the relationship of Esau to Seir.

Observation 4: The Chronicler felt free to draw upon material from different locations within his source to create a genealogy.[48]

THE CHRONICLER AS INTERPRETER OF HIS SOURCE MATERIAL

There are several instances where the Chronicler, instead of directly copying his source, appears to have interpreted his source, and substituted a word or phrase of his own for an original word or phrase in his source. For example, there are two instances where the Chronicler substitutes one name for the other.

First Chronicles 1:34 records the sons of Isaac as "Esau and Israel" rather than "Esau and Jacob" as found in his source.[49] It must be recognised that the Chronicler only refers to "Jacob" on two occasions (1 Chr 16:13, 17), both in a quote from Ps105:6, 10, and in both places in Chronicles it is in parallel to "Israel."[50] This simply reflects the Chronicler's preference for one term over the other and is not an updating or interpretation of the birth account. It must also be recognised that "Israel" is a major theme of the Chronicler and that he is here possibly also seeking to give an indication of where Israel, the people, fit into the genealogy of the world, rather than simply relating where Jacob/Israel, the man, fits.

In 1 Chr 1:51 the Chronicler lists "the chiefs of Edom" whereas Gen 36:40 speaks of the "chiefs of Esau." There are several possible reasons for this change:
1) To finish off a list which begins with the kings of Edom (1:43–51a).
2) For matters of consistency, because this list concludes with "the chiefs of Edom" (1:54)
3) To distance Esau, the relative (1:34), from Edom, the enemy (1 Chr 18:11–13; 2 Chr 20:2; 21:8–10; 25:14–20; 28:17). The Chronicler's work nowhere associates Esau with Edom. The change from Esau to Edom in 1:51 further distances Esau from the people of Seir (1:38–42), who are elsewhere in Chronicles identified as Edomites (2 Chr 25:11–19).

---

[48] Wilson notes that on occasion "genealogies in which both names and kinship links are taken from narrative traditions" do occur and tend to be brief, as these segments in 1 Chronicles also are, *Genealogy*, 201.

[49] Genesis 25:26 and throughout all of the Genesis narrative until Jacob's name change in Gen 32:28. Even after the name change, he is called "Jacob" (77X), more frequently than "Israel" (43X).

[50] However, while Ps 105:6 reads, "O seed of Abraham his servant, sons of Jacob, his chosen ones," 1 Chr 16:13 has "O seed of Israel his servant, sons of Jacob, his chosen ones." In this instance it would appear that the Chronicler altered his source to bring greater prominence to Jacob/Israel.

In contrast to the Genesis text, which discusses Esau on either side of Seir and Edom, Chronicles discusses Esau, Seir and Edom (both kings and chiefs), without returning to Esau. Edom the enemy, then, along with Seir, is not to be identified with Esau the brother, fellow descendant of Abraham, who received the promise.[51] This change, however, is a product of interpretation. What the text means *within the context* of the community in which it was produced. If the community felt pressure or threat from Edom/Seir in their day, it is likely that the Chronicler would not wish to identify the threat giver as "brother" and so interpreted his source in another direction.

It was previously stated that the Chronicler included the phrase, "and Hadad died" (1:51a). The Chronicler's distancing of Esau from Edom/Seir, gives two possible (and not mutually exclusive), interpretations of this phrase. Part of the reason for this interpretation of the text is the need to show the transition from kings to chiefs within the society of a traditional enemy. If a king is still recorded as living, this transition is not effected. The inclusion of the phrase, "and Hadad died," implicitly indicates that it was the death of the king that brought about the transition from one form of leadership to another. Kingship, as such, no longer exists within Edom, they instead are led by "chiefs." In line with the Chronicler's statement about the rise of Israelite kingship (1:43a), this ties the fall of Edomite kings to the rise of Israelite kings.[52] The Chronicler implies that Edom's kings fell because Israel's kings arose and, consequently, that Israel is both independent of, and superior to, Edom.

Another contributing reason for this addition is the need to maintain consistency within the accounts of Edom's kings. Each of the statements regarding a king's reign ends with "and X died." It was upon the death of "X" that the next king rose to power. To be consistent with the other accounts Hadad must have died, which in turn leads to the rise of the chiefs.

In each case of interpretive change, the Chronicler amended the text in line with his own bias or preference. There was no internal demand or inconsistency within the wider text for these changes, the impetus for alteration coming as a consequence of the Chronicler's own viewpoint which was shaped by his own historical circumstances.

---

[51] In this regard it is interesting to note that three times in Gen 36, Genesis clearly identifies Esau and Edom (36:1, 8, 19), twice makes Esau the "father of the Edomites" (36:9, 43), and indicates that he lived in "Seir" (36:8–9). Each of these identifications are omitted by the Chronicler.

[52] Japhet, *Chronicles*, 64. This can also be observed in the transition from Saul to David (1 Chr 10:13–14), and the Davidic monarchy to Cyrus (2 Chr 36:15–23).

Observation 5: The Chronicler felt free to amend the text to conform either to his own preference for wording or to reflect his interpretation of the text in light of the political realities of his own day.

One other act of interpretation is found in the transformation of Keturah from a wife to a concubine. Genesis 25:1 indicates that Keturah was a אִשָּׁה (wife), although 1 Chronicles refers to her as a פִּילֶגֶשׁ (concubine). Further, the status of Keturah's sons is impacted when the Chronicler changes the emphasis of his source from the sons "she bore to him (i.e. Abraham)" to "the sons of Keturah ... she bore" (1 Chr 1:32). Consequently the descendants listed in Chronicles are Keturah's sons rather than Abraham's sons. Genesis 25:6 indicates that Abraham had "concubines" (plural), whose sons were "sent away" while Abraham still lived. Genesis 25:9 further says that Abraham's "sons Isaac and Ishmael buried him" in his family burial ground, while nothing is said about Keturah's sons who, supposedly, were not present. This would suggest that they had been sent away, and were, therefore, the sons of a concubine. The transition of Keturah from wife to concubine then probably took this form:
1) Keturah is called a wife in the source and has sons.
2) The sons of concubines were sent away.
3) Isaac and Ishmael were present when Abraham was buried, so neither was the son of a concubine.
4) The sons of Keturah were not present at the funeral, so they must have been sent away.
5) Consequently, if her sons were sent away, Keturah must have been a concubine not a wife.[53]

This transition, however, occurred through the interpretation of the text, an attempt to make clear and consistent what otherwise appeared obscure or contradictory. The change in the term from "wife" to "concubine" is then not necessarily an attack on the sons to reduce their status, but is a reflection of the interpretative process while reading the source text.[54]

---

[53] See further Braun, *1 Chronicles*, 22. He concludes, "the terminology of v 32 does represent an interpretative viewpoint of the writer." See also Gary N. Knoppers, "Shem, Ham and Japheth: The Universal and the Particular in the Genealogy of Nations," in *The Chronicler as Theologian: Essays in Honor of Ralph W. Klein* (ed. M. Patrick Graham, et al. *Journal for the Study of the Old Testament Supplement 371*; London: T&T Clark International, 2003), 14 note 4.

[54] Williamson suggests that the list of the sons of Keturah was "added later to the Chronicler's composition," *Chronicles*, 43. He suggests this because, 1) the list is out of place between the lists of Ishmael and Isaac on the basis of 1:28; 2) "their genealogies" (1:29 – NIV 'descendants'), presupposes the descendants of Isaac and Ishmael just listed; 3) the changes to the text are "out of character" with what the Chronicler does elsewhere in

Observation 6: The Chronicler interpreted his sources to smooth out potential inconsistencies, and in so doing modified their terminology in line with his interpretation.

THE CHRONICLER: CHANGING THE EMPHASIS OF HIS SOURCE MATERIAL

Observation 5, above, indicates that the Chronicler had his own biases and concerns which impacted upon how he utilised his sources. This, however, extends not simply to what he included, or how he presented data, but also to what he excluded from his account.

The table of nations in Gen 10, which is substantially reproduced by the Chronicler, not only mentions lists of descendants but also refers to their land (אֶרֶץ), language (לָשׁוֹן),[55] family (מִשְׁפָּחָה), and nation (גּוֹי) All of these, except two

---

this chapter; 4) in Gen 25, the list of Keturah's offspring precedes that of Ishmael while in 1 Chronicles it follows Ishmael. In response I would suggest, 1) the list of Keturah does not stand between that of Ishmael and Isaac, but between Ishmael and another introduction to the descendants of Abraham (1:34), which introduces Isaac and his offspring Esau and Israel; 2) "their genealogies" are in fact taken directly from the source (Gen 25:13), but the Chronicler omits the phrase "the names of the sons of Ishmael by their names." In Genesis it only introduced one genealogy, that of Ishmael, which it does here in Chronicles, not two (i.e. Isaac and Ishmael); 3) While the changes may be "out of character" with what the Chronicler does in 1 Chr 1, they are not out of character with his work elsewhere in Chronicles, where he reshapes his sources to suit his purposes; 4) while it is true that this is one of only two places in 1 Chr 1 where the Chronicler alters the order of his source, that he does change the order in one place, allows for changes in another. As was observed in the genealogies of Israel in 1 Chr 2–8, the Chronicler does not always follow the expected order (and gives reasons on one occasion for this, 1 Chr 5:1–2). A further question that arises, however, is where else could this list of Keturah's sons go? Placing it before Ishmael, with no introduction, would be equally out of place. Placing it after Isaac would mean relocating it to the end of 1 Chr 1 (but before Isaac's other son Jacob/Israel). The relocation of Keturah to after Ishmael could be in reality the logical location unless the Chronicler desired, by means of explanation, to include the narrative regarding the death of Sarah and the marriage of Isaac which led up to this account in his source.

[55] The "language" of foreigners is also an issue in Neh 13:24 where Nehemiah expresses his concern that the children of "mixed" marriages are unable to speak the language of Judah, but instead only speak the language of Ashdod, Ammon and Moab. In the Chronicler's presentation, the languages of these groups do not exist. On the significance of language and identity see A. Helman, "'Even the Dogs in the Street Bark in Hebrew': National Ideology and Everyday Culture in Tel-Aviv," *JQR* 92 (2002): 359–382.

references to "land," are omitted in the Chronicler's account.[56] Omitted from Genesis 25:16 are references to חָצֵר (villages) and טִירָה (camps), and the areas settled by Ishmael (25:18). Omitted from Gen 36:1–9 are Esau's settlements in Seir and from 36:43 reference to אֶרֶץ and אֲחֻזָּה (possessions). In all of 1 Chr 1, the only persons or groups recorded as possessing lands are the kings of Edom who "died" and consequently lost these possessions.

By contrast, Judah's list contains details of their towns and territories (1 Chr 2:50b–55; 4:9–10, 21–23). The lists of Simeon and the Transjordanian tribes consist of settlements (1 Chr 4:28–33; 5:8b–9, 16, 23), or expansion of territory (1 Chr 4:41–43; 5:10, 18–22). Levi has its allotted settlements (1 Chr 6:39–66 [6:54–81]). Ephraim has its lands and settlements (1 Chr 7:28–29). Benjamin's second listing centres on land, particularly land in the vicinity of Jerusalem (1 Chr 8:6, 13, 28, 29, 32), and the people, either as original settlers or returnees, returned to their possessions (אֲחֻזָּה),[57] or lived in Jerusalem (1 Chr 9:2–3).

The Chronicler systematically removes land from everyone except Israel. Israel, and Israel alone, are possessors of land, dwellers in land, expanders of land, or able to return to a land from which they were exiled. All other nations, if they are mentioned as having possessions at all, die and lose their land, or have their land taken from them by one of Israel's tribes. This use of his sources indicates a clear and deliberate attempt by the Chronicler to present his "theology of land" to his readers. It is important, however, to note that he does this in 1 Chr 1 not through new material, but through his use (or non-use), of existing material. He presents his theology by deliberately editing the data available to him. While this is another example of the Chronicler as interpreter of his sources, it goes beyond the subtle changes previously noted. Instead, the Chronicler deliberately and blatantly manipulated his sources to present his vision of reality of what the community is, or should be.

The Chronicler's methods may be further exhibited by his treatment of Abraham in his genealogies. It has been noted that almost all the genealogies in Genesis are reproduced in Chronicles, except for those of Cain and two of the sons of Terah.[58] As mentioned, while it is possible that the descendants of Lot (Moab and Ammon), were omitted for current polemical purposes, the reason for the omission of the descendants Nahor is less certain. While there is genealogical material recorded in Genesis for Nahor, son of Terah (Gen 22:20–24), and other

---

[56] אֶרֶץ (10:5, 10, 11, 20, 31, 32); לָשׁוֹן (10:5, 20, 31); מִשְׁפָּחָה (10:5, 18, 20, 31, 32); גּוֹי (10:5 [2X], 20, 31, 32 [2X]). אֶרֶץ is used in a general sense in Gen 10:8, 25 // 1 Chr 1:10, 19. Other terms dealing with land and settlement in Gen 10 omitted by the Chronicler are פּוּץ (scattered; 10:18); גְּבוּל (border; 10:19), and פָּרַד (spread out; 10:5, 32).

[57] In Chronicles only in 1 Chr 7:28 (Ephraim and Manasseh), and 9:2.

[58] See note 20, above.

relationships are established within the narrative of Genesis,[59] none of this material is related by the Chronicler, nor is there any mention of Nahor and Haran, Abraham's brothers, in Chronicles.[60]

The genealogies in Gen 5 and 11 also both end with a prominent person (Noah and Terah), and their three sons. Following each of them, in either list or narrative form, are the accounts of the descendants of these three sons, with only the narrative of Genesis indicating the rising prominence of Abraham over his brothers.

The narrative in Genesis could be viewed as genealogically ambiguous. Although Abraham's son Isaac becomes the father of Esau and Jacob, the latter becoming the father of the twelve patriarchs, the narrative does not demand that any of these be viewed in one genealogical manner only. It is equally possible to list genealogically Israel and Esau as descendants, not of Abraham, but of Nahor through Rebekah. It is also possible to list the twelve patriarchs, not as descendants of Abraham, but as descendants of Nahor through Rachel and Leah, daughters of Laban, grandson of Nahor.[61]

It is probable then, in order to remove any ambiguity, and to show that Israel was descended from the man of promise (1 Chr 16:16; 2 Chr 20:7), that all other possible readings were eliminated. The omission of Nahor, brother of Abraham, places Israel as the descendant of Abraham (and no one else), and therefore Israel is the inheritor of the promise and the rightful inheritor of the land. Furthermore, the omission of the descendants of Lot son of Haran, son of Terah also eliminates any rival claimants (i.e. Moab and Ammon), to the land.

As land has been seen to be a focus of the Chronicler, the promise of land and the right to land has to be firmly established. This is accomplished by removing all other ancestors of Israel, and therefore any competing claims either to the land or rights to the land. This may further explain why the link provided in Genesis between Esau, Edom and Seir is not carried into the Chronicler's genealogies. In 1 Chr 1:51 the Chronicler changes עֵשָׂו (Esau; Gen 36:40), to אֱדוֹם

---

[59] Laban as Rebekah's brother (Gen 24:29), Rachel and Leah as daughters of Laban (Gen 29:16).

[60] Two other persons with the name "Haran" are recorded in 1 Chr 2:46; 23:9. A Nahor is mentioned (1 Chr 1:26 // Gen 11:24), as the father of Terah, although Terah's son Nahor is not alluded to.

[61] The genealogies of Genesis would then read: "Nahor, the father of Bethuel the father of Rebekah who was given to Isaac, the mother of Jacob the father of the twelve Patriarchs"; or "Nahor the father of Bethuel the father of Laban the father of Rachel & Leah who were given to Jacob, the mothers of the twelve Patriarchs" See also 1 Chr 2:34–41 where the descendants of a daughter given to a "servant" (cf. Jacob as Laban's hired help in Gen 29:14b–30; 30:25–43), as being counted in the lineage of the woman's father rather than of the woman's husband.

(Edom). Esau, as a son of Isaac may have been able to claim land, but because there is no recorded link between Esau and Edom/Seir in the Chronicler's genealogies, these latter have no claim to land. The Chronicler, by his deliberate omissions, exalts Abraham as the link to Israel and also affirms Israel's right to land through Abraham.

Yet Abraham is not the goal of the genealogies. It has already been noted that, when quoting Ps 105:6, the Chronicler omits reference to Abraham and substitutes "Israel," forming a parallelism between Jacob and Israel in his text (1 Chr 16:13).[62] While it is possible to view this as a reflection of stylistic choices,[63] or even that the Psalm was later altered from Israel to Abraham,[64] it is more probable that the Chronicler sought to enhance "Israel" the person and by extension the nation. This should not be taken to indicate a denigration of Abraham, but should be seen in the light of the Chronicler's emphasis on Israel as the sole possessor of land. Abraham was the father of "many nations" (Gen 17:4–5), a fact confirmed in 1 Chr 1:29–37. However, "many nations" are not the inheritors of land, only Israel. Ishmael, Keturah's sons and Esau are not recorded in Chronicles as possessing land. It is Israel that the Chronicler seeks to draw his focus upon regarding the possession of land. The Chronicler therefore presents Abraham as merely a link, although an important link,[65] leading to one of the Chronicler's primary concerns, Israel's right to land.

In Genesis, Abraham is dominant, even through the lives of Isaac and Jacob. It is the promise to him that is paramount.[66] God is the God of Abraham.[67] In Chronicles, it is Israel that is dominant, and God is the God of Israel.[68] While

---

[62] Note, however, that the Chronicler does not omit reference to Abraham from Ps 105:9 // 1 Chr 16:16. In 1 Chr 16:16–17 all the founders are listed, "Abraham, Isaac, Jacob, Israel," thus making a change in content both unnecessary as well as awkward.

[63] "Israel was doubtless substituted for Abraham, since it makes a more obvious, though less poetic, parallel" Curtis and Madsen, *Chronicles*, 223. What he fails to address, however, is why it is obvious to the Chronicler but not to the Psalmist.

[64] Japhet indicates that Willi states that the reading in Chronicles is the original, *Chronicles*, 318. Kraus, however, says that while "individual manuscripts follow 1 Chron. 16:13" this reading is "probably not original," *Psalms 60–150* (CC; trans. Hilton C. Oswald; Minneapolis: Fortress Press, 1993), 307.

[65] As evidenced by his being the end of one genealogy (1 Chr 1:27), and the beginning of two (1 Chr 1:28, 34). Even the presence of both forms of his name Abram/Abraham point to Yahweh's call and the change of name accompanied with the promise.

[66] Genesis 26:3–5; 28:4; 35:12; 50:24

[67] Genesis 26:24; 28:13; 31:42; 32:9; 48:15

[68] 1 Chronicles 4:10; 5:26; 15:12; 15:14; 16:4; 16:36; 22:6; 23:25; 24:19; 28:4; 29:18; 2 Chr 2:12; 6:4; 6:7; 6:10; 6:14; 6:16; 6:17; 11:16; 13:5; 15:4; 15:13; 20:19; 29:7; 29:10; 30:1; 30:5; 30:6; 32:17; 33:16; 33:18; 34:23; 34:26; 36:13. Only Jeremiah (49X), has more

Genesis indicates that everybody has land, in Chronicles, only Israel possesses the land. Even after the exile, the people return to בַּאֲחֻזָּתָם (their possessions; 1 Chr 9:2), which suggests that the land is still theirs, even though they had been exiled from it.

These alterations indicate that in various ways, sometimes subtle, sometimes overt, the Chronicler deliberately manipulated his source to highlight and emphasise his primary concerns. Although it is clear that he does this for theological and polemical purposes, this is not to say that he was not "historical" in his presentation. If history is simply presenting the past in light of the present, then the Chronicler's manipulation of the sources was "historical," in that it sought to give meaning and understanding to present realities, values and expectations.[69]

> *Observation 7: The Chronicler was not a passive copier of his sources, but took deliberate and calculated action to manipulate the presentation of his sources in such a manner as to present his view of the historical and theological realities of the people. That his sources were the accepted story of his community, and did not disappear, may indicate that he was less concerned with being contradicted by his sources or by the community than he was in presenting his own story, message, and vision to the community.*[70]

---

occurrences of "the God of Israel." Twice the Chronicler records references to "Yahweh, the God of Abraham, Isaac and Israel" (1 Chr 29:18; 2 Chr 30:6), a phrase found elsewhere only in 1 Kgs 18:36 (non-synoptic passage). Only in Exod 3:6, 15, 16; 4:5 is God/Yahweh called "the God of Abraham, Isaac and Jacob." The phrase is used several times in the New Testament: Matt 22:32 // Mark 12:26 // Luke 20:37; Acts 3:13; 7:32. In every instance except Acts 7:13, the narrative of Exodus lies behind the reference.

[69] A recent editorial regarding Australian history and identity, and the clash between politicians and historians over that history and identity, indicates that the manipulation of history for present ends and in light of present views is not an ancient art but also a present reality. "[Then Australian Prime Minister] Keating mined history and spun his myths. Often his history was bad . . . [he made] a claim on Australia's future by offering a commanding re-interpretation of its past . . . Keating used history as no PM has used it before—as a weapon to legitimise his vision," Paul Kelly, "Our Rival Storytellers," *The Weekend Australian*, September 27–28 2003.

[70] Whether the Chronicler was seeking to replace an older account with his own or was presenting a parallel, yet different, version of the past and vision for the future is uncertain. That the Deuteronomistic accounts of Samuel and Kings still exist indicates that if the former was his purpose, he failed miserably. "I do not suppose that they necessarily wished to replace or suppress writings which were concerned with other matters than specifically the events and protagonists of the monarchical period. But when it comes to

CONCLUSIONS AND IMPLICATIONS

This study of the Chronicler's use of Genesis has indicated certain tendencies regarding his utilization of his sources. At times he is extremely careful, recreating portions of his source exactly. The Chronicler is also selective, including only those portions of his source which are consistent with his overall picture and purpose, while eliminating those portions which are contrary or irrelevant to what he desires to present. He also feels free to alter his text through the addition of new words or supplying alternate words in order to remove any potential ambiguities. Further, he sometimes repositions portions of his source in a way that suits his purposes and presentation, even if that presentation provides a different emphasis or a totally different viewpoint than did his source.

Overall, it is the Chronicler's purposes which determine the content and shape of his material. It is ultimately his purposes which determine what is included as well as what is excluded. This last point is very significant. No longer is it reasonable to assume that it is merely the non-synoptic portions of the text which are significant for understanding the Chronicler's theology. Not only is his synoptic portion of great importance, being a reflection of his purposes, but so also are those portions which he omits from an otherwise parallel passage. It is only in examining the omissions from the sources utilised in 1 Chr 1 that his emphasis on Israel as the sole possessor of land is highlighted. It is only through the observation that Nahor and Terah are omitted that it is recognised that the shift of focus is away from Abraham and onto Israel.[71] This indicates that future study of the Chronicler's theology and purpose must look wider than his text. It must delve into how his sources are used, manipulated, adjusted and presented by the Chronicler.[72] Future studies must look at what is included as well as excluded.

---

the telling of the tale of the House of David, I imagine that the Annalists would indeed have wished for no rival storytellers," John Jarick, *1 Chronicles* (London: Sheffield Academic Press, 2002), 3.

[71] It is, in many ways, only the Pentateuch that informs us of the importance of Abraham. If all we possessed was Chronicles, it is unlikely that Myers would have said that Abraham "was the center of interest for the writer and who marks the end of the main line—Adam, Noah, Abraham," *1 Chronicles*, 7. It is only the source that clearly informs us of the importance of Abraham, while in the Chronicler's genealogies, he is only another name.

[72] In this regard, see especially, Kalimi, *Reshaping*.

Types of Differences between 1 Chronicles 1 and Genesis

Figure 11.7: Plené Spelling

1 Chr		Gen		1 Chr	Gen
תוגרמה	ו	תגרמה		1:6	10:3
רודנים	ו	דדנין		1:7	10:4
נמרוד	ו	נמרד		1:10	10:8
גבור	ו	גבר		1:10	10:8
לודיים	י	לודים		1:11	10:13
צידון	ו	צידן		1:13	10:15
אופיר	י	אופר		1:23	10:29
בכור	ו	בכר		1:29	25:13
נביות	ו	נבית		1:29	25:13
תלדותם	ו	תולדתם		1:29	25:13
תלדותם		תולדתם	ו	1:29	25:13
חנוך	ו	חנך		1:33	25:4
דישׁן	י	דשׁון		1:38	36:21
דישׁן		דשׁון	ו	1:38	36:21
דישׁון	י	דשׁן		1:41	36:25
דישׁון	ו	דשׁן		1:41	36:25
דישׁון	ו	דישׁן		1:41	36:26
דישׁון	ו	דישׁן		1:42	36:28
חומשׁ	ו	חמשׁ		1:45	36:34
חומשׁ	ו	חמשׁ		1:46	36:35

Figure 11.8: Misread Letters

1 Chr		Gen		1 Chr	Gen
דיפת	ד	ריפת	ר	1:6	10:3
רודנים	ר	דדנים	ד	1:7	10:4
עיבל	י	עובל	ו	1:22	10:28
יעוש	ו	יעיש	י	1:35	36:14
צפי	י	צפו	ו	1:36	36:11
עלין	י	עלון	ו	1:40	36:23
שפי	י	שפו	ו	1:40	36:23
חמרן	ר	חמדן	ד	1:41	36:26
יעקן	י	ועקן	ו	1:42	36:27
הדד	ד	הדר	ר	1:50	36:39
פעי	י	פעו	ו	1:50	36:39
עליה	י	עלוה	ו	1:51	36:40

Figure 11.9: Conjunction ו

1 Chr	Gen	1 Chr	Gen
	ו	1:8	10:6
	ו	1:8	10:6
	ו	1:29	25:13
	ו	1:30	25:14
ו		1:35	36:14
ו		1:36	36:11
	ו	1:36	36:11
ו		1:36	36:12
	ו	1:37	36:13
ו		1:38	36:20

Four occurrences with "these" (Gen. 36:13, 23, 24, 25)

Figure 11.10: Transposed Letters

1 Chr		Gen		1 Chr	Gen
עיות	יו	עוית	וי	1:46	36:35

Figure 11.11: Alternate Word Endings

1 Chr		Gen		1 Chr	Gen
תרשישה	ה	תרשיש		1:7	10:4
סבתא	א	סבתה	ה	1:9	10:7
רעמא	א	רעמה	ה	1:9	10:7
רעמא	א	רעמה	ה	1:9	10:7
משך	ד	מש		1:17	10:23

Figure 11.12: Preposition

1 Chr	Gen		1 Chr	Gen
תלדותם	לתולדתם	ל	1:29	25:13

Figure 11.13: Direct Object Marker

1 Chr	Gen	1 Chr	Gen
	את	1:32	25:2 (X5)
	את	1:32	25:3 (X2)
	את	1:35	36:14 (X3)

Figure 11.14: "These"/ אֵלֶה

1 Chr	Gen	1 Chr	Gen
	ואלה	1:37	36:13
	אלה	1:38	36:20
	ואלה	1:40	36:23
	ואלה	1:40	36:24
	ואלה	1:41	36:25
	אלה	1:41	36:26
	אלה	1:42	36:27
	אלה	1:42	36:28

Figure 11.15: Additional Words

1 Chr	Gen	1 Chr	Gen
	בני	1:4	10:1
	בני אדם	1:17	10:23
ובני		1:32	25:1
	ושמה	1:32	25:1
	ויקח	1:32	25:1
	ויסף	1:32	25:1
	לו	1:32	25:2
	ויהיו	1:36	36:11
	יהיו	1:39	36:22
	וימלך באדום	1:43	36:32
	בן עכבור	1:50	36:39
וימת הדד		1:51	36:39
	למשפחתם למקמתם בשמתם	1:51	36:40

Figure 11.16: Alternate Words

1 Chr	Gen	1 Chr	Gen
בני	ילד	1:32	25:3
פילגש	אשה	1:32	25:1
ילדה	ויל ד	1:32	25:2
אדום	עשו	1:51	36:40
ויהיו	ואלה שמות	1:51	36:40

CHAPTER 12
A: 1 CHRONICLES 1:1–54
THE WORLD BEFORE ISRAEL

INTRODUCTION

First Chronicles 1 begins the Chronicler's genealogical section, as well as his overall work. As has been established,[1] the Chronicler had the text of Genesis before him as he wrote, and he copied much of the data contained in 1 Chr 1 from it. Although at times the Chronicler slightly modified his source, he did not substantially change any of the content which he found within Genesis. While it is clear that he altered the emphasis of the text in order to present his own historical picture, he did not add personal names to his text, nor did he substantially change the relationships which existed between persons, except in certain defined cases, often for clearly polemical reasons.

Although Chapter 11 presented some of the Chronicler's emphases, such as the recognition that in the genealogies only Israel possesses land, as well as the break in the relationship between Esau and Edom/Seir, this does not fully address the overall purpose for which this chapter was included by the Chronicler. It is that purpose which is under investigation here.

A simple reading of the text of 1 Chr 1 portrays genealogy at its most foundational. First Chronicles 1 presents a series of linear and segmented genealogies containing an overview of humanity from the creation until the time of the patriarchs: Abraham, Isaac, and Israel. First Chronicles 1 does not extend into the period when the people dwelt in Egypt, the Exodus, or the conquest of Canaan. First Chronicles 1 contains no Judges or Israelite kings.[2] Israel itself does not properly exist as a people, but only as one man, the son of Isaac and grandson of Abraham (1 Chr 1:34). Israel, as a distinct family, only begins in 1 Chr 2:1–2. First Chronicles 1 then, records social structures prior to Israel, while 1 Chr 2–8 records the genealogies of Israel.

First Chronicles 1 contains the genealogies of three families and the leadership of a fourth group: the family of Adam (1 Chr 1:1–23); the family of

---

[1] See Chapter 11, above.
[2] Although it does contain a reference to Israelite kingship (1 Chr 1:43).

Shem (1 Chr 1:24–37); the family of Seir (1 Chr 1:38–42); and the leaders, both kings and chiefs, of Edom (1 Chr 1:43–54). Although there are clear connections between the families of Adam and Shem,[3] the text does not indicate any genealogical connection between Seir and Edom, or between Seir/Edom and the families of Adam or Shem. Although commentators often portray such a connection on the basis of the Chronicler's source in Genesis, the text of Chronicles does not give these connections.[4] As the text stands, the Chronicler indicates that neither Seir nor Edom originates in either the Adamic or the Semitic lines. While it can be concluded that the Chronicler may have assumed that his readers would understand that connection based upon their familiarity with the source, just as he could omit the kinship terms in 1 Chr 1:1–4, 24–27, if the Chronicler deliberately omitted the genealogical connections with the anticipation that his readers would not, or could not, supply this genealogical connection, then this would suggest that the Chronicler was seeking to disassociate the Edomites and Seirites from any genealogical connection to the descendants of Shem, and thus to Israel through Abraham.

What 1 Chronicles 1 Is Not

Before investigating what 1 Chr 1 is within the Chronicler's scheme, it would be helpful to determine what 1 Chr 1 is not. Various proposals have been put forward to explain the inclusion of this material, many of which do not take account of the issues facing the Chronicler at his time of writing, or the text as it stands.

---

[3] The first five names of the family of Shem (Shem, Arphaxad, Shelah, Eber, Peleg), are also found in 1 Chr 1:17–19.

[4] Braun divides the text into two sections: 1:1–23 "from Adam to Noah," and 1:24–54, "from Shem to Abraham and his sons," even though 1 Chronicles does not indicate any kinship relationship between Seir or Edom with Abraham, *1 Chronicles*, 13. Japhet says "chapter 1 is composed of three parts, clearly distinguishable by content and formal elements"; 1:1–27 "from Adam to Abraham," 1:28–34a "the descendants of Abraham," 1:34b–2:2 "the descendants of Isaac," *Chronicles*, 53. However, it is clear that 1:28 is a continuation of 1:27 through the repetition of Abraham, an identification made plain in 1:27, "Abram, that is Abraham," while 1:24 begins a new genealogy with Shem as the head. Although some of the names in the family of Shem are contained in 1 Chr 1:17–23, many others are new, indicating a different genealogy. McKenzie is similar to Japhet. He has 1:1–27 "from Adam to Abraham" and 1:28–54 "from Abraham to Israel," *Chronicles*, 62–67.

FIRST CHRONICLES 1 AS COMMENTARY

Selman suggests that 1 Chr 1 is "in effect a brief commentary on Genesis."[5] This is clearly overstating the case. Although the Chronicler has drawn upon Genesis, he has offered no comments upon nor has he sought to explain Genesis to his readers. There are no amplifications or clarifications of data, although, as seen in the case of Keturah there is some interpretation. In his narrative, the Chronicler often amplifies, clarifies, and modifies his source. Therefore, in certain respects, his narrative does act as a commentary on his sources. The Chronicler, however, has not sought to explain the content of Genesis, but he simply uses data from Genesis to further his own purposes. First Chronicles 1 is, therefore, not "commentary."

FIRST CHRONICLES 1 AS PRESENTING "DIVINE ELECTION"

Several commentators suggest that 1 Chr 1 was included to indicate that Israel was the subject of divine election. The narrowing focus of the Chronicler from Adam, through the seventy nations, and ultimately to Israel is said to point to that divine choice. Pratt states:

> The first task before the Chronicler was to establish that his readers were descendants of a divinely selected people. To accomplish this end he drew from several chapters in Genesis to demonstrate that God had chosen the twelve tribes of Israel for special privileges and responsibilities which now belonged to his readers . . . [they] were not like other nations; they were beneficiaries of a divine program of narrowing selection.[6]

Although Yahweh's choice of Israel is mentioned in other writings of the Hebrew Bible,[7] the divine election of Israel is never mentioned in Chronicles. Israel is often called עַמִּי (my people) by Yahweh in Chronicles (1 Chr 11:2; 17:6, 7, 9, 10; 2 Chr 6:5, 6; 7:13, 14), but it is unclear whether this is the result of Yahweh's choice of the people (cf. Deut 7:7), or the people's choice of Yahweh (cf. Josh 24:15; 1 Kgs 18:21). Examples of divine choice are present in Chronicles, but not of the people as a whole, but of individuals or smaller groups within society. Even in these instances, choice is to a particular function or role. In Chronicles, David is chosen to be king (1 Chr 28:4; 2 Chr 6:5–6), Solomon is chosen to be the temple builder (1 Chr 28:5, 6, 10; 29:1), while the Levites are specifically chosen for their tasks in respect to the cult (1 Chr 15:2; 2 Chr 29:11). Jerusalem (2 Chr 6:5, 6, 34, 38; 33:7) and the temple are chosen as the place for

---

[5] Selman, *1 Chronicles*, 89.
[6] Pratt, *Chronicles*, 63. Cf. Braun, *1 Chronicles*, 14; Williamson, *Chronicles*, 40.
[7] Deuteronomy 7:6, 7; 10:15; 14:2; Isa 14:1; 44:2; 49:7; Jer 33:24; Ezek 20:5.

Yahweh's name (2 Chr 7:12, 16; 12:13). Israel, however, is never said to have been "chosen" (בחר) by Yahweh. If the declaration of the chosen status of Israel was the purpose of the lists in 1 Chr 1, this unwillingness on the part of the Chronicler to state the chosen status of Israel in the remainder of his work would be surprising, particularly in light of the continuity of thought expressed elsewhere between the genealogical and narrative portions of his work.

Pratt's statement that one purpose of 1 Chr 1 was to demonstrate that, "God had chosen the twelve tribes of Israel for special privileges and responsibilities which now belonged to his readers," must also be challenged.[8] The privileges and responsibilities of the worshiper of Yahweh are made clear within the Chronicler's work. Also clear are the consequences, good or ill, for the people's obedience to or failure in their worship of and service to Yahweh. This, however, is not mentioned or suggested in 1 Chr 1 which contains no mention of God, cult, or cultic ritual. It contains no references to the Levites or their cultic duties. There are no references to Yahweh's powerful acts on behalf of, or in judgement upon, the people. While it is correct to say that the genealogies as a whole speak of such things, particularly with the emphasis on the cult in 1 Chr 6, the references to answered prayer, blessings for faithfulness as well as exile for unfaithfulness, it is also correct to say that 1 Chr 1 contributes nothing to that understanding.

FIRST CHRONICLES 1 AS ENCOURAGEMENT TO THE POSTEXILIC COMMUNITY

Thompson suggests that the purpose of 1 Chr 1 is based upon the need of the postexilic people to be encouraged through the recognition of their past. He says, "the generations after the exile needed a sense of history and legitimacy. In other words, they needed roots."[9]

Although it may be true that those who returned to the land required both history and legitimacy, what is unclear is how the genealogies of 1 Chr 1 would provide that. If the genealogies of 1 Chr 1 were solely concerned with Israel, then they could legitimately be said to display Israel's history and legitimacy to the people in the Chronicler's time period. Pratt says that, "by tracing the special roots of Israel, the Chronicler demonstrated that Israel held a privileged relationship with the Creator."[10]

However, 1 Chr 1 concerns itself not only with "the special roots of Israel," but with all the ancient peoples. Israel is in fact only a very minor portion of 1 Chr 1, which pays more attention to Esau, Seir, and Edom than to Israel. In 1 Chr

---

[8] Pratt, *Chronicles*, 63.

[9] Thompson, *Chronicles*, 49. Cf. Michael Wilcock, *The Message of Chronicles* (Leicester: Inter-Varsity Press, 1987), 19–31; De Vries, *Chronicles*, 34.

[10] Pratt, *Chronicles*, 64.

1, Cush, Egypt, and Canaan also receive more attention than Israel. If 1 Chr 1 is assumed to legitimise Israel or show Israel's "privileged relationship with the Creator," then it must also be concluded that it legitimises these other peoples as well, for they also gain a portion of the Chronicler's attention.

Furthermore, to establish someone's "roots," a direct connection between that person with those roots must be established. In order to legitimise an individual in the present, a genealogy must connect the present with the past.[11] This is not accomplished through the inclusion of 1 Chr 1. While a potential connection through the name "Israel" may be suggested (1 Chr 1:34), a name which is used in the postexilic lists of community members to define those in the community who were not cultic officials (Ezra 2:2, 70; 6:16; 7:7; 9:1; 10:5, 25; Neh 11:3, 20), how the "Israel" of the Chronicler's present connects with the "Israel" of 1 Chr 1 is not indicated. Closer examination of the Chronicler's genealogical section indicates that the only genealogies that are seen to carry the potential to connect a person in the Chronicler's present with persons in the past are those of the family of Sheshan (1 Chr 2:34–35), David (1 Chr 3), and Saul (1 Chr 8:33–40).

Finally, Pratt states that, "the post-exilic readers of Chronicles had faced discouragements that caused many of them to wonder if God had utterly rejected them."[12]

The fundamental premise which underlies Pratt's suggestion is that the understanding of Yahweh's relationship with, and attitude towards, his people was identical at every point of time after the first group of people returned to the land and the temple was rebuilt, up until the time when the Chronicler produced his work. While this premise is a common one, and appears to underlie many of the suggestions of the purpose of the genealogical section, in general, and 1 Chr 1, in particular, it overlooks the extent of the time period from the destruction of the temple (587 B.C.E.), authorisation of the temple rebuilding under Cyrus (538 B.C.E.), completion of the second temple (515 B.C.E.), and the writing of the Chronicler's work (circa 350 B.C.E.). This span of over 200 years makes it unlikely that the first to return to the land had the same outlook and

---

[11] In respect to the politico-jural function of genealogies, Wilson says, "whenever the authority of an officeholder is questioned, genealogies may be cited both by the incumbent, who seeks to justify his position, and by the challenger, who wishes to show that his own claim is more valid than that of his rival . . . A second situation in which genealogies play an important role occurs when the office in question becomes vacant, and it becomes necessary to choose a successor. In cases where the new officeholder must have a particular kinship relation to the former incumbent, the genealogies serve to show who the next officeholder should be, and at the same time they rule out a number of other possible candidates," *Genealogy*, 42.

[12] Pratt, *Chronicles*, 63–64.

understanding of Yahweh's attitude towards the people as those to whom the Chronicler addressed his work. Consequently, those who were the first to return would require a different message than those who were part of a society which had lived in the land for over 150 years.

It is clear that the issues and concerns which were current during the administrations of Ezra and Nehemiah during the reign of Artaxerxes (464–423 B.C.E.),[13] were not the same as those of the Chronicler several generations later.[14] This would be even more true of the people in the Chronicler's day, some 150–180 years after the return and the building of the second temple. It is, therefore, not safe to transpose the outlook of one time period onto another, particularly when the social, political, and religious situations that existed in these two time periods were not the same. It is only through the understanding of the Chronicler's own time period, and the circumstances which prevailed in that time period rather than in an earlier period, that a complete understanding of the Chronicler's purposes can be determined.

It can be concluded then that 1 Chr 1 is not commentary, nor is it concerned with the divine election of Israel, or with Israel's privileges, responsibilities, and legitimacy. It does not appear to concern itself with connecting the present people of Yehud with the "Israel" of the past or to encourage the people of the present that Yahweh had accepted them. Having addressed what 1 Chr 1 is not, we must now determine what it is.

What 1 Chronicles 1 Is

First Chronicles 1:1–42, through its linear and segmented genealogies, is a list that is made up primarily of fathers and sons. While there are some references to women,[15] almost all of the references are to males, although "son" may also used in the broader sense of "descendant." This is in stark contrast to the lists of Judah, Ephraim, Manasseh, and Benjamin where women play a much more significant role.

In 1 Chr 1 one finds no wars or muster lists. There are no totals of warriors or officials which play such an important part in some of the Israelite lists. While it

---

[13] I am working here on the assumption that the Artaxerxes of Ezra is Artaxerxes I, and that Ezra preceded Nehemiah.

[14] The difference in the attitudes expressed towards intermarriage in Ezra/Nehemiah and Chronicles is a significant example.

[15] Keturah the concubine of Abraham (1 Chr 1:32); Timna the sister of Lotan (1 Chr 1:39); and Mehetabel, daughter of Matred, daughter of Me-Zahab (1 Chr 1:50). While Gen 36:12 records Timna as the concubine of Esau's son Eliphaz, 1 Chr 1:36 lists Timna under the "sons of Eliphaz."

is observed that Nimrod is a גִּבּוֹר (mighty warrior; 1 Chr 1:10), a term which occurs elsewhere in the genealogies (1 Chr 5:24; 7:2, 5, 7, 9, 11, 40; 8:40; 9:13, 26), he is the only one so recorded in 1 Chr 1, and here it seems to have no particular significance for the Chronicler. Nowhere else in the genealogical section does a גִּבּוֹר appear alone. Elsewhere, they are always recorded as part of a group.

First Chronicles 1:1–42 contains few "historical notes." First Chronicles 1:19 refers to a time when נִפְלְגָה הָאָרֶץ (the earth was divided) which became the basis for the naming of פֶּלֶג (Peleg) son of Eber. To these may be added the Edomite king list (1 Chr 1:43–51a), which records the death of the various kings as well as the cities from which they reigned.

Other than these brief comments, the genealogical information contained in 1 Chr 1 is barren. It is purely names. This is particularly striking in light of what is known of the Chronicler's source in Genesis. Totally absent are references to land, languages, clans and cities, apart from those of the Edomite kings (Gen 10:5, 10–12, 18b–20, 30–32). Also absent are known references to marriages, wives (Gen 12:5; 25:1, 20; 28:6; 29:21, 28; 30:4, 9), deaths (Gen 25:8; 35:18, 29; 49:33), and the birth of children (Gen 16:15; 21:1–3; 25:21–26; 29:31–30:24; 35:16–18). First Chronicles 1 contains no wars or conflicts, although these occur within the Chronicler's source material (Gen 14; 34:25–29; 48:22).

Even more significant is the total absence of cultic worship, even though several of the persons mentioned in Genesis are recorded as building altars, offering sacrifices, and worshipping (Gen 8:20–21; 12:7–8; 22:9; 26:25; 33:20; 35:1, 3, 7). It may be objected that the Chronicler did not wish to portray the ancients as sacrificing in any location except for Jerusalem, however, in his narrative the Chronicler does have Solomon sacrificing at the high place of Gibeon (2 Chr 1:3), although it must be conceded that this is because, in the Chronicler's scheme, the tabernacle is located at Gibeon (cf. 1 Kgs 3:2–4 where the tabernacle is not mentioned). There should, however, be no objection to the recording of Abraham's "sacrifice" of Isaac in the "region of Moriah" (Gen 22:2), for the Chronicler portrays this as being the site of the temple in Jerusalem (2 Chr 3:1), and the place where David himself offered sacrifices (1 Chr 21:26, 28). If Abraham's sacrifice had been included, this would heighten the Chronicler's vision of Jerusalem as the one authorised place for the cultic worship of Yahweh. Yet, it is not mentioned, thus leaving the patriarchs without cult or sacrifice.[16]

It is this "barrenness" which helps to identify the purpose of 1 Chr 1, but this barrenness of life prior to the enumeration of the sons of Israel must be viewed in contrast with, and not isolated from, the life and vitality of the Chronicler's

---

[16] It should be noted that the Chronicler may have omitted this reference because of the issue of child sacrifice.

portrayal of the sons of Israel in 1 Chr 2–8 in general, and specifically with the Chronicler's portrayal of returned Israel in 1 Chr 9. This is particularly the case when it is observed that 1 Chr 9 is located on the same chiastic level as 1 Chr 1, and is therefore structurally placed to extend, heighten and to contrast with 1 Chr 1.

THE BARRENNESS OF 1 CHRONICLES 1

First Chronicles 2–8 has already been dealt with at length, so it is not necessary to review these chapters. First Chronicles 9, however, sharing the same chiastic level as 1 Chr 1, is markedly different when compared to 1 Chr 1. These contrasts heighten the barrenness of 1 Chr 1 while emphasising the vitality of 1 Chr 9, and with it, the restored community.

One of the most striking observations when 1 Chr 1 and 1 Chr 9 are compared, as already suggested, is the complete absence of any cultic activity in 1 Chr 1, while 1 Chr 9 is taken up almost entirely with cultic personnel, their duties and function. First Chronicles 9 contains lists of priests (1 Chr 9:10–13), Levites (1 Chr 9:14–16), and gatekeepers (1 Chr 9:17–22). It further contains descriptions of the duties of the gatekeepers (1 Chr 9:23–29), priests (1 Chr 9:30), Levites (1 Chr 9:31–32), and musicians (1 Chr 9:33). As mentioned above, the Chronicler's source in Genesis contains numerous references to cultic activity, none of which were incorporated into 1 Chr 1, even though cultic activity was included in some of the genealogies of the tribes in 1 Chronicles (1 Chr 4:10; 5:20; 5:27–6:66 [6:1–81], and especially 6:33–34 [6:48–49]). The community that is portrayed in 1 Chr 9, which is on the same chiastic level as 1 Chr 1 and concludes the Chronicler's genealogies, is shown to be the complete opposite of the community portrayed in 1 Chr 1. Whereas the cult is absent in 1 Chr 1, it dominates 1 Chr 9. In 1 Chr 9, the cult is established and organised, with distinct divisions of labour between defined groups.[17] First Chronicles 9 indicates not only the presence of cultic officials, but also a designated cultic place (1 Chr 9:11, 13, 19, 21, 23, 26, 27, 29, 33). All such cultic references, either to duties or place, are absent in 1 Chr 1.

The focus of 1 Chr 9 on the cult and cultic place, also draws attention to the city of Jerusalem where the cultic place is located (1 Chr 9:3, 34). As previously mentioned, such a reference would have been totally appropriate for Abraham, particularly with the Chronicler's connecting the location of the temple with the

---

[17] First Chronicles 9:10–22 indicates the different cultic groups, while 1 Chr 9:23–33 indicates some of the different duties that they performed. The Chronicler specifically states that the task of mixing the spices was the duty of the priests (1 Chr 9:30).

location of Abraham's sacrifice of Isaac, although he does not make this connection explicit (Gen 22:2; 2 Chr 3:1).[18] This connection is not made by the Chronicler in 1 Chr 1. The society of 1 Chr 1, including Abraham, Isaac and Israel, is cultless. It lacks cultic personnel as well as a cultic place.

What is also noteworthy is that the kings who are listed in 1 Chr 1 rule from their cities, die, and are replaced. While these kings are said to rule, they are given no connection with a cult, even in their own towns. First Chronicles 9:22, however, mentions the central role of David in organizing at least some of the cultic officials, a task which is further highlighted in 1 Chr 23–26. This is consistent with other portrayals of David throughout Chronicles, which indicates the interest that David, and other Judahite kings, such as Hezekiah and Josiah, took in all aspects of the cult.

David, however, is not alone in his work for the cult in 1 Chr 9. Samuel is portrayed as a co-founder of the gatekeepers, along with David. The actions of Samuel as co-founding cultic functions with David indicate the joint actions of king and prophet in proper cultic formation.[19] This is highlighted by the reference in 2 Chr 35:18:

> The Passover had not been observed like this in Israel since the days of the prophet Samuel; and none of the kings of Israel had ever celebrated such a Passover as did Josiah, with the priests, the Levites and all Judah and Israel who were there with the people of Jerusalem.

Although Japhet suggests that the mention of Samuel in 2 Chr 35:18 is the Chronicler's method of referring to the period of the judges,[20] it is better to understand Samuel here as Yahweh's prophetic representative who helped to initiate certain cultic functions, and the actions of 1 Chr 9:22 as the joint actions of Yahweh's representatives who formulate a cultic office. In Chronicles, the king sits on the throne of Yahweh's kingdom (1 Chr 17:14; 28:5; 29:23), and is, therefore, Yahweh's executive representative. Likewise, the prophets speak Yahweh's message to the people (2 Chr 20:20; 21:12; 24:19; 25:15; 28:9; 34:23), demanding their obedience. That the gatekeepers were appointed by both king and prophet points to the divine origins of this office, and demands that this office

---

[18] See further Japhet, *Chronicles*, 551–552; Williamson, *Chronicles*, 204–205.

[19] The historicity of this statement is doubtful. First Samuel 25:1 indicates that Samuel died during the reign of Saul, well before David brought the ark to Jerusalem (2 Sam 6), making it impossible for David and Samuel to cooperate in this action. In 1 Chr 15:18; 16:38 the Chronicler indicates that the position of gatekeeper came into being when David brought the ark to Jerusalem, while 1 Chr 26 shows David as organising the gatekeepers into divisions.

[20] Japhet, *Chronicles*, 1055.

must be upheld and maintained.[21] A similar example is found in 2 Chr 29:25, where the Levites are stationed with the musical instruments in, "the way prescribed by David and Gad the king's seer and Nathan the prophet; this was commanded by the LORD through his prophets."

In these texts, the Chronicler indicates that the cultic officials are assigned and organised by the joint actions of Yahweh's representatives: king and prophet. This does not occur in 1 Chr 1. Although there are kings, they establish no cult. Neither are there any prophets who speak the word of Yahweh to inform the kings or the people of Yahweh's cultic order. There is, therefore, no cult, and no cultic officials performing the required duties for Yahweh, and as a result, life is barren, as the genealogy suggests. When it is recognised that cults, cultic places, cultic worship, and the possession of land were present in the Chronicler's source, and that the Chronicler stripped them all away in his presentation in 1 Chr 1, the absence of these becomes even more significant.

The barrenness of 1 Chr 1 is how the tradition described Judah during its exilic period: no temple, no cult, no officiating cultic officials, no land. The Ezra narrative indicates that the later, dominant tradition maintained that each of these was rebuilt or restored only in the postexilic period (Ezra 1–3), that is, these institutions did not exist while Judah was in exile. This suggests that life in 1 Chr 1 was lived in a type of "exile," an exile that was removed only when Israel settled into its land (1 Chr 2–8), just as the exile of Israel ended with the return to, and resettlement of, Judah and Jerusalem.

If 1 Chr 1 is a portrayal of exile, and the barrenness that comes from that exile, this highlights some of the other details and contrasts in 1 Chr 1, 9. First Chronicles 1:43–51a indicates that those in exile may have cities. It should be noted, however, that only kings live in cities, and these cities are cities where death occurs. Although the cities have kings, those kings die and kingship is acquired by a different king in different city. By contrast, in 1 Chr 9:2 the people

---

[21] This suggests that the Chronicler's community was facing some form of controversy regarding the gatekeepers. It is possible that this issue arose because the gatekeepers had only recently gained Levitical status, or because an issue had arisen within the postexilic society which made the people question the Levitical status which the gatekeepers had long maintained and received. Whichever it was, and I favour the latter, the Chronicler was firm in asserting the Levitical status of the gatekeepers and also that that status was ancient, with their origins as a group dating back to Samuel and David. Although 1 Chr 9:22 indicates that the origins of the gatekeepers as a group were to be found in the actions of David and Samuel, 1 Chr 9:20 also acknowledges that there were "gatekeepers" of indeterminate origin and organization prior to this time who were under the supervision of Phinehas son of Eleazar. On the struggle over the legitimate Levitical claims of the gatekeepers, see Olson, "Gatekeepers." For the role of the gatekeepers in Chronicles, see Wright, "Guarding the Gates."

have their own property and towns (בַּאֲחֻזָּתָם בְּעָרֵיהֶם) rather than the ongoing singular of the kings in 1 Chr 1. While the people of 1 Chr 9 may not currently have an indigenous king, they are still guided by the principles of an ancient king, that is David, and an ancient prophet (1 Chr 9:22). The society of 1 Chr 9 also has Jerusalem, a city alive with people and with an active purpose as the centre for the cult. While the cities of the kings of 1 Chr 1 only had the king recorded (or in the case of Hadad, also the name of his wife, 1 Chr 1:50), thus suggesting an empty and barren city, the city of Jerusalem and the towns surrounding it in 1 Chr 9 teem with the living.

Those who settle in their towns and property are "Israelites, priests, Levites and temple servants." This suggests a large, rather than a small, number, and that when the people returned from exile to their land, they returned to life, growth and prosperity. Also, those who dwelt in Jerusalem are said to number at least 3,410, with other gatekeepers living in the surrounding villages (1 Chr 9:25).[22] Irrespective of the accuracy of these numbers, the picture given in 1 Chr 9 is that of a large, well populated city. This is in clear contrast to the picture of 1 Chr 1 which lists the barest of names, gives no totals for the various groups, and where even the kings lived alone. While in 1 Chr 9 there are totals for Judah (690), Benjamin (956), priests (1,760), and gatekeepers (212), there are no group totals in 1 Chr 1. In 1 Chr 1, each person, even the person named Israel, is presented as part of a small clan, or as a lone individual.

The Chronicler thus portrays life in postexilic Yehud, with its centre in Jerusalem, as well ordered, well structured, and growing. People have land, possessions, and towns. Each of these things are missing in 1 Chr 1. This contrast between the two societies is designed to portray the concept that life in the present is far better than life in the past, even the ancient past. As the Chronicler indicates that life under the kings of Israel/Judah only led to exile (1 Chr 3), an understanding which he will further clarify in his narrative section, so here in 1 Chr 1 he is suggesting that life before Israel was the equivalent of exile. There is thus no "idyllic" age to look back upon, there is only the present necessity to continue to live in Jerusalem, with its cult, cultic officials, and cultic place, as the centre of the community. This indicates that it is only the cult centred in Jerusalem that gives life and vitality to the society.

It is only as the community continues to live in proper relationship to the cult that the community will continue to prosper and avoid another exile. This is further established in the narrative where Hezekiah makes it plain that just as the people had gone into exile for their rebellion against Yahweh (2 Chr 29:6–10), so

---

[22] No number is given for the total number of Levites, unlike the similar text in Neh 11:18 which lists the total as 284. However, it must be noted that the totals in 1 Chr 9 and Neh 11 do not agree. For a discussion of the relationship between Neh 11 and 1 Chr 9, see the following chapter.

also if they will return to Yahweh, Yahweh's wrath will be turned aside (2 Chr 29:10),and those who have been exiled will be returned (2 Chr 30:9). Hezekiah indicates that to receive this restored community, the people, including those of the former kingdom of Israel, must remake Jerusalem, with its cult, their central focus (2 Chr 30:5–12). The Chronicler indicates that his society has followed in that same path instigated by David, and continued by Hezekiah, but he also asserts that they must maintain the centrality of the cult in order to continue in the land.

The Chronicler's portrayal may further point to an overall concern that he has in the production of his work. If fullness and vitality are only to be found within a restored Israel, it then becomes necessary for those who are outside of the province of Yehud to return, and become a part of this vital, living community. The Chronicler's final word וְיָעַל (and let him go up; 2 Chr 36:23), taken from Ezra 1:3,[23] becomes an invitation to those still outside the land to leave the land of exile, and come and participate in this restored, vital, cult centred community.

It may be objected that such an understanding of 1 Chr 1 by someone reading Chronicles for the first time would be impossible, as first time readers could not come to this conclusion about 1 Chr 1 until they came to 1 Chr 9.[24] While this is a valid observation, it also fails to recognise that the reading of authoritative texts was neither a "one off," nor were such readings done independently. Ben Zvi has strongly argued that, "the book was meant to be read, reread, and most likely read to others. It cannot be overstressed that reading of the book by the literati of Yehud were rereadings of the book."[25]

He further states that

> Given the social and socializing roles fulfilled by authoritative books in ancient Israel in general, and the clear didactic tone of Chronicles, one can assume confidently that the ancient literati emphasized in their readings questions such as what is the point of the story? Why is it told? What does it say about us . . . and

---

[23] The exact relationship between 2 Chr 36:22–23 and Ezra 1:1–3 is disputed. Japhet, *Chronicles*, 1076 and Martin J. Selman, *2 Chronicles* (TOTC; Leicester: Inter-Varsity Press, 1994), 551, hold that the Chronicler himself included this in his text, utilising Ezra as his source, while Williamson, *Israel*, 7–10, maintains that they are a later addition to Chronicles, which properly ended at 2 Chr 36:21; cf De Vries, *Chronicles*, 13–14. In light of his focus on the restored community in the genealogies, the idea that the inclusion of Ezra 1:1–3 by the Chronicler as an encouragement to those outside the land to migrate to this restored community in Yehud, is reasonable.

[24] H. G. M. Williamson, personal correspondence.

[25] Ben Zvi, "Observations," 67, n. 1.

about our behaviour? In other words, these communities of readers approached the book and its subunits with point-driven strategies.[26]

This suggests that the reading of the genealogies, like the reading of the work as a whole, was guided and informed by the reading community. Further, the observation that the book was not simply read, but reread, suggests the ongoing didactic function contained within the rereadings. This therefore allows that such an interpretation of 1 Chr 1 would not need to be "discovered" by the reader, but would be pointed out by the reading community.

CONCLUDING OBSERVATIONS

First Chronicles 1 is the opening, barren, portrayal of life lived in exile. It is a life without Yahweh, his cult, or any of the prosperity which faithfulness to Yahweh brings. First Chronicles 2–8 presents the opening picture of a society which begins to emphasise the centrality of Yahweh, through prayer (1 Chr 4:10; 5:20), mourning over evil (1 Chr 7:22), and the proper cultic officials, performing the proper cultic duties in the proper cultic place (1 Chr 5:27–6:66 [6:1–81]). Even here, however, there is imperfection, with the people being unfaithful to Yahweh (1 Chr 2:3, 7; 5:25), and being exiled (1 Chr 5:41 [5:26; 6:15]; 9:1). The genealogies culminate, however, in the Chronicler's portrayal of the postexilic community in 1 Chr 9. A community settled, growing, and prosperous, with Yahweh, his cult, cultic officials, and cultic place as the centre of their lives.

Oeming is therefore essentially correct when he observes a progression in the Chronicler's portrayal of society in the genealogies. He suggests that there is a narrowing focus in the genealogies from the world, to Israel, Jerusalem, and finally the temple.[27]

---

[26] Ben Zvi, "Observations," 44.
[27] Oeming, *Das wahre Israel*, 210. See Figure 12.1.

Figure 12.1: Oeming's Narrowing Focus on the Temple

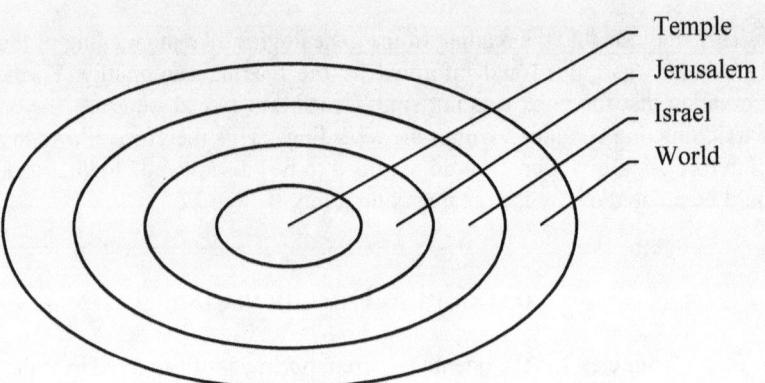

It can now be seen, however, that the genealogies portray much more than this, for there is not simply a narrowing focus upon the temple, but a growing focus on a well ordered, faithful society. While the pre-Israelite society may have been barren, even "Israel" is shown to be unfaithful, by failing to maintain the centrality of the cult. As a consequence, Israel suffers the same fate of the barrenness of exile as does the pre-Israelite society. In effect, in 1 Chr 2–8 Israel had come out of the exile of 1 Chr 1 into a life of vitality centred upon the cult. However, due to its own unfaithfulness, it returned to that barrenness of exile. This situation, however, is shown to be rectified in the Chronicler's community which has returned to vitality of life with life centred on the temple cult in Jerusalem. The Chronicler's society is one which does what not even monarchic Israel could do, it maintains the centrality of the cult, supports its personnel, and prospers in its land. The Chronicler, therefore, portrays his own society as different to that found in Israel (1 Chr 2–8), and the complete opposite to the barrenness which is found in 1 Chr 1.

It is now to the portrayal of his own society in 1 Chr 9 that we must turn.

CHAPTER 13
A1: 1 CHRONICLES 9:1B–34
ISRAEL RE-ESTABLISHED

INTRODUCTION

There are two issues which must be considered in order to understand the Chronicler's portrayal of society in 1 Chr 9. The first is the identification of his source and his use of that source. Is the Chronicler merely copying a source (and thus the meaning of that source), without imposing his own ideology onto the source? If this is the case, and our previous investigations have shown that this has not been the Chronicler's practice, then no special meaning is to be derived from 1 Chr 9. If, however, the Chronicler formulated his material himself, or transformed his source into its current shape, then it can be inferred that in so doing he had a specific purpose(s) in mind in line with his own ideological viewpoint. Once this is investigated and determined, then the second question, "What is the purpose of his text?," can be investigated fully.

DETERMINING THE CHRONICLER'S SOURCE

Any careful reading of the text of Chronicles forces one to confront the traditions and texts which lie behind this work. In addition to the Chronicler's unique material there are clear affinities to a number of other works within the Hebrew Bible.[1] The exact relationship between the texts of Chronicles and these other works has, however, been the subject of debate. Keil postulated that both Samuel/Kings and Chronicles utilised an essentially common source which each author used in accordance with their own purposes. In this way he sought to account for the variations between the two texts.[2] However, the majority view

---

[1] In addition to the more obvious parallels with the texts of Samuel and Kings, Chronicles exhibits clear literary parallels to Genesis, Numbers, Joshua, Ruth, Ezra, Nehemiah, Psalms, Isaiah, Jeremiah (the latter two in material also shared with Kings).

[2] Keil, *Chronicles*, 30–31. For an overview of debate regarding the sources and historicity of Chronicles in the nineteenth century see John W. Wright, "From Center to Periphery: 1 Chronicles 23–27 and the Interpretation of Chronicles in the Nineteenth

today is that the Chronicler used the canonical books of the Hebrew Bible and sources no longer available, his own interpretations of these texts, as well as other traditions in the production of his work.[3]

As indicated previously, the work by McIver and Carroll has aided in developing criteria for determining any direct literary relationship between two works.[4] In Chapter 11 the application of their findings to the text of 1 Chr 1 helped to support the conclusion that the textual relationships that had been assumed between 1 Chr 1 and Genesis can now be affirmed.

The question, however, is still uncertain in those passages which contain fewer than sixteen identical consecutive words and yet have portions which are very similar or identical to another text. Are these shorter passages still evidence of copying? Did the writer of Chronicles have this alternate text available to him, yet for purposes of his own, chose not to duplicate it in full? Was the writer of Chronicles simply acquainted with these alternate texts, but had no access to them at the time of writing? Or was the Chronicler working from an alternate source (either oral or written), which had similarities to, but important differences from, the alternate text in the Biblical material?[5]

First Chronicles 9:2–34 and Neh 11:1–35 are two texts where these questions are applicable.[6] Both profess to be lists of Jerusalem dwellers in the postexilic province of Yehud (1 Chr 9:3; Neh 11:3), and both contain smaller portions of

---

Century," in *Priests, Prophets and Scribes: Essays on the Formation and Heritage of Second Temple Judaism in Honour of Joseph Blenkinsopp* (ed. Eugene Ulrich, et al. *Journal for the Study of the Old Testament Supplement 149*; Sheffield: Sheffield Academic Press, 1992); and Graham, *Utilization*. Recently, Auld has encouraged a return to the common source hypothesis, *Kings Without Privilege: David and Moses in the Story of the Bible's Kings* (Edinburgh: T&T Clark, 1994).

[3] In this regard, note particularly the words of Knoppers that the Chronicler is "an interpreter . . . exegete . . . independent writer," "Hierodules," 69.

[4] McIver and Carroll, "Experiments."

[5] It is important to remember that in their experiments McIver and Carroll distinguished between three separate groups. 1) Those who had knowledge of an event, but no access to written material. 2) Those who had read and were acquainted with written material but at the point of writing did not have that written material available. 3) Those who had read and were acquainted with written material and had that material available while they wrote, "Experiments," 668–673. They concluded that the greater the availability of written sources at the time of writing, the greater the likelihood of copying and identical texts.

[6] See Figure 13.1 for an English comparison of the parallel portions of these texts. Figure 13.1 is based upon the NRSV, yet modified in points to better reflect the Hebrew text.

identical text. Both, however, exhibit significant differences when compared to one another.[7]

Figure 13.1: 1 Chronicles 9 // Nehemiah 11

1 Chr 9	Neh 11
2 Now the first to live again in their possessions in their towns were Israel, priests, Levites, and temple servants.	3 These are the leaders of the province who lived in Jerusalem; but in the towns of Judah all lived on their possessions in their towns: Israel, priests, Levites, temple servants, and the descendants of Solomon's servants.
3 And in Jerusalem lived some of the people of Judah, Benjamin, Ephraim, and Manasseh	4 And in Jerusalem lived some of the people of Judah and Benjamin.
4 Uthai son of Ammihud, son of Omri, son of Imri, son of Bani, from the descendants of Perez son of Judah.	Of the sons of Judah: Athaiah son of Uzziah son of Zechariah son of Amariah son of Shephatiah son of Mahalalel, from the descendants of Perez; 5 and Maaseiah son of Baruch son of Col-hozeh son of Hazaiah son of Adaiah son of Joiarib son of Zechariah
5 And of the Shilonites: Asaiah the firstborn, and his sons. 6 Of the sons of Zerah: Jeuel and their kin, six hundred ninety.	son of the Shilonite. 6 All the descendants of Perez who lived in Jerusalem were four hundred sixty-eight valiant warriors.
7 Of the Benjaminites: Sallu son of Meshullam, son of Hodaviah, son of Hassenuah,	7 And these are the Benjaminites: Sallu son of Meshullam son of Joed son of Pedaiah son of Kolaiah son of Maaseiah son of Ithiel son of Jeshaiah.

---

[7] For a detailed analysis of the similarities and differences and the relation of the MT of the two works to their respective LXX editions see Gary N. Knoppers, "Sources, Revisions, and Editions: The Lists of Jerusalem's Residents in MT and LXX Nehemiah 11 and 1 Chronicles 9," *Textus* 20 (2000): 141–168.

1 Chr 9	Neh 11
8 Ibneiah son of Jeroham, Elah son of Uzzi, son of Michri, and Meshullam son of Shephatiah, son of Reuel, son of Ibnijah;	
	8 And his followers Gabbai, Sallai:
9 and their kindred according to their generations, nine hundred fifty-six. All these were heads of families according to their ancestral houses.	nine hundred twenty-eight.
	9 Joel son of Zichri was their overseer; and Judah son of Hassenuah was second in charge of the city.
10 Of the priests: Jedaiah, Jehoiarib, Jachin,	10 Of the priests: Jedaiah son of Joiarib, Jachin,
11 and Azariah son of Hilkiah, son of Meshullam, son of Zadok, son of Meraioth, son of Ahitub, the chief officer of the house of God;	11 Seraiah son of Hilkiah son of Meshullam son of Zadok son of Meraioth son of Ahitub, chief officer of the house of God,
	12 and their associates who did the work of the house, eight hundred twenty-two; and Adaiah son of
12 and Adaiah son of Jeroham,	Jeroham son of Pelaliah son of Amzi son of Zechariah
son of Pashhur, son of Malchijah, and	son of Pashhur son of Malchijah, 13 and his associates, heads of ancestral houses, two hundred forty-
Maasai son of Adiel, son of Jahzerah, son of Meshullam, son of Meshillemith, son of Immer; 13 besides their kindred, heads of their ancestral houses, one thousand seven hundred sixty, qualified for the work	two; and Amashsai son of Azarel son of Ahzai son of Meshillemoth son of Immer, 14 and their kindred,
of the service of the house of God.	valiant warriors, one hundred twenty-eight; their overseer was Zabdiel son of Haggedolim.
14 Of the Levites: Shemaiah son of Hasshub, son of Azrikam, son of Hashabiah, of the sons of Merari;	15 And of the Levites: Shemaiah son of Hasshub son of Azrikam son of Hashabiah son of Bunni; 16 and Shabbethai and Jozabad, of the leaders of the Levites, who were over the outside work of the house of God;
15 and Bakbakkar, Heresh, Galal,	

1 Chr 9	Neh 11
and Mattaniah son of Mica, son of Zichri, son of Asaph;	17 and Mattaniah son of Mica son of Zabdi son of Asaph, who was the leader to begin the thanksgiving in prayer, and Bakbukiah, the second among his associates; and Abda son of Shammua son of Galal son of Jeduthun.
16 and Obadiah son of Shemaiah, son of Galal, son of Jeduthun, and Berechiah son of Asa, son of Elkanah, who lived in the villages of the Netophathites.	
	18 All the Levites in the holy city were two hundred eighty-four.
17 The gatekeepers were: Shallum, Akkub, Talmon, Ahiman; and their kindred	19 The gatekeepers, Akkub, Talmon and their kindred, who kept watch at the gates, were one hundred seventy-two.
Shallum was the chief,	

THE RELATIONSHIP BETWEEN 1 CHRONICLES 9 AND NEHEMIAH 11

There are a number of theories regarding the relationship between these passages:
1) Nehemiah 11 is dependent upon 1 Chr 9.[8]
2) First Chronicles 9 is dependent upon Neh 11.[9]
3) Both Neh 11 and 1 Chr 9 are dependent upon a common source.[10]

---

[8] Payne, "Chronicles," 365.

[9] First Chronicles 9 "may be dependent . . . on Neh xi," Myers, *I Chronicles*, liii, 67. However, Myers elsewhere says that "it is fairly clear that neither list was copied from the other; there are too many differences," *Ezra Nehemiah*, 185. Braun states that "the author of 1 Chr 9 had before him Neh 11 *in its present form*" (italics mine) although "these divergences . . . rule out the possibility of direct borrowing," *1 Chronicles*, 133–134.

[10] Williamson, *Chronicles*, 88. Although he says "evidence for a firm decision on the matter is thus lacking" he also says, "it is difficult now to be sure that the original list did not itself have a heading which could have given rise independently to both 1 Chr 9:2 and Neh 11:3" which indicates his allowance for a common source. See further Williamson, *Ezra, Nehemiah*, 344–350. Japhet indicates that Neh 11 "constitutes a fuller and more authentic version of the document, while Chronicles is actually an abridgement" Japhet, *Chronicles*, 203. Curtis suggests that, if these lists did utilise a common source, then "the

4) First Chronicles 9 "interpolates" or "fills out" Neh 11.[11]

Any theory of the origins of or interrelationship between these texts must address three separate issues:
1) The similarities exhibited between the texts.
2) The differences between the texts.
3) The common form of the texts.

In this chapter I investigate these issues in respect to the texts of 1 Chr 9 and Neh 11. It is my contention that the differences in the texts speak against either a common source or one text using the other as a source. Instead I suggest that both lists share a common form of reporting which had become reasonably standardised in the postexilic period lists recording the leaders of the community. Since a standard form was utilised, the similarities in the lists of 1 Chr 9 and Neh 11 are not due to copying, but to the utilisation of a common genre in the time period in which they were compiled.

THE SIMILARITIES BETWEEN THE TEXTS

Myers points out that thirty-five of the names in the two lists "are the same or nearly so."[12] At first sight, this may indicate great similarity between the texts until it is recognised that Neh 11 contains eighty-one names and 1 Chr 9 seventy-one, that is, less than half of the names in each text are located in the other.[13] Similarly, 1 Chr 9:2–17, 34 contains 191 words of which only ninety-three are reflected in Neh 11, while the parallel text in Neh 11:3–19 contains 227 words, eighty-eight of which are reflected in 1 Chr 9.[14]

---

differences between them may be due to changed conditions of population in Jerusalem" at the times of their different authors, *Chronicles*, 168.

[11] Kidner, *Ezra and Nehemiah*, 117. Curtis also suggests this possibility, *Chronicles*, 168 because 1) the Chronicler has already treated all of the tribes, as well as the priests and singers, in 1 Chr 1–8 and, 2) "he systematically considers the duties of the Levites and gatekeepers" rather than the persons of the priests and Levites as in 1 Chr 6.

[12] Myers, *I Chronicles*, p 67.

[13] Forty-three percent of the names in Neh 11; forty-nine percent of the names in 1 Chr 9. The differences prompt Myers to conclude that "the compiler of our list either had another purpose in mind and deliberately excluded some of the names or had other information at hand," *I Chronicles*, 67.

[14] Forty-nine percent of the words in 1 Chr 9:2–17, 34 are reflected in Neh 11 while thirty-nine percent of the words in Neh 11:3–19 are reflected in 1 Chr 9. The difference of five similar words between the two texts is the result of the Chronicler's general practice in this passage of not assimilating the *nun* of the preposition מן to the following consonant in contrast to the practice of the author of Nehemiah. See further Waltke and O'Connor, *Introduction*, 11.2.11.

It is also recognised that while some verses in 1 Chr 9 are almost exactly paralleled in Neh 11,[15] the removal of these verses from consideration results in the correlation between the two passages dropping to only 37percent for 1 Chr 9 and 29percent for Neh 11. This indicates that, while the two texts contain significant similarities, they also contain significant differences.

There are certain names in the text which, while not identical, may represent variations in spelling.[16] That these persons may be identified with one another can be determined through the genealogical relationships stated within the list:

- Asaiah // Maaseiah (1 Chr 9:5; Neh 11:5), both of whom are identified as being "Shilonites" within the tribe of Judah.
- Obadiah son of Shemaiah // Abda son of Shammua (1 Chr 9:16; Neh 11:17), both are indicated as "son of Galal, the son of Jeduthun."

Figure 13.2: Similar Names in the Lists

1 Chr 9		Neh 11	
4	עותי	4	עתיה
5	עשיה	5	מעשיה
7	הודויה	9	יהודה
10	יהויריב	10	יויריב
11	עזריה	11	שריה
12	מעשי	13	עמשסי
12	עדיאל	13	עזראל
12	משלמית	13	משלמות
16	עבדיה	17	עבדא
16	שמעיה	17	שמוע

It is reasonably certain that these refer to the same person. More contentious is the relationship between:
- Maasai son of Adiel // Amashsai son of Azarel (1 Chr 9:12; Neh 11:13). Although both are said to be from the line "Meshillemith/ Meshillemoth, the son of Immer," the intermediate ancestor(s) cannot be correlated (the son of Jahzerah, the son of Meshullam in 1 Chr 9:12; the son of Ahzai in Neh 11:13).

---

[15] 1 Chronicles 9:2 // Neh 11:3; 1 Chr 9:10–11 // Neh 11:10–11; 1 Chr 9:14 // Neh 11:15. The first passage is the introduction to the lists, the latter three cover the priests and the Levites.

[16] See Figure 13.2.

While ancient and modern tribal genealogies may change to reflect changes in status, politics, and intertribal affiliations, it is uncertain as to what would cause such alterations in this text. Genealogical change often results in the current generation being newly related to a different "founding ancestor."[17] This is not the case here, for it is instead the middle ancestors in the list which are altered. This is contrary to normal genealogical practice where middle ancestors of lesser importance are omitted, rather than changed, resulting in "telescoping." If these were to refer to the same individual, it would be a striking example of difference. It is therefore better to suppose here a genealogy of different individuals, with similar names.

A final consideration which has suggested to some that one of the texts was dependent upon the other is the form which they share. Both texts deal with settlers in Jerusalem, and give details of this group in the order Judah, Benjamin, priests, Levites, gatekeepers. This aspect of their similarity will be further explored later.

THE DIFFERENCES BETWEEN THE TEXTS

Although it was certainly the similarities between the texts which suggested to many some type of dependence of one text upon the other, the differences between the texts speak against such dependence.

The Different Contexts of the Lists

Neh 11:1–3 indicates that this is a list of those selected by lot to live in Jerusalem following the building of the walls, while 1 Chr 9:2 states that this is a list of the initial resettlers of Jerusalem following the return from exile.[18] Additionally, although the first part of the lists are very similar, the latter part of the lists bear no relation to each other. First Chronicles 9:18–34 refers primarily to the gatekeepers and their duties, while Neh 11:20–24 indicates the officials in charge

---

[17] Cf. 1 Chr 9:7 where Sallu son of Meshullam is connected to Hassenuah (Neh 11:9) while in Neh 11:7 he is part of the line from Jeshaiah while Hassenuah is simply another member of the larger tribal unit of Benjamin.

[18] Japhet, however, suggests that instead of being a list of "resettlers" after the exile, it is rather a list of the first settlers of Jerusalem with no indication in the text of a "return," *Chronicles*, 207–208. She is followed in her interpretation by Johnstone, who indicates that the idea of "to dwell 'again'" is governed by the mention of exile in 1 Chr 9:1 and knowledge of a "return," from other sources. The text itself neither mentions nor directly suggests such a return. Johnstone, *Chronicles: Volume 1*, 120. So also earlier Keil, *Chronicles*, 153–154. This issue is addressed later, and while the details are not essential to our purpose here, what is important is the recognition that the Chronicler does not place this list at the rebuilding of the walls, but either at the "return" or at the prior settlement of Jerusalem.

of various groups, and Neh 11:25–36 is a list of the towns in which the people of Judah and Benjamin lived.[19]

The Different Totals in the Census of the Various Groups.

Each of the groups mentioned in 1 Chr 9 and Neh 11 begins with a list of names followed by a numerical total for that group. None of the numbers in the two lists correspond to each other.[20] Likewise, for the priests in 1 Chr 9, only one total is given (1 Chr 9:13), while in Nehemiah totals are given after each sub-group, although even here the total does not correspond to that of 1 Chr 9.[21] These differing totals suggest that the two lists originated in different time periods. The higher numbers contained within 1 Chr 9 may reflect the numerical growth of the Jerusalem community over that time period as a consequence of Nehemiah's actions in repopulating Jerusalem.[22]

---

[19] The Judahite towns list bears many similarities to the settlement list of Josh 15, but the Benjaminite list has few points of contact with Josh 18. Janzen sees the town list of Neh 11 as the borders of the Temple community in the postexilic period, "Politics, Settlement, and Temple Community in Persian-Period Yehud," *CBQ* 64 (2002): 490–510.

[20] See Figure 13.3. No total is given for the Levites in 1 Chr 9:14–16.

[21] Note also that neither total is in agreement with the lists of Ezra 2:36–39 // Neh 7:39–42 which give a total of 4,289 priests. This difference could reflect different time periods, different counting methods (i.e. the lists in Ezra 2 // Neh 7 could reflect all descendants, or all male descendants, while the lists of Nehemiah and 1 Chr 9 could reflect only those actively serving in the temple, the other being excluded through age or other restrictions), or the reluctance of the majority of priests to live within Jerusalem.

[22] Selman, *1 Chronicles*, 124, suggests that the slightly higher numbers and the similarity of names suggests a partial transition of leadership "perhaps half a generation later than Nehemiah 11." He also uses the higher numbers as one of his proofs that the Chronicler borrowed from Nehemiah (page 123). It must be admitted that it is equally possible that the higher numbers in Chronicles reflects the population of Jerusalem a half generation before Nehemiah, i.e. at the time of Ezra's "reforms." It is possible that as a consequence of the social upheaval caused by Ezra's reforms, and the political retaliation of the families of the dispossessed wives (Ezra 10:18–44), through their objections to a first attempt to build the walls of Jerusalem (Ezra 4:7–23. esp. 4:12 and Nehemiah's reactions in Neh 1:3), that the population of Jerusalem decreased which necessitated Nehemiah's attempt to repopulate the city and the numbers in his list of Neh 11. In this regard it is significant that the assumed higher population of Jerusalem as indicated in Ezra 10:1 has been used to suggest that the work of Ezra was subsequent to that of Nehemiah because Nehemiah's work resulted in the increase of population in Jerusalem. My suggestion is that the work of Ezra resulted in a decrease in the population of Jerusalem, a situation rectified by Nehemiah. This is not to suggest, however, that the numbers in 1 Chr 9 are from the period of Ezra, only that the higher numbers do not demand, of themselves, that they be from a later time period. For the issues in the debate regarding the order of

Figure 13.3: Group Totals

	1 Chr		Neh	
Judah	9:6	690	11:6	468
Benjamin	9:9	956	11:8	928
Priests	9:13	1760	11:12	822
			11:13	242
			11:14	128
			Total	1192
Levites			11:18	284
Gatekeepers	9:22	212	11:19	172

The "Elimination" of Leaders

The list of Neh 11 is focussed upon the leadership in the community (Neh 11:3). Nehemiah's list speaks of:

- ראש (head/leader): 11:3, 16, 17
- אַנְשֵׁי־חַיִל (valiant warriors): 11:6, 14[23]
- אַחֲרָיו (followers): 11:8
- נְגִד בֵּית הָאֱלֹהִים (chief officer of the house of God): 11:11
- פָּקִיד (supervisor): 11:9, 14, 22
- עַל־הָעִיר מִשְׁנֶה (district leader): 11:9
- מִשְׁנֶה מֵאָחִיו (second in charge): 11:17
- רָאשִׁים לְאָבוֹת (heads of fathers): 11:13
- עַל־הַנְּתִינִים (those who are in charge of the Nethinim): 11:21

The Chronicler's list does not contain most of these leadership references, leaving only the reference to "chief officer of the temple" (1 Chr 9:11), the priests who were "valiant warriors/able men" (1 Chr 9:13), and the "heads of families" (1 Chr 9:13). When the Chronicler inserts a term for authority into this text, he uses "head of the father's [house]" (1 Chr 9:9, 33, 34), or simply "head" or "chief" (1 Chr 9:17, 34).[24]

Ezra and Nehemiah see further the discussion in J. Stafford Wright, *The Date of Ezra's Coming to Jerusalem* (London: Tyndale Press, 1958).

[23] The phrase גִּבּוֹרֵי חַיִל occurs also in 1 Chr 5:24; 7:2; 7:9; 9:13; 12:22, 26, 31 [12:21, 25, 30]; 26:6,:31, 2 Chr 13:3; 14:8 [14:7];. 17:13,:14, Neh. 11:14. In a war context it always has the meaning of "valiant warrior" or "fighting man," in a non-conflict situation it takes the meaning of one capable at their duties.

[24] The first is Shallum, the "head" of the gatekeepers who follows in the footsteps of Phinehas as the person responsible for the gatekeepers (1 Chr 9:20), the second is the "heads" of the Levites.

If this text is a compilation by the Chronicler, this may suggest that for him the only legitimate authority is that connected with the temple or with the extended family unit. This may reflect the ongoing shift in power and control within the community from the secular to the cultic. Over time in the Second Temple period the High Priest became the *de facto* leader of the community even in the face of imperial appointments of governors. This omission of leaders may reflect a step in this transition.

The Alternate Genealogies

Although the lists of the Chronicler and Nehemiah share a similar overall form, dealing with the people in the order: Judah, Benjamin, priests, Levites, gatekeepers, the genealogical information contained in these lists is often different. As such, we have genealogies or individuals found only in 1 Chronicles (1 Chr 9:4, 6, 8, 15, 16, 17), and genealogies or individuals found only in Nehemiah (Neh 11:4, 5, 7, 8, 9, 14, 16, 17). These represent leaders within the clans of Judah and Benjamin as well as priests, Levites and gatekeepers. These differences indicate that while some leaders retained their position, new persons have arisen to take leadership positions within the community. These lists suggest some continuity in leadership, particularly in the cult. Although there are changes in both minor and major positions, there was significant change within the leadership of the laity. It is uncertain, however, whether this reflects generational change or factors of social disruption within the community which resulted in the loss of status of certain individuals.

The Descendants of Judah

Nehemiah lists two primary descendants of Judah, Athaiah from Perez (Neh 11:4), and Maaseiah from "the Shilonite" (Neh 11:5).[25] The Chronicler lists three lines of descent, through Perez, the Shilonite, and Zerah (1 Chr 9:4–6). Perez and Zerah were the twin sons of Judah and Tamar (Gen 38:29–30), and Shelah was the third son from a previous marriage (Gen 38:1–5). That the Chronicler introduced Zerah into his list while retaining Perez suggests that he considered the "Shilonite" of his source to be "Shelah," son of Judah. As a result, he then produces in this list is a representation of all the sons of Judah, just as he had previously done in his genealogy of Judah (1 Chr 2–4). In the context of "resettlement" this has the effect of indicating that all of Judah is in the land,

---

[25] The Hebrew here is הַשִּׁלֹנִי. This could mean "the Shilonite" (so NRSV, JPS), or be a reference to "Shelah" (NIV). It is my contention that "Shilonite" is here meant and that this "Shilonite," on the basis of the tribal total in Neh 11:6, was descended from Perez. The Chronicler, however, interpreted his source so as to indicate a reference to "Shelah" son of Judah, and included it into his list on this basis.

none remains in exile.[26] This perception is further intensified by the inclusion of "Ephraim and Manasseh" as part of those who lived in Jerusalem (1 Chr 9:3), even though no descendants of these tribes are recorded. The inclusion of the northern tribes into the community and cultic life of Jerusalem is a major theme of the Chronicler (2 Chr 30:10–11, 18; 31:1; 34:9).[27]

Although it has been suggested that the Uthai of 1 Chr 9:4 refers to the same individual as the Athaiah of Neh 11:4, this is not demanded.[28] Genealogies can show variations in order to exhibit changes in family, political, and social ties. There is no reason here to demand such variation in the text other than to seek to correlate the lists of 1 Chr 9 and Neh 11.

The Descendants of Benjamin

The genealogy of Sallu (1 Chr 9:7), may reflect a later transfer for, uncertain reasons, of Sallu's heritage from Jeshaiah to Hassenuah. As is often noted, בֵּן (son), may refer to a descendant or it may refer to a successor in an office. It is possible, therefore, that while Nehemiah lists Sallu according to one purpose, the Chronicler lists him according to a different one. Thus, Sallu may be listed as a biological son in one list, while the other list records him as a holder of a particular office, and he is, therefore, now the "son" of his predecessor. Another possibility is that the Chronicler telescoped the material that is also contained in Neh 11:7–9 into this one phrase in 1 Chr 9:7.[29] Significantly, however, the Chronicler includes the ancestry of Ibneiah, of whom both he and the Mesh-

---

[26] The use of the terms "resettlement" and "return" are not meant to imply that the land was empty during the Babylonian period, or that every Judahite was exiled (cf. Jer 40–43 where many were left in the land, while others fled to neighbouring countries, although it must be noted that a significant number of these went to Egypt). It is a term which speaks from the perspective of those whose ancestors had been transported to Babylon and in whose self understanding were now "returning" to "resettle" their ancestral land.

[27] When the text of Chronicles is correlated with the text of Kings, this inclusion of the northern tribes can be seen to be prominent after the fall of Samaria. However, as the Chronicler does not mention the fall of Samaria, it is probable that he considered the potential inclusion of the northern tribes in Jerusalem's cultic life to be an ongoing possibility. The Chronicler's insistence that the northern tribes are in rebellion against David is not the same as their being excluded from Israel for they are still "brothers" (2 Chr 11:4).

[28] Japhet suggests the identification of Uthai and Athaiah on the basis of the similarity of the names (Hebrew: עותי and עתיה) and that the other differences in the genealogy are due to "textual corruption or . . . different selections from still longer pedigrees, now lost," *Chronicles*, 209.

[29] "The son of Hodaviah . . . can hardly be other than a different presentation of the name 'Jehudah' . . . the son of Hassenuah" in Neh 11:9, Japhet, *Chronicles*, 210.

ullamite clan founder, Ibnijah, occur only here in the Hebrew Bible. These, as well as the ancestry of Elah and Meshullam (1 Chr 9:8), are not contained in Neh 11.

What is clear is that the presentation of the Benjaminite list contains four families to Nehemiah's one, and that the focus of the list is not on the "followers,"[30] "overseers" or those "in charge" within the tribe, but is instead the "heads of families." This suggests that for the Benjaminite list, as for the Judahite list, some sense of the entire tribe dwelling in Jerusalem is intended rather than simply Nehemiah's leaders. Sallu and his ancestry, then, are possibly less important than what they represent: Benjamin is no longer in exile but dwelling in the land.

The Priests

Whether the names of the priests Azariah/Seraiah (1 Chr 9:11; Neh 11:11), are to be considered as variants is uncertain. Ezra 7:1 indicates Ezra's ancestry as "Ezra son of Seraiah, the son of Azaraiah, the son of Hilkiah."[31] What may be of significance is that only in Neh 11:11 and 1 Chr 9:11 is the ascending order Zadok, Meraioth, Ahitub located. The lists of 1 Chr 6 and Ezra 7 do not locate a

---

[30] The precise meaning of אַחֲרָיו in Neh 11:8 is uncertain. Batten says that the text is corrupt and suggests amending to read "his brother" (LXX[L] here reads "his brothers"), *Ezra/Nehemiah*, 268–269, so also Williamson, *Ezra, Nehemiah*, 343, BHS, NRSV. Ralf's edition of the LXX of Neh 11:8 has οπισω αυτου, which is used in the LXX (1 Sam 14:13) and NT (Mark 1:20) for following someone. It is used in Neh 3:16–17 for those who worked beside one another on the wall, and in both instances translates אַחֲרָיו (the Hebrew term is used sixteen times in Neh 3 to list successive workers on the wall). אַחֲרָיו is used 100 times in the MT. In Lev 20:5 it is used for one who follows another into a practice or behaviour, and in Num 16:25 for following a leader along a path, or following the ark of the covenant across the Jordan (Josh 3:3). It is also used for one's later descendants (Num 25:13; Deut 4:37) and a later time period (Exod 10:14). Any of these would be applicable in the context of Neh 11. It is probable then that Neh 11 is here referring to Gabbai and Sallai as subordinates of Sallu, and possibly those who would be expected to "follow" him in his office of authority. Consequently the NIV is probably correct in indicating Gabbai and Sallai as "followers" of Sallu, in whatever form that "following" occurred.

[31] For Ezra's genealogy, see Figure 3.3 and the discussion there. Interestingly, Ezra's list has Shallum as a variant of the Chronicler's Meshullam, but whereas the Chronicler only takes the genealogy to Ahitub, Ezra 7:5 takes his genealogy back to Aaron. Further, Ezra makes no reference to any ancestor after the exile. It is probably the Seraiah, high priest at the destruction of the temple (2 Kgs 25:18), who is indicated. Hilkiah was the high priest during Josiah's reforms (2 Kgs 22:8–12). Jehozadak, son of Seraiah, was the father/ancestor of Joshua the high priest at the construction of the second temple (Hag 1:1, 12).

Meraioth in this position, although both have a Meraioth as a son of Zerahiah.[32] The exact reasons for these differences between 1 Chr 9/Neh 11 and 1 Chr 6/Ezra 7 have already been discussed.[33] What is significant is that only 1 Chr 9 and Neh 11 share this variation. This indicates some relationship between these parts of the lists, although the precise nature of that relationship cannot be determined at this stage. It is probable, then, that the priestly lists in 1 Chr 9:11; Neh 11:11 represent a tradition of the preexilic priesthood that had not yet been telescoped with the deletion of Meraioth. Ezra's list, being later, would have omitted this name as this individual was not "significant" enough to be retained.

The Levites

In his discussion of the Levites, the Chronicler includes representatives from each of the clans which made up the cultic musicians, thus indicating that all of the clans of cultic musicians which were present prior to the exile, were also present within the postexilic community. This is an expansion upon the presentation found in Nehemiah. Nehemiah refers to descendants of Bunni (Neh 11:15), Asaph (Neh 11:17), and Jeduthun (Neh 11:17). The Chronicler's genealogy of Shemaiah, instead of containing "Bunni" indicates "a Merarite" (1 Chr 9:14), while retaining references to the descendants of Asaph (1 Chr 9:15), and Jeduthun (1 Chr 9:16). He incorporates three unidentified persons (1 Chr 9:15), as well as including a reference to descendants of Elkanah and the curious reference to Elkanah living "in the villages of the Netophathites" (1 Chr 9:16).

Although in one census (Ezra 2:41; Neh 7:44), only Asaph is mentioned among the singers, for the Chronicler Asaph, Jeduthun, Heman, Ethan and their descendants are presented as the leaders, under the appointment of David, of music in the temple worship. In his list in 1 Chr 9, the Chronicler presents representatives of Asaph and Jeduthun. In addition, Ethan is a descendant of Merari (1 Chr 6:29 [6:44]), while elsewhere the line of Heman runs through three persons named Elkanah (1 Chr 6:19–21 [6:34–36]). Finally, it must be remembered that the villages of the Netophathites (1 Chr 9:16), are cited elsewhere as the dwelling places of the singers within the postexilic community (Neh 12:28–29).

In this manner the Chronicler has incorporated all the families of musicians, irrespective of status, into the Jerusalem community. However, it is important to note that the Levitical duties in 1 Chr 9 only deal with music. This is in contrast to the list in Nehemiah which, although containing "the leader to begin the thanksgiving in prayer" (Neh 11:17), shows that the Levitical duties also incorporated "the outside work of the house of God" (Neh 11:16). In Chronicles,

---

[32] 1 Esdras 8:1–2 omits the sequence "Azariah son of Meraioth son of Zerahiah" found in Ezra 7:3–4.

[33] See previous discussion in chapter 3.

the duties which Nehemiah relates to the Levites fall to the gatekeepers in their status as Levites.

The Gatekeepers

The other significant difference in the texts concerns the leaders of the gatekeepers (1 Chr 9:17; Neh 11:19). The Chronicler mentions four (Shallum, Akkub, Talmon, Ahiman[34]), while Nehemiah records only two (Akkub and Talmon). The Chronicler also indicates that Shallum is their "chief/head." Shallum, Akkub, and Talmon occur in the census list of Ezra 2:42 // Neh 7:45 along with Ater, Hatita, and Shobai, who are not mentioned elsewhere. Akkub and Talmon are two of the six gatekeepers in both the time of Joiakim, the High Priest, as well as the time of Nehemiah (Neh 12:26). This may indicate that the clan was present rather than the individuals, as these are in different generations.[35] Why 1 Chr 9 lists more gatekeepers than Neh 11 is uncertain, although it could be related to the general trend of 1 Chr 9 to higher totals.

Although much of the material common to 1 Chronicles and Nehemiah is significant because of its differences, the material the Chronicler includes in 1 Chr 9:18–34 is also of great significance. The Chronicler's unique material declares the antiquity of the gatekeepers both in their task and in their Levitical connections (1 Chr 9:19–21), their appointment to their task in the temple by David and Samuel (1 Chr 9:22), duties of guarding the temple (1 Chr 9:23–27), responsibilities for both buildings and supplies (1 Chr 9:28–29), and the baking of the ritual bread (1 Chr 9:31–32).[36] The gatekeepers subordination to Phinehas, son of Eleazar (1 Chr 9:20), is consistent with the portrayal of Eleazar as the one responsible for the tabernacle and its contents (Num 4:16). The Chronicler's understanding of the role of gatekeepers is therefore integrated into the priestly understanding of the rights and duties of the priests.

---

[34] Braun suggests that Ahiman occurs through a confusion with the following "their brothers" which is similar in form, although in the current context is to be understood as a proper name on the basis of "the four principal gatekeepers" (1 Chronicle 9:26), *1 Chronicles*, 136.

[35] It has been suggested by Williamson that Meshullum (Neh 11:25), is a variant of Shallum. *Ezra, Nehemiah*, 358. He further suggests that this is a variant of Shelemiah/Meshelemiah, who is the head of the gatekeepers in 1 Chr 26:1–2, 14.

[36] However, the Chronicler is very clear that although the gatekeepers had certain responsibilities, other duties, such as the mixing of incense, were totally the responsibility of the priests (1 Chr 9:30).

CONCLUDING OBSERVATIONS ON THE SIMILARITIES AND DIFFERENCES

In his work, the Chronicler's lists are fuller and more expansive than the lists contained in Nehemiah. Through this expanded list, the Chronicler has indicated that "all Israel" (as represented by the presence of Judah, Benjamin, Ephraim and Manasseh), dwelt in Jerusalem. Jerusalem was also home to a complete Levitical cultic institution consisting of priests, Levites, musicians, and gatekeepers who can trace their status as Levites back to Korah, and their position in the temple to David. The Chronicler desires "all Israel" to be present, and shapes his list to ensure that "all Israel" is present.

What can be concluded from these observations is that although the lists of 1 Chr 9 and Neh 11 bear some similarities, the differences between them are such to indicate that these lists:

- were produced at different times as evidenced by the different totals as well as the different leaders of the varying groups.
- reflect a number of different leaders within the community, indicating a change in leadership over time.
- reflect different views of leadership at their times of production, from individuals as leaders of clans, groups or guilds in Nehemiah, to leaders as "heads of families" and/or cultic leaders in Chronicles.
- reflect a change in the population of the community, with a general growth in the Jerusalem population between the two lists.

These differences suggest that either:

1) If the Chronicler did make use of the list in Neh 11, he simply selected some information, while greatly modifying or omitting many other parts of his source, while also incorporating material from some source unknown to us, or;
2) If the Chronicler and Nehemiah utilised a common source, with each author selecting material according to their own purposes, then this list must have either been internally inconsistent in terms of numbers of people, leaders, status of individuals and groups so as to result in the variations present in these two texts, or each author selected only a small portion of the available material.[37]

Knoppers correctly observes:

---

[37] Knoppers suggestion that the LXX of Nehemiah, MT Chronicles and MT Nehemiah "represents a revision of and a development from an older source" also falls into this category. Merely contextualizing, editing and supplementing an original catalogue by three documents instead of two does not adequately address the vast differences between these texts, "Sources," 167.

The many incidental, but not insignificant, dissimilarities between Nehemiah and Chronicles make it difficult to derive one list from the other. One can readily understand why tradents would provide their own editorial comments on sources in their employ, but it seems unlikely that they would randomly alter kinship relationships, excise genealogies, delete administrative functions, and arbitrarily change, supplement, or excise numerical totals.[38]

Consequently, it is more probable to conclude either that the Chronicler utilised a different list to that found in Neh 11, or that the list of 1 Chr 9 is the product of the Chronicler himself, using whatever sources may have been available, in line with his own polemical purposes. This latter option appears to fit best the details of his list unless we assume that the separate list he incorporated just happened to coincide with his own theological and social outlook as typified in the rest of his writing.

THE COMMON FORM OF THE TEXTS

One of the arguments which has been utilised to suggest direct or indirect use of Neh 11 by the Chronicler is the common form of the two texts. Since they share a common form and order, the two texts must be related. It is indisputable that the order of presentation in the texts (Judah, Benjamin, priests, Levites, gatekeepers), is the same. This, however, is not conclusive evidence of literary dependence, for an investigation of other lists of persons and duties in the postexilic literature reveals that this is a common pattern, as has been previously demonstrated.[39]

As was observed, what this indicates is that within the postexilic period a general pattern had developed which was utilised in referring to those who made up the second temple community. This pattern clearly distinguished between lay and clergy (with the lay members normally having the priority), but also distinguishing between members of the clergy on the basis of their function,

---

[38] Knoppers, "Sources," 166–167. Note in this regard the comments of Wilson who, while acknowledging that in *oral* genealogies such factors as telescoping and fluidity are present, when a genealogy becomes a written text it becomes fixed and less susceptible to alteration to meet changes in status or power within a society; "when a genealogy is made part of a written document, the possibility of continual formal change is severely limited, with the result that a number of genealogical functions that require such change are proscribed or at least severely hampered," *Genealogy*, 55. This statement is often overlooked in seeking to understand the Chronicler's genealogies, often with the assumption that the Chronicler severely altered *written* sources. According to Wilson, this type of change, although not impossible, is less likely.

[39] See the discussion in Chapter 4 as well as Figure 4.2.

giving higher status to the priests over the Levites and expressing the relative status between Levitical groups (i.e. singers and gatekeepers).

This suggests that in compiling their lists the Chronicler and the author of Nehemiah gathered their material from any source(s) available to them, included and shaped the material according to their own purposes (Nehemiah to show the leaders who lived in Jerusalem; Chronicles showing the presence of all Israel, lay and clergy in all its forms), and presented these in the form that was both familiar and expected. It is this common form which provides much of the similarity between the lists of 1 Chr 9 and Neh 11. The similar data that the lists contain may reflect the use of a common source or tradition, while the differences reflect a change in leadership or personnel over the time period in which the two lists were compiled.

Consequently, on the basis of content and form, it can be concluded that there is no longer any reason to demand either a direct or indirect literary relationship between 1 Chr 9 and Neh 11. It is more reasonable to conclude that the author of Nehemiah and the Chronicler compiled their own lists, on the basis of the data available to them, and in line with their own purposes, both utilising the form of presentation typical in their community.

THE PURPOSE OF 1 CHRONICLES 9

In previous chapters, several observations have been made with regard to 1 Chr 9, which need to be brought together.

First, it is noticed that 1 Chr 9:1b–34 consists of three sections:
First Chronicles 9:1b – Judah (and Israel) taken into Exile.
First Chronicles 9:2 – The (re)settlement of the people.
First Chronicles 9:3–34 – Those who dwell in Jerusalem.

The last section is the largest, and most encompassing of all, dealing with the leadership of Judah, Benjamin, and the cultic officials. Not only are the cultic officials listed genealogically, but some of their duties are also recounted. In this it is interesting to note that the primary duties recorded are those of the gatekeepers, although some priestly or musical duties are mentioned (1 Chr 9:30, 33). While this clearly emphasises the role of the gatekeepers, it must be remembered that the duties of the priests, Levites and musicians were dealt with in some detail in 1 Chr 6:16–17, 33–34 [6:31–32, 48–49], where these cultic officials were first mentioned. The inclusion of the gatekeeper's duties may, then, be nothing more than an attempt to show here, at their first mention, what "gatekeepers" actually did.

ISRAEL RE-ESTABLISHED 351

Second, the third section is bracketed by the phrase, they dwelt in Jerusalem (וּבִירוּשָׁלַםִ יָשְׁבוּ; 1 Chr 9:3), or (יָשְׁבוּ בִירוּשָׁלָםִ; 1 Chr 9:34).[40] This phrase acts like an *inclusio* around the entire list, and seeks to emphasise that all those incorporated by it (Judah, Benjamin, Ephraim, Manasseh, priests, Levites and gatekeepers) dwelt in Jerusalem. This is shown to be the rightful dwelling place not just of some, but of "all Israel." Jerusalem, and the cult which it contains, is not simply the possession of the cultic officials, it belongs instead to all of the people, and therefore all of the people must give their attention to it.

Third, dwelling in Jerusalem, with the presence of the cultic officials, is shown to be the opposite of, and the solution to, being in exile. First Chronicles 9:1b–3 presents a clear progression: unfaithfulness, exile, (re)settling in their own possessions, and finally dwelling in Jerusalem. This suggests that, for the Chronicler, a mere return to the land, i.e. living "on their own property," is insufficient to the maintenance of social stability, or for ensuring that the people remain in the land, while preventing a return to exile. Jerusalem and its cult cannot simply exist, it must become and remain the focus of the community. This is highlighted by the Chronicler's last word, וְיָעַל (and let him go up; 2 Chr 36:23), which is spoken in the context of the "house in Jerusalem" that Cyrus orders built for Yahweh. What the Chronicler expresses as a hope in 2 Chr 36:23, he indicates is a present reality in 1 Chr 9. Although the population of Jerusalem is small, with only 3,618 persons indicated, and some of the gatekeepers included in this list living outside of Jerusalem (1 Chr 9:25), the community is nonetheless progressing towards the ideal that the Chronicler believes should exist.[41]

Fourth, the Chronicler presents not simply all Israel as present in Jerusalem, but also all Levi. Jerusalem is inhabited by representatives of all of the sons of Judah (1 Chr 9:3–6), as well as the sons of Benjamin (1 Chr 9:7–9). There are in fact more Benjaminites (956) listed in Jerusalem than there are Judahites (690). Furthermore, all of Levi is also present in Jerusalem. Jerusalem contains priests (1 Chr 9:10–13), Levites, who are made up of the representatives of the musical

---

[40] In respect to the reverse order, Kalimi says, "presenting the concluding words in the inverse order of the introduction stresses this literary structure and binds the component parts of the list together with even more strength," *Reshaping*, 321.

[41] This raises questions as to whom the Chronicler directed his work. If he sought to instill a focus upon Jerusalem, to whom was he writing? This message would be applicable to those who dwelt in postexilic Yehud who, perhaps, had grown neglectful of Jerusalem and its temple (cf. Neh 13:10–12; Mal 3:6–9). It is also possible that the Chronicler directed his work to those who still remained in Babylon and other parts of the Persian empire. He possibly wanted these people to migrate to Yehud, thus strengthening the province numerically and making it more economically viable, or to show their devotion to Yahweh and his temple by contributing funds for its upkeep and maintenance (cf. 1 Chr 29:6–8; 2 Chr 24:8–12; 34:9).

guilds of Asaph, Jeduthun, Ethan through Shemaiah the Merarite, and Kohath through Elkanah (1 Chr 9:14–16). Also present are the gatekeepers (1 Chr 9:17–22), whose tasks also include caring for the equipment and materials which will be used in the cultic ritual (1 Chr 9:28–32). These three groups appear to correspond with those mentioned in 1 Chr 6:33 [6:48], with the gatekeepers being the group "assigned to all the duties of the tabernacle," that is, those that do not involve sacrifice or music.

Fifth, although not having a recorded genealogy, 1 Chr 9:3 emphasises the presence of Ephraim and Manasseh in the postexilic Jerusalem community. "Israel" is not to be thought of as being made up of Judah, Benjamin and Levi alone. Instead, all of the tribes have the right, opportunity, and responsibility to come and make Jerusalem their home, and the cult of Yahweh the focus of their lives. This is reiterated throughout the narrative where all of the tribes are invited to come and participate in the worship of Yahweh (1 Chr 13:2–5; 15:3; 2 Chr 15:9; 30:1, 10, 11, 18; 34:9). Judah and Benjamin stand on the outside levels of the Chronicler's description of the sons of Israel, and theirs is not a position of prominence. They are not listed in superior positions to the other tribes, but in inferior ones. Judah and Benjamin are on the outside, furthest away from the leaders of the cult, while the other tribes are listed closer to the cult and the cultic tribe in 1 Chr 6, probably signifying the opportunity for these other tribes to access the cult and not be restricted by their non citizenship within the tribes of Judah or Benjamin. This indicates that the Chronicler's appeal to וְיָעַל (let them go up) is open to all who would come, rather than just a select group.

It is interesting to note that, although the decree of Cyrus indicated that all those who professed to be Yahweh's people could participate in the building of the temple (Ezra 1:3), when certain groups sought to participate in this project, they were called the "enemies of Judah and Benjamin" (Ezra 4:1). Even though these groups fulfilled the requirements of Cyrus for being the people of Yahweh, for "we seek your God and have been sacrificing to him since the time of Esarhaddon" (Ezra 4:2), and therefore should have been permitted to participate, "Judah and Benjamin" considered them enemies and refused them permission. Here in the genealogies, it is Judah and Benjamin who are placed on the outside of the chiastic structure, while those who had been previously excluded are placed on the inside of that structure, closest to the cult. It is possible, albeit unprovable, that part of the Chronicler's purpose was to encourage his own community to be accepting of those who professed the worship of Yahweh, yet did not "belong" to the accepted or acceptable tribes, and is opposing the perspective contained in Ezra.[42]

---

[42] Trotter has rightly noted the difficulties encountered when trying to reconstruct the history of the early postexilic period utilising the text of Ezra as the primary chronological marker, "Was the Second Jerusalem Temple a Primarily Persian Project?," *SJOT* 15

SETTLERS OR RESETTLERS?

The question remains, however, as to which time period is being indicated in 1 Chr 9. Some translations render the term וְהַיּוֹשְׁבִים הָרִאשֹׁנִים, (1 Chr 9:2), with the sense of a resettlement upon, or dwelling again in the land (NIV, NRSV, GNT, NCV, CEV, God's Word). This translation is often guided by the context of "exile" in which the verse is found (1 Chr 9:1b). If the people had been exiled, then the following verse which speaks of "dwelling," must be in reference to a return from exile, and thus a "resettlement." Other translations render the term with a sense of "the first settlers" (KJV, NASB, JPS). If this translation is followed, then this suggests that this is a list not of those who returned, but of those who dwelt in Jerusalem when it was first occupied.

Commentators are also divided in their interpretation of this phrase and its meaning. Although the majority conclude that this refers to postexilic dwellers in the land,[43] there are some who favour the idea that a preexilic group is intended.[44]

Japhet has strongly argued for the understanding that "the first dwellers" refers to the monarchic period.[45] She indicates that the idea of a "resettlement" or people "dwelling again" is "not inherent in the text," but is only assumed on the basis of the mention of an exile in 1 Chr 9:1b.[46] She further indicates that "dwelling" (יָשַׁב) is an important theme in 1 Chr 2–8, and as the Chronicler had summed up the genealogical emphasis of his genealogies in 1 Chr 9:1 by stating

---

(2001): 276–294. It is clear that the final author of Ezra sought to exclude those groups whose origins were external to either Judah, Benjamin or Levi. The Chronicler, however, is clearly more inclusive in his approach, and could be deliberately opposing the view expressed in Ezra. On the exclusion of "foreigners" in the postexilic period, see further Lester L. Grabbe, "Triumph of the Pious or Failure of the Xenophobes? The Ezra-Nehemiah Reforms and their *Nachgeschichte*," in *Jewish Local Patriotism and Self-Identification in the Graeco-Roman Period* (ed. Siân Jones and Sarah Pearce *Journal for the Study of the Pseudepigrapha Supplement 31*; Sheffield: Sheffield Academic Press, 1998).

[43] Allen, *Chronicles*, 75; Goettsberger, *Chronik*, 89; Hill, *Chronicles*, 179; Klein, *1 Chronicles*, 266; Knoppers, *1 Chronicles 1–9*, 500; Myers, *1 Chronicles*, 63, 67; Oeming, *Das wahre Israel*, 182; Pratt, *Chronicles*, 94; Rothstein and Hänel, *Chronik*, 171; Rudolph, *Chronikbücher*, 84; Selman, *1 Chronicles*, 123–124; Thompson, *Chronicles*, 105; Tuell, *Chronicles*, 41; Williamson, *Chronicles*, 88. Rudolph suggests emending the text to read הַשָּׁבִים, "those who returned," *Chronikbücher*, 82; cf. Braun, *1 Chronicles*, 130.

[44] Braun, *1 Chronicles*, 129; Curtis and Madsen, *Chronicles*, 169; De Vries, *Chronicles*, 89; Japhet, *Chronicles*, 207–208; Johnstone, *Chronicles: Volume 1*, 119–121; Keil, *Chronicles*, 153–154. It must be noted that Curtis allows for both options, but prefers "first to dwell."

[45] Japhet, *Chronicles*, 207–208.
[46] Japhet, *Chronicles*, 208.

that "all Israel was listed," so here in 1 Chr 9:2 he is dealing with his territorial theme by indicating that the people and cultic officials lived "on their own property in their own towns." Finally, Japhet suggests that the term, וְהַיּוֹשְׁבִים הָרִאשֹׁנִים, which she translates as "the old dwellers" or the "dwellers of old," finds its closest comparisons in references to "the former prophets" (Zech 1:4; 7:7), and "the former days" (Ecclesiastes 7:10), and therefore refers to the distant past.

Johnstone, like Japhet, says that the idea of "dwelling again" comes only through reading 1 Chr 9:2 as the continuation of 1 Chr 9:1.[47] He contends that 1 Chr 9:2 is not referring exclusively to postexilic society, even though some postexilic personages are recorded. He suggests instead that 1 Chr 9 is seeking to "portray the population of Jerusalem in terms of the Davidic ideal"[48] Although acknowledging that some of the persons mentioned are postexilic, he contends:

> By relating these contemporaries of Nehemiah to the Davidic era, C is throwing a bridge across the generations. All are involved in the one perpetual cult of the Temple, whether in the age of David in the tenth century or of Nehemiah in the fifth. In a global way, past and present are combined in timeless contemporaneity in order to express in the most adequate way possible—the solidarity that integrates the disparate generations across the ages—the enduring status and function of Jerusalem.[49]

In response, it must be recognised that Japhet's primary assertion cannot be sustained. Her claim that "nothing in the context in fact indicates a 'return' or 'restoration'" is abrogated by her own acknowledgement that this understanding is based upon the context found in 1 Chr 9:1b, which mentions the exile of Judah.[50] The mention of "those who dwell" immediately after the mention of an "exile" would automatically connect the two events in the minds of the readers/hearers, and would suggest that a resettlement or return is to be understood here. There is, in fact, nothing to suggest that a preexilic settlement is here in view. First Chronicles 9:1a has already presented a summation of the genealogical section with "all Israel" being recorded. Within the listing of the various tribes in 1 Chr 2–8, the land and territory which a number of the tribes had occupied had been already recorded, including gains and losses of territory. This indicates that in the phrase "all Israel," not only were the genealogies included, but also the land where these persons had dwelt. The phrase "all Israel" would therefore encapsulate both people and land, just as the lists of the individual tribes had both people and land listed. Japhet's assertion that 1 Chr 9:2

---

[47] Johnstone, *Chronicles: Volume 1*, 120.
[48] Johnstone, *Chronicles: Volume 1*, 120.
[49] Johnstone, *Chronicles: Volume 1*, 121.
[50] Japhet, *Chronicles*, 208.

is merely the summation of that data is therefore unnecessary. Instead, it is more reasonable to conclude that just as 1 Chr 9:1b has presented Judah being exiled for its unfaithfulness, so now 1 Chr 9:2 is recording the return of those who were exiled to dwell again in their land.

Further, while it is true that הָרִאשֹׁנִים, can refer to a former time period, this is simply a past time period which is viewed from the perspective of the author. It can thus refer to either the distant, or the recent, past. Thus Zechariah 1:4; 7:7, 12 refer to הַנְּבִיאִים הָרִאשֹׁנִים (former/earlier prophets) that is, to prophets who preceded Zechariah. Likewise, כַּיָּמִים הָרִאשֹׁנִים (the former days; Zech 8:11), refers to the days which preceded this particular pronouncement; הַמְּלָכִים הָרִאשֹׁנִים (the former kings; Jer 34:5), refers to the kings which preceded Zedekiah; and הַפַּחוֹת הָרִאשֹׁנִים (the former governors; Neh 5:15), refer to those governors which preceded Nehemiah. Each of these speak of those who preceded from the perspective of the speaker/author. This suggests that, although the Chronicler referred to הַיּוֹשְׁבִים הָרִאשֹׁנִים, he only meant those who dwelt in Jerusalem prior to his own time period. There is nothing inherent in the term that demands that these be preexilic inhabitants of Jerusalem. Consequently, the Chronicler could talk about הַיּוֹשְׁבִים הָרִאשֹׁנִים (the former dwellers) that is, those who dwelt in Jerusalem in the past, while still signifying those who returned from exile.[51]

Johnstone's suggestion is also unacceptable. He suggests that the Chronicler is indicating not the inhabitants of Jerusalem at a set time, but all those who have dwelt in Jerusalem from the past until the present. The foundation of his argument is the mention of David in 1 Chr 9:22. While Hill states that 1 Chr 9:2

---

[51] So also Knoppers, *1 Chronicles 1–9*, 500. Keil rejects the argument of Berthau that Neh 5:15 could be used as a corollary to 1 Chr 9:2. He summarises Berthau as suggesting "the time between Zerubbabel and Ezra is called the time of the former governors (הַפַּחוֹת הָרִאשֹׁנִים), with whom Nehemiah contrasts himself, the later governor, to prove that according to that the former inhabitants in our passage may very well denote the inhabitants of the land in the first century of the restored community." In dismissing this argument, Keil goes on to say, "the governors were changed within short periods, so that Nehemiah might readily call his predecessors in the office 'former governors;' while the inhabitants of the cities of Judah, on the contrary, had not changed during the period from Zerubbabel to Ezra, so as to allow of earlier and later inhabitants being distinguished," *Chronicles*, 154. It is clear that Keil's objections are based upon his assumption that Ezra was the author of Chronicles (see further his argument, *Chronicles*, 22–27), but even if that were the case, it would not be correct to assume that the same persons who dwelt in Jerusalem at the building of the second temple (515 B.C.E.), were still alive and dwelling in the city at the time of Ezra (458 B.C.E.). Further, that Ezra himself was a later migrant to Jerusalem, he would be correct in referring to the "earlier dwellers," that is, those who lived there before himself. That the Chronicler probably wrote his work in the mid- to late-fourth century B.C.E., further undermines Keil's objections.

"confirms the linkage of the postexilic Jewish community with earlier national Israel,"[52] this is not the same as Johnstone's attempt to incorporate "past and present . . . in timeless contemporaneity."[53] As Klein has noted, dependence upon the reference to David here is weak, for, "it indicates that the gatekeepers were installed in their office by David, but that does not mean the present list is meant to refer to that time."[54]

Klein's objections are further enhanced when it is recognised that the text refers not only to David, but also Samuel. David and Samuel are put forward as joint organisers of the gatekeepers, yet nowhere is it suggested that Samuel dwelt in Jerusalem. This undermines Johnstone's suggestion that "the enduring status and function of Jerusalem" is here in view.[55]

Johnstone's position is further challenged by Oeming's observation that 1 Chr 9:2 does not refer to Jerusalem at all. He says, "1 Chronicles 9:2 does not mention those who dwell in Jerusalem, but is placed in apposition to those in verse 3, marked by the *waw* which opens verse 3; the renewed ישבו are clearly two groups."[56]

Oeming goes on to say, "this means that those named in the list of the dwellers in Jerusalem were not the first dwellers."[57]

In other words, "the former settlers" or "the first settlers" of 1 Chr 9:2 does not refer to those who lived in Jerusalem, but only to those who lived in their possessions and towns. This clearly makes the reference to a "return" more likely, for the concept of a "return" places the dwelling in towns and possessions into a living context. It is only when Israel dwell in their towns and possessions that those who dwell in Jerusalem are mentioned. The Chronicler is perhaps suggesting that it is only as the people again dwelt in the land, that they began to make "any significant move to inhabit Jerusalem."[58]

This is also consistent with the observation of Oeming, that in the genealogies as a whole, the Chronicler has a narrowing focus from world, to Israel, to Jerusalem, to temple.[59] Judah (and Israel) are taken into exile (1 Chr

---

[52] Hill, *Chronicles*, 179.
[53] Johnstone, *Chronicles: Volume 1*, 121.
[54] Klein, *1 Chronicles*, 266, note 22.
[55] Johnstone, *Chronicles: Volume 1*, 121.
[56] "1 Chr 9,2 erwähnt die Bewohner Jerusalems nicht, sondern stellt sie mit V.3 als Neueinsatz den Vorhergehenden geradezu entgegen, markiert jedenfalls mit dem Waw das V,3 eröffnet, und dem erneuten ישבו deutlich zwei Gruppen," Oeming, *Das wahre Israel*, 182.
[57] "Das bedeutet, daß die in der Liste V.3ff genannten bewohner Jerusalems nicht die *ersten* Bewohner sind," Oeming, *Das wahre Israel*, 182.
[58] Selman, *1 Chronicles*, 126.
[59] Oeming, *Das wahre Israel*, 210, and my Figure 12.1.

9:1b), which as 1 Chr 1 indicates is the equivalent of the barrenness of life for The world before Israel. They are then allowed to return to their land, that is, the former land of Israel/Judah, where they dwell in their possessions and towns (1 Chr 9:2). Following that, there is a move to Jerusalem (1 Chr 9:3), where the numbers increase. Finally, there is the focus upon the temple and its personnel (1 Chr 9:10–34).

While the idea that 1 Chr 9:2 refers not to the return from exile but to the original settlement of the land may be initially attractive, several observations have made this untenable. The position of 1 Chr 9:2 within the context of exile suggests a resettlement, while "the earlier/former dwellers" is to be taken as referring to a time prior to the Chronicler, but does not require so ancient a time as the preexilic period, and certainly not the time period of David.

CONCLUDING OBSERVATIONS

The Chronicler concludes his genealogies on a positive note. Often in his genealogies there had been negative portrayals or outcomes, from the barrenness of 1 Chr 1 (which is here contrasted with the fullness of 1 Chr 9),[60] to the various tribal defeats and exiles due to unfaithfulness. The Chronicler does not conclude his genealogies in that way. Although this section itself begins with the negative of exile (1 Chr 9:1b), it concludes with all Israel back in their own possessions in their own land and with Jerusalem settled by all Israel, including the full complement of cultic officials.

The conclusion to the Chronicler's genealogies are hopeful. They speak of the promise of an ongoing possession and occupation of their ancestral properties, of community growth and stability. The conclusion to the genealogies seeks to ensure a place in the land not just for the prominent tribes, but for all who worship Yahweh. It is a call for the acceptance by the majority (Judah, Benjamin and Levi), of the minority, those who profess membership of the community by other genealogical means, but are yet the worshipers of Yahweh. It is also a call to the minority to become full participants in the postexilic community. Finally, it is an invitation to those who have not yet migrated to Yehud to "go up" to Jerusalem, and to make it the focus of their own cultic devotion.

In this, it must be recognised that the conclusion to the Chronicler's genealogies is the same as the centre. Just as the majority of the content of 1 Chr 9 is taken up with the cultic officials and their duties, so also the focus of the genealogies as a whole is the centrality of the cult and its officials in the performance

---

[60] On the contrasts that exist between 1 Chr 1 and 1 Chr 9, see "The Barrenness of 1 Chronicles 1," in Chapter 12, above.

of their duties. In this way, in both the middle and the end, the Chronicler emphasises the necessity for the centrality of the cult, not only for the nation as a whole as the twelve tribes, but also for their own present reality as a small province within the greater empire of Persia.

CHAPTER 14
CONCLUSION

INTRODUCTION

In the introductory chapter it was proposed that 1 Chr 1–9 is a deliberately constructed chiasm which, through the placing of the main idea, the thesis, or the turning point at its centre, was presenting the meaning of both the chiastically structured genealogical section as well as the Chronicler's work as a whole.

Having investigated each of the individual sections, it is now necessary to draw these observations together to determine if the thesis has been established, and, if so, what are the implications for further study not only of the Chronicler's genealogies, but of the work as a whole.

THE CHIASTIC STRUCTURE OF 1 CHRONICLES 1–9

Welch has suggested that a true chiasm requires three separate elements: balance, inversion, and intensification.[1] In chapter 1 it was proposed that the Chronicler's genealogies largely exhibit these phenomena. Having investigated the genealogies in detail, it is necessary to revisit this assertion to see if it has, in fact, been established.

BALANCE

A chiastic structure is "in balance," when the two halves contain the same, or nearly the same, number of elements and when the two halves, and perhaps the various elements within those halves, are similar in the quantity of their content. This investigation of the proposed chiastic structure has established that the two halves of the Chronicler's genealogies are balanced. Both halves contain the same number of elements, and each of these elements (with the exception of C // C^1), is reasonably similar in the quantity of its content. Thus, B // B^1 represent the shortest elements of the genealogy, while the longer sections are also balanced against one another in terms of the quantity of material they contain. As

---

[1] Welch, "Introduction," 9–10.

mentioned, only levels C // C¹ are not balanced against one another, an imbalance which results in the first half of the Chronicler's genealogies being somewhat longer than the second half.

This, however, should not negate the overall conclusion that the Chronicler's genealogies are "balanced" and are thus presented chiastically. Levels C // C¹ are, in fact, the only levels in the structure that are not balanced, and on the basis of the investigation of 1 Chr 2:3–4:23 in Chapter 8, it can be concluded that the additional length of level C was the result of the particular theological purpose of the Chronicler in that section. He sought to contrast the way of the monarchy, which led to exile, to the way of Jabez, which led to honour, answered prayer, and the expansion of land. In the Chronicler's theology, seeking Yahweh, as exemplified in the prayer of Jabez, is the solution to the problem of unfaithfulness within the community.

INVERSION

The second requirement for the identification of a text as chiastic is that it exhibit "inversion," or "the appearance of the same or related terms in the two halves, however in reverse order." While it is true to say that the same "terms" were not always identified in the parallel sections, it would also be true that the same ideas or themes were located within the parallel levels. Thus, A // A¹ dealt with those persons who came either before Israel existed, or after they returned from exile. B // B¹, dealt with the descendants of Israel, albeit in different contexts. C // C¹ were complementary through their mention of Israelite kings, as well as the focus on prayer and Jerusalem. Levels D // D¹ through mention of various tribes either engaged in, or prepared for, warfare. Levels E // E¹ both dwelt with the Levites, while levels F // F¹ focussed on the cultic officials, either their duties or their identity.

It is further observed that these parallel themes were presented in an inverted order, with the first named in the first half, being the last named in the second half. There was also a very clear pivot point where the presence of the inversion would be recognised, and the central theme, that of the identity and duties of the cultic personnel, would also be recognised. All data prior to this pivot point is repeated in some form in inverse order after this pivot point.

INTENSIFICATION

The final element that is required to identify a text as chiastic is *intensification*, or the idea that words and ideas are not stated once, but are repeated in such a way that the fundamental ideas that the author seeks to relate are reemphasised for the sake of his readers/hearers.

Intensification is related to "inversion." While inversion indicates that there is a reversal of order in the general theme and content of the various levels, intensification indicates that that theme is emphasised and extended in some way.

In the Chronicler's genealogies, intensification occurs in three ways. First, the thought contained in the second section essentially repeats and/or extends the same idea(s) contained in the first. Thus B // B^1 both refer to "Israel." Level B refers specifically to the person, while B^1 refers to "all Israel," to those who could be considered to have descended from Israel. While level B refers to Israel's descendants when it lists the twelve sons of Israel, Level B^1 intensifies B by expanding beyond the twelve sons to all the descendants. Level D refers to the wars and warriors of various tribes, including both their victories and defeats. Level D^1 extends this by not only recording the warriors of certain tribes, but also placing towards the centre of these tribes the greatest pre-monarchic military leader, Joshua. Further, while level D indicates that there had been unfaithfulness leading to exile, D^1 extends the discussion on the results of unfaithfulness by indicating that mourning before Yahweh over past unfaithfulness results in restoration, with children being born and towns being built. In this way, both levels B^1 and D^1 repeat and/or extend what was found in levels B and D.

Levels C // C^1 also use repetition and extension in their presentation. Both of these sections mention the families of the royal lines of David and Saul, including the lines of both until long after the end of the Davidic and Saulide dynasties. Both levels also present alternatives to monarchy as the means of enabling the ongoing survival of the community. Level C proposes the way of Jabez, who focussed upon prayer to Yahweh, while level C^1 identifies the focus on dwelling in Jerusalem as being paramount.

The second means of intensification which was observed in the Chronicler's genealogies is the use of expansion. This is observed not through repeated data, but simply more data related to the same general issue. In level E, the descendants of Levi are recorded, while in level E^1 the lands of the descendants of Levi are recorded. A similar example is found in F // F^1. In level F cultic duties are indicated, with the declaration that certain duties were the right of the "sons of Aaron," while in level F^1 the identity of these "sons of Aaron" are indicated. In both of these examples, the terms and themes of the first section are not simply repeated in the second, but new data is provided. It must be noted that data is repeated on occasion. Level E has lists of the primary sons of Levi, which are repeated in level E^1. Likewise, the "sons of Aaron" are mentioned in both F // F^1. What is important is that the second section is not a mere repetition of the themes, but an expansion of them.

The third means of intensification is through the provision of contrasts. This was observed in A // A^1. Level A presented the barrenness of a society devoid of the Yahwistic cult. Level A^1 contrasts this by presenting the fullness of the Chronicler's postexilic society with its full complement of cultic officials, as well as the presence of the full complement of the clans of both Judah and Benjamin. This contrast is further emphasised through the mention of the presence of both Ephraim and Manasseh, tribes which had once departed from the true worship of Yahweh, but who were now reincorporated into the postexilic cultic community.

OBSERVATION

As the preceding overview indicates, each of the necessary criteria indicated by Welch for the identification of a chiasm is present within the Chronicler's genealogies. This can only lead to the conclusion that the proposed thesis is correct, and that the Chronicler's genealogies are presented chiastically.

IMPLICATIONS FOR FUTURE RESEARCH

The implications of this finding are far reaching. If, as has been observed, the genealogies are in fact a chiasm, this negates the possibility that the genealogies are a haphazard conglomeration of unrelated materials which have been placed piecemeal into Chronicles by various editors over a long period of time. On the contrary, if the genealogies are a chiasm, this demands that they be the intentional work of an author who was working to an identifiable purpose and goal. A chiasm of this magnitude could not have been produced accidentally, but would require deliberate thought and structuring to make the chiasm possible. Although it does not exclude the possibility of minor additions to, or alterations of, the text of the genealogies, the recognition of the chiastic structure of the genealogies should end the debate regarding the proposed wholesale additions to and alterations of the text of the genealogies which was so dominant throughout the twentieth century.

The recognition of the chiastic structure of the genealogies does not resolve the debate regarding the unity of the text of Chronicles. While the relationship between the genealogies and the narrative of Chronicles was not the primary focus of this work, such a relationship could be established through a fuller comparison of the themes and outlook of the genealogies with the remainder of the work. This investigation has been undertaken to a limited extent, where required to understand the genealogies themselves, and this limited investigation does give some indication of a consistency of theme and outlook between the genealogies and the narrative, a consistency which points to the unity of the genealogical section with the narrative of Chronicles, and thus, to the strong probability that the Chronicler is the author of the genealogical section.

However, while a consistency of theme and outlook may point to a common author, it may also suggest a common "school." There is also the possibility that the "Genealogist" was himself the final redactor of Chronicles who shaped the entire work: including material consistent with his position; deleting material inconsistent with that position; while rearranging other material to produce Chronicles as it now stands.[2] If this is the case, then the "Genealogist" could rightly be termed the author of the work, and bear the name "Chronicler."

If it were concluded that the "Genealogist" is not the author of Chronicles, but merely added the genealogies to a pre-existent work, then the similarities and contrasts upon which that conclusion is reached would form the basis for ongoing investigation into the varying theologies and ideologies which were present in Yehud during the late Persian and early Greek period. If, however, it were concluded that the "Genealogist" is the author of Chronicles, then this presents further implications and avenues for investigation.

THE PRIORITY OF THE CULT

The chiastic structure of 1 Chr 1–9 pivots on 1 Chr 6:33–38 [6:48–53]. This section emphasises on the one hand the joint role in the cult of all the Levites, and on the other, the priority of the sons of Aaron within the cult as the only persons authorised to offer burnt offerings and to make atonement.

This chiastic structuring indicates that the theme of Chronicles, if considered to be a unified text, is the cult as a whole. The Chronicler's purpose is to ensure that the proper cultic officials are offering the proper cultic offerings in the proper cultic place, and that the people are supporting the cult so as to maintain its proper functioning. This centrality of the cult within Chronicles may require that all else be made subservient to that theme. The actions of kings, prophets, soldiers, and people which are recorded within Chronicles must be investigated as to how those actions support or undermine the place of the cult and the cultic officials, with the appropriate warning in relation to the Chronicler's own day and community.

Second, although it is common to speak about a "pro-Levitic" or a "pro-priestly" redaction of Chronicles, these paradigms may be inappropriate in light of the pro-cultic viewpoint of the Chronicler. The genealogies indicate that it is the cult that is central to the ongoing life of the nation. They also indicate that all of the Levites are essential to the proper functioning of the cult. While the genealogies give a place of priority to the sons of Aaron in respect to the task that they perform, the genealogies also make plain that all the Levites, of whom the sons of Aaron are only a part, are vital to the functioning of the cult. The implication of this is that if all of the Levites are not present, then the cult does not function properly, an observation born out in the remainder of the work.

---

[2] It is, of course, obvious that Chronicles is such an editing and rearrangement of Samuel/Kings. What is meant here is the possibility that the Chronicler possessed an intermediate text, or an earlier edition of "Chronicles," which he then shaped into the text which now exists.

It is therefore unnecessary to suggest that a later editor(s) sought to exalt or denigrate the Levites or the priests. It is also equally unnecessary to suggest that supporters of individual Levitical groups (i.e. gatekeepers or cultic musicians), sought to elevate their particular group within the community. The genealogies indicate that each group was present in the Chronicler's time, and each group had a vital and necessary task within the postexilic temple community, while the absence of any one group would have resulted in the collapse of the whole, with devastating results for the community at large.

COMMUNITY SUPPORT FOR THE CULT

That the Chronicler felt compelled to write a book which promoted the necessity of community support for the cult strongly suggests that this had become an issue within the Chronicler's community. Other postexilic literature indicates that, at times, community support for the cult had waned, with the result that the cultic officials were not supported materially. This led some to abandon their cultic duties so as to provide for themselves (Neh 13:10-13; Mal 3:6-12). While Chronicles lays no specific charges in this regard, there would be no reason to either encourage faithfulness to the cult or to portray the consequences of unfaithfulness to the cult, if these issues or problems were not making an impact of some kind within the Chronicler's community.

This is not to say that the issue had reached the stage presented in Neh 13:10 where both Levites and cultic musicians had abandoned their duties to "go back to their own fields." It does suggest that Chronicles was written because, at a minimum, the tendency to abandonment of the cult was starting to become an issue which had gained the notice of those in power. It is therefore possible that Chronicles was a type of pre-emptive action by those in authority to arrest these early signs of cultic abandonment or neglect.

In many respects the "pastoral" manner in which Chronicles addresses this issue is suggestive that such abandonment was only in the early stages. The narrative contains positive portrayals of faithfulness to the cult as well as warnings which display the consequences of abandonment of the cult. Unlike the Deuteronomistic History, however, it does not portray irreversible condemnation because of these actions, but extends an invitation to return to the cult of Yahweh with the assurance that forgiveness, acceptance, and blessing awaited those who did return. Chronicles gives the impression of a stern, yet early warning to those who were wavering in their loyalty to Yahweh. It is not, however, a Deuteronomistic pronouncement of judgment upon those who had already abandoned Yahweh.

These warnings, however, also have an applicability to a readership outside of postexilic Yehud. It was stated previously that 2 Chr 36:23 may be an invitation to those who remained in Babylon and the other provinces of Persia to migrate to Jerusalem and make its temple the central focus of their cultic observance. If this is correct, it suggests that by remaining outside the land, these people are guilty of ignoring the cult and are potentially bringing further judgment upon Jerusalem. The Chronicler then is encouraging these people to return to Jerusalem from their exile, just as both Hezekiah and Josiah encouraged the remnant of the northern tribes to return to the temple cult in Jerusalem.

THE DAVIDIC KINGS

If the primary theme of the genealogies, and therefore of the work as a whole, is the promotion of the cult, its rites, and officials, then it necessarily follows that the Davidic kings are not the primary theme of the work. Without doubt, the Chronicler holds the Davidic kings, particularly David, Solomon, and Hezekiah, in high esteem, and presents them as examples of faithfulness to Yahweh to be emulated. This is not, however, an indication that the Chronicler, or his community, either anticipated or even wanted a return to an indigenous king in general, or to a Davidic king in particular. It is fair to say that much study of Chronicles has sought to maintain the ongoing importance of the Davidic monarchy. This is, no doubt, due in part to the pronouncements contained in the Deuteronomistic History and some of the prophets on this matter. It may also reflect the impact of messianism, and, in the Christian tradition, the impact of the New Testament's teaching on Jesus as the son of David (Matt 9:27; 15:22; 20:30-31; 21:9, 15), who takes up the throne of David (Luke 1:32).

The genealogies themselves, however, indicate that David, although important for his contribution to the cultic life of Israel, and having an example of cultic devotion which should be emulated, is of no greater importance for the Chronicler's community than Saul. Neither is the focus of the genealogies, for both are located on lower, supporting, genealogical levels. The lines of both ended, and, as the narrative clearly indicates, the royal authority of both was given to another.

This is not to deny the importance of both persons to Yehud's past. This is not, however, the same as suggesting that either of these lines had a significance to Yehud's present.

Chronicles as a whole indicates that the kings are presented primarily in their relationship to, and their actions for or against the cult, the cultic place, and the cultic officials. It is this that marks the importance of the kings for the Chronicler's community, and nothing more. The kings are presented in Chronicles as examples of contemporary responses to the cult, portray warnings against neglecting the cult, and encouragements for the full support of the cult.

THE PLACE OF THE PERSIAN KINGS IN THE CHRONICLER'S YEHUD

The genealogies portray both the Davidic and Saulide kings, important as they may have been, as having no ongoing relevance and importance. What is central is the cult. The narrative, however, extends this and presents some intriguing avenues for investigation.

The narrative indicates that as a result of Saul's unfaithfulness, his kingdom was given to David (1 Chr 10:13–14). Upon his accession to the throne, David brought the ark to Jerusalem, provided a tent for it, as well as providing and organising cultic officials. Further, although forbidden to personally build the temple, he made provisions for its construction, including materials, labour and detailed plans. Chronicles also indicates that as a result of the unfaithfulness of the Davidic kings the kingdom was given to Cyrus (2 Chr 36:22–23). Upon his accession to the throne, Cyrus gives an order for a new temple to be built.

The parallel between these presentations cannot be accidental. It is clear that the Chronicler is portraying the Persian kings as the rightful successors to the Davidic kings, just as David was the rightful successor to Saul. The Persian kings received the kingdom from Yahweh, and they have authorised the building of the second temple, just as David received the kingdom and proceeded to prepare for the building of the first temple.

This observation begs the question of what the Chronicler felt was the required response and attitude of the people toward the Persian kings. If rebellion against, or rejection of, the Davidic kings was seen as rebellion against Yahweh (2 Chr 13:8), what would rebellion against or rejection of the Persian kings be, if not the same thing?

This also raises the question as to the historical context in which these things were written. Why were these things written? Was there rebellion against Persia in Yehud? Or was Yehud being influenced in a particular way because of the political troubles emanating from Greece and Egypt in the mid- to late-fourth century B.C.E.? If the Chronicler was advocating loyalty to Persia, does this indicate that there were factions within the society which were advocating rebellion, or perhaps a pro-Egyptian or pro-Greek policy? Were there agents of these countries present in Yehud who were fomenting rebellion?

Further, what does this imply as to the date of writing? If the Chronicler was encouraging loyalty to Persia, does this not suggest that the Persian empire still existed, at least in some form, and therefore a date of composition prior to the death of Darius III in 330 B.C.E. is required.

It is equally possible that a date of composition prior to the surrender of Jerusalem to Alexander's army several years earlier is in view. It is clear from the manner in which Chronicles treats Saul and David that the end of a dynasty marks Yahweh's removal of royal power from one line, and its transference to another. If Persia had already fallen to Alexander, it would be unlikely that loyalty to the Persian kings would be promoted. Instead, as with David and later with Cyrus, loyalty to the new monarchy would be encouraged, for it would be seen to be established by Yahweh. If loyalty to the Persian kings is being promoted, then this suggests that Persia had not yet fallen. Consequently, a date prior to 330 B.C.E. would be in view for the production of Chronicles.

ALL ISRAEL

Finally, the Chronicler's genealogies raise important questions in relation to the status of non Judahites/Benjaminites within the post exilic community. This is true not only from the presence of foreigners in the Judahite genealogy itself, but also the inclusion of those tribes which made up "Israel," the traditional Deuteronomistic enemy of Judah. Were there those who still claimed descent from these groups who sought to attach themselves to the postexilic temple community. Was this, in fact, an attempt to include worshippers of Yahweh from Samaria who, in some way, professed to be the religious, if not the physical, descendants of Israel (2 Kgs 17:24–41; Ezra 4:2)? This is suggested not only in the genealogies (1 Chr 9:3), but also in the narrative of Chronicles (2 Chr 30:1, 10, 18; 31:1; 34:9). Who was this "Ephraim and Manasseh" who were part of the postexilic community if not those who worshipped Yahweh in the territory once known by that name. And if they worshipped Yahweh in that territory, does not that make them part of "all Israel," and therefore entitled to enter into the community, and worship Yahweh in the temple?

FINAL COMMENTS

This study was begun with a simple question in mind: "why would anyone in their right mind begin a book with nine chapters of names?" Having addressed that one question has opened up many more. At the same time, it has answered the seemingly complicated one of "why the genealogies." For the Chronicler, the answer would have been far simpler. This study has made clear that the purpose of the genealogies, indeed the purpose of the book of Chronicles as a whole, is to encourage and support the work of the proper cultic officials, performing the proper cultic duties, in the proper cultic place.

BIBLIOGRAPHY

Abba, Raymond. "Priests and Levites in Ezekiel." *Vetus Testamentum* 28 (1978): 1–9.
Ackroyd, Peter R. "Chronicles-Ezra-Nehemiah: The Concept of Unity." Pages 344–359 in *The Chronicler in His Age*. Journal for the Study of the Old Testament Supplement 101. Sheffield: Sheffield Academic Press, 1991.
Adeyemo, Tokunboh, ed. *Africa Bible Commentary*. Nairobi: WordAlive Publishers, 2006.
Allen, Leslie C. *1, 2 Chronicles*, The Communicator's Commentary 10. Waco: Word, 1987.
Andersen, Francis I. and David Noel Freedman. *Hosea*, The Anchor Bible 24. Garden City: Doubleday, 1980.
Anderson, Arnold A. *2 Samuel*, Word Biblical Commentary 11. Dallas: Word, 1989.
Andriolo, Karin R. "A Structural Analysis of Genealogy and Worldview in the Old Testament." *American Anthropologist* 75 (1973): 1657–1669.
Ashley, Timothy R. *The Book of Numbers*, The New International Commentary on the Old Testament. Grand Rapids: Eerdmans, 1993.
Auld, A. Graeme. "The Cities in Joshua 21: The Contribution of Textual Criticism." *Textus* XV (1990): 141–152.
———. "Cities of Refuge in Israelite Tradition." *Journal for the Study of the Old Testament* 10 (1978): 26–40.
———. *Joshua Retold: Synoptic Perspectives*. Edinburgh: T&T Clark, 1998.
———. *Kings Without Privilege: David and Moses in the Story of the Bible's Kings*. Edinburgh: T&T Clark, 1994.
———. "The 'Levitical Cities': Texts and History." *Zeitschrift für die alttestamentliche Wissenschaft* 91 (1979): 194–206.
———. "Textual and Literary Studies in the Book of Joshua." *Zeitschrift für die alttestamentliche Wissenschaft* 90 (1978): 412–417.
Averbeck, Richard E. "כפר." Pages 689–710 in *New International Dictionary of Old Testament Theology and Exegesis, Volume 2*. Edited by Willem A. VanGemeren. Grand Rapids: Zondervan, 1997.
———. "ברר." Pages 772–774 in *New International Dictionary of Old Testament Theology and Exegesis, Volume 1*. Edited by Willem A. VanGemeren. Grand Rapids: Zondervan, 1997.
Baker, David W. "Further Examples of the *Waw Explicativum*." *Vetus Testamentum* 30 (1980): 129–136.
Barrick, W. Boyd. "Genealogical Notes on the 'House of David' and the 'House of Zadok'." *Journal for the Study of the Old Testament* 96 (2001): 29–58.

Bartlett, J. R. "The Edomite King-List of Genesis XXXVI. 31–39 and 1 Chron I. 43–50." *Journal of Theological Studies* 16 (1965): 301–314.

Bartusch, Mark W. *Understanding Dan: An Exegetical Study of a Biblical City, Tribe and Ancestor*, Journal for the Study of the Old Testament Supplement 379. London: Sheffield Academic Press, 2003.

Batten, Loring W. *A Critical and Exegetical Commentary on The Books of Ezra and Nehemiah*, The International Critical Commentary. Edinburgh: T&T Clark, 1913.

Begg, Christopher. "'Seeking Yahweh' and the Purpose of Chronicles." *Louvain Studies* 9 (1982): 128–141.

Ben Zvi, Ehud. "The List of the Levitical Cities." *Journal for the Study of the Old Testament* 54 (1992): 77–106.

———. "Observations on Ancient Modes of Reading of Chronicles and Their Implications, with an Illustration of Their Explanatory Power for the Study of the Account of Amaziah (2 Chronicles 25)." Pages 44–77 in *History, Literature and Theology in the Book of Chronicles*. London: Equinox, 2006.

Bendavid, Abba. *Parallels in the Bible*. Jerusalem: Carta, 1972.

Blenkinsopp, Joseph. *Ezra-Nehemiah*, Old Testament Library. Philadelphia: Westminster/John Knox Press, 1988.

Block, Daniel I. *The Book of Ezekiel Chapters 25–48*, The New International Commentary on the Old Testament. Grand Rapids: Eerdmans, 1998.

Boda, M. J. "Chiasmus in Ubiquity: Symmetrical Mirages in Nehemiah 9." *Journal for the Study of the Old Testament* 71 (1996): 55–70.

Boling, Robert G. "Levitical Cities: Archaeology and Texts." Pages 23–32 in *Biblical and Related Studies Presented to Samuel Iwry*. Edited by Ann Kort and Scott Morschauser. Winona Lake: Eisenbrauns, 1985.

Botterweck, G. Johannes and Helmer Ringgren. *Theological Dictionary of the Old Testament*. Translated by John T. Willis. Vol. 1. Grand Rapids: Eerdmans, 1974.

———. *Theological Dictionary of the Old Testament*. Translated by David E. Green. Vol. 4. Grand Rapids: Eerdmans, 1980.

Braun, Roddy L. *1 Chronicles*, Word Biblical Commentary 14. Waco: Word, 1986.

———. "A Reconsideration of the Chronicler's Attitude toward the North." *Journal of Biblical Literature* 96 (1977): 59–62.

———. "Solomon, the Chosen Temple Builder: The Significance of 1 Chronicles 22, 28, and 29 for the Theology of Chronicles." *Journal of Biblical Literature* 95 (1976): 581–590.

———. "Solomonic Apologetic in Chronicles." *Journal of Biblical Literature* 92 (1973): 503–516.

Budd, Philip J. *Numbers*, Word Biblical Commentary 4. Waco: Word, 1984.

Butler, Trent C. *Joshua*, Word Biblical Commentary 7. Waco: Word, 1983.

Campbell, Antony F. and Mark A. O'Brien. *Sources of the Pentateuch: Texts, Introductions, Annotations*. Minneapolis: Fortress Press, 1993.

Carter, Charles E. *The Emergence of Yehud in the Persian Period: A Social and Demographic Study*, Journal for the Study of the Old Testament Supplement 294. Sheffield: Sheffield Academic Press, 1999.

Chapell, Bryan. *Christ-Centered Preaching: Redeeming the Expository Sermon*. Grand Rapids: Baker Books, 1994.

Clines, David J. A. *Ezra, Nehemiah, Esther*, The New Century Bible Commentary. Grand Rapids: Eerdmans, 1984.

———. ed. *The Dictionary of Classical Hebrew*. Vol. 1 Sheffield: Sheffield Academic Press, 1993.

Corduan, Winfried. *I & II Chronicles*, Holman Old Testament Commentary 8. Nashville: Holman Reference, 2004.

Cross, Frank M. "Reuben, First-Born of Jacob." *Zeitschrift für die alttestamentliche Wissenschaft* 100 (sup; 1988): 46–65.

———. *Canaanite Myth and Hebrew Epic: Essays in the History of the Religion of Israel*. Cambridge: Harvard University Press, 1973.

———. "A Reconstruction of the Judean Restoration." *Journal of Biblical Literature* 94 (1975): 4–18.

Curtis, Edward L. and Albert A. Madsen. *A Critical and Exegetical Commentary on the Books of Chronicles*, The International Critical Commentary. Edinburgh: T&T Clark, 1910.

de Vaux, Roland. *Ancient Israel: Its Life and Institutions*. Translated by John McHugh. London: Darton, Longman & Todd, 1961.

De Vries, Simon J. *1 and 2 Chronicles*, The Forms of the Old Testament Literature 11. Grand Rapids: Eerdmans, 1989.

———. *1 Kings*, Word Biblical Commentary 12. Waco: Word, 1985.

———. "Moses and David as Cult Founders in Chronicles." *Journal of Biblical Literature* 107 (1988): 619–639.

Dillard, Raymond B. "The Chronicler's Solomon." *Westminster Theological Journal* 43 (1981): 289–300.

———. "The Literary Structure of the Chronicler's Solomon Narrative." *Journal for the Study of the Old Testament* 30 (1984): 85–93.

———. "Reward and Punishment in Chronicles: The Theology of Immediate Retribution." *Westminster Theological Journal* 46 (1984): 164–172.

Driver, S. R. *A Critical and Exegetical Commentary on Deuteronomy*, The International Critical Commentary. Edinburgh: T&T Clark, 1902.

———. *An Introduction to the Literature of the Old Testament*, The International Theological Library. Edinburgh: T&T Clark, 1892.

Duke, Rodney K. *The Persuasive Appeal of the Chronicler: A Rhetorical Analysis*, Journal for the Study of the Old Testament Supplement 88. Sheffield: Almond Press, 1990.

———. "Punishment or Restoration? Another Look at the Levites of Ezekiel 44.6–16." *Journal for the Study of the Old Testament* 40 (1988): 61–81.

Durham, John I. *Exodus*, Word Biblical Commentary 3. Waco: Word, 1987.
Dyck, Jonathan E. *The Theocratic Ideology of the Chronicler*, Biblical Interpretation Series 33. Leiden: Brill, 1998.
Endres, John C., William. R. Millar, and John Barclay Burns. *Chronicles and Its Synoptic Parallels in Samuel, Kings, and Related Biblical Texts*. Collegeville: The Liturgical Press, 1998.
Fensham, F. Charles. *The Books of Ezra and Nehemiah*, The New International Commentary on the Old Testament. Grand Rapids: Eerdmans, 1982.
Freedman, David N. "The Chronicler's Purpose." *Catholic Biblical Quarterly* 23 (1961): 436–442.
Fried, Lisbeth S. *The Priest and the Great King: Temple-Palace Relations in the Persian Empire*, Biblical and Judaic Studies 10. Winona Lake: Eisenbrauns, 2004.
Friedman, Richard Elliott. *Who Wrote the Bible?* New York: HarperSanFrancisco, 1997.
Galil, Gerson. "The Chronicler's Genealogy of Ephraim." *Biblische Notizen* 56 (1991): 11–14.
Geoghegan, Jeffrey C. ""Until This Day" and the Preexilic Redaction of the Deuteronomistic History." *Journal of Biblical Literature* 122 (2003): 201–227.
Gese, Hartmut. "Zur Geschichte der Kultsänger am zweiten Tempel." Pages 147–158 in *Vom Sinai zum Zion: Alttestamentliche Beiträge zur biblischen Theologie*. Beiträge zur evangelischen Theologie 64. München: Chr. Kaiser, 1974.
Goettsberger, Johann. *Die Bücher der Chronik oder Paralipomenon*, Die Heilige Schrift des Alten Testamentes. Bonn: Peter Hanstein, 1939.
Grabbe, Lester L. "Triumph of the Pious or Failure of the Xenophobes? The Ezra-Nehemiah Reforms and their *Nachgeschichte*." Pages 50–65 in *Jewish Local Patriotism and Self-Identification in the Graeco-Roman Period*. Edited by Siân Jones and Sarah Pearce. Journal for the Study of the Pseudepigrapha Supplement 31. Sheffield: Sheffield Academic Press, 1998.
———. ed. *Leading Captivity Captive: 'The Exile' as History and Ideology*. Journal for the Study of the Old Testament Supplement 278. Sheffield: Sheffield Academic Press, 1998.
Graham, M. Patrick. "Aspects of the Structure and Rhetoric of 2 Chronicles 25." Pages 78–89 in *History and Interpretation: Essays in Honour of John H. Hayes*. Edited by M. Patrick Graham, William P. Brown, and Jeffrey K. Kuan. Journal for the Study of the Old Testament Supplement 173. Sheffield: Sheffield Academic Press, 1993.
———. *The Utilization of 1 and 2 Chronicles in the Reconstruction of Israelite History in the Nineteenth Century*, Society of Biblical Literature Dissertation Series 116. Atlanta: Scholars Press, 1990.
Gray, George Buchanan. *A Critical and Exegetical Commentary on Numbers*, The International Critical Commentary. Edinburgh: T&T Clark, 1903.
Hallo, William W. and K. Lawson Younger. *The Context of Scripture Volume 2: Monumental Inscriptions from the Biblical World*. Leiden: Brill, 2003.

Halpern, Baruch. *David's Secret Demons: Messiah, Murderer, Traitor, King*. Grand Rapids: Eerdmans, 2001.
Haran, Menahem. "Studies in the Account of the Levitical Cities: I. Preliminary Considerations." *Journal of Biblical Literature* 80 (1961): 45–54.
———. "Studies in the Account of the Levitical Cities: II. Utopia and Historical Reality." *Journal of Biblical Literature* 80 (1961): 156–165.
———. *Temples and Temple-Service in Ancient Israel: An Inquiry into Biblical Cult Phenomena and the Historical Setting of the Priestly School*. Winona Lake: Eisenbrauns, 1985.
Hartman, Thomas C. "Some Thoughts on the Sumerian King List and Genesis 5 and 11B." *Journal of Biblical Literature* 91 (1972): 25–32.
Hauer, Christian E. "David and the Levites." *Journal for the Study of the Old Testament* 23 (1982): 33–54.
———. "Who Was Zadok?" *Journal of Biblical Literature* 82 (1963): 89–94.
Heard, R. Christopher. *Echoes of Genesis in 1 Chronicles 4:9–10: An Intertextual and Contextual Reading of Jabez's Prayer* 2002 [cited August 21, 2006]. Available from www.purl.org/jhs.
Heath, Elaine. "Jabez: A Man Named Pain: An Integrative Hermeneutical Exercise." *Ashland Theological Journal* 33 (2001): 7–16.
Helman, A. "'Even the Dogs in the Street Bark in Hebrew': National Ideology and Everyday Culture in Tel-Aviv." *Jewish Quarterly Review* 92 (2002): 359–382.
Hertzberg, H. W. *I & II Samuel*. Translated by John Bowden, Old Testament Library. London: SCM Press, 1964.
Hess, Richard S. *Joshua*, Tyndale Old Testament Commentary. Leicester: Inter-Varsity Press, 1996.
Hill, Andrew E. *1 & 2 Chronicles*, The NIV Application Commentary. Grand Rapids: Zondervan, 2003.
———. "Patchwork Poetry or Reasoned Verse? Connective Structure in 1 Chronicles XVI." *Vetus Testamentum* 33 (1983): 97–100.
Hill, Andrew E. and John H. Walton. *A Survey of the Old Testament*. 2d ed. Grand Rapids: Zondervan, 2000.
Hoffmann, Rudolt-E. "Eine Parallele zur Rahmenerzählung des Buches Hiob in I Chr 7:20–29." *Zeitschrift für die alttestamentliche Wissenschaft* 92 (1980): 120–132.
Hogg, Hope W. "The Genealogy of Benjamin: A Criticism of 1 Chronicles VIII." *Jewish Quarterly Review* 11 (1898): 102–114.
Hurowitz, Victor (Avigdor). *I Have Built You an Exalted House: Temple Building in the Bible in Light of Mesopotamian and Northwest Semitic Writings*, Journal for the Study of the Old Testament Supplement 115. Sheffield: Sheffield Academic Press, 1992.
Janzen, David. "Politics, Settlement, and Temple Community in Persian-Period Yehud." *Catholic Biblical Quarterly* 64 (2002): 490–510.

Japhet, Sara. "Conquest and Settlement in Chronicles." *Journal of Biblical Literature* 98 (1979): 205–218.

———. *I & II Chronicles*, Old Testament Library. Louisville: Westminster/John Knox Press, 1993.

———. *The Ideology of the Book of Chronicles and Its Place in Biblical Thought*. 2nd revised ed, Beiträge zur Erforschung des Alten Testaments und des antiken Judentums 9. Frankfurt am Main: Verlag Peter Lang, 1997.

———. "The Supposed Common Authorship of Chronicles and Ezra-Nehemiah Investigated Anew." *Vetus Testamentum* 18 (1968): 330–371.

———. "The Relationship between Chronicles and Ezra-Nehemiah." Pages 298–313 in *Congress Volume: Leuven 1989*. Edited by J. A. Emerton. Leiden: Brill, 1991.

Jarick, John. *1 Chronicles*, Readings: A New Biblical Commentary. London: Sheffield Academic Press, 2002.

Johnson, Marshall D. *The Purpose of the Biblical Genealogies with Special Reference to the Setting of the Genealogies of Jesus*. Second ed. Eugene: Wipf and Stock, 2002.

Johnstone, William. *1 and 2 Chronicles Volume 1: 1 Chronicles 1–2 Chronicles 9: Israel's Place Among the Nations*, Journal for the Study of the Old Testament Supplement 253. Sheffield: Sheffield Academic Press, 1997.

———. *Chronicles and Exodus: An Analogy and Its Application*, Journal for the Study of the Old Testament Supplement 275. Sheffield: Sheffield Academic Press, 1998.

———. "Guilt and Atonement: The Theme of 1 and 2 Chronicles." Pages 113–140 in *A Word in Season: Essays in Honour of William McKane*. Edited by James D. Martin and Philip R. Davies. Journal for the Study of the Old Testament Supplement 42. Sheffield: JSOT Press, 1986.

Kalimi, Isaac. *An Ancient Israelite Historian: Studies in the Chronicler, His Time, Place and Writing*, Studia Semitica Neerlandica 46. Assen: Konninklijke Van Gorcum, 2005.

———. *The Reshaping of Ancient Israelite History in Chronicles*. Winona Lake: Eisenbrauns, 2005.

Kallai, Zecharia. "The System of Levitic Cities and Cities of Refuge: A Historical-Geographical Study in Biblical Historiography." Pages 23–62 in *Biblical Historiography and Historical Geography: Collection of Studies*. Edited by Beiträge zur Erforschung des Alten Testaments und des antiken Judentums 44. Frankfurt am Main: Peter Lang, 1998.

Kartveit, Magnar. *Motive und Schichten der Landtheologie in I Chronik 1–9*, Coniectanea biblica: Old Testament Series 28. Stockholm: Almqvist & Wiksell International, 1989.

Katzenstein, H. J. "Some Remarks on the Lists of the Chief Priests of the Temple of Solomon." *Journal of Biblical Literature* 81 (1962): 377–389.

Keil, C. F. *The Books of the Chronicles*. Translated by Andrew Harper, Commentary on the Old Testament 3. Grand Rapids: Eerdmans, 1976.

Keil, C. F. and F. Delitzsch. *Joshua*. Translated by James Martin, Commentary on the Old Testament 2. Grand Rapids: Eerdmans, 1976.
Kelly, Brian E. *Retribution and Eschatology in Chronicles*, Journal for the Study of the Old Testament Supplement 211. Sheffield: Sheffield Academic Press, 1996.
Kelly, Paul. "Our Rival Storytellers." *The Weekend Australian*, September 27–28 2003, 27–28.
Kidner, Derek. *Ezra and Nehemiah*, Tyndale Old Testament Commentary. Leicester: Inter-Varsity Press, 1979.
Kiuchi, N. *The Purification Offering in the Priestly Literature: Its Meaning and Function*, Journal for the Study of the Old Testament Supplement 56. Sheffield: JSOT Press, 1987.
Klein, Ralph W. *1 Chronicles*, Hermeneia. Minneapolis: Fortress Press, 2006.
———. "How Many in a Thousand?" Pages 270–282 in *The Chronicler as Historian*. Edited by M. Patrick Graham, Kenneth G. Hoglund, and Steven L. McKenzie. Journal for the Study of the Old Testament Supplement 238. Sheffield: Sheffield Academic Press, 1997.
Knoppers, Gary N. *1 Chronicles 1–9*, The Anchor Bible 12. New York: Doubleday, 2004.
———. *1 Chronicles 10–29*, The Anchor Bible 12A. New York: Doubleday, 2004.
———. "Great Among His Brothers," but Who is He? Heterogeneity in the Composition of Judah 2000 [cited August 21, 2006]. Available from www.purl.org/jhs.
———. "Greek Historiography and the Chronicler's History: A Reexamination." *Journal of Biblical Literature* 122 (2003): 627–650.
———. "Hierodules, Priests, or Janitors? The Levites in Chronicles and the History of the Israelite Priesthood." *Journal of Biblical Literature* 118 (1999): 49–72.
———. "Intermarriage, Social Complexity, and Ethnic Diversity in the Genealogy of Judah." *Journal of Biblical Literature* 120 (2001): 15–30.
———. "Sources, Revisions, and Editions: The Lists of Jerusalem's Residents in MT and LXX Nehemiah 11 and 1 Chronicles 9." *Textus* 20 (2000): 141–168.
———. "Shem, Ham and Japheth: The Universal and the Particular in the Genealogy of Nations." Pages 13–31 in *The Chronicler as Theologian: Essays in Honor of Ralph W. Klein*. Edited by M. Patrick Graham, Steven L. McKenzie, and Gary N. Knoppers. Journal for the Study of the Old Testament Supplement 371. London: T&T Clark International, 2003.
———. "The Relationship of the Priestly Genealogies to the History of the High Priesthood in Jerusalem." Pages 109–133 in *Judah and the Judeans in the Neo-Babylonian Period*. Edited by Oded Lipschits and Joseph Blenkinsopp. Winona Lake: Eisenbrauns, 2003.
Knoppers, Gary N. and Paul B. Harvey. "Omitted and Remaining Matters: On the Names Given to the Book of Chronicles in Antiquity." *Journal of Biblical Literature* 121 (2002): 227–243.
Koch, Klaus. "Ezra and Meremoth: Remarks on the History of the High Priesthood." Pages 105–110 in *Sha'arei Talmon: Studies in the Bible, Qumran, and the*

Ancient Near East Presented to Shemaryahu Talmon. Edited by Michael Fishbane and Emmanuel Tov. Winona Lake: Eisenbrauns, 1992.

Kraft, Charles H. *Christianity in Culture: A Study in Dynamic Biblical Theologizing in Cross-Cultural Perspective*. Maryknoll: Orbis Books, 1979.

Kraus, Hans-Joachim. *Psalms 60–150*. Translated by Hilton C. Oswald, A Continental Commentary. Minneapolis: Fortress Press, 1993.

Laato, Antti. "The Levitical Genealogies in 1 Chronicles 5–6 and the Formation of Levitical Ideology in Post-exilic Judah." *Journal for the Study of the Old Testament* 62 (1994): 72–99.

Labahn, Antje and Ehud Ben Zvi. "Observations on Women in the Genealogies of 1 Chronicles 1–9." *Biblica* 84 (2003): 457–478.

Lemke, Werner E. "The Synoptic Problem in the Chronicler's History." *Harvard Theological Review* 58 (1965): 349–363.

Levine, Baruch A. "The Netinim." *Journal of Biblical Literature* 82 (1963): 207–212.

———. *Numbers 1–20*, The Anchor Bible 4. New York: Doubleday, 1993.

Longman, Tremper. "גדד." Page 821 in *New International Dictionary of Old Testament Theology and Exegesis: Volume 1*. Edited by Willem A. VanGemeren. Grand Rapids: Zondervan, 1997.

Maass, F. "כפר *kpr* pi. to atone." Pages 624–635 in *Theological Lexicon of the Old Testament*. Edited by Ernst Jenni and Claus Westermann. Peabody: Hendrickson, 1997.

Madvig, Donald H. "Joshua." in *The Expositor's Bible Commentary Volume 3*. Edited by Frank E. Gaebelein. Grand Rapids: Zondervan, 1992.

Malamat, Abraham. "King Lists of the Old Babylonian Period and Biblical Genealogies." *Journal of the American Oriental Society* 88 (1968): 163–173.

———. "Tribal Societies: Biblical Genealogies and African Lineage Systems." *Archives Europeennes de Sociologie* 14 (1973): 126–136.

Margolis, Max L., ed. *The Book of Joshua in Greek: Part V: Joshua 19:39–24:33*. Philadelphia: Annenberg Research Institute, 1992.

Marquart, J. "The Genealogies of Benjamin." *Jewish Quarterly Review* 14 (1902): 343–351.

Mauchline, John. *1 and 2 Samuel*, New Century Bible. London: Oliphants, 1971.

Mazar, Benjamin. "The Cities of the Priests and the Levites." Pages 193–205 in *Congress Volume*. Supplements to Vetus Testamentum VII. Leiden: Brill, 1960.

McConville, J. G. *Deuteronomy*, Apollos Old Testament Commentary. Leicester: InterVarsity Press, 2002.

McIver, Robert K. and Marie Carroll. "Experiments to Develop Criteria for Determining the Existence of Written Sources, and Their Potential Implications for the Synoptic Problem." *Journal of Biblical Literature* 121 (2002): 667–687.

McKenzie, Steven L. *1–2 Chronicles*, Abingdon Old Testament Commentaries. Nashville: Abingdon Press, 2004.

Michalowski, Piotr. "History as Charter: Some Observations on the Sumerian King List." Pages 237–248 in *Studies in Literature From the Ancient Near East by Members of the American Oriental Society Dedicated to Samuel Noah Kramer*. Edited by Jack M. Sasson. New Haven: American Oriental Society, 1984.

Millard, Alan R. "Large Numbers in the Assyrian Royal Inscriptions." Pages 213–222 in *Ah, Assyria . . . Studies in Assyrian History and Ancient Near Eastern Historiography Presented to Hayim Tadmor*. Edited by Mordechi Cogan and Israel Eph'al. Jerusalem: Magnes Press, 1991.

Miller, J. Maxwell. "Rehoboam's Cities of Defense and the Levitical City List." Pages 273–286 in *Archaeology and Biblical Interpretation: Essays in Memory of D. Glenn Rose*. Edited by Leo G. Perdue, Lawrence E. Toombs, and Gary L. Johnson. Atlanta: John Knox, 1987.

Myers, Jacob M. *Ezra Nehemiah*, The Anchor Bible 14. Doubleday: Garden City, 1965.

———. *I Chronicles*, The Anchor Bible 12. Garden City: Doubleday, 1965.

———. *II Chronicles*, The Anchor Bible 13. Garden City: Doubleday, 1965.

Na'aman, Nadav. "Sources and Redaction in the Chronicler's Genealogies of Asher and Ephraim." *Journal for the Study of the Old Testament* 49 (1991): 99–111.

Nelson, Richard D. *Joshua*, Old Testament Library. Louisville: John Knox Press, 1997.

Newsome, James D. "Toward a New Understanding of the Chronicler and His Purposes." *Journal of Biblical Literature* 94 (1975): 201–217.

Noth, Martin. *The Chronicler's History*. Translated by H. G. M. Williamson, Journal for the Study of the Old Testament Supplement 50. Sheffield: Sheffield Academic Press, 1987.

———. *The Deuteronomistic History*. Translated by Jane Doull and John Barton, Journal for the Study of the Old Testament Supplement 15. Sheffield: JSOT Press, 1981.

Oeming, Manfred. *Das wahre Israel: die "genealogische Vorhalle" 1 Chronik 1–9*, Beiträge zur Wissenschaft vom Alten (und Neuen) Testament 128. Stuttgart: Kohlhammer, 1990.

Oliver, Anthony. "אבל." Pages 243–248 in *New International Dictionary of Old Testament Theology and Exegesis: Volume 1*. Edited by Willem A. VanGemeren. Grand Rapids: Zondervan, 1997.

Olivier, J. P. J. "סלח." Pages 259–264 in *New International Dictionary of Old Testament Theology and Exegesis Volume 3*. Edited by Willem A. VanGemeren. Grand Rapids: Zondervan, 1997.

Olson, Dan. "What Got the Gatekeepers into Trouble?" *Journal for the Study of the Old Testament* 30 (2005): 223–242.

Olyan, Saul. "Zadok's Origins and the Tribal Politics of David." *Journal of Biblical Literature* 101 (1982): 177–193.

Payne, J. Barton. "1, 2 Chronicles." Pages 301–562 in *The Expositor's Bible Commentary Volume 4*. Edited by Frank E. Gaebelein. Grand Rapids: Zondervan, 1988.

Pechawer, Larry. *The Lost Prayer of Jabez*. Second, revised and expanded, 2002 ed. Joplin: Mireh, 2001.

Poirier, John C. "Memory, Written Sources, and the Synoptic Problem: A Response to Robert K. McIver and Marie Carroll." *Journal of Biblical Literature* 123 (2004): 315–322.

Pratt, Richard L. *1 and 2 Chronicles*, A Mentor Commentary. Fearn, Ross-shire: Christian Focus Publications, 1998.

Radday, Yehuda T. "Chiasmus in Hebrew Biblical Narrative." Pages 50–117 in *Chiasmus in Antiquity*. Edited by John W. Welch. Hildesheim: Gerstenberg Verlag, 1981.

Rendsburg, Gary A. "The Internal Consistency and Historical Reliability of the Biblical Genealogies." *Vetus Testamentum* 40 (1990): 185–206.

Rooke, Deborah W. *Zadok's Heirs: The Role and Development of the High Priesthood in Ancient Israel*, Oxford Theological Monographs. Oxford: Oxford University Press, 2000.

Rothstein, J. Wilhelm and D. Johannes Hänel. *Das erste Buch der Chronik übersetzt und erklärt*. Leipzig: Deichertsche Verlagsbuchhandlung, 1927.

Rudolph, Wilhelm. *Chronikbücher*, Handbuch zum Alten Testament 21. Tübingen: Paul Siebeck, 1955.

———. "Lesefrüchte." *Zeitschrift für die alttestamentliche Wissenschaft* 93 (1981): 291–292.

Sasson, Jack M. "A Genealogical 'Convention' in Biblical Chronography?" *Zeitschrift für die alttestamentliche Wissenschaft* 90 (1978): 171–185.

Selman, Martin J. *1 Chronicles*, Tyndale Old Testament Commentary. Leicester: Inter-Varsity Press, 1994.

———. *2 Chronicles*, Tyndale Old Testament Commentary. Leicester: Inter-Varsity Press, 1994.

Smith, Henry Preserved. *A Critical and Exegetical Commentary on the Books of Samuel*, The International Critical Commentary. Edinburgh: T&T Clark, 1899.

Snyman, Gerrie F. "A Possible World of Text Production for the Genealogy in 1 Chronicles 2.3–4.23." Pages 32–60 in *The Chronicler as Theologian: Essays in Honor of Ralph W. Klein*. Edited by M. Patrick Graham, Steven L. McKenzie, and Gary N. Knoppers. Journal for the Study of the Old Testament Supplement 371. London: T&T Clark International, 2003.

Stinespring, W. F. "Eschatology in Chronicles." *Journal of Biblical Literature* 80 (1961): 209–219.

Sugimoto, Tomotoshi. "The Chronicler's Techniques in Quoting Samuel-Kings." *Annual of the Japanese Biblical Institute* 16 (1990): 30–70.

Suh, Myung Soo. *The Tabernacle in the Narrative History of Israel from the Exodus to the Conquest*, Studies in Biblical Literature 50. New York: Peter Lang, 2003.

Syren, Roger. *The Forsaken First-Born: A Study of a Recurrent Motif in the Patriarchal Narratives*, Journal for the Study of the Old Testament Supplement 133. Sheffield: JSOT Press, 1993.

Talmon, Shemaryahu. "Ezra and Nehemiah (Books and Men)." Pages 317–328 in *The Interpreter's Dictionary of the Bible (Supplementary Volume)*. Edited by George A. Buttrick. Nashville: Abingdon, 1976.
Thompson, J. A. *1, 2 Chronicles*, The New American Commentary 9. Nashville: Broadman & Holman, 1994.
Throntveit, Mark A. "Linguistic Analysis and the Question of Authorship in Chronicles, Ezra and Nehemiah." *Vetus Testamentum* 32 (1982): 201–216.
———. *When Kings Speak: Royal Speech and Royal Prayer in Chronicles*, Society of Biblical Literature Dissertation Series 93. Atlanta: Scholars Press, 1987.
Torrey, Charles C. *Ezra Studies*. New York: KTAV Publishing House, 1970.
Tov, Emmanuel. "The Nature and Background of Harmonizations in Biblical Manuscripts." *Journal for the Study of the Old Testament* 31 (1985): 3–29.
Trotter, James M. "Was the Second Jerusalem Temple a Primarily Persian Project?" *Scandinavian Journal of the Old Testament* 15 (2001): 276–294.
Tuell, Steven S. *First and Second Chronicles*, Interpretation: A Bible Commentary for Teaching and Preaching. Louisville: John Knox Press, 2001.
Van Seters, John. "The Chronicler's Account of Solomon's Temple Building: A Continuity Theme." Pages 283–300 in *The Chronicler as Historian*. Edited by M. Patrick Graham, Kenneth G. Hoglund, and Steven L. McKenzie. Journal for the Study of the Old Testament Supplement 238. Sheffield: Sheffield Academic Press, 1997.
von Rad, Gerhard. *Das Geschichtsbild des chronistischen Werkes*, Beiträgen zur Wissenschaft vom Alten (und Neuen) Testament 3. Stuttgart: Kohlhammer, 1930.
Wakely, Robin. "חיל." Pages 116–126 in *New International Dictionary of Old Testament Theology and Exegesis: Volume 2*. Edited by Willem A. VanGemeren. Grand Rapids: Zondervan, 1997.
———. "גבר." Pages 806–816 in *New International Dictionary of Old Testament Theology and Exegesis: Volume 1*. Edited by Willem A. VanGemeren. Grand Rapids: Zondervan, 1997.
Waltke, Bruce K. and M. O'Connor. *An Introduction to Biblical Hebrew Syntax*. Winona Lake: Eisenbrauns, 1990.
Watson, Wilfred G. E. "Chiastic Patterns in Biblical Hebrew Poetry." Pages 118–168 in *Chiasmus in Antiquity*. Edited by John W. Welch. Hildesheim: Gerstenberg Verlag, 1981.
Watts, James W., ed. *Persia and Torah: The Theory of Imperial Authorization of the Pentateuch*. Society of Biblical Literature Symposium Series 17. Atlanta: Society of Biblical Literature, 2001.
Weanzana, Nupanga. "1 and 2 Chronicles." Pages 467–530 in *Africa Bible Commentary*. Edited by Tokunboh Adeyemo. Nairobi: WordAlive Publishers, 2006.

Weinberg, Joel. *The Citizen-Temple Community*. Translated by David L. Smith-Christopher, Journal for the Study of the Old Testament Supplement 151. Sheffield: Sheffield Academic Press, 1992.
Welch, Adam C. *Post-Exilic Judaism: The Baird Lecture for 1934*. Edinburgh: William Blackwood & Sons, 1935.
———. *The Work of the Chronicler: Its Purpose and Its Date: The Schweich Lectures 1938*. London: Oxford University Press, 1939.
Welch, John W. "Introduction." Pages 9–16 in *Chiasmus in Antiquity*. Edited by John W. Welch. Hildesheim: Gerstenberg Verlag, 1981.
———. ed. *Chiasmus in Antiquity*. Heldesheim: Gerstenberg Verlag, 1981.
Wellhausen, Julius. *Prolegomena to the History of Israel*. Atlanta: Scholars Press, 1994.
Wenham, Gordon J. *The Book of Leviticus*, The New International Commentary on the Old Testament. Grand Rapids: Eerdmans, 1979.
———. *Genesis 1–15*, Word Biblical Commentary 1. Dallas: Word, 1987.
———. *Numbers*, Tyndale Old Testament Commentary. Leicester: Inter-Varsity Press, 1981.
Wenham, J. W. "Large Numbers in the Old Testament." *Tyndale Bulletin* 17 (1967): 19–53.
Wilcock, Michael. *The Message of Chronicles*, The Bible Speaks Today. Leicester: Inter-Varsity Press, 1987.
Wilkinson, Bruce H. *The Prayer of Jabez*. Sisters: Multnomah, 2000.
Williamson, H. G. M. *1 and 2 Chronicles*, The New Century Bible Commentary. Grand Rapids: Eerdmans, 1982.
———. "The Ascension of Solomon in the Book of Chronicles." *Vetus Testamentum* 26 (1976): 351–361.
———. "The Composition of Ezra 1–6." Pages 244–270 in *Studies in Persian Period History and Historiography*. Forschungen zum Alten Testament 38. Tübingen: Mohr Siebeck, 2004.
———. "Eschatology in Chronicles." Pages 162–198 in *Studies in Persian Period History and Historiography*. Forschungen zum Alten Testament 38. Tübingen: Mohr Siebeck, 2004.
———. *Ezra, Nehemiah*, Word Biblical Commentary 16. Waco: Word, 1985.
———. *Israel in the Books of Chronicles*. Cambridge: Cambridge University Press, 1977.
———. "A Note on 1 Chronicles VII 12." *Vetus Testamentum* 23 (1973): 375–379.
———. "The Origins of the Twenty-Four Priestly Courses: A Study of 1 Chronicles 23–27." Pages 126–140 in *Studies in Persian Period History and Historiography*. Forschungen zum Alten Testament. Tübingen: Mohr Siebeck, 2004.
———. "Sources and Redaction in the Chronicler's Genealogy of Judah." Pages 106–114 in *Studies in Persian Period History and Historiography*. Forschungen zum Alten Testament 38. Tübingen: Mohr Siebeck, 2004.
Wilson, Robert R. "Between 'Azel' and 'Azel': Interpreting the Biblical Genealogies." *Biblical Archeologist* 42 (1979): 11–22.

―――. *Genealogy and History in the Biblical World.* New Haven: Yale University, 1977.
―――. "The Old Testament Genealogies in Recent Research." *Journal of Biblical Literature* 94 (1975): 169–189.
Woudstra, Marten H. *The Book of Joshua*, The New International Commentary on the Old Testament. Grand Rapids: Eerdmans, 1981.
Wright, J. Stafford. *The Date of Ezra's Coming to Jerusalem.* London: Tyndale Press, 1958.
Wright, John W. "The Legacy of David in Chronicles: The Narrative Function of 1 Chronicles 23–27." *Journal of Biblical Literature* 110 (1991): 229–242.
―――. "The Fight for Peace: Narrative and History in the Battle Accounts in Chronicles." Pages 150–177 in *The Chronicler as Historian.* Edited by M. Patrick Graham, Kenneth G. Hoglund, and Steven L. McKenzie. Journal for the Study of the Old Testament Supplement 238. Sheffield: Sheffield Academic Press, 1997.
―――. "From Center to Periphery: 1 Chronicles 23–27 and the Interpretation of Chronicles in the Nineteenth Century." Pages 20–42 in *Priests, Prophets and Scribes: Essays on the Formation and Heritage of Second Temple Judaism in Honour of Joseph Blenkinsopp.* Edited by Eugene Ulrich, John W. Wright, Robert P. Carroll, and Philip R. Davies. Journal for the Study of the Old Testament Supplement 149. Sheffield: Sheffield Academic Press, 1992.
―――. "Guarding the Gates: 1 Chronicles 26:1–19 and the Roles of the Gatekeepers in Chronicles." *Journal for the Study of the Old Testament* 48 (1990): 69–81.
Wyckoff, Chris. "Have We Come Full Circle Yet? Closure, Psycholinguistics, and Problems of Recognition with the *Inclusio.*" *Journal for the Study of the Old Testament* 30 (2006): 475–505.

INDEX OF AUTHORS

Abba, Raymond 69, 135
Ackroyd, Peter 1, 36
Adeyemo, Tokunboh 5, 11
Allen, Leslie 36, 66, 239, 353
Andersen, Francis 67
Anderson, Arnold 80
Andriolo, Karin 9
Ashley, Timothy 137–139, 157
Auld, A. Graeme 128, 130–36, 139, 140, 143–45, 147–52, 162, 334
Averbeck, Richard 46, 47, 192
Baker, David 252
Barrick, W. Boyd 75
Bartlett, J. R. 9
Bartusch, Mark 210
Batten, Loring 112, 345
Begg, Christopher 187
Ben Zvi, Ehud 127, 206, 218, 330, 331
Bendavid, Abba 135
Blenkinsopp, Joseph 1, 64, 334
Block, Daniel 69, 70, 285
Boda, M. J. 23, 26
Boling, Robert 127
Botterweck, G. Johannes 188, 191
Braun, Roddy ... 36, 54, 57, 64, 66, 75, 103, 108, 114, 129, 130, 134, 148, 156, 175, 179, 180, 191, 194, 196, 198, 204, 210, 232, 240, 252, 269, 271, 307, 320, 321, 337, 347, 353
Budd, Philip 38
Butler, Trent 143
Campbell, Antony 138, 300
Carter, Charles 179
Chapell, Bryan 26
Clines, David 72, 73, 75, 93, 246

Corduan, Winfried 198
Cross, Frank ... 3, 6, 7, 9, 80, 82, 247, 286
Curtis, Edward ... 27, 29, 35, 45, 80, 95, 98, 103, 108, 115, 130, 152, 155, 163, 165, 179, 189, 192, 197, 198, 202, 230, 231, 238, 240–42, 247, 252, 274, 275, 283, 300, 311, 337, 338, 353
de Vaux, Roland 227
De Vries, Simon ... 28, 36, 51, 57, 59, 61, 130, 227, 269, 283, 322, 330, 353
Dillard, Ray 27, 57, 203, 204
Driver, S. R. 139, 286
Duke, Rodney 69, 187
Durham, John 193, 198
Dyck, Jonathan 180
Endres, John 55, 135, 303
Fensham, F. Charles 112
Freedman, David 6, 7, 9, 67
Fried, Lisbeth 127
Friedman, Richard 42, 43
Galil, Gerson 197, 201
Geoghegan, Jeffrey 167
Gese, Hartmut 99
Goettsberger, Johann 135, 229, 238, 272, 353
Grabbe, Lester 187, 353
Graham, M. Patrick ... 1, 6, 23, 42, 174, 178, 307, 334
Gray, George 58, 137, 138
Hallo, William 167, 241
Halpern, Baruch 69
Haran, Menahem 38, 126, 296, 310
Hartman, Thomas 9
Harvey, Paul 1

Hauer, Christian 81, 127
Heard, R. Christopher 2, 177, 238, 239, 241
Heath, Elaine 2
Helman, A. 308
Hertzberg, H. W. 80
Hess, Richard 191
Hill, Andrew ... 27, 36, 45, 46, 108, 166, 189, 192, 198, 231, 240, 269, 353, 355, 356
Hoffman, Rudolt 188
Hogg, Hope 263
Hurowitz, Victor 246
Janzen, David 341
Japhet, Sara 1, 4, 32, 36, 41, 54, 58–60, 74, 95, 108, 111, 114, 116, 130, 156, 173, 179, 188, 191, 197, 201, 202, 210, 229, 230, 236–38, 240, 242, 247, 252, 269, 273, 277, 283, 287, 302, 306, 311, 320, 327, 330, 337, 340, 344, 353, 354
Jarick, John 313
Johnson, Marshall 9, 13, 75, 96, 97, 98, 189, 190, 194, 295
Johnstone, William ... 28, 36, 37, 38, 49, 50, 51, 118, 119, 121, 156, 179, 180, 183, 229, 269, 272, 293, 340, 353–356,
Kalimi, Isaac ... 27, 29, 130, 133, 182, 238, 313, 351
Kallai, Zecharia 126
Kartveit, Magnar 1, 8, 30, 153
Katzenstein, H. J. 110, 112, 114
Keil, C. F. 80, 108, 117, 118, 130, 148, 198, 199, 210, 212, 240, 271, 275, 283, 333, 340, 353, 355
Kelly, Brian 312
Kelly, Paul 312
Kidner, Derek 112, 338
Kiuchi, N. 48
Klein, Ralph 6, 64, 108, 109, 111, 112, 126, 128, 153, 157, 178, 221, 230, 231, 237, 238–40, 247, 252, 254, 269, 271, 307, 353, 356
Knoppers, Gary 1, 3, 15, 28, 31, 36–38, 64, 67, 71, 74–76, 94, 101, 108, 115, 116, 130, 218, 224, 225, 227, 229–31, 235–37, 240, 247, 252, 254, 270–72, 300, 307, 334, 335, 348, 349, 353, 355
Koch, Klaus 113
Kraft, Charles 3, 4
Kraus, Hans-Joachim 311
Laato, Antti 82, 98
Labahn, Antje 218
Lemke, Werner 294
Levine, Baruch 38, 137
Longman, Tremper 127, 193
Maass, F. 46
Madvig, Donald 191
Malamat, Abraham 9, 15
Margolis, Max 134
Marquart, J. 263
Mauchline, John 80
Mazar, Benjamin 126, 130, 148
McConville, J. G. 286
McIver, Robert ... 172, 291–98, 300, 334
McKenzie, Steven 2, 231, 320
Michalowski, Piotr 9
Millard, Alan 178
Miller, J. Maxwell 127
Myers, Jacob 36, 40, 75, 112, 126, 197, 199, 202, 210, 233, 240, 272, 283, 313, 337, 338, 353
Na'aaman, Nadav 197, 199
Nelson, Richard 143
Newsome, James 6, 7, 9
Noth, Martin 1, 8, 9, 12, 14, 22, 32, 64, 75, 139, 188, 228, 229, 295, 300
Oeming, Manfred ... 1, 28, 36, 128, 288, 331, 332, 353, 356
Oliver, Anthony 188
Olivier, J. P. J. 46
Olson, Dan 94, 328

Olyan, Saul............................80, 82, 108
Payne, J. Barton... 40, 67, 198, 211, 337
Pechawer, Larry 2, 238, 240, 241
Poirier, John 291, 293, 295
Pratt, Richard.........2, 3, 28, 35, 36, 98, 163, 233, 269, 321–23, 353
Radday, Yehuda.............. 26–28, 32, 235
Rendsburg, Gary 199, 203
Rooke, Deborah 82
Rothstein, J. Wilhelm........1, 35, 36, 67, 105, 135, 269, 271, 300, 353
Rudolph, Wilhelm..........8, 9, 12, 14, 36, 41, 73, 75, 95, 97, 103, 106, 108, 115, 127, 188, 198, 199, 212, 229, 233, 237, 240, 247, 252, 271, 283, 300, 353
Sasson, Jack 9
Selman, Martin..........36, 180, 199, 231, 235, 269, 272, 321, 330, 341, 353, 356
Smith, Henry 38, 80, 192
Snyman, Gerrie 5, 16, 19
Stinespring, W. F. 203
Sugimoto, Tomotoshi.......................134
Suh, Myung.......................................43
Syren, Roger....................................247
Talmon, Shemayahu........113, 231, 236, 335, 347
Thompson, J. A....36, 46, 64, 231, 233, 322, 353
Throntveit, Mark 1, 27
Torrey, Charles.........................275, 276
Tov, Emmanuel........................113, 134
Trotter, James...............................1, 352
Tuell, Steven 3, 30, 36, 353
Van Seters, John........................42, 168

von Rad, Gerhard 99, 283
Wakely, Robin 190, 191
Waltke, Bruce......................... 272, 338
Walton, John 166
Watson, Wildred 24, 27
Watts, James.................................297
Weanzana, Nupanga......................5, 11
Weinberg, Joel........ 38, 90, 92, 172, 220
Welch, Adam................... 6, 7, 9, 102
Welch, John......23–26, 28–31, 65, 116, 235, 359, 362
Wellhausen, Julius...5, 6, 9, 10, 38, 79, 80, 108, 116–18, 126, 166, 228
Wenham, Gordon... ......23, 47, 139, 303
Wenham J. W. 178
Wilcock, Michael 322
Wilkinson, Bruce..........................2, 238
Williamson, H. G. M...........1, 2, 8, 23, 27–30, 36, 41, 57, 64, 72–75, 93, 95, 98, 103, 108, 112, 117, 163, 165, 170, 175, 180, 181, 188, 192, 197–199, 202–05, 210–12, 230–38, 244, 247, 248, 252, 254, 269, 272, 275, 276, 283, 284, 300, 302, 303, 307, 321, 327, 330, 337, 345, 347, 353
Wilson, Robert..........9–21, 64, 73, 82, 105–107, 110, 114, 115, 117, 196, 215, 222, 245, 262–64, 285, 286, 295, 296, 303, 305, 323, 349
Woudstra, Marten.....................143, 191
Wright, J. Stafford............................342
Wright, John.........2, 94, 174, 175, 177, 186, 197, 328, 333
Wyckoff, Chris................................230

www.ingramcontent.com/pod-product-compliance
Lightning Source LLC
Chambersburg PA
CBHW021351290426
44108CB00010B/198